MW00358849

— ISLAMIC ANTICHRIST

— MIDEAST BEAST

JOEL RICHARDSON

FREE Ⓐ JOELSTRUMPET.COM

UNDER FREE RESOURCES

— DANIEL REVISITED

MARK DAVIDSON

FOURSIGNPOSTS.COM

Revelation Deciphered

Revelation Deciphered

by

Nelson Walters

Ready for Jesus
Publications

"To the angel of the church in Philadelphia *write . . .*"

(Rev. 3:7 NASB)

Join the movement to awaken the Church:

Ready for Jesus Ministries

www.TheGospelInTheEndTimes.com

nelson@thegospelintheendtimes.com

ACKNOWLEDGMENTS

Jesus, I have never had a more intimate time of fellowship with you than during the writing of this book. I have enjoyed each moment immersed with you in your Word. I am so grateful for the privilege of knowing you deeper. Lord, let me know you deeper still!

Laura, thank you for your patience and unending support throughout this ministry. You are the love of my life and God's greatest gift.

Joseph Lenard, thank you for your tireless devotion to this project, your insights, your love of Jesus and his followers, and most of all your friendship. This book would not have been the sweet aroma it is before our Lord without you.

Joel Richardson, thank you for sparking the interest in me to pursue the Word of God wherever it goes, and for your patient support of my ministry. You have been a great mentor.

John Preacher, thank you for all your advice, encouragement, and assistance. Additionally, thank you for the dramatic, rocking book-cover art! Your talent is amazing.

All those who read the book and provided insights, thank you for listening to the Spirit and for providing me with "course corrections" that have made this book what it is.

To all of you who have published and shared my writings on-line, thank you for your support.

Ready For Jesus Ministries, thanks to all of you for your voluntary efforts to prepare the world for the return of our King and Savior.

PRAISE FOR *REVELATION DECIPHERED*

I truly appreciate Nelson Walters' thoroughly Gospel-centered approach to understanding the Book of Revelation. *Revelation Deciphered*, like his previous works, is a fantastic contribution to the study of Revelation. This book will no doubt help prepare the Body of Christ for the return of their glorious King Jesus."

Joel Richardson

Author, *New York Times* Bestseller, *Mideast Beast*

Revelation Deciphered by Nelson Walters will knock the spiritual "socks" off the Church! These are exciting times. We are on the cusp of a new scripturally-sound, integrated understanding of the prophecies of Daniel and Revelation. Truly letting *scripture-interpret-scripture* provides unique insights into God's prophetic Word. The Church needs this teaching to *wake-up* and *properly prepare* for events during each year of the 70th Week of Daniel, up until the Rapture. You will receive a "strange stirring of the heart" as you read this account of Jesus' overall plan of redemption. Amazing new insights. Perfect timing for the Church. Highly recommended!

Joseph Lenard

Co-author (with Donald Zoller) of *The Last Shofar!—What the Fall Feasts of the Lord Are Telling the Church* (2014)

Revelation Deciphered is a monumental work, worthy of serious consideration. Nelson Walters illuminates prophecy not just from the book of Revelation but throughout the Bible. This is one of the finest treatments of end-time prophecies I have come across, Now more than ever, the church needs to hear what God is saying concerning the events of the end days. Nelson is an author who is willing to put aside all the popular theories concerning the end-times and allow God's Word to speak for itself.

John Preacher

Publisher, *Armageddon News*

Nelson Walters has taken on the monumental task of bringing the understanding of the Book of Revelation up-to-date. He has copiously compared Scripture with Scripture, and all who read *Revelation Deciphered* will have their minds and hearts opened to understand the Scriptures, which are truly written for us living at the end of the age. Nelson's deep concern is that believers in Jesus would all be overcomers through the coming 70th Week of Daniel. May it be so!

Howard Bass

Pastor, Yeshua's Inheritance Congregation, Beer Sheva, Israel

Revelation Deciphered is the best and most interesting commentary on Revelation I have ever read. Its strength lies in its approach — Scripture interpreting Scripture. I'm looking forward to helping spread the message of being ready for Jesus here in Australia.

Steve Müller

Pastor, Faith Baptist Church, Gladstone, Queensland, Australia

Refreshing and Solid! In *Revelation Deciphered*, Nelson Walters provides an intriguing and powerful thesis on the Book of Revelation. He proves it cannot be read as a stand-alone section of scripture, but demonstrates instead that it must be understood through the prophetic cypher of the Old and New Testaments. This, he contends, provides the Key to the enigma and allows for the full disclosure of the often hard to understand, misinterpreted, and symbolic language. To decipher Revelation any other way is to completely distort the meaning and end up inside a delusional paradigm that is much of what we see in end time teaching today. Nelson provides an essential bridge back to reality that encourages us to journey again into this mystery book with confidence.

Katie Griffith

Publisher, *Daily Prophecy Digest*

Nelson Walter's new book, *Revelation Deciphered,* is a refreshing and in-depth study of The Revelation and how it is rooted in the writings of the Hebrew prophets of the Old Testament. Walter's insights into Daniel's 70th Week will provoke students of God's Word to take a new look at some familiar passages... and some not so familiar.

Greg Maxwell

The Issachar Mandate

In his book *Revelation Deciphered,* Nelson Walter's interpretation of Revelation is amazing. He explains this complex book in the simplest and most scriptural way so that even a new Christian can grasp the keys to unlocking coming Biblical prophecy.

Shauna Stephens

Publisher, *Revelation Revealed*

CONTENTS

Part Three: The Book of Daniel, Underpinning of Revelation

Part Four: THE LETTERS TO THE SEVEN CHURCHES

Part Five: OVERCOMING THE 70TH WEEK OF DANIEL

A Beginning Word

OFF THE CLOCK

I believe you are about to embark on an exciting journey into the most controversial book of the Bible — the Book of Revelation; the book of the Bible that best explains God's plan to bring about the return of Jesus. Being of a category of biblical literature called "apocalyptic literature," much like the book of Ezekiel or Daniel, Revelation features visions of strange colored horses, dragons, thrones in heaven, scenes in the starry sky, etc. God has placed them in Revelation as a message to us. What do they all mean? In *Revelation Deciphered*, we are going to visit and make sense of these things.

But I don't want them to just make sense to you in some "academic," "head-knowledge" way. Head-knowledge is interesting, but knowledge we can *apply* is useful. Knowledge we can apply *in the Love of Jesus* will minister. I want this book to affect the very core of your being, to affect your relationship with the risen Jesus, King of the Universe. I wrote this book to change your life. Let me tell you a brief story about an event that just happened in my life, and how life change can happen. I use stories like this throughout *Revelation Deciphered* as metaphors of the biblical passages and ideas this book explains.

I glanced down at my watch. The battery was dead. With as many things as had just happened to me and around me, I wasn't surprised.

August 5th was my day off. Even though it was only 6:30 AM, the Carolina sun promised it would be a great morning. I was sitting outside of the office of my Primary Care Provider awaiting my yearly physical, and even the thoughts of being prodded and poked weren't upsetting me that fine morning.

My PCP went over my blood test results, perfect, perfect, perfect. I was really feeling blessed until he said, "Everything is about as good as could be expected, but you have a low grade fever. Do you feel alright?" I told him I felt good, not just okay. The only thing bothering me was my left elbow was warm. I had a cyst on that elbow that my PCP and I had watched slowly grow over the past month.

"Let me send you over to the orthopedic surgeon and have her drain it," he suggested. "Then we can put you on some antibiotics. It's probably infected."

On my way to the Orthopedic Surgeon for this "minor procedure," I began to feel worse. By the time I got to her office which is next to the hospital, my fever was 103°. She immediately admitted me to the hospital for intravenous antibiotics. Despite her immediate action, my blood had become infected and one of my heart valves was damaged.

Compared to the hospitalizations and open heart surgery that ensued, a dead watch battery was nothing. This was the first time I was able to wear a watch since that fateful day. "It must have been dead for a while," I thought. Then I glanced at the time the watch died: 6:30 AM August 5th. The exact moment that my odyssey had begun! What kind of crazy co-incidence was this? Or was God sending me a sign?

God had saved me, of that there was no doubt. What if I hadn't had my regular yearly physical scheduled on that exact day? What if my PCP had only placed me on a mild antibiotic instead of referring me? Would I have survived or would I have been as motionless as my watch? God showed his infinite grace to me. He holds the entire universe together, each atom and each proton. Every breath we take is his grace after all, and by his grace he allowed me to live on for his purposes.

What were the odds of me being in my PCP's office at the exact hour my infection became noticeable; approximately 1 in 10,000 (about 365x24)? What were the odds of my watch stopping at that exact moment as well; also approximately 1 in 10,000? Combined the odds are 1 in 100 Million. Those are odds to make even the staunchest atheist take notice.

What are the odds of the prophecies in the Book of Revelation occurring in the exact order and timing God has ordained? Is the universe large enough to contain this number? Yet with God, the odds of my event occurring as it did was 100%, and the odds of Revelation's prophecies being fulfilled is also 100%. Are we willing to live in the reality of those odds?

I realized a possible second meaning in the stopped watch. Did God "take me off the clock?" All of us would probably say we are living sold-out lives for Jesus, but had I been partially living on the world's time instead of 100% on God's time? This event was certainly a wake-up call; a time to reflect and re-evaluate my life. This is an aspect of God's grace as well.

This event has also been an enormous source of testimony for me about God's grace. In Luke, Jesus spoke about the coming persecutions and hard times that will come upon the earth and said, "They will lay their hands on you and will persecute you, delivering you to the synagogues and prisons, bringing you before kings and governors for my name's sake. It will lead to an opportunity for your *testimony*." Can reading and studying Revelation help us re-evaluate our lives to better use them for his glory?

I pray that this book will do for you what my infection did for me: take you off the world's clock and put you on God's clock 100%. Time is short; God has an incredible plan proposed that will lead to the glorious return of his Son as King of the Earth. He wants every one of his bond-servants to buy into his plan 100%. He wants us all to be a *part* of His plan.

For that reason, you will find that this book (*Revelation Deciphered*) is different than every other commentary on Revelation. Indeed, the Book of Revelation itself is unlike any other book of the Bible. It is not a stand-alone book, but rather acts as a *compendium* of the other end-time prophecies found throughout the Bible. It is the revelation of Jesus Christ and by Jesus Christ to us his bond-servants, but was written down by John to organize and chronologically arrange these other end-time prophecies. It accomplishes this by quoting them within the text of Revelation. There are hundreds of Old and New Testament references found in its pages that point the reader to these other prophecies, and these references give Revelation a Bible-wide-panoramic scope. In addition, of course, Revelation expands these other prophecies gives some new insights not contained in other scripture.

Most commentaries on Revelation are organized as a verse-by-verse description. That approach might work for commentaries on other books of the Bible, but there are inherent problems with that method for deciphering Revelation. A verse-by-verse approach adds to the confusion caused by Revelation's scripture-wide basis for its teachings. Attempting to jump back and forth from a verse in Revelation to a reference in another book of the Bible and back again to Revelation can be hopelessly perplexing. Additionally, the Book of Revelation is *not* totally chronological in its layout, but, as is common in Hebrew literature, some later chapters are *further descriptions* of previously described events.

Hence, *Revelation Deciphered* is not a verse-by-verse traditional commentary on Revelation, but rather it provides an all-encompassing, sweeping canvas of the end times. I think you will appreciate this difference. Because it is not a verse-by-verse view of Revelation, as you read through *Revelation Deciphered*, it is helpful to have in mind the overall organization of this book. It is primarily organized around the *Pattern of Seven Events*; the seven events that chronologically define the "end times." This commentary will assist the reader in uncovering and understanding this new insight of a foundational, chronological configuration of *seven events* or occurrences found throughout scripture that describe the period our culture calls "The Tribulation." Amazingly, this *Pattern of Seven Events* shows up over and over in scripture.

Following this introduction is a summary of each of the five **Parts** and all the **Chapters** of this book. These summaries provide a feel for how this commentary is put together and how the *Pattern of Seven Events* is crucial to deciphering Revelation. This organizational understanding will assist you in reading through the text.

As stated, *Revelation Deciphered* is unlike any other commentary — organized in a different way, as well as having hundreds of unique and helpful insights into Revelation. These insights help us understand the message that Jesus is giving to the Church during the last days. In essence, the following summary of the **Chapters** of this book allows you to see the "forest among the trees" and how all the insights, relating to the rest of the Bible, are connected together in understanding the amazing Book of Revelation. This chapter summary explains these unique "pieces of the puzzle." This is helpful in *deciphering Revelation*.

My great desire is that through this study of Revelation, you come to know and love Jesus more; that you go "off the clock" to become completely sold-out for him, and then that you become part of his plan to return and restore the world.

SUMMARY OF PARTS AND CHAPTERS

Part One: REVEALING REVELATION

Part One of **Revelation Deciphered** introduces the main themes discussed in the book and provides detailed analysis of Revelation Chapters 1, 4, and 5.

CHAPTER ONE   A PRINCESS, A DRAGON, AND SPIDERMAN

Chapter One introduces the readers to the idea that the human brain is hard-wired to understand and desire the return of Jesus. Humans express this inherent desire as a metaphor in most of our fairy tales and stories where a hero (*Jesus*) saves a maiden (*the Church*) from a dragon or villain (*Satan*.) The Chapter also acts as an introduction in which I discuss my motivation in writing the book, my philosophies related to eschatology, and my methodology of writing.

CHAPTER TWO   UNCOVERING THE KEYS

In Chapter Two, the book introduces the readers to the *five biblical interpretation "keys"* we utilized to decipher prophecy. The book compares the use of these five "keys" to the "code" of the famous German Enigma Typewriter used to encrypt *and de-encrypt* messages in WWII. Only when all five wheels of that typewriter were set in position could sense be made out the scrambled code.

CHAPTER THREE   A TREASURE MAP (REVELATION 6, MATTHEW 24)

The most logical way to begin looking for treasure is with a treasure map. If you know where to look, the chances of you discovering treasure is greatly enhanced! Such a map exists for the 70th Week of Daniel; it is a series of seven events found throughout scripture that chronologically mark that period of time. In this Chapter we biblically demonstrate that pattern of events (the *Pattern of Seven Events*) and as an added benefit, definitely identify the timing of the Rapture.

CHAPTER FOUR BOOKENDS (REVELATION 1-3)

Chapter Four begins the process of interpreting the text of Revelation. The book first demonstrates the importance John (the writer of Revelation) places on quoted phrases from elsewhere in the Bible. We then discover that the *Book of Revelation* opens and closes (like a *"bookend"*) with a phrase quoted from the *Book of Daniel.* The book then helps the reader discover a second bookend using a quote from Jesus's *Olivet Discourse.* We then demonstrate what John meant by the intentional use of these *"bookends,"* and link the *"bookends"* to proof that the *Letters to the Seven Churches* are prophetic (based on the *Pattern of Seven Events*) and not simply historic letters.

CHAPTER FIVE   SIGNED, SEALED, AND DELIVERED (REVELATION 4-5)

The central event in Revelation is the opening of the *Seven Sealed Scroll.* Chapter Five uncovers the multi-part identity of the *Scroll* and demonstrates the link between it and the resurrection and *Rapture.* The Chapter concludes by validating the relationship between this *Scroll* and the *Pattern of Seven Events:* 1) deception by false messiahs, 2) bloodshed, chaos, and war, 3) famine and economic collapse, 4) abomination and death, 5) martyrdom and apostasy, 6) celestial signs, and 7) rapture then wrath.

Part Two: *THE PATTERN OF SEVEN EVENTS*

Having introduced the insight of the *Pattern of Seven Events* in Part One of **Revelation Deciphered**, Part Two proves how this pattern is essential to understanding the end times by presenting the seven events of the pattern in prophetic books throughout the Bible. These examples not only prove the existence of the pattern, but also give insights of one of the most detailed chronological descriptions of the end times in literature. Although some of these Chapters are based on books of the Bible other than Revelation, all the sections and Chapters are used to explain themes and passages in Revelation. Additionally, all of the Chapters in Part Two support themes that build throughout **Revelation Deciphered** about *Rapture Timing* and the *Islamic* nature of the Antichrist.

CHAPTER SIX   THE WALLS CAME TUMBLING DOWN   (JOSHUA 6,

JUDGES 6-8)

Chapter Six initiates the examination of the *Pattern of Seven Events* by exploring the related accounts of Jericho and Gideon. The Chapter first demonstrates that these accounts are both allegories of end time events, and then shows how they demonstrate the *Pattern.*

CHAPTER SEVEN   A HORSE OF A DIFFERENT COLOR (REVELATION 6:1-8)

Chapter Seven explores the *Four Horsemen of the Apocalypse* that "ride" during the opening of the first four seals on the *Seven Sealed Scroll.* The Chapter demonstrates that the horsemen are not "men," but rather events in the *Pattern of Seven Events.* Unique to this book is the true purpose of the horsemen which is deciphered along with their essential Islamic nature, which supports an *Islamic Antichrist.*

CHAPTER EIGHT   EVENT ONE: DECEPTION BY FALSE MESSIAHS

Chapter Eight looks at the *First Event* in the *Pattern of Seven Events:* Deception by False Messiahs. The Chapter carefully examines what Jesus taught about the nature of the deception and also scans Islamic and Jewish eschatology for possible candidates for these False Messiahs. The Chapter also references Old Testament passages that linked to this *First Event.*

CHAPTER NINE   EVENT TWO: WAR, BLOODSHED, AND CHAOS

Chapter Nine looks at the *Second Event* in the *Pattern of Seven Events:* War, Bloodshed, and Chaos. The Chapter examines Jesus's teaching on this event and specifically on his command to not be terrified when these events begin. The Chapter concludes with a reference to Isaiah made by Jesus in the *Olivet Discourse* that clearly identifies the "wars" being referenced by this event.

CHAPTER TEN   EVENT THREE: FAMINE AND ECONOMIC COLLAPSE

Chapter Ten looks at the *Third Event* in the *Pattern of Seven Events:* Famine and Economic Distress. Particular attention is given to prophecies in Isaiah and Ezekiel that involve events in Israel that will occur during this event; specifically the "siege" that takes place over 430 days.

CHAPTER ELEVEN   EVENT FOUR: ABOMINATION AND DEATH

Chapter Eleven looks at the *Fourth Event* in the *Pattern of Seven Events:* Abomination and Death. The Chapter looks at the Midpoint of the 70th Week from both the perspective of earth and the perspective of heaven. It further references Old Testament passages that refer to this central event when the Antichrist sits in the Temple of God.

CHAPTER TWELVE   EVENT FIVE: MARTYRDOM AND APOSTASY

Chapter Twelve looks at the *Fifth Event* in the *Pattern of Seven Events:* Martyrdom and Apostasy. This Chapter looks at how God will use the faithfulness of his servants to witness to a fallen world and to their weaker brothers and sisters as part of his Divine plan. The Chapter also examines the Great Falling Away that will accompany the Great Tribulation, and also examines the Flight of the Faithful who escape into the wilderness.

CHAPTER THIRTEEN   EVENT SIX: THE CELESTIAL EARTHLY DISTURBANCE

Chapter Thirteen looks at the *Sixth Event* in the *Pattern of Seven Events:* The Celestial Earthly Disturbance. This Chapter compares and contrasts five passages of scripture that describe "the sign" that precedes the coming of our Lord. This comparison delineates the effects of the event on the unrighteous and the righteous, and also speculates on effects this event may have on the length of the solar year and the calendar.

Chapter Fourteen looks at the *Seventh Event* in the *Pattern of Seven Events:* Rapture and Wrath. The Chapter demonstrates how the Rapture and the beginning of God's Wrath will occur on the same exact day. The Chapter examines Ezekiel's vision of the resurrection and the Gospel's analogies of the Flood and Sodom and Gomorrah in explaining the twin events. The Chapter then provides an in depth study of the Day of the Lord and God's Wrath as seen in the *Trumpet and Bowl Judgements.*

Part Three: THE BOOK OF DANIEL, UNDERPINNING OF REVELATION

Chapter Fifteen examines the Book of Daniel and the central role it plays in the *Pattern of Seven Events.* The Chapter looks at many various prophecies about the Beast and the Beast Empire and also provides an in-depth look at Daniel's Great Vision Prophecy.

Part Four: LETTERS TO THE SEVEN CHURCHES

After having demonstrated the overwhelming evidence for the *Pattern of Seven Events* in Part Two, in Part Four we return to the *Letters to the Seven Churches* of Revelation. Now that the reader is intimately familiar with the *Pattern*, the book demonstrates how the *Letters to the Seven Churches* of Revelation reflect this same pattern! In this way, the book concludes that the *Seven Churches of Revelation* are pictures of *THE CHURCH* of Jesus Christ as it endures and overcomes the "Tribulation" in each of its seven years! The *Letters* are Jesus's advice to the Church during each of those years.

Chapter Sixteen examines Jesus's letter to the Church of Ephesus that will endure Event One: Deception by False Messiahs. Ephesus means "desired one" and the Antichrist and Jesus will vie for the love and worship of this Church. AGAPAO love for Jesus is the key for this Church overcoming the Antichrist and his "Nicolaitans."

Chapter Seventeen examines Jesus's letter to the Church of Smyrna that will endure Event Two: War, Bloodshed, and Chaos. The name Smyrna is derived from the myrrh, the spice used for embalming. The great physical difficulties of the Church will begin during Event Two.

CHAPTER EIGHTEEN   THE CHURCH OF PERGAMUM (REV. 2:12-17)

Chapter Eighteen examines Jesus's letter to the Church of Pergamum that will endure Event Three: Famine and Economic Collapse. This Church is warned against eating food sacrificed to idols during the Mark of the Beast.

CHAPTER NINETEEN   THE CHURCH OF THYATIRA (REV. 2:18-29)

Chapter Nineteen examines Jesus's letter to the Church of Thyatira that will endure Event Four: Abomination and Death. This Church whose name means "graveyard," is promised to inherit the "authority" that is originally given to the Antichrist during this event.

CHAPTER TWENTY   THE CHURCH OF SARDIS (REV. 3:1-6)

Chapter Twenty examines Jesus's letter to the Church of Sardis that will endure Event Five: Martyrdom and Apostasy. Sardis is derived from the Sardonyx stone that is white with red streaks; reminders of the purity of the saints who are martyred.

CHAPTER TWENTY-ONE THE CHURCH OF PHILADELPHIA (REV. 3:7-13)

Chapter Twenty-One examines Jesus's letter to the Church of Philadelphia that will endure Event Six: The Celestial Earthly Disturbance. This is the Church awaiting the Rapture when Jesus will open the door of heaven and keep them from the coming trial of the Wrath of God.

CHAPTER TWENTY-TWO   THE CHURCH OF LAODICEA (REV. 3:14- 22)

Chapter Twenty-Two examines Jesus's letter to the Church of Laodicea that will endure Event Seven: Rapture and Wrath. These former churchgoers are the Foolish Virgins who are left behind by the Rapture. Jesus still desires they come to repentance so he stands at the door and knocks.

Part Five: OVERCOMING THE 70TH WEEK OF DANIEL

After concluding Part Four and its exhaustive review of the *Letters to the Seven Churches,* Part Five applies those prophecies so that the readers are prepared for what is going to occur in the future and what they can do to be victorious during those times.

CHAPTER TWENTY-THREE   APPOINTMENTS

Chapter Twenty-Three discusses the most revolutionary teaching in **Revelation Deciphered**: that each of the events in the *Pattern of Seven Events* are timed to coincide with one the seven Old Testament *Feasts of the Lord!* The book demonstrates that not only will these fulfillments on Feast Days take place in order (one for each year of the

"Tribulation,") but also that each consecutive *Feast* is itself a picture or metaphor of the related event from the *Pattern of Seven Events!* The Chapter concludes by decoding the mysterious *"Days of Daniel" (1260, 1290, 1335, and 2300)* and demonstrating that all of these will also fall on perfectly appropriate Old Testament *Feast Days* or historic events! In this way, Chapter Twenty-Three provides an incredibly specific timeline of the entire "Tribulation" period.

CHAPTER TWENTY-FOUR   TO HIM WHO OVERCOMES

Finally in Chapter Twenty-Four, **Revelation Deciphered** applies the advice given by Jesus himself in the *Letters to the Seven Churches* of Revelation. At this point in the book, the readers are intimately familiar with the events of the "Tribulation" and their timing. Jesus's advice, which appears random in other, traditional interpretations of the *"Letters,"* is found in this Chapter to be amazingly appropriate for dealing with and overcoming each of the Seven Events of the *Pattern of Seven Events.*

PART ONE:

Revealing Revelation

Chapter One

A PRINCESS, A DRAGON, AND SPIDERMAN

Why are both Christians and non-Christians fascinated with the time period our culture commonly calls "the Tribulation?" Non-Christians don't believe the Bible is truth, and most Christians now believe they will be raptured off the earth before this period begins. Yet, images from the Book of Revelation dot our literature and movies about apocalyptic themes fill our theatres. Part of the answer is that an obsession with *how* the world as we know it will "end" seems to be hard-wired into our sub-conscious mind.

Even our children's "fairy tales" reflect this fascination. Take a moment and reflect back on the bedtime stories you heard as a child or read to your children. How many involve the rescue of a helpless "damsel in distress?" Have you considered that this timeless theme is essentially the retelling of the story of the Bible? A young maiden (the Bride of Christ or the Church) is captured by an evil dragon (Satan). A brave knight (Jesus) comes to her aid, and after an epic battle, he overcomes and kills the dragon. The happy couple then marries (the *Wedding of the Lamb/Marriage Supper of the Lamb*) and lives happily ever after. "Happily ever after" is an odd phrase. No human lives "ever after" unless they are redeemed by the blood of Christ. So even this phrase that occurs at the end of many fairy tales is a reflection of the ultimate redemption reality the Bible portrays in its pages. The next time you read a fairy tale to your children or grandchildren, think about the religious analogy that it might contain. You will be surprised at what you might find.

As we begin to physically mature, we move away from fairy tales and frequently develop an interest in superheroes. Have you considered how these stories also reflect the timeless story of Jesus coming to rescue his Bride and defeating Satan? We can consider two specific superhero stories to see this analogy. *Superman* was born on another planet and came to earth with super powers (Jesus came from heaven and was enabled by the Spirit's power to do many miracles). Superman frequently would save his love interest, Lois Lane, from the clutches of his arch enemy, Lex Luther. *Spiderman* was born as a normal human but after a bite from a radio-active spider, he acquired super powers. Aren't these perfect pictures of the Holy Spirit infilling a person and enabling them to accomplish his will?

If you think about it, most of the "hero stories" we watch as adults are analogies of the greatest story ever told as well. The hero in these stories usually represents Jesus, the villain is Satan, and the helpless damsel is the Church. Have fun with this the next time you watch a movie with a "hero" theme and see if you can find overtones of Jesus's story in it. It seems even the most committed atheist author is hard-wired to long for the Savior to return to redeem the world, even if it is at a sub-conscious level. In their creative process, they can't help but express this longing, even if it is conveyed by a hero in tights and a mask. We can't help but think that way because we know the world is messed up and we can't fix it. It's full of sex trafficking, cancer, divorce, parents with Alzheimer's disease, abused children, terrorists, and a host of other injustices that are far beyond our ability to fix. But into this junk-yard of a world comes a hero. It is the consummation of the story we long for.

Ed Catmull, President of Walt Disney Animation Studios, says that all education is "story-telling", and story-telling is a means to change the world[i]; I agree with him. The Bible is primarily a collection of stories, so it appears the Holy Spirit agrees as well. This book that you are now reading is full of these stories, many of which have a *prophetic aspect* to them. We plan to voice those aspects.

DECIPHERING REVELATION

Because we are hard-wired to long for the coming of our hero, Jesus, all of us have an inborn desire to understand Revelation. We are drawn to it. Unfortunately, Revelation is the last book in the canon of scripture intentionally, and understanding it is a bit like a final exam in High School. It will take all our previous understanding of scripture to uncover the meaning of all its various metaphors and strange language.

The purpose of this book is to help you jump-start your understanding of this key section of scripture — Revelation.

I think you'll enjoy the process. The process of understanding Revelation is a bit like reading a "who-done-it" mystery or cracking a cryptogram. Most of us are designed with a brain that loves to solve mysteries. When I was in seventh grade, I had quite an interesting Health Teacher. He was a World War II vet and had a passion for code-breaking and cryptograms. This interest was based on his military service in the department charged with breaking the Japanese and German codes. He founded a Cryptography Club at my middle school, and after school a dozen of us would sit enraptured hearing about his military stories of breaking codes. He also taught us how to uncover the keys to simple cryptograms ourselves. I remember a time when I "intercepted" a note between two girls in my seventh grade class, broke the simple code it was written in, and learned the identity of the boys each one of them secretly liked — much to their horror. Seventh grade boys are like that. I should know. I lead a church-based, middle-school small group of 17 of them.

Breaking earthly ciphers requires one or more "keys." For instance, if you are faced with a cryptogram of HGTMT, it would be impossible to solve without a key. But once you know that H=J, G=E, T=S, and M=U, solving the cryptogram is easy. The solution is JESUS. This is a rather simple cryptogram with a single key. More complex cryptograms use multiple keys that make their codes much harder to break. The famous German "Enigma" code in World War II used a typewriter to encrypt the code. The Enigma typewriter scrambled a message by means of three, four, or five notched wheels which displayed the letters of the alphabet. The wheels could be set in multiple positions. We should think of each of the wheels (up to five) as a "key." In order to unscramble the code, the wheels needed to be set in their exact original settings. A British spy was able to photograph the instruction manual of the Enigma typewriter which led to the British being able to break the code.[ii]

Deciphering the book of Revelation, however, isn't something you can learn in a class. It isn't a mental exercise or simply the expression of logical processes.

Computers won't untangle it. "Systems" won't unravel it. The book opens this way, "The Revelation of Jesus Christ, which *God gave Him* to show to His bond-servants, the things which must soon take place; and He sent *and communicated it by His angel* to His bond-servant John" (Rev. 1:1 NASB, emphasis mine). Revelation is written spiritually, and *only by God's Holy Spirit can we uncover what it means*. Even with the greatest supercomputer in the world, if we approach this book from a *fleshly* point of view, we will fail to understand it. That doesn't mean, however, that we should not use multiple "keys" to help us uncover its true meaning. The next Chapter (Chapter Two: "Uncovering The Keys") will help us uncover five of these "keys" (the *Five "Keys"*). We can think of them as *five wheels* on an Enigma typewriter. When we set these wheels in proper alignment, we are able to see the text with new eyes.

THE SLEEPING CHURCH

This brings up an interesting question: *haven't millions of followers of Christ, empowered by the Spirit, tried to unlock its secrets before? What makes this book different?* Frankly, although this commentary on Revelation is, indeed, *distinctly different* from all other commentaries, nothing *earthly* makes this book different than the dozens of others that I've read on Revelation. And certainly, nothing separates me spiritually from the other authors. Although I love my Lord with all my heart and desire to follow him, I am probably no more spiritual or Godly than many who have come before. They may have been *more* devoted to our Lord. Additionally, I am certainly no more intelligent than these saints. If there is any truth at all in this book (and I believe there is), it is because the *Spirit of the Living God chose to reveal it and put it here.* Why now? We are closer to the return of our Lord than at any other time in history, and, perhaps, *the truth in this book is needed now more than at any time in history.* Will there be further deciphering of Revelation in the future by other more-gifted men and women? Undoubtedly so! This book is built on the shoulders of giants of the faith who have gone before. Others will come after. It is the process Jesus has chosen. And sometimes he chooses the foolish things of this world to confound the wise.

In this book, you are going to find many *new interpretations* of passages of Revelation that differ from familiar, traditional interpretations; *be prepared for them.* They will most likely shock and surprise you. Does that mean that the Church and all those beloved commentators of the past have been *wrong* about these passages all these years, and just now, we suddenly understand them? Hardly; it *may* mean the Church and those commentators have been *asleep*, however. There is a huge difference between *wrong* and *asleep*. Jesus prophesied about this very thing in the *Parable of the Ten Virgins*, "While the bridegroom was delaying, they *all* got drowsy and began to *sleep*" (Matt. 25:5 NASB, emphasis mine). Here Jesus tells us that *all* the virgins (churchgoers) will be sleeping prior to his return; including the *wise* virgins. This is an incredible prophecy; one that has been overlooked by nearly the entire Church. It is the *Emperor's New Clothes* of the New Testament. Who wants to admit they are asleep? Yet, Jesus says *we are all snoozing*; including the wise virgins who have written commentaries in the past.

Might "sleeping" include not utilizing all "keys" in interpretation? As we saw with the Enigma Typewriter, if all five "keys" were not set in the exact correct position, proper interpretation was impossible. So, when you read the new interpretations of Revelation in this book, please remember the *Parable of the Ten Virgins* and the Enigma typewriter, and then *carefully* look at what the Bible passage *itself* is truly saying — not just what you've always *thought* it was saying. Remember that past interpretations were given by those who were led by the Holy Spirit and who the Church respected greatly, but they may have been asleep. But now, God is doing something new; he is preparing his Bride, the Church, for what is to soon come.

THE *PATTERN OF SEVEN EVENTS*

One of the things I learned while preparing to write this book is that the time period right before Jesus's return (which our culture calls the "Tribulation") contains a *Pattern of Seven Events* (see Appendix A for a summary of these key seven events). This *Pattern of Seven Events* is an interesting chronological "fingerprint" of happenings that identifies "The Tribulation." When this pattern of events is recognized *in chronological order* in a passage of scripture, it identifies the prophetic passage as being about "The

Tribulation" period. These seven important events are: *1) deception by false messiahs, 2) bloodshed, 3) famine, 4) abomination and death, 5) apostasy and martyrdom, 6) heavenly signs, and 7) rapture* and then *wrath*. These events are found in chronologic order in the petitions of the Lord's Prayer, in the order and meaning of the "Jewish" Feasts of the Lord, and in prophetic passages in Matthew, Mark, Luke, Revelation, Psalms, Joshua, and Daniel.

This *Pattern of Seven Events* is best exemplified in the events that surround the opening of the *Seven Seals* in Rev. 6-8 (see Chapters Six and Seven). The Gospel of Luke mentions the first six events of the pattern in Luke 21:8-11.

Understanding the *Pattern of Seven Events* is of *extreme* importance, yet I believe the uncovering of this pattern (and its frequent use throughout scripture) is unique to this book. Studying this book will help you identify the pattern, and by so doing, it will help you "time stamp" prophetic passages about the end times. We will begin to discuss this pattern of events in enormous detail in every chapter of Part Two: "The *Pattern of Seven Events*," Part Four: "*Letters to the Seven Churches*," and Part Five: "Overcoming the 70th Week of Daniel."

KNOWLEDGE

During this process, we have to beware of a trap. We must not acquire knowledge for the sake of knowledge alone. God's Word is clear that knowledge without love is worthless: "If I have the gift of prophecy and know all mysteries and all knowledge, and if I have all faith so as to remove mountains, but do not have love, I am nothing" (1 Cor. 13:2 NASB). It is tempting to believe that understanding and deciphering Revelation, in and of itself, is a worthy goal. It is not. The purpose of our quest is to apply the Word of God *in love*. In Part Five: "Overcoming the 70th Week of Daniel," we will attempt to do just that. In the meantime, let's endeavor to not become "puffed up" by the knowledge we attain, but rather let's always keep our eyes on the final goal.

Our goal is to apply God's Word *in love*.

WRITE . . .

Christians frequently mention a "call" from God for their ministry. I feel this is a good place to mention mine. In December, 2013, I had no interest or inclination to write a book. I had never written a book before, and the prospects seemed daunting. During that month, however, a Bible verse became imprinted on my consciousness:

> And to the angel of the church in Philadelphia *write*: he who is holy, who is true, who has the key of David, who opens and no one will shut, and who shuts and no one opens, says this . . . (Rev. 3:7 NASB; emphasis mine)

When I'm studying the Word of God, it isn't unusual for a particular verse to "jump out at me," to almost "glow" as I read it. To me, this is a signal from the Holy Spirit to pay particular attention to that verse. Most times, these verses instruct me to "clean up my act," turn away from unrighteousness, and become more like Jesus. This verse was different. I knew God wanted to say something to me, but I wasn't sure what it was.

Over the following days and weeks, that verse resounded in my subconscious mind like a broken record. Within my mind, it had shortened to ". . . to the angel of the church in Philadelphia *write* . . ." Over and over, this section of the verse came to my consciousness. Finally, it focused on one word: *"write."* I prayed, *Lord, do you really want me to write?* I felt like Moses making up all kinds of excuses why I wasn't hearing clearly. I didn't know how to write prose, I don't have the proper education, I'm a terrible speller, I don't this and I don't that. God was persistent: *"write."* So I did. I wrote a brief "article" on this verse and sent it to a brother in Christ who I consider a great and gifted writer, Greg Maxwell. Greg encouraged me. The article became the first post in a blog, *The Gospel in the End Times* (www.thegospelintheendtimes.org). The blog website became the basis for my first book, *Are We Ready for Jesus?: How to Prepare for His Return* (Seraphina Press, 2015).

Now, just because I have a "call" doesn't mean I think of myself too highly. I am just a writer with a call like many thousands of others. Every word I write isn't God breathed. I hold my opinions of the end times loosely, as I believe all of us should. Indeed, we "see through a glass darkly." I make mistakes as we all do.

Ch. 1: A Princess, A Dragon, and Spiderman

After I finished my first book, I thought God's call might be complete, but it wasn't. As soon as my first book was completed and before it was out in stores, a second call came. God further expanded my understanding of the verse he had given me, ". . . to the *angel* of the *church in Philadelphia* write . . ." What is the church in Philadelphia and who is its angel? As you will learn later in this book, Philadelphia is the church that Jesus raptures out of the *Great Tribulation*. We will also discuss how the word "angel" in scripture can mean messenger. So I was to write to the church that is raptured and its messenger(s). What should I write about? What would be the most important aspects that church will need to know? They will need to understand the times they will live in, and they will need to know how to "overcome" during that period. Those are the things I decided to write about.

You may have picked this book up "hot off the presses," and the time period that our culture calls "the Tribulation" may not have started yet. Or you may be reading this book during that particular period, and I may have long since died or been martyred. In either case, this book is for you, the blessed Church; the Church that Jesus opens the door of heaven for that no one can shut.

This is a lofty goal. I have tried to take the writing of this book as seriously as its goal. Remember, I am not a prophet. This book is not inerrant. The scriptures within it *are inerrant*, however. Let them speak to you, and let the Holy Spirit interpret them for you. He is faithful to correct my errors and get his message across to you.

I need to warn you that this book will challenge your thinking. You may be a student of the Word and the end times in particular. Despite that (or possibly because of that), I am certain that many elements within this book will be contrary to your current understanding. The main theses of this book are contrary to what *my* understanding of the Book of Revelation was only a few short years ago. I invite you on the same journey I took; look at the same scriptures that led me to these new conclusions. Let the Holy Spirit guide you. I emphatically implore you to not abandon the journey until you have completed at least Part Two: "The *Pattern of Seven Events*." A unique interpretation of familiar scripture requires development. Allow this book to amplify those new ideas and show you their validity before you dismiss them out of hand.

SUMMARY

We have seen that we all are created with an innate longing for the return of our Redeemer. This longing has found its way into our fairy tales and stories in the form of a metaphorical retelling of God's plan of redemption. This is true even if the longing is sub-conscious. This book is arranged to reveal the Book of Revelation and the seven-year period our culture calls "The Tribulation." In order to accomplish this goal, the book is organized into **Five Main Parts:**

- **Part One**: "Revealing Revelation": where we discover the *Five "Keys"* necessary to decipher the book, and where we examine the main themes of Revelation.
- **Part Two**: "The *Pattern of Seven Events*": where we examine the *Pattern of Seven Events;* chronological events that scripture has provided us of the seven year "Tribulation" period.
- **Part Three**: The Book of Daniel, Underpinning Revelation: where we examine the Book of Daniel upon which so much of Revelation was based.
- **Part Four**: "*Letters to the Seven Churches*": where we examine the prophetic nature of the *Letters to the Seven Churches* based on the *Pattern of Seven Events*.
- **Part Five**: "Overcoming the 70th Week of Daniel": where we **apply what we've learned** in order to prepare ourselves and the Church for the trials yet to come.

In the next Chapter, we will uncover the *Five "Keys"* that are used to help decipher Revelation.

Chapter Two

UNCOVERING THE "KEYS"

I grew up in the coal-mining region of Pennsylvania. Little wood frame homes were nestled into the valleys of softly rolling hills that we called "mountains." After I saw the Rockies, I realized they were only hills, but without that frame of reference, they sure seemed mountainous to my young eyes. Every Sunday, my family would make the ten-mile trek south on the river to another small coal-mining town where my Grandmother lived. As we left the valley we lived in, we would go through a section known as "The Narrows." After I learned to paddle a canoe, I discovered that the river passed through a tapered gorge at this point and formed some small, class-two rapids. It was a good spot to throw in a fishing line as well.

In the spring of my Seventh Grade year, my Health teacher (the same teacher mentioned in Chapter One: "A Princess, A Dragon, And Spiderman") brought some freshly uncovered Native American *arrowheads* into class. He explained that he found them at "the Narrows." To a thirteen year-old, arrowheads were just about as cool as Civil War memorabilia and classic baseball cards. My teacher informed us that they were building a new shopping center in the Narrows area, and he found the arrowheads in the excavation. He believed there must have been an Indian village there at one time.

That evening I begged my father to take me arrowhead hunting over the weekend. My dad was pretty excited about the idea as well. Bright and early Saturday morning, we were digging through the fresh earth finding spear points and arrowheads galore. The prize of the morning's find, however, was a rock mortar and pestle used for grinding corn. Flush with our success, my dad and I climbed in the car the next Saturday for more treasure hunting, but the buildings' foundations were already poured. Time had covered over the past once again; unfortunately, permanently this time.

After I learned to drive a car, I would frequently steer into the Narrows Shopping Center. I'd sit and think about that Saturday morning with my Dad and what probably still lay beneath the foundations of the buildings. I'd remember: *Wow, when I was a kid we drove by this spot a hundred times on my way to my Grandmother's house, never realizing what treasures laid beneath the surface.* Occasionally, I'd stop at other locations in that area and look around for arrowheads, hoping there was another village I had overlooked. But there was never another treasure-hunting day like that one Saturday.

Bible study can be like that, especially the study of prophecy. Two thousand years of cultural and language differences can cover up the true, ancient meanings just like five centuries of topsoil can cover an ancient Indian village. If we only look at the surface, we tend to view passages of scripture through the lens of our 21st century world and discern what they might mean in our modern culture. But beneath the layers of time lays the languages and culture of an ancient world in which those passages were written. Discovering the true meaning of some passages requires "digging" to uncover what they meant in that ancient society, and sometimes it requires a fellow enthusiast telling you where to look for "arrowheads."

In this Chapter Two: "Uncovering the Keys", we will discover the *Five "Keys"* that are used to help decipher Revelation.

Key # 1: The *First Key to Deciphering Revelation* is that language and cultural differences between the first century and now can obscure the meaning.

Before we begin to look at the next four "Keys," I'm sure some of you are thinking of skipping this Bible interpretation "stuff," and just start by examining something "exciting" like the *Four Horsemen* or the *Beast.* Let me answer that concern. First, there is some very interesting "stuff" to be uncovered in this Chapter. By the time you complete it, you will have discovered a simple but elegant proof of what the true timing of the Rapture will be. This proof has the power to potentially end most "Rapture" controversies. You will have also discovered that the Creation account in Genesis functions as a prophecy of all the years from Adam to the return of Jesus. I promise that

14

you will find this Chapter *interesting*. But the most important reason we examine prophecy interpretation methodologies is that we must see Bible passages the same way the original writer intended us to see them. In order to truly understand the symbolism of the *Four Horsemen*, we must view the passages that John wrote as he would have seen them through his first-century "eyes." Becoming familiar with the "Keys" presented in this Chapter will help us do that. Then, when we reach Chapter Six: "Horse of a Different Color (Rev. 6:1-8,)" the symbolism of the *Four Horsemen* that John intended will spring to life before *your* eyes.

THE REVEALING

Revelation (Gk: APOKALYPSIS) means the "revealing" or the "uncovering." The title comes from the first verse of the book: "The Revelation of Jesus Christ" (Rev. 1:1 NASB). This phrase is in reference to the revealing of Jesus that will occur when he comes on the clouds with great glory and the whole world beholds him. It also refers to the sequence of events that will lead up to that revealing.

To me "the revealing" has a personal meaning as well. Throughout my walk with God, he has slowly but surely revealed the meaning of Revelation to me; layer by layer. I don't consider this a finished work by any means! We are all pilgrims on this walk. God chooses to reveal different things to each of his servants at different times, and complete "revelation" will only come to His Body as a whole when we stand before him and he explains all things. We are all just parts of that Body. My personal uncovering is like my discovery of the Indian Village at the Narrows. I've read passages in Revelation many times overlooking their deeper meaning. Then with a whisper of God's Spirit, my eyes opened and I found "arrowheads."

Revelation was not the first book of the Bible I decided to study. Frankly, it was the last. I was scared to study Revelation as a new Christian. It has a reputation for being, well, "weird." It is littered with strange images of beasts and horsemen, and strewn with language that seems odd. I remember having read Revelation for the very first time. I cracked Revelation open, determined to finish it. By the time I did, I could honestly say that I was confused and didn't understand it at all. It would be years before I'd attempt to read it again.

Ch. 2: Uncovering the "Keys"

Revelation is a difficult book, but by reading it we earn a promise, "Blessed is he who reads and those who hear the words of the prophecy, and heed (Gk: TEROUNTES, meaning "guard") the things which are written in it; for the time is near" (Rev.1:3 NASB). The blessing is extended to those who read, hear and guard the words of prophecy in Revelation. We may struggle with its difficult language and its meaning, but God has promised a blessing to those who persevere and study it. He also blesses those who "guard" its meaning. This book is my humble attempt to *guard* from misunderstanding and misinterpretation what the Holy Spirit has given us. My prayer is that through this writing, the Church will be better equipped to *overcome* the time of testing that is yet to come. That is yet another way we keep or guard its meaning.

Returning to my story about studying Revelation, for all these reasons, I tried to tackle Revelation again. If you've had trouble understanding the book as I did, don't give up. God will help you understand it. For my second reading I decided to utilize a commentary. I can't remember which specific commentary I chose that time (I've consulted dozens and dozens at this point), but at least I finished my study with some sense of the flow of the book and a rudimentary grasp of what it said.

During the years that followed, a wonderful change began to happen within me. At that point, I had spent years studying the Bible, and although I only had a very elementary understanding of Revelation, I was becoming familiar with much of scripture. The next time I tackled Revelation, I began to notice *themes* that I recognized from other books of the Bible. The Old Testament prophets spoke of harlots, beasts, and lampstands; and the landscape of Revelation was packed with these images. That time as I read, I began to check out these references to these same things. Amazingly, the Book of Revelation began to open up to me as the Old Testament references brought the text to light. I realized I had discovered another one of Revelation's "Keys."

I had been misunderstanding the book in the same way many English-speaking Christians not familiar with the Old Testament misunderstand it. I was trying to comprehend it on its own *as an independent book*, when it actually is *a reference book* to what the rest of the Bible has to say about the time before Jesus's return. It is, basically, a book of quotes.

Key # 2: *Sense and Reference* — **One of the "keys" to understanding Revelation is to see it as a compendium of reference quotes, organizing and expanding upon other biblical prophecies.**

The idea that the Holy Spirit has spread "breadcrumbs" (quoted words and phrases) throughout scripture to help us find our way (discover the meaning of passages) is actually a very old and trusted method of Bible interpretation. It was first established as a principal of Jewish scripture interpretation by Hillel the Elder (110 – 10 BC). He called this methodology *gezerah shavah* [iii] or literally "equal laws/equal verdicts." This methodology teaches that a symbol or quoted passage in scripture means the same thing everywhere it is found. It is extremely likely that John was highly aware of this methodology. A modern Bible study discipline known as *"Sense and Reference"* is almost identical. This discipline teaches that every Bible passage has a "sense" which is its obvious meaning upon reading; what the text actually says. The passage may also have a "reference," however, which is another Bible passage(s) that it quotes or refers to that helps expand the meaning. [iv] At that point in my walk, I may not have known the technical terms for these disciplines, but I had discovered them.

This newly found knowledge was at once liberating and daunting. I realized I now had one of the tools I needed to better understand the book of Revelation, but that a thorough knowledge of *all* the other books of the Bible was necessary for me to really uncover it secrets. At that point, I began to appreciate the Psalmist's advice to be a man whose "delight is in the law of the Lord, and in His law he meditates *day and night*" (Psalm 1:2 NASB, emphasis mine). It was going to take night and day study of the scriptures to understand Revelation. Fortunately, this book you are reading has conveniently gathered a number of these references to other scripture passages together to help you begin your own personal understanding. The references are not complete! It is for you to take what this book has begun and add to it.

From this knowledge of the importance of the quotes found in Revelation, I also gained a sense of what separated a good commentary on Revelation from a poor one — did the commentator recognize this aspect of the Book? Did he understand the other scripture references and utilize them in their exegesis (determining meaning *from* the scripture)? Sadly, I can say only a handful of the dozens of commentaries I've utilized recognize this key factor. I highly recommend you consider this "gauge" for yourself when weighing the value of a commentary on Revelation. No matter how well known the author, if they don't have an understanding of this "Key," much of the commentary may just be the author's opinion. Rather than deciphering Revelation, they may be adding to the confusion. They may be commenting while they are "sleeping."

BEGIN AT THE BEGINNING

Before we flip to the last chapters of the Bible and delve into studying the end of the Book (Revelation), let's take a brief moment to look at the beginning of the Book (Genesis). We can't understand the climax of the story unless we understand how the plot developed up until that point. In fact, the history of the world as given to us in God's Word will reveal a great deal about the future of that same world:

> Remember the *former things long past*, for I am God, and there is no other; I am God, and there is no one like me, *declaring the end from the beginning* (Heb: BRESHIT, meaning "in the beginning"), and from ancient times things which have not been done, saying, "My purpose will be established and I will accomplish all My good pleasure." (Isa. 46:9-10 NASB, clarification and emphasis mine)

God expects us to recall *the things long past* because he is going to declare the end of all things from *the beginning*. The Hebrew word BRESHIT which we translate as the title of the opening book of the Bible, "Genesis," is actually the Bible's opening phrase "*in the beginning.*" This is the same Hebrew root word used by Isaiah in the above passage, so it is incumbent on anyone who wants to understand the events that will occur at the end of the time to understand the events that occurred at the beginning of time; *in the beginning.*

Notice I say "events." I believe God's Word is inerrant and without error. It has become "fashionable" for even churchgoers to believe that the accounts in the Old Testament are simply "fairy tales" or at best allegories to explain deeper spiritual truths. These churchgoers don't believe the events described there actually happened as written. They don't believe in a literal six day creation or a literal man named Adam. I do. I trust 2 Tim. 3: 15-17 that states that *all* scripture is "God breathed." I trust Jesus who stated in Luke 16:31 that if someone doesn't trust Moses (who wrote Genesis) and the prophets, he won't trust one who rises from the dead (Jesus himself). In Matt. 23: 35 Jesus also referred to "righteous Abel," who was Adam's son, as a historical figure. The writers of the epistles refer to Adam, Noah, Abraham, and numerous other individuals from Genesis as historical. To not believe in the literal Genesis accounts is to not believe in the validity of the words of Jesus and the Apostles. So I believe. And an amazing thing occurs when you view the Genesis accounts as historical records. You begin to see the greater plan that God has designed for his creation.

DECLARING THE END FROM THE BEGINNING

As we begin to study Genesis, we learn that God created the world and heavens as we know them in six literal days. In the account given to Moses by the Holy Spirit, God is careful to let us know that they were literal days. In Genesis 1:5, 8, 12, 19, 23, and 31 the phrase ". . . there was evening and there was morning, day (one, two, three, etc.)…" appears. This phrase tells us without doubt that God created in *six days* that had an evening and a morning. (Jewish understanding of a "day" is that it begins at sundown not sunrise.) Yes, this contradicts the false teaching of "evolution." It is far beyond the scope of this work to scientifically prove creationism so I refer you to the ministries Answers in Genesis (www.answersingenesis.com) and the Institute for Creation Research (www.icr.org). The resources on these sites will lead you to a full understanding of why we can trust God's Word about creation and why macro-evolution as classically presented is impossible.

Besides contradicting the secular-humanistic theory of evolution, the historical account of creation acts as the very first prophecy in the Bible. Yes, it will amaze you to learn that the creation account is *prophecy* that "declares the end from the beginning." It

19

is known as the *"Great Creation Prophecy."* Details about the first week of history give us particulars about all of human history, and relevant to our purposes in this book, information about the "Tribulation" period to come. Look back carefully at the passage I quoted from Isaiah. It states God declared the end from "the beginning" (Heb.: BRESHIT, meaning "in the beginning"). Literally, God is saying he declared the end from "in the beginning," or from the creation account itself.

We are made in God's image, but he is different than we are. His ways are higher than ours. I think that is one of the major factors why scripture is sometimes hard for us to understand. God said he was declaring the end from "in the beginning" but what did this mean?

We first need to understand how God tells time. As can be expected, it is not the same way we look at time. Let us examine a 2000 year old section of scripture with new eyes:

> Know this first of all, that *in the last days* mockers will come with their mocking, following after their own lusts and saying, "Where is the promise of His coming? For ever since the fathers fell asleep, all continues just as it was from the beginning of creation." For when they maintain this (that Jesus is not returning soon), it escapes their notice *that by the word of God the heavens existed long ago and the earth was formed out of water* … But do not let this one fact escape your notice, beloved, *that with the Lord one day is like a thousand years, and a thousand years like one day.* The Lord is not slow about His promise, as some count slowness, but is patient toward you, not wishing for any to perish but for all to come to repentance. But the day of the Lord will come like a thief. (2 Pet. 3:3-5, 8-10 NASB, clarification and emphasis mine)

This is a section of scripture where the Apostle Peter is clearly instructing us on Jesus' Second Coming. First he shows us how in the *last days* there will be mockers who doubt that the return of Jesus is "right around the corner." These mockers are non-believers and some are believers. A large portion of the church already acts as if Jesus' coming is not close at hand. This includes believers who are living as if they have their whole, normal lifetimes in front of them and pastors who are not preparing their flock for the trials that lie ahead.

Peter then helps us understand why the mockers mock: they don't understand God's way of telling time! The modern Church has focused on the verse that says that God wishes all to come to repentance. This *is* a wonderful picture of God's grace, and we should focus on it. But prior to that verse is the phrase that explains it all. *"One day is like a thousand years."* This is the key to this entire passage, but it has been misunderstood. This is not some general statement like: "God is eternal so long periods of years are like a day to Him." No, this is a specific instruction. *It means when we see the word "day" in the account of creation, it refers to a thousand-year period prophetically!* Notice that prior to this instruction about the thousand-year equivalent, Peter carefully mentions creation, *"by the word of God the heavens existed long ago and the earth was formed out of water."* Why does Peter mention the creation? What does it have to do with the return of Jesus? *The Creation account is mentioned so the reader will understand that the day-equals-a-thousand-years formula is to be inserted into it.* If Peter did not mean for us to insert the formula into the creation account, why did he mention the creation? This is an awesome key to understanding. It helps show us in the scriptures how God tells time.

IS THE CREATION NARRATIVE A PROPHECY?

Now how does Peter want us to apply this principle so we won't be like the mockers who think Jesus is delayed in his coming? God created over six days and on the seventh he rested. Applying the principle of *a day = a thousand years*, God is declaring that *6000 years have been appointed to Satan's dominion over the earth, then on the seventh day we will enter Jesus's thousand-year rest, the millennial kingdom,* where the dominion is returned to Jesus.

This is a pretty radical concept. What does Peter say about it? He confirms it! In verse 5 of the passage in 2 Peter, we find "for when they maintain this (the idea that Jesus is not coming soon) *it escapes their notice that by the word of God the heavens existed long ago and the earth was formed out of water*" (2 Peter 3:5 NASB, clarification mine). Peter validates that the reason that scoffers don't understand when

Jesus will return is that they don't understand *that the creation narrative gives us the approximate timing of the Lord's return*. They don't understand that the principle of *a day = a thousand years* is to *apply prophetically to the creation account.*

In looking at the fall of man, it is interesting how God also used the *day = a thousand years* formula immediately. God spoke to Adam and said, "Of the tree of the knowledge of good and evil you shall not eat, for in the *day* that you eat of it you shall surely die" (Gen. 2:17 NKJV, emphasis mine). Adam lived 930 years as recorded in Genesis 5:5. Thus God was correct, Adam died on the *same day* (same thousand years) that he sinned. Adam died *spiritually* immediately upon consuming the fruit, but God's principle of a thousand years equaling a day fulfilled Adam's *physical* death as well.

THE AGES OF CREATION

In the *Great Creation Prophecy,* God has laid out the history of man into seven 1000-year periods we call *ages.* Into each age, God placed an aspect of his redemptive plan. In this way, the Creation Narrative is also a prophecy foretelling the events in the entire Bible. It also explains why the order of the creative acts don't make sense to a human mind. Theologians have long questioned why plants (which require sunlight) were created on the *third day* before the Sun, Moon and stars, which were created on the *fourth day*[v]. Human logic can't fathom this. Men of faith have simply trusted God's Word as true, and rightly so. But if Jesus had it in mind to order his creative acts in such a way that the narrative of these events would act as a *prophecy*, then of course it makes perfect sense. To me this is yet another proof of Divine influence in the inspiration of scripture. Only a God whose ways are higher than man's could possibly conceive creating an order of creation that seems *illogical* to men, even ancient men, but yet when we finally understand it, the order declares his infinite mind and power. All of creation declares your worth, Lord Jesus. I am in awe of you!

The following table shows the beauty of the *Great Creation Prophecy*, and how the creative events foretell God's redemptive plan in each of these ages (one thousand years). As you study this table, please notice how the creation events exactly match the major redemption event in God's great plan. The "Years from Creation" column is based on the genealogies from the book of Genesis and later from other Old Testament books. A reference that mathematically calculates these "days from creation" is *The Time of The End* by Tim Warner (Thomas Nelson, Inc. 2012). A second reference that also mathematically calculates the days from creation is *Ezekiel 4: The Master Key to Unlock the Bible's Chronology* by Yves Peloquin (Unpublished 2004)[vi]. Although these chronologies were independently calculated without knowledge of the other, both agree that Jesus was crucified at the same point (3993 years after creation.) God has *very* carefully recorded these years through the bloodline of his Messiah, Jesus.

This table shown below [Figure 1: *Great Creation Prophecy* (Days of Creation Related to the Chronology of the Earth)] allows us to see a beautiful picture of God's plan with every thousand-year period exactly matching its day in creation. Not surprisingly, the Biblical genealogies and time lines add up to six thousand years just as *the Great Creation Prophecy* predicts.

Day of Creation	Creation Event	Major Redemption Event	Years from Creation
1	Light and Darkness	Knowledge of Good and Evil	0- 1000
2	Separation of Waters	The Flood	1000 – 2000
3	Separation of Dry Land, Creation of Plants and Trees	Exodus and Creation of the Nation of Israel	2000 – 3000
4	Sun and Moon	Jesus and the Church	3000 – 4000
5	Birds and Fish Multiply	Multiplication of God's People into Jews and Christians	4000 – 5000
6	Land Creatures and Man	Dominion of Man over Creation, Tribulation	5000 – 6000
7	God Rested	Millennial Kingdom	6000 – 7000

Figure 1: The Great Creation Prophecy

Let's take a brief moment to look at the beauty of this prophecy. It is truly amazing. Frankly, it is beyond human comprehension. The symbols are stunning that God used in the creation story to represent the major works of redemption he was to do.

On the *first day*, God separated light from darkness. In scripture, light signifies good and darkness evil. During that first thousand-year period of man's history, the fall of man occurred and Adam and Eve came to know good and evil. Light and dark were separated.

During the *second day*, God separated the waters beneath from the waters above. During the second thousand-year period on earth, God caused the waters above and below to come crashing down in a worldwide flood when the floodgates of the deep were opened and rain fell for forty days and nights.

On the *third day*, God separated the waters and created land, plants, and trees. During the third thousand-year period God separated the waters of the Red Sea and created dry ground so the Israelites could cross during the Exodus. He also created their nation when he brought them into the Promised Land. In my first book, *Are We Ready for Jesus?* (Seraphina Press, 2015), we learned that God's symbol for the nation of Israel is the *fig tree*. In Luke 21:29, Jesus refers to Israel as the fig tree and also mentions "all the trees." God's symbol for each nation is a tree. God created trees on the *third day* of creation, and planted the nation Israel in the Promised Land during the third thousand years.

On the *fourth day*, God created the lights in the sky. The sun represents Jesus and the moon, who reflects the light of the sun, is his bride, the Church. Each of us individually "shine like the stars in the world" (Phil. 2:15). Four thousand years from the creation event, Jesus came to dwell among his people and the Church was born.

On the *fifth day*, God multiplied the fish of the sea and the birds of the air. These symbols are a bit more obtuse. In the ancient *Mazzaroth* (the Hebrew name for the constellations of the Zodiac), Pisces, the fish, symbolizes the nation of Israel, divided into two kingdoms, Israel and Judah. Although far beyond the scope of this book, the *Mazzaroth* constellations detail *in order* God's redemptive plan for creation. A great resource on this topic is *The Mystery of the Mazzaroth — Prophecy in the Constellations* by Tim Warner (Thomas Nelson, Inc., 2013). I highly recommend this book.

Returning to the Creation Prophecy, birds fly on wings like eagles which are a picture of the Holy Spirit from Isaiah 40:31. During the first thousand-year period after the death of Jesus (related to the *fifth day* of creation), God's people were now divided into two groups, Christians who had the Holy Spirit represented by the birds and the Jews represented by the fish. God multiplied them both.

THE DOMINION OF MAN

Finally, we come to the *sixth day*. God says:

> So God created man in His own image; in the image of God He created him; male and female He created them. Then God blessed them, and God said to them, "Be fruitful and multiply; fill the earth and *subdue it; have dominion* over the fish of the sea, over the birds of the air, and over every living thing that moves on the earth." (Genesis 1:27-28 NKJV, emphasis mine)

This is such a perfect picture of what man has been able to do in the last thousand years. Man has *subdued* the earth as never before with automobiles, planes, nuclear power, television, and computers. It is also a picture of what the Antichrist will do. He will *subdue* the earth and have *dominion* over it; at least for a short period.

Finally on the *seventh day*, the seventh age of a thousand-years duration, we will enter God's rest. In Hebrews 4:8-9 (NASB) it says, "For if Joshua had given them rest, He would not have spoken of another *day* after that. So there remains a Sabbath rest for the people of God." Notice how the writer of Hebrews says "another *day*." God's Word is so specific and consistent. A day equals a thousand years prophetically. The Millennial Kingdom, the coming Sabbath rest alluded to, will be a thousand-years long.

If you were not aware of this great prophecy, I am sure you are as amazed as I was when I became aware of it. It is no wonder that Satan would want to do everything in his power to obstruct this message from getting out. With this in mind, he schemed up the *theory of evolution* with its assumed long ages of millions and billions of years. This evil theory not only attempts to deny Jesus' creative power, but also attempts to obscure this wonderful prophecy.

If we are going to decipher Revelation we need to know where the events in that book fall in regard to God's overall plan of redemption. This prophecy helps us put God's plan and the Book of Revelation in perspective.

CHARACTERS IN THE STORY

God declared the end (Revelation) from the Beginning (from Genesis), and the characters and accounts found there are foundational for what will happen at the end. I highly recommend you re-read Genesis before continuing on with this book to recall these characters and their history.

If we don't fully understand the fall of Adam, we won't understand that God originally gave him dominion over the earth; a dominion that Satan tricked him out of. Not understanding this essential truth will make it difficult to comprehend the *7 Sealed Scroll* that Jesus opens in Revelation. If we don't understand Noah, we won't fully appreciate Jesus's statement that his coming and the rapture of the church and his Wrath will be like the days of Noah. If we don't understand Lot, we won't see the connection that Jesus plainly made between the days of Lot and the pouring out of his wrath upon the earth in Revelation. If we don't understand Jacob and Esau, we won't see the link between this account and what is known as the *"Time of Jacob's Trouble."* We also won't realize why the second horseman of Revelation rides a "fiery red" horse. God truly has declared the end from the Book of Genesis. It is an important link that we all must understand.

Throughout this book, you will see us make reference to the *"Law of Primacy."*[vii] This is a law of biblical interpretation that states the first use of a symbol in the Bible is what that symbol will mean in all of its future uses. Most of these symbols occur in Genesis. This is yet another way that God has declared the end from the beginning.

Key # 3: God declared the end (Revelation) from the beginning (Genesis) — Another "key" to understanding the Book of Revelation is that Genesis will help explain many of the metaphors and symbols.

BROTHERS

The accounts of two sets of brothers found in Genesis are immensely critical to understanding the Time of the End, and "why" events will unfold the way they will. The first set of these brothers is Ishmael and Isaac (sons of Abraham). The second set of twin brothers is Esau and Jacob (sons of Isaac).

Isaac and Jacob carried the promises made to Abraham. Ishmael and Esau, who were both the older brothers, lost their birthrights and their inheritances. The current conflict in the Middle East is a result of the ancestors of these four men struggling over the lost blessings and inheritance. The events foretold in Revelation that will take place are the final chapter in this 4000-year old struggle. The prophecies analyzed in this book reflect that struggle as well. We must understand it to understand the prophecies.

The first set of these brothers was Ishmael and Isaac; and Abraham was the father of both boys. God had promised to make Abraham's descendants as numerous as the stars in the sky. God's timetable for blessing Abraham with a son took a lot longer than Abraham had expected, so he and his wife Sarah took matters into their own hands. Sarah asked Abraham to impregnate her maid servant, Hagar, so as to provide a son. As soon as Hagar conceived, a jealousy developed between her and Sarah, an animosity that would continue throughout the rest of their relationship. When Abraham was 86 years old, Hagar bore him a son whom the Angel of the Lord told her to name Ishmael. This was God's prophecy about him:

> He will be a *wild donkey of a man*, his hand will be against everyone, and everyone's hand will be against him. (Gen. 16:12 NASB, emphasis mine)

When Ishmael was fourteen years old, Sarah finally bore the son of God's promise to Abraham, Isaac. After the birth of Isaac, the old jealousy between Sarah and Hagar rose up again. Their sons carried on this feud:

> Now Sarah saw the son of Hagar the Egyptian, whom she had borne to Abraham, *mocking*. Therefore she said to Abraham, "Drive out this maid and

her son, for the son of this maid shall not be an heir with my son Isaac." (Gen. 21:9-10 NASB, emphasis mine)

At the Lord's command, Abraham listened to Sarah and drove Hagar and Ishmael from their home. Ishmael was fourteen. Only a year earlier, he had been the heir, imagining a great future for himself. Now, after being driven away by his father, both he and his mother were homeless.

A similar loss of inheritance occurred in the very next generation. Isaac had two twin sons, Jacob and Esau. Esau foolishly sold his birthright to Jacob for a pot of stew. Later, Jacob, the younger brother, tricked Isaac into passing the Abrahamic blessing to him rather than Esau. This was within God's providence and election. Esau was so mad he threatened to kill Jacob. This is a grudge that the descendants of Esau hold to this day in the Middle East. Interestingly, Esau married the daughter of Ishmael (Gen. 28:9) and the bloodlines of the two disinherited and bitter brothers were forever joined.

We will learn considerably more about Esau in Chapter Seven: "A Horse of a Different Color (Revelation 6:1-8)." Suffice it to say at this point, however, that the loss of inheritance (the Land of Israel) has created an animosity between the descendants of Ishmael and Esau (the Islamic peoples) and the descendants of Jacob (the Jews). All the future events foretold in Revelation describe how this animosity will play out in the Time of the End.

THE *SEPTUAGINT*

Yet another key to my understanding of Revelation came as I dutifully studied many of the scripture references found in the Old Testament. Many of them didn't exactly match quoted passages in Revelation. I thought that odd. Why didn't New Testament quotes of the Old Testament say the same thing when I referenced the passage *in the same Bible*? Were the New Testament writers using a different set of scriptures than I was?

The shocking answer is that they were! They were primarily quoting from the *Septuagint* Old Testament. The New Testament is written in Koine (or common) Greek[viii]. Nearly all of our current English Bibles, the NASB, the NIV, the ESV, etc., utilize a *Hebrew text* in translating the Old Testament. The Septuagint[ix] is the *Greek translation* of the Old Testament and uses the same Koine Greek as the New Testament. This is a key understanding. Legend has it that in the third century BC, Ptolemy II of Egypt had the Hebrew text of the scriptures translated into Greek by seventy Hebrew scholars so his Alexandrian Jewish residents, who were more familiar with Greek than Hebrew, could read the Bible. The name *Septuagint* comes from "seventy" and the abbreviation of this translation (LXX) also means seventy in reference to the seventy scholars.

The burning question is: Which is more accurate, the Greek text or the Hebrew? Without question, the early Christians utilized the Greek *Septuagint* text. Only five New Testament quotes of the Old Testament are considered to come from the Hebrew Scriptures[x], and all of the Old Testament quotes from Revelation are thought to come from the *Septuagint*. This clearly shows that the Apostles who wrote the New Testament books felt that the *Septuagint* was also the inspired Word of God, and as they wrote their New Testament Books in Greek, they invariably used the *Septuagint* as their reference source for Old Testament passages.

Another question may be popping into you mind, "Weren't the writers of the New Testament all Jews, and wouldn't they be using Hebrew Old Testament texts?" Most of the writers were Jews and most had memorized much of the Hebrew Old Testament Scriptures. Unfortunately, the Hebrew manuscripts of those days no longer exist today! A leader of the early Church, Irenaeus, was bold enough to claim that the Hebrew texts of his era (second century) were "manipulated" by the Jews to make them "less Christ-like."[xi] The surviving Hebrew manuscripts we use for our current English translation Bibles date to approximately AD 1000 while surviving *Septuagint* manuscripts date to approximately 200 BC. These factors in combination with the similarities of the LXX with newly discovered and translated Dead Sea Scrolls[xii], leads me to believe they are no less accurate than the Hebrew texts we are all familiar with. They *may even be more accurate* in some instances. Using and comparing *both* Hebrew and Greek texts is suggested. In this book, we utilize both translations of the Hebrew text (NASB and NIV) and the Greek text (LXX).

What is of *greatest* interest in Bible study, however, is the use of the *Septuagint* in word studies. Greek words found in the New Testament cannot really be compared with the Hebrew words of the Old Testament. That is, unless we use the *Septuagint* as our Old Testament source. *By using the Septuagint, we can compare Greek words and phrases from the New Testament to the Old and vice versa.* This is of incredible value if we study a book like Revelation that has hundreds of Old Testament references.

Key # 4: Old Testament text — Another "key' to understanding Revelation is that Old Testament quotes within Revelation are from the Greek *Septuagint*, not our standard Hebrew Translations.

A Proper Theology of the Time of the End

Personally, I don't like the term, "The Tribulation." I prefer "The *70th Week of Daniel.*" The term "The Tribulation" isn't used in the Bible to describe that period. The seven-year time period immediately before the physical return of Jesus is properly called the *70th Week of Daniel*, which is derived from a passage in Daniel 9. For those not familiar with this term, it is a seven-year period set aside by God. It is called a "Week" because the Bible on occasion measures time in seven-year increments called "shabua" that mimic the six days of work and a Sabbat, comprising a week. In ancient Hebrew culture, God commanded Israel to cultivate the land for six years and then allow their land to remain fallow in the seventh year (Lev. 25:3-4, 8), just as work was not permitted on the Sabbath. This seventh year of the seven-year cycle is called the *Shemitah*. In Daniel Chapter 9, the Angel Gabriel told Daniel:

Seventy weeks (SHABUA) have been decreed for your people and your holy city, to finish the transgression, to make an end of sin, to make atonement for iniquity, to bring in everlasting righteousness, to seal up vision and prophecy and to anoint the most holy place. (Dan. 9:24 NASB, clarification mine)

This famous passage indicates that God has ordained 70 *shabua* for the Jews and Jerusalem. A reasonable question to ask at this point is: *If the 70th Week of Daniel was ordained for the Jews, what does it have to do with Christians?* This is a legitimate question. Let me answer that question with another question. In Jeremiah 31:31, God states that he will make the New Covenant with the house of Israel and the house of Judah (the Jews). Is the New Covenant not to apply to Christians because it was specifically made with the Jews? No, of course it is to apply to Christians as well because they have been "grafted in" to the roots of Israel (Rom. 11:17-24). If Christians have been grafted into the New Covenant, isn't it logical they have been grafted into the 70th Week as well? The Church was a mystery in the days of Daniel when this prophecy was given. The angel not mentioning the Church in no way means this prophecy is also not for the Christians as well as Jews.

Returning to the prophecy of the 70 Weeks, we see that at its completion almost all prophecy will be completed, all sin will be atoned for, and an ever-lasting righteousness will be obtained for those who are in Jesus. This will be fulfilled upon the Second Coming of the Lord. During his earthly ministry, Jesus indicated to us that this period of 70 Shabua (70 Weeks which is *seventy times seven* years = 490 years) is a time period during which forgiveness will be granted:

> Then Peter came and said to Him, "Lord, how often shall my brother sin against me and I forgive him? Up to seven times?" Jesus said to him, "I do not say to you, up to seven times, but up to *seventy times seven*." (Matt 18: 21-22 NASB, emphasis mine.)

After this period of *seventy times seven* years, the judgment of God will have come upon the unrepentant, right before the end of that period.

The passage in Dan. 9 indicates that 69 of these shabua have already occurred. This period began with the decree to rebuild Jerusalem, following the Babylonian destruction. There is some controversy among commentators about the exact events that frame the *beginning* of this time period. Some say the period started with King Cyrus's decree in Isaiah 44:28, others say a later Persian king's decree started the period, while still others claim that the period does not begin with a decree, but rather with the actual construction that the decree authorized.

Some say the 69 shabua ended with the baptism of Jesus by John the Baptist, with his anointing by the Holy Spirit descending as a dove. Others say it ended with Jesus's entry into Jerusalem seated on a donkey, while still others state that the 69 weeks ended with Jesus' announcement in Matt. 23:37-39, "I shall go and return unto My place" (Hosea 5:15), which was six months before the crucifixion. Regardless of which measurement proves correct, one "week" still remains. That final shabua, the *70th Week of Daniel*, is pictured in these verses:

> The people of the prince who is to come will destroy the city and the sanctuary. And its end will come with a flood; even to the end there will be war; desolations are determined. And he will make a firm covenant with the many for *one week*, but *in the middle of the week* he will put a stop to sacrifice and grain offering; and on the wing of abominations will come one who makes desolate, even until a complete destruction, one that is decreed, is poured out on the one who makes desolate. (Dan. 9:26-27 NASB, emphasis mine)

Most Bible commentators believe this seven-year period is marked by two halves separated by a *Midpoint.* Each half of the period will be 3 ½ years long. The first half was called "*The Beginning of the Birth Pangs*" by Jesus (Matt. 24:8). Many commentators call the second half of the period the "*Great Tribulation*" (Matt. 24:21), however, Jesus never called the second half the "*Great Tribulation*;" he only stated that after the *Midpoint* there would *be* "great tribulation." In my opinion, the Rapture truncates the *Great Tribulation*, as it is "cut short" for believers. In Luke 21:24, Jesus actually named the second half of Daniel's 70th Week "*the Times of the Gentiles*." We will discuss this time period ("*the Times of the Gentiles*") and why it specifically applies to the second half of Daniel's 70th Week in much greater detail in Chapter Eleven: "Event Four: Abomination and Death."

At the *Midpoint* that separates the two halves, several important events occur. The man who is known as the Antichrist is revealed by him sitting in the newly constructed Temple of God in Jerusalem (2 Thess. 2:3-4). He will also set up an idol known as the *Abomination of Desolation* within the Temple (Matt. 24:15). Immediately after these *Midpoint* events, the Antichrist begins the greatest period of persecution the world has ever known — the *Great Tribulation*. At the end of the *Great Tribulation*, Jesus returns to resurrect the righteous and delivers his Church at the Rapture. He will later redeem and save the Jews who repent and judge the Antichrist and the False Prophet at an event known as the physical Second Coming (the term "Second Coming" is used to refer to both the Rapture and the physical coming of Jesus to earth with his Church). A graphic of these events follows (Figure 2: The 70th Week of Daniel):

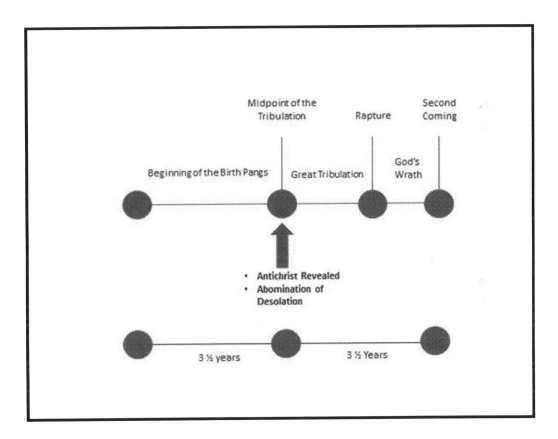

Figure 2: The 70th Week of Daniel

We will explain all these events in significantly more detail in subsequent Chapters.

PROOF OF RAPTURE TIMING

"Figure 2: the *70th Week of Daniel*" has probably prompted a question: *Why do you have the rapture pictured as occurring at the end of the Great Tribulation? I thought the Church was raptured prior to the 70th Week of Daniel even starting.* Statistics show that over 61% of American Christian leaders believe in a Rapture, which means a "catching away" of believers by Jesus and His Holy Angels into the air.[xiii] (I also believe in the Rapture, which is a biblical teaching). Of that number, the overwhelming majority believe it will occur *prior* to the *70th Week of Daniel*. We call this a *Pre-Tribulation Rapture*. So, it is likely you may hold this belief (I do not). A minority of Christians believe that the Rapture occurs on the very last day of the 70th Week. We call that a *Post-Tribulation Rapture*. (I do not hold this view either.) It is far beyond the scope of this book to discuss this topic in any depth at this point. I do recommend my book, *Rapture Debate Over? – Stunning New Biblical Evidence*, which may be the most complete biblical treatment of this topic.

This commentary does, however, present *proof after proof after proof* of proper rapture timing as they relate to the scripture text being discussed at that point in the book. There are more than a dozen proofs throughout this book that the rapture occurs as it is pictured in "Figure 2: the *70th Week of Daniel*." If you want to learn more about why it is likely that the Rapture occurs *during* the *70th Week of Daniel* and not before it (nor at its *Midpoint* or at its completion), please consult these other wonderful books, which I highly recommend:

- *Antichrist Before the Day of the Lord* by Alan Kurschner (Eschatos Publishing, 2013; 238 pages);
- *Prewrath: A Very Short Introduction* by Alan Kurschner (Eschatos Publishing, 2014; 119 pages);
- *The Rapture Question Answered — Plain & Simple* by Robert Van Kampen (Fleming H. Revell, 1997; 211 pages);
- *The Pre-Wrath Rapture of the Church* by Marvin Rosenthal (Thomas Nelson, 1990; 320 pages);

- *The Last Shofar!* by Joseph Lenard and Donald Zoller (Xulon Press, 2014; 319 pages);
- *Are We Ready For Jesus?* by Nelson Walters (Seraphina Press, 2015; 200 pages); particularly Chapter 5 (38 pages).

I am sure you are sitting there stunned and amazed. I realize a *Pre-Tribulation Rapture* is one of the most highly-treasured, popular beliefs in the Church today; highly treasured, taught by many respected Bible teachers and theologians, yet completely inaccurate and dangerous. If you have been taught this belief and hold to it, please do not be "put off" and lay this book aside! We are looking at new insights.

To believe that you will avoid the *70ᵗʰ Week of Daniel* is to not prepare for it. If you don't prepare, you may not "overcome" and may be subject to deception and apostasy. In addition, the belief that everything will just "pan out" will also not be sufficient for you to prepare for these times. (One of the stated purposes of this book is to help believers "overcome" the *70ᵗʰ Week of Daniel*.) Please, stay with us for the full presentation of this book. Your very life might depend on it.

Note: Because of the hidden danger of a *Pre-Tribulation Rapture* position, unless it can be proven without doubt to be 100% accurate and accepted without question, all believers should be taught how to prepare to overcome during the 70ᵗʰ Week.

If you assume a *Pre-Tribulation* or a *Post-Tribulation* timing for the Rapture, *you will also not be able to properly decipher Revelation*. This is a major factor in why so few commentaries on Revelation are accurate. If you try to superimpose a false doctrine like the *Pre-Tribulation or Post-Tribulation Rapture* on a Book of the Bible you will misinterpret it. This is a serious problem. If you do that with Revelation, it will seem a most confusing hodgepodge of non-sequential, random prophecies. I know as I used to believe the false doctrine of the *Pre-Tribulation Rapture*.

The purpose of this book is to decipher Revelation, it does *not* present a comprehensive explanation of proofs that the Rapture does in fact occur during the

Sixth Year of the 70th Week and not prior to the 70th Week beginning or concluding.

I also realize that many of the readers of this book may not be able or willing to set this book aside and undertake a comprehensive examination of Rapture timing. With that in mind, in the next Chapter I will present you with a short but elegant proof that disproves both the *Pre-Tribulation* and *Post-Tribulation* theories of Rapture timing! For some, this might be the single most important insight in this entire book.

SUMMARY

The following graphic (Figure 3: Five Keys to Deciphering Revelation) illustrates the *"Five Keys"* that are the five wheels on the "Enigma typewriter" in my brain that I use to help me decipher New Testament texts.

Keys	Explanation
1) Language and cultural differences between the first and twenty-first centuries must be uncovered	John's cultural background of Jewish idioms and customs influence the text of Revelation
2) Sense and Reference	Revelation is a book of reference quotes that guide us to Old Testament passages, organizing and expanding on them.
3) God declared the end (Revelation) from the beginning (Genesis)	Genesis provides a foundation of symbolic and metaphorical material to understand Revelation.
4) Old Testament text	John used the *Septuagint* Old Testament for his reference quotes. We should use the *Septuagint* for most word studies and references.
5) Understanding of the 70th Week of Daniel and the Rapture	A proper theology of the 70th Week of Daniel and the Rapture is necessary to properly understand Revelation

Figure 3: Five Keys to Deciphering Revelation

Chapter Three

A TREASURE MAP
(THE *PATTERN OF SEVEN EVENTS*)

In my first formative years as a believer, I sat under the teaching of a wise older, pastor who had the saying, "the *main thing* is to keep the *main thing* the *main thing*." In other words, concentrate on what is most important. Understanding Revelation requires the same emphasis. Once we understand the *main thing*, this confusing book populated by beasts and colored horses comes into sharp focus.

In order to do just that (focus on the *main thing*), we are going to begin our study of Revelation in a most unorthodox way; by studying Rev. 6 and Matt. 24!! Practically every other commentary on Revelation begins with Rev. 1:1 and precedes from there. That would be true for this commentary as well if we didn't have a "treasure map." If you have a map of where the treasure is buried, you always begin there.

The novel *Treasure Island* by Robert Louis Stevenson popularized the concept of a treasure map with a ubiquitous "X marks the spot" over the treasure's location. The discovery of the map by young hero, Jim Hawkins, in an old captain's sea chest, sets the plot in motion. Greed overcomes the villagers and pirates as they all seek the fortune "under the X." The treasure map was the *main thing* in the novel, *Treasure Island*.

Is there a "map" of Revelation with a clearly marked "X" that helps us interpret the Book? Will this *main thing* lead us to a vast spiritual treasure? The answers are "yes" and "yes." The *main thing* is the *Pattern of Seven Events*. You may be unaware of this pattern, but once you discover it, all end time prophetic passages "open up" and their meanings and chronology can be understood. It is a treasure map of infinite worth.

JESUS GAVE US THE *PATTERN*

If the treasure map of the end times and Revelation is the main thing, then doesn't it make sense that Jesus himself should deliver it to us! And he did. Something of great value has lain hidden in the middle of one of the most famous end-time passages in the Bible. For millennia, Christians have passed over this treasure map and missed it. The setting was so familiar it was passed right over — literally, hidden in plain sight. Since it is only logical that Jesus himself would provide his Church with this map, it only makes sense that it would be found in Jesus's great teaching on end-times: the *Olivet Discourse* (Matt. 24-25, Mark 13, and Luke 21).

At this moment, I am sure that every proponent of the *Pre-Tribulation Rapture* is taking exception to my claim that the treasure map is found in the *Olivet Discourse*. If you are not aware, *Pre-Tribulation Rapture* advocates claim that the *Olivet Discourse* in Matt. 24 was given only for the Jews. They have constructed an elaborate set of evidences to confirm this. We will discuss these evidences later in the book. At this point, however, we do not need to evaluate the validity of these claims. The treasure map presented in this Chapter is totally *independent* of the intended audience of the *Olivet Discourse*. It is even valid if the audience *was* exclusively meant to be the Jews!

The fact that it's found in the *Olivet Discourse*, however, is pertinent. Because *Pre-Tribulation Rapture* theorists have discounted the *Discourse* as relevant for the Church, it has lain under-examined for decades. Imagine that you are listening to Jesus's words for the very first time without the layers of baggage that endless end time arguments have created. After you have heard the argument with fresh ears, only then do I ask you to re-engage your mind to explore it and contest it.

THE OLIVET DISCOURSE — A SPRING AFTERNOON

Let us first set the context for Jesus's sermon on end-times: the *Olivet Discourse* (Matt. 24-25, Mark 13, Luke 21). Jesus gave this sermon on one of the last afternoons before he was betrayed. He had just had a heated exchange with the established Jewish leaders in Jerusalem. As our Lord and his disciples left the temple area, the disciples were stunned by the interchange they had just witnessed. They tried to break the tension by commenting on the majestic temple architecture, but Jesus rebuffed them by saying that soon not one of those magnificent stones would stand upon another.

On their way back to their "camp" on the Mount of Olives, Jesus' disciples tried to put the day's events in perspective. After his triumphant entry on Palm Sunday, they had expected Jesus to be recognized as Messiah and king. Now everything was falling apart. Jesus and the leaders of the nation had just had a knock-down war-of-words from which there was no going back. Not only that, Jesus had just prophesied that the temple where the Messiah would someday sit as king would soon be destroyed. How could Jesus be crowned king after that day's events? Their vision of the future had just been smashed into a million pieces like Jesus' prophecy about the temple stones.

I can imagine Jesus' closest disciples whispering under their breath, "If Jesus isn't going to become king, what will happen to us?" They finally got up the nerve to ask their master about the future. Jesus responded with the *Olivet Discourse*, an amazing prophetic sermon about his return (Second Coming). It began with the simple question that was quoted at the beginning of this Chapter:

> As he was sitting on the Mount of Olives, the disciples came to Him privately, saying, 'Tell us, *when will these things happen, and what will be the sign of your coming, and of the end of the age?*'"(Matt. 24:3 NASB, emphasis mine)

The disciples question was the same as ours is today, "When will these things happen?" Jesus wants his listeners to understand the timing of events. He went into great detail about the signs that would precede his return. That return is pictured dramatically at the climax of the *Discourse*:

> The sign of the Son of Man will appear in the sky, and then all the tribes of the earth will mourn, and *they will see the Son of Man coming on the clouds of the sky with power and great glory.* And He will send forth His angels with a great trumpet and they will gather together His elect from the four winds, from one end of the sky to the other. (Matt. 24:30-31 NASB, emphasis mine)

This is the "X that marks the spot;" the return of our Savior and King.

SIGNS OF HIS RETURN

The *Olivet Discourse* (in Matt. 24) is organized as *a series of signs* that precede the return of Jesus (Matt. 24:30-31). Pictorially, this might look like the following graphic (Figure 4: "The Olivet Discourse"):

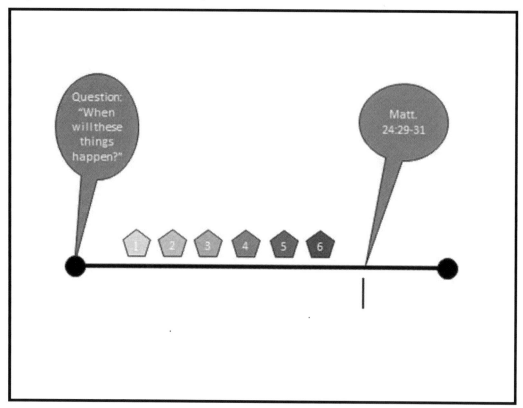

Figure 4: The Olivet Discourse

The Discourse begins with the disciples' question, "When will these things happen and what will be the sign of your coming?" It ends with the event depicted in Matt. 24:30-31, the of Jesus. In between are *six signs* that Jesus gives to his disciples that precede his return. These signs were given in direct response to the question they asked about what would be the sign of his coming. They asked for one sign, Jesus gave them six.

These six prophetic events are listed below (Figure 5: "*Six Signs* in the Olivet Discourse"):

Sign	Description	Reference (Matt. 24)	Additional Clarification References
1	Deception by False Messiahs	vv. 4-5	vv. 23-26
2	Wars and Chaos	vv. 6-7	
3	Famine and Economic Collapse	v. 7	
4	Abomination and Death	vv. 9	vv. 15-21
5	Martyrdom and Apostasy	vv. 9-12	
6	Celestial Signs	v. 29	

Figure 5 Six Signs in the Olivet Discourse

These *six signs* are represented by the six numbered pentagonal boxes in Figure 4: "The Olivet Discourse." When viewed in this manner, the organization of the Olivet Discourse jumps to life. Jesus gave his disciples the first five signs in exact order in Matt. 24:4-12. He then expounded on two of these signs in Matt. 24:15-26, and then he gave the final sign in Matt. 24:29. After this series of six signs, Jesus described his return to the disciples in Matt. 24:30-31.

In combination these six signs plus the return of Jesus *are* the *Pattern of Seven Events.*

The six signs are not unique to Matt. 24. This assessment may be new to you, but Bible commentators have long been aware of the amazing parallel between Matt. 24 and the first six *Seals* of Rev. 6. Both *Pre-Tribulation Rapture* and *Post-Tribulation Rapture* proponents seem to agree on the comparison.

In his commentary on Revelation, *Pre-Tribulation Rapture* supporter John Walvoord along with his editors Mark Hitchcock, and Phillip Rawley state, "There is a remarkable parallel between the progress of chapter 6 (Revelation) as a whole and the description given by our Lord of the end of the age in Matthew 24:4–31"[xiv]. Other *Pre-Tribulation Rapture* supporters Andreas J. Köstenberger, L. Scott Kellum, and Charles L Quarles present an impressive table showing the exact mirror image between prophecies of the *Seals* of Rev. 6 and the *Olivet Discourse* on page 834 of their classic book *The Cradle, the Cross, and the Crown* (B&H Academic, Nashville, 2009)[xv]. Ron Bigalke of the Pre-Trib. Research Center also supports this view[xvi], and in a recent debate, Thomas Ice, Director of the Pre-Trib. Research Center, confirms that the signs in Matt. 24 are equivalent to the Six Seals in Rev. 6[xvii].

Post-Tribulation Rapture supporter William Jack Kelley also points out the amazing parallels of the six signs in Matt. 24 to the Six Seals in Rev. 6 in his book *Shadow of Things to Come* (Westbow Press, Bloomington, 2013)[xviii]. Another *Post-Tribulation Rapture* exponent, David Berg, acknowledges this link as well[xix]. The academic and theological community is mostly unified in its acceptance of this comparison. The following graphic (Figure 6: "*Six Signs* in Matt. 24 and Rev. 6") summarizes these comparisons.

Sign	Description	Reference (Matt. 24)	Additional Clarification References	(Rev. 6)
1	Deception by False Messiahs	vv. 4-5	vv. 23-26	vv. 1-2
2	Wars and Chaos	vv. 6-7		vv. 3-4
3	Famine and Economic Collapse	v. 7		vv. 5-6
4	Abomination and Death	vv. 9	vv. 15-21	vv. 7-8
5	Martyrdom and Apostasy	vv. 9-12		vv. 9-11
6	Celestial Signs	v. 29		vv. 12-17

Figure 6: Six Signs in Matt. 24 and Rev. 6

Because there is perfect parallelism with the first six events found in Matt. 24 and Rev.6, it is our hypothesis that there will be perfect congruence with the seventh event as well. We will prove that hypothesis shortly, but for now, let's examine the other versions of the Olivet Discourse found in Mark and Luke to see if they also contain this *Pattern.*

Sign	Description	Matt. 24	Rev. 6	Mark 13	Luke 21
1	Deception by False Messiahs	vv. 4-5, 23-26	vv. 1-2	vv. 5-6, 21-23	v. 8
2	Wars and Chaos	vv. 6-7	vv. 3-4	vv. 7-8	vv. 10-11
3	Famine and Economic Collapse	v. 7	vv. 5-6	v. 8	v. 11
4	Abomination and Death	vv. 9, 15-21	vv. 7-8	vv. 13-20	vv. 17, 20-24
5	Martyrdom and Apostasy	vv. 9-12	vv. 9-11	vv. 9-13	vv. 12-19
6	Celestial Signs	v. 29	vv. 12-17	vv. 24-25	vv. 25-26

Figure 7: The First Six Events

Examining this table of the same six, parallel events in the exact chronology in four separate books of the Bible establishes the first six events as a *Pattern*. And as we have already seen, the eschatological community agrees. The only question that remains is whether there is a seventh event in the *Pattern*: the *Pattern of Seven Events*.

In Chapter One: "A Dragon, a Princess, and Spiderman," we theorized that this seventh event would be *Rapture and Wrath*. This is *highly* controversial. Those who

44

believe in a *Pre-Tribulation Rapture* imagine the *Wrath of God* to begin at the *First Seal* of Revelation and the Rapture to occur before this. *Post-Tribulation Rapture* enthusiasts imagine the Rapture will occur at the very end of Daniel's 70th Week. Only a tiny minority of Christians imagine a *Seventh Event* of *Rapture and Wrath* occurring soon after the *Sixth Event*, the *Sixth Seal*. But what others believe is not as important as what scripture teaches. Only the Word of God has the authority to decide this issue. If we *are* able to resolve this issue we will determine the timing of the Rapture (one of Christianity's most contentious issues) and will also establish the *Pattern of Seven Events*. We will have our "treasure map" to all of the end times and Revelation.

THE SEVENTH EVENT

Let us recall the return of Jesus pictured in the *Discourse*:

> The sign of the Son of Man will appear in the sky, and then all the tribes of the earth will mourn, and *they will see the Son of Man coming on the clouds of the sky with power and great glory*. And He will send forth His angels with a great trumpet and they will gather together His elect from the four winds, from one end of the sky to the other. (Matt. 24:30-31 NASB, emphasis mine)

This event is believed to be the physical Second Coming of Jesus by 96% of the Church. Both the *Pre-Tribulation Rapture* and the *Post-Tribulation Rapture* camps believe that. They believe the same events are also depicted in Revelation in the following passage:

> I saw heaven opened, and behold, a white horse, and He who sat on it is called Faithful and True, and in righteousness He judges and wages war. His eyes are a flame of fire, and on His head are many diadems; and He has a name written on Him which no one knows except Himself. He is clothed with a robe dipped in blood, and His name is called The Word of God. And *the armies which are in heaven, clothed in fine linen, white and clean were following Him on white horses*. From His mouth comes a sharp sword, so

that with it He may strike down the nations, and He will rule them with a rod of iron; and He treads the wine press of the fierce wrath of God, the Almighty. And on His robe and on His thigh He has a name written, "King of Kings, And Lord of Lords" . . . And I saw the beast and the kings of the earth and their armies assembled to make war against Him who sat on the horse and against His army. (Rev. 19:11-16, 19 NASB, emphasis mine)

Both the *Pre-Tribulation Rapture* camp and the *Post-Tribulation Rapture* camp consider this second passage where Jesus rides a white horse and comes to do battle with the Antichrist at Armageddon to be the physical Second Coming. I agree with them. Both camps also claim the event in depicted in Matt. 24:30-31 is *this same event.* But what if they are both *mistaken*? What if the event in Matt. 24:30-31 is something else? In fact, the events as they are portrayed in scripture couldn't be more dissimilar! These differences are seen in following graphic (Figure 8: "Contrasts in Matt. 24:30-31 and Rev. 19:11-16, 19")

Events in Matt. 24:30-31	Events in Rev. 19:11-16,19
Jesus comes on the clouds	Jesus rides a white horse
Jesus blows a trumpet	Jesus has a sword coming from his mouth
Jesus comes with his angels	Jesus is followed by the saints on white on horses
Jesus comes to gather the elect	Jesus comes to destroy the Antichrist

Figure 8: Contrasts in Matt. 24:30-31 and Rev. 19:11-16, 19

This obvious disparity with traditional interpretation is *why I am recommending you set aside all your pre-conceived notions about timing and events and hear Jesus's words as if for the first time*. If you haven't done that yet, now is the time.

What Jesus Didn't Say

Jesus gave us Six Events that will occur prior to his return in Matt. 24:30-31. We now know these events are the first Six Seals, and that nearly the entire eschatological community agrees. Of greater interest to me however, is what Jesus *didn't say* were signs. On that spring afternoon, this was all new information to the disciples; they did not have the Book of Revelation so they had no basis on which to question the signs. But fifty to sixty years later, Jesus gave the visions found in Revelation to John the Revelator which provided much more detail about end-time events. We now have this additional information at our fingertips. We have *References*.

In that vision in Revelation, Jesus provided John with 21 major end-time prophetic events or signs: seven *Seals* (found in Rev. 6-8:1 that we already have seen include the *six events* of the *Olivet Discourse*), seven *Trumpet Judgments* (Rev. 8-11), and seven *Bowl Judgments* (Rev. 16). The *Trumpet and Bowl Judgments* contain extremely severe punishments. The *First Trumpet Judgment* for instance, includes fire, blood, and hail which burn 1/3 of the land and grass on the planet (Rev. 8:7). The *Fifth Trumpet Judgment* lasts 5 months and includes what appear to be demonic stinging locusts that cause many of the inhabitants of the earth to wish for death that doesn't come (Rev. 9:1-6). The *Sixth Trumpet Judgment* results in the death of a 1/3 of mankind (Rev. 9:18). The *Bowl Judgments* which directly follow are even more severe than the *Trumpet Judgements*.

These judgments would be undeniable signs of the soon return of Jesus; yet, he chose to ignore them and *did not list a single one as a sign* of his coming in the *Olivet Discourse*. What are we to make of this? Why is the *Olivet Discourse* silent on the *Trumpet and Bowl Judgments* and only lists the first six *Seals* as signs? Obviously, Jesus and the Holy Spirit were omniscient and fully aware of these coming plagues. So we must conclude Jesus *intentionally* did not include the *Trumpet and Bowl Judgements* in the *Olivet Discourse* as "signs." Also even more obviously, Jesus would not purposely mislead the Church (or even the Jews) by giving an incomplete list of signs. No, Jesus has left us with *only one possible conclusion*:

> The *Trumpet and Bowl Judgments* are not given as signs of the coming of our Lord because these judgments occur *after* his coming. His coming *precedes* them.

The disciples asked Jesus what would be the sign of his coming. Jesus responded with all six events (the first six *Seals* of Rev. 6:1-17) that would *precede* it; and he didn't give a single sign that would *follow* it (the *Trumpet and Bowl Judgments*).

Let's take a moment to consider the implications of what we have just uncovered. We know from Revelation that the Battle of Armageddon and the physical Second Coming take place sometime *after* the *Sixth Bowl*:

> The sixth angel *poured out his bowl* on the great river, the Euphrates and its water was dried up so that the way would be prepared for the kings from the east . . . "Behold, *I am coming* like a thief. Blessed is the one who stays awake and keeps his clothes so that he will not walk about naked and men will not see his shame." And they gathered them together to the place which in Hebrew is called Har-Magedon. (Rev. 16:12, 15-16 NASB, emphasis mine)

From this passage, we learn that Jesus is still "coming" (*"I am coming"*) *after* the *Sixth Bowl* is poured out. From this we can deduce without a doubt that the *physical* Second Coming occurs *after* the *Trumpet and Bowl Judgments*. Yet, we have just learned that the event in Matt. 24:30-31 occurs *before* the *Trumpet and Bowl Judgments*. What event is it? It obviously cannot be the physical Second Coming. Jesus again, has left us only one option: it's the *Rapture!* *This is radical new understanding for the Church!* The Rapture is a HARPAZO, a forceful, visible, and sudden rescue, and that is exactly what is depicted in Matt. 24:30-31.

This new information is hard to assimilate all at once. Let's return to our previous graphic of the *Olivet Discourse* and add what we have learned, shown in the following graphic (Figure 9: "The *Olivet Discourse* with *Trumpets* and *Bowls* Added"), so we can visualize it.

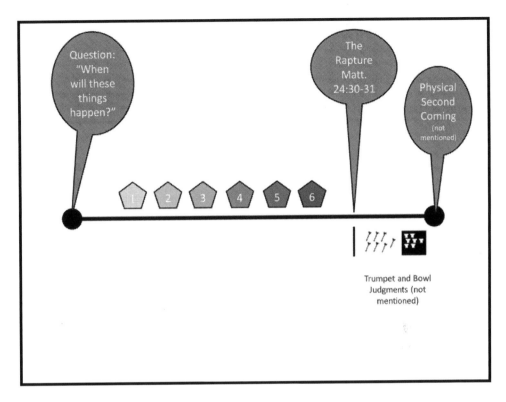

Figure 9: The Olivet Discourse with Trumpets and Bowls Added

This graphic helps our understanding. Let's look at the structure of the *Olivet Discourse:*

- The disciples initiate the *Discourse* by asking "When will these things happen and what will be the sign of your coming?"
- Jesus then responds with the *six events* that precede his coming that are the same as the first six *Seals* of Rev. 6:1-17.
- Jesus then depicts his coming in graphic terms that are forceful, visible, and sudden.

Jesus does <u>not</u> depict the *Trumpet Judgements* or *Bowl Judgments* or the physical Second Coming in the *Olivet Discourse* because these events come *after* his arrival (his PAROUSIA), at the Rapture.

THE *OLIVET DISCOURSE* = THE *PRE-WRATH RAPTURE*

I don't know if you have noticed it yet, but the *Olivet Discourse* is an exact depiction of the *Pre-Wrath Rapture*. The pre-Wrath Rapture is claimed by its proponents to happen after the Sixth Seal and prior to the *Trumpet and Bowl Judgements*. Let us overlay a graphic of the *Pre-Wrath Rapture* on the one we have now developed for the *Olivet Discourse* so you can see the perfect fit of this Rapture theory with the model of the *Discourse*. This graphic (Figure 10: "Perfect Match of The *Olivet Discourse* and the *Pre-Wrath Rapture*") appears below:

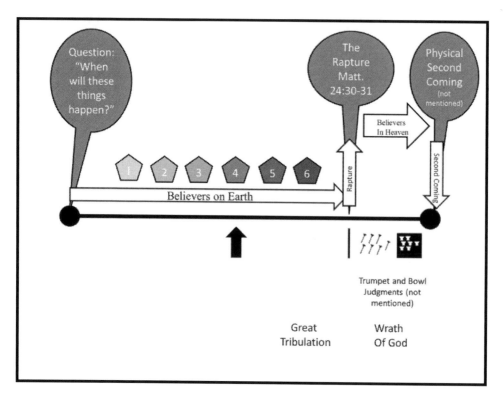

Figure 10 The Olivet Discourse and the Pre-Wrath Rapture

The first *six events* occur while the believers are still on the earth (so they can see the signs of his coming!) The last three of the six signs perfectly match the timing of the *Great Tribulation*, which follows the Midpoint (black arrow) of the 70th Week, just as depicted in the graphic. Note that *the Rapture occurs after the Sixth Sign,* just as it does in Matt. 24:29-31. The believers are insulated from the *Wrath of God* (the *Trumpet and Bowl Judgments*) by the Rapture, just as prophesied by 1 Thess. 1:10 and 1 Thess. 5:9.

> The *Olivet Discourse* is the *ultimate and definitive proof of Rapture timing*. It makes mute all other Rapture theories and proofs.

In summary, the Olivet Discourse is the ultimate and definitive proof of Rapture timing. It makes mute all other Rapture theories and proofs. This alone should end the "Rapture Timing Debate." Admittedly, entrenched doctrine positions are very difficult to change, and additional biblical evidence is helpful for some to change their position. Let's demonstrate in the section below some sample arguments from the other Rapture theory camps to show how this is true.

CONTRARY RAPTURE TIMING POSITIONS:

1) *PRE-TRIBULATION RAPTURE* ARGUMENTS

Pre-Tribulation Rapture proponents will be quick to point out that they also believe the Rapture occurs before the *Trumpet and Bowl Judgments*; long before. This is correct; however, they must then identify the event taking place in Matt. 24:30-31. We have conclusively shown it cannot be the physical Second Coming of Jesus, as it is stated in Rev. 16:12, 15-16 that *"I am coming"* after the *Sixth Bowl* is poured out. If it isn't the physical Second Coming, and if they say it isn't the Rapture, what event is it? They have no answer for this argument. A great weakness of the *Pre-Tribulation Rapture* position is that it is an inferred position, and they cannot point to a single passage of scripture that clearly depicts the Rapture happening before the so-called "Tribulation." This proof shows that the depiction of the Rapture was always there in Matt. 24:30-31; unfortunately, most have missed it — hidden in plain sight.

A few *Pre-Tribulation Rapture* supporters claim that the reason Jesus didn't list the *Trumpet and Bowl Judgments* is that they are "spiritual" and won't be physically realized. However, Revelation is incredibly specific in terms of what these judgments will entail: fire, hail, and blood that burn 1/3 of the land and trees, the poisoning of 1/3 of the fresh water, the death of 1/3 of the population of the earth. These are not "spiritualized" judgments, but very explicit physical judgments. So, this "spiritualized" reasoning does not hold up.

2) *POST-TRIBULATION RAPTURE* ARGUMENTS

Many *Post-Tribulation Rapture* proponents believe the *Seals, Trumpets,* and *Bowls* happen concurrently; that is, at the same time. They do not believe that the *Trumpet and Bowl Judgments* only occur at the end of the *70th Week of Daniel* as pictured in the preceding graphics. We will present numerous proofs that their theory on Concurrent *Seals, Trumpets,* and *Bowls* is incorrect. However, for the purposes of this Chapter Three, those proofs are *unnecessary*. All we need to understand at this point is that Jesus did not mention the *Trumpet and Bowl Judgments* as a sign of his return in the *Olivet Discourse*. Thus, he must return *before* a single *Trumpet* is sounded and before a single *Bowl* is poured out or the *Discourse* has seriously misled the Church. It is important to note that whether the *Seals, Trumpets,* and *Bowls* are concurrent or consecutive is *immaterial to this proof of Rapture timing*. This is the elegance of this Rapture Proof.

SEALS, TRUMPETS, AND BOWLS

One of the reasons that Revelation is difficult to outline and decipher is the organization of the 7 seals, 7 trumpets, and 7 bowls. There is great debate within the Church as to whether they are all *concurrent* (they all happen throughout the seven year period) or whether they are *consecutive* (the Seals occur first, the Trumpets second, and the finally the Bowls). I must thank Alan Kurschner[xx] for his outstanding investigation into this issue which conclusively shows they are *consecutive* (they happen one after another). A graphic of each of the two views (Figure 11: *Concurrent* Seals, Trumpets, and Bowls Model; and Figure 12: *Consecutive* Seals, Trumpets, and Bowls Model) follows:

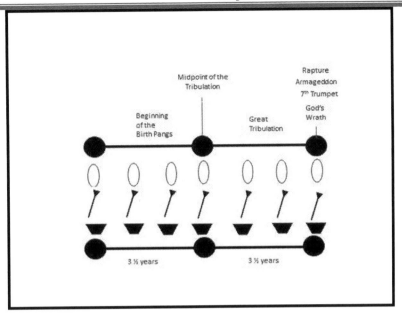

Figure 11: Concurrent Seals, Trumpets, and Bowls Model

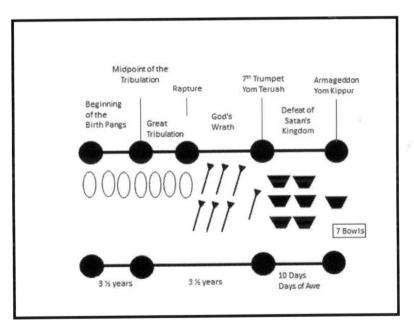

Figure 12: Consecutive Seals, Trumpets, and Bowls Model

The "concurrent" theory is consistent with what is known as a *Post-Tribulation Rapture*. This theory states that Jesus will return at the very end of the *70th Week of*

Daniel, save all of Israel on that last day, and fight the battle of Armageddon. This *Post-Tribulation Rapture* theory *requires* that the *Seventh Seal*, the *Seventh Trumpet*, and the *Seventh Bowl* all occur at about the same time (essentially on the last day of the 70th Week) to mitigate inconsistencies in their position and the obvious sense of Scripture that the Resurrection and Rapture occur after the *Sixth Seal*, and that the Day of the Lord (God's Wrath) unfolds before the Battle of Armageddon. Most believers in a "concurrent" theory of the Seals, Trumpets, and Bowls believe that the *Seventh Trumpet* is the *last trumpet* referred to by Paul in 1 Cor. 15 that accompanies the Rapture. We discuss the *last trumpet* and its true identity in Chapter Six: "The Walls Came Tumbling Down (Joshua 6, Judges 6-8)."

The "consecutive" theory of Seals, Trumpets, and Bowls is consistent with a *Pre-Wrath Rapture* as is taught in this book. When the *Seventh Seal* is opened, it reveals the 7 trumpet judgments. When the *Seventh Trumpet* is blown, it reveals the 7 bowl judgments. The *Seventh Seal and Seventh Trumpet* are like "nesting dolls" that contain the next series of events within them. This is further developed in my first book, *Are We Ready for Jesus?*

THE EVIDENCE

The simplest approach to understand this issue about the *consecutive* occurrence of the seals, trumpets, and bowls is to examine the *Olivet Discourse* as we just did earlier in this Chapter Three: "A Treasure Map." We learned that these first seven events in the *Pattern of Seven Events are* the *Seven Seals*. As we stated in that Chapter, the fact that the *Olivet Discourse doesn't* present the *Trumpet and Bowl Judgments* is an enormous clue about Rapture timing. Jesus's PAROUSIA (or "coming") must precede the *Trumpet and Bowl Judgments* because Jesus does *not* give the Trumpets or Bowls as *signs* of his coming in his answer to the Disciples as to this exact question about the signs of his second coming! Both *Pre-Tribulation* and *Post-Tribulation* Rapture timing theories are disproven by this one simple proof.

I think what else is absolutely logical is that *only the seals* are broken prior to the PAROUSIA (the "Rapture part" of Jesus's second coming at the breaking of the

Seventh Seal. The Seals break first, only then are the Trumpets blown. This is also overwhelming proof that the Seals and Trumpets are not concurrent.

There are other proofs of a consecutive timing of seals, trumpets, and bowls as well. The following graphic gives most of Alan Kurschner's published reasons why the Seals, Trumpets, and Bowls must be consecutive and not current:

Reason	Implication
Rev. 15:1 claims the 7 Bowls are the *last* aspect of God's Wrath.	If the 7 Bowls are the "last" aspect of God's Wrath, another aspect (the Trumpet Judgments) must precede them
Rev. 8:1 clearly shows that the 7 Trumpets are given to the angels after the *seventh seal* is broken	If the 7 Trumpets are blown after the seventh seal, the Seals obviously precede the Trumpet Judgments
Silence occurs *after* the *seventh seal* is broken. In Zeph. 1:7, silence is shown to precede the Day of the Lord (God's Wrath)	If silence must precede the Day of the Lord (God's Wrath), all of the Seals must precede God's Wrath as well. By extension, the Seals must precede the Trumpets and Bowls which are God's Wrath
Each of the septets (Seals, Trumpets, and Bowls) are progressively worse than the preceding	This implies a progressive worsening order of events
At the *fifth seal*, the martyrs under the altar are told to wait for God's avenging of their murder	By extension, God's Wrath (the Trumpets and Bowls) cannot have occurred before the *fifth seal*
The Celestial Earthly Disturbance Event occurs at the *sixth seal*. In Joel 2:30-31 we are told this precedes the Day of the Lord (God's Wrath)	By extension, God's Wrath (the Trumpets and Bowls) cannot have occurred before the *sixth seal*.
In Rev. 7:3, God instructs his angels to not damage the earth or the seas or the trees prior to sealing the 144,000	The first three trumpets damage the earth, the sea, and the trees. By extension the Trumpet Judgments must follow this sealing event

Figure 13: Evidence for Consecutive Seals, Trumpets, and Bowls

This is additional conclusive evidence that the seals, trumpets and bowls are *consecutive* and not concurrent.

Ch. 3: A Treasure Map

This book is about Revelation and not the Rapture per se, so if you still have questions about Rapture timing, please read *Rapture Debate Over?* which provides dozens of additional proofs for the *Pre-Wrath Rapture* and disproves all of the primary proofs for the other Rapture positions. If you have Rapture questions, this is the reference to check out.

GOD'S WRATH

It is our thesis that the *Seventh Event* includes not only the Rapture, but the *Wrath of God* as well. There is a plethora of evidence in the seminal texts we have looked at for this. Both the Rapture and Wrath are symbolically shown to occur together in the *Olivet Discourse* by Jesus employing the historic account of Noah and the Flood (The First Wrath of God) as a foreshadow of what will occur at the Second Wrath of God in the end times:

> For the coming (Gk: PAROUSIA) of the Son of Man will be just like the days of Noah. For as in those days before the flood they were eating and drinking, marrying and giving in marriage, *until the day that Noah entered the ark*, and they did not understand *until the flood came and took them all away*; so will the coming of the Son of Man be. (Matt. 24:37-39 NASB, emphasis mine)

Jesus is clear that on the *very day* Noah entered the Ark, the Flood came and took all the unrepentant away. He is also clear that his PAROUSIA and the Second Wrath will be the same! The Second Wrath will take place on the exact day of the Rapture.

Revelation supports this position as well. After the *Fifth Seal* we are told the judgment and Wrath of God has not yet begun:

> When the Lamb broke the *Fifth Seal*, I saw underneath the altar the souls of those who had been slain because of the word of God, and because of the testimony which they had maintained; and they cried out with a loud voice, saying, "*How long, Oh Lord, holy and true, will You refrain from judging and*

56

avenging our blood on those who dwell on the earth?" (Rev. 6:9-10 NASB, emphasis mine)

This is an extremely direct statement that God's Wrath has not begun yet as of the Fifth Seal. Yet after the Sixth Seal we read that it has begun as the inhabitants of the earth cry out:

Fall on us and hide us from the presence of Him who sits on the throne, and from the wrath of the Lamb; for the great day of their wrath has come, and who is able to stand? (Rev. 6:16-17 NASB, emphasis mine)

This is another very direct statement. The *Wrath of God* obviously begins after the *Sixth Seal*, which co-incidentally is the timing of the Rapture. These scriptural passages fit together like pieces of a puzzle. The only "missing" piece, supposedly, is an explicit depiction of the Rapture after the *Sixth Seal*. That piece isn't missing, however. The vast multitude in Rev. 7:9-17 who have come out of the Great Tribulation are the Raptured saints. The book *Rapture Debate Over?* proves this point with an elegant set of evidences found in its Fourth Chapter. Anyone interested in examining that proof in detail is referred to that book.

THE PATTERN OF SEVEN EVENTS

We have now demonstrated the entire seven event pattern. We have found the treasure map first given by Jesus in the *Olivet Discourse* and then expanded upon in the vision he gave John. The complete set of Seven Events is listed in the graphic on the next page:

Sign	Description	Matt. 24	Rev. 6	Mark 13	Luke 21
1	Deception by False Messiahs	vv. 4-5, 23-26	vv. 1-2	vv. 5-6, 21-23	v. 8
2	Wars and Chaos	vv. 6-7	vv. 3-4	vv. 7-8	vv. 10-11
3	Famine and Economic Collapse	v. 7	vv. 5-6	v. 8	v. 11
4	Abomination and Death	vv. 9, 15-21	vv. 7-8	vv. 13-20	vv. 17, 20-24
5	Martyrdom and Apostasy	vv. 9-12	vv. 9-11	vv. 9-13	vv. 12-19
6	Celestial Signs	v. 29	vv. 12-17	vv. 24-25	vv. 25-26
7	Rapture and Wrath	vv. 30-31, 37-39	vv. 10-11, 17; 7:9-17	vv. 26-27	vv. 27-28, 34-36

Figure 14: The Pattern of Seven Events in the Gospels and Revelation

SUMMARY

Now the real fun begins! We have been given a treasure map (The *Pattern of Seven Events*). If we apply it in the Old Testament, end time prophecies found in Psalms and the Prophets can be chronologically ordered. We will do just that in Part Two of this book.

If we apply the treasure map to the Book of Revelation, it helps us chronologically sort the various chapters. We will establish the chronological ordering of the Book of Revelation at the end of Chapter Four: Bookends."

Perhaps of even greater value, this Chapter has helped us solve one of the greatest contentions in Christianity today: the timing of the Rapture! In the final Chapter of this book we examine the implications of this knowledge for our churches.

Chapter Four

BOOKENDS
(REVELATION 1 – 3)

With our treasure map of the *Pattern of Seven Events* firmly in hand, we are now ready to return to the beginning: Rev. 1:1. Revelation is a great book and great books have great beginnings. Many of the most memorable quotes from literature are actually the very first sentence of the book they are taken from. Consider some of these famous first lines; can you identify the book from the quote?

1) "It was the best of times; it was the worst of times."
2) "Call me Ishmael."
3) "In the beginning God created the Heavens and the earth."
4) "It was a bright cold day in April, and the clocks were striking thirteen."
5) "Whether I shall turn out to be the hero of my own life, or whether that station will be held by anybody else, these pages must show."

In case you missed one or two, here are the answers: 1) *A Tale of Two Cities*/Charles Dickens, 2) *Moby Dick*/Herman Melville, 3) *The Holy Bible*, 4) *1984*/George Orwell, and 5) *David Copperfield*/Charles Dickens.

THINGS THAT MUST TAKE PLACE

The Apostle John considered the first verse of the books of the Bible that he wrote to be very important as well. Not only did he consider the first verses important, but careful study shows he frequently quoted other Biblical passages in these initial verses of his books. In fact, "Sense and Reference" is a common theme in all of John's writings. The

Gospel of John begins with the words, "In the beginning," an obvious reference to Genesis 1:1. With these three words, John immediately placed the reader at the moment of creation when he further stated, "In the beginning was the Word, and the Word was with God and the Word was God" (John 1:1 NASB). By this, John was letting us know that Jesus (the LOGOS or the Word) was present at the creation with the Father and that he and the Father were one. The reason for this reference deepens as John continues, "He was in the beginning with God. All things came into being through Him, and apart from Him nothing came into being that has come into being" (John 1:2-3 NASB). Here we see the creation process and learn that Jesus himself was the Creator!

The question arises: Why didn't John simply reference the passage (example: "See Gen. 1:1") as we might do today? The answer is that our chapter and verse divisions did not exist in John's day. The Book of Genesis was a continual scroll without any verse or chapter numbers. If John wanted the reader to recall a passage of scripture, he had to quote it. John's readers had memorized huge sections of the Old Testament by the time of their Bar Mitzvah at age 13. When John quotes these scriptural passages, he assumes the reader will know them by heart. Unfortunately, most modern readers of scripture don't know the quotes. This is where a good Bible software package complete with the Greek-translation *Septuagint* Old Testament comes in handy. I highly recommend you purchase one to search for phrases and words and make connections with what the New Testament writers like John might be referring to. It will greatly deepen your understanding of the New Testament. Personally, I use *Logos Bible Software*® with a *Septuagint* add-on. It is somewhat pricey, but in my mind is well worth the investment.

Now the big question arises, does Revelation, written by John, begin with a similar, famous quote just as the Gospel of John does? Twenty-first century English-speaking eyes might not notice, but it does! Revelation begins:

The Revelation of Jesus Christ, which God gave Him to show to His bond-servants the *things which must* soon *take place*. (Revelation 1:1 NASB, emphasis mine)

"Things which must take place" is not a familiar phrase to our ears, but it was to the young Christian Church undergoing persecution in John's day. Although it only occurs twice in the Old Testament, the phrase *"things which must take place"* (Gk: HA DEI GENESTHAI) is one of the most famous phrases of deliverance in scripture. Both Old Testament uses of this Greek phrase are found in the *Septuagint* account of Daniel Chapter 2, in verse 29 and then again in verse 45. These two uses of the phrase act as *"Bookends"* for the interpretation of Nebuchadnezzar's dream of the statue of four metals. By "bookend," I mean that the phrase is *both* the first and the last phrase in that portion of scripture.

> O king: thy thoughts upon thy bed arose as to *what must come to pass* hereafter; and he that reveals mysteries has made known to thee *what must come to pass* (Gk: HA DEI GENESTHAI). (Dan. 2:29 LXX, clarification and emphasis mine)

> The great God has made known to the king *what must happen* hereafter (Gk: HA DEI GENESTHAI): and the dream is true, and the interpretation thereof sure. (Dan. 2:45 LXX, clarification and emphasis mine)

Also notice that if you are looking at the English translation you totally miss the "bookend" phrase. It only appears in the Greek. John was obviously very aware of this "bookend" phrase as we will soon learn.

This famous prophetic dream of the statue of Dan. 2 was given to Nebuchadnezzar, King of Babylon, to help him (and Bible students later) understand the history of world empires from the vantage point of Babylon right up to the return of Jesus. The young, persecuted Church would have been hungry for an explanation of how Jesus would deliver them from the succession of evil empires that had oppressed the people of God throughout the ages. By opening Revelation with the phrase *"things that must take place,"* John was telling the Church *this book will explain the Book of Daniel and will show you how Christ will deliver us.* To make this point crystal clear, John used the phrase as bookends for the entire Book of Revelation! The phrase opens the book in Rev. 1:1 and closes the book in Rev. 22:6 as well, just as the phrase in Daniel 2 acted as bookends for the interpretation of Nebuchadnezzar's dream. Amazing. This cannot be coincidence.

I must take time to thank Pastor David Bielby[xxi] for his writing about this use of the above Greek phrase *which is absolutely critical to understanding Revelation*. It was his understanding of this aspect of Revelation that led me to the rest of my "deciphering" of this Book of the Bible.

IMAGES FROM DANIEL

Immediately after announcing to his readers that one of the purposes of Revelation was to explain the *Book of Daniel*, the Holy Spirit through the inspired pen of John, quotes another of the most famous prophecies from the *Book of Daniel*, "*Behold, he is coming with the clouds*, and every eye will see Him, even those who pierced Him; and all the tribes of the earth will mourn over Him" (Rev. 1:7 NASB). This time the quote is from Daniel 7:13:

> I beheld in the night vision, and, lo, *one coming with the clouds of heaven* as the Son of man, and he came on to the Ancient of days, and was brought near to him. And to him was given the dominion, and the honor, and the kingdom; and all nations, tribes, and languages, shall serve him: his dominion is an everlasting dominion, which shall not pass away, and his kingdom shall not be destroyed. (Dan. 7:13-14 LXX, emphasis mine)

By quoting from Daniel 7, John is telling his readers that the book of Revelation will explain that famous prophecy of Daniel 7 as well.

As if these are not enough references to Daniel in Revelation, John then immediately records his vision of the risen Jesus *which is an exact fingerprint match* with Daniel's encounter with the pre-incarnate Jesus found in Daniel 10 (Jesus appeared to Daniel more than 400 years before he humbled himself and became man). Why does our Lord appear to Daniel and John? First, they are both dearly loved, but secondly,

Jesus' appearance lends credibility to the visions. It re-enforces that Revelation was dictated by our Lord himself. Third and *most* importantly, as we will learn in Part Four of this book ("*Letters to the Seven Churches*"), the various aspects of Jesus' appearance have important symbolic meaning.

The similarities between Daniel's and John's vision of the Lord are striking. Let's compare these two visions of Jesus in Daniel 10 and Revelation 1, shown in Figure 15: "Jesus' Appearance in Daniel and Revelation::

Feature	Daniel 10	Revelation 1
Jesus' Clothing	Fine linen v.5	A long robe v.13
Jesus' Belt	A golden belt v.5	A golden sash v. 13
Jesus' voice	Like a great multitude v. 6	Like a trumpet and the sound of many waters vv. 10,15
Jesus' Face/Hair	Like lightening v. 6	Hair white like wool, snow v.14
Jesus' Eyes	Like torches v. 6	Like a flame of fire v.14
Jesus' Arms and Legs	Like polished bronze v. 6	Like burnished bronze v.15
Seer's Reaction	Fainted v.9	Fainted v.17

Figure 15: Jesus's Appearance in Daniel and Revelation

There can be no question that these visions are of the same person. Since Revelation identifies him as the Lord Jesus, we know that *Daniel* also saw the Lord.

This vision in Daniel 10 opens the *Book of Daniel*'s most detailed prophecy of events to occur during what an Angel calls *"the time of the end."* We refer to this vision that stretches over three chapters (Dan. 10, 11, 12) as "*Daniel's Great Vision Prophecy,*" and we will discuss it at great length in Chapter Fifteen: "Overcoming Lions." By quoting this vision reference from Daniel 10, John is now telling the reader that what they are about to learn about in Revelation will further explain *Daniel's Great Vision Prophecy,* which primarily prophesies about the period we know as the *70th Week of Daniel.*

Revelation explains what will occur during the *70th Week of Daniel.*

THINGS THAT ARE ABOUT TO TAKE PLACE

John was not done providing scripture references so the reader would know what the visions he was about to write entailed. We have seen how John used the phrase *"Things that must take place"* taken from the *Book of Daniel* as bookends for the entire Book of Revelation, locating them at the beginning and end of the book (Rev. 1:1 and Rev. 22:6). We already discussed that this reference informed readers that the Book of Revelation was an explanation of the *Book of Daniel* and would reveal how Jesus would deliver his people.

Amazingly, these two references to this phrase are not the only use of it in Revelation. John quotes it again in Rev. 4:1 and quotes *a related phrase* in Rev. 1:19. Do these phrases act as bookends for any other famous passage of scripture? They do! They appear in the first and last verse of the enigmatic passage about the *Letters to the Seven Churches* found in Rev. 2 and 3! This is of amazing importance. If we understand *this related phrase* found in Revelation 1:19, we might gain insight into what John is telling us about the meaning of the whole passage about the *Seven Churches.*

The related phrase in Rev. 1:19 differs from the original found in Daniel 10 by only one Greek word (DEI vs. MELLEI). The two phrases from Rev. 4:1 and Rev. 1:19 appear below:

From Rev. 4:1:	HA	DEI	GENESTHAI
	Things	that must	take place

From Rev. 1:19:	HA	MELLEI	GENESTHAI
	Things	that *are about to*	take place

It is noted that this related phrase (*"Things that are about to take place"*) occurs in *two other places* in the New Testament. It is found in the question that the Disciples ask Jesus that prompts him to explain the signs of his return and the end of the age (Luke 21:7). It is also found in the final phrase of the same passage (Luke 21:36), which is Jesus's response to the Disciples: the famous *Olivet Discourse* which we looked at in Chapter Three: "A Treasure Map." This is another "bookend," but this time using the related phrase *"Things that are about to take place,"* as shown:

> They questioned Him, saying, "Teacher, when therefore will these things happen? And what will be the sign when *these things are about to take place*? (MELLEI GENESTHAI)" (Luke 21:7 NASB, clarification and emphasis mine)

> But keep on the alert at all times, praying that you may have strength to escape all these *things that are about to take place* (MELLEI GENESTHAI) and to stand before the Son of Man. (Luke 21:36 NASB, clarification and emphasis mine.)

This repetition of the same phrase can be no accident or coincidence. Clearly, John in Revelation is referencing the opening and closing verses of the most famous teaching of Jesus on the end times, the *Olivet Discourse*.

So what does this second set of bookend phrases in Rev. 1:19 and Rev. 4:1 tell us? In my opinion, John is informing us that the passage about the *Letters to Seven Churches* that begins immediately after this reference and is contained within the bookend phrases is going to give us further understanding of the period at the end of the age which Jesus discusses in the *Olivet Discourse*. The *Olivet Discourse* gives us details about the *70th Week of Daniel* including *the Pattern of Seven Events*; so in essence, the Holy Spirit is telling us that the passages about the *Letters to the Seven Churches* are about the *70th Week of Daniel* and the *Pattern of Seven Events* in particular. This provides us the context to understand why the *Letters to the Seven Churches* are contained as they are in the beginning section of the book of Revelation — they relate to the seven years at the end of the age as discussed in the rest of Revelation. This is a very helpful insight in understanding Revelation.

The *Letters to the Seven Churches* describe the *70th Week of Daniel* and the Pattern of Seven Events

I realize these "bookend" quotes may be somewhat difficult to follow and understand. Perhaps this graphic [Figure 16: Bookend Quotes of Dan. 2, Rev., and *Olivet Discourse*] will help visualize these bookend quotes:

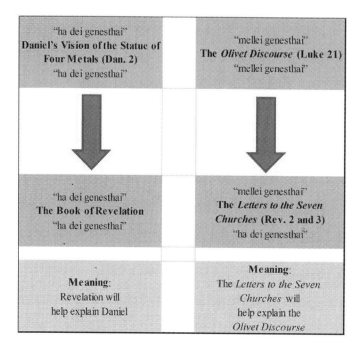

Figure 16 Bookend Quotes of Dan. 2, Rev. and Olivet Discourse

As can be seen in this graphic, the Holy Spirit inspired the writers of scripture to place "bookend" quotes around these four great messages about the return of Jesus. The two uses of these bookend quotes in Revelation have the purpose of directing the reader's attention back to the original passages (Daniel 2 and Luke 21) so the reader can understand what the visions in Revelation are about.

Three of the four uses of these bookend quotes are perfect; they use the exact same phrase at the beginning of the passage and at its end. The fourth, the *Letters to the Seven Churches*, starts with one of the quotes "HA MELLEI GENESTHAI" and ends with the other "HA DEI GENESTHAI." Why is that? The reason John uses a different quote at the end of the passage of Revelation 3, as we will learn in the next chapter [Chapter Five: "Signed, Sealed, and Delivered (Revelation 4-5)"], is to refer the reader's attention away from the *Olivet Discourse* (the subject of the *Letters to the Seven Churches*) and back to the *Book of Daniel*. The second quote, which refers the reader back to Daniel, "HA DEI GENESTHAI," appears in Rev. 4:1; after that, all of Revelation 4 and 5, which follow it, concern a reference to Daniel 7. We will learn a great deal more about this in Chapter Five: "Signed, Sealed, and Delivered."

This concept of the usage of *Bookend Scripture Verses* to give us understanding of related links to other scripture is revolutionary. I have read dozens and dozens of commentaries on Revelation. None of them say the *Letters to the Seven Churches* refer to the *70th Week of Daniel*. But also none of these commentaries recognize the concept of references acting as bookends at the beginning and end of Revelation (Rev. 1:1, Rev. 22:6) *and* at the beginning and end of the passage about the *Seven Churches* (Rev. 1:19, Rev. 4:1) to show the linkages. Indeed, some of the topsoil of two thousand years of language and cultural differences has been removed to find the valued "arrowheads."

The concept that the *Letters to the Seven Churches* are prophetic and about the *70th Week of Daniel* is revolutionary understanding.

THE THINGS THAT ARE

Before we move on, we should take time to look at what older commentaries have had to say about the meaning of the passages about the *Letters to the Seven Churches*. Most of the commentaries teach that the letters to the Churches of Revelation are historic, and they base this upon a verse we have already looked at:

Therefore write the *things which you have seen*, and *the things which are*, and *the things which will take place after these things*. (Rev. 1:19 NASB, emphasis mine)

Most of these commentaries claim John is instructed in Revelation to write down three things:

- What he saw in the vision in Rev. 1 (the appearance of Jesus),
- What was currently happening in John's first century world, and
- What will happen in the future.

If this interpretation of Rev. 1:19 was correct, the only section of Revelation which could really fit into the category of "what's currently happening in John's first century world" (the *things that are*) would be the *Letters to the Seven Churches* of Chapters 2 and 3. And for centuries many commentators stopped right there. They assumed they had the outline of the Book of Revelation figured out, as follows:

1) "Things which you have seen":   Chapter 1
2) "Things that are":   Chapters 2 and 3
3) "Things that are about to take place"   Chapters 4-22

If the *Letters to the Seven Churches* were intended to be only related to events that occurred in John's day, they would merely have been letters of advice from Jesus to seven real churches in Asia Minor (current-day Turkey). Most commentators have then taken this idea a step further and expanded the letters' meaning to *modern churches* as well. These commentators say that the advice Jesus gives the churches in Revelation is timeless and can be applied to any church, because these ancient churches are indicative of the types of problems from which all churches suffer. I have heard many sermons preached from this exact point of view.

Although this thinking isn't "*wrong*," and seems reasonable, there are several serious problems with this interpretation. Obviously, these are not your average letters of advice to churches. The other epistles are full of advice from the Apostles to many of the early churches, but none are written quite like the *Letters to the Seven Churches.* The following points are key understandings related to these *Letters:*

- The *Letters to the Seven Churches* were written in "apocalyptic" language; no other section of the Bible related to Christian living is couched in this type of language.

- The *Letters to the Seven Churches* contain numerous Old Testament and New Testament references and symbols which apply to the end times.

- The concept of including advice to local churches is out of place in a Revelation whose expressed purpose is to explain the *Book of Daniel*, the *Olivet Discourse*, and our deliverance by Jesus. This is especially true given the reference phrases that the Holy Spirit (through the pen of John) chose as bookends verses for this passage that point to the *70th Week of Daniel.*

- There were many more than just seven churches in Asia Minor at this time, some larger and more influential. Why were only these seven chosen to receive a letter from Jesus?

- The advice from Jesus does not seem to match our historical knowledge of the churches. Jesus's letter to Philadelphia does not contain any critiques, yet in the letter to this church from Ignatius (an early Church Father), a number of issues were mentioned in regard to members causing unrest and trusting Jewish Law rather than Christ's grace[xxii]. If the *Letters to The Seven Churches* were meant to impart real time advice to historic churches, Jesus's guidance would match the historic accounts.

- The order of the letters is not random, but occurs in a very specific sequence. The end time symbolism of events found in each of the letters *exactly* matches the order of the *Pattern of Seven Events* found in other portions of scripture describing the *70th Week of Daniel.* Chapter Three: "A Treasure Map" has established this Pattern and all of Part Two of this book

("The *Pattern of Seven Events*") re-enforces it. Part Four: "*Letters to the Seven Churches* (Revelation 2-3)" then demonstrates how the *Letters to the Seven Churches* exactly matches this pre-established pattern of events.

These bullet points cast serious doubt on the theory that the *Letters to the Seven Churches* are meant *solely* as advice to historic or even modern churches. The only solid, biblical basis for considering the *Letters to the Seven Churches* as being historic is the phrase "The things that are" in Rev. 1:19. But what if that phrase means something different than what has been thought? Let's investigate. This phrase is a translation of the Greek words HA EISIN. Literally, this means "things that *they* are" (3rd person plural), or as noted theologian and New Testament translator Henry Alford[xxiii] translated it: "things that they *signify;*" and I think this is exactly how the words should be translated. The word EISIN is plural; the currently popular translation "things that are" would require a singular verb. So why do *all* major translations ignore the literal meaning of the words? The usual reasoning given is that within the context, if we translate the words as "things that are," the result creates a balanced "things that were, are and will be" type of phrase. It also supports the theology of the translators that the *Letters to the Seven Churches* are historic and supports their *preconceived* outline of the Book of Revelation.

But if we substitute Henry Alford's literal translation back into Rev. 1:19, it would read: "Write the things which you have seen (the vision of my appearance), and the things that *they signify*." If the various aspects of Jesus's appearance have *symbolic meaning* (and they do), this phrase would make complete sense. Interestingly, in most of the letters Jesus wrote to the seven churches, a different aspect of Jesus' appearance (the double edged sword, his feet like burnished brass, etc.) is present. This supports this *symbolic* view of Jesus's appearance.

By using a literal translation of the Greek words, Alford's translation makes more sense than the traditional interpretation. Jesus instructs John to write what he had seen. Up to this point, all that John had seen was the vision of the risen Christ. Why is Jesus instructing him to record this? Is he asking John to write this vision down because it's a reference to the *Book of Daniel*? Perhaps, but let's look again at the command

Jesus gives John and substitute the literal translation, "Write the things that you have seen and the things which *they signify*." This interpretation gives us a *reason* why John is being instructed to record Jesus's appearance because *each aspect of Jesus' appearance has a symbolic meaning*. Jesus wants John to record this so when we study the *Letters to the Seven Churches*, many of which include one or two aspects of Jesus's appearance, we will understand the meaning of those aspects. Doesn't this make much more sense?

As if to prove this point, immediately after this phrase of Rev. 1:19, Jesus interprets what two of the symbols mean! The *lampstands* are the seven churches and the *stars* are the angels of the churches. The placement of the interpretation of symbols by Jesus is not random, but supports our new thesis about the Letters and Alford's century-old translation.

The idea that the *Letters to the Seven Churches* are simply advice to historic or even modern churches does not make sense in context, linguistically, or logically. This passage on the *Seven Churches* is *not* meant solely as advice to those churches *nor* meant solely to instruct our modern churches on Christian living. Can we apply this passage on the Letters as advice to our current churches? Yes, of course we can (and should!). But the primary meaning of the *Letters to the Seven Churches* in Revelation is much deeper than that.

SEVEN CHURCH AGES

Many others in the Church assume that the *Seven Churches* of Revelation are seven church "ages." What is amusing is that most of those who hold this position of *Seven Church Ages* believe in a *Pre-Tribulation Rapture*. If this passage referred to Church eras, it would contradict the theory of "imminence" (no prophecy must be fulfilled prior to the coming of Jesus for the Rapture) which is necessary for their *Pre-Tribulation Rapture* theory. Obviously, a "church age or era" would be a fulfilled prophecy. I find that dichotomy both illogical and amusing. The view of *Seven Church Ages* isn't correct, but not exclusively because of that reason. The following are the reasons this theory is flawed:

- There is absolutely *no scriptural basis* for this theory of *Seven Church Ages*. God does nothing without first telling his prophets. Where is the biblical evidence? If this were a biblically accurate view, there would be at least one other "witness" scripture to testify to the validity of coming "church ages". We have seen how John uses hundreds of Old Testament references in Revelation, yet not one reference to Church Ages exists. There are literally dozens of references within the *Letters to the Seven Churches* to the exact order of the *Pattern of Seven Events* that scripture gives to describe the *70th Week of Daniel*, but not one to a "church age."

- These seven church "ages" are totally arbitrary. Internet searches for what various writers thought the ages were are different. Without any basis in scripture, this view floats on the opinions of men.

- If these churches truly are "types" of church ages, they should be unique to a period of history. All seven church types existed in the first century, existed throughout the last two thousand years, and exist currently. There was never a time when one "type" of church was dominant.

- Just like the previous theory of merely the description of seven actual historic churches, the *Seven Church Ages* theory ignores the references within the Book of Revelation that testify that the book is meant to explain the *Book of Daniel*, and that *the passage about the Seven Churches explains the 70th Week of Daniel*. Indeed, this is a *key understanding*.

SEVEN CHURCHES *WITHIN* THE *70TH WEEK OF DANIEL*

Now that we have eliminated the *traditional* interpretations of the *Letters to the Seven Churches* as illogical and unbiblical, let's consider the remaining theory, proposed here, that the *Letters to the Seven Churches describe the Church of Jesus Christ as it endures and overcomes each of the seven years of the 70th Week of Daniel*. Here are the reasons this interpretation of the passages is the best fit with scripture:

- It is a perfect match with the scriptural references that act as bookends for this passage that tell us it will be an explanation of the *70th Week of Daniel*.

- It is a perfect match with the reference to Jesus coming on the clouds and the *Vision of the Risen Christ* in Rev. 1 that points us to Dan. 7 and Dan. 10-12.

- It is consistent with the overall theme of the Book of Revelation which is meant as an explanation of the *Book of Daniel* and our deliverance by Christ at the end of the age. It does not arbitrarily interject information about Christian living into an apocalyptic book. Viewed this way, the Book of Revelation is a consistent whole.

- The numerous references within the *Letters to the Seven Churches* to end-time events make sense and are now easily understood.

- References within the *Letters to the Seven Churches* exactly match the order of the *Pattern of Seven Events* that is established in other parts of scripture to describe the *70th Week of Daniel*.

- It answers the question asked by all those favoring a *Pre-Tribulation Rapture* as to where the Church is during Revelation's description of what they call "the Tribulation." (Although there are many other references to the Church in Rev. 4 -22, obviously the references to the *Seven Churches* are the most clear — the fact is that the Church goes through most of the "Tribulation," yet escapes God's wrath during the last year! This fits the *Pre-Wrath Rapture* model.)

Based on these facts, we can safely place the passages about the *Seven Churches* within the *70th Week of Daniel*, at the End of the Age. The question now becomes: *What are the modeled seven churches and how are they related to the 70th Week of Daniel?* The thesis this book will put forward is shocking, stunning and mind blowing! In my opinion, the *Seven Churches* are *pictures of each successive year* (approximately)*of the 70th Week of Daniel*, and what the Church of Jesus Christ must overcome *each year* to be victorious. This is, indeed, a *critical key* to correctly understanding Revelation, and this understanding is uniquely revealed here for your consideration.

> **The *Letters to the Seven Churches* are pictures of the Church enduring and overcoming each of the 7 years of the 70th Week.**

If this thesis is correct, understanding of the *Letters to the Seven Churches* will arm the Church with the information it needs to overcome the time of testing that lies ahead during the *70th Week of Daniel*. This is not a trivial point of who is right and who is wrong. It is a question of eternal significance for the members of Jesus' Church as they go through this time period.

You are probably thinking *that is all well and good, but is there any proof of this thesis*? Amazingly the answer is a resounding: *yes*. There is overwhelming proof. In fact, once the *Letters to the Seven Churches* are viewed in this way, I believe it is impossible to correctly view them any other way. All of Part Two: "The *Pattern of Seven Events*" will present that evidence.

SUMMARY

In the last two Chapters of this commentary, we have established the two *primary* facets for understanding and deciphering Revelation: 1) that there is a *Pattern of Seven Events* that acts like a Treasure Map allowing us to chronologically date events in the *70th Week of Daniel*, and 2) that the *Letters to the Seven Churches* are prophetic of that period and exactly match the *Pattern of Seven Events*. It is our belief that without these two foundational understandings, a complete grasp of Revelation is absolutely impossible. If you are still struggling with either of these concepts, please consider re-reading the appropriate Chapters.

Based on these factors, we would now like to propose an explanation of each chapter of the Book of Revelation and how they fit in the overall timeline of the 70th Week of Daniel. Feel free to refer back to this graphic as needed during your study. These graphics appear on the next page.

Revelation Chapter	Purpose	Events in the Pattern of Seven Events	
1	Introduction		
2 and 3	Letters to the Seven Churches	All 7	
4 and 5	Vision of the Throne in Heaven		
6	Opening the 7 Sealed Scroll	① ② ③ ④ ⑤ ⑥	
7	Protection of the Jewish Remnant and the Saints	7	
8 and 9	The Wrath of God: the Trumpets	7	
10	The Seven Thunders		
11	The Two Witnesses and the *Seventh Trumpet* (Coronation of Jesus as King)		
12	The Dragon and the Woman	Events 4-5	
13	The Two Beasts	Events 1-4	
14	Three Visions	7	
15	The Throne in Heaven after the Seventh Trumpet	7	
16	The Wrath of God: the Bowls	7	
17 and 18	Mystery Babylon		
19	Preparation for the Marriage of the Lamb and Armageddon	7	
20	The Millennial Kingdom and the Great White Throne Judgment		
21	The Eternal State		
22			

Figure 17: Organization of Revelation

Ch. 4: Bookends

By adding the icons for each of the events in the *Pattern of Seven Events*, the full scope of Revelation can be seen.

- Chapters 4-11, 15-16, and 19-21 represent the ongoing narrative of the Book on how Jesus will defeat the powers of evil and save his saints. All other chapters provide supplemental material.

- Chapters 2-3 explain how churchgoers are to overcome each of the events in the *Pattern of Seven Events*.

- Chapters 12-14 concern a number of complementary visions that that are not part of the chronological narrative, but that provide additional information about the *Pattern of Seven Events* from diverse perspectives.

In the next chapter, Chapter Five: "Signed, Sealed, And Delivered (Revelation 4-5)," we will examine the enigmatic *7 Sealed Scroll* and how identifying it helps us understand the purposes of the Lord in the *70th Week of Daniel*.

Chapter Five

SIGNED, SEALED, AND DELIVERED
(REVELATION 4 – 5)

As you may have noticed, we have temporarily skipped commentary on Revelation 2-3 which concern the *Letters to the Seven Churches*. We will return to these letters for an in-depth study later in this book. Instead we will first undertake an examination of the *Pattern of Seven Events* as detailed in Revelation (and throughout the rest of scripture) until we have established an incredibly thorough biblical understanding of these events. Then we will return to the letters equipped to uncover the *Pattern of Seven Events* within them and how Jesus instructs churchgoers to overcome these events.

At this point, we will begin our study in Rev. 4 where the ongoing, chronological narrative of Revelation begins. This narrative involves the opening of a mysterious *7 Sealed Scroll*. This scroll is mysterious because the Church has forgotten the meaning of the scroll; the Church has amnesia.

Having one of their main characters develop *amnesia* is a commonly used devise by novelists. This plot twist automatically provides the story of their book with mystery and intrigue as the character struggles to regain knowledge of his past life. Jason Bourne is the main protagonist in the popular book *The Bourne Identity* by Robert Ludlum (Bantam Books, New York 1980), which was also made into a movie series. In the book, the main character is a CIA assassin who must regain memory of who he was. Believe it or not, Bourne's last name was inspired by a real-life amnesia patient, Ansel Bourne. Ansel was an evangelical preacher in the 1880's who intentionally left from his hometown in Rhode Island to assume a new life as a shopkeeper in Norristown, PA. In Pennsylvania, he assumed the name Albert Brown and lived there for two months. One morning, he woke up with no memory of "Albert Brown" or his time in Norristown. This created confusion for both him and his neighbors who only knew him as Albert

Brown. Disoriented, he returned to Rhode Island and never assumed the alter-ego Albert Brown again.[xxiv]

There are many cases of biblical-amnesia in the Church. Portions of the Bible that were once understood are now clouded over as forgotten memories. The identity of the *7 Sealed Scroll* seen opened in Revelation is one of those cases. The opening of the scroll is one of the central events of the Book of Revelation and thus the *70th Week of Daniel*. The seals on the Scroll *are* the *Pattern of Seven Events*. Obviously, this is a very important scroll, and understanding it is absolutely key to end-time understanding *and* timing.

John knew exactly what this *Scroll* was. He cried when initially no one was found worthy to open it (Rev. 5:4). He was so sure his readers would also understand its identity; he didn't identify it by name. Centuries of misconception have followed, and now guesses abound as to what it is and the writings it contains. But fortunately, the Bible has left us plenty of clues to solve this mystery. In fact, we can know the identity of the *Scroll* with certainty. This Chapter Five: "Signed, Sealed, And Delivered (Revelation 4-5)" is especially rich with unique insights, and the logic inherent in the insights needs to be uncovered slowly for optimal understanding. Take your time reading this Chapter Five.

THE FIRST CLUE: A BOOKMARK IN REVELATION

John left a "bookmark" for us on one of the pages in Revelation. This bookmark is of extreme importance if we are going to solve this mystery of the identity of the *Scroll*. We have already learned about this bookmark in Chapter Four: "Bookends (Revelation 1-3)." It is the phrase *"things that must take place"* which is a quote from Dan. 2. As mentioned previously, this phrase occurs in the very first verse of Revelation, in the last chapter of Revelation, and then occurs again in Rev. 4:1. Wherever this reference phrase is found within Revelation, it acts as a bookmark to indicate *John is referring to a passage in Daniel.*

Immediately after the use of that bookmark phrase in Rev. 4:1, John is called up to heaven in a vision. He sees the throne room of God and God the Father seated on the throne. The fact that this is a vision of Heaven is of extreme importance. Revelation may seem strange and symbolic (it is), however, part of the reason for these strange symbols may be that we are looking at demons and angelic beings *as they really are*; from Heaven's perspective. When we observe the great, red seven-headed dragon and are told this is Satan (Rev. 12:9), perhaps we are seeing Satan as he really is. We are told he is the "dragon, the serpent of old." This reference to Genesis clearly equates the serpent in the garden with the dragon. Did Eve's encounter with the "serpent" involve a creature with seven heads? Perhaps it did. We will not return to this point again, but I want to express it here, because it assists me in deciphering Revelation to remember that this vision is from *Heaven's* perspective.

Now immediately after the use of the "bookmark" phrase, *things that must take place*, we encounter this vision which I believe is without question another reference to Daniel. In Dan. 7, the prophet experienced a nearly identical *Vision of the Throne Room of God*. Are these throne-room visions in Revelation and Daniel one and the same?

John has established a pattern — first we see the "bookmark," and then we see a vision. This is exactly what happened in Rev. 1. John quoted this same bookmark phrase and only a few verses later we see the vision of the Risen Lord which was identical with the vision in Dan. 10. Now in Rev. 4, we see the phrase again and immediately thereafter we see the *Vision of the Throne in Heaven*. In both cases, the visions John saw in Revelation bear an uncanny resemblance to the ones in the *Book of Daniel*. In Chapter Four: "Bookends (Revelation 1-3)," we saw that the two *Visions of Christ* in Revelation and Daniel were actually one and the same. My thesis is that it is also true of the two visions of the *Throne in Heaven* (in Dan. 7 and Rev. 4-5).

Before we examine the link between the two *Throne in Heaven* visions, let's look at the Daniel scene more closely.

THE THRONE ROOM OF DANIEL

Daniel's *Vision of the Throne in Heaven* in Dan. 7 is incredible. It is broken up into three segments (vv. 9-10, vv. 13-14, and then an angelic explanation in vv. 26-27). Interspersed between the segments of these heavenly visions are the events that are occurring on the earth. So, we first are given a view of events on the earth, then we see heaven's reaction, we view more events on the earth, and again we see heaven's explanation. Let's examine the first segment of Daniel's heavenly vision:

> I beheld until the thrones were set, and the Ancient of days sat; and his raiment was white as snow, and the hair of his head, as pure wool: his throne was a flame of fire, and his wheels burning fire. A stream of fire rushed forth before him: thousand thousands ministered to him, and ten thousands of myriads, attended upon him: *the judgment sat, and the books were opened.* (Dan. 7:9-10 LXX, emphasis mine)

We see that the focus of the first part of this vision is on a heavenly court being seated and books (*scrolls*) being opened. Does Dan. 7 give us further information about one of these scrolls and what results follow after it is opened? It does. Only a few verses later, the result of the judgment of the court is made known. We will learn in Chapter Fourteen: "Event Seven: Rapture and Wrath" that this following scene is the *Coronation of King Jesus* which occurs at the *Seventh Trumpet* (compare the language to Rev. 11:15-16):

> I beheld in the night vision, and, lo, one coming with the clouds of heaven as the Son of Man, and he came on to the Ancient of days, and was brought near to him. *And to him was given the dominion*, and *the honor, and the kingdom*; and all nations, tribes, and languages, shall serve him: *his dominion is an everlasting dominion*, which shall not pass away, and *his kingdom shall not be destroyed.* (Dan. 7:13-14 LXX, emphasis mine)

It is very clear that a transfer of power has occurred, and the kingdom has passed to "the Son of Man." The passage also indicates that this is the last time that power will transfer. Jesus's dominion will be everlasting. Daniel was confused and asked the angel giving him the vision for an explanation. The angel then replied, and it is recorded later in the chapter:

And *the judgment has sat,* and *they shall remove his (Satan and the Antichrist's) dominion to abolish it, and to destroy it utterly. And the kingdom and the power and the greatness of the kings that are under the whole heaven were given to the saints* of the Most High; *and his (Jesus's) kingdom is an everlasting kingdom,* and all powers shall serve and obey him. (Dan. 7:26-27 NASB, clarification and emphasis mine)

The angel's explanation makes it clear to Daniel that one focus of the heavenly judgment is on transferring the dominion *from Satan and the Antichrist to Jesus and the saints.* The opening of the scrolls pictured in Dan 7:10 seem to be the impetus of this transfer of power. In order to further understand Daniel, we need to examine the Revelation account because it gives us far greater detail.

A TALE OF TWO VISIONS

First, let's compare the *Visions of the Throne in Heaven* in Daniel and Revelation to see if they are truly one and the same. Figure 18: Visions of a *Throne in Heaven* in Dan. and Rev. provides this summary of the two visions of the *Throne:*

Element of the Vision	Daniel 7	Revelation 4-5
Thrones for the elders	Thrones were set up (v. 9)	24 thrones with 24 elders (4:4)
Throne for God	The Ancient of Days took His seat (v. 9)	A throne in heaven and one sitting on the throne (4:2)
God's Appearance	Hair like wool (v. 9) Body like Beryl (10:6)	Hair like wool (1:14) Body like jasper, sardius (4:3)
Throne's Appearance	A river of fire coming out before him (v. 10)	Flashes of lightening from out of the throne (4:5)
God's Attendants	Thousands upon thousands and myriads upon myriads (v. 10)	The number of them were myriads upon myriads and thousands upon thousands. (5:11)
The Scroll	The book(s) were opened (v.10)	Jesus opens the *Scroll with 7 Seals* (6:1)
The Son of Man	one coming with the clouds of heaven (v. 13)	He is coming with the clouds (1:7)
The Transfer of the Kingdom	All the kingdoms of the whole earth given to the saints and Christ (v.27)	The kingdom of this world has become the kingdom of our Lord and of His Christ (11:15)
Extent of the Kingdom	His dominion is an everlasting dominion (v.14)	He will reign for ever and ever (11:15)

Figure 18: Visions of a Throne in Heave in Dan. and Rev.

Again, as we saw in Chapter Four: "Bookends (Revelation 1-3)" with the *Vision of the Risen Christ*, the *Vision of a Throne in Heaven* [found in Rev. 4 and 5 (and continuing with its judgments through Chapter 11)] is a perfect fingerprint match for the vision of Daniel. The use of the exact quote "thousands upon thousands and myriads upon myriads" (Gk: CHILIOI CHILIAS KAI MURIOS MURIAS) in Dan. 7:10 and Rev. 5:11 is John's way of telegraphing his intentions to the readers of his day that these visions are *one and the same*. As we have seen, the *use of exact quotes from the Old Testament* (in Greek from the *Septuagint*) is incredibly important in Revelation. As we stated in Chapter Two: "Uncovering the Keys," it is a Revelation "key" for correct interpretation.

TIMING OF THE OPENING OF THE SCROLL

Knowing that the two *Visions* of the *Throne in Heaven* are truly one and the same is important because the vision in Daniel gives us a sense of the timing of when these events occur. Prior to Daniel's *Vision of the Throne in Heaven* we read:

> I noticed his horns, and behold, another *little horn* came up in the midst of them, and before it three of the former horns were rooted out: and, behold, *there were* eyes as the eyes of a man in this horn, and a mouth speaking great things. I beheld until the *thrones were set, and the Ancient of days sat.* (Dan. 7:8-9 LXX, emphasis mine)

Nearly all commentators on Daniel believe that the *"little horn"* pictured in this passage is the Antichrist. From this passage we learn that the Antichrist is active prior to the *Throne in Heaven* scene (". . . thrones were set, and the Ancient of days sat."). The Antichrist has arisen *prior* to the judgment taking place. Immediately after the first segment of the *Vision of the Throne in Heaven* we read:

> I beheld then because of the voice of the great words which *that horn* spoke, until the wild beast was slain and destroyed, and his body given to be burnt with fire. (Dan. 7:11 LXX, emphasis mine)

We now see that after the first *Throne in Heaven* scene in Daniel 7:9-10, the Antichrist is still active for a time. He is then destroyed along with his Beast kingdom after this first scene. This chronological ordering of events allows us to know that the *Visions of the Throne in Heaven* in both Daniel and Revelation (we have proven they are one and the same) occur *after* the Antichrist first arises and *before* he is judged and destroyed.

This analysis, which I believe is unique to this book, is incredibly important because *it allows us to chronologically "time stamp" the opening of the 7 Seals of Revelation.* The *7 Sealed Scroll* is opened at the end of the first segment of the *Throne in Heaven* scene ["the books were opened" (Dan. 7:10)]. There are many who teach that the 7 Seals of Revelation are opened prior to the rise of the Antichrist. *We have proven that that is impossible.* We know with certainty that the seals cannot be opened prior to the court being seated, and this doesn't happen until the Antichrist has arisen. It is most likely that the *seals* of the *7 Sealed Scroll begin to be opened* at the very beginning of Daniel's 70th Week. In Part Two: "The *Pattern of Seven Events*," we will provide significantly more evidence that all the seals open during the 70th Week.

> **The Seals of the *7 Sealed Scroll* of Revelation begin to be opened at the commencement of Daniel's 70th Week.**

PURPOSES OF THE JUDGMENT

We have just discovered that the opening of the *7 Sealed Scroll* in Revelation is the same event pictured in Dan. 7: 9-10 and that it occurs *during* the *70th Week of Daniel*. Now we must determine *what kind of judgment(s)* the heavenly court decides and what the *identity of the books* that are opened? We have already determined that Daniel 7:9-10 is the same vision as found in Rev. 4-6. Our working hypothesis, therefore, is that the *7 Sealed Scroll* opened in the second vision is one of the "books."

There are several other biblical texts which highlight judgments and God's Throne. Psalm 9 is the primary Old Testament passage picturing these events:

> You have *sat on the throne judging righteously.* You have *rebuked the nations.* You have *destroyed the wicked*; you have *blotted out their name* forever and ever. The enemy has come to an end in *perpetual ruins,* And You have *uprooted the cities*; The very memory of them has perished . . . He has established His *throne for judgment,* and He will judge the world in righteousness; *He will execute judgment for the peoples with equity . . .* And those who know Your name will put their trust in You, For You, O Lord, have not forsaken those who seek You. Sing praises to the Lord, who dwells in Zion. Declare among the peoples His deeds. For *He who requires blood* remembers them. *(Psalm 9: 4-5, 7-8. 10-12* NASB, emphasis mine)

I recommend you review this entire Psalm, but I have delineated the four main aspects of judgment the Psalm outlines: 1) rebuking of the nations, 2) destruction of the wicked, 3) uprooting of cities, and 4) judgment *for* the righteous. Our theory is that this judgment is the same judgment as in both *Throne in Heaven* visions. In Psalm 9, we learn the judgment of the wicked is *perpetual* and the memory of the cities of the world has *perished*. Based on these facts, this judgment will occur at the return of Jesus. Since we know that both *Throne in Heaven* visions take place during the *70th Week of Daniel*, we can be confident that all three of these biblical references are picturing the same judgment. This is important because that means the four purposes of the judgment in Psalm 9 will also apply to both *Throne in Heaven* visions. We will return to these four aspects of judgment later in this Chapter as we explore the identity of the *7 Sealed Scroll*.

We also notice that at the judgment of the wicked they have their names "blotted out." What are their names blotted out *from*? Psalm 69 tells us:

> May they be *blotted out of the book of life* and may they not be recorded with the righteous (Psalm 69:28 NASB, emphasis mine)

This use of the *Book of Life* in God's judgment is confirmed by Psalm 9:12, "he who requires blood remembers them." A person's faith in Jesus's *blood sacrifice* allows our names to not be blotted out from the "*Book of Life*."

In Revelation, we find yet another reference to the use of the *Book of Life* during one of God's judgments:

> Then I saw *a great white throne and Him who sat upon it . . . the books were opened*; and another book was opened, which is *the book of life;* and the dead were judged from the things which were written *in the books, according to their deeds . . .* And if anyone's *name was not found written in the book of life, he was thrown into the Lake of Fire. (Rev. 20: 11,12, 15* NASB, emphasis mine*)*

This judgment (*The Great White Throne Judgment*) occurs *after* the end of the thousand year Millennial Kingdom reign of Jesus. It is not the same judgment as seen in Dan. 7 which occurs prior to Jesus's return, however, it is the same *type* of judgment. God's judgment and justice is "immutable" and unchanging. *The way he will judge at the return of Christ is the same way he will judge a 1000 years from now.*

If we study the Judgment in Rev. 20: 11-15, God first sits on his throne and then uses two sets of "books." The first are the books which have our deeds recorded in them. The second is the "*Book of Life*" which has our names written in it if we are saved. All humans are first judged by their deeds. None are found righteous by deeds alone, so only those made righteous by the *blood sacrifice* of Jesus (Psalm 9:12) are saved from the Lake of Fire. This is God's unchanging system of justice. When the books of our deeds are opened, the *Book of Life* is opened as well. They are used together.

God's immutable system of justice used in Rev. 20: 11-15 is the same system as the one that will be used in Dan. 7:9-10; and not surprisingly, the Rev. 20 passage directly quotes Dan. 7:10 that the "*books were opened.*" This confirms that the same sort of judgment is taking place. When we read that "the books were opened" in Dan. 7:10, it refers to both the "books" which contain our deeds *and* the "*Book of Life*" even though the later book is not specifically mentioned. *This is an incredibly important nuance of interpretation.*

Earlier in Rev. 20, another earlier judgment which involves thrones is also pictured:

> *Then I saw thrones, and they sat on them, and judgment was given to them.* And I saw the souls of those who had been beheaded because of their testimony of Jesus and because of the word of God, and those who had not worshiped the beast or his image, and had not received the mark on their forehead and on their hand; and they came to life and reigned with Christ for a thousand years. The rest of the dead did not come to life until the thousand years were completed. *This is the first resurrection.* (Rev. 20: 4-5 NASB, emphasis mine)

In my opinion, this judgment *is* the same judgment as the one found in Dan. 7:9-10. We see thrones and judgment, but this time we are told what we are witnessing is the judgment prior to the *First Resurrection*. The other judgment we just looked at in Rev. 20: 11-15 occurs *after* the Millennial Kingdom (The Great White Throne Judgment) and happens after the *Second Resurrection* (after the thousand years.) Thus both judgments occur in conjunction with a Resurrection! It makes perfect sense that the "books" seen in Dan. 7:10 (man's deeds and the *Book of Life*) would be opened at each Resurrection. How else would the dead be judged as righteous or unrighteous?

RESURRECTIONS

Because these two judgments are associated with Resurrections, we need to pause and examine what a resurrection is and what it isn't. The Bible describes a number of people who were raised back to life in both the Old and New Testaments. Most of these were raised to life only to die again. My definition of a Resurrection is the raising of the righteous back to *eternal life en mass in what could be termed a "harvest"*. Raising the dead is temporary; Resurrection is permanent. The graphic on the next page is the list of saints (Figure 19: Raised to Life) who were raised back to life only to die again. These are not included in what I term a Resurrection:

Saint Raised to Life	Reference
Son of Zarephath's Widow	1 Kings 17:17-24
Son of Shunammite Woman	2 Kings 4:35
Man who touched Elisha's bones	2 Kings 13:21
Widow's son at Nain	Luke 7:13-15
Jairus's Daughter	Matt. 9:25
Lazarus	John 11:43-44
Eutychus	Acts 20:9-12

Figure 19: Raised to Life

Some people also consider Paul as raised from the dead in Acts 14:19-20, but the Bible doesn't explicitly say so. Also notice that all of these were individual cases, all eventually died again (the raising to life was temporary), and all await a permanent Resurrection at the *"First Resurrection."*

We are now ready to begin to examine Resurrections rather than just the raising of individuals. Jesus frequently compared the Resurrection(s) to a *harvest*. Because the Hebrew harvest was divided into three parts, my theory is the Resurrection will be divided into exactly three parts as well. Here is a brief explanation of the *Three-Part Harvest*:

- *First Fruits Harvest*: a limited, preliminary harvest which was presented to YHWH as an offering
- *Primary Harvest*: the harvest when the majority of the grain was reaped
- *Gleanings Harvest*: a final sweep through the fields to reap any remaining grain

If this theory is correct, we should find evidence in scripture for these same three parts of the harvest. That is exactly what we see:

> In Christ all will be made alive. But each in his own order: *Christ the first fruits*, after that *those who are Christ's at His coming* (the primary harvest)" (1 Cor. 15:22-23 NASB, clarification and emphasis mine).

This verse in 1 Corinthians accounts for the first two harvests: the *First Fruits Harvest* and the *Primary Harvest*. The *Gleanings Harvest* and the *Primary Harvest* are found in this other verse in Revelation we just studied above:

> And I saw the souls of those who had been beheaded because of their testimony of Jesus and because of the word of God, and those who had not worshiped the beast or his image, and had not received the mark on their forehead and on their hand. *They came to life* and reigned with Christ for a thousand years. *The rest of the dead did not come to life until the thousand years were completed.* This is the *first* (Gk: PROTOS, meaning first or primary) resurrection. (Rev. 20:5-6 NASB, clarification and emphasis mine)

Here in Rev. 20:6 we see two resurrection harvests being referred to. The *primary one* includes those who did not take the Mark of the Beast, did not worship the Beast, and those who were beheaded for the testimony of Jesus and the Word of God. This resurrection includes only the righteous. A *secondary resurrection* is mentioned as well. This one will include all the rest of the dead (righteous and unrighteous) and will happen *after* the Millennium. This *second resurrection* is the *Gleanings Harvest*.

These *three resurrections* pictured above perfectly fit the picture of the *Three Part Hebrew Harvest*. Let's assemble a summary graphic [Figure 20: Resurrections (Three)] to see what groups of people might be resurrected in each resurrection.

Harvest	Those Resurrected	Timing
First Fruits	Jesus Many Bodies of the Saints (at Crucifixion of Jesus; Matt. 27:52-53)	After the Crucifixion of Jesus
Main Harvest (First Resurrection) Rev. 20: 4-6	Old Testament saints (Abraham, Daniel, etc.) Dead in Christ prior to the Rapture The Two Witnesses (see Chapter Twelve)	At the end of the sixth year of the 70th Week
Gleanings Harvest (Second Resurrection) Rev. 20:11-15	Dead in Christ after the Rapture (during 7th year of 70th Week and the Millennial Kingdom) Unrighteous Dead from all of history	After the end of the Millennial Kingdom

Figure 20: Resurrections (Three)

FIRST FRUITS HARVEST

We have already seen that Jesus is referred to as the "first fruits." We also know *his resurrection* occurred three days and three nights after his crucifixion (on the *Feast of First Fruits* by the way). In Matthew, we learn that many Old Testament saints were raised to life immediately after Jesus rose from the dead:

> And behold, the veil of the temple was torn in two from top to bottom; and the earth shook and the rocks were split. The tombs were opened, and *many bodies of the saints who had fallen asleep were raised*; and coming out of the tombs after His resurrection they entered the holy city and appeared to many. (Matt. 27:51-53 NASB, emphasis mine)

These were obviously saints who were entombed near Jerusalem. Did they ascend to heaven with Jesus? Were they also part of the "first fruits" resurrection? Scripture doesn't tell us, but I think we can assume they did ascend and were part of this preliminary harvest. A good discussion of how this all fits with the *Feast of First Fruits* is contained in Chapter 6 of the book, *The Last Shofar!* by Lenard and Zoller.

Who these saints might have been leads to highly interesting speculation. Since they presented themselves in Jerusalem after Jesus's resurrection, we can assume they died and were buried in that area. Was one of them John the Baptist? Were some of them prophets like Zechariah? Were others kings like David and Solomon? Are they *the 24 Elders* who are mentioned in Revelation as being in Heaven before the *Main Harvest* resurrection? Someday, we may know for certain.

THE PRIMARY HARVEST

Since the *Primary Harvest* (*Main Harvest*) is the "primary" (Gk: PROTOS) one, it must include most of the saints. Revelation pictures this harvest in vivid agricultural terms:

> Then I looked, and behold, a white *cloud*, and sitting on the cloud was one like a son of man, having a golden crown on His head and a sharp sickle in His hand. And another angel came out of the temple, crying out with a loud voice to Him who sat on the cloud, "Put in your sickle and reap, for the hour to reap has come, *because the harvest of the earth is ripe*." Then He who sat on the cloud swung His sickle over the earth, and the earth was reaped. (Rev. 14:13-16 NASB, emphasis mine)

We already know from Rev. 20:4-6 that this harvest includes all the martyrs of the *70th Week of Daniel*. We also know from 1 Cor. 15:23 that all those who are "Christ's at his coming" are in this harvest as well. This includes all the dead in Christ throughout the Church age. What about Old Testament saints like Daniel and Abraham who were buried away from Jerusalem? If we examine Dan. 12, we will find the answer.

> But at that time (after the Great Tribulation) your people—*everyone whose name is found written in the book*—will be delivered. *Multitudes who sleep in the dust of the earth will awake*: some to everlasting life, others to shame and everlasting contempt. Those who are wise will shine like the brightness of the

heavens, and those who lead many to righteousness, like the stars for ever and ever. (Dan. 12:1b-3 NIV, clarification and emphasis mine)

After the Great Tribulation, all of Daniel's people (Jews) whose names are written in "the book" will be delivered (resurrected). Later in this Chapter we will examine whether "the book" referenced in Dan. 12:1-3 is the *Book of Life*. At this point, however, we can see that Old Testament saints are written in it and are resurrected in the *Primary Harvest*.

This harvest should also include the *Two Witnesses* whose resurrection is recorded in Rev. 11. The career of the *Two Witnesses* creates a great deal of contention among Bible scholars. We know from Rev. 11:3 that their ministry is 1260 days long. At the end of their ministry, we learn that *the Beast* that comes out of the Abyss will kill them and their bodies will lie in the streets of Jerusalem for 3 1/2 days. At that point they will be resurrected:

But *after the three and a half days, the breath of life from God came into them (the Two Witnesses), and they stood on their feet*; and great fear fell upon those who were watching them. And they heard a loud voice from heaven saying to them, "Come up here." Then they went up into heaven in the cloud, and their enemies watched them. (Rev. 11:11-12, clarification and emphasis mine)

Some commentators claim the ministry of the *Two Witnesses* occurs during the first half of Daniel's 70th Week. Some claim it is the last half. Everyone has an opinion on their ministry and almost all of them are different. In Part Four, I propose a unique theory that their ministry overlaps both halves of the 70th Week, extending from the *Third Year* to 3 1/2 days before the Resurrection at the end of the *Sixth Year*. If my theory is correct, the resurrections of these *Two Witnesses* will take place with all the other saints martyred by *the Beast* at the *Primary Harvest Resurrection*.

GLEANINGS HARVEST

The *Gleanings Harvest* (the "second resurrection") will occur after the conclusion of the 1000-year Millennial Kingdom and will include all the unrighteous dead throughout all the ages and some righteous dead. All of them are ". . . judged from the things which were written in the books according to their deeds . . . and if anyone's name was not found written in the *Book of Life*, he was thrown into the Lake of Fire" (Rev. 20:12, 15 NASB, emphasis mine). The limited number of righteous in this resurrection (it is a "gleaning") will include those who repent and die in Christ in the final year of the 70th Week (*after* the Rapture) and all the repentant Jews and Gentiles *who die in Jesus* during the 1000 year Millennial Kingdom. These are the survivors of the 70th Week (having human bodies and not resurrection bodies) and children born to them during the Millennium.

TIMING OF THE PRIMARY HARVEST

Based on these explanations above, all people who will be resurrected can be fit within the framework of a Hebrew *Three-Part Harvest*. This is very strong evidence that this is in fact how the resurrections will take place. Let's now look at the timing of the *Primary Harvest Resurrection* because it will also give us the *timing of the Rapture* that directly follows this main Resurrection.

> Then I saw thrones, and they sat on them, and judgment was given to them. And I saw the souls of those who had been beheaded because of their testimony of Jesus and because of the word of God, and those who had not worshiped the beast or his image, and had not received the mark on their forehead and on their hand; and *they came to life* and reigned with Christ for a thousand years. The rest of the dead did not come to life until the thousand years were completed. *This is the first resurrection.* (Rev. 20:4-5 NASB, emphasis mine)

We have already learned that the first verse of this passage pictures the opening of *the 7 Sealed Scroll*. The thrones are set up at the very beginning of Daniel's 70th Week and the judgment is passed for the Resurrection once the names of all those written in *"the Book"* (Dan. 12:1) are exposed; this "time stamps" the passage. This interpretation can be confirmed by the other passage in Revelation that clearly shows this *Primary Harvest*, which is followed by a second "reaping" (of the ungodly) which is the Wrath of God:

> Then I looked, and behold, a white cloud, and sitting on the cloud was one like a son of man, having a golden crown on His head and a *sharp sickle* in His hand . . . Then He who sat on the cloud *swung His sickle over the earth, and the earth was reaped.* And another angel came out of the temple which is in heaven, and he also had a sharp sickle. Then *another angel, the one who has power over fire*, came out from the altar; and he called with a loud voice to him who had the sharp sickle, saying, "Put in your sharp sickle and gather the clusters from the vine of the earth, because her grapes are ripe." So the angel swung his sickle to the earth and gathered the clusters from the vine of the earth, and *threw them into the great wine press of the wrath of God*. And the wine press was trodden outside the city, and blood came out from the wine press, up to the horses' bridles, for a distance of two hundred miles. (Rev. 14:14, 16-20 NASB, emphasis mine)

This passage clearly shows that the Wrath of God during the *Day of the Lord* (which begins after the *Seventh Seal*) chronologically follows the *Primary Harvest Resurrection*. A second set of scriptures will confirm this. The reference to the *Wine Press of God* in Rev. 14: 17-20 comes from Isaiah:

> Who is this who comes from Edom, with garments of glowing colors from Bozrah; this One who is majestic in his apparel, marching in the greatness of his strength? "It is I who speak in righteousness, mighty to save." (It is Jesus) Why is your apparel red, and your garments like the one who *treads in the wine press*? "I have trodden the wine trough alone, and from the peoples there was no man with me. I also trod them in my anger and trampled them

in *my wrath; their lifeblood is sprinkled on my garments*, and I stained all My raiment. "For the *day of vengeance was in my heart, and my year of redemption* has come. . . And I poured out their lifeblood on the earth." (Isa. 63:1-4, 6 NASB, clarification and emphasis mine)

This is an incredible passage for many reasons.

    1) The direct reference to the *wine press* and *pouring out of blood upon the ground* in Rev. 14 are directly made from this passage in Isaiah.

    2) The passage clearly refers to this event as *God's Wrath*.

    3) It clearly gives the time of this period as *a day* and *a year*. So Jesus treads the wine press of his Wrath for one year.

Some might argue that this passage in Isaiah depicts the physical Second Coming. "See (they might say), Jesus is marching from Edom and Bozrah, he is upon the earth." Yes, that is true. The first verse involves the events upon the physical return of Jesus, but the *treading of the wine press* happens earlier. Jesus's stained garment proves this.

And I saw heaven opened, and behold, a white horse, and He who sat on it is called Faithful and True, and in righteousness He judges and wages war. His eyes are a flame of fire, and on His head are many diadems; and He has a name written on Him which no one knows except Himself. *He is clothed with a robe dipped in blood*, and His name is called The Word of God. (Rev. 19:11-13)

Nearly all commentators agree that this passage in Rev. 19 depicts Jesus *just prior* to his physical Second Coming. But notice something interesting that is missed by almost all: *his garments are already dipped in blood!* This is not something that happens upon the earth *after* his physical Second Coming, but something that happens before it during the one year Wrath of God. So in Isaiah 63:1 when Jesus is marching from Edom in garments dipped in blood, they didn't get stained in Edom; they already were stained. *This is an enormously important prophecy insight!*

This is consistent with a *Pre-Wrath* timing for the Resurrection; that the *Primary Resurrection* will precede the Wrath of God, beginning after the *Seventh Seal.*

We know from 1 Thess. 4:17 that during the "first resurrection," the dead in Christ rise first, and then the saints who are alive are caught up together with them in the air; the Rapture immediately follows the Resurrection. If the *Primary Harvest Resurrection* includes saints who by faith do not take the Mark of the Beast, the Resurrection (and thus the Rapture) must occur *after* the Mark of the Beast is institutionalized! The Rapture cannot happen prior to the *70th Week of Daniel* as a *Pre-Tribulation Rapture* position presupposes. It must occur during the 70th Week (near the end of the *Sixth Year* of the 70th Week.) The saints will toil for six years of "tribulation" and rest in Heaven during the seventh year of the "week," much as the Sabbath provides rest in a calendar week.

It should be noted that this analysis of the Resurrection authoritatively proves there isn't a *Pre-Tribulation Rapture.* It is impossible to study Revelation with an open mind and still accept that theory. I have, however, read some explanations from *Pre-Tribulation Rapture* theorists who try and explain away this clear teaching by saying there are as many as seven resurrections and even multiple "first resurrections." They claim that is why those who have refused the Mark of the Beast are included in the first resurrection; that the Primary Resurrection happens before the 70th Week and then again during it. However, these theorists are unable to provide scriptural support for their unorthodox positions. The Bible is clear: there is only one *Primary Harvest* (the "first resurrection") and it takes place at the end of the *Sixth Year* of the 70th Week. There are *not two* "primary" resurrections! First is first.

> **This passage (Rev. 20:4-5) about the *Main Harvest Resurrection* authoritatively *proves* there isn't a *Pre-Tribulation Rapture.***

WHO'S NOT HOME YET?

Before we uncover the identity of this incredibly important *Scroll*, the two visions of the *Throne in Heaven* provide us other timing details of two events during the 70th

Week that are critically important — the Resurrection and the Rapture. First, let's take a brief look around the *Throne Room of God.* As we look around the *Throne Room* in Rev. 5, we see:

- God the Father on his throne (verse 1)
- A strong angel (verse 2)
- The *24 Elders*, the 4 living creatures, the Seven Spirits of God, and the Lamb (verse 6)
- A great multitude of angels (verse 11)

What we don't see are the redeemed saints of God. If we look ahead to Rev. 7, John is able to see the saints at that point, in fact he asks who they are and he is told the following:

> These are they which came out of *great tribulation*, and have washed their robes, and made them white in the blood of the Lamb. Therefore are they before the throne of God, and serve him day and night in his temple: and he that sitteth on the throne shall dwell among them. (Rev. 7:14-15 NASB, emphasis mine)

Why does John see the saints in Rev. 7 and not in Rev. 5? The answer strikes us in the face: the saints are not in heaven yet in Rev. 5 (they are not raptured yet!) at the beginning of the Period many call "the Tribulation" (the *70th Week of Daniel*).

I know many readers may have believed that the Rapture happens before the *70th Week of Daniel* in what is called the *Pre-Tribulation Rapture*. This vision of John's is pretty conclusive proof that the Rapture does *not* happen before that period (the *70th Week of Daniel*) begins. Why would John not see the multitude of saints as Jesus begins to open the seals of the *7 Sealed Scroll*? Why wouldn't they be praising God with all their might? The reason is obvious: they aren't in heaven yet — there is no *Pre-*

Tribulation Rapture. When they finally arrive in Rev. 7, *after* the *Seventh Seal* is broken, John then sees the multitude in heaven and asks about them.

This is another amazing proof that there is no *Pre-Tribulation Rapture*

THE *7 SEALED SCROLL*

Let's now return to the identity of the *7 Sealed Scroll,* which is so prominently featured in Revelation. We have learned that John's vision of the *Throne in Heaven* in Rev. 4-11 is the same vision as Daniel had in Dan. 7. Both visions include the opening of a *Scroll* which we learned results in the transfer of power and the kingdom *from* Satan and the Antichrist *to* Jesus and His saints. We have also just learned that the *Throne in Heaven Vision* and the opening of this *Scroll* are related to the *"Primary Harvest"* and the *first resurrection* of the dead as well. In Revelation, we learn the *Scroll* has *seven seals* and that it is written on both sides.

> I saw in the right hand of Him who sat on the throne a book *written inside and on the back*, sealed up with *seven seals*. (Rev. 5:1 NASB, emphasis mine)

Because the Church now has "amnesia," it has forgotten the identity of the *Scroll*. There has been great speculation as to what this *Scroll* is and about its seals. Some have claimed it is the sealed *Book of Daniel* (Dan. 12:4), others claim it is the sealed Wrath of God, while still others insist it is the Title Deed to the Earth. Finally, we are proposing here yet a fourth possibility for this *Scroll* (unique to this book): that it is *Mans' Inheritance* that includes salvation of the righteous, punishment for the wicked, and the transfer of dominion back to the rightful owners of the earth. This final concept is a combination of three of the other ideas *and* uniquely matches the purposes of God's judgment listed in Psalm 9 that we studied earlier in this Chapter.

If we are going to identify the *7 Sealed Scroll*, we will need to look at the clues we are given. The clues found in this chapter should be consistent with our thesis that it is *Mans' Inheritance* if we are correct in our assumptions. Let's look at the clues:

- The scroll is written on both sides (Rev. 5:1). Scrolls were usually only written on one side because the grain of the papyrus only allowed easy writing on one side. For this reason, there were very few scrolls, books, or tablets written on both sides.

- The Greek word translated "scroll" specifically means a papyrus scroll.

- The scroll is sealed with *seven seals*, all of which are visible to John (Rev. 5:1). Some claim that as each seal is broken, a little more of the scroll is revealed. This is disproven by the fact that *all seven seals must be on the outside of the scroll in order to be visible to John.*

- John cries when no one is initially found worthy to open the scroll (Rev. 5:4). This indicates that seeing the scroll opened is something that John desired a great deal. Would John desire the Wrath of God to be poured out? Probably not. Might he be emotionally upset if the *Book of Daniel* wasn't unsealed? Again, probably not. Might he be upset if the dominion of the earth stayed with Satan and didn't revert back to the saints of God? Yes! Would he cry if the righteous weren't resurrected and rewarded? He would absolutely be devastated!

- Jesus is found worthy to open the *Scroll* because the angels and elders said, "Worthy are you to take the book (scroll) and break its seals *for you were slain* and *purchased* for God with your blood men from every tribe and tongue and people and nation" (Rev. 5:9 NASB, clarification and emphasis mine). Jesus is *specifically* worthy because he was slain and because he purchased our redemption with his blood. Redemption by a "kinsman redeemer" was necessary to buy back a piece of property. Jesus fulfilled all these requirements by his death on the cross where he willingly paid the redemption price for our sins.

A proper identification of the *Scroll* will be consistent with each one of these clues. Let us examine a graphic (Figure 21: Features of Revelation's *Scroll* and Correlations) that details how each theory of the scroll's identity matches the clues:

Feature of the Scroll	Book of Daniel	God's Wrath	Title Deed to the Earth	Man's Inheritance
Written on both sides	No	Yes	Yes*	Yes
Paper Scroll	Yes	Yes	Yes	Yes
Sealed	Maybe***	Maybe**	Yes	Yes
Source of John crying	No	No	Yes	Yes
Requires redemption by means of Jesus' blood	No	No	Yes	Yes

Figure 21: Features of Revelation's Scroll

*Title deeds were first sealed and then signed by witnesses on the outside of the scroll. This would entail writing on both sides. This is pictured in Jeremiah 32:10.

** There are two visions of an unsealed scroll of lamentations and woes written on both sides in Ezekiel and Zechariah. They are unsealed in the visions but that does not mean they weren't sealed at one time.

*** A scroll is sealed in Dan. 12:4. We are unsure at this point what that scroll is — this is discussed in the section below.

THE BOOK OF DANIEL

Let's first examine whether the *7 Sealed Scroll* is the *Book of Daniel*. This choice should be *eliminated* from consideration immediately because the *Book of Daniel* was not described as written on both sides nor did scripture say that opening it required

102

redemption by means of Jesus' blood. Further, John would have no reason to cry if it remained sealed.

In Daniel 12:4 we do see that a "book" or scroll *is* sealed, however. For this reason, many commentators have long believed this was the *Book of Daniel*. But let's look at what the text actually says:

> And at that time Michael the great prince shall stand up, that stands over the children of thy people: and there shall be a time of tribulation, such tribulation as has not been from the time that there was a nation on the earth until that time: at that time thy people shall be delivered, even every one that is written in *the book*. And many of them that sleep in the dust of the earth shall awake, some to everlasting life, and some to reproach and everlasting shame. And the wise shall shine as the brightness of the firmament and some of the many righteous as the stars for ever and ever. And thou, Daniel, close the words, and *seal the book* to the time of the end; until many are taught, and knowledge is increased. (Dan. 12: 1-4 LXX, emphasis mine)

This famous passage contains two references to *"the book."* Are they the same book? The use of the definitive article, "the" in both instances means either it's the same book as one referred to earlier in scripture or the most significant book of its type. These two references to *"the book"* only a few verses apart *must* refer to the same book. Because the *Book of Daniel* obviously does not contain the names of the righteous who will be resurrected, this is further proof that the *Book of Daniel* is *not sealed* in Dan. 12:4, contrary to the view of many commentators.

THE *BOOK OF LIFE*

Is "the book" sealed in Dan. 12:4 the *Book of Life*? Although the sealed scroll in Dan. 12 is not referred to as the *Book of Life* directly, I conclude it is. The *Book of Life* is referenced by name no less than eight times in scripture. It is certainly the most well-known scroll in scripture, and it certainly can be referred to as *"the book."* The first direct mention of this book by name is found in Psalms in a prophetic passage about the Jews who would encourage the crucifixion:

> Let them be blotted out of *the book of the living*, and let them not be *written with the righteous*. (Psalms 69:28 LXX, emphasis mine)

Based on this reference from the days of King David, Daniel would certainly be aware that this book existed and could describe it as *"the book."* Also notice that the righteous are *written* in this book just as Daniel's vision describes.

A second reference to the names of the righteous being written in the *Book of Life* is made by Paul in his Letter to the Philippians: ". .. the rest of my fellow workers, whose *names are in the book of life"* (Phil. 4:3 NASB, emphasis mine).

After the Millennium (after the 1000 year reign of Christ's Kingdom), a judgment will take place called the *Great White Throne Judgment* (we have learned this takes place after the "second resurrection"). Notice what John relates in Revelation about that judgment:

> I saw the dead, the great and the small, standing before the throne, *and books were opened*; and another book was opened, which is *the book of life*; and the dead were judged from the things which were written in the books, according to their deeds. And if *anyone's name* was not found *written* in the *book of life*, he was thrown into the Lake of Fire. (Rev. 20:12 NASB, emphasis mine)

Again, a third time we learn that the names of the saved are written in the *Book of Life*. Can the reference in Dan 12:4 of the names of the righteous being written into *"the book"* refer to anything else but the *Book of Life*? *"The book"* is obviously and definitively the *Book of Life*.

Now that we have determined that the sealed *Scroll* in Dan. 12:1-4 is indeed the *Book of Life*, let's examine how it is used in God's immutable system of judgment. In the passage in Rev. 20:12 above, we see that "the books were opened" and that the *Book of Life* is opened with "the books." As we have already learned in this Chapter, the "books" record our deeds. The *Book of Life* records whether or not someone is saved by the Blood of Jesus. We also learned the process of the judgment of souls by God is the same whether during the *70th Week of Daniel* or a thousand years later. *God's justice is immutable and unchanging.*

Isn't it then logical that God's unchanging justice will prevail prior to the Resurrection and Rapture? Isn't it logical that the heavenly court will be seated, "the books" (man's deeds) will be opened, the *Book of Life* (salvation) will also be opened, and a "judgment" of souls will be rendered prior to these events? We already know from the *Throne in Heaven Vision* in Dan. 7 that a court is seated, books are opened, and a judgment rendered during Daniel's 70th Week. Because God's justice is immutable, we know without question that the *Book of Life* must also be opened at that time as well. It is the only way under God's unchanging system of justice that He determines who the righteous are. The *Book of Life* cannot *only* be opened a thousand years after Christ's return. It must *also* be opened prior to the Resurrection and Rapture. Anytime souls are judged, it must be opened. Dan. 7:10 doesn't directly refer to the *Book of Life*, however. It says "the books were opened," but we have already seen the *Book of Life* is opened in Daniel 12: 1-4, so Daniel pictures all the books opening, only God's system of progressive revelation revealed it in separate visions.

THE *BOOK OF LIFE* IS SEALED

> And thou, Daniel, close (Gk: ENPHOBOS, meaning fill with Holy fear) the words, *and seal the book to the time of the end* (Gk: SUNTELEIA meaning "payment" or "completion of multiple parts"); until many are taught, and knowledge is increased. (Dan. 12:1-4 LXX, clarification and emphasis mine)

Dan. 12:4 tells us the *Scroll* (the *Book of Life*) will be sealed. The most significant sealed scroll in the Bible is the *7 Sealed Scroll* seen in Rev. 5:1. Could these two scrolls, actually be one and the same? Several old commentaries on Revelation consider that it may be—*Jamieson-Fausset- Brown's Commentary* and the *Cambridge Bible for Schools and Colleges* both elude that it is[xxv].

In my opinion, careful examination of the text indicates that the 7 Sealed Scroll opened in Rev. 6-11 may include the *Book of Life* (but not be solely the *Book of Life*). Dan. 12:4 indicates the *Scroll* (the *Book of Life*) will be sealed until the *"time of the end."* The Holy Spirit through the pen of Daniel uses a very specific term to designate the word "end" in the phrase "time of the end." This Greek word is SUNTELEIA which means *"completion of multiple parts."* This is entirely consistent with the seven seals (many parts) of the *Scroll* in Revelation.

The completion will come after the *multiple parts* (7 seals) are opened. The term, SUNTELEIA also has a meaning of *"payment"* or *"consummation of a deal"* which also matches perfectly with the payment Jesus made on behalf of those being saved. We learned in Rev. 5:5-10 that this payment is required of the one worthy to open the *7 Sealed Scroll*. This specific term, SUNTELEIA, was also used by the disciples in the question which launched the Olivet Discourse, "As he was sitting on the Mount of Olives, the disciples came to him privately, saying, 'Tell us, when will these things happen, and what will be the sign of Your coming, and *of the end* (Gk: SUNTELEIA) of the age" (Matt. 24:3 NASB, clarification and emphasis mine). This is a very particular Greek word. In the New Testament it is *always* used in reference to the return of Jesus and the end of the age. In every case, it is referring back to this use in Dan. 12:4.

The dual concepts of a *"payment"* and the *"completion of many parts"* found in the word SUNTELEIA are found in one verse in Revelation:

> Worthy are you (Jesus) to take the book and to break its seals (seven seals which when open are the completion of multiple parts); for you were slain and *purchased for God with Your blood* (the payment) men from every tribe and tongue and people and nation. (Rev. 5:9 NASB, clarification and emphasis mine)

This is the time of the end Daniel was referring to—the breaking of the seven seals on the *7 Sealed Scroll*. When all *Seven Seals* are broken, we will reach the completion of multiple parts, the SUNTELEIA. Only Jesus is worthy to break the seals and reveal the names of the righteous because of the payment he made with his blood on our behalf to purchase men from every tribe. *This purchase of man's salvation by Jesus's blood also definitively identifies the 7 Sealed Scroll as the Book of Life.*

Some question how a sealed scroll can be the *Book of Life*. They ask: If names of the saved are constantly being added to it, how it can be sealed? This is a very good question. The answer is found in the Psalms.

> In *your book* were all written *the days that were ordained for me*, when as yet there was not one of them. (Psalm 139:16 NASB, emphasis mine)

The all-knowing God, who exists outside of the constraints of time, has written the names and all the days of the righteous into *"the book"* ahead of time. Hence, he already knows who will come to salvation and has already written their names in the *Book of Life,* to be revealed at the end. Truly, we serve an omnipotent, omniscient God.

Others ask how a human like Daniel could be worthy to seal the *Book of Life*. Frankly, he is not. In my opinion, Dan. 12:4 pictures a symbolic sealing. The Prophets were frequently asked to perform symbolic acts. Ezekiel and John were each asked to symbolically "eat" the *7 Sealed Scroll*. Rather, the sealing of the Scroll in Dan. 12:4 is symbolic of the time the Scroll was sealed. In the immediately preceding passage (Dan. 11:21-Dan. 3), the Angel Gabriel gave Daniel the first completely chronological account of the *Pattern of Seven Events* which culminates with the Resurrection and Rapture! (We will study this additional account of the *Pattern of Seven Events* later in PART TWO of the book.) However, at this point, our theory is that once Gabriel gave Daniel the *Pattern*, he asked him to symbolically place the events as *Seals* on the Scroll to be opened at the SUNTELLIA; the time of the end. Once the *Pattern of Seven Events* takes place and all the *Seals* are removed from the Scroll, it will open to reveal the names of the righteous.

Finally, others ask the completely logical question, "If the Resurrection and Rapture take place at the *Seventh Seal*, how can the raptured saints be pictured in Rev. 7:9-17 prior to the opening of the Seventh Seal at Rev. 8:1?" This is a very good question and I don't have a complete answer.

We know that the Resurrection and Rapture and the Wrath of God in the form of fire falling from heaven happen on the same day. The fire from heaven is the *First Trumpet Judgement* that occurs just after the *Seventh Seal*. It is possible the Rapture occurs just slightly before the opening of the *Seventh Seal* and the *First Trumpet Judgment* (fire falling from heaven) happens. However, it is also possible that the events of Rev. 6:12 – 8:1 all take place in a very short period of time and the exact chronology is not expressed in the text; that this section of Revelation is by topic not exact chronology. My personal opinion is that the most important events happen on the 7's (*Seventh Seal, Seventh Trumpet, and Seventh Bowl*) and the most elegant and logical solution is that the *Seventh Seal* opens into the *Day of the Lord* which contains Rapture and Wrath. However, I admit that the opening of the *Book of Life* and thus the Resurrection and Rapture may happen just prior to the opening of the *Seventh Seal*. In either case (whether the Rapture occurs just prior to the *Seventh Seal* or just after), both events happen on the same physical day.

WORDS OF HOLY FEAR

Dan. 12:4 also discusses the *"closing of the words"* and not just the sealing of *"the book."* This has confused commentators. The reason is the underlying Greek word that is translated "closing" doesn't mean that at all! It actually means *"filling with Godly fear."* This is the same Greek word (Gk: ENPHOBOS) used in the New Testament when the women encountered the angels at Jesus's tomb after his Resurrection and bowed before them. It is highly consistent with the Holy and frightening eternal nature of the words on the *7 Sealed Scroll*.

After giving Daniel the prophecy in Dan. 12:1-4, the angel is joined by two others and they further clarify its meaning. Daniel is confused even by the further explanation and they respond accordingly:

I heard, but *I understood not*: and I said, O Lord, what will be the end (PERAS, meaning "boundary" or "limit") of these things? And he said, Go, Daniel: for the words are closed (Gk: ENPHOBOS; *"filling with Godly fear:"*) and sealed up to the time of the end (Gk: PERAS) . . . and thou shalt stand in thy lot at the end (Gk: SUNTELEIA) of the days. (Dan. 12:8-9, 13 LXX, clarification and emphasis mine)

Again the angel uses the same two Greek words in his explanation: ENPHOBOS and SUNTELEIA. Daniel is told that the words on the scroll are *"filled with Godly fear"* and sealed until the time of the *"limit or boundary."* Then Daniel is told he will stand in his *"lot"* at the SUNTELEIA which we now know is when the Resurrection happens. So we are told Daniel will be resurrected and stand with his lot (the tribe of Judah) at the breaking of the *Seventh Seal*.

Based on all of this evidence, I think we can say with a good degree of confidence that *"the book"* that is sealed in Dan. 12 is the *Book of Life,* and it is also the *7 Sealed Scroll* seen in Revelation. These are wonderfully helpful insights into understanding this prophetic scripture.

IS THE *BOOK OF DANIEL* SEALED?

One unexpected outcome of proving that *"the book"* sealed in Dan. 12 is actually the *7 Sealed Scroll* is discovering that it is *not* the *Book of Daniel*. Hundreds of prophecy teachers and commentaries on Daniel assume that his book is supernaturally sealed based on Dan. 12. The analysis in the preceding sections, however, proves that is not the case.

Some commentators believe another chapter in Daniel also seems to refer to sealing (Dan. 8:26), but upon examining the *Septuagint*, the Greek text seems to explain that passage better than the Hebrew as well; and without supernatural sealing. The Greek text reads:

> And the vision of the evening and morning that was mentioned *is true*: and do thou *seal* (Gk: SPHRAGIZO, meaning *"to seal or to set a signet ring seal **to certify**"*) *the vision*; for it is for many days. (Dan. 8:26 LXX, clarification and emphasis mine)

The meaning here in the Greek can mean to *"certify"* the vision. This fits perfectly with the beginning of the verse which states that the timing of the evenings and mornings was true. The angel is essentially saying, *"This is true and here is God's signet ring seal to certify it."* Thus, contrary to the opinion of many commentators, it appears that the *Book of Daniel* and the specific vision in Dan. 8 are *not* sealed in a supernatural way that limits our understanding of them. The visions are *open* and able to be interpreted. We will discuss them in depth in Chapter Fifteen: "Overcoming Lions (Daniel 1-12)."

Now, it is true that the proper understanding of many of Daniel's prophecies are only recently coming to light (*this book explains some of this new understanding*), but this is not due to an "unsealing" of prophecies. New understanding of eschatology is now being uncovered in many different books of the Bible. Consider all the new insights into Revelation also found in this book, yet John specifically says Revelation is not sealed. Uncovering of new insights does not require an "unsealing" of a book of the Bible. Undoubtedly, new insights are coming to light, and we can thank the Holy Spirit for uncovering these new insights into the meaning of prophetic scripture for the benefit of the Church. It is needed now as we get closer to the end times.

LAMENTATIONS, MOURNING AND WOE

After determining that the *7 Sealed Scroll* contains the *Book of Life*, are there things other than the names of the saints written onto the *Scroll* as well? In Rev. 20:12, John refers to the *Book of Life* directly, yet he never refers to the *7 Sealed Scroll* as the *Book of Life*. Might this be because the *7 Sealed Scroll* contains more than just the *Book of Life*?

Some commentators have expressed the theory that the *7 Sealed Scroll* is the Wrath of God. The scroll cannot solely be one of lamentation and woe (the Wrath of

God) because this definition would not result in John crying that it couldn't be opened and it wouldn't require redemption by Jesus' blood to open it. It is possible, however, that the lamentations and woes found on the scrolls pictured in Ezek. 2: 9-10 and Zech. 5:1-3 *are* written onto this *Scroll* in addition to the names of the righteous, as we just learned above. It is possible the *7 Sealed Scroll* has multiple meanings and purposes. This idea of multiple meaning is re-enforced by the direct quote from Ezek. 2 found in Rev. 5; both scripture passages are shown below:

> Then I looked, and behold, a hand was extended to me; and lo, *a scroll* was in it. When He spread it out before me, it was *written on the front and back*, (Gk: GEGREMMANON ESOTHEN KAI OPISTHEN) and written on it were *lamentations, mourning and woe*. (Ezek. 2:9-10 NASB, clarification and emphasis mine)

> I saw in the right hand of Him who sat on the throne *a book written inside and on the back* (Gk: GEGRAMMENON ESOTHEN KAI OPISTHEN), sealed up with *seven seals*. (Rev. 5:1 NASB, clarification and emphasis mine)

Again, as we have seen previously, direct quotes from the Old Testament (specifically, from the Greek *Septuagint*) are identification markers in Revelation that the passage is related to the Old Testament reference. This is direct proof that the scroll contains lamentations. This makes sense because the *seven trumpets* found when the *Scroll* opens are part of the Wrath of God. The idea that the *Scroll* could contain both the names of those to be delivered *and* the curses to be poured out on the unrighteous is re-enforced by two parallel passages in Revelation and Ezekiel:

> Go; take *the book* which is open (Gk: ENEOGMENON meaning *"having been opened"*) in the hand of the angel who stands on the sea and on the land. So I went to the angel, telling him to give me the little book. And he said to me, "Take it and eat it; it will make your stomach bitter, but in your mouth it will be *sweet as honey* (Gk: GLYKY HOS MELI)." I took the little book out of the

angel's hand and ate it, and in my mouth it was sweet as honey; and when I had eaten it, my stomach was made bitter. (Rev. 10:8-10 NASB, clarification and emphasis mine)

And I looked, and behold, a hand stretched out to me, and in it a volume of *a book*. And he unrolled it before me: and in it the *front and the back were written upon*: and there was written in it *Lamentation, and mournful song, and woe* . . . Thy mouth shall eat, and thy belly shall be filled with this volume that is given to thee. So I ate it; and it was in my mouth as *sweet as honey* (Gk: GLYKY HOS MELI). (Ezek. 2:9, 3:3 LXX, clarification and emphasis mine)

Once again we see a direct Old Testament quote in the passage in Revelation which positively identifies *the Scroll* as one and the same as Ezekiel's scroll. Interestingly the passage from Ezekiel is a continuation of the same passage that identifies the *Scroll* as the *7 Sealed Scroll*. Also notice in the Revelation passage that *the Scroll* is listed as just *"having been opened."* This is the process John witnessed in Revelation Chapters 6 – 8 as the *7 Sealed Scroll* was opened.

From these two passages, we learn that *the Scroll* is both sweet ("good") and sour ("bad"). The order of the sweetness and sourness is important. At first it is sweet. When the *Scroll* is initially opened, the names of the redeemed are seen ("good news"). The dead in Christ rise first and those who survive the *Great Tribulation* are gathered together, and they meet their Lord in the air. This is the Rapture. Immediately after the Rapture, the Wrath of God is poured out ("bad news"). It is at this point (after the sweetness of the Rapture) that the sourness of the Wrath of God (the start of the Day of the Lord) is delivered on the unrighteous.

A TITLE DEED HIDDEN IN A JAR

Now that we've established that *the Scroll* contains the sweetness of the Rapture (the deliverance of the saints) and the sourness of the Wrath of God, let's continue to examine the theory that the *Scroll* in Rev. 5 is also the *Title Deed to Earth*. If this is true, the opening of this title deed would be the transference of dominion that we already saw pictured in the *Throne in Heaven Vision* in Dan. 7.

The possibility that the *7 Sealed Scroll* contains the *Title Deed to the Earth* requires some explanation. Man was originally given dominion over the earth in the garden (Gen. 1:26-30). However, Satan obtained that dominion after the fall. We know that for certain, because in the Gospel of Luke Satan makes this statement:

> And he (Satan) led Him (Jesus) up and showed Him all the kingdoms of the world in a moment of time. And the devil said to Him, "I will give you all this *domain* (dominion) and its glory; for it has been *handed over to me*, and I give it to whomever I wish. Therefore if you worship before me, it shall all be yours." (Luke 4:5-7 NASB, clarification and emphasis mine)

In Dan. 7 we learned that this dominion that is currently controlled by Satan will be transferred to Jesus and his saints after the judgment that occurs in the *Throne in Heaven Vision*.

In Old Testament Israel, title transfers of land required a *title deed* that indicated the details of the transfer, and also how the land might be redeemed by the original owner. This *title deed* was then sealed. If Satan obtained dominion over the earth from Adam, then a *title deed* most probably would have been written. In this deed Satan would have been given dominion, but the details of how that dominion might transfer back to its original owners would also be recorded. We know from Daniel that this dominion will be returned to the saints and Jesus once the events of Dan. 7 and Rev. 4-11 are complete. So, might the *7 Sealed Scroll* contain the *Title Deed to the Earth*? It very well might.

In Jeremiah there is an account of the prophet purchasing a property from Hanamel, his nephew. This was not an ordinary property purchase. Jeremiah was commanded by God to purchase the property during Nebuchadnezzar's final siege of Jerusalem. This meant that Jeremiah was purchasing land that he would never use because it would soon fall into the hands of the Babylonians. God informed Jeremiah that the purchase was symbolic and that Jeremiah was to "'Take these deeds, this *sealed* deed of purchase and this open deed, and put them in an earthenware jar, that they may last a long time.' for thus says the Lord of hosts, the God of Israel, 'Houses and fields and vineyards will again be bought in this land'" (Jer. 32:14-15 NASB, emphasis mine). The sealed deed was symbolic of a coming day when the land would once again return to the ownership of the Jews. Jeremiah could safely purchase the land, because God was promising to restore it someday. If the *7 Sealed Scroll* contains the *Title Deed to the Earth*, it is symbolic of the coming restoration of all things when the earth is given back to Jesus and his saints. God has promised that, just as assuredly as he promised Jeremiah that his land would be restored.

The Greek word HYPOSTASIS is an interesting key to further understanding *title deeds*. This word is traditionally translated "substance" or "assurance" throughout the New Testament as it is in this verse from Hebrews, "Now faith is the assurance (Gk: HYPOSTASIS) of things hoped for, the conviction of things not seen" (Heb. 11: 1 NASB, clarification mine). A recent archeological discovery of a chest with many title deeds inside it was made in northern Israel. On the outside of the chest was the title "HYPOSTASIS." Did this Greek word have a relationship to *title deeds*? Did they call the deeds "assurances?" The owner of the properties might never have seen the land for which they had the deeds, but had "assurance" that they owned them by means of these deeds.[xxvi] If we substitute the words *"title deed"* into the famous verse in Hebrews we get this paraphrase: "faith is the *'title deed'* of things hoped for." We might die before Jesus restores the kingdom to the saints, but we have the *assurance* of Rev. 4-11 that Jesus will do just that. We can have faith in what will someday be because of that *7 Sealed Scroll*.

PSALM 9 AND MAN'S INHERITANCE

At the beginning of this Chapter, we discussed Psalm 9 and the judgment of God pictured there. Having determined that the *7 Sealed Scroll* opened at that judgment is Man's Inheritance, let's examine how the purposes of that judgment found in Psalm 9 and the purposes written into *7 Sealed Scroll* are the same:

Purpose	Psalm 9	7 Sealed Scroll
Transfer of the Kingdom	You have rebuked the nations, v. 5	Transfer of the Title Deed of the Earth
Punishment of the Wicked	You have destroyed the wicked, v. 5 You have uprooted the cities, v. 6	The Wrath of God
Reward of the Righteous	For He who requires blood remembers them; He does not forget the cry of the afflicted, v. 12	The Resurrection and Rapture

Figure 22: Comparison of the Judgments in Psalm 9 and the *7 Sealed Scroll*

The writer of Hebrews testifies to this promise of eternal inheritance:

> For this reason he is the mediator of a new covenant, so that, since a death has taken place for *the redemption of the transgressions* that were committed under the first covenant, those who have been called may receive the promise of the *eternal inheritance.* (Heb. 9:15 NASB, emphasis mine)

Notice how the writer of Hebrews links the *redemption of transgressions* that was paid for by Jesus' death to this *inheritance.* This is the same concept as seen in Rev. 5, that our Messiah is worthy to open the scroll because he paid the price. In Ephesians we read:

> After listening to the message of truth, the gospel of your salvation—having also believed, you were *sealed in Him with the Holy Spirit of promise,* who is

given as a pledge of our *inheritance*, with a view to *the redemption* of God's own possession. (Eph. 1:13-14 NASB, clarification and emphasis mine)

Again, in this above passage from Ephesians, redemption and eternal inheritance are intimately linked.

> The *7 Sealed Scroll* is *"Man's Inheritance"*: 1) deliverance for the saints, 2) punishment for the wicked, and 3) a return of the dominion of the kingdoms of this world to their rightful owners: Jesus and His saints.

DANIEL 7 AND THE *7 SEALED SCROLL*

Having identified the *7 Sealed Scroll*, I'd like to take a brief moment to once again examine how the events of Dan. 7 relate to this scroll. We now know that when Dan. 7:10 states that "the books were opened," one of those books will be the *7 Sealed Scroll*. The Scroll begins to be opened when the Heavenly Court is seated in Dan. 7:9 and we have found this occurs at the beginning of Daniel's 70th Week. The *seventh seal* is broken at the conclusion of Daniel 7:10, and at this point the Resurrection and Rapture occur and immediately after that the Wrath of God is poured out in the form of the Trumpet judgments. In Dan. 7:11, we learn that the Beast continues his boastful words even after the opening of the *7 Sealed Scroll* and the pouring out of God's Wrath. This is completely consistent with a Pre-Wrath Rapture. Finally in Dan. 7:13-14, we see Jesus's coronation as King and his receiving the dominion and the Kingdom. We will learn in Chapter Fourteen: "Event Seven: Rapture and Wrath" that this occurs at the *seventh trumpet*.

We began our study in this Chapter with Daniel's *Throne in Heaven* vision in Dan. 7, and now we have circled back to this vision again to find that all the major events of the *70th Week of Daniel* are highlighted in this vision!

I realize there is a lot of content packed into the above sections. Do not worry if you were not able to fully grasp the concepts yet. In future chapters, we will continue to unpack these ideas with other explanations.

SUMMARY:

We have re-learned two important facts that we forgot during the Church's *amnesia* about the correct definitions of important terms used in Daniel and Revelation. First, we have learned that the *7 Sealed Scroll* will be opened *during* the *70ᵗʰ Week of Daniel*. Second, we learned that the *7 Sealed Scroll* is *Mans' Inheritance* containing deliverance for the righteous, punishment for the wicked, and a return of the dominion of the earth to its rightful owners—Christ and His saints. Once we were able to re-establish these facts, we were able to properly outline Revelation.

We have now begun to analyze the first five chapters of Revelation. Before we move on to analyze the rest of the book of Revelation, let me explain how we will proceed. Revelation is written with a "main story line" and "side stories" that explain various elements of the main story. The main story line flows from Rev. 4-11 (the opening of the *7 Sealed Scroll*), then it picks up again in Rev. 15-16 (the Bowl Judgments), and it concludes in Rev. 19-22 (the return of Christ, the Millennial Kingdom, and the Eternal State). Because Revelation is *not written as a continuous saga*, we will not analyze it verse by verse and chapter by chapter. Instead, we will discuss the main story line in depth in Chapters Seven: "A Horse of a Different Color (Revelation 6)" and Chapters Twelve, Thirteen, and Fourteen. The *supplemental information* found in Rev. 12-14 and Rev. 17-18 will be covered in the remaining Chapters of Part Two ("The Pattern of Seven Events") of this book at appropriate points in our discussion. Rev. Chapters 2-3 are covered in depth in Part Four. Although this may seem confusing at first, it will allow for a better flow and understanding of the ideas in Revelation.

PART TWO:

The *Pattern of Seven*

Events

Chapter Six

THE WALLS CAME TUMBLING DOWN
(JOSHUA 6, JUDGES 6 – 8)

When something is important, *really* important, it is repeated over and over. Ideas which at first may seem strange become clear and understandable with repeated exposure. We see this in American elementary school curriculums where math tables are repeatedly studied. In music, repetition is a key element. Crucial musical and lyrical phrases repeat over and over throughout the song and are known as "hooks."

When the important factor is presented in slightly different ways, we can gain additional information about it from these slight differences. In Steven Spielberg's secular, science fiction movie, "Close Encounters of the Third Kind" (EMI Films, 1977)[xxvii] a wonderful depiction of this effect occurs at the beginning of the film. A number of ordinary people begin doing unusual things after an initial alien encounter. Some paint, some sculpt, some bring dirt into their homes to build a small mountain. All of them are trying to create a "picture" of a mesa in Wyoming known as Devil's Tower. In the fictional movie, all of these ordinary people were given a vision of this location where the aliens would finally reveal themselves. Eventually, from the combination of these different impressions of Devil's Tower, many of these ordinary people, who were "invited" by the aliens, are able to locate it. Several of them are then able to travel to Devil's Tower and be there for the aliens' arrival.

As strange as this secular movie plot seems, it actually is very similar to the technique employed by the Holy Spirit in inspiring parts of the Bible. In the Bible, a truly important theological idea may be presented in different "pictures" of the idea. These pictures may be located throughout the Bible in different books. Paul points out the value of these Old Testament depictions:

Ch. 6: The Walls Came Tumbling Down

> Now these things happened to them (Israel) as an example, and they were written for our instruction, upon whom the ends of the ages have come. (1 Cor. 10:11 NASB, clarification mine)

Jesus's redemptive work on the cross, for instance, was "pictured" in the Old Testament a number of times so that when the Jews saw it happening, they would, hopefully, understand it. In the book of Exodus it was presented through the Passover story. The blood of a lamb (representing the blood of Jesus) was painted on the door frame of Jewish homes to protect them from the angel of death.

Psalm 22 presented a vivid *prophetic picture* of Jesus's time on the cross including the gambling for his clothes (v.18), his bones being out of joint (v.14), the piercing of his hands and feet (v.16), etc. As he was hanging on the cross, Jesus referenced this Psalm 22 ("Sense and Reference") by quoting its first verse, "My God, my God, why have you forsaken me?" Unfortunately, the Jews within hearing distance misunderstood Jesus's reference thinking he was calling on Elijah. By missing this reference, they also missed its messianic message of deliverance.

In Isaiah 53, we see another picture of Jesus's suffering on the cross. We learn that he was pierced for our transgressions and crushed for our iniquities (v.4). He was scourged for our healing (v.5), did not open his mouth to defend himself (v.7) and was given a grave of a rich man (v. 9). In this case related to Isaiah 53, the Ethiopian eunuch to whom this passage was explained by Phillip (who was an *accurate* commentator of scripture!) did not miss the messianic message, and he was baptized and saved (Acts 8:26-40).

If the *70th Week of Daniel* is important (and it obviously is), doesn't it make sense that the Bible will also contain numerous "pictures" of this time period in the Old and New Testaments? Is the Church missing these references to the *70th Week of Daniel* today? It is easy for us to find depictions of Jesus's time on the cross in the Old Testament because this event has already taken place. It is much more difficult for us to find those pictures of the *70th Week of Daniel* in the scriptures because they are all still to be fulfilled in the future. We don't have hindsight about the details of that time. But when we do find these pictures, they are a treasure of infinite worth because they will help us know in advance what is to occur. We must be like the Ethiopian eunuch and not miss the message our Messiah and his Word have for us, as it is explained to us.

Most of the references to the *70ᵗʰ Week of Daniel* in scripture refer to it generally or refer solely to the Day of the Lord, which occurs at the end of the time period. There are a special group of these pictures, however, that refer to the 70ᵗʰ Week in *chronologic order*. These pictures are *extremely valuable* because they help us organize and sequence what is to occur. The *Letters to the Seven Churches*, the *Olivet Discourse*, and the opening of the *7 Sealed Scroll* in Revelation are among these pictures, but there are others. We are able to identify these priceless pictures because they form a "pattern" of events with a specific order—the *Pattern of Seven Events* (see Appendix A for a summary of these seven events). When we learn to identify that configuration, we can align future passages we discover with it. All of these pictures involve *a sequence of seven specific events*. Deception comes first, then bloodshed, then famine, then death, etc. The pattern is extremely precise as we will uncover in this Part of the book. Just like the picture of Devil's Tower in the movie, each of these pictures gives us a different glimpse of that time. Taken in their totality, however, a very detailed picture of the *70ᵗʰ Week of Daniel* emerges. This is a picture we can *apply* in order to prepare to overcome the tribulation of the 70ᵗʰ Week.

The purpose of these pictures in the *Letters to the Seven Churches, etc.* is to inform the Church so it can overcome the *70ᵗʰ Week of Daniel*.

One of the first 'pictures" of the *70ᵗʰ Week of Daniel* occurs in the Biblical account of the *conquest of Jericho*. The early church fathers knew this account prophesied the 70ᵗʰ Week, but the majority of the modern Church has forgotten this message (amnesia)[xxviii].

In the last chapter [Chapter Five: "Signed, Sealed, and Delivered (Revelation 4-5)"], we learned that the opening of the *7 Sealed Scroll* of Revelation will cause the dominion and kingdoms of this world to revert to their rightful owners, Jesus and His saints, during a seven year "battle." In the *conquest of Jericho*, Joshua and the Israelites won the dominion and kingdom of Jericho through a *seven-day* battle. There are numerous other direct parallels that clearly define the Old Testament story as "metaphor" of the future account in Revelation.

THE CHIEF CAPTAIN OF THE HOST OF THE LORD

Joshua received his battle orders about Jericho and other battles directly from Jesus in the form of a *Christophany*. A *Christophany* is a physical appearance of Jesus in the Old Testament. The passage makes it very clear that the "chief captain of the host of the Lord" is Jesus. If there was any doubt, the command that Joshua remove his shoes because he was on Holy ground guarantees that Joshua was in the presence of the divine:

> And it came to pass when Joshua was in Jericho, that he looked up with his eyes and saw a man standing before him, and there was a drawn sword in his hand; and Joshua drew near and said to him, Art thou for us or on the side of our enemies? And he said to him, I am now come, the chief captain of the host of the Lord. And Joshua fell on his face upon the earth, and said to him, Lord, what commandest thou thy servant? And the captain of the Lord's host said to Joshua, *Loose thy shoe off thy feet, for the place whereon thou now standest is holy.* (Josh. 5:13-16 LXX, emphasis mine)

It is obvious that this is the Lord. The command to remove his shoes is identical to the command Moses received at the burning bush.

This vision is one of Jesus himself. The instructions he is about to give Joshua in this portion of scripture are very unusual. Why did he give Joshua these bizarre marching orders? Did he give them to test Joshua's faith? Certainly only a man of faith would trust that walking around the city, blowing on trumpets and shouting would bring about a military victory. Might Jesus have had another motive as well? Might he had chosen these specific orders so that the "picture" symbolically painted by the account would help us understand a *future event*? My study of the Bible has taught me that God frequently gave his people "odd" instructions to paint a picture. For example, Noah was given strange instructions to build a boat in the desert. We know from Matt. 24:37-41 that the account of Noah is a picture of the *Rapture*. Jonah was swallowed by a great fish. We know from Luke 11:29 that the Sign of Jonah was given to illustrate the time Jesus would spend in the grave. We have already seen how Passover is a picture of Jesus's redemptive work on the cross. In my previous book, *Are We Ready for Jesus?*, we discuss a number of other Old Testament characters that have end time meanings: Joseph, Lot, Gideon, Elijah, etc. It should not be surprising to us then, when an Old Testament account has a dual meaning. The *conquest of Jericho* is one of these stories.

JERICHO

Just like the pictures and sculptures that the characters in *Close Encounters* constructed, each of the pictures of the *70th Week of Daniel* that we will examine in Part Two: "The *Pattern of Seven Events*" will help provide us with clues to what that period will be like. All of these pictures are organized around the *Pattern of Seven Events* (see Appendix A for full summary of these seven events). In summation, these pictures will arm us with the information we will need to *endure and overcome* during those seven years. This is an incredibly important insight for the Church to understand. The Old Testament account of the *Conquest of Jericho* gives us information about the transfer of the kingdom and the timing of the opening of the 7 seals. The Chief Commander of the Host of the Lord (Jesus) said to Joshua:

> Now Jericho was tightly shut because of the sons of Israel; no one went out and no one came in. The Lord said to Joshua, "See, I have given Jericho into your hand, with its king and the valiant warriors. You shall march around the city, all the men of war *circling the city once. You shall do so for six days.* Also *seven priests shall carry seven trumpets* of rams' horns before the ark; then *on the seventh day you shall march around the city seven times,* and the *priests shall blow the trumpets.* It shall be that when they make a *long blast with the ram's horn,* and when you hear the sound of the trumpet, all the *people shall shout*

with a great shout; and the wall of the city will fall down flat, and the *people will go up* every man straight ahead." (Joshua 6:1-5 NASB, emphasis mine)

At first glance, this account has nothing to do with Revelation. We see "circling," "priests with trumpets," and the "Ark of the Covenant," and we don't find these symbols in Revelation. So let's dig a little deeper and remove some topsoil so we can reveal the meaning of these ancient symbols. First, let's examine the very obvious parallel symbolism in the two accounts in a chart (Figure 23: *Conquest of Jericho Symbols in Revelation*):

Joshua	Revelation
Led by Yeshua	Led by Yeshua
2 spies	2 witnesses
Spies hidden 3 1/2 days	Witnesses dead 3 1/2 days
Rahab is a harlot	Israel is a harlot
Rahab saved by red cord	Israel saved by Jesus's blood
Jordan River parted	Mount of Olives parted
Israel "shows" Ark of the Coveant to Jericho for 7 days	Church "shows" Jesus to the world for 7 years
Trumpets sound	Jesus's voice like a trumpet
Jericho's walls fall	1/10 of Jerusalem's walls fall
7 priests blow 7 trumpets	7 angels blow 7 trumpets
Jericho is burned	Jesus burns the world with fire
Isrel will rule Canaan	Israel will rule again

Figure 23: Conquest of Jericho Symbols in Revelation

These multiple commonalities reveal a direct link between the story of Jericho and Revelation. Without the Book of Revelation, the account of the *Conquest of Jericho* would seem like a confused story of incomprehensible commands from Jesus. Without the *Jericho account*, Revelation seems a jumbled story of odd events. But when the two accounts are merged into a single picture of the *70th Week of Daniel*, the interplay of the symbols in the two accounts give us tremendous insight into the proper interpretation of Revelation.

YEHOSHUA

Notice the name of the leader in Table 16 (Yehoshua or the shortened "Yeshua") above is the same in both accounts. Both *Joshua* and *Jesus* share the same name (in Hebrew) which means "YHWH (Jehovah) is salvation." Amen, he is. The writer of Hebrews recognized this and claimed that Jesus was a better "Yeshua" than Joshua because the "rest" that Jesus leads us into will remain:

> For if Joshua had given them *rest*, He would not have spoken of another day after that. So there remains a *Sabbath rest* for the people of God. (Heb. 4:8-9 NASB, emphasis mine)

This *rest* that the writer of Hebrews refers to is the *Millennial Kingdom* of Jesus on earth. The Sabbath and the seventh day of Creation all foreshadow this coming Kingdom. Jesus's struggle to wrest the Kingdom from Satan during the *70th Week of Daniel* is what leads us into this *rest* with him. As we have mentioned previously, the *Sabbath rest* will also occur *during* the *70th Week of Daniel*. Just as with any calendar week, there will be six days (years) of laborious toil (tribulation) for the saints of God, then on the seventh day (year), they will *rest* in Heaven with Jesus after the Rapture. This is a beautiful parallel picture.

127

Ch. 6: The Walls Came Tumbling Down

THE BATTLE PLAN OF THE LORD

The most important symbol in the *Conquest of Jericho* account is the Ark of the Covenant. Jesus is the final fulfillment of every "ark" found in the Bible. He is Noah's Ark that symbolizes our deliverance in the Rapture. He is Moses' Ark that saved that Hebrew baby from the river of Satan's fury. He is the Ark of the Covenant that held back the Jordan and allowed Israel to enter the promised-land. Thus, it is Jesus who leads the campaign against the evil fortress (Jericho) that Satan has constructed *and* Jesus who is carried around the city by his followers. Joshua displayed the Ark of the Covenant as he marched around Jericho. With each day's encircling, he showed the residents of that city the Lord. As we enter into the 70th Week, *this will be our job* as saints, to circle the globe showing the world Jesus in us, the love of Jesus. It's our Great Commission (Matt. 28:18-20). This is the battle plan of the Lord, both for Jericho and for the Church during the *70th Week of Daniel.* In my opinion, this is an aspect of it the Church misses completely. Our posture towards evil should be *offensive* not defensive. Jesus said:

> Upon this rock I will build my church; and the *gates of Hades* will not overpower it. (Matt. 16:18-19 NASB, emphasis mine)

Gates are defensive structures not offensive. It is the Church who will storm their gates. In this passage in Matt. 16, Jesus was perhaps alluding to this very *Jericho account.* The walls of Satan's evil fortress (Jericho) will fall again in the near future.

Rev. 12:11 says the saints "*overcame* him (Satan) because of the blood of the Lamb and because of the word of their testimony, and they did not love their life even when faced with death." Again this connotes being on the offensive. Most in the Church today fear persecution and are hoping a *Pre-tribulation Rapture* excuses them from front-line duty. This passage in Rev. 12, however, seems to indicate that persecution even unto death is *a means of victory.* The Church currently sees those who will go through what they call the "Tribulation" period as needing to cower in fear, but it will be the time of the Church's greatest offensive attack on Satan. I absolutely believe in the allegory of Jericho—the saints are outside the walls storming the gates. It is not a time of defense. It is a time of offense.

While the children of Israel walked around the walls, they appeared defenseless, and I'm sure the Jericho defenders shot arrows at them constantly. This is yet another picture of the 70th Week. Christians will appear defenseless as they are "shot" at by the forces of the Antichrist, but that is an illusion. Spiritually, they are winning by testifying about the Ark of the Covenant (Jesus) and by laying their lives down. They will trust the Chief Commander of the Host of the Lord who gives them their orders, and they will be victorious. The Children of Israel followed the seemingly crazy battle plan they were given by God and the walls came tumbling down. The "walls" will fall again.

SEVEN SEALS

In regard to the link between the *Seven Seals* (*Pattern of Seven Events*) and the seven day *Conquest of Jericho*; notice the seventh day of the battle is different. On that day seven priests blow seven trumpets. In Revelation we read: "When the Lamb broke the *Seventh Seal*, there was silence in heaven for about half an hour. And I saw the *seven angels* who stand before God, and *seven trumpets* were given to them" (Rev. 8: 1-2 NASB, emphasis mine). The circling of the city during the first six days in the *Conquest of Jericho* symbolizes the first six years of the *70th Week of Daniel*. During that time six seals (a *circle* around the city is *similar in shape to a seal!*) will be broken. Notice that on the seventh day of the battle of Jericho, the children of Israel circle the city seven times. Remember from the last chapter, we learned that the *Seventh Seal* is like a nesting doll containing the seven trumpets. This is the symbolism of circling the city seven times while blowing seven trumpets. The symbolism is exact; the seals come first, then the trumpets.

In regard to timing of the seven seals, just as there was one circling of the city per day in the first six days, I believe *a seal may break every year* of the *70th Week of Daniel*. This concept is a bit hard to grasp. This graphic (Figure 24: 7 Years and 7 Seals) might help visualize it.

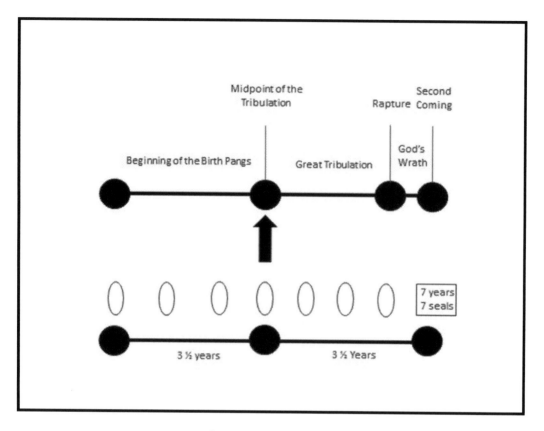

Figure 24: 7 Years and 7 Seals (not to scale)

With this graphic it is easier to see that if the *First Seal* is broken at the beginning of this period (*Year Zero*) seven seals can be broken in the first six years. Following this logical pattern, the Midpoint of the 70th Week will fall in the middle of the *"Fourth Year"* and the Rapture, most likely, will occur at the very end of the *"Sixth Year"* of this period, at the *Seventh Seal* initiating the Day of the Lord when God's Wrath, is unleashed on earth. It is easy to think the *Seventh Seal* occurs at the very end of the period, but this is not so. See *The Last Shofar!* by Lenard and Zoller for the case for this proposed timing of the Rapture and start of God's Wrath, as an enhancement of the *Pre-Wrath Rapture* position.

Now I am *not* saying that each seal will break at the beginning of each year. The seals may break at the beginning of each year, or they may break during the year. It is interesting to consider that there are Seven Jewish Feast Days (Lev. 23), and, perhaps, a seal will break on a different Feast Day each year. I rather like this idea, but it is just a theory at this point. In Chapter Twenty-Three: "Appointments," we discuss this theory in considerably more depth. Until that point we will use the convention of a seal breaking "each year" of the *70ᵗʰ Week of Daniel* because it provides a very useful chronological framework. Also please remember the concept of seven seals breaking one per year during the 70ᵗʰ Week is still just a thesis based on the *Conquest of Jericho* account and we are not attempting to prove these ideas yet. The Jericho account supports this logic, but we will not have "proved" this theory of the breaking of each of the seals during each of the seven years of the 70ᵗʰ Week until the completion of this book.

7 TRUMPETS

As we stated previously, the Jericho account also confirms that the Trumpet Judgments (the *seven trumpets*) follow *after* the first six years of the *70ᵗʰ Week of Daniel* (after the *Seventh Seal*, at the start of the *Seventh Year*), just as the Book of Revelation states:

> When the Lamb broke the *seventh seal*, there was silence in heaven for about half an hour. And I saw the seven angels who stand before God, and seven trumpets were given to them. (Rev. 8:1-2 NASB, emphasis mine)

> Also seven priests shall carry seven trumpets of rams' horns before the ark; then on the *seventh day* you shall march around the city seven times, and the priests shall blow the trumpets. (Josh. 6:4 NASB, emphasis mine)

In the last chapter [Chapter Five: "Signed, Sealed, and Delivered (Revelation 4-5)"], we presented this graphic (Figure 25: 7 Trumpets) of how this looks in relation to the *70ᵗʰ Week of Daniel*:

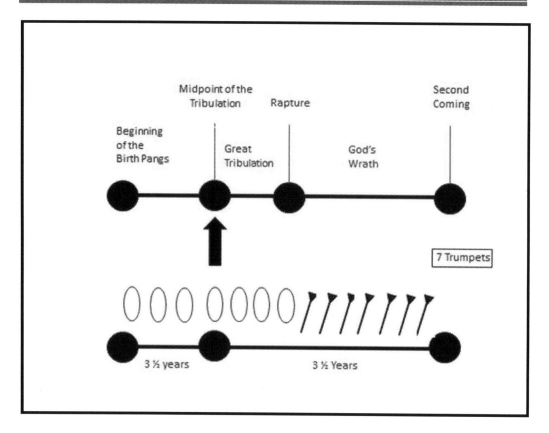

Figure 25: 7 Trumpets (not to scale)

As can be seen in this graphic, all *seven trumpets* are blown during the *Seventh Year* of the 70th Week, just as the *seven trumpets* were blown on the seventh day of the *Conquest of Jericho*. This period is also known as "The Day of the Lord," and it is the time period when God pours out his wrath on the ungodly.

GIDEON

In the very next book of the Bible, in Judges (following Joshua), there is another parallel account—that of Gideon. His story also includes trumpets, a great shout and unusual battle orders. From this we can surmise that the *Gideon Account* may be another picture provided by the Lord of the final struggle between good and evil, also shown in the *70th Week of Daniel* per the account in Revelation. Let's look at a graphic (Figure 26: Joshua Gideon Comparison) of the comparisons between Joshua and Gideon:

Joshua Account (Joshua 6)	Gideon Account (Judges 6,7)
Battle was 7 days	Midian persecuted Israel for 7 years
Joshua met Jesus	Gideon met Jesus
Two spies are sent into Jericho	Gideon and his servant spy on the Midian camp
Joshua consecrated the people by means of circumcision	Gideon consecrated the people by destroying the altar of Baal
Unusual battle orders requiring faith	Unusual battle orders requiring faith
Walls of Jericho fall	In the dream of a Midianite, the Midian camp tents fall down after being crushed by a barley loaf that rolls down the hill
Enemy was defeated by the blowing of trumpets and a great shout	Enemy was defeated by the blowing of trumpets and a great shout

Figure 26: Joshua Gideon Comparison

There can be very little doubt that the *symbolism* of the conquests of the *Jericho Account* and the *Gideon Account* are one and the same. If you have any doubt that the Gideon account is also to apply to the *70th Week of Daniel*, the Book of Isaiah clarifies this doubt:

> For you shall break the yoke of their burden and the staff on their shoulders. The rod of their (Israel's) oppressor, *as at the battle of Midian*, for every boot of the booted warrior in the battle tumult and cloak rolled in blood, will be for burning, fuel for the fire. For a child will be born to us, a son will be given to us; and the government will rest on his shoulders; and his name will be called Wonderful Counselor, Mighty God, Eternal Father, Prince of Peace. *There will be no end to the increase of his government* or of peace, on the throne of David and over his kingdom to establish it and to uphold it with justice and

righteousness *from then on and forevermore.* (Isa. 9: 4-7 NASB, clarification and emphasis mine)

Most Christians are familiar with this passage which is frequently read at Christmas, however, the link to the battle of Midian (*the Gideon Account*) and the end times where Jesus establishes his eternal Kingdom is not frequently understood.

This is a crucial insight because the *Gideon Account* provides additional details that the *Jericho Account* does not. First, the *Gideon Account* lists the enemies of Israel as the Midianites, the Amalekites, and the sons of the east (Judges 6:1-3). Who were the Midianites? We know that Moses' father-in-law Jethro was from Midian and that Midian was located in what is current day Saudi Arabia[xxix]. We learn in Jud. 8:24 that they were descendants of Ishmael. The Amalekites were descendants of Esau[xxx] [we will learn in Chapter Seven: "A Horse of a Different Color (Revelation 6)" that both groups are current day *Islamists*]. The nations east of Israel are Jordan, Iraq, and Iran. It is likely the "sons of the east" came from these regions. If we assemble all the nations together, and if we assume Midian (Saudi Arabia) was the controlling partner nation, we have a reasonable picture of the Islamic nations. In Joel Richardson's book, *Mideast Beast* (WND Books, 2012), and in my previous book, *Are We Ready For Jesus?* (Seraphina Press, 2015), a strong case is made that the coming empire of *the Beast* will be *Islam.* This grouping of nations in the Gideon account re-enforces that opinion. Later in Judges, we read this passage: "So Gideon arose and killed Zebah and Zalmunna, and took the *crescent ornaments* which were on their camels' necks" (Judges 8:21 NASB, emphasis mine). The *crescent* is a symbol of *Islam.* The kings of the Midianites were wearing crescents, so this aspect of the Gideon account strengthens the assertion that Islam is the Beast Empire as well. Zebah and Zalmunna (along with other Midianite rulers Oreb and Zeeb) are also mentioned in Psalm 83. In this Psalm, a future assembly of nations (all of which are currently Islamic) conspires to destroy Israel, but is defeated by the Lord. The Psalmist asks that this assembly and their leaders be dealt with by God like the Midianites (Ps. 83:9) and these Midianite kings (Ps 83:11). Most commentators believe Psalm 83 is about Armageddon, so this is a clear indication of the *prophetic nature* of the *Gideon Account.*

In Judges 6:2 we learn that Israel was hiding in the clefts of the rocks and in caves due to Midian (Islam). This is entirely consistent with the picture we are about to draw of the *70ᵗʰ Week of Daniel*. After the *Midpoint* of that seven year period, Israel will flee to the mountains as Jesus instructs in the Olivet Discourse, "But when you see Jerusalem surrounded by armies, then recognize that her desolation is near. Then those who are in Judea must flee to the mountains, and those who are in the midst of the city must leave, and those who are in the country must not enter the city" (Luke 21:20-21 NASB).

We also learn from the *Gideon Account* that Midian (Islam) will devastate the future food supply of Israel:

> So they would camp against them and *destroy the produce of the earth* as far as Gaza, and *leave no sustenance in Israel* as well as no sheep, ox, or donkey. For they would come up with their livestock and their tents, they would come in *like locusts* for number, both they and their camels were innumerable; and they came into the land to devastate it. So Israel was brought very low because of Midian, and the sons of Israel cried to the Lord. (Judges 6:4-6 NASB, emphasis mine)

We will learn in Chapter Seven: "A Horse of a Different Color (Revelation 6)" that disruptions of the food supply is an integral part of the Antichrist's plan for the *70ᵗʰ Week of Daniel*. Here in the *Gideon Account*, we see disruption of food as integral as well. We also notice the forces of the enemy are compared to *locusts*. We will see this in additional accounts of the *70ᵗʰ Week of Daniel* as well.

THE LORD'S BATTLE PLAN

God's battle plan for Gideon is very similar to what occurs in the *Jericho Account*:

> When the three companies blew the *trumpets* and broke the pitchers, they held the torches in their left hands and the trumpets in their right hands for blowing,

135

and cried, "A sword for the Lord and for Gideon!" Each stood in his place around the camp; and all the (Midian) army ran, crying out as they fled. When they blew 300 trumpets, the Lord set the sword of one against another even throughout the whole (Midian) army; and the army fled. (Judges 7:20-22 NASB, clarification and emphasis mine)

In the battle plans of both Joshua and Gideon, *trumpets* are blown and the people *shout*. There is one difference in the Gideon battle plan as compared to the Jericho plan: Gideon's army carries torches (Gk: LAMPAS) concealed by jars made of clay. At Gideon's signal, the Israelites broke the jars of clay and exposed the torches. This lit up the hillside Gideon's forces were on and is part of what scared the Midianites.

What is the symbolism of these torches? There are three Greek words for lamps or torches. The word LYCHNOS means an individual oil lamp. When this word is used, it symbolizes an individual's witness or the Word of God (Psalms 119:105). LYCHNIA is a lampstand or a collection of individual lamps. Lampstands symbolize churches or groups of individual lamps. The final word is LAMPAS which is used in the *Gideon Account*. The first appearance of LAMPAS in the Old Testament is in a very famous passage:

And when the sun was about to set, there was a flame, and behold a smoking furnace and lamps (LAMPAS) of fire, which passed between these divided pieces. In that day the Lord made a covenant with Abram, saying, to thy seed I will give this land, from the river of Egypt to the great river Euphrates. (Gen. 15:17-18 LXX, clarification mine)

Here God (Jesus and the 7 Spirits of God) are symbolized as LAMPAS or torches. I find it amazingly interesting that the LAMPAS passed between the cut pieces of animals in Abraham's vision above and confirmed the Abrahamic Covenant which ceded the land to Abram and his seed. In Judges we see a symbolic picture of that final battle that wins that land as an everlasting inheritance for the Israelites.

If LAMPAS is the *Messiah*, what is the symbolism of the jars of clay? Paul spoke of these same jars:

> For God, who said, "*Light* shall shine out of darkness," is the One who has shone in our hearts to give the Light of the knowledge of the glory of God in the face of Christ. *But we have this treasure in earthen vessels*, so that the surpassing greatness of the power will be of God and not from ourselves. (2 Cor. 4:6-7 NASB, emphasis mine)

According to Paul, *we are the jars of clay* that when broken, expose the bright light of the LAMPAS (Jesus.) This is a very similar picture to the one painted in the *Jericho Account* where the children of Israel carried the Ark of the Covenant (Jesus) around the city for 7 days while being shot at by the city dwellers. In Judges we see the jars of clay being broken (persecuted or killed) and then the light (of Jesus) shining brightly. Part of God's battle plan for us, especially in the 70th Week, is persecution. As the clay jars break (representing the persecution of the saints), the Messiah's light will shine brighter.

Interestingly, Jesus also referred to the saints exposing the LAMPAS during the *70th Week of Daniel* in the *Parable of the Ten Virgins*. This parable is found in the parables section of the Olivet Discourse in which Jesus further clarified the End of the Age to his disciples:

> But at midnight there was a shout, 'Behold, the bridegroom! Come out to meet him.' Then all those virgins rose and trimmed their *lamps* (Gk: LAMPAS meaning torches). The foolish said to the prudent, 'Give us some of your oil, for our lamps (torches) are going out.' But the prudent answered, 'No, there will not be enough for us and you too; go instead to the dealers and buy some for yourselves.' And while they were going away to make the purchase, the bridegroom came, and those who were ready went in with him to the wedding feast; and the door was shut. Later the other virgins also came, saying, 'Lord,

lord, open up for us.' But he answered, 'Truly I say to you, I do not know you.' (Matt. 25:6-12 NASB, clarification and emphasis mine)

Most commentators (me included) used to think of the virgins' lamps as individual lamps. They are not! They are the LAMPAS or *our testimony about the Messiah.* These torches are fed by oil (the Holy Spirit). The foolish virgins don't have enough oil to keep their testimony bright during the persecution. When Jesus returns for the rapture of the Church, they are left behind. We will learn significantly more about this when we read Part Four. This new insight about our testimony about the Messiah being the virgin's lamps was given to me by Mark Davidson, author of *Daniel Revisited.* This insight provides us with valuable information as to how we as believers should prepare for the days of persecution ahead—keep our testimonies strong in the Holy Spirit.

GIDEON'S ARMY

The Midianite army numbered 135,000 while Gideon's Israelites had 32,000 men. The Lord's comment to Gideon about this mismatch is one of my *favorite* Bible verses:

> The people who are with you are *too many* for me to give Midian into their hands (Judg. 7:2 NASB, emphasis mine).

Gideon must have thought, *too many? We are outnumbered four to one!* But God's will is utterly independent of natural laws. While Gideon looked at physical numbers, God looks at the hearts of those he uses for his glory. Not only would God get the glory, but God desired the right men to accomplish his mission. He saw many who were unfit for the task before them. Soldiers with the wrong spirit would only get in the way.

God's first layoff was based on fear. Two-thirds of Gideon's force left because they were afraid. I anticipate that at least two-thirds of the church goers in the 70th *Week of Daniel* will be afraid to take a stand on the return of Jesus. Should we fear this "layoff?" No, God is choosing his army.

Next, God made a strange request. He asked Gideon to lead his men to the water and watch how they drank. Those who cupped their fingers and drank from their hands were to be retained. All those who lapped up the water directly from the stream were excused. Only 300 men drank from their hands and remained.

What does this mean? Those who drank from their hands were able to remain *watchful*. Their eyes were not fixed on the water around them, but rather they scanned the horizon while their hands held the water. Those who lapped up the water took their eyes off events around them. God's command for all us before Jesus' return is "Therefore *keep watch*" (Matt. 25:13 NIV, emphasis mine). Only those keeping a watch on the events prophetically unfolding will be helpful to God in the final battle. This is how God will choose his army.

Let us now return to the *Jericho Account* to learn about a critical final piece of the end time picture.

THE RAPTURE

If we read the *Conquest of Jericho* account closely we'll notice that the timing of the Rapture is given:

> It shall be that **when they make a long blast with the ram's horn**, and **when you hear the sound of the trumpet**, all the people shall **shout with a great shout**; and the wall of the city will fall down flat, **and the people will go up**. (Joshua 6:5 NASB)

This passage bears amazing similarity to Paul's accounts of the Rapture:

> For the Lord Himself will descend from heaven with a **shout**, with the voice of the archangel and with **the trumpet of God**, and the dead in Christ will rise first. Then **we who are alive and remain will be caught up** together with them in the clouds to meet the Lord in the air (1 Thess. 4:16-17 NASB).

We will all be changed in a moment, in the twinkling of an eye, *at the last trumpet*; for the trumpet will sound, and *the dead will be raised imperishable* (the Resurrection), and *we will be changed* (the Rapture). (1 Cor. 15:51-52 NASB, clarification and emphasis mine)

Many commentators believe that the "last trumpet" is the *seventh trumpet* blown by an *angel* during the Trumpet Judgments. This is probably incorrect for two reasons. First, the "last trumpet" is called *"the trumpet of God" (1 Thess. 4:16)*. Jesus blows this trumpet not an angel as the prophet says "the Lord blows the *trumpet*" (Zech. 9:14). Also the phrase the *"last trumpet"* is a Jewish *idiom* that means a specific trumpet blast on the Jewish Feast of Yom Teruah (Feast of the Blowing of Trumpets).[xxxi] When this is understood, the picture comes into focus. The "last trumpet" is the final *"long blast with a ram's horn"* on Yom Teruah just like the quote above from the *Jericho Account*. This is truly amazing. At the breaking of the *Seventh Seal*, Jesus will blow the trumpet of God and a great shout will go out. The dead in Christ will rise first, and, as the *Jericho Account* states, "the people will go *up*." Just as in the seven-day battle of Jericho, the "symbolic Rapture" occurs after encircling the city for six days (six seals), at the very end of the *Sixth Year* of the *70th Week of Daniel*, the Rapture will occur at the *seventh seal* (encircling the city seven times). The saints will be gathered together by the angels to our Lord and will enter a Sabbath rest in Heaven.

You are probably thinking, *Nelson how can you state something like this with this little proof?* This isn't "little proof," it's actually fairly substantial. But there is more, much more. As we continue through the rest of the scriptural "pictures" of the *70th Week of Daniel*, *the Rapture always occurs at the end of the Sixth Year*. It is like a fingerprint. As we continue through this book, the evidence for the Rapture at the end of the 6th year of the 70th Week will accumulate.

ADDITIONAL BATTLES

Both the *Jericho* and *Gideon Accounts* detail additional battles after the initial victories over the main opponents. Joshua conquered a number of other cities after Jericho, and

Gideon chased the Midianites and killed their two kings. These are both pictures of *what occurs in the 30 days* that follow the Second Coming at the end of the 70th Week that we discussed above. It is during this time, after the physical return of Jesus that the *Goat and Sheep Judgment* takes place; and it is likely during this time that Jesus throws the Antichrist and False Prophet (two kings) into the *Lake of Fire*. We discuss the timing of this event in Chapter Twenty-Three: "Appointments."

In both accounts, we also learn of those who even after these great victories are tempted by the riches of their enemy. After the defeat of Jericho, Achan kept bars of silver and gold and a "Babylonian" garment buried in his tent. Gideon collected gold as spoil and made it into a breastplate which scripture declares became a snare for Gideon and all Israel. These vignettes give us insight that even after Jesus's great victory over the Antichrist during the Day of the Lord, there may be those among the Jews who still look back and long for the materialism of the kingdom of Satan.

SUMMARY

The accounts of the *Conquest of Jericho* and *Gideon* are interrelated and can be viewed as two pictures of the same future battle. We have shown that *this battle is symbolic of the 70th Week of Daniel*.

In the next Chapter, we will begin to examine the first four events in the *Pattern of Seven Events*: *the Four Horsemen*. God's Word has chosen to group these first four events into one category, thus it is critical that we begin our study with the common purpose of these events that are the reason for their grouping.

Chapter Seven

A HORSE OF A DIFFERENT COLOR
(REVELATION 6:1-8)

Before we begin our detailed, focused study of each of the separate events in the *Pattern of Seven Events*, we need to examine the "Four Horsemen" of Rev. 6. These horsemen are loosed upon Jesus breaking each of the first four *Seals*. These first four events are grouped together by divine inspiration; they are different than the other events in the *Pattern*. We need to understand why they are different before we examine them separately. You see, these four events are used by Satan to try and retain his power.

How does a dictator retain power? In most of their reigns, there's a moment when they sense a threat from within their nation or from without. What steps do they take? In the 1980's, Mikhail Gorbachev realized the power of the Soviet Union was crumbling. He attempted to reform the Soviet politico-economic system. It backfired. Within a decade, the Soviet Empire crumbled. Reform only leads to the people desiring more. Most dictators create a police state. In East Germany during the cold war, every citizen knew that anyone, literally anyone, could be an informant for the *Stasi* (the East German security force.) Even members of one's own household could betray you. Fear is a powerful weapon in the hands of a dictator.

The following list of *ten steps* has been proposed as *means of keeping dictatorial power*[xxxii]:

1) Do not reform
2) Create a police state
3) Give your subjects bread and circus (gladiator games)
4) Lie
5) Engage in name calling
6) Blame foreigners

7) Make friends with big Nation States

8) Time events for maximum impact

9) Strengthen your military

10) Develop a nuclear weapon

After Jesus breaks the *First Seal* on the *7 Sealed Scroll*, Satan will know his dictatorship of this world is about to end. He will most likely strike out against Jesus by taking these exact *ten steps* of a typical dictator outlined above to try and hold on to his dominion. As we work through Satan's reaction to the opening of each of the first four seals, keep this list of *ten steps* in mind. It is eerie how similar the events that follow each seal match this list.

In Chapter Five: "Signed, Sealed, and Delivered (Revelation 4-5)," we learned that this *7 Sealed Scroll* is most likely *Mans' Inheritance*. The opening of this *Scroll* is pictured in Rev. 6-11 and is the Bible's most detailed "picture" of the *Pattern of Seven Events* (see Appendix A for a summary of these seven key events) . Satan realizes that once this *Scroll* is opened, his dominion over both the earth is lost and that the dead in Christ Jesus will rise to spend eternity with Him. Satan will attempt to thwart its opening at all costs. As Jesus opens each of the first four seals, Satan attacks the saints with cunning and malicious intent. The reaction to the opening of these first four seals represents Satan's attempt to cause the Bride of Christ to commit apostasy. If he cannot do this, he attempts to kill her. As we learn about each of these seals, we must remember that *it is not God's Wrath* being poured out yet; it is *Satan fighting back against Jesus.*

Many in the Church, however, teach that the events surrounding the opening of the seals are God's Wrath to punish those on the earth. They say this because it is Jesus who breaks the seals. *Although Jesus opens the seals, the riders of the horses themselves cause all the events*. The rider of the *white horse* carries a bow and is intent on conquering. The rider of the *red horse* takes peace of mind from the earth. The rider of the *black horse* sets the high price for grain, and the rider of the *green horse* is death itself. Jesus opening the seals is not proof that these events are the Wrath of God.

Others say that the *Living Creatures* who say "come" prior to each horse emerging are calling out the horses and their riders. The word spoken by the four *Living Creatures*, "*come*," is very reminiscent of the epilogue to the Book of Revelation (Chapter 22) where we also hear a fourfold call for Jesus to "come": "The Spirit and the bride say, '*Come*.' And let the one who hears say, '*Come*'. . . Amen, *Come, Lord Jesus*" (Rev. 22:17, 20 NASB, emphasis mine). This is entirely consistent with the purpose of the opening of the *Scroll*. The *Living Creatures* are anticipating and praying for the return of Christ as each seal is broken. They are literally asking Jesus to "come," not the riders of the horses.

The events that surround the opening of the *Fifth Seal* that follows the four horsemen, however, prove unequivocally that the horsemen are not the Wrath of God. After the *Fifth Seal* opens, the martyrs under the altar cry out for God's vengeance. God tells them to wait a little while. Obviously then, God's Wrath (vengeance on the unrighteous), had not yet begun at that point (the *Fifth Seal*). God is telling the martyrs to wait before his Wrath is poured out. *If God's Wrath had not begun by the Fifth Seal, it had not begun during the first four seals as well. This is an incredibly important nuance to understand.* The events that follow the seals are not God's doing and are not the Wrath of God; *God is simply allowing these events caused by Satan to occur on earth.* In the Book of Job, we learn of a similar process. Satan requests God's permission to test Job. God grants Satan permission within certain parameters. God is always in charge, but the actual events are Satan's doing.

> **The events following the opening of the first four seals are not God's Wrath. They are Satan's reaction to the breaking of the seals, which God allows.**

The *seven seals* are broken in the first six years of the 70th Week of Daniel, and the *seven trumpets* are blown in the final year after the scroll is opened. The *seven seals* are divided into the following groups:

145

- Three seals opened before or at the *Midpoint* of Daniel's 70th Week,
- One seal opened at the *Midpoint*,
- Three seals opened after the *Midpoint*.

It is important to understand the *Midpoint* before we proceed. It is one of the most crucial dates in the history of the world. Once we understand the *Midpoint*, we can better understand why the seals (the *Pattern of Seven Events*) are divided into these groups.

THE *MIDPOINT* OF THE TRIBULATION

Time is like a merchant's scale. Events pile up on the lighter end of the scale until the accumulated weight of them unbalances it. We have come to call this the "tipping point." The *70th Week of Daniel* is divided into two halves of 3 ½ year durations. Events leading up to the *Midpoint* will tip the scale of world history. When this point is reached, we will descend into a period of unspeakable horror known as the *Great Tribulation* (Matt. 24:21), which is also called the *Time of Jacob's Distress* (Trouble) as mentioned in Jeremiah:

> I have heard a sound of terror, of dread, and there is no peace. Ask now, and see if a male can give birth. Why do I see every man with his hands on his loins, as a woman in childbirth? And why have all faces turned pale? 'Alas! For that day is great, there is none like it; and it is *the time of Jacob's distress*, but he will be saved from it. (Jer. 30:5-7 NASB, emphasis mine)

I think that right now events are already being piled on the scale of time. Within the last 65 plus years since the recreation of the nation of Israel in 1948, we have seen the world steadily darkening. The fifties saw the advent of television (which permits mass deception), the sixties saw the sexual revolution, the seventies saw the resumption of child sacrifice (abortion), the eighties saw the growth of materialism (idolatry), the nineties witnessed the emergence of the internet, denial of absolute truth and the advent of "political correctness," and the twenty-first century saw the rise of Islam and the homosexual revolution. Each subsequent weight has brought us closer to the tipping point of world events.

These events are only preliminary. The heftiest weights to be placed upon the scale of time will be those that are prophesied in Daniel 8 (the vision of the Ram and the Goat), Daniel 11, Revelation 6 (the first four seals) and Matthew 24 and Luke 21 (the *Beginning of the Birth Pangs* in the *Olivet Discourse*). These events include deception by false messiahs, war, rumors of war, disturbances, economic collapse, famine, plagues, death, and "seismos" (either earthquakes or nuclear explosions). The combined chaos of these world-wide events will finally tip the scale and usher in the Great Tribulation.

FOUR HORSEMEN, YET SEVEN SEALS

Now that we understand the importance of the *Midpoint* of Daniel's 70th Week, we can better understand why the seals are divided into groups: a first group of four seals (before or at the *Midpoint*) and a latter group of three seals. A graphic of this division of the seven seals during the 70th Week is shown below (Figure 27: Division of the Seals):

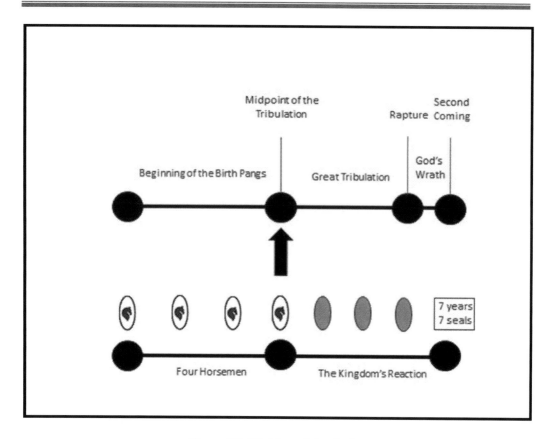

Figure 27: Division of the Seals

Commentators have long wondered why the first four seals feature horses and riders and the remaining seals do not. This difference (horsemen or no horsemen) demonstrate that they comprise *two separate groups of seals*, possibly with two purposes. Once we understand that a seal is broken during each year of the 70th Week, however, the reason for the difference becomes obvious: the *Midpoint* of Daniel's 70th Week divides them. As we learned earlier in this chapter, the horses and horsemen that come out with the opening of the *first four seals* represent Satan's attempts to disrupt God's plan to redeem the world. This makes complete sense. Satan cannot stop the *Scroll* from opening. His only strategy will be to take as many Christians down with him as possible. These attempts cumulate in the events of the *Midpoint*. Satan's best efforts fail, though, and the seals continue to open.

After the *Midpoint*, three additional seals are opened. We will learn that this *last set of three seals* is *God's reaction to Satan's horsemen* in Chapters Twelve, Thirteen, and Fourteen.

ZECHARIAH'S HORSES

The picture of the four horses in Rev. 6 is not the first time these four horses appear in scripture. By mentioning them, the Holy Spirit is *referring us back to Zechariah 6*. One cannot surmise about the *Four Horsemen of Revelation* without understanding this Old Testament reference. As we have stated many times previously, Revelation is a book of references. In the following verse of Zechariah we see the Horses come out:

> Now I lifted up my eyes again and looked, and behold, four chariots were coming forth from between the two mountains; and the mountains were bronze mountains. With the first chariot were *red horses*, with the second chariot *black horses*, with the third chariot *white horses*, and with the fourth chariot *strong dappled horses*. (Zech. 6:1-3 NASB, emphasis mine)

Can we be sure these are the same horses? Three of the four horses of Zechariah are listed by color and these match the color of the first three horses in Rev. 6 (white, red, and black). The final horse is listed as *strong* and *dappled*. Dappled is a pattern (spotted) rather than a specific color so it isn't inconsistent with Revelation's horses. The *Fourth Horse* of Revelation may well be spotted with colored spots. John simply didn't see or report that aspect of the horse.

Second, Zechariah's horses are paired and have a chariot associated with them. It is not unusual for one witness of an event to see more or less than a second witness. In the gospel accounts of the empty tomb, some of the writers report a single angel while another reports two. This doesn't make them different accounts, simply a different perspective. The same is true for these horses. John may have only seen one horse and Zechariah more than one.

Ch. 7: A Horse of a Different Color

The use of a chariot in Zechariah is consistent with other divine horses and chariots found in the Old Testament such as the chariots that God revealed to Elisha's servant (2 Ki. 6:17) or the chariot that carried Elijah from Elisha's presence (2 Ki. 2:12). Interestingly, the cherubim (the four living creatures) are described as having wheels (Ezek. 10:2, 6, 13). The cherubim are even described *as* chariots, "and for the altar of incense refined gold by weight; and gold for *the model of the chariot, even the cherubim* that spread out their wings and covered the ark of the covenant of the Lord" (1 Chron. 28:18, NASB emphasis mine). Knowing this, I ask, *were the riders of Revelation's horses seated on the horse itself or in a chariot that was a cherubim*? Is this why the four living creatures (cherubim) are involved in the first four seals, because they were carrying the riders? We cannot be sure, but it is interesting to consider.

Returning to Zechariah, we notice that the horses come out from between two mountains of bronze. If we can determine what these are and when they arise, we'll know the location and timing of the horses. Mountain is a symbol of a kingdom (Dan. 2:35). Bronze is a metal and also a symbol found in the exact same dream interpretation, ". . . Then another third kingdom of *bronze*, which will rule over all the earth." (Dan. 2:39, emphasis mine). Nearly every commentator on this passage agrees that this kingdom was the Hellenistic (Greek) Kingdom.

By combining these symbols, we can *easily* see that the two mountains of bronze are two sub-kingdoms that came out of the Bronze (Greek) Kingdom. We know from history that the *Seleucid Empire* and the *Ptolemaic Empire* were the two dominant empires that came out of Alexander the Great's Hellenistic Empire. The Bible refers to them as the King of the North (Seleucid) and King of the South (Ptolemaic). Interestingly, Dan. 11 clearly states that these empires will rise again *in the end times*: "*At the end time* the king of the South will collide with him, and the king of the North will storm against him" (Dan. 11:40 NASB, emphasis mine). If we return to Zechariah 6 we see references to the "north country' and the "south country" ["the *black horses* are going forth to the north country; and the *white ones* go forth after them, while the *dappled ones* go forth to the south country" (Zech. 6:6 NASB)]. This reference in Zechariah completely supports a theory that the mountains of bronze are the modern inheritors of the King of the North and King of the South (Seleucid and Ptolemaic empires). *This is the third proof that the Four Horsemen "ride" during the 70ᵗʰ Week of Daniel and not before it.* The re-formation of the kingdoms of the King of the North and the King of the South happens shortly *before* the 70ᵗʰ Week.

Now that we have determined what the two mountains of bronze are, we can know *where* each of the horses will ride:

> The *black horses* are going forth to the *North Country*; and the *white ones* go forth after them, while *the dappled ones* go forth to the *South Country*. (Zech. 6:6 NASB, emphasis mine)

Zechariah tells us the *black* and *white horses* are going north to the *King of the North*, and that the dappled horses are going south to the *King of the South*. What about the *red horses*? They are not mentioned so we can only surmise. Most likely, they are staying where they came forth, on the border between the two mountains of bronze. We will see how this is important as we continue to study the horses. Finally, Zechariah shows us that *these horses* are spiritual beings sent by God:

> Then I spoke and said to the angel who was speaking with me, "What are these, my lord?" The angel replied to me, "These are *the four spirits of heaven*, going forth after standing before the Lord of all the earth. (Zech. 6:4-5, emphasis mine)

This is important because it shows the horses are *heavenly* spirits, not demonic. As we stated before, this indicates that God is *permitting* the riders of the horses to come forth. The riders most likely are not divine messengers, but they utilize the help of God's spirit-beings to come upon the world stage. [This re-enforces a comment we made in Chapter Five: "Signed, Sealed, and Delivered" that what appear to be strange symbols (horses and horsemen, a dragon, etc.) are actually more than symbols and are the *actual* appearance of spiritual beings. These beings are invisible to humans, but visible from heaven's perspective.]

This timing for the re-formation of the kingdoms of the *King of the North* and the *King of the South* before the 70ᵗʰ Week starts is necessary for them to be in place related to the riding of the *Four Horsemen* described in Zechariah and Revelation, which occurs during the 70th Week, as has been shown. The start of the 70th Week (and, hence, the Rapture) is *not* "imminent," as these re-formation events must occur before the 70th Week starts and the first horseman rides—this further argues against the *Pre-Tribulation Rapture*, which holds to an "imminent" return of Jesus at the Rapture (without any prophesized events happening) before the start of the 70th Week.

THE COLOR OF THE HORSES

We are told the color (and pattern) of each of the horses, and these are very important and descriptive. This is shown in this graphic (Figure 28: Color of the Horses of Zechariah and Revelation).

Tribulation Year	Zech. 6 Color	Rev. 6 Color	Greek Word
First	White	White	LUEKOS
Second	Red	Red	PURRHOS
Third	Black	Black	MELAS
Fourth	Dappled	Green	CHLOROS (green) POIKILOS (various) PSALMOS (psalm like) (Heb.) BAROD (spotted)

Figure 28: Color of the Horses

As we can see, the first three horses have identical colors in Zech. 6 and in Rev. 6. The *Fourth Horse*, however, is described by no less than three Greek words and a fourth word in the Hebrew. As we will soon see, the use of all four words to describe the *Fourth Horse* is significant. The most unusual of these colors/patterns of the *Fourth Horse* is CHLOROS which means green. This Greek word is the root word of our

English "chlorophyll" which is the substance within a plant that makes it green. The Greek word CHLOROS, therefore, is not a pale green, but a *deep, vibrant green*. Why then do Bible translations render CHLOROS as "pale?" Frankly, I believe it is because they do not understand the significance of this Greek word that the Holy Spirit chose for this horse. The horse is known as the "death" horse, and "pale" seemed a better word to these translators. I believe they were wrong, however.

If we examine the four colors found in Rev. 6 in combination, they create an interesting pattern, *white, red, black, and green*. If we examine the flags of *Islamic nations* in the Middle East, *all* of them contain only these four colors. Some contain two, some contain three, and some contain all four, but none of the flags contain other colors. Green itself was Mohammed's favorite color, and it is considered the *color of Islam*. In my previous book, *Are We Ready For Jesus?—How to Prepare for His Return* (Seraphina Press, 2015), we discussed at length how the *Antichrist* will be *Islamic* in Chapter Six. We do not have space here to discuss this lengthy topic, but if you have interest, the best book available on this topic is Joel Richardson's *Mideast Beast* (WND Books, Washington D.C., 2012).

If this concept is new to you and you have held the traditional view that the Antichrist will be European ("Roman"), please read these books. Before you have the chance to read them, however, consider the Holy Spirit's use of the color *vibrant green* for the *Fourth Horse*. This use makes total sense if Rev. 6 is signaling that *Islam* will be involved in the first four seals. It makes no sense at all if it is being used as a symbol for death independent of *Islam*. Vibrant green is the color of life not death. That is why traditional translations of the Bible mistranslate CHLOROS as "pale." Although the color choice of *vibrant green* for the *Fourth Horse* is far from the only proof that the *Antichrist* and his empire will be Islamic, it certainly supports that view.

We will look at other significances of the horses' colors as we look at each of the individual horses and their riders, in the following sections.

Ch. 7: A Horse of a Different Color

YEAR ONE: EVENT ONE (DECEPTION BY FALSE MESSIAHS)

THE *WHITE HORSE* AND RIDER

There are hundreds of theories about who will ride the *white horse* of Rev. 6. Billy Graham claims it will be the *Antichrist*, some say he has already ridden and he was Saddam Hussein, Mohammed or Hitler. Irenaeus thought it would be Jesus, some have pictured Obama on that horse, Muslims attribute this passage to their Mahdi, the Hindu see Krishna, and some consider the rider impersonal—that "pestilence" rides the horse.[xxxiii] However, in spite of these various speculations, we can know with certainty the *purpose* of the rider. We don't have to guess.

Let's first look at the color of the horse which is LEUKOS (white) in the Greek. In Rev. 19:11 we see Jesus riding a *white horse*. This has led many to believe that the rider of the *white horse* in Rev. 6 is also Jesus. However, there are several differences that make this very, very, unlikely.

White horse in Rev. 6	White Horse in Rev. 19
Rider has a bow without arrows	Rider has a sword
Rider was "given" a victor's crown (stephanos)	Rider "has" royal crowns (diadems)
Goes out conquering and "to conquer" (incomplete)	Will subdue the entire earth
Peace taken from the earth by the red horse that follows	Peace brought to the earth by the rider on the white horse

Figure 29: The White Horses in Rev. 6 and 19

We can see that the rider of the *white horse* looks like Jesus but isn't Jesus. This exactly mirror the events in the *Pattern of Seven Events*. Here is the portion of Matthew that coincides with the rider of the *white horse*:

154

And Jesus answered and said to them, "See to it that no one *misleads you*. For many will come in my name, saying, 'I am the Christ,' and will *mislead* many. (Matt. 25:4-5 NASB, emphasis mine)

The rider of the *white horse* is a *deceiver*, just as Jesus prophesied would be the case. He wants to appear as a messiah so he rides a *white horse*. But as we look at the additional aspects of this rider, we will see he is only an *imposter*.

Zechariah 6:6 tells us that the *black horses* go forth to the "North Country" and the *white horses* "goes forth after them." This is significant because it tells us this deceiver on the *white horse* will arise from the revived Seleucid Empire that the Bible calls "the King of the North." This is another good indicator that the *Antichrist*, the deceiver, will be *Islamic*.

He Had a Bow

If we look into scripture for the first use (Law of Primacy) of the word "bow" (Gk: TOXON) we find it in an unusual place:

I set *my bow* in the cloud, and it shall be *for a sign of a covenant* between me and the earth. (Gen. 9:13 NASB, emphasis mine)

At first glance this seems like it doesn't fit. *This can't be the reference John was alluding to* in Revelation, you might say: ". . . there before me was a *white horse*! Its rider held a *bow* (Rev. 6:2 NIV, emphasis mine). Many English translations even mis-translate "bow" of Gen. 9 as "rainbow," but that is *not* what the word is. The Holy Spirit chose the word "bow." It is a picture of God hanging up his weapon in the sky as *a sign of a covenant* that he would *not destroy the earth* with water again, as God did with the Flood of Noah's day. Yes, it is word-play with "rainbow," but the Greek word is "bow."

If John was referring to this verse in Genesis, and I believe he absolutely was, it would imply that the rider of the *white horse* was "hanging up his weapons and entering into a covenant." This is a key understanding. Most prophecy students are intimately familiar with these passages about a *false covenant*:

> Because you have said, "We have made *a covenant with death*, and with Sheol we have made a pact. The overwhelming scourge will not reach us when it passes by; for we have made falsehood our refuge and we have concealed ourselves with deception. (Isa. 28:15 NASB, emphasis mine)

> And he will make *a firm covenant with the many* for one week, but in the middle of the week he will put a stop to sacrifice and grain offering; and on the wing of abominations will come one who makes desolate, even until a complete destruction, one that is decreed, is poured out on the one who makes desolate. (Dan. 9:27 NASB, emphasis mine)

Amazing! If "*bow*" truly does equate with a "*covenant*" (and God's Word says it does), this passage related to the *white horse* in Rev. 6 would be pointing us to these famous references of a *deceptive covenant* entered into by the *Antichrist*! Not only does "bow" equate with a *covenant*, but scripture shows us it equates with *deception* as well. "They are a *deceptive bow*; their princes fall by the sword" (Hos. 7:16 NASB, emphasis mine). This is completely consistent with what we have already learned about the rider of the *white horse* being a *deceiver*.

HE WAS GIVEN A CROWN

Because many commentators don't understand that Revelation is a book of references pointing back to the Old Testament, most miss what this crown (Gk: STEPHANOS or victor's crown) is referring to which is given to the rider of the *white horse* (Rev. 6:2), and simply guess at what it means. I believe the correct reference is found in the *same passage as the white horse*; in Zechariah 6:

> Take silver and gold, make an ornate *crown* (Gk: STEPHANOS) and set it on the head of Joshua the son of Jehozadak, the high priest. Then say to him, 'Thus

says the Lord of hosts, "Behold, a man *whose name is Branch*, for He will branch out from where He is; and He will build the temple of the Lord. Yes, it is He who will build the temple of the Lord, and He who will bear the honor and sit and rule on His throne. Thus, He will be a priest on His throne, and the counsel of peace will be between the two offices. (Zech. 6: 11-13 NASB, emphasis mine)

This passage is universally known to be symbolic of Jesus, who shares the same Hebrew name as this Joshua (Yehoshua). Jesus is also known as *the Branch*, will build the Millennial Temple in Jerusalem, and will be both King and Priest. By referencing this verse from Zechariah, John in Revelation is showing us that the rider of the *white horse* will deceptively appear as Jesus or a messiah figure, and will be both the religious and political leader at that time. Again this is amazing symbolism of the *deceiver*, the *Antichrist*.

CONQUERING AND TO CONQUER

I must admit that for my entire Christian life I have thought of this phrase ("conquering and to conquer") as a military phrase referring to conquering countries and planning to conquer them. I was wrong. That is not how the word is used in scripture. It is used in connection with a *spiritual* conquering. In fact, the Greek word NIKAO found in this phrase is usually translated "overcoming." I am sure you know many of the verses where this Greek word is used by heart:

Do not be *overcome* by evil, but *overcome* evil with good. (Rom. 12:21 NASB, emphasis mine)

In the world you have tribulation, but take courage; I have *overcome* the world. (John 16:37 NASB, emphasis mine)

> For whatever is born of God *overcomes* the world; and this is the victory that has *overcome* the world—our faith. (1 John 5:4 NASB, emphasis mine)

Based on this word study, we can see that it is not a physical conquering, but a *spiritual* conquering that the rider of the *White Horse* is attempting! This is revolutionary understanding. Again, as with each of the previous symbols in this passage, deception, especially *spiritual deception*, is the theme.

THE NICOLAITANS

Earlier in Revelation, Jesus wrote letters to the Seven Churches of Asia Minor. To most he says "to he who *overcomes . . .* " This is the same Greek word, NIKAO. Interestingly, in two of those letters, John addresses a group of people that historians have had trouble identifying. This group might be related to this word as well:

> Because you have there some who hold the teaching of *Balaam*, who kept teaching Balak to put a stumbling block before the sons of Israel, to eat things sacrificed to idols and to commit acts of immorality. So you also have some who in the same way hold the teaching of the *Nicolaitans*. (Rev. 2:14-15 NASB, emphasis mine)

The *Nicolaitans* appear only in Revelation. Irenaeus (who we saw also mis-identified the rider of the *white horse* as Jesus) believed they were a gnostic sect who followed Nicolas (Acts 6:5) of Antioch.[xxxiv] This view is highly discounted today, and frankly, the group remains unknown. Some have looked at the meaning of the two Greek words used in constructing the name "Nicolaitans" and surmise it may be a code word for the followers of the coming *Antichrist*. They consider these followers to be those who try to "overcome the people of God" (NIKAO meaning "overcome" plus LAO meaning "people of God").

Balaam is linked as a false (deceptive) teacher in this passage in 2 Peter:

They count it a pleasure to revel in the daytime. They are stains and blemishes, reveling in their deceptions, as they carouse with you, having eyes full of adultery that never cease from sin, enticing unstable souls, having a heart trained in greed, accursed children; forsaking the right way, they have gone astray, having followed *the way of Balaam*, the son of Beor, who loved the wages of unrighteousness; but he received a rebuke for his own transgression, for a mute donkey, speaking with a voice of a man, restrained the madness of the prophet. These are springs without water and mists driven by a storm, for whom the black darkness has been reserved. For speaking out arrogant words of vanity they entice by fleshly desires, by sensuality, those who barely escape from the ones who live in error, promising them freedom while they themselves are slaves of corruption; for *by what a man is overcome* (NIKAO), *by this he is enslaved.* (2 Pet 2:13-19 NASB, emphasis mine)

Notice the passage ends with the word "*overcome*." This word is intimately tied to *deception* and defeating deception. The rider of the *white horse* is a type of *Balaam*, a false prophet; deceiving and trying to deceive.

The picture is complete; the rider of the *white horse* is a *deceiver*. He carries a false peace treaty, and his crown and *white horse* show he is trying to appear as a messiah in Jesus's place. Finally, he is trying to conquer (overcome) the souls of men. All these descriptions fit the *Antichrist* very well, who is the rider of the *white horse*.

THE PURPOSE OF THE WHITE HORSEMAN

At the beginning of this Chapter, we discussed that Satan's purpose in sending the horsemen will be to cause the inhabitants of the world to worship *the Beast*. Now that we have undertaken an exhaustive study of the *white horse*, we are ready to examine how it fits into Satan's plan to create *apostasy*. We have seen that Satan will empower the Antichrist and the False Prophet. The *False Prophet* is Satan's primary tool in trying to cause the Bride of Christ to commit apostasy and thus undo Christ's plan of redemption that will consummate when the *Scroll* opens. We learned the *False Prophet* "makes the earth and those who dwell in it to worship the first beast." (Rev. 13:12) The *False Prophet* does this by utilizing four main techniques:

1) Signs and Lying Wonders
2) Warfare
3) The Mark of the Beast
4) Persecution unto death

It is my belief that the *False Prophet* will undertake these four aspects of his unholy ministry in the *exact order* listed above which perfectly aligns with the first four seals on the *7 Sealed Scroll* (and the first four events in the *Pattern of Seven Events*). First, as the *white horse* rides, the *False Prophet* most likely will proclaim to be the historic Jesus and will perform wondrous, lying signs to "prove" it. Second, as the *red horse* rides, the *False Prophet* and *Antichrist* will both call Muslims to incredibly successful jihads which will cause all to be in awe of them. Third, as the *black horse* rides, the *False Prophet* will institute the *Mark of the Beast* causing many to deny Christ in order to feed their families. Finally as Death rides the *green horse*, the *False Prophet* will make it mandatory that everyone prostrate themselves before the image of *the Beast* or be killed. These four methodologies accomplished in this exact order will result in *the Great Apostasy. This parallel between the ministry of the False Prophet and the four horsemen is uncanny.* It cannot be coincidence. It also shows that these works are orchestrated by Satan and fit perfectly with the scenario of Revelation.

Let's look at specific scriptures related to the *white horse* (related to the *first event* in the *Pattern of Seven Events*—see Appendix A for a summary of these seven key events) and see how they align with the ministry of the *False Prophet* found in Rev. 13. We will look at parallel passages in the *Olivet Discourse* which also outlines the *Pattern of Seven Events*. The graphic below (Figure 30: White Horse Related to the *First Event*) introduces these parallel passages:

Year of 70th Week of Daniel	Pattern of Seven Events	Rev. 6	Matt. 24	Rev. 13
First Year	1) Deception by False Messiahs	A *white horse* (to mimic Jesus's horse), and he who sat on it had a bow (False Covenant); and a *crown* (Messiah's crown) was given to him, and he went out conquering and to *conquer (Gk: NIKAO meaning "spiritually overcome")* (Rev. 6:2 NASB)	For many will *come in My name*, saying, '*I am the Christ*,' and will *mislead many* . . . For *false Christs and false prophets* will arise and will show *great signs and wonders*, so as to mislead, if possible, even the elect." (Matt. 24: 5, 24 NASB)	He (False Prophet) *performs great signs*, so that he even makes fire come down out of heaven to the earth in the presence of men. And *he deceives those who dwell on the earth because of the signs* which it was given him to perform. (Rev. 13: 13-14 NASB)

Figure 30: White Horse Related to the First Event

As we examine these three parallel passages (Rev. 6, Matt. 24, and Rev. 13), we see great similarity of themes and even exact wording between them: *a spiritual deception* (NIKAO, "will mislead many," "he deceives those who dwell on the earth."), *the use of signs and wonders* ("show great signs and wonders," "performs great signs"), and a *deception that he is the historical Jesus* (messiah's horse and crown, "come in my Name," "I am the Christ," "false Christs and false prophets").

Hence, the purpose of the *white horse* is to undermine confidence in the true Messiah, and to deceive the world by means of a false messiah, the *Antichrist*, who can negotiate a peace accord and a *false prophet* who can perform signs and wonders. Most of these signs will be supernatural, but the negotiation of the prophetic *Covenant with Death* ("he had a bow") that is "enforced" on Israel will also likely be a sign to the entire world of the prowess of the Antichrist. The purpose of this multi-faceted deception will be to cause the inhabitants of the world to doubt the true Messiah and to have confidence in and worship *the Beast*, the empowered *Antichrist*.

Ch. 7: A Horse of a Different Color

YEAR TWO: EVENT TWO

THE *RED HORSE* AND ITS RIDER

Sometime within the *Second Year* of the 70th Week, the *red horse* and its rider will come forth. Red is an interesting color. This horse isn't just "red," it is a "fiery red" (Gk: PURRHOS). It is the same color that Zechariah's *red horse* is described and the same color as the dragon (Satan) is described in Rev. 12. Genesis describes the stew that Jacob tempted Esau with as "fiery red." This is the stew that led to Esau giving Jacob his birthright. After this event, Esau was known as "Edom" which meant "red." This use of the color "fiery red" in Genesis is the first mention of PURRHOS in the Bible (Greek from the *Septuagint*). We know from the law of primacy, that this first mention has meaning in future symbolic uses of the word. For this reason we need to examine the story of *Esau and Jacob*.

ESAU, EDOM, AND "THE TIME OF JACOB'S TROUBLE"

The "*Time of Jacob's Trouble* (or distress)" is a term that is familiar to most. It is found in Jeremiah and is a reference to the *Great Tribulation*, the period of the *70th Week of Daniel* from the *Midpoint* up to the Rapture. We have examined this verse in Chapter Two: "Uncovering the Keys":

> "For behold, days are coming," declares the Lord, "when I will restore the fortunes of my people Israel and Judah." The Lord says, *I will also bring them back to the land* that I gave to their forefathers and they shall possess it." Now these are the words which the Lord spoke concerning Israel and concerning Judah: "For thus says the Lord, I have heard a sound of terror, of dread, and there is no peace. Ask now, and see if a male can give birth. Why do I see every man with his hands on his loins, as a woman in childbirth? And why have all faces turned pale?" "Alas! For that day is great, there is none like it; and it is *the time of Jacob's distress*, but he will be saved from it. It shall come about on that day," declares the Lord of hosts, "that I will break *his* yoke from off *their*

162

neck and will tear off their bonds; and strangers will no longer make them their slaves." (Jer. 30:3-8 NASB, emphasis mine

The passage above in Jeremiah begins with an event ("*I will bring them back to the land*") that occurred in 1948, the restoration of the nation of Israel. Please note that God tells us that *both* Israel and Judah were to be restored to the land, so the current occupiers of Israel probably include representatives from all 12 tribes. Also note the reference to labor pains. This is what Jesus was referring to in the *Olivet Discourse* as the "*Beginning of the Birth Pangs*" in Matt. 24: 4-8.

While most prophecy teachers notice these things, few seem aware that this passage in Jeremiah is itself a reference to a much older section of scripture from Genesis. Understanding the *70th Week of Daniel* requires knowledge of this earlier "type" or picture of the *Great Tribulation* found in Genesis*:*

> Then God said to *Jacob*, "Arise, go up to Bethel and live there, and make an altar there to God, who appeared to you *when you fled from your brother Esau.*" So Jacob said to his household and to all who were with him, "Put away the foreign gods which are among you, and purify yourselves and change your garments; and let us arise and go up to Bethel, and I will make an altar there to God, who answered me in *the day of my distress* and has been with me wherever I have gone." (Gen. 35:1-3 NASB, emphasis mine)

This above passage in Genesis reveals several important aspects of the 70th Week. First, notice that the type or picture in Jer. 30 *refers to Israel by his older name, Jacob.* After Jacob wrestled with the pre-incarnate Jesus, the Lord changed his name *from Jacob to Israel*. The name *Jacob* means "he who grasps the heel" or "supplanter." It is interesting how the opinion of the nations of the world is that the Nation of Israel is not entitled to the land, that they are *supplanters* of the Palestinian people. After the Nation of Israel wrestles with God during the 70th Week, the land's name will be changed again to *Beulah* (Isa. 62:4) which means 'bride." This new name pictures the day when all Israel will gaze upon the one they pierced (Jesus), repent and be saved—at the physical return of Jesus to earth. At that point, they will no longer be viewed as "supplanters" but rightful heirs.

Second, notice that the passage in Genesis claims Jacob flees from "Esau." There are two aspects to this. First it pictures *the flight of Israel* that Jesus commanded upon their seeing the *Abomination of Desolation* set up (Matt. 24:15). This flight is also pictured in Rev. 12:6. Most intriguing to me though, is that Jacob is fleeing from *Esau.*

Very few commentators have discussed *Esau* as a picture of the *Antichrist* and his empire, but in the above verse we can clearly see the *Time of Jacob's Trouble* is tied to *Esau.* His nickname, *Edom,* means "red" and it is interesting that Satan, the Beast of Rev. 13, and the *red horse* we are studying, are all this color. The links are unmistakable.

If *Esau is a picture of the Antichrist and his Beast Empire,* we need to learn more about him. We remember from Genesis that Esau was Jacob's older brother. Esau traded Jacob his birthright for a bowl of fiery red (PURRHOS) soup. Not only did Esau lose his *birthright* (the land of Israel) but Jacob also stole *Esau's blessing* (the Abrahamic Covenant) by disguising himself as Esau to his blind father Isaac when Isaac gave his blessing, which he intended for Esau (Gen. 27). This helps explain a lot about why the land of Israel today is so contentious for those in the Middle East. Esau became furious about his stolen blessing and begged his father to bless him as well, which Jacob could not do:

> Isaac replied to *Esau,* "Behold, I have made him (Jacob) your master and all his relatives I have given to him as servants; and with grain and new wine I have sustained him. Now as for you then, what can I do, my son?" Esau said to his father, "Do you have only one blessing, my father? Bless me, even me also, O my father." So Esau lifted his voice and wept. Then Isaac his father answered and said to him, "Behold, away from the fertility of the earth shall be your dwelling, and away from the dew of heaven from above. *By your sword you shall live,* and your brother you shall serve; but it shall come about when you become restless, that *you will break his yoke from your neck*" (Gen. 27:37-40, NASB, clarification and emphasis mine.)

From this passage in Gen. 27 we can see Esau's descendants will always be a violent people and live by the sword. It is also *their destiny to die by that sword* as Jesus has instructed Peter, "Put your sword back into its place; for all those who take up the sword shall perish by the sword" (Matt. 26:52 NASB). Revelation further clarifies the idea in this verse, "if anyone kills with the sword, with the sword he must be killed" (Rev. 13:10 NASB).

For most of history Edom has been secondary to Jacob, but someday they *will break the yoke from around their necks.* This is exactly what God said in Jer. 30 that we studied at the top of this section. This is yet another reference to Edom. Many think that it's solely a reference to Jacob for whom Jesus breaks the yoke of the Antichrist, but it isn't. It's also a reference to *the people of Esau* as well. They will break Israel's yoke around *their* necks (conquer Israel) and launch the *Time of Jacob's Trouble.* The quoted passage in Jer. 30 has a double meaning. Yes, it refers to the people of Esau breaking Israel's yoke at the *Midpoint* of the 70th Week and it also refers to Jesus breaking the Antichrist's yoke around Israel's neck.

Immediately, after receiving his father's secondary blessing, Esau desired to kill Jacob:

> So Esau bore a grudge against Jacob because of the blessing with which his father had blessed him; and Esau said to himself, "The days of mourning for my father are near; *then I will kill my brother Jacob.*" (Gen. 27:41 NASB, emphasis mine)

Jacob then fled from Esau just as Gen. 35 tells us. *This is the picture of the future flight of Israel during Jacob's Trouble.* It was on this flight from Esau that Jacob had his dream we now know as "Jacob's Ladder" where he saw the pre-incarnate Christ as a ladder with the Angels ascending and descending upon him. So, this is some background on Jacob and Esau, which is further described in the next section below; it has quite a history, which has ramifications down to today in the Middle East.

Ch. 7: A Horse of a Different Color

ESAU THROUGHOUT HISTORY

Who are famous descendants of Esau? One of the first is Doeg. When King Saul was pursuing David, Saul discovered that the priests of Nob had given David food and shelter. Saul became angry and ordered his army officers to kill all the priests of Nob. None of Saul's men (Israelites) would obey this diabolical order. It was then that Doeg the Edomite stepped forward. He not only killed all the priests of Nob, he also killed all the women and children in the city and every animal (see 1Sam.22:16-19). This is the legacy of Esau; living by the sword and more than willing to kill the descendants of Jacob.

Haman who tried to eliminate all the Jews during the time of Queen Esther was an Edomite (being related to Agag, the king of the Amalekites-Edomites); as was Herod the Great, who slaughtered the innocents in his attempt to kill Jesus. Edom has a violent past and will continue to hate Jacob until the end, as illustrated by these passages from Ezekiel and Amos:

> Because you (*Edom) have had everlasting enmity* and have delivered the sons of Israel to the power of the sword *at the time of their calamity, at the time of the punishment of the end*, therefore as I live," declares the Lord God, "I will give you over to bloodshed, and bloodshed will pursue you; since you have not hated bloodshed, therefore bloodshed will pursue you. (Ezekiel 35:5-6 NASB, clarification and emphasis mine)

> Thus says the Lord, "For three transgressions of Edom and for four I will not revoke its punishment, *because he pursued his brother* (Jacob) *with the sword* while he stifled his compassion; his anger also tore continually, *and he maintained his fury forever.* So I will send fire upon *Teman* and it will consume the citadels of *Bozrah*." (Amos 1:11 NASB, clarification and emphasis mine)

So who are these violent people today? If Haman was living in Persia, as is assumed, some of the *Iranians* today might be Edomites. Others have claimed the *Turks* are

166

Edomites, and certainly nearly all commentators feel the modern *Palestinians* are Edomites. This broad spectrum of possibilities shows no human really knows for sure. My opinion is that the modern *Islamists* are Edomites.

I find Jer. 49 interesting. In this chapter of Jeremiah, the cities of Esau are listed as Teman (v. 7), Dedan (v.8), and Bozrah (v.13). We also see two of these cities mentioned in the citation from Amos above. The first two cities are part of *Saudi Arabia*. Might descendants of Esau inhabit Saudi Arabia? Personally, because these cities associated with Saudi Arabia are specifically mentioned here and in other places in the Bible in reference to Esau and Edom, I support a position that Edom is presently *western Saudi Arabia, perhaps containing Medina and Mecca.*

GOD'S PLAN FOR EDOM

God plans to totally destroy Edom and the Edomites, as mentioned in Jeremiah and Obadiah:

> Edom will become an object of horror; everyone who passes by it will be horrified and will hiss at all its wounds. Like the overthrow of Sodom and Gomorrah with its neighbors," says the Lord, "*no one will live there, nor will a son of man reside in it.*" (Jer. 49:17-18 NASB, emphasis mine)

> Then the house of Jacob will be a fire and the house of Joseph a flame; but the house of Esau will be as stubble. And they will set them on fire and consume them, so that there will be *no survivor* of the *house of Esau*," For the Lord has spoken. (Obad. 1:18 NASB, emphasis mine)

God will completely wipe violent Esau off the face of the earth, and the land of Edom will be like Sodom and Gomorrah. These are very strong words.

After this lengthy but necessary study on Esau, we now understand that the *red horse* and his rider are associated with *Esau and his violent descendants.* We saw in Zech. 6 that the *red horse* most likely stayed on the border of the "North Country"

(Seleucid Empire) and the "South Country" (Ptolemaic Empire). So it is likely the bloodshed in the *Second Year* of Daniel's 70th Week will involve these future revived empires.

TO TAKE PEACE FROM THE EARTH

As we return to Rev. 6, we read that the rider of the *red horse* is granted three things:

> A *red horse*, went out; and to him who sat on it, *it was granted* to *take peace from the earth*, and that men would *slay one another*; and *a great sword was given* to him. (Rev. 6:4 NASB, emphasis mine)

These three things granted are:

- the ability to take peace (Gk: EIRENE) from the earth,
- that men might slay (Gk: SPHAZO) one another, and
- a great (Gk: MEGAS) sword

All three of these descriptions are consistent with the violent Edomites.

The first thing the rider of the *red horse* is given is the ability to take peace from the earth. This peace is the Greek word EIRENE which can mean "lack of conflict" or "peace of mind." In my opinion, it carries both meanings. Jesus foresaw that during this *Second Year* of the 70th Week, his followers would be concerned by the conflict that was to come upon the earth so he told them, "You will be hearing of wars and rumors of wars. *See that you are not frightened*, for those things must take place, but that is not yet the end for nation will rise against nation and kingdom against kingdom" (Matt. 24:6-7 NASB, emphasis mine). *Jesus specifically tells us to not be frightened*. It is for this reason that I believe the "peace" that is taken away is primarily *peace of mind*. During the *First Year* of the 70th Week, the Antichrist appears as a man of peace and confirms the false covenant with the "many." Now in the *Second Year*, he mounts a *red war horse*, removes that peace, and the world is horrified.

The world has seen many wars and struggles. Why might this year of conflict be different and cause the whole world to be frightened? The first reason is the Greek word translated "slays" (SPHAZO). This word means to butcher and can even mean to sacrifice. The first use of this word (law of Primacy) is found in Genesis 22:10 when Abraham prepared to sacrifice Isaac. Although all wars involve bloodshed, this particular war will involve a killing that is different. It will involve killing that is done as a religious sacrifice. Isn't this what we are currently seeing in the Middle East with ISIS beheading those it calls apostates and infidels?

Second, the rider of the *red horse* is given a great (Gk: MEGAS) sword. The word MEGAS means "the ultimate." What weapon is the ultimate in our world? A *nuclear bomb* is the most fearful weapon of all time. Might this war involve nuclear weapons? Jesus in the *Olivet Discourse* used an interesting term in the signs he instructed us to watch for in the *"Beginning of The Birth Pangs"* (Matt. 24:8). The word translated "earthquakes" in Matthew, Mark and Luke means "a literal shaking." The Greek word SEISMOS *may* be an earthquake or any natural or man-made disaster. The storm on the Sea of Galilee that Jesus calmed was described as a SEISMOS. A *nuclear explosion* would certainly also classify as a SEISMOS, so this is possibly what the Scripture is speaking of. A nuclear blast is certainly a great shaking and a disaster. I think it is likely that the great sword of Rev. 6:4 is a *nuclear missile*.

PURPOSE OF THE RED HORSEMAN

As we learned in the previous section about the *white horse*, Satan's overall purpose for the *Four Horsemen* is to cause the inhabitants of the world to worship *the Beast*. Let's examine parallel scriptures related to the *red horse* and see Satan's specific methodology in regard to this horseman. The graphic below related to the *red horse* (Figure 31: Red Horse Related to the *Second Event*) shows the parallel passages in Revelation and Matthew:

Year of 70th Week of Daniel	Pattern of Seven Events	Rev. 6	Matt. 24	Rev. 13
First Year	1) Deception by False Messiahs	A *white horse* (to mimic Jesus's horse), and he who sat on it had a bow (False Covenant); and a *crown* (Messiah's crown) was given to him, and he went out conquering and to *conquer (Gk: NIKAO meaning "spiritually overcome")* (Rev. 6:2 NASB)	For many will *come in My name*, saying, '*I am the Christ*,' and will *mislead many* . . . For *false Christs and false prophets* will arise and will show *great signs and wonders*, so as to mislead, if possible, even the elect." (Matt. 24: 5, 24 NASB)	He (False Prophet) *performs great signs*, so that he even makes fire come down out of heaven to the earth in the presence of men. And *he deceives those who dwell on the earth because of the signs* which it was given him to perform. (Rev. 13: 13-14 NASB)

Figure 31: Red Horse Related to the Second Event

As we focus on these passages, we see an emphasis on *war* and *bloodshed*. The purpose of that warfare, however, is explained in Rev. 13:4; it causes those on the earth to respect the might of *the Beast* and his military prowess, eventually leading to worship. This will not be a worship based on *love*, but rather one based on *fear*; fear of *the Beast's* power to kill and destroy. This is why Jesus *specifically* instructs us in Luke 21:9 to *"not be frightened"* when the *red horse* rides.

YEAR THREE: EVENT THREE

THE *BLACK HORSE* AND ITS RIDER

Today at lunch time I heard, "I'm starving." "Me too, I'm famished." These co-workers had just had a meal less than five hours earlier, but our American lifestyle is conditioned to not do without. A time is coming, however, when all that will change. What will it be like when Jesus breaks the *Third Seal* on the *Scroll* and the *black horse* of Revelation rides?

The Bible is clear that there is a *coming famine*; one of world-wide proportions. Revelation pictures this coming famine as a *black horse:*

170

I looked, and behold, a *black horse*; and he who sat on it had a pair of scales in his hand. And I heard *something like a voice* in the center of the four living creatures saying, "A quart of wheat for a denarius, and three quarts of barley for a denarius; and do not damage the oil and the wine." (Rev. 6:6-7 NASB, emphasis mine)

We are building a thesis that one seal is broken during each of the 7 years of the *70^(th) Week of Daniel*. If that thesis is correct, this famine occurs in the *Third Year*. As we have seen with the previous two horses, the color of the horse is symbolic of the event occurring. In this case it's black, representing *economic turmoil* and subsequent *famine*. The following passage in Exodus is pertinent:

> So Moses stretched out his staff over the land of Egypt, and the Lord directed an east wind on the land all that day and all that night; and when it was morning, the east wind brought the *locusts*. The locusts came up over all the land of Egypt and settled in all the territory of Egypt; they were very numerous. There had never been so many locusts, nor would there be so many again. For they covered the surface of the whole land, so that the land was *darkened* (*blackened*); and *they ate every plant of the land and all the fruit of the trees* that the hail had left. Thus nothing green was left on tree or plant of the field through all the land of Egypt. (Exod. 10:13-15 NASB, clarification and emphasis mine)

The picture here is of so many locusts that the land of Egypt became *blackened*. After the locusts invaded, the *famine* began. Another famine is coming upon the earth. Jesus prophesied it will occur after the *Third Year* of the 70^(th) Week begins:

> In various places there will be *famines* and earthquakes. But all these things are merely the *Beginning of Birth Pangs*. (Matt. 24:7-8 NASB, emphasis mine)

Notice how Jesus places the *famines* during the "*Beginning of The Birth Pangs* period." (The first 3 1/2 years of the *70th Week of Daniel*.)

WHAT THE LOCUSTS HAVE EATEN

The prophet Joel prophesied about a *famine and locusts* as well. Joel 1:1-14 gives the account of an ancient famine caused by locusts. Joel then uses this ancient account as an analogy about the 70th Week. Just as we have seen in Revelation, Joel uses a direct quoted reference as a "bookend" at the beginning and end of the prophetic passage: "*Consecrate a fast, proclaim a solemn assembly; gather the elders.*" This passage occurs in Joel 1:14 and Joel 2:15-16. These two verses form a "bookend" just as we learned about in Chapter Four: "Bookends (Revelation 1-3)." Within the "bookend" we learn the timing of when Israel is to call this assembly: it is when the invading army is so great "*there has never been anything like it*" (Joel 2:2 NASB). This verse echoes Dan. 12:1 which speaks of the *Great Tribulation*, "There will be *a time of distress such as never occurred* since there was a nation until that time," and Jesus's words, "For then there will be a *great tribulation*, such as *has not occurred since the beginning of the world* until now, nor ever will" (Matt. 24:21 NASB).

In Joel 1:15 and Joel 2:1, the prophet also tells us that the *Day of the Lord* (God's Wrath) is near. The references to the *Day of the Lord* being imminent indicate that the events portrayed happen *before the Seventh Year* of the *70th Week of Daniel*, when God's Wrath is poured out. This is also consistent with the references to the famine in Revelation and the *Olivet Discourse*.

What causes the famine? In the *Septuagint* (Greek) translation of Joel Chapter 1, we see three types of insects descend on the crop (caterpillars, locusts and grasshoppers). Blight, drought and fire (possibly from warfare) also affect the crops. In Joel Chapter 2 we are told about what appear to be the Antichrist's soldiers, "A fire consumes before them and behind them a flame burns. The land is like the garden of Eden before them but a desolate wilderness behind them" (Joel 2:3 NASB). So, apparently *warfare* has an effect on the vegetation of the landscape. It appears a *drought* is partially responsible as well.

Even the beasts of the field pant for you; for *the water brooks are dried up* and fire has devoured the pastures of the wilderness. (Joel 1:20 NASB, emphasis mine)

In Isaiah we learn that a *drought* will last during the occupation of Jerusalem that occurs during the *Great Tribulation*:

So now let me tell you what I am going to do to my vineyard (Jerusalem): I will remove its hedge and it will be consumed; I will break down its wall and it will become trampled ground. I will lay it waste; it will not be pruned or hoed, but briars and thorns (Gentile nations) will come up. *I will also charge the clouds to rain no rain on it.* (Isa. 5:5-6, clarification and emphasis mine)

Revelation shows us that it is the *Two Witnesses* who cause the drought, "These have the power to shut up the sky, so that rain will not fall during the days of their prophesying" (Rev. 11:6 NASB). God tells us through Joel that the drought is only for a season, however:

So rejoice, O sons of Zion, and be glad in the Lord your God; for He has given you the early rain for your vindication. And He has poured down for you the rain, the early and latter rain as before. *The threshing floors will be full of grain, and the vats will overflow* with the new wine and oil. *Then I will make up to you for the years that the swarming locust has eaten.* (Joel 2:23-25 NASB, emphasis mine)

SCALES IN HIS HAND

The rider of the *black horse* (the *Antichrist*) is seen holding a pair of merchant's scales in his hand. We know the rider is the Antichrist because the *black horse* is sent to the "North Country" (Seleucid Empire) in Zech. 6, and the Antichrist is the "King of the

North." The voice from amongst the living creatures (is this the voice of Antichrist?) calls out a price for grain, "A quart of wheat for a denarius, and three quarts of barley for a denarius." It appears the Antichrist is using the famine to his advantage and is selling food. A denarius was a coin common in the Roman world of John's day. It was equivalent to a worker's wages for one day, but the amount of grain purchased by this wage is hardly sufficient to sustain a single person let alone a family.

Is it during this famine that the *False Prophet* begins to require the Antichrist's *Mark of the Beast*? We know from Rev. 13 that he will institute an economic program where the inhabitants of the earth are not able to *buy or sell* without this mark.

> He causes all, both small and great, rich and poor, free and slave, to receive *a mark on their right hand or on their foreheads*, and *that no one may buy or sell except one who has the mark* or the name of the beast, or the number of his name. (Rev. 13:16, 17 NASB, emphasis mine)

A world that is in the midst of the worst famine in history would be an easy target for the Antichrist. Is it his offer of food to a hungry world that finally leads him to wide-spread power?

There was a famine in Joseph's day as well. During that famine, Joseph advised the Egyptian Pharaoh to take some economic steps *to leverage the value of the food* Joseph had stored up during the seven years of plenty:

> Now there was no food in all the land, because the *famine* was very severe, so that the land of Egypt and the land of Canaan languished because of the famine. *Joseph gathered all the money* that was found in the land of Egypt and in the land of Canaan for the grain which they bought, and Joseph brought the money into Pharaoh's house. When the money was all spent in the land of Egypt and in the land of Canaan, all the Egyptians came to Joseph and said, "Give us food, for why should we die in your presence? For our money is gone." Then Joseph said, "*Give up your livestock*, and I will give you food for your livestock, since your money is gone." So they brought their livestock to

Joseph, and Joseph gave them food in exchange for the horses and the flocks and the herds and the donkeys; and he *fed them with food in exchange for all their livestock* that year. (Gen. 47:13-17 NASB, emphasis mine)

First, Joseph sold the food for *cash*. When the Egyptians' money was gone, he traded the food for their means of business (*livestock*). Next, he bought their *land*:

So Joseph *bought all the land* of Egypt for Pharaoh, for *every Egyptian sold his field, because the famine was severe* upon them. (Gen. 47:20 NASB, emphasis mine)

Finally, with no worldly possessions, the people traded themselves as *slaves* to Pharaoh:

So they said, "You have saved our lives! Let us find favor in the sight of my lord, and *we will be Pharaoh's slaves*." (Gen. 47:25 NASB, emphasis mine)

This is only conjecture, but I fully expect *the same pattern* to occur as the *Antichrist* assumes global power during the period of severe drought and famine.

WHAT SHOULD WE THEN DO?

Understanding what is coming so we can prepare emotionally and physically is one of the main purposes of prophecy. Those who have read my previous book, *Are We Ready For Jesus?—How to Prepare for His Return* (Seraphina Press, 2015), are already aware that God desires that we prepare for the famine that is coming. Unfortunately, many in the Church miss this key teaching of the "faithful and wise servant" Jesus mentioned in his *Olivet Discourse*, as we discussed in my previous book:

Who then is the *faithful and sensible slave* whom his master put in charge of his household *to give them their food* at the proper time (KAIROS meaning "appointed time")? Blessed is that slave whom his master finds so doing when he comes. Truly I say to you that he will put him in charge of all his possessions. (Matt. 24:45-47 NASB, clarification and emphasis mine)

The first part of the above passage is a riddle, and Jesus asks "who is the faithful slave?" There are three clues to the riddle:

- He is a faithful and wise slave

- His master put him in charge of his household

- He provides food for his household at the "appointed time."

Have you guessed yet? *It's Joseph.* Jesus wants his leaders to be *like Joseph* during Daniel's 70th Week; he wants us to provide food for his household, and the first step is as Joseph did—to *store food* for the upcoming days. Now he isn't commanding us to gather food for "*our*" household, it's *his* household he wants us to prepare for. His household is the Church and the Jews. Both are our brothers and sisters. So is Jesus telling us to be "preppers?" Yes, shockingly he is, but not for ourselves, it's for our neighbors and our community of Christians and Jews.

WHAT WILL GOD DO?

God has promised to take care of his remnant. Some may be cared for by those who are prepared, the "*Josephs*" among us. God will also provide miraculously for others. We know he provides for the future Jewish remnant, after the *Midpoint* of the 70th Week:

> Then the woman (Israel) fled into the wilderness where she had a place prepared by God, so that *there she would be nourished* for one thousand two hundred and sixty days (3 ½ years). (Rev. 12:6 NASB, clarification and emphasis mine)

In Jesus' letter to the Church of Pergamum, he tells us of his provision for that church:

To him who overcomes, to him I will give some of the *hidden manna.* (Rev. 2:17 NASB, emphasis mine)

We will study this section of scripture related to Jesus's *Letters to the Seven Churches* in depth in Part Four: *"Letters to the Seven Churches."*

Should we also be prepared for the worst? God has told us *not* to take the *Mark of the Beast*; it is equivalent to *eternal damnation.* It's not an option. All Christians must be mentally prepared to *refuse even if that means starvation or martyrdom* by the sword! We know this will happen to some as we will learn in the next section. This can't be emphasized enough—do NOT take the *Mark of the Beast*!

PURPOSE OF THE BLACK HORSEMAN

As we have seen in the previous two sections about the *white horse* and the *red horse*, Satan's purpose for all the horsemen is to *deceive* the inhabitants of the world into worshiping *the Beast.* Let's examine parallel scriptures related to this horseman of the *black horse*, to see how Satan utilizes him to this end. The following graphic (Figure 32: Black Horse Related to the *Third Event* of the *Pattern of Seven Events*) shows the parallel passages from Revelation and Matthew:

Year of the 70th Week of Daniel	Pattern of Seven Events	Rev. 6	Matt. 24	Rev. 13
Third Year	3) Famine and Economic Collapse	A *black horse* and he who sat on it had a pair of scales in his hand. And I heard something like a voice in the center of the four living creatures saying, *"A quart of wheat for a denarius, and three quarts of barley for a denarius; and do not damage the oil and the wine."* (Rev. 6:5-6 NASB)	And in various places there will be *famines* (Matt. 24: 7 NASB)	And he causes all, the small and the great, and the rich and the poor, and the free men and the slaves, to be given a mark on their right hand or on their forehead, and he provides that *no one will be able to buy or to sell, except the one who has the mark.* (Rev. 13: 16-17 NASB)

Figure 32: Black Horse Related to the Third Event

In this set of passages from Revelation and Matthew, we observe a cause and effect of events that surround the famine of the *Third Year* of the 70th Week. First there is *famine* and the price of food greatly escalates. Finally, in response, the *False Prophet* initiates the *Mark of the Beast* so that the inhabitants of the earth can provide for their families. The evil purpose of this *Mark*, however, is to cause all of those who take it to worship *the Beast*, and, thereby, reject God. Once again, taking the *Mark of the Beast* is described as an unforgivable sin, and that person faces eternal damnation and separation from God (Rev. 14:11). This is a serious warning from God and calls for "patient *endurance* on the part of the saints who obey God's commandments and remain faithful to Jesus" (Rev. 14:12, emphasis mine). God, through the Holy Spirit, the Comforter, will help us to endure and *not* take the *Mark of the Beast*.

YEAR FOUR: EVENT FOUR

THE GREEN "DEATH" HORSE AND ITS RIDER

As we have already discussed, as Jesus breaks each of the first four seals on the *Scroll*, Satan and his earthly agent the Antichrist will respond by trying to prevent the scroll from opening. After the *Fourth Seal* is broken, Satan unleashes his ultimate attempt; his last ditch, nothing-held-back effort to retain his dominion. Jesus tells us this time during the *Fourth Year* of the 70th Week will be like nothing the world has ever experienced. It will be *"great" tribulation.*

The rider of the *white horse* at the beginning of the 70th Week will bring deception. This deception will open the opportunity for war and bloodshed in the *Second Year*. The warfare will lead to economic chaos and famine in the *Third Year*. Finally, world-wide hunger will assist the rider of the *green horse* to assume great global power during the *Fourth Year* of the 70th Week. This will happen at the *Midpoint* of this period. In Chapter Eleven: "Event Four: Abomination and Death" we will look at the following events that occur at the *Midpoint* of the *70th Week of Daniel*:

- Michael the Archangel rises to fight Satan and his angels,
- Satan is cast down to the earth and is filled with rage,

- By rising, Michael releases *the Beast* which subsequently possesses the *Antichrist*,
- The demon-assisted *Antichrist* invades Jerusalem, kills many and sends the Jewish survivors into captivity "into all nations," and
- Flush with his victory and with the power he has assumed from implementing the *Mark of the Beast*, the *Antichrist* sits in the temple of God and proclaims himself God.

It is at this point, he begins the *Great Tribulation*, the most wide-spread persecution of Christians and the Jews that the world has ever seen. We have already seen what Daniel and Matthew have to say about this time but are listed here for review:

> And there will be a time of distress such *as never occurred since there was a nation until that time.* (Dan. 12:1 NASB, emphasis mine)

> For then there will be a *great tribulation,* such *as has not occurred since the beginning of the world until now, nor ever will.* (Matt. 24:21 NASB, emphasis mine)

Revelation pictures this persecution as the *green horse* and his rider:

> An ashen (Gk: CHLOROS meaning *vibrant green*) horse; and he who sat on it had the name Death; and Hades was following with him. Authority was given to them over a fourth of the earth, *to kill with sword and with famine and with pestilence and by the wild beasts of the earth.* (Rev. 6:8 NASB, clarification and emphasis mine)

We have already discussed that the purpose of the *vibrant green* color is to represent *Islam,* the religion of death. In my opinion this can be the only meaning of vibrant, summer green as the color of the "death" horse. This color has confused Bible translators for years who have mistranslated CHLOROS as "pale." These translators couldn't figure out why a "lively" green was used for a "death" horse. The colors of Zechariah's corresponding "fourth" horse have significant additional meaning:

- In Hebrew, the words are translated as strong, speckled (Heb: AMUSSIM BERUDDIM). The *strong, spotted horse* reminds me of Nebuchadnezzar's statue of the four metals. The *toes of that statue* which represent the final human kingdom were iron and clay mixed. The iron was "strong," and the mixture of two materials is "speckled" in a way.

- In Greek, the words are translated as "various colored" and "psalm-like" (Gk: POIKILOS PSALMOS). "Various colored" describes the various ways that the Antichrist will persecute the Church: through sword, famine, pestilence, and wild beasts. "Psalm-like" is quite a strange word to describe a horse. In my opinion this is a reference to being like Psalms 14, which is also about this *Fourth Year* of the *70th Week of Daniel*.

HE HAD THE NAME "DEATH"

The rider of the vibrant *green horse* is named "Death" and he is followed by "Hades." These two characters, *Death* and *Hades* are a reference to a very famous Old Testament passage:

> Because ye (Israel) have said, "We have made a covenant with *Hades*, and agreements with *Death*; if the rushing storm should pass, it shall not come upon us: we have made falsehood our hope, and by falsehood shall we be protected." (Isa. 28:15 LXX, clarification and emphasis mine)

The *Covenant with Death and Hades* pictured above is the peace covenant signed by Israel and the Antichrist that launches the *70th Week of Daniel*. This same covenant is broken at the midpoint (Dan. 9:27). When Rev. 6:8 refers to these characters (*Death* and *Hades*), John is indicating to us that the *green horse* will be involved in the breaking of this peace covenant. This clear reference is a "time stamp" confirming that the *green horse* will ride at the *Midpoint* of Daniel's 70th Week during the *Fourth Year*. This is an important nuance of interpretation.

The passage (Rev. 6:8) then says that authority was given to them (to *Death* and *Hades* by God) over a quarter of the earth to kill. A quarter of the earth could mean two things. It could mean they had power to kill a quarter of the population or it could mean their power to kill was restricted to 25% of the earth's land mass. Mark Davidson, author of the landmark book *Daniel Revisited* (Westbow Press, 2013) has shown how Islam controls 25 % of the land mass and population of the world,[xxxv] and he suggests that the killing will be restricted to that area. Either position is scripturally possible. It is my opinion that the Antichrist is given authority to kill a quarter of the world's total population, of which declared Christianity (not all "born-again" believers) represents approximately 31%. If the *Great Tribulation* is as severe as Daniel and Jesus tell us, then it appears that the death toll should *not* be limited to the Muslim realm and could easily extend to 25% of the world's population. After all, Jesus tells us unless he was to shorten the days of the *Great Tribulation*, "no life would have been saved" (Matt. 24:22 NASB). This is highly consistent with a global massacre.

The Antichrist's various means of killing deserve examination. There are actually only three means of killing in that passage not four as the English translation of Rev. 6:8 implies. Let's carefully review it again:

> He who sat on it had the name Death; and Hades was following with him. Authority was given to them over a fourth of the earth, to kill with (Gk: EN) sword and with (Gk: EN) famine and with (Gk: EN) pestilence and by (Gk: HYPO) the wild beasts (Gk: THERION) of the earth. (Rev. 6:8 NASB, emphasis mine)

Examination of three Greek words in the passage will unlock the meaning of this verse for us. The first word we will examine is THERION which here is translated "wild beasts." It occurs 30 times in the Revelation. In every instance other than this one, it refers to either the Antichrist or the False Prophet. It is my opinion that it should be translated "beasts" here, and implies both of these demonically-empowered beings.

Ch. 7: A Horse of a Different Color

Providing further substantiation of this opinion are the two Greek prepositions used in the verse: EN and HYPO. The Greek word EN precedes the three means of killing (sword, famine, and pestilence) and it carries the meaning of "in or within the sphere of." The English renders this "with" and that is an adequate translation. These are the means of killing. The preposition that precedes "beasts," however is a different Greek word (HYPO) that means "under or under the authority of." Proper translation of the verse, therefore, strictly implies that the killing is under the authority of the beasts. This cannot be lions or wolves, but must mean the demonic-empowered beasts mentioned 29 more times in Revelation (the Antichrist and False Prophet.)

This proper translation eliminates the chance that this killing is due to natural disasters (pestilence or famine), and requires us to view the three means of killing as forms of persecution. The Greek word for sword (Gk: RHOMPHAIA) means a two-edged *scimitar*. Although this certainly *may be a symbol to denote war*, it also can be a weapon for *beheading*. We notice Islamic extremists already murdering by this means at an alarming rate. Famine will occur during the ride of the *black horse*, and can be a means of persecution if food is denied to a population. If the only people given access to food are those who pledge allegiance to the Antichrist, famine can be a means of execution. Pestilence or illness can be natural (lack of sanitation, etc.) or man-created via biologic weapons. Ezekiel speaks of four plagues, "For thus says the Lord GOD, 'how much more when I send my four severe judgments against Jerusalem: *sword, famine, wild beasts and plague* to cut off man and beast from it! Yet, behold, survivors (a remnant) will be left in it who will be brought out, both sons and daughters'" (Ezek. 14:21-22 NASB; clarification and emphasis mine). This helps re-enforce the idea that God does not cause these plagues but is still in control. *Authority* is given to the Antichrist to kill in this way. That is why the Greek proposition "HYPO" is used to denote the Beast's authority. Nothing will happen that God does not permit; it is all part of his ultimate plan, and believers can take comfort in that the Holy Spirit will be with us through whatever happens.

Jesus gives us a vivid picture of what the *Great Tribulation* will be like, "Then they will deliver you to tribulation, and will kill you, and you will be hated by all nations because of my name. At that time many will fall away *and will betray one*

182

another and hate one another" (Matt. 24: 9-10 NASB; emphasis mine). I think the saddest part of this passage is the betrayal by other Christians. We will discuss this aspect at length in Chapter Twelve: "Event Five: Martyrdom and Apostasy."

PURPOSE OF THE GREEN HORSEMAN

As with each of the previous three sections, Satan's purpose for the *green horse* is to cause the inhabitants of the world to worship *the Beast*. Let's see how Satan accomplishes this evil purpose, summarized in the following chart (Figure 33: Green Horse Related to the *Fourth Event*):

Year of the 70th Week of Daniel	Pattern of Seven Events	Rev. 6	Matt. 24	Rev. 13
Fourth Year	4) Abomination and Death	An ashen *(Gk: CHLOROS, meaning "green") horse*; and *he who sat on it had the name Death; and Hades was following with him*. *Authority was given to them* over a fourth of the earth, *to kill with sword and with famine and with pestilence and by the wild beasts* of the earth. (Rev. 6:7-8 NASB)	Then they will *deliver you to tribulation*, and *will kill you*, and you will be *hated by all nations because of My name*. At that time *many will fall away* and will betray one another and hate one another . . . Therefore when you see the *abomination of desolation* which was spoken of through Daniel the prophet, standing in the holy place (Matt. 24: 9-10, 15 NASB)	They worshiped the dragon because *he gave his authority to the beast* . . . and it was given to him to give breath to the image of the beast, so that the image of the beast would even speak and *cause as many as do not worship the image of the beast to be killed*. (Rev. 13: 4, 15 NASB)

Figure 33: Green Horse Related to the Fourth Event

This group of passages from Revelation and the *Olivet Discourse* from Matthew clearly focuses on the *authority given to the Beast* ("authority was given to them," "gave his authority to the beast"), *the image of the Beast* ("the abomination of desolation," "the image of the beast"), and the *persecution unto death* that will result from remaining true to Jesus ("to kill with sword and famine and pestilence", "will kill you and you will be hated by all nations because of my Name," "cause as many as do not worship the image of the beast to be killed"). Hence, the purpose of the rider of the *green horse* is to force the inhabitants of the earth to *worship the Beast* by means of a "covert or die" policy.

SUMMARY

The parallels between the ministry of the *False Prophet* and the events surrounding the opening of the first four seals show these events are not random, but rather are a well-orchestrated plan of Satan to deceive unbelievers *and* believers into worshiping *the Beast*. This obvious case of scripture-interpreting-scripture proves that the events brought on by the *Four Horsemen* are Satan's doing and not God's. Additionally, they add further overwhelming weight to the theory that the horsemen ride *during* the *70th Week of Daniel* and not before it. *Satan releases one horseman during each of the first four years*. These horsemen then ride God's spirit beings (the horses) onto the world stage. This represents God's granting Satan permission to send out his horsemen throughout the earth, to further God's purposes to bring about the end of the age and his final justice upon the earth.

To view a summary graphics of all the aspects of the first four events ("the Four Horsemen") in the *Pattern of Seven Events*, please turn to Appendix A.

Chapter Eight

EVENT ONE: DECEPTION BY FALSE MESSIAHS

In the preceding Chapter, we examined the "Four Horsemen" that ride immediately after the opening of each of the first four Seals on the *7 Sealed Scroll* as described in Rev. 6. These "Horsemen" are the first four events in the *Pattern of Seven Events*, and we just learned Satan's purpose for each of these events is to cause the inhabitants of the world to worship the Beast. The first of these events is *deception by False Messiahs*. As we have already discovered, Satan will send out the Antichrist and False Prophet in the first year of the *70th Week of Daniel*. One of them may very well claim to be the historical Jesus, and they will perform amazing signs and wonders. By these means, Satan hopes to cause the world to worship the Beast by means of *deception*.

The rider of the *green horse* is Death. This is not a man, but apparently a demonic force. Isn't it likely the riders of the other *horses* are demonic forces as well? Might the rider of the *white horse* be Deception? Might the red horse be Fear and the black horse be Want? Those titles are my best understanding of the riders.

The *First Event* then, brings forth Deception. As humans we are easily deceived; especially by what we see. But sight is the opposite of faith which is what pleases God. After all "faith is the assurance of things hoped for, the conviction of things *not seen*" (Heb. 11:1 NASB, emphasis mine).

Harry Houdini is one of the most famous illusionists of all time. But only three short years after his death, his associates began to de-mystify his illusions. In 2004, an exhibition "spilled the beans" on all his secrets[xxxvi]. But what if a demonically empowered individual burst on the scene performing signs and wonders that were real? What if the greatest of his signs is a Mideast Peace Agreement that seemed to work?

Who will believe their eyes (what they see) and who will believe the Spirit that lives within them? This will be the conflict of the *First Event.*

In addition to the passage we studied in Rev. 6:1-2, numerous other scriptures in the Old and New Testaments testify about this event.

THE *OLIVET DISCOURSE* (MATT. 24, MARK 13, LUKE 21)

Jesus gave his disciples (and us) and amazingly clear and unambiguous description of this first event. This first event, however, falls within a series of the first three events that Jesus termed "the Beginning of the Birth Pangs." When Jesus referred to "*birth pangs*" he was making reference to several Old Testament passages that compare the *Great Tribulation* period to labor pains of a pregnancy. We have already looked at the passage in Jeremiah that refers to this period as the "*Time of Jacob's Distress (or Trouble)*."

> I have heard a sound of terror, of dread, and there is no peace. Ask now, and see if a male can give birth. Why do I see every man with his hands on his loins, *as a woman in childbirth*? And why have all faces turned pale? Alas! for that day is great, there is none like it; and it is *the time of Jacob's distress (trouble)*, but he will be saved from it. (Jer. 30:5-8 NASB, clarification and emphasis mine)

We can see that the pain of this time is equivalent to *childbirth* for the nation of Israel. Isaiah then shows the result:

> O Lord, they sought you in distress; they could only whisper a prayer, your chastening was upon them. As the *pregnant woman approaches the time to give birth*, she writhes and cries out in her *labor pains*, thus were we before You, O Lord. We were pregnant, we writhed in labor, we gave birth, as it seems, only to wind. We could not accomplish deliverance for the earth, nor were inhabitants of the world born. Your dead will live; their corpses will rise. You who lie in the dust, awake and shout for joy, for your dew is as the

186

dew of the dawn, and *the earth will give birth to the departed spirits*. (Isa. 26:16-19 NASB, emphasis mine)

The result of the time of distress is the resurrection; the departed souls are the "baby!" This is a wonderful picture that scripture has given us. Many people view the approaching time of trouble with dread. We should be viewing it as the end of a pregnancy: difficult, but the end result is a wonderful miracle. This picture is what Jesus was alluding to in Matthew 24:8 when he gave us the signs that mark the beginning of these labor pains.

The events Jesus foretold in the "*Beginning of The Birth Pangs*" period match up exactly with the events occurring when the *First Three Horsemen* of Rev. 6 "ride." As we have seen in Chapter Three: "A Treasure Map" and in the graphic "Figure ", there are unmistakable fingerprint parallels between the three "Birth Pangs" and the first three "Horsemen." These events all occur *prior* to the midpoint of the 70th Week.

SPECIFIC OR GENERAL?

An important question to consider before we begin to look at the details of the *Beginning of the Birth Pangs* period is this: Are these general conditions that will exist or are they specific events to watch for? For instance, there have been literally hundreds of individuals who have claimed to be messiah over the last 2000 years.[xxxvii]. There have been hundreds of wars and rumors of wars. These are general conditions. Jesus's followers asked what will be the sign of his return. In order for the *Beginning of the Birth Pangs* period to be a sign, they must be *specific events* not general conditions. A woman's birth pangs during a natural pregnancy don't begin months ahead of time, rather they begin right at the end. The same will be true of *the Pattern of Seven Events*. This is incredibly important understanding related to the timing of these *specific* events.

FALSE MESSIAHS

Luke tells us that *false messiahs* will arise in Jesus's name and seek to mislead many.

And He said, "*See to it that you are not misled*; for many will come in My name, saying, 'I am He,' and, 'The time is near.' Do not go after them. (Luke 21:8 NASB, emphasis mine)

The rider of the *white horse* of Revelation 6 is obviously one of these false messiahs. But Jesus makes it clear that "*many*" will claim to be messiah. It seems that every year, dozens of potential "antichrists" are identified. None of these to date have claimed to be savior of the world. However, might there be false Jewish, Muslim and Christian messiahs who claim to be our savior during this *First Year* of the 70th Week? That is entirely possible. Jewish end time eschatology looks forward to a Messiah Bar Joseph and Messiah Bar David[xxxviii]. The fact that Jewish false prophets will be in the land is supported by Zechariah: "'It will come about in that day,' declares the Lord of hosts, 'that I will cut off the names of the idols from the land, and they will no longer be remembered; and I will also *remove the prophets* and the unclean spirit from the land'" (Zech. 13:2 NASB, emphasis mine). In addition to the Jews, Muslims look forward to a Mahdi and Isa (a non-divine false Jesus). The rider of the *white horse* is the one we need to watch closely, but Jesus indicates many will come in His name. Might they all be on the world stage at the same time? They might.

One interesting point that may be confusing is how a Muslim messiah can come "in Jesus's name." Muslims do believe in *a* Jesus—a Muslim one. The heretical Quran teaches that the biblical Jesus was a prophet (not divine and did not die on the cross) and will return in the end times to bring the world to a common faith in Allah. The Mahdi and the Muslim version of Jesus will both claim our biblical Jesus is *Islamic*. In their heretical view, his full name is Isa son of Mary (not the son of God.) This name is fascinating because it is pronounced "Esau." Yes, like that Esau, son of Isaac. Famous Muslim apologist, Ahmad Deedat wrote:

"The Holy Quran refers to Jesus as 'Yesu,' and this name is used more times than any other title, because this was his 'Christian' name. Actually, his proper name was 'Eesa' (Arabic), or 'Esau' (Hebrew); classical 'Yeheshua', which the Christian nations of the West Latinized as Jesus. Neither the 'J' nor the second 's' in the name *Jesus* is to be found in the original tongue - they are not found in the Semitic language. The word is very simply – 'E S A U.'"[xxxix] — Ahmad Deedat

This clarification further strengthens the links between Edom and *Islam* and the prophecies about Edom we learned about in the last chapter.

The Qur'an gives the Muslim Jesus titles like "Word from God", "Messiah" (Âl 'Imran 3:45), "sign for all peoples" (al-Anbiya' 21:91). It also *claims he will return on judgment day*, "And (the Muslim Jesus) *shall be a Sign* (for the coming of) the Hour (of Judgment): therefore have no doubt about the (Hour), but follow ye Me: this is a Straight Way" (az-Zukhruf 43:61). Notice how Islamists expect the return of the Muslim Jesus to be *a sign of the hour of judgment*. This parallels the Luke account that says the false messiahs will say *"the time is near."* Can you see how this will be *satanic deception* and will influence many to mistakenly think this is the return of the *biblical* Jesus?

Of greater importance than what the heretical Islamic texts say about the Muslim Jesus is what they don't say. They *deny* he is the Son of God: "It befits not (the Majesty of) Allah that He should beget a son" [Quran (Surah Maryam, Verse 350]. Muslims totally misinterpret the meaning of "only begotten son" in our scriptures to mean a biologic type of conception through God himself —-rather than *divine* conception through the Holy Spirit. Obviously, Christians don't believe there was physical union between God and Mary either. "Only begotten son" is the English translation from the Greek word, *MONOGENES,* meaning "pertaining to being the only one of its kind or class, unique in kind," as Jesus is *both God and man* and is *uniquely* God's divine Son. This misconception has led Muslims to deny the divinity of Jesus.

Who is the liar but the one who denies that Jesus is the Christ? This is *the antichrist,* the one *who denies the Father and the Son.* (1 John 2:22 NASB, emphasis mine)

Ch. 8: Event One: Deception by False Messiahs

The Islamic view of the unholy ministry of Isa is interesting. This view includes the following points:

- Allah's Apostle said, "The Hour will not be established until the son of Mary (i.e. Jesus) descends amongst you as a just ruler, he will *break the cross, kill the pigs (Jews)*, and abolish the Jizya tax. Money will be in abundance so that nobody will accept it (as charitable gifts)." (*Sahih Bukhari 3.656*, also *Sahih Bukhari 4.657*)

  The usage of the term "break the cross" indicates he will attempt to abolish Christianity. The Jizya tax is tax imposed on "infidels" that allows them to continue to practice their religion. Abolishing this tax will be the equivalent of abolishing all religions except Islam. The Jizya tax currently allows Christians living under Muslim law and authority to avoid the punishment for not accepting Islam: *death*. After Isa returns, Muslims believe he will kill all who reject Islam.

- Allah's Apostle said, "How will you be when the son of Mary (i.e. Jesus) descends amongst you and he will judge people by the Law of the Quran *and not by the law of Gospel*" (*Fateh-ul Bari page 304 and 305 Vol 7*) (*Sahih Bukhari 4.658*)

This passage shows Muslims expect Isa will institute Sharia Law (the law of the Quran) and eliminate all Judeo-Christian laws. This echoes Daniel's prophecy related to the Antichrist, ". . . he will intend to make alterations in times and *in law*." (Dan. 7:25 NASB, emphasis mine)

This book has quoted a number of Islamic writings in this section. Muslim writings are *heretical*; they are not divinely inspired and not inerrant like the Bible. Although they are not prophecies, these writings are interesting in that if a demonically-possessed and empowered individual arises who seems to fulfill these "prophecies" about Isa, the Muslims of the world (and sadly many churchgoers) will follow him to damnation.

If you wish to learn more about these Muslim traditions, the book *The Islamic Antichrist* (WND Books, 2009) by Joel Richardson details the amazing similarities between Muslim "prophecies" and the revealed Word of God.

IS ISA THE *FALSE PROPHET* OR THE ANTICHRIST?

We can't know with certainty that Isa will be the *False Prophet*. We can't know that a man with this name and fitting this description will even arise, but scripture gives us clues. In the *Olivet Discourse* as recorded in the Gospel of Matthew, Jesus tells us false messiahs *and* false prophets will arise.

> Then if anyone says to you, "Look, here is the Christ!" or "There!" do
> not believe it. For false Christs *and* false prophets will rise and show
> great signs and wonders to deceive, if possible, even the elect. *See, I*
> *have told you beforehand.* Therefore if they say to you, "Look, He is in
> the desert!" do not go out; or "Look, He is in the inner rooms!" do not
> believe it. (Matt. 24:4-5, 23-25 NASB, emphasis mine)

This is Jesus' most stern warning in the entire *Olivet Discourse*, and it mirrors his warning in Luke's account not to go "after them." He first says the false messiah and the *False Prophet* will show great signs that could deceive the elect in Jesus. He then emphasizes this by saying, "See I have told you beforehand."

Revelation appropriately refers to a *False Prophet* (since Muslims consider Isa a prophet and a miracle-worker, but not the Son of God).

> He exercises all the authority of the first beast in his presence, and
> causes the earth and those who dwell in it to worship the first beast,
> whose deadly wound was healed. *He performs great signs, so that he*
> *even makes fire come down from heaven on the earth in the sight of*
> *men.* And *he deceives those who dwell on the earth by those signs*
> which he was granted to do in the sight of the beast, telling those who

191

dwell on the earth to make an image to the beast who was wounded by the sword and lived. He was granted power to give breath to the image of the beast, *that the image of the beast should both speak* and cause as many as would not worship the image of the beast to be killed. He causes all, both small and great, rich and poor, free and slave, to receive *a mark on their right hand or on their foreheads*, and that no one may buy or sell except one who has the mark or the name of the beast, or the number of his name. (Rev. 13:12-17 NASB, emphasis mine)

We have already seen in Chapter Seven: "A Horse of a Different Color (Revelation 6)," the *False Prophet* has four main missions all aligned with the first four events in the *Pattern of Seven Events*. The purpose of these *four missions* is to cause the world to worship the Beast:

- To perform great lying signs and to present himself as the historic Jesus
- To assist the Beast in calling the Islamic world to jihad
- To cause all men to receive the Mark of the Beast
- To make the image of the Beast and cause it to speak

What are the *great signs* that the *Antichrist* and the *False Prophet* will be given authority to do? It is suspected that the Antichrist *may appear* to be healed of a fatal head wound (not actually healed, only the *appearance* of it). We also see from Revelation that the *False Prophet* will be able to call down *fire from heaven*. Are these signs the "great delusion" referred to by Paul? "For this reason God will send upon them a deluding influence so that they will believe what is false" (2 Thes. 2:11 NASB). These great signs will be powerful signs which will appear to be from God, but they are not. They will cause many to be lead astray. Christians need to be ready for witnessing these false signs as part of the *delusion*.

In summary, although this book has concentrated on the Islamic messiah (the Mahdi) and the False Prophet (Isa), the *Olivet Discourse* accounts in Luke and Matthew indicate "many" will claim to be messiahs. Many are more than two. I firmly expect a number of false messiahs to arise in the 70th Week.

THE BOOK OF DANIEL

Other than Revelation and the *Olivet Discourse*, the Book of Daniel is the Church's greatest source of prophecies about the 70th Week. As we learned in Chapter Four: "Bookends," one of the expressed purposes of Revelation was to explain the Book of Daniel, and the very term the "*70th Week of Daniel*" comes from this ancient book (as we saw in Chapter Two: "Uncovering the Keys"). One would expect Daniel to have something to say about this first event, *deception by False Messiahs*, and he does.

Daniel is very clear that a "deceiver" will initiate the 70th Week by negotiating a treaty with "the many."

> And he (the Antichrist) will make *a firm covenant with the many for one week.* (Dan. 9:27 NASB, clarification and emphasis mine)

In Daniel 9:27 the word translated "covenant" is the Hebrew word BERITH. This same word is found in a passage in Isaiah that most likely refers to this same covenant that Israel will enter into: the Covenant with Death and Sheol. Israel will trust Antichrist rather than the Most High.

> Therefore, hear the word of the Lord, O scoffers, who rule this people who are in Jerusalem, because you have said, "We have made *a covenant* (Heb.: BERITH) *with death*, and with *Sheol we have made a pact.* The overwhelming scourge will not reach us when it passes by; for we have made falsehood our refuge and we have concealed ourselves with deception." (Isa. 28:14-15 NASB, clarification and emphasis mine)

Israel will make this Covenant with *Death and Sheol*. In Chapter Seven: "Horse of a Different Color (Revelation 6)," we learned these same two figures, *Death and Sheol*, will ride and follow the *green horse* at the *Midpoint* of Daniel's 70th Week (Rev. 6:7-8). It is at this exact moment that the *Covenant with the Many* is broken. This is substantial proof that all these passages refer to the same Covenant and events. It is also substantial proof that the *Fourth Seal* is broken at the *Midpoint* of the 70th Week, just as we have surmised.

In Isa. 28:15, we also understand that *Israel* will make falsehood their refuge instead of God. Israel will choose this false peace over trusting in Jesus and will, hence, be "disturbed."

> Therefore thus says the Lord God, "Behold, I am laying in Zion a stone, a tested stone, *a costly cornerstone* for the foundation, firmly placed. He who believes *in it* will *not be disturbed*. (Isa 28:16-17 NASB, emphasis mine)

Israel will trust the rider of the *white horse* (Rev. 6: 1-2) rather than Jesus, *the costly cornerstone*. Elsewhere in Daniel we learn that: "seven periods of time (seven years) will pass over you, until you recognize that the Most High (Jesus) is ruler over the realm of mankind" (Dan. 4:16 NASB, clarification mine). Not recognizing this essential truth will cost Israel dearly:

> Then hail will sweep away the refuge of lies and *the waters will overflow the secret place*. Your covenant with death will be canceled, and your *pact with Sheol* will not stand; *when the overwhelming scourge passes through, then you become its trampling place*. (Isa. 28:17-18 NASB, emphasis mine)

When we look at this passage we see "waters will overflow the secret place." This is nearly identical language to Rev. 12:5 (NASB) where Satan pursues Israel *after* the *Midpoint*: "And the serpent poured water like a river out of his mouth after the woman, so that he might cause her to be swept away with the flood." The Antichrist will break Israel's covenant with Death and Sheol, invade at the *Midpoint* of Daniel's 70th Week, desecrate Jerusalem and the Temple, and initiate the Great Tribulation.

But there is an even more important aspect to the Covenant with Death and Sheol than the peace accord. There have been many false peace treaties in the past; why is this one different? I believe it's different because this one will involve the return of the sacrificial system! The Jews will trust the *sacrifice of a lamb* to cause the *angel of death* (the overwhelming scourge) to pass over them. This is a picture of Passover. God has provided the true Passover Lamb, Jesus, as our only means of salvation. In AD 70, God allowed the destruction of the Temple to eliminate the opportunity of Jews to rely on the old system. He built a new system on the cornerstone of Jesus; a new temple in our hearts. When the Jews rebuild what God has torn down and reinstitute the sacrifice of animals to achieve atonement, they will in essence say that they can provide their own salvation, both in terms of physical peace and in terms of spiritual peace with God. It will be a great sacrilege; trusting in the old Mosaic Covenant not the New Covenant in Jesus's blood! *This is an incredibly important new understanding for the Church.*

WHO NEGOTIATES THE COVENANT WITH THE MANY?

The *Covenant with the Many* that is strengthened at the very beginning of Daniel's 70th Week is of incredible importance. It marks the beginning of the Week and the breaking of this Covenant appears to allow the Antichrist the ability to invade Israel.

There are two main thoughts about who ratifies the *Covenant with the Many*. Up to this point in time, we have assumed it is negotiated by the Antichrist, but this is somewhat ambiguous because the "he" in "he will strengthen" of Dan. 9:27 could be Jesus or the Antichrist. It isn't clear. Some commentators believe it will be the *Mosaic Covenant* that Jesus will strengthen with the Jews. Most, however, believe it is an alliance between the Antichrist and the Jews (and possibly other nations as well). As we examined previously, if the Covenant in view truly is the *Mosaic Covenant*, the question must be asked: "Why would Jesus strengthen this covenant and how would it be strengthened?" I don't have a good answer for this, nor have I seen a satisfactory answer. Some have additionally thought the covenant might refer to the *New Covenant* in Jesus's blood, but Jesus won't apply that to the Jews *until the end of the 70th Week.* Additionally, this passage pictures events during the 70th Week which include the

Abomination of Desolation and the elimination of the sacrifice and offerings. Both of which are actions of the Antichrist. It is inconsistent that Jesus would establish the covenant and then it would be broken by the Antichrist. The Man of Sin can break it only if he establishes it. Finally, in Chapter Seven: "A Horse of a Different Color (Revelation 6)," we learned that the rider of the *white horse*, the Antichrist, carries a "bow" which is symbolic of a false covenant. I personally conclude that it is the *Antichrist* who *strengthens* the covenant.

It is essential that the Church understands that the Covenant with the Many isn't "made" by the Antichrist, rather it is the strengthening of an existing covenant. "And he will make (Heb. GABAR, meaning "strengthen") a firm covenant with the many for one week" (Dan. 9:27 NASB). The most famous existing, secular covenant made with Israel is United Nations Resolution 181, ratified in November 1947, which partitioned Palestine into Arab and Israeli States. Although accepted by Israel, this plan was rejected by the Arabs and resulted in the Israeli War for Independence. This partition plan has *never* been recognized by the Arab states[xl]. Perhaps, this famous covenant or the Oslo Accords will be "strengthened," accepted by all parties, and finally become the *Covenant with the Many*.

In Chapter Fifteen: "Overcoming Lions," we will take a detailed look at a very, very special prophecy: Daniel's Great Vision Prophecy (Dan. 10-12). That prophecy contains six of the seven events in the *Pattern of Seven Events* in exact order, and provides astonishing insights not found elsewhere in scriptures.

THE BOOK OF ISAIAH

The ancient, Old Testament Book of Isaiah has much to say about the *Pattern of Seven Events*. As we have just learned, it is the primary text for the Covenant with Death and Sheol which Israel will enter as part of the deception of the First Event when Israel will "strike *bargains* with the children of foreigners" (Isa. 2:6). We have also learned that true sacrilege of this Covenant is not that Israel will trust in the Antichrist to provide safety, but that as part of this Covenant, Israel will re-establish the sacrificial system from the Old Testament whereby they will trust the "blood of bulls" rather than the

Blood of the Lamb (Jesus) for the remission of their sins. Isaiah opens with this prophetic announcement by God about this:

> "What are your multiplied sacrifices to me?" says the Lord. "I have had enough of burnt offerings of rams and the fat of fed cattle; and I take no pleasure in the blood of bulls, lambs or goats. When you come to appear before me, who requires of you this trampling of my courts? Bring your worthless offerings no longer." (Isa. 1: 11-13 NASB)

God considers Israel's sacrifices a "trampling" of his courts. God's solution is clear:

> "Come now, and let us reason together," says the Lord, "Though your sins are as scarlet, they will be as white as snow" (Isa. 1:18 NASB)

Only by washing their garments in the blood of Lamb (Rev. 7:14) can Israel's sin be "white as snow."

THE ASSYRIAN

Isaiah is the first prophet to also clearly identify the geographic home of the Antichrist: Assyria.

> For *a complete destruction, one that is decreed*, the Lord God of hosts will execute in the midst of the whole land. Therefore thus says the Lord God of hosts, "O My people who dwell in Zion, *do not fear the Assyrian* who strikes you with the rod and lifts up his staff against you, the way Egypt did. For in a very little while my indignation against you will be spent and my anger will be directed to their destruction." The Lord of hosts will arouse a scourge against him *like the slaughter of Midian at the rock of Oreb*; and His staff will be over the sea and He will lift it up the way He did in Egypt. So it will be in that day, that *his burden will be removed from your shoulders and his yoke from your*

neck, and the yoke will be broken because of fatness. (Isa. 10: 23-27 NASB, emphasis mine)

There are those who claim that this passage only refers to the historic invasion of Israel by Assyria. Nothing could be further from the truth. There are no less than three end time references within this passage! The phrase "a complete destruction, one that is decreed" is quoted in Dan. 9:27 with specific reference to the 70th Week. As we learned in Chapter Six: "The Walls Came Tumbling Down (Jos. 6, Jud. 6-8)," Midian is a picture of the 70th Week, and as we saw in Chapter Two: "Uncovering the Keys," breaking of the Antichrist's yoke is quoted in Jer. 30 in regard to the time of Jacob's trouble.

The prophet Micah is just as clear about the Antichrist being from the geographic realm of Assyria.

> Now muster yourselves in troops, daughter of troops; they have laid siege against us; with a rod they will smite the judge of Israel on the cheek. But as for you, Bethlehem Ephrathah, too little to be among the clans of Judah, from you One will go forth for Me to be ruler in Israel. His goings forth are from long ago, from the days of eternity . . . This One will be our peace when *the Assyrian* invades our land, when he tramples on our citadels. (Mic. 5:1-2, 5 NASB, emphasis mine)

This passage is frequently quoted at Christmas, but it has more to do with the 70th Week than it does with Christmas. Notice the passage begins with reference to a siege. This is the siege of the Antichrist that begins at the midpoint of the 70th Week. Only Jesus (born in Bethlehem) will be able to overcome the Assyrian (the Antichrist).

THE BOOK OF EZEKIEL

Ezekiel's visions as described in Ezek. 13 and Ezek. 38 give two references that *allude* to the event that opens Daniel's 70th Week in *Year One*:

My hand will be against the prophets who see false visions and utter lying divinations. They will have no place in the council of my people, nor will they be written down in the register of the house of Israel, nor will they enter the land of Israel, that you may know that I am the Lord God. It is definitely because *they have misled my people by saying, 'Peace!' when there is no peace.* And when anyone builds a wall, behold, they plaster it over with whitewash. (Ezek. 13: 9-10 NASB, emphasis mine)

You (the Antichrist) will say, 'I will go up against the land of un-walled villages. *I will go against those who are at rest, that live securely,* all of them living without walls and having no bars or gates, to capture spoil and to seize plunder, to turn your hand against the waste places which are now inhabited, and against the people who are gathered from the nations, who have acquired cattle and goods, who live at the center of the world.' (Ezek. 38:11-12, clarification and emphasis mine)

The first passage above is from Ezekiel's first vision in Ezek. 1 -15. It teaches that Israel's false prophets will proclaim "peace." We already know that this deceptive peace is the result of a *False Peace Treaty* that is signed by the Antichrist with Israel during the *First Year* of Daniel's 70th Week.

The second passage above is from the vision of the *Gog of Magog War*. Here again, we learn that Israel will be living in false security prior to the invasion that will occur at the *Midpoint* of the 70th Week. Although Ezekiel doesn't clearly delineate the signing of the deceptive *Covenant with Sheol*, we can assume its signing from these passages that support the concept.

SUMMARY

The *Pattern of Seven Events* is unmistakably written across the pages of the Bible, both in the Old and New Testaments. This event will be marked by deception by False

Ch. 8: Event One: Deception by False Messiahs

Messiahs and Prophets who will claim to be the historic Jesus, perform signs and wonders, and also sign the Covenant with the Many with Israel that inaugurates the 70th Week of Daniel. Please turn to Appendix A for a summary of all the aspects of Event One: Deception by False Messiahs.

In the next Chapter we will examine Event Two: War, Bloodshed, and Chaos.

Chapter Nine

EVENT TWO: WAR, BLOODSHED, AND CHAOS

In Chapter Seven: "Horse of Different Color (Rev. 6)," we introduced the Second Event in the *Pattern of Seven Events* as the rider of the *red horse* that rides after the breaking of the *Second Seal*. In the previous Chapter we further identified the rider of this horse as Fear. Revelation tells us this rider will be granted three things. He will be allowed to take peace from the earth, he will be allowed to cause men to kill one another, and he will be given a "great sword."

Fear is one of Satan's greatest weapons. It is contrasted with love. "There is no fear in love; but perfect love casts out fear" (1 John 4:18 NASB). Just like trusting what we see, fear is part of the fallen human nature we all possess. Being anxious about something by its very nature is not trusting that God is in control of everything we face in life. Faith is believing God is in ultimate control of all things and causes all things to work together for our good.

THE *OLIVET DISCOURSE* (MATT. 24, MARK 13, LUKE 21)

A week or two ago, I watched an amazing "domino" demonstration on the internet. As the dominoes fell, they "climbed" steps, split, turned on appliances, etc. It must have taken days for the filmmaker to set up what only took 5 minutes to fall in sequence.

Events in the world have taken 2000 years to "set up," but when the *white horse* rides, the dominoes will begin to fall. The events of *Year Two* of the 70th Week of Daniel will be the direct result of *Year One*—the Mahdi and Isa coming upon the world stage. News reports tell us that terrorist "sleeper cells" exist all over the world. This terrorism risk is an incredible *underestimate*. The risk is much greater than a few sleeper cells. Many, many currently peace-loving Muslims will join the effort to dominate the world once these Muslim leaders are in place. As we learned in the last section, the rise of Isa is *the* "sign" to Muslims that judgment day has come. It is incredibly likely that *most Muslims* will rise to fight when the see the prophetic signs in *their* scriptures revealed. Luke's account of this period says:

> "When you hear of wars and disturbances (Gk: AKATASTASIAS, meaning "riots", "chaos," "anarchy," or "revolutions"), do not be terrified; for these things must take place first, but the end does not follow immediately." Then He continued by saying to them, "Nation (Gk: ETHNOS, meaning "people group") will rise against nation and kingdom against kingdom (Gk: BASILEIAN EPI BASILEIAN), and there will be great earthquakes (Gk: SEISMOS, meaning "shaking")." (Luke 21: 9-11 NASB, clarification mine)

At the beginning of the *Olivet Discourse*, Jesus gave the Church two commands in the first two verses: *do not be misled* and *do not be terrified*. The reason he gives us these commands is that it will be *very easy* to be misled or terrified. In regard to the command to not be terrified, in Rev. 6 which foretells the same time period, we learn that the rider of the *red horse* takes peace from the earth. The *Second Year* of the 70th Week of Daniel will be a terrifying time, but Jesus wants us to know that He is still in control and what we see with our eyes is *not to terrify us*.

During the *Second Year*, wars and riots will break out. It is likely that the Mahdi and Isa will drive the process as they encourage Muslims world-wide to revolt and join the Jihad. Muslims who are currently living peaceful lives in their communities might turn to violence overnight once they believe they are in the last days. The phrase "people group against people group" might also imply racial warfare. Might terrorist acts and riots explode across most of the cities of the world? It might. Jesus knows this will *terrify* most people as the world will become a very unsafe place. We are to stay focused on *our mission*, however, to present the love of Jesus to the world. Unfortunately, most Christians will be *unprepared* for this moment, and as Jesus says in Matthew, "Because lawlessness is increased, most people's love will grow cold." We need to continue to live our lives as a testimony to Jesus regardless of the peril around us. We need to *prepare ourselves* for this. In summary, we need to *get ourselves emotionally and spiritually ready* for these coming events.

Jesus gives us a specific clue on how to prepare for these events.

> Do not be terrified; for these things must take place (HA DEI GENESTAI) first (Luke 21:9 NASB)

Jesus says that we are not to be terrified because these are the "things that must take place;" Jesus quotes Dan. 2:29, 45 just as Rev. 1:1 does. In essence, Jesus tells us these are the things decreed to happen prior to his return. We are not to be terrified because this is all part of his divine plan.

THE BOOK OF ISAIAH

In the *Olivet Discourse*, Jesus also drops a huge clue about the *war* that is to begin during this described *Second Year*. He uses the phrase "kingdom against kingdom" which is a direct quote from Isaiah. Christopher Mantei of Voice of the Martyrs ministry made me aware of the following reference from Isaiah related to this:

> So I will incite Egyptians against Egyptians; and they will each fight against his brother and each against his neighbor, city against city and *kingdom against kingdom* (Gk: BASILEIAN EPI BASILEIAN). (Isa. 19:2 NASB, emphasis mine)

This passage from Isaiah mentions a civil war in Egypt that takes place close to the return of Jesus and spreads into a war between kingdoms. Two verses later we learn who the antagonist is (the *Antichrist*). "'Moreover, I will deliver the Egyptians into the hand of a cruel master, and a mighty king (the *Antichrist*) will rule over them,' declares the Lord God of hosts (Isa. 19:4 NASB, clarification and emphasis mine)." This is the same war between the King of the North (Assyrian Kingdom) and the King of the South (Egyptian Kingdom) mentioned in Zech. 6, which we have studied previously. We will study this war more extensively in Chapter Fifteen: "Overcoming Lions (Daniel 10-12)." Daniel's Great Vision Prophecy contains additional new insights into the *Second Event*.

SUMMARY

Because Israel has negotiated a false peace treaty with the Antichrist, most of the aspects of the *Second Event* will not affect Israel. For this reason there are limited references to the *Second Event* in Old Testament. To view a graphic that summarizes this event, please review Appendix A.

In the next Chapter, we will examine the *Third Event* in the *Pattern of Seven Events*.

Chapter Ten

EVENT THREE: FAMINE AND ECONOMIC COLLAPSE

The *Third Event* in the *Pattern of Seven Events* most likely occurs during the third year of the 70th Week. This event is described in Revelation as the rider of the *black horse* that we discussed in detail in Chapter Seven: "Horse of a Different Color (Rev. 6)." In Chapter Eight: "Event One: Deception by False Messiahs," we identified the rider of this horse as Want.

Our human bodies require food, water, and shelter. When we are deprived of these things we "Want." Jesus was obviously aware of how he created us:

> Do not worry then, saying, 'What will we eat?' or 'What will we drink?' or 'What will we wear for clothing?' For the Gentiles eagerly seek all these things; for *your heavenly Father knows that you need all these things*. But seek first his kingdom and his righteousness, and all these things will be added to you" (Matt. 6:31-33 NASB, emphasis mine)

The Third Event will also be a test of faith. Will we seek God's Kingdom first and trust him to "add all these things" to us? Or will we trust our human instincts and the economic systems of this world?

Prior to Jesus feeding the 5000, he asked the disciples to feed them. Perplexed they trusted in what they saw with their eyes. They didn't have enough money to feed the multitude, and the only food available to them was a little boy's lunch of five loaves and two fish. But this lunch, given to Jesus in faith, was enough. The little boy is a hero of this story. He planned in advance, yet he surrendered all he had to Jesus. In turn, our Savior multiplied this offering and fed all those who followed him. In Chapter

Eighteen: "To Him Who Overcomes," we will learn more about providing for the faithful during the *Third Event*.

THE *OLIVET DISCOURSE* (MATT. 24, MARK 13, LUKE 21)

The *Olivet Discourse* is remarkably silent on the *Third Event*. All three versions simply mention that there will be "famines." Matthew's Gospel also relates the *Parable of the Wise and Foolish Servants* which does discuss providing food for God's household at the appointed time. If you desire to review this parable, refer to Chapter Seven: "Horse of a Different Color (Rev. 6)."

I want to stress one thing about Jesus's simple statement that there will be famines, however. This statement is clear: there will be famines! If we know this in advance (and we do), shouldn't we be doing something about that *now*, just as Joseph did?

THE BOOK OF EZEKIEL

Ezekiel has quite a bit to say about the *Third Event*, and his testimony forms a great deal of our understanding of how this event will impact Israel. Consistent with the pattern of events we have already seen in multiple other pictures of Daniel's 70th Week, a *food shortage* is pictured. Interestingly, this food shortage seems to begin with the *siege of Jerusalem*. Is this the same siege pictured in Micah 5:1 that we discussed earlier? It most likely is the same:

> Now you son of man, get yourself a brick, place it before you and inscribe a city on it, Jerusalem. *Then lay siege against it*, build a siege wall, raise up a ramp, pitch camps and place battering rams against it all around. Then get yourself an iron plate and set it up as an iron wall between you and the city, and set your face toward it so that it is under siege, and besiege it. This is *a sign to the house of Israel*. (Ezek. 4:1-3 NASB, emphasis mine)

Then, incredibly, God's words to Ezekiel, tell us the length of the siege the future Antichrist forces will bring siege against *Jerusalem*:

> As for you, lie down on your *left side* and lay the iniquity of the house of Israel on it; you shall bear their iniquity for the number of days that you lie on it. For I have assigned you a *number of days corresponding to the years* of their iniquity, *three hundred and ninety days* (390 days); thus you shall bear the iniquity of the house of Israel. When you have completed these, you shall lie down a second time, but on your *right side* and bear the iniquity of the house of Judah; I have assigned it to you for *forty days* (40 days), a *day for each year*. Then you shall set your face toward the siege of Jerusalem with your arm bared and prophesy against it. Now behold, I will put ropes on you so that you cannot turn from one side to the other until you have completed the days of your siege. (Ezek. 4:4-8 NASB, clarification and emphasis mine)

Commentators have wondered for years about the "sin" of Israel and the "sin" of Judah that resulted in days of this siege. A most satisfactory answer was provided by Yves Peloquin[xli]. He proposes that the 40 years of Judah's sin were the *40 years* King Manasseh had an abomination—an idol *in the Temple*. He proposes that the *390 years* of Israel's sin were the 390 years that the *Ark of the Covenant* was in the city of Gibeah.

There was a strange sinful happening in Gibeah which seems to figure into this explanation. Mr. Peloquin points out that in Judges 19 a woman was horribly sexually defiled by evil men and killed in Gibeah. Her body was cut up into pieces by her Levite "husband" (she was his concubine), and her body pieces sent out to the twelve tribes in Israel as a witness to her defilement and murder by the men of Gibeah. This sin is mentioned again in Hos. 9:9 and Hos. 10:9 as "days of deep corruption."[xlii] In both cases, the sins are abominations against the Tabernacle and then later the Temple.

If we add the total days of the siege together we determine a siege of *430 days*. This is incredible information; absolutely incredible.

Many other commentators believe this siege only applied to the days of Ezekiel, but there is a *"time stamp"* that proves any previous fulfillment was simply the "near" fulfillment of a *"near/far"* prophecy. *Final fulfillment will take place at the time of the end.* The Prophet Ezekiel, who prophesied during the Babylonian captivity, was given a vision of a "unique disaster" coming upon the Jewish people at *"the end."* This vision stretches from Ezekiel 1 through 15. Ezekiel's initial vision is very similar in structure to Daniel's initial vision and John's. It begins with a vision of the Lord upon his throne. "Now it came about in the thirtieth year (593 BC), on the fifth day of the fourth month, while I was by the river Chebar among the exiles, the heavens were opened and I saw visions of God" (Ezek. 1:1 NASB, clarification mine). Ezekiel saw the living creatures, and he saw the Lord upon his throne. The appearance of the Lord was similar to those described by Daniel and John. The Lord then gave Ezekiel a *Scroll written on both sides.* We have already studied this scene in Chapter Five: "Signed, Sealed, and Delivered (Revelation 4-5)." As we have already seen, this is the *same Scroll* that John eats in Revelation 10: the *7 Sealed Scroll* which is also the *Book of Life.* This reference definitively "time stamps" the vision (in Ezekiel 1-15) as being related to the 70th Week of Daniel. Other references to "the end" and "the day is coming" also confirm this as being about this time period.

Also notice that the number of days involves punishment for *Israel* and *Judah.* In Ezekiel's day, northern *Israel* had been punished and taken into exile. Of course, only Jews (Judah) were in Jerusalem. Hence, this siege spoken of by Ezekiel can't refer exclusively to Ezekiel's day.

We have learned that Jerusalem is defeated and the *Abomination of Desolation* is set up at the *Midpoint* of the 70th Week. This new information tells us that the *siege of Jerusalem* begins nearly a year and a half earlier during the *Third Year* of the 70th Week of Daniel. As we continue to read, we learn that *food shortage* is a feature of the siege:

> He said to me, "Son of man, behold, I am going to break the staff of bread in Jerusalem, and they will *eat bread by weight* and with anxiety, and *drink water by measure* and in horror, because *bread and water will be scarce*; and they will be appalled with one another and waste away in their iniquity." (Ezek. 4:16-17 NASB, emphasis mine)

This passage mentions eating bread by *weight*. This is an exact parallel to Rev. 6: 5-6 where the Rider of the *black horse* sells a specific weight of grain for a day's wages. From this we know that we are reading about the same period of time, the *Third Year* of the 70th Week of Daniel.

THE BOOK OF ISAIAH

Isaiah speaks of the Third Event as well.

> These two things have befallen you; who will mourn for you? The devastation and destruction, *famine* and sword; how shall I comfort you? Your sons have fainted; they lie *helpless* at the head of every street, like an antelope in a net, full of the wrath of the Lord, the rebuke of your God. Therefore, please hear this, you afflicted, *who are drunk, but not with wine*: thus says your Lord, the Lord, even your God who contends for His people, "Behold, I have taken out of your hand the cup of reeling, the chalice of my anger; *you will never drink it again.* I will put it into the hand of your tormentors" (Isa. 51:19-21 NASB, emphasis mine)

God clearly says that after the 70th Week Israel will never drink the cup of his Wrath again that includes this famine; so obviously, this is the famine of the Third Event!

SUMMARY

The Third Event in the Pattern of Seven Events is summarized in a graphic in Appendix A. If you desire to view all the aspects of this event, please refer to that graphic.

Chapter Eleven

EVENT FOUR: ABOMINATION AND DEATH

The *Fourth Event* of the *Pattern of Seven Events* takes place at the Midpoint of the 70th Week and marks the beginning of the *Great Tribulation*. The *Fourth Event* is equivalent to the *Fourth Seal* and the rider of the *green horse* that we examined in Chapter Seven: "Horse of a Different Color (Rev. 6)."

Rev. 6:8 is unambiguous that the rider of the *green horse* is Death. During the *Fourth Event*, the Antichrist will be unambiguous about who he is as well. He will sit in the Temple of God and defile it. He will demand worship from the inhabitants of the world. It will be a "submit or die" scenario. Satan will have attempted to deceive as many as possible during the first three events. In this *Fourth Event*, however, there is no deception. Satan will attempt to kill all those who do not bow to his Antichrist (and by extension to him.)

As we learned in Chapter Eight: "Deception by False Messiahs," if Isa (the false Muslim Jesus) appears, the time that Muslims will tolerate Jews and Christians will be over. In today's current environment, the "people of the book" (Jews and Christians) are somewhat tolerated and allowed to pay a tax in some nations rather than being forced to covert. All Muslims, however, believe that when Isa comes, this will change. It will be "convert or die" for all inhabitants of earth. In this way they expect Isa will create a "pure" Islamic world. This certainly parallels what we anticipate in the *Fourth Event*.

THE *OLIVET DISCOURSE* (MATT. 24, MARK 13, LUKE 21)

In the Gospel of Luke, Jesus presents a brief passage about what to expect during the *Great Tribulation*, which starts at the *Midpoint* of the 70th Week:

But before all these things (before the completion of the *Pattern of Seven Events*), they will lay their hands on you and will *persecute you*, delivering you to the synagogues and prisons, bringing you before kings and governors for my name's sake. It will lead to *an opportunity for your testimony*. So make up your minds not to prepare beforehand to defend yourselves; for I will give you utterance and wisdom which none of your opponents will be able to resist or refute. But *you will be betrayed* even by parents and brothers and relatives and friends, and they will *put some of you to death*, and you will be *hated by all* because of my name. Yet not a hair of your head will perish. *By your endurance you will gain your lives*. (Luke 21:12-19 NASB, clarification and emphasis mine)

This passage has been attributed by many exclusively to the ministry of the Apostles. Certainly the first several verses apply equally well to the Apostles who were persecuted for their testimony. The last several verses, however, don't apply well to their ministry. We have no record of them being betrayed by friends and relatives, and they were not hated by *all* because of Jesus's name. The question also must be asked, why would Jesus include a passage about the persecution of the Apostles in response to their question about signs leading to His second coming? It is more likely that this passage has a "near/far" interpretation. It was foreshadowed in the ministry of the Apostles, but its final fulfillment will be during the 70th Week of Daniel when the whole world *will* hate the Church because of Jesus's name. In 2016, this is beginning to become evident but has not yet come to full fruition. This passage from Luke is parallel to a similar passage in Matthew:

Then they will *deliver you to tribulation*, and will *kill you*, and *you will be hated by all nations* because of my name. At that time many will fall away and will *betray* one another and hate one another. Many false prophets will arise and will mislead many. Because *lawlessness is increased, most people's love will grow cold*. But the one who endures to the end, he will be saved. This gospel of the kingdom shall be preached in the whole world as a testimony to all the nations, and then the end will come. (Matt. 24:9-14 NASB, emphasis mine)

The parallels are obvious. We will be "delivered" (this word occurs in both passages) to persecution. We will be "betrayed" (this word also occurs in both passages) by family and friends. We will be "hated" (this word occurs in both passages as well) by all.

In Matthew, the verse *immediately following* this passage shown above (Matt. 24:9-14) begins with "therefore."

> *Therefore* when you see the *abomination of desolation* which was spoken of through Daniel the prophet, standing in the holy place (let the reader understand), then those who are in Judea must flee to the mountains. (Matt. 24:15-16 NASB, emphasis mine)

"Therefore" is always "there for" a reason! It means that the verse further explains the preceding passage. These following verses shown above are clearly about the *Great Tribulation*, thus the preceding verses (Matt. 24:9-14) are as well, and since we proved Luke's account is parallel, all these verses involve the last 3 1/2 years of Daniel's 70th Week, which contain the *Great Tribulation*.

I realize this analysis was a bit complex, but establishing that these passages are about the *Great Tribulation* is of extreme importance because they explain *the purpose* of that period of time. Many who believe in the theory of a *Pre-Tribulation Rapture* claim the purpose of the *Great Tribulation* is to bring the *Jews* to repentance, as they incorrectly believe that the Rapture occurs before it and, therefore, incorrectly believe that the Church won't go into the *Great Tribulation*—-hence, they believe that these passages must only be referring to the Jews. Bringing the Jews to repentance is *one* of its purposes, but these passages in Matthew and Luke show another critical purpose—- for Christians to preach the Gospel and give testimony of Jesus. The Luke passage says, "*It will lead to an opportunity for your testimony*" (Luke 21:13 NASB). Matthew says, "This gospel of the kingdom shall be preached in the whole world as a *testimony* to all the nations, and then the end will come" (Matt. 24:14 NASB). Testimony of the saints is a *primary* rationale behind the *Great Tribulation*. As we have repeatedly stated, during this period the saints are figuratively circling Jericho showing the inhabitants the Ark of the Covenant (Jesus) despite being shot at with flaming darts. But the walls will fall. The kingdoms of the world will become the kingdoms of our Lord and of His Christ.

In the *Fourth Year* of the 70th Week of Daniel we will reach the significant *Midpoint*.

THE *MIDPOINT* FROM HEAVEN'S PERSPECTIVE

Because the *Midpoint* of the 70th Week of Daniel is such a pivotal moment in the history of man, the Bible "time stamps" that moment in several passages. Daniel views this time at the *Midpoint* from the perspective of heaven:

> Now at that time *Michael*, the great prince who stands guard over the sons of your people, *will arise*. And there will be *a time of distress* such as never occurred since there was a nation until that time. (Dan. 12:1 NASB, emphasis mine)

Revelation also views this important moment:

> And there was war in heaven, *Michael* and his angels waging war with the dragon (Satan). The dragon and his angels waged war, and they were not strong enough, and there was no longer a place found for them in heaven. And *the great dragon was thrown down*, the serpent of old who is *called the devil and Satan*, who deceives the whole world; he was thrown down to the earth, and his angels were thrown down with him. Then I heard a loud voice in heaven, saying, now the salvation, and the power, and the kingdom of our God and the authority of His Christ have come, for the accuser of our brethren has been thrown down, he who accuses them before our God day and night. And they overcame him because of the blood of the Lamb and because of the word of

their testimony, and they did not love their life even when faced with death. For this reason, rejoice O heavens and you who dwell in them. *Woe to the earth and the sea, because the devil has come down to you,* having great wrath, knowing that he has only a short time. (Rev. 12:7-12 NASB, clarification and emphasis mine)

Notice both Daniel and Revelation show that Michael the Archangel arises at this time (the *Midpoint*). We learn from Revelation that Michael stands up to do battle with Satan, overcomes him and casts the devil and his demon followers to the earth. Daniel clarifies that this event ushers in the *Great Tribulation* which means that *Satan is cast down at the Midpoint* of the 70th Week of Daniel.

I also notice with great interest the role that current day Christians play in the fall of Satan. Just as we discussed in Chapter Six: "The Walls Came Tumbling Down (Joshua 6, Judges 6-8)," they help overcome him by the blood of the Lamb, their testimony, and their willingness to face death. This is the struggle that will primarily occur during the *first half* of the 70th Week of Daniel as the saints figuratively circle the earth showing Satan's forces the Ark of the Covenant (Jesus).

THE RESTRAINER

Another question we must ask about *Michael* is what does he arise *from*? What has he been *doing*? Might he be "the restrainer" from 2 Thess. 2: 6 who currently is *holding back the Antichrist*? His rising to fight Satan and his demons ushers in the *Great Tribulation*. Might his rising also allow the Antichrist to be revealed? In Daniel 10 we learn *spiritual warfare* is a major function of Michael's ministry. Michael had been fighting the Prince of Persia, a demonic being, as explained in Daniel 10: "But the prince of the kingdom of Persia was withstanding me (Daniel) for twenty-one days; then behold, Michael, one of the chief princes, came to help me, for I had been left there with the kings of Persia" (Dan. 10:13 NASB, clarification mine).

Michael is a spiritual being. As such he is seen struggling with other spiritual beings, the Prince of Persia (in Dan. 10) and Satan (in Rev. 12). Is it likely that who or what he is restraining is also a spiritual being? I believe it is. I believe it's *the Beast that rises from the abyss* (Rev. 11: 7, Rev. 17:8). *This Beast,* a demon, is a mirror image of Satan, and it is released from the abyss as Michael leaves to do war with Satan and his demons. Once free, *this Beast* directly possesses the man who will be *Antichrist* and empowers him to accomplish the unspeakable evil of the *Great Tribulation,* which is unleashed upon the Jews and Christians. This is entirely consistent with Revelation 12, which shows the *Great Tribulation* begins *after* Satan is cast down:

> And when the dragon (Satan) saw that he was thrown down to the earth, he persecuted the woman (Israel) who gave birth to the male child (Jesus). . . . So the dragon was enraged with the woman (Israel; the Jews), and went off to make war with the rest of her children, who keep the commandments of God and hold to the testimony of Jesus (Christians). (Rev. 12:13, 17 NASB, clarification mine)

AT THE *MIDPOINT* FROM EARTH'S PERSPECTIVE

After Satan is cast down to the earth in the spiritual realm, two main events will happen on earth. The Beast-empowered *Antichrist* will capture Jerusalem, and then he will sit in the Temple of God and proclaim himself to be God. The capture of Jerusalem is pictured in Luke. Many prophecy teachers wrongly assume this passage from Luke applies exclusively to the destruction of Jerusalem and the Temple in 70 AD. It does not. Those events foreshadow what is to come, but *final fulfillment* still awaits us (*near/far* fulfillment of prophecy).

> But when you see Jerusalem surrounded by armies, then know that its desolation is near. Then let those who are *in Judea* flee to the mountains, let those who are in the midst of her depart, and let not those who are in the country enter her. For these are the *days of vengeance* (Gk: EKDIKESIS, meaning "*justice* or avenging"), *that all things which are written may be fulfilled.* But woe to those who are pregnant and to those who are nursing

babies in those days! For there will be *great distress* in the land and *wrath* upon this people. And they will fall by the edge of the sword, and be led away captive into all nations. And Jerusalem will be trampled (Gk: PATESOUSIN) by Gentiles *until the times of the Gentiles are fulfilled.* (Luke 21:20-24 NASB, clarification and emphasis mine)

There are three things which indicate future fulfillment of Luke 21. *First*, notice the Greek word translated "vengeance" actually means *justice*. Earlier in Luke's Gospel we find this word used in the following verse that highlights its meaning: "Will not God bring about *justice* (EKDIKESIS) for His elect who cry to Him day and night" (Luke 18:7 NASB). This justice is a legal term. The justice will occur when the *7 Sealed Scroll* is opened, bringing reward for the righteous, punishment for the wicked, and a return of the dominion of the earth to the rightful owners (Christ and the saints).

Second, how can we be sure these are future events? First notice the verse "for these are the days of vengeance that *all things which are written* may be fulfilled." Obviously *all prophecy* wasn't fulfilled in 70 AD. In addition, notice the exact parallelism of these three verses from Luke, Matthew and Mark:

But when you see Jerusalem surrounded by armies, then know that its *desolation* is near. *Then let those who are in Judea flee to the mountains.* (Luke 21:20 -21 NASB, emphasis mine)

So when you see the '*abomination of desolation*,' spoken of by Daniel the prophet, standing where it ought not (let the reader understand), *then let those who are in Judea flee to the mountains.* (Mark 13:14 NASB, emphasis mine)

Therefore when you see the '*abomination of desolation*', spoken of by Daniel the prophet, standing in the holy place (whoever reads, let him understand), *then let those who are in Judea flee to the mountains.* (Matt. 24:15-16 NASB, emphasis mine)

All three verses speak of the *desolation of Jerusalem and fleeing to the mountains*. Luke 21 simply gives an earlier look at what will be a singular future event, the capture of Jerusalem and the Abomination in the temple.

Third, if the events in Luke truly were uniquely in regard to 70 AD, Jesus was giving his followers terrible advice[xliii]. The Roman armies slowly approached Jerusalem starting in 66 AD. By the time they encircled the city, it was too late to escape. Many were slaughtered at this time trying to slip through the Roman lines. Obviously Jesus would not give such poor advice. Hence, Jesus was *not* referring exclusively to the situation in 70 AD.

Now that we are sure that Luke 21 has future fulfillment, let's carefully look at what it prophesies. It clearly states that many will die in the siege of Jerusalem and that many will be taken as captives into "all the nations." This imprisonment of the Jews (and Jesus' subsequent setting the captives free) is found in numerous scriptures. (Psalm 14:7; 102:13,19, 20; Isaiah 11:11-12,15-16; 27:12-13; 35:5-6; 42:6-7,16; 52:11-12; 61:1-3; Jeremiah 31:8-10; Ezekiel 39:25-28; Joel 2:32-3:1; Hosea 11:11; Micah 2:12-13; 4:6-7; 5:6; 7:12; Zechariah 10:6-11). In my book, *Are We Ready for Jesus? How to Prepare for His Return* (Seraphina Press, 2015), I discuss how Jesus wants his Church to prepare for this horrific future event and how he wants us to care for our brother Jacob (Israel; the Jews) at that time.

THE TIMES OF THE GENTILES

The passage in Luke 21 then concludes by saying that *Jerusalem will be trampled until the "Times of the Gentiles" are complete* (Luke 21). What does *"the Times of the Gentiles"* mean? The traditional view of many commentators is that it refers to the time that Gentiles (non-Jews) controlled all or part of Jerusalem (from AD 70 on). Some commentators have dated Gentile control all the way back to Babylonian days. Still others have suggested it is the time that the Dome of Rock has been present on the Temple Mount. The problem with all of these views is that they rely solely on what we as commentators "think" it means, rather than relying on what *the Bible says* it means.

218

The "sense" of the passage in Luke 21:20-24 is that it refers to the time period immediately after the *Midpoint* of Daniel's 70th Week and nothing more. Let's see if we can find further clues in "reference" passages that may give us further hints as to what the "Times of the Gentiles" means. The primary references to these verses are found in Daniel:

> Seventy weeks have been decreed for your people and your holy city . . . *to seal up vision and prophecy* . . . (Dan. 9:24 NASB, emphasis mine)

> These are days of vengeance so that *all things which are written will be fulfilled*. (Luke 21:22 NASB, emphasis mine)

This first parallel reference implies that Jesus is explaining Daniel's prophecy about *the seventy sevens* or *Shabua*. The following second reference deepens the connection between the passages:

> *The people of the prince who is to come will destroy the city* and the sanctuary. And its end will come with a flood; even to the end *there will be war*; *desolations are determined*. (Dan. 9:26 NASB, emphasis mine)

> But when you see *Jerusalem surrounded by armies*, then recognize that *her desolation is near*. (Luke 21:20 NASB, emphasis mine)

You are probably saying "wait a minute, Daniel 9:26, related to the "people of the prince," it's talking about AD 70." Is it really? Are we making the same mistake commentators previously made about Luke 21:20-24—that it referred to AD 70? The first sixty-nine weeks (Shabua) of Daniel's vision *end* with Jesus's death. The destruction of the Temple in AD 70 happened forty years *after* the "pause" of Daniel's 70 weeks, after the 69th Week, so how can Dan. 9:26 be part of the prophecy which is *about* the 70 weeks? I believe Dan. 9:26 also speaks of the destruction yet to come in the future.

There is another parallel showing Jesus is explaining the 70 Weeks in Luke 21:20-24 in the following passage in Daniel 9:27:

> In the ***middle of the week*** he will put a stop to sacrifice and grain offering; and on the wing of abominations will come one who makes desolate. (Dan. 9:27 NASB, emphasis mine)

We have already shown that the events of Luke 21:20-24 happens at the ***Midpoint of Daniel's 70th Week*** so this confirms the timing:

> ***Until*** a complete ***destruction***, one that is decreed is poured out on the one who makes desolate. (Dan. 9:27 NASB, emphasis mine)

> ***Until*** the ***times*** of the Gentiles are fulfilled. (Luke 21:24 NASB, emphasis mine)

The perfect parallelism continues through the end of both passages. It appears the end point of the *Times of the Gentiles* is the *destruction of the Antichrist*. What is the link between "Times of the Gentiles" and "the destruction of the Antichrist?" The following verse in Daniel provides us the link:

> They (the saints) will be given into his (Antichrist's) hand for a ***time, times, and half a time***. But the court will sit for judgment and his dominion will be taken away, annihilated and ***destroyed*** forever. (Dan. 7:25-26 NASB, clarification and emphasis mine)

This above verse in Dan. 7 is the linking verse that I think Jesus had in mind. The words "*times*" and "*destruction*" both appear in this one passage. So, are the "*Times of the Gentiles*" the same as "*time, times, and half a time*?" Yes, I believe they are. Is there more proof? Yes, there is, as follows:

Jerusalem will be *trampled (Gk: PATEO)* under foot by the Gentiles until the times of the Gentiles are fulfilled. (Luke 21:24 NASB, clarification and emphasis mine)

It has been given to the nations; and they will *tread (Gk: PATEO)* underfoot the holy city for forty-two months. (Rev. 11:3 NASB, clarification and emphasis mine)

We can see that the *trampling* of Jerusalem is *42 months*. We already know that "*time, times, and half a time*" is 1260 days, 3 ½ years or *42 months*. We have a match. We can now say with fair certainty that the "*Times of the Gentiles*" is equal to *the last half of Daniel's 70th Week* (42 months) and *not* the time from the Babylonian invasion and *not* the time since AD 70, as are so frequently taught.

TIMES

What did Jesus mean by "*times*" when he used this word? We have already seen that the Greek word translated "times" is KAIRON meaning "*appointed times.*" In the Hebrew this word is MO'EDIM which also can mean "*Feasts of the Lord.*" Could Jesus have been talking about the Feasts of the Lord? Since we know each "time" is a year, was Jesus talking about a cycle of all seven Feasts that take a year to complete? It is very likely. We also know that the primary fulfillment of the first four spring Feasts have already taken place during Jesus' first coming. Three more Feasts (*Yom Teruah, Yom Kippur, and Tabernacles*), the fall feasts, still remain to be prophetically fulfilled, and will occur during Jesus' second coming. It is incredibly likely these three fall Feasts will be fulfilled during the 70th Week of Daniel. (This case is fully explained in the book, *The Last Shofar!* by Lenard and Zoller). So, when Jesus referred to the "Times" of the Gentiles," was he also referring to Feasts of the Lord that will be fulfilled when the Gentiles are in control of Jerusalem? He may have been. In Chapter Twenty-Three: "Appointments," we discuss this connection in substantially more depth.

THE DESOLATION OF THE ABOMINATION

After the Antichrist captures Jerusalem, he is ready to take his seat in the Temple of God and proclaim himself as God. This is the event known as the *Abomination of Desolation*. The actual Abomination may be the "image of the Beast" referred to in Revelation 13 or may be a combination of that and the Antichrist proclaiming he is God.

Jesus refers to this event which was named by Daniel as "the *Abomination of Desolation*." The Greek word translated desolation is EREMOSIS which means *devastation, desolation, barren, and isolated*. This refers to the Temple of God *and* to the city, I believe. The temple is made barren as it is desecrated by the Abomination. God presence will not enter the temple with this horrid sacrilege in its midst. The city is made barren after the Jews are taken into captivity.

THE BOOK OF DANIEL

In Daniel Chapter 2, we find the story of Nebuchadnezzar's dream of a huge *metal statue*. We will discuss that dream and what it means in Chapter Fifteen: "Overcoming Lions (Daniel 1-12)." For our purposes here, God helped Daniel interpret the dream. He informed Nebuchadnezzar that Babylon was the *head of gold* of the statue and that other Kingdoms, inferior to Babylon, represented by other inferior metals, would assume pre-eminence after Babylon fell. Nebuchadnezzar obviously didn't like what God revealed to him in his dream. He didn't want Babylon's kingdom to end, so he made his *own statue* in defiance of God's revealed Word. Nebuchadnezzar's statue was *all gold* (the metal representing Babylon) rather than multiple metals. He was in essence defiantly saying to God, *you may have a statue of different metals and think other kingdoms will replace Babylon, but my statue is only gold—Babylon will last forever.* In Dan. 3 we learn more about this statue constructed by Nebuchadnezzar:

> Nebuchadnezzar the king made an *image of gold*, the height of which was *sixty cubits* and its width *six cubits*; he set it up on the plain of Dura in the province of Babylon. (Dan 3:1 NASB, emphasis mine)

This statue definitely is a foreshadow of the Abomination. First, it is *an image of the Beast*. We know that ancient Babylon was the first of four beasts that Daniel prophesied. In Nebuchadnezzar's dream, gold was the color of the Babylonian portion of the statue which was associated with the first beast, so an image of gold was an image of the first beast. We know from Rev. 13:14 that the final Abomination will be an image of the fourth beast. From the description of the statue which Nebuchadnezzar built, we also see the numbers *60* and *6* in the above passage in association with his statue. The number of the *final Beast Empire* will be *600, 60, and 6* (the infamous "666"). God's Word is telling us Nebuchadnezzar's image is *like the final one* that is to come, but it is not evil to the same extreme as the final version, as ~~it~~ the statue which Nebuchadnezzar built lacks the *600*.

After the image was set up, Nebuchadnezzar commanded everyone to bow to the image. In the *Septuagint* Old Testament, the Greek word for bow down is PROSKUNEO which is the identical Greek word translated in Revelation as "worship" in the following passage about the *Abomination of Desolation*:

> And it was given to him to give breath to the image of the beast, so that the image of the beast would even speak and cause as many as do not *worship* (PROSKUNEO) the image of the beast to be killed. (Rev. 13:15 NASB, clarification and emphasis mine)

This Greek word PROSKUNEO literally means "to kiss the ground in reverence to something greater." This is a perfect picture of how Muslims bow to Mecca to worship Allah (Satan). We also see in Dan. 3 that Nebuchadnezzar ordered a call to worship to be played by an orchestra of instruments. It was upon that signal that the bowing was to take place. This is also a perfect picture of the Muslim "call to prayer," that plays from their minarets prior to each of these prayer sessions. In my previous book, *Are We Ready For Jesus?*, and has been discussed in this book, I presented the case that it is likely that the Abomination itself will be the Muslim's Kaaba's Black Stone, possibly set up *on* the Temple, and it will be the object of worldwide worship. It too is demonically inspired.

THE BOOK OF EZEKIEL

Immediately after the 430-day siege we discussed in the previous Chapter, in the *Fourth Year* of Daniel's 70th Week, we learn that the Antichrist will overcome Jerusalem and *2/3 of the inhabitants of Jerusalem will be killed by fire and sword and the remaining 1/3 shall be exiled:*

> As for you, son of man, take a sharp sword; take and use it as a barber's razor on your head and beard. Then take scales for weighing and divide the hair. *One third you shall burn in the fire at the center of the city*, when the days of the siege are completed. Then you shall take one third and strike it with the sword all around the city, and one third you shall scatter to the wind; and I will unsheathe a sword behind them. . . *One third of you will die by plague or be consumed by famine* among you, *one third will fall by the sword* around you, and *one third I will scatter to every wind*, and I will unsheathe a sword behind them. (Ezek. 5:1-2, 12 NASB, emphasis mine)

The passage clarifies that the third that is *burned in the fire* actually *die of disease or starvation*. I assume this fire is the means the remaining inhabitants will use to dispose of the bodies. This passage (Ezek. 5:1-2, 12), about *2/3 of the inhabitants dying after the siege*, is a perfect match with Zech. 13:8-9, which also prophesies that 2/3 of the population will be "cut off" and die. God will, however, refine the remaining third as precious metal through fire. That is his purpose.

> However, I will leave a *remnant*, for you will have those who escaped the sword among the nations when you are scattered among the countries. Then those of you who escape will remember me among the nations to which they will be carried captive, how I have been hurt by their adulterous hearts which

turned away from me, and by their eyes which played the harlot after their idols; and they will loathe themselves in their own sight for the evils which they have committed, for all their abominations. Then they will know that I am the Lord; I have not said in vain that I would inflict this disaster on them. (Ezek. 6: 8-10 NASB, emphasis mine)

God chose this *remnant* and marked them, which we see in the passage shown below (Ezek. 9:3-6). Is this the same *144,000 Jews* we see marked in Rev. 7? I believe it might be. If that is true, the marking of the 144,000 occurs *before Antichrist's siege of Jerusalem*. This is new interpretation as most commentators, only studying Revelation, teach that the marking of the Jews happens after the *Sixth Seal* rather after the *Fourth Seal*, which I am proposing. Here is Ezekiel's vision of this marking:

And He called to the man clothed in linen at whose loins was the writing case. The Lord said to him, "Go through the midst of the city, even through the midst of Jerusalem, and *put a mark on the foreheads of the men* who sigh and groan over all the abominations which are being committed in its midst." But to the others He said in my hearing, "Go through the city after him and strike; do not let your eye have pity and do not spare. Utterly slay old men, young men, maidens, little children, and women, but do not touch any man *on whom is the mark*." (Ezek. 9:3-6 NASB, emphasis mine)

God's temple will then be profaned by the people of the Antichrist:

I will give it (the *temple*) into the hands of the *foreigners* as plunder and to *the wicked of the earth* (the people of the Antichrist) as spoil, and they will profane it. I will also turn my face from them, and they will profane my secret place; then robbers will enter and profane it. Make the chain, for the land is full of bloody crimes and the city is full of violence. Therefore, I will bring the *worst of the nations*, and they will possess their houses. (Ezek. 7:21-24 NASB, clarification and emphasis mine)

Ch. 11: Event Four: Abomination and Death

This passage says that the city is given to the people of the Antichrist as "*spoil*." This is the plan that Gog of Magog, "to capture *spoil* and seize plunder" (Ezek. 38:12 NASB, emphasis mine). This common theme shows the connection between the two prophetic passages.

Finally, God shows Ezekiel his ultimate plan for the remnant of Israel that will be in captivity:

> I will gather you from the peoples and assemble you out of the countries among which you have been scattered, and I will give you the land of Israel. When they come there, they will remove all its detestable things and all its abominations from it. And I will give them one heart, and *put a new spirit within them*. And *I will take the heart of stone out of their flesh and give them a heart of flesh*, that they may walk in my statutes and keep my ordinances and do them. Then *they will be my people, and I shall be their God*. (Ezek. 11: 17-20 NASB, emphasis mine)

God's words to Ezekiel show that the captives will cleanse the land from its abominations. God also promises to save them. This is the time they (the remnant of the Jews alive at the time) look upon Jesus, the one they pierced, repent, and are saved (Zech. 12:10), which occurs when Jesus physically returns to earth *at the very end* of the 70th Week of Daniel (at end of *Seventh Year*). They will then inherit the New Covenant:

> I will take you from the nations, gather you from all the lands and bring you into your own land. Then I will sprinkle clean water on you, and you will be clean; I will cleanse you from all your filthiness and from all your idols. Moreover, *I will give you a new heart and put a new spirit within you*; and I will remove the heart of stone from your flesh and give you a heart of flesh. I will *put my Spirit within you* and cause you to walk in my statutes, and you will be careful to observe my ordinances. You will live in the land that I

gave to your forefathers; so you will be my people, and I will be your God. (Ezek. 36:24 – 28 NASB, emphasis mine)

PSALMS

Psalm 14 is incredibly rich in meaning and provides an exact fingerprint of this *Fourth Event* of the 70th Week.

> The fool has said in his heart, "There is no God." They are corrupt; they have committed *abominable deeds.* . . They have *all turned aside*, together they have become corrupt; there is *no one who does good*, not even one. (Psalms 14:1, 3 NASB, emphasis mine)

This passage may be familiar. Verses 1- 3 of this Psalm are quoted directly by Paul in Romans 3:10-12 to prove that all have sinned and fallen short of God's Glory.

This passage is a clear reference to the *Abomination of Desolation* that is set up in the *Fourth Year* of Daniel's 70th Week and to the *Great Apostasy*—the "turning aside" or "falling away." The word this Psalm uses is translated "corrupt." This is the same word used in Gen. 6:11 for the condition of the world before the Flood. This word also means "destroy" and is the same word the angels of God used when speaking of the destruction of Sodom and Gomorrah. Both uses of the Greek form of this word from the *Septuagint* are found in Revelation:

> And the nations were enraged, and Your wrath came, and the time came for the dead to be judged, and the time to reward Your bond-servants the prophets and the saints and those who fear Your name, the small and the great, and to *destroy(corrupt)* those who *destroy(corrupt)* the earth. (Rev. 11:18 NASB, clarification and emphasis mine)

Psalm 14 then presents the persecution of the Jews and Christians, the "*Great Tribulation*," which begins in this *Fourth Year*:

> Do all the workers of wickedness not know, who *eat up my people* as they eat
> bread? (Psalms 14: 4 NASB, emphasis mine)

We quoted this verse in Chapter Seven: "A Horse of a Different Color (Revelation 6)"
when we discussed Balaam. Balaam is a foreshadow of the *False Prophet*, and his name
means "he who consumes." In this verse, the people of the *Antichrist* are said to "eat
up" God's people.

In the final verse of this short Psalm 14, we see the captivity of the Jews which
is detailed in many places including Luke 21: 24. We also studied this captivity, which
occurs at the *Midpoint* of the 70th Week of Daniel, in the last chapter, Chapter Eight.

> Oh, that the salvation of Israel would come out of Zion! When the Lord restores
> his *captive people*. (Psalm 14: 7 NASB, emphasis mine)

It is incredible that all these aspects of the *Fourth Year* of Daniel's 70th Week are found
in this one Psalm (Psalm 14) containing only seven verses.

THE BOOK OF ZECHARIAH

The Prophet Zechariah confirms Ezekiel that 2/3 of the population of Jerusalem
(possibly Israel) will perish:

> "It will come about in all the land," declares the Lord, "That two parts in it will
> be cut off and perish; But the third will be left in it. And I will bring the third
> part through the fire, refine them as silver is refined, and test them as gold is
> tested. They will call on my name, and I will answer them; I will say, 'They
> are my people,' and they will say, 'The Lord is my God.'" (Zech. 13:8-9
> NASB)

God's Word to Zechariah also confirms the taking of spoil by the Antichrist armies and
the captivity of the survivors:

Behold, a day is coming for the Lord *when the spoil taken from you* will be divided among you. For I will gather all the nations against Jerusalem to battle, and *the city will be captured, the houses plundered, the women ravished and half of the city exiled*, but the rest of the people will not be cut off from the city. (Zech. 14: 1-2 NASB, emphasis mine)

THE BOOK OF ISAIAH

Isaiah's account of the fall of Jerusalem at the midpoint of the 70th Week begins with the siege:

For behold, the Lord God of hosts is going to remove from Jerusalem and Judah both supply and support, the whole supply of bread and the whole supply of water . . . And the people will be oppressed, each one by another, and each one by his neighbor; the youth will storm against the elder and the inferior against the honorable. When a man lays hold of his brother in his father's house, saying, "You have a cloak, you shall be our ruler, and these ruins will be under your charge," (Isa. 3:1, 5-6 NASB)

During the siege, we observe that food and water will be cut off, and great unrest and lack of leadership will prevail. After that, God will permit his vineyard (Israel) to be trampled by removing the hedge of protection he had placed around it:

So now let me tell you what I am going to do to my vineyard: *I will remove its hedge* and it will be consumed; I will break down its wall and *it will become trampled ground*. I will lay it waste. It will not be pruned or hoed, but briars and thorns (the Gentiles) will come up. I will also charge the clouds to rain no rain on it." (Isa. 5:5-6 NASB, clarification and emphasis mine)

SUMMARY

The Fall of Jerusalem and the setting up of the abomination of Desolation as part of the Fourth Event will change the world forever. First dramatically for the worst; but as this is also part of God's ultimate plan, for the better as Jesus returns and defeats the powers of evil.

In Appendix A, a graphic presents all the aspects of this event in the *Pattern of Seven Events*.

Chapter Twelve

EVENT FIVE: MARTYRDOM AND APOSTASY

On December 15, 1944, Christmas was only ten days away. American forces were closing in on the German Border, and the reign of Adolph Hitler (a foreshadow of the Antichrist) was all but over. Certainly, total victory would soon be theirs. The next day, December 16th, 200,000 German troops and over 600 armored vehicles and tanks roared through the heavily forested areas of the Ardennes. Hitler had realized that since D-Day his empire had begun to crumble. Only a surprise attack of epic proportions could save it. He gambled everything on this shocking offensive. With luck, the Germans would push the Allied forces back to the sea. This time if Hitler was again able to corner them in Dunkirk[xliv], he would not let them escape as they did in 1940.

Maps on evening news shows in the United States began to show a bulge in the allied lines as the German forces swept their way into Belgium, France and Luxemburg. The name, the Battle of the Bulge, was coined.[xlv] Prayer vigils were held as the world held its breath. Freedom as we knew it was at stake. The Allies, although amazingly successful in the months since their landing in Normandy had significant supply problems. The German Blitzkrieg showed the Allied defenses were a house of cards.

In order to reach Dunkirk before the Allies regrouped, the German forces needed to control the small town of Bastogne, Belgium. All seven major roads in this country converged there. Overwhelming German forces were brought to bear on the town, and day after day they pounded the small American forces within. Finally on December 22nd, the German commander sent a humanitarian appeal for surrender of the allies:

Ch. 12: Event Five: Martyrdom and Death

There is only one possibility to save the encircled U.S.A. troops from total annihilation: that is the honorable surrender of the encircled town. In order to think it over a term of two hours will be granted beginning with the presentation of this note. If this proposal should be rejected one German Artillery Corps and six heavy A. A. Battalions are ready to annihilate the U.S.A. troops in and near Bastogne. The order for firing will be given immediately after this two hours term. All the serious civilian losses caused by this artillery fire would not correspond with the well-known American humanity.

The German Commander.[xlvi]

American General Anthony McAuliffe's response is legendary:

NUTS!

The Allied Commander[xlvii]

Despite the overwhelming odds against it, the will of the 101st Airborne which protected the town, totally disrupted the German advance and boosted American morale throughout the region. On the day after Christmas, General George Patton arrived on the scene to repulse the Germans. Only a few months later, the German "1000 year Reich" collapsed and surrendered.

When our Lord breaks the *first seal* of the scroll, Satan, like Hitler, will realize that his empire is collapsing. He will strike out with a surprise offensive, sending out the *Four Horsemen*, one by one, as each of the first four seals is being opened. When the *Fourth Horse*, the *Green Death Horse*, rides, appearances will be that the forces of our King might be crushed. It will be a time of tribulation like the world has never seen.

Just as Hitler dreamed of a second chance to drive the Allies into the sea at Dunkirk, Satan will remember all of his failed attempts to defeat God's plan. He'll recall Moses' narrow escape in the basket in the Nile, Pharaoh's missed chance at the Red Sea, Sennacherib's near defeat of Jerusalem, Haman, Nero, Hitler, and Mohammed. This time he'll think he has the perfect plan.

But against overwhelming odds, a battered and besieged little band of Christians will stand up and say a spiritual "NUTS!" They will scream this with their testimony and their blood. Those are weapons Satan will not expect nor be able to defeat. The *Fourth Horseman*, the *Green Death Horse*, is Satan's ultimate attack. At that point, he has nothing more. He'll continue to persecute the Jews and the Church unto death, but that is all he can do. He will have played all his cards. Then Jesus will break the *Fifth Seal*. SNAP! The sound will be spiritually deafening. Only two seals left to go before Satan's empire crumbles.

MARTYRS UNDER THE ALTAR

We have seen how the sequential opening of the first four seals on the *Scroll* result in a sequential counter-offense by Satan in the form of the *Four Horsemen*. It is our thesis that a seal breaks during each year of the *70th Week of Daniel*. In total these seven seals represent the *Pattern of Seven Events*. When the *Fifth Seal* breaks in the *Fifth Year*, the Antichrist will still be pursuing his mad scheme to hunt down and kill all of God's people, but he has nothing new to add, so there are no more horsemen. Now it is God's turn. The remaining three seals on the *Scroll* represent His inevitable plan to return the dominion of the earth to Jesus and his saints coming to fruition.

> When the Lamb broke the *fifth seal*, I saw underneath the altar the *souls of those who had been slain* because of the word of God, and because of the testimony which they had maintained; and they cried out with a loud voice, saying, "How long, O Lord, holy and true, will You refrain from judging and avenging our blood on those who dwell on the earth?" And there was given to each of them a white robe; and they were told that they should rest for a little while longer, until the number of their fellow servants and their brethren, who were to be killed even as they had been, would be completed also. (Rev. 6: 9-11 NASB, emphasis mine)

To fleshly, human eyes this is a strange way to reclaim dominion. I am sure 99% of Christians read this passage and don't see it as an *offensive* affront on Satan. But it is.

Martyrdom is nothing new. One of my favorite books on my bookshelf is a little-known volume, *Jesus Freaks* (Albury Publishing, Tulsa, 1999) by the former members of DC Talk (a Christian Music Group from the 90's) and The Voice of the Martyrs ministry organization. It is not the book you'd expect from a Christian rock band. It has nothing to do with music; rather it's similar to *Fox's Book of Martyrs* (Wilder Publications, Blacksburg, 2009). It gives the account of the lives and deaths of martyrs of the Church down through the ages.

Certainly, those who follow the news media are shocked and disgusted nearly weekly by one or more new, horrific, murder videos of Christians being butchered by Islamists. The number of those "under the altar" grows daily. In 2010 it was estimated that 160,000 Christians died for their faith[xlviii] and these statistics were prepared prior to the rise of ISIS. So the question asked by the martyrs under the altar lingers in the air, "How long, Lord?" and also the unspoken, "Why Lord?"

Jesus had this to say to his disciples:

> If they have called the head of the house Beelzebul, how much more will they malign the members of his household! *Therefore do not fear them*, for there is nothing concealed that will not be revealed, or hidden that will not be known. What I tell you in the darkness, speak in the light; and what you hear whispered in your ear, proclaim upon the housetops. *Do not fear those who kill the body but are unable to kill the soul*; but rather fear Him who is able to destroy both soul and body in hell. (Matt 10:25-28 NASB, emphasis mine)

Jesus's instructions sound strange to our fleshly ears. Don't fear those that can kill the body? For most of us, that is our greatest fear. Jesus' instructions, however, are the exact opposite. Don't be surprised when you're persecuted and don't fear it, even to death. You can hear him saying, "I've got this under control. This is all within the plan." Implicit in his warning in Matt. verse 28 is the hope that the Deliverer is coming. He is right at the door. During the *Fifth Year* of the 70th Week of Daniel, his return is less than two years away. Not only is the Holy Spirit with us in all we go through, but *our eternity with Jesus is our ultimate future*; so even if death comes, He has us covered, and we will have a reward from Him for our suffering. However, just knowing the timeframe of the persecution will be a comfort to those going through it. Paul's instruction to the Church at Philippi echoes Jesus's instructions:

> Conduct yourselves in a manner worthy of the gospel of Christ . . . standing firm in *one* spirit, with *one* mind striving *together* for the faith of the gospel; in no way alarmed by your opponents—*which is a sign* of destruction for them, but of salvation for you, and that too, from God. For to you it has been granted for Christ's sake, not only to believe in Him, but also to suffer for His sake. (Phil. 1:27-29 NASB, emphasis mine)

In this passage, Paul builds on Jesus's instructions to be fearless in the face of persecution. First, he admonishes us to stand firmly *together* as a unit. It is this unity in the faith that accomplishes God's goal: to act as a *sign*; a sign of our opponents' coming destruction and our salvation. Standing firm in persecution, a unified Church is living in a manner worthy of the gospel. Earlier Paul states that "to live is Christ, to die is gain" (Phil. 1:21 NASB). If we truly believe that Gospel message, what will we fear? When persecutors see Christians standing in absolute faith that a better life and reward is coming, it is a witness to the persecutors of both of their coming judgment and the sure salvation of God. This is God's battle plan. How many millions of our opponents will see this and be converted by this faithful act of witness? Thus Paul is able to say, "It has been granted for Christ's sake, not only to believe in him, but also to suffer for his sake." What a statement! It is our special *privilege* to suffer for Christ because his reward is with him, and this life is nothing compared to awesomeness of what is to come.

Ch. 12: Event Five: Martyrdom and Death

Two Numbers

Returning to the cry of the Martyrs in Rev. 6, let's look at the Messiah's response in that context:

> And there was given to each of them a *white robe*; and they were told that they should rest for a little while longer, until *the number* of their fellow servants and their brethren who were *to be killed even as they had been would be completed* also. (Rev. 6:10-11 NASB, emphasis mine)

The first thing Jesus does is reward and recognize them. They are given *white robes* as a sign of purity. Their trial is over; they have *overcome*. But what comes next is alarming and upsetting. Jesus tells them to wait a while longer until the *number* of their fellow servants who are to be martyred are killed! This is very strange to our earthly minds.

There are *two numbers* which are to be completed prior to Christ's return. 1) One is the culmination of the Great Commission: the *Gospel is to be preached to all nations* (Matt. 24:14). This number we can understand. Bringing lost souls into the Kingdom is wonderful. 2) The second number is almost incomprehensible. There are a *specific number of martyrs who must be killed for the faith*. How can that be? Isn't God a God of peace and love? How can he set a pre-determined number of martyrs?

We don't understand this concept because we don't understand the horror of sin, we don't understand the war we are in against Satan, and we don't understand the weapons of this warfare. In Chapter Six: "The Walls Came Tumbling Down (Joshua 6, Judges 6-8)," we discussed the offensive nature of our combat. We are encircling the city just like Joshua. The enemy may be firing flaming darts at us, but it is our encircling of Jericho presenting Jesus to a dying world that overcomes the enemy. This is what Jesus means by being unafraid, presenting the gospel even in the midst of persecution. But how does martyrdom fit this picture?

And they *overcame him* (Satan) because of the blood of the Lamb and because of the word of their testimony, and they did not love their life *even when faced with death*. (Rev. 12:11 NASB, clarification and emphasis mine)

We discussed this martyrdom in Chapter Six: "The Walls Came Tumbling Down (Joshua 6, Judges 6-8)." Satan is cast down from heaven by Michael. This verse makes it clear, however, that the saints play a part in overcoming him through their testimony and martyrdom. How does this work? God's ways are not our ways. I don't have any idea how it works, but because God's Word says so, I know that it does. This doesn't make martyrdom easy, but it makes it easier, knowing that we can join with Christ to defeat the enemy of our souls. If it is our calling, we are to walk in it. We aren't to look for it! Heaven forbid, but if God has ordained it, we are not to fear. As a final note, let's return to the initial passage we looked at:

When the Lamb broke the *fifth seal*, I saw underneath the altar the souls of those who had been *slain because of the word of God, and because of the testimony which they had maintained*. (Rev. 6:9 NASB, emphasis mine)

Even in our current culture, the Word of God is coming under attack. The Martyrs later seen under the altar are going to die for God's Word and their testimony. They will maintain their testimony unto death. Will you? Will I? *We must emotionally prepare to face these challenges*. The Bible tells us they are coming.

> **Churches need to emotionally prepare their members for the coming days of severe persecution.**

THE APOSTASY

The second aspect of the Fifth Event is *the* Apostasy. Faced with the choice of *persecution unto death* or *apostasy*, many churchgoers may, unfortunately, choose *apostasy*. They will deny Jesus is the son of God and live for a short period of time longer than their faithful brothers. In previous passages in Luke and Matthew, we learned they will even *betray* their brothers and sisters who remain faithful. This is a horrible and almost unthinkable situation. Jesus says the love of "most" will become cold. This means *most* churchgoers we know will choose *apostasy* rather than martyrdom. *At greatest risk* may be those Christians who were expecting to be "snatched away" in a *Pre-Tribulation Rapture*. They won't be emotionally or spiritually prepared for the choice set before them. Joshua laid this choice out for all generations:

> Choose for yourselves today whom you will serve: whether the gods which
> your fathers served which were beyond the River, or the gods of the Amorites
> in whose land you are living; but *as for me and my house, we will serve the
> Lord.* (Jos. 24:15 NASB, emphasis mine)

Some Christians will escape, however. They will heed Jesus's warning in Matthew 24:15 and will flee to the mountains. There God may protect and provide for them. In my previous book, I discuss God's protection of his people in the "Secret Place" at some length, and I refer interested readers to that book.

THE *GREAT TRIBULATION*: PERSPECTIVE OF THE UNRIGHTEOUS

Although Christians and Jews will be martyred in numbers which this earth has never seen, the *Great Tribulation* will not seem like such a great tribulation to the *unrighteous*. Let's contrast two verses given by the Lord which illustrate this:

> For then there will be a *great tribulation*, such as has not occurred since the
> beginning of the world until now, nor ever will. (Matt. 24:21 NASB, emphasis
> mine)

> The coming of the Son of Man will be *just like the days of Noah*. For as in
> those days before the flood they (the unrighteous) were eating and drinking,
> marrying and giving in marriage, until the day that Noah entered the ark, and

they did not understand until the flood came and took them all away; so will the coming of the Son of Man be. (Matt. 24: 38-39 NASB, clarification and emphasis mine)

How is it possible that although the *Great Tribulation* is occurring, the *unrighteous* will be living life as if nothing had happened? There are several reasons:

- The *unrighteous* are not the ones being persecuted. We see this effect in western nations today. Although mass slaughter of Christians is presently occurring in the Middle East (in 2015), western nations don't seem to notice.
- They will have plenty of food because they have taken the *Mark of the Beast*.
- They will have become "conditioned" or desensitized by years of murder and war to not notice the horrific events around them.
- The news media will present the Christians and Jews as the enemies of freedom and safety. In Revelation 11:10-11, we learn the peoples of the world will *rejoice* and exchange gifts when the *Two Witnesses* of God are murdered.

PSALMS

The *Fifth Year* of Daniel's 70th Week is *a year of martyrdom* for most of God's people as the *Great Tribulation* rages on. The *Fifth Seal* of Revelation which also pictures this year directly quotes Psalm 13 when these already martyred saints cry out: "How long, Oh, Lord?" There is another aspect to this *Fifth Year*, however, the *protection of God's remnant*. Psalm 15 focuses on this facet of the *Fifth Year*:

> O Lord, who may *abide in your tent*? Who may dwell on your holy hill? (Psalm 15:1 NASB, emphasis mine)

The *"tent of the Lord"* is also seen as a place of refuge in Psalms 27, 61 and 90. Psalm 27, which is read during the Jewish month of Elul, links this *tent of refuge* with God's "secret place" detailed in Psalm 91. It is during this time that God will hide Israel's remnant. Revelation refers to this hiding in Rev. 12 where "the woman" is Israel:

Then the *woman* (Israel) fled into the wilderness where she has a place prepared by God, so that there she would be nourished for one thousand two hundred and sixty days (3 ½ years). (Rev. 12:6 NASB, clarification and emphasis mine)

The remainder of Psalm 15 lists the righteous that will enter God's tent of refuge.

I find the use of the word *"tent"* here to be interesting. Might Israel again live in literal tents in the wilderness, as was the case in the Exodus? Is this how God will preserve them from the Antichrist? Only time will tell.

Psalm 91 talks about the secret place of the Most High that has been a refuge for believers throughout the ages of the Church. This special psalm promises God's protection in times of trouble. Millions have turned to it for strength and encouragement. Close examination of the words of this psalm show it has special meaning for the "time of Jacob's trouble" (the 70th Week of Daniel). *Psalms 91 is a wonderful scripture to memorize to use in time of trouble.* A famine of God's Word is coming (Amos 8:11–12). There will be a day when the only scripture we have to guide us and comfort us is *what we have memorized* or that we hide in our shoes. (In the concentration camp, the family of Corrie ten Boom famously hid pages torn from their Bible in their shoes.)

Our times are not yet that desperate, but many of us could yet experience the 70th Week; let's take a look at Psalm 91:

He who dwells in the *secret place* of the Most High shall abide under the shadow of the Almighty. I will say of the Lord, "*He is my refuge and my fortress*; My God, in Him I will trust." (Psalm 91:1–2 NKJV, emphasis mine)

I have always been fascinated with the concept of a *secret place*. In Hebrew the word means "the hidden place, the hiding place, the covered place, or the covert place." It is mentioned numerous times in scripture. Psalms 27 also speaks specifically of the *secret place* during time of trouble:

For in the *time of trouble* He shall hide me in His *pavilion* (*tent*); in the *secret place* of His tabernacle He shall hide me; He shall set me high upon a rock. (Psalm 27:5 NKJV, clarification and emphasis mine)

Psalm 31 is also specific about hiding us from the conspiracies of men. This passage reminds me of Psalm 2, when the nations rage against God and his Messiah: "Why do the *nations rage* and the peoples plot in vain?" (Psalm 2:1 NIV, emphasis mine). This is also alluded to in Psalm 31:

You shall hide them in the *secret place* of your presence from the *plots of man*; you shall keep them secretly in a *pavilion* from the *strife of tongues*. (Psalm 31:20 NKJV, emphasis mine)

Although we may *dwell* in the secret place, we shall *abide* in the shadow of the Almighty. The Hebrew word translated "shadow" means "under the protection of." Some scriptures picture this type of protection as the shelter provided by a roof or *pavilion*. Other more intimate analogies show a mother bird's wings covering her young. All of these are pictures of how God will protect us, his people, at that time before Jesus's return.

In Isaiah is a very special picture of how God hid Jesus in the shadow of his hand until he was ready for ministry:

And he has made my mouth like a sharp sword; *in the shadow of His hand He has hidden me*, and made me a polished shaft; *in His quiver He has hidden me*. (Isaiah 49:2 NKJV; emphasis mine)

I believe, in the same way, God's hand might hide his people from the Antichrist. Despite all the drones and GPS systems available, God's hand can block and frustrate the Antichrist, making him unable to hunt down the elect. However, even in martyrdom, if that is what he has called us to, he has promised to be with us always, even to the end of the age (Matthew 28:20), and the Holy Spirit is ever our Comforter.

God's presence is the safest possible place to be. I don't believe we need to begin scouting out mountain retreats in which to hide. If God desires us to hide at that time, we might be given eagles' wings (Revelation 12:14; Exodus 19:4; Isaiah 40:31). What we do need to do immediately, however, is to place all our trust in God alone. *"He is my refuge and my fortress; My God, in Him I will trust"* (Psalm 91:2 NKJV, emphasis mine). God is our fortress whether he hides us or walks with us to face our adversary. Either way, we are completely safe with him. Eternity with him is our perspective and heaven is our home, no matter what happens to us before he comes.

SUMMARY

During the Great Tribulation, the *Fifth Event*, there will be a choice that every inhabitant of the earth will need to make. They will either worship the Antichrist or Jesus, The righteous choice may lead to martyrdom, but the unrighteous choice will lead to eternal damnation.

In Appendix A, there is a graphic for your review of all major aspects of the *Fifth Event* in the *Pattern of Seven Events*.

Chapter Thirteen

EVENT SIX: THE CELESTIAL EARTHLY DISTURBANCE

What is the scariest event you have ever encountered? A couple years ago, I felt a "tremor" of 5.5 on the Richter scale. Those of you who have experienced a *real* earthquake probably laugh that this could be scary, but not being able to trust the ground beneath your feet is frightening. We are accustomed to the natural world being very stable and consistent, but an event, a *terror*, is coming that will rock everyone's world, literally.

> I will display *wonders in the sky and on the earth*, blood, fire and columns of smoke. The sun will be turned into darkness and the moon into blood before the great and awesome Day of the LORD come. . . . the earth and the sky will *tremble*. (Joel 2:30-31, 3:16b NASB, emphasis mine)

God has said an event will occur that theologians call the *"Celestial Earthly Disturbance Event."* This event is not a ho-hum, everyday occurrence. God says he will display "wonders" in the sky and on the earth. This Hebrew word found in Joel is the same Hebrew word used in Exodus for the signs and judgments God brought against Egypt and Pharaoh. This event will be unmistakably a "God thing." It will not be a collection of eclipses or similar natural phenomenon. It will be wondrous and terrifying.

The *Celestial Earthly Disturbance Event* is detailed in several other scriptural passages. One of these passages shows the event occurs after the *Sixth Seal* of the *Scroll* is broken. We already know from the thesis we have established that this "time stamps" this event as occurring during the *Sixth Year* of the 70th Week of Daniel, and makes it the *Sixth Event* in the *Pattern of Seven Events*.

I looked when He broke the *sixth seal*, and there was a great *earthquake*; and
the *sun became black* as sackcloth made of hair, and the whole *moon became
like blood*; and the stars of the sky fell to the earth, as a fig tree casts its unripe
figs when shaken by a great wind. The sky was split apart like a scroll when it
is rolled up, and every mountain and island were moved out of their places.
(Rev. 6:12-14 NASB, emphasis mine)

In my previous book, I assembled five scripture passages describing this *Celestial
Earthly Disturbance Event* in a single table. I'd like to re-present that table (Figure 34:
The Celestial Earthly Disturbance Event) because it is highly instructive.

Column1	Joel 2:30–31	Isa. 13:6–13	Matthew 24:29	Luke 21:25–26	Rev. 6:12–14
Sun	Darkness	Dark when it rises	Darkened	Signs in the sun	Black as sackcloth
Moon	Color of blood	Not shed its light	Not give its light	Signs in the moon	Color of blood
Stars		Not flash forth light	Fall from the sky	Signs in the stars	Fall from the sky
Heavens		Heavens tremble	Powers of the heavens will be shaken. Sign of the Son of Man will appear.	Powers of the heavens will be shaken.	Sky split and rolled up like a scroll
Seas				Roaring of the waves (tsunami?)	
Earth	Blood, fire, and columns of smoke (volcanoes?)	Earth shaken			Earthquake; every mountain and island moved
Righteous				Lift your head; your redemption is near.	
Wicked		Hands go limp; hearts melt		Perplexity among the nations; men fainting	Hid in caves and asked rocks to fall on them
What Precedes	Pouring out of God's Spirit		The Great Tribulation	Jerusalem trampled at the Midpoint of the 70th Week	Fifth seal broken at Fifth Year of the 70th Week
What Follows	Day of the Lord, the wrath of God	Day of the Lord, the wrath of God	Son of Man comes on the clouds with great glory and his angels gather the elect.	Son of Man comes on the clouds with great glory.	Wrath of the one who sits on the throne and the Lamb has come.

Figure 34: The Celestial Earthly Disturbance Event

What is immediately obvious from studying this table is all five scripture passages picture the same event. They are so similar, it is like a fingerprint. No one who is honestly examining these passages can deny they are not the same event. After all, how many *sun darkening, moon to blood,* and *stars falling from the sky* events do we expect? And what an awesome and terrifying event it will be. In addition to the sun and moon being darkened, meteors will fall, and there will be an incredible earthquake, volcanoes and tsunamis. The hearts of the wicked will melt at the sight, and they will hide themselves in caves. Anyone who claims the "blood moon tetrad" experienced in 2014 and 2015 fulfills these scriptures is not reading all the related passages. This will be a *one-of-a-kind* event.

It is obvious from Joel, Isaiah and Revelation that the Day of the Lord, God's Wrath, follows this event. Very interestingly, it is also apparent from Matthew and Luke's accounts that prior to God's Wrath being poured out, Jesus returns on the clouds and his angels gather the elect. This is the *Rapture*! Placing all five visions of this same event side by side gives us this amazingly comprehensive look at the events surrounding Jesus' return, and reveals details not normally seen in one passage standing alone.

These facts are all consistent, however, with the *Jericho Model* we constructed in Chapter Six: "The Walls Came Tumbling Down (Joshua 6, Judges 6-8)." Both the Rapture and then the Wrath of God (the 7 Trumpets and 7 Bowls) occur *after* the seals of the *Scroll* are opened.

THE PURPOSE

Who can know the mind of God and determine his purposes? If he doesn't specifically mention his rationale in his Word, we can only speculate. I can see four reasons for the *Celestial Earthly Disturbance Event.* There are probably many more.

- To set the stage for the return of Jesus, providing cosmic and earthly signs of his coming.
- To give hope to the righteous.
- To give one last chance for repentance.

- To begin to restore the Earth to its natural state (we will explain this further below.)

In my part of the country, electrical storms are commonplace. One night a couple of years ago, I was standing in my driveway. Out over the ocean, cloud-to-cloud lightening was lighting up the sky. The dark thunderclouds would "glow" as the lightening flashed. You couldn't see the actual bolts, but the flashes were awe-inspiring. It struck me in that moment that I was watching a mini-preview of the "sign of the Son of Man," at his second coming.

> For just as the *lightning* comes from the east and flashes even to the west, so will the coming of the Son of Man be. (Matt. 24: 27 NASB, emphasis mine)

I realized that during the *Celestial Earthly Disturbance Event*, God will dim the lights (the sun and the moon) so that the Shekinah Glory of Jesus can put on a show when he returns on the clouds! I ran inside and brought my family out to the driveway to watch this object lesson on the return of the Messiah. One purpose of the event is to set the stage for Jesus' return.

A second purpose is to give hope to the righteous. The *Celestial Earthly Disturbance Event* will also be the sign that Jesus is at the door.

> But when these things begin to take place, straighten up and lift up your heads, because your redemption is drawing near." (Luke 21:28 NASB)

The rest of the world will be hiding in caves, but the Christians will be lifting their heads, watching for Jesus. Additionally, while the nations are hiding, they will be unable to continue to persecute Christians. It is likely that this event is what cuts the days of the *Great Tribulation* short. This will encourage the saints as well.

A third purpose will be to grant the world a chance at repentance. Who will be able to deny that this is of God?

Then the kings of the earth and the great men and the commanders and the rich and the strong and every slave and free man *hid themselves in the caves and among the rocks of the mountains*; and they said to the mountains and to the rocks, "Fall on us and hide us from the presence of Him who sits on the throne, and from the wrath of the Lamb; for the great day of their wrath has come, and who is able to stand?" (Rev. 6:15-17 NASB, emphasis mine)

To me, this is a very sad passage. Even after such an obvious "God" event, the hearts of the wicked will be so hardened, they will be unable to repent.

THE 360 DAY YEAR

The final purpose of the *Celestial Earthly Disturbance Event* may be to begin to restore the earth to its original orbit and length of year. Peter spoke of this time:

And that He may send Jesus, the Christ appointed for you, whom heaven must receive *until the period of restoration of all things* about which God spoke by the mouth of His holy prophets from ancient time. (Acts 3:20-21 NASB, emphasis mine)

If God is going to restore "*all things,*" does that include restoring the earth back to a year of 360 days? Up until this point in the book, I have attempted to not be overly speculative. However, this section is highly speculative to attempt to explain the *Celestial Earthly Disturbance Event,* which is totally miraculous. Changing the number of days in the year, certainly qualifies as a miraculous event.

Before we examine *whether* God changes the length of the year, let's first explore why I suspect that he might. The most famous time period in all of history is given in the *Book of Daniel* and Revelation: "*time, times, and half a time.*" This period is known to be 3 1/2 years, and it is considered to represent the last half of the 70th Week of Daniel. This period is also given to us as 42 months and 1260 days. It is the period of time that the Antichrist will rule, as recorded in Daniel and Revelation:

They will be given into his hand for a *time, times, and half a time* (3 ½ years). (Dan. 7:25 NASB, clarification and emphasis mine)

There was given to him (the Antichrist) a mouth speaking arrogant words and blasphemies, and authority to act for *forty-two months* was given to him. (Rev. 13:5 NASB, clarification and emphasis mine)

And he will make a firm covenant with the many for one week (7 years), *but in the middle of the week* (3 ½ years) he will put a stop to sacrifice and grain offering." (Dan 9:27 NASB, clarification and emphasis mine)

Then the woman fled into the wilderness where she had a place prepared by God, so that there *she would be nourished* for *one thousand two hundred and sixty days* (3 ½ years) . . . But the two wings of the great eagle were given to the woman, so that she could fly into the wilderness to her place, *where she was nourished* for a *time and times and half a time* (3 ½ years), from the presence of the serpent. (Rev. 12:6, 14 NASB, clarification and emphasis mine)

This final passage shows that 1260 days is identical to the time period: "*time, times and half a time.*" John demonstrates this by using the repeated phrase "where she was nourished."

What is interesting to me is that 1260 days do not equal 42 months nor do they equal 3 1/2 years during our current solar year of 365.242 days. Three and a half years are 1277.5 days, and 42 Jewish months of 29.5 days (alternating 29 day and 30 day months) are 1239 days. How can this be? Commentators have noticed that if the year was 360 days and each month was 30 days, these numbers of days, months, and years would add up perfectly. Prophecy teachers have come to call this 360-day-year a "prophetic year." The question comes to my mind, why did God create a prophetic year of 360 days and make it different than a present natural solar year of 365.242 days? The prophetic community is largely silent on this issue. What adds to the mystery is that it appears that at one time, the natural year and the prophetic year were both 360 days with 30 day months!

> In the six hundredth year of Noah's life, in the *second month, on the seventeenth day of the month,* on the same day all the fountains of the great deep burst open, and the floodgates of the sky were opened . . . The water prevailed upon the earth *one hundred and fifty days* . . . In the *seventh month, on the seventeenth day of the month,* the ark rested upon the mountains of Ararat. (Gen. 7:11, 24, 8:4 NASB)

From this passage we can see that water prevailed on the earth exactly *5 months* and this was a period of *150 days.* This is the original 30 days-per-month calendar. There are other passages as well that imply an exact 30 day month: (Deut. 34:8 and 21:13, and Num. 20:29 where mourning for the dead is ordered for a "full Month," and is carried on for thirty days).

HISTORIC BASIS FOR A 360 DAY YEAR

I found this scriptural basis for a 360 day year very interesting. After a little exploration, I discovered that not only did the ancient Jews observe a 360 day year [30-day months, as in account of Noah (Gen. 7:11 and 8:3-4)], but so did the ancient Egyptians, Babylonians, and Mayans.[xlix] Also the Chinese[l], Hindu, and Assyrians[li] had an identical 360-day calendar. The use of this type of calendar in these widely divergent groups cannot be coincidence. Many of these ancient civilizations had advanced knowledge of astronomy. Could they have been that wrong about the length of a year? It is also interesting that a circle is 360 degrees in circumference. Why was this number chosen in antiquity? Was it to match the number of days it took for the earth to circle the sun in a solar year?

Some might say the idea that the Earth once had 360-day year is nonsense, but Kepler's laws actually support this view[lii] with math that is far beyond my comprehension. It appears that if the earth had a 360-day year, it would be spherical instead of ovoid and the circumference in miles would exactly equal the number of arc seconds in a circle! (21, 600) Also the orbit of the moon would automatically be 30 days (a month). These are amazing coincidences, if they are coincidences. If the earth did indeed move from a 360-day year to our current calendric year of 365.242 days, how did it happen? There are many ideas. Danny R. Faulkner[liii] , Immanuel Velikovsky[liv], and Walter T. Brown[lv] have all proposed their theories that involve events of cataclysmic proportions: events related to the flood or a near collision of planets.

If one of these theories proves correct; Noah would have been *unaware* of the changes to the length of day and the length of the year when he left the Ark. His children and grandchildren would have kept the same 360-day calendar they used when they entered it. This original 360-day calendar would have then been dispersed across the earth with the migration of people separated at the Tower of Babel when God confused their languages. The ancient calendars of all those civilizations listed in the section above were likely the same calendar Noah used. For years these calendars probably seemed to work, but eventually as the length of the year continued to increase, the disparity between their calendars and the actual seasons became apparent. At that time a need arose to develop new calendars based on the new length of a year[lvi].

THE *CELESTIAL EARTHLY DISTURBANCE* AND THE 360 DAY YEAR

Now how does this theory of the length of the year relate to the *Cosmic Earthly Disturbance Event*? Jesus made an interesting statement in the Olivet Discourse:

> For then there will be a *great tribulation*, such as has not occurred since the beginning of the world until now, nor ever will. *Unless those days had been cut short*, no life would have been saved; but for the sake of the elect *those days will be cut short*. (Matt. 24:21-22 NASB, emphasis mine)

How will these days be cut short? Will the length of *Great Tribulation* be shortened? Yes, most likely it will be by the advent of the Rapture, when the believers will be removed from the tribulation——hence, the tribulation is "cut short" for them. Will the *Celestial Earthly Disturbance Event* disrupt the Antichrist's plans to end life as we know it on earth? We do know that when the *Celestial Earthly Disturbance Event* takes place, the wicked will hide in caves. Will their hiding effectively end the *Great Tribulation* by the removal of the persecutors? Yes, this is likely.

In addition will this event shorten *the number of days* in the year? Are the numbers of days in the year restored to God's ideal at the same time the *Great Tribulation* is cut short? We can't know for sure, but it is interesting to consider it. We noted earlier that if the length of the year changed, it took an event of cataclysmic proportions (the Flood or a near collision of a planet) to do it. During the *Celestial Earthly Disturbance Event*, there will be very significant cataclysmic events. Might God actually move the earth at that time to cause the type of earth shaking consequences we read about in the prophetic literature? At the same time, might this change the length of the year?

> For the stars of heaven and their constellations will not give their light; the sun will be darkened in its going forth, and the moon will not cause its light to shine . . . therefore I will shake the heavens, *and the earth will move out of her place.* (Isa. 13:10, 13 NKJV, emphasis mine)

It appears that God intends to change the orbit of the earth; *possibly* moving it slightly closer to the sun and thus shortening the length of the year. When the prophet Joel wrote that God will show "wonders" in the sky above, he meant exactly what he wrote.

Jesus's words are ringing in my ear as I write about this event, "But when these things begin to take place, straighten up and lift up your heads, because your redemption is drawing near" (Luke 21:28 NASB). While the people of the *Antichrist* are cowering in caves, God's people lift their heads watching for the return of the *Messiah*.

SUMMARY

The Sixth Event is the "sign" of God's impending Salvation (for the righteous) and Wrath (for the non-repentant.) After this sign, the return of our Savior truly becomes imminent.

In Appendix A, you can refer to a graphic that presents the major aspects of this *Sixth Event* in the *Pattern of Seven Events*.

Chapter Fourteen

EVENT SEVEN: RAPTURE AND WRATH

My Grandfather moved to this country from Wales when he was eleven years old. His parents said goodbye, packed him on a steamer ship, and he never saw them again! I find this so foreign to our current way of thinking. I can't imagine sending my ten year old to another country to never see her again. She is so unready for a trip like that. There is still so much I want to teach her about Jesus and life. But my great grandparents felt they needed to give my Grandfather the opportunities that America offered.

As I alluded to above, there was a price to pay for this opportunity. To the best of my understanding, without the spiritual influence of his parents, my Granddad died an unbeliever. My Dad and his five brothers and sisters were raised in an unbelieving household, and except for Dad, I believe they all passed away without a saving knowledge of Jesus. My mother was also born into an unbelieving household, and after they married, they raised my brother and me as unbelievers as well. Except for a miracle, Dad would have died without Jesus, just as his father, brothers and sisters did. However, God had other plans. I am blessed that I was included in that miracle.

People find it hard to comprehend, but I had never heard the gospel until the day I was saved in June, 1992. Most Christians probably believe there isn't an American who doesn't know that Jesus died on the cross for our sins, but I am living proof that there was at least one. I would love to tell you my conversion story, but this is about Dad's miracle, not mine.

Suffice it to say that I began praying for the salvation of my Mom, Dad, and brother from the day I was saved. Satan had a hard grip on them. If not for Dad's miracle, none of them would have been transformed. Just to explain how hard-hearted they were toward God, the story of my wife and my first Christmas together still makes me shake my head.

My parents decided to come and visit my wife and me in our new apartment for Christmas. As a relatively new Christian (18 months at that point), naturally I invited them to our church's Christmas Eve service. Good ol' Pastor Witt never missed an opportunity to present the Gospel, and that night was no different. He laid out God's plan of redemption in all its glory. I was so excited. I was sure my parents would "get it" when they heard the Gospel just as I had. I was so wrong.

When we got back to our apartment, my parents were furious that we had taken them "someplace like that." They told my wife and me exactly what they thought of Christians. My dad said Christians were hypocrites, slave owners, and crusaders, and that he couldn't believe in a God with followers than that. He then asked me a question, "If Adolph Hitler repented and asked for salvation, would your Jesus save him?" (Dad fought in WWII against Hitler.) "Of course," I said.

That was the wrong answer to Dad. He and Mom packed their bags and left in the middle of the night, on a Christmas Eve no less. My wife's and my relationship towards them was strained from that point on. That didn't stop us from praying for them, however.

Twenty years later, Dad required back surgery. He had traveled from their small coal-mining community to Philadelphia to have the surgery at a "big city hospital." Unfortunately, he had a heart attack in his room prior to surgery. After bypass surgery, his sternum was infected with MRSA, a "flesh-eating" bacterium which is resistant to antibiotics. Dad spent six months in intensive care and rehabilitation hours away from family and friends. We were told Dad's prognosis was very bad. Not knowing if he would live or die, I traveled the five hours from my home across the state to see Dad every other weekend.

On the day Dad was saved, I knew something was different the moment I walked into room. "Nelson, I had a dream last night." Dad never talked about dreams. "Really, Dad, what was it about?" I asked. Dad was animated like I had not seen him in years. "There was a lion. He was sitting up on top of a ladder," Dad explained. "Were you afraid of it?" I asked. "No," he said, "Somehow I knew he was there to *help* me."

In an instant the entire meaning of Dad's dream flashed into my mind. It was a God-thing. I had never interpreted a dream before and have never interpreted one since, but I knew what this one meant. "Dad, would you like to know what it means?" I asked. "Absolutely," Dad replied. "Do you know who the lion is, Dad?" I asked. "No," he said. "He's Jesus. The Bible calls him the 'Lion from the Tribe of Judah,'" I said. "That's why you knew he was there to *help you* and not hurt you." Dad was silent.

I knew what the ladder meant as well. In "Evangelism Explosion"[lvii] training, I had learned about an illustration that used a ladder. So I continued, "Dad, Jesus is at the top of the ladder because he is totally righteous, totally sinless, totally Holy. All of us want to climb the ladder, but we can't." I asked, "Dad, who is the most righteous person alive today?" Dad immediately responded, "Mother Theresa." I answered, "She is on the *third rung* of the ladder, Dad. Jesus is way up on the one hundredth rung, but even the most righteous among us is only on the third rung." "Who is the most unrighteous?" I asked. Dad responded without hesitation, "Adolph Hitler." I knew this would be his response, and maybe this was why God chose the ladder, so Dad would learn this analogy. "Adolph is on the lowest rung of the ladder," I told him. "And you and I are on the *second* rung. We're not as high as Mother Teresa and not as low as Adolph. But, Dad, when Jesus looks down at us from the hundredth rung, we all look about the same." Dad was quiet. "There is only one way for us to get to the top of the ladder. Jesus has to come down, put us on his back, and carry us to the top. We can't do it on our own," I explained. Dad's eyes began to tear up. He finally got it, but he wasn't ready to commit just yet. Dad didn't want to talk about his dream any more. He refused. In retrospect, I realize it was because it was me, his son, there in the room with him. His last tiny bit of pride prevented him from committing in front of me.

The rest of that day was long and quiet. When it was time for me to leave, I was desperate. I couldn't leave without knowing if Dad was saved or not. I didn't know if I'd ever see him again. I quickly shot up a short prayer, "Jesus, please give me a sign. Let me know my Dad is yours." Instantly a 300 lb. nurses' aid walked into the room. Around her neck was a necklace with a name dangling from it in two inch letters. The name stretched all the way to her waist. It said: JESUS. I laughed to myself and shot up a second prayer, "Jesus, when I asked for sign, I didn't expect a literal one! But thank you." That night Dad entered the salvation of Jesus, and God was merciful and allowed him to live on.

Dad lived another five years. My wife and I had taken our children to the "happiest place on earth," Disney World, of course. In the middle of an Indiana Jones enactment, my brother phoned me, "Dad is in a coma. Come home immediately." "Put the phone up to Dad's ear," I instructed him. My brother said, "It's pointless, he's in a coma." "Give it a try," I said. My brother held the phone to my Dad's ear, and I told him everything a son wants to say to his Dad. I was just about finished, but God wasn't. He had one final miracle. For a brief moment, Dad opened his eyes and, with his last bit of strength, said his last words, "Nelson, I'll see you when you get to heaven."

Today we are one day closer, Dad. I can't wait to see you again. The Resurrection has a very special meaning to all of us who await reunions such as what I anticipate.

EZEKIEL'S VALLEY OF DRY BONES

Ezekiel was given the most amazing and detailed *vision of the resurrection* in the Bible, the famous *Vision of the Dry Bones* in Ezek. 37:

> There was a noise, and behold, a rattling; and the bones came together, bone to its bone. And I looked, and behold, sinews were on them, and flesh grew and skin covered them; but there was no breath in them. Then He said to me, "Prophesy to the breath, prophesy, son of man, and say to the breath, 'Thus says the Lord God, "*Come from the four winds, O breath, and breathe on these slain, that they come to life.*" So I prophesied as He commanded me, and the breath came into them, and they came to life and stood on their feet, an exceedingly *great army.* Then He said to me, "Son of man, these bones are the whole house of Israel; behold, they say, '*Our bones are dried up* and our hope has perished. We are completely cut off.' Therefore prophesy and say to them, 'Thus says the Lord God, "Behold, *I will open your graves and cause you to come up out of your graves, my people; and I will bring you into the land of*

Israel. Then you will know that I am the Lord, when I have *opened your graves and caused you to come up out of your graves*, my people. *I will put my Spirit within you and you will come to life*, and I will place you on your own land. Then you will know that I, the Lord, have spoken and done it," declares the Lord." (Ezek. 37:7-14 NASB, emphasis mine)

Right now, my Dad's body is nothing but dry bones. Soon, at the resurrection, those bones will spring to life just like those in this vision.

It is my opinion that *all the dead who have trusted God for their salvation (Christians and many Old Testament Jews) rise at one time at the Seventh Seal.* We saw in Chapter Five: "Signed, Sealed, and Delivered (Revelation 4-5)" that this is the "Main Harvest" and the *first resurrection.* We know without a doubt that the righteous Jews who have trusted in their Messiah (trusting in him even before his birth, ministry, death, and resurrection) will themselves be resurrected. Daniel was told:

But go thou, and rest; for there are yet days and seasons to the fulfillment of the end (Gk: SUNTELEIA, meaning *"payment, or completion of many parts"*); and thou shalt stand in thy lot (Gk: KLEROS, meaning "assigned portion") at the end (Gk: SUNTELEIA) of the days. (Dan. 12:13 LXX, clarification and emphasis mine)

First of all, it is abundantly clear that Daniel is being told *he will be resurrected.* Second, there is a subtle hint that the resurrection happens at the *Seventh Seal.* We studied the Greek word SUNTELEIA in Chapter Five: "Signed, Sealed, and Delivered (Revelation 4-5)." In that chapter, we showed that the *"completion of many parts"* likely referred to the opening of the *7 Sealed Scroll.* At the *Seventh Seal*, Jesus's *payment* (with his blood) for the souls of the righteous is deemed worthy, the *Scroll* is opened, and the names of *all* righteous are revealed. It just makes sense that the Jewish righteous rise with the Christian righteous; all of whom have trusted in their Messiah. This is not definitive proof, but I think it makes the most sense and is consistent with the theory of only three resurrections (*first fruits, first resurrection, and second resurrection*).

Other commentators believe that the Jews who have died holding a saving faith in God (David, Daniel, Abraham, etc.) will rise *when the nation of Israel is saved in one day*, at the Second Coming. (Rom. 11:26). This alternative theory would necessitate an extra "resurrection" which is not supported by the Bible.

Others question the word *"army"* in the passage from Ezekiel: ". . . they came to life and stood on their feet, an exceedingly great *army"* (Exek. 37:10 NASB, emphasis mine) and why the resurrected would be referred to as an *army*. In my opinion, this is a direct reference to Rev. 19:14 and are the *armies of the Lord* that follow Christ back to the earth at the Second Coming: "And the *armies* which are in heaven, clothed in fine linen, white and clean, were following Him on white horses." These are the *resurrected saints* now in their "resurrection bodies" ('fine linen, white and clean') who comprise the armies of the Lord. Some commentators hold that *this army* are an *army of angels*, but I think this position that they are the *Church* and the saints returning with Jesus aligns with all scripture.

THE *SEVENTH EVENT* AND THE *SEVENTH SEAL*

How much time elapses between the *Sixth Seal* and *Seventh Seal* is not known (I propose a theory in Chapter Twenty-Three: "Appointments"). But, before Jesus leaves heaven, he breaks the *Seventh Seal*. Once that final seal is broken, the *Book of Life* opens and the names of the elect can be read.

> When the Lamb broke the *seventh seal*, there was silence in heaven for about half an hour. And I saw the seven angels who stand before God, and *seven trumpets* were given to them. Another angel came and stood at the altar, holding a golden censer; and much *incense was given to him, so that he might add it to the prayers of all the saints on the golden altar which was before the throne.* And the smoke of the incense, with the prayers of the saints, went up before God out of the angel's hand. (Rev. 8:1-4 NASB, emphasis mine)

Many commentators believe all of Rev. 7 (the sealing of the Jewish elect and the rapture of the Church) comes before the *Seventh Seal*. This is inaccurate if the *Scroll* truly contains the *Book of Life* and the names of those to be rescued, it needs to be open prior to him rescuing them!

Also notice that after the *Seventh Seal* is broken, there is silence in heaven for a half an hour. Zephaniah prophesied this would happen prior to the pouring out of God's Wrath: "Be silent before the Lord God; for the *day of the Lord* is near" (Zeph. 1:7 NASB, emphasis mine). Why is there silence? Commentators have made guesses for centuries. *The Pulpit Commentary*[lviii] suggests it may be the congregation of heaven being quiet while the angel appears before God to present incense and the prayers of the saints. *The Ellicott Commentary*[lix] suggests that the groans of the persecuted are stilled. *Meyer's NT Commentary*[lx] suggests it is a moment of reverence because the Wrath of God is about to be poured out.

While all three of these older commentaries may contain an element of truth, they miss the point that prior to the silence there was praise; constant praise. Why would the praise of the Elders and the Living Creatures of the Father and Son cease? In my opinion, there *is only one logical reason: one object of their praise is missing!* Jesus will have left heaven to go get his Bride – the Rapture! David prophetically has written:

> There will be *silence* before you (in heaven), and praise in Zion (on earth), O God, and to you the vow will be performed. O you who hear prayer (Rev. 8:4), to you all men come. Iniquities prevail against me; as for our transgressions, you forgive them. How blessed is the one whom you choose and bring near to you to *dwell in your courts* (in heaven). (Psalm 65: 1-4, clarification and emphasis mine)

This amazing passage shows the contrast of silence in heaven and praise on earth at the Rapture that happens at the *seventh seal* which aligns with the *Pre-Wrath Rapture* position, supported by this book.

259

The prayers of the saints rising in incense before the Father are prayers for deliverance and retribution from intense persecution. The Father and Son will shortly answer them. Before they do, all the peoples of the earth will witness the return of the Messiah. They will see his glory, as described in Jesus' Olivet Discourse:

> But immediately *after the tribulation of those days* the sun will be darkened, and the moon will not give its light, and the stars will fall from the sky, and the powers of the heavens will be shaken. And then the sign of the Son of Man will appear in the sky, and *then all the tribes of the earth will mourn, and they will see the Son of Man coming on the clouds of the sky with power and great glory.* And He will send forth His angels with a great trumpet and they will *gather together His elect* from the four winds, from one end of the sky to the other [the Rapture]. (Matt. 24:29-31 NASB, clarification and emphasis mine)

Jesus is clear in this passage that *all* peoples will see him coming on the clouds (this is not a silent rapture) and they will mourn and wail, but again, the wailing is not for repentance. This is truly heartbreaking that they are that hard-hearted.

But while the inhabitants of the earth mourn, the Bride of Christ, the Church, rejoices as the Angels gather the saints together to meet the Lord in the sky. This is the *Rapture*, at the *Seventh Seal* of Revelation at the conclusion of the *Sixth Year*. Just like a calendar week, the final year, during the *Seventh Year* of the 70th *Week* of Daniel, God will give Sabbath rest to the saints from their *laborious work* (tribulation) in the first six years. This places the following events in heaven following the Rapture, as listed in Rev. 7, in perspective:

> A great multitude which no one could count, *from every nation and all tribes and peoples and tongues*, standing before the throne and before the Lamb, clothed in white robes, *and palm branches were in their hands*; and they cry out with a loud voice, saying, "Salvation to our God who sits on the throne, and to the Lamb." And all the angels were standing around the throne and around the elders and the four living creatures; and they fell on their faces before the

throne and worshiped God, saying, "Amen, blessing and glory and wisdom and thanksgiving and honor and power and might, be to our God forever and ever. Amen." (Rev. 7:9-12 NASB, emphasis mine)

Heaven isn't silent anymore, it is rocking with praise! The Messiah has returned to heaven with his bride. What is this event we are observing in Rev. 7:9-17? Could it possibly be the *Wedding Supper of the Lamb*? Is this the celebration of saints who have just been married to the Lamb? This is a very controversial and complex subject. There are some hints in the text, however. The first clue is that we notice the saints are *wearing* white garments. These garments are mentioned numerous times in Revelation, and there is a progressive nature to these white robes: 1) they are promised while the saints are on earth, 2) they are given to the saints in heaven, and 3) they are finally worn. So what are these garments? I believe they are a reference to the wedding garments worn at the *Wedding Supper of the Lamb*. Jesus's *Parable of the Wedding Feast* is the first mention of these garments:

> But when the king came in to look over the dinner guests, he saw a man there who was not dressed in *wedding clothes*, and he said to him, 'Friend, how did you come in here without *wedding clothes*?' And the man was speechless. Then the king said to the servants, 'Bind him hand and foot, and throw him into the outer darkness. (Matt. 22:11-13 NASB, emphasis mine)

It appears that the wearing of these garments is required to be a guest at the *Wedding Supper of the Lamb*. In my opinion, when we look at all the references to white garments (wedding clothes) in Revelation they are referring back to this parable. Simply being promised or given the garments is not enough; saints must *wear* the garments. We know that these white garments are the "righteous deeds of the saints" (Rev. 19: 8). This righteousness comes only from faith in Jesus; no one has this righteousness themselves. It is the free gift of God.

SAINTS IN WHITE GARMENTS

In the Book of Revelation we are given multiple visions of saints in heaven dressed in white robes. What these visions say about the timing of the Rapture is profound. These visions are listed in "Figure 35: Saints in White Garments in the Book of Revelation":

Saints and their activity	White Garments	Reference
Saints in Sardis are on earth during the Great Tribulation	The ones who overcome are promised White garments	Rev. 3:4-5
Inhabitants of Laodicea are on earth during the Wrath of God	Jesus advising them to buy white garments to cover their nakedness	Rev. 3:18
The 24 elders are before the throne upon the opening of the *Seven Sealed Scroll*	The elders are wearing white garments	Rev. 4:4
Saints are found UNDER the altar. They are listed as "souls" not embodied beings	Saints are given white garments but asked to wait. They are not wearing the garments	Rev. 6:9-11
Saints are before the throne of Jesus waving palm branches. We are specifically told they "came out of the Great Tribulation."	Saints are wearing their white robes	Rev. 7:9-17
A vast multitude praises God	White garments are given to the Bride of Christ to wear for the Wedding of the Lamb	Rev. 19:1-10
The Armies of heaven accompany Christ back to the earth	They are wearing white garments	Rev. 19:14

Figure 35: White Garments in the Book of Revelation

Initially in the first two references, these white garments are promised to saints still upon the earth; both in the *Letter to Sardis* and the *Letter to Laodicea*. These passages re-enforce the imagery of the white clothes being a righteousness that is put on only in heaven.

Whether the "white garments" are being worn or not helps us assemble the occurrences chronologically. If you notice there appears to be an order to the use of these white garments. In two of the passages, we see that the saints are "given" their garments, and in two other passages they are already wearing their garments. This will help us chronologically list the passages. As you can see according to this methodology, the reference towards the end of Revelation in 19:1-10 actually occurs much earlier in the narrative than where it is placed in Revelation. *This is a tremendously important insight!!* Let's now look at each individual reference and what it says about Rapture timing.

REV. 6:9-11

The first two references to white garments are made in two of the *Letters to the Seven Churches* as we have just seen. The next reference is to the elders wearing white robes (we will discuss the elders later in this Chapter.) After the reference to the elders, the next occurrence of the saints in heaven with white garments is found at the opening of the *Fifth Seal*.

> When he opened the fifth seal, I saw under the altar the *souls* of those who had been slain because of the word of God and the testimony they had maintained. They called out in a loud voice, "How long, Sovereign Lord, holy and true, until you judge the inhabitants of the earth and avenge our blood?" Then each of them was given a *white robe*, and they were *told to wait a little longer*. (Rev. 6:9-11 NASB, emphasis mine)

There are several crucial points to be made about this passage. The first is that the saints are "under the altar" and are referred to as "souls" (not yet in human bodies.) From this we can tell that the Resurrection has not happened yet. In Rev. 20:4, the saints are also called "souls" prior to the Resurrection. They are given their white robes that they will wear after the Resurrection, but are told to wait a little while longer to wear them. The saints don't have bodies to wear the white robes on yet! They are also told to wait for God's vengeance (God's Wrath) because obviously that has not happened at that point either. For all these reasons we know that the Rapture has not occurred yet at the *Fifth Seal.*

REV. 19: 1-10

The next picture of the saints in heaven is found towards the end of Revelation. We know it is the next chronological step however, because the saints are *given* their white garments but are not yet wearing them. This is a crucial insight!

> Then I heard what sounded like a great multitude, like the roar of rushing
> waters and like loud peals of thunder, shouting: "Hallelujah! For our Lord God
> Almighty reigns. Let us rejoice and be glad and give him glory! For the
> *wedding of the Lamb has come*, and his bride has made herself ready. *Fine
> linen, bright and clean*, was given her to wear. (Rev. 19:6-8 NASB, emphasis
> mine)

This scene is immediately upon the Rapture. The saints appear to be in heaven in human bodies and appear to no longer be under the altar of God. They are also no longer told to wait to put on their white garments. This indicates the Resurrection has taken place and the wedding of the Lamb is about to take place. The saints have not put on their white garments yet, however, but the *Wedding of the Lamb* seems tied to the wearing of these garments.

REV. 7:9-17

The fourth scene is immediately *after* the *Wedding of the Lamb*. The saints have put on their white garments! They are now wearing the righteousness of Jesus!

> After this I looked, and there before me was a *great multitude* that no one could
> count, from every nation, tribe, people and language, standing before the throne
> and before the Lamb. They were *wearing white robes* and were holding palm
> branches in their hands. And they cried out in a loud voice: "Salvation belongs

to our God, who sits on the throne, and to the Lamb." (Rev. 7:9-10 NASB, emphasis mine)

Here we see the same "great multitude" as in Rev. 19 now wearing their robes and holding Palm Branches. The *Wedding of the Lamb* has taken place in heaven signified by the wearing of the garments.

REV. 19:14

The final event that pictures the saints in heaven and white garments is controversial. It is controversial because of the preconceived notions of some commentators. Let's look at two parallel passages only a few verses apart.

> His bride has made herself ready; *fine linen, bright and clean*, was given her to wear. (Rev. 19:7-8 NASB, emphasis mine)

> The armies of heaven were following him, riding on white horses and dressed in *fine linen, white and clean*. (Rev. 19:14 NASB, emphasis mine)

These passages only 6 verses apart both refer to *"fine linen (bright or white) and clean."* Can this obvious reference in the same chapter mean anything other than these are the same garments and the same individuals? Many commentators claim the armies of heaven referred to in verse 14 are angels not the Bride of Christ. These commentators make this assumption because of a theology that can't accept that the Bride of Christ is in heaven and returns to the earth *with Jesus prior* to Armageddon; when the obvious reading is that these armies are the Resurrected and Raptured bride.

INTERPRETATION

In my opinion, evaluating all these passages leaves only one possible interpretation: the Rapture is neither Pre-Tribulation nor Post-Tribulation, but rather is Pre-Wrath. As we have seen, the saints under the altar clearly show that the Rapture has not happened by the *Fifth Seal*. Thus Pre-Tribulation Rapture theory is eliminated from consideration. The numerous references to saints being given white robes and then putting them on *while in heaven* during the 70th Week of Daniel is direct proof that the Rapture happens prior to the end of the Week. How else are the saints given Resurrection bodies, come out from under the Altar of God, and able to "wear" the righteousness of Christ in heaven? Thus the Post-Tribulation Rapture theory is also eliminated from consideration as well.

Now that we have examined the wedding clothes of the saints, we have a working theory that the *Wedding of the Lamb* occurs at the *Seventh Seal* upon the Rapture of the Church. As we continue to examine the rest of scripture, however, we will see this is a much more complex subject, and that this working theory may not be completely accurate.

PARABLE OF THE WEDDING FEAST

The *Parable of the Wedding Feast* in Matt. 22 was the third in a series of three parables Jesus taught the day after his entrance into Jerusalem on "Palm Sunday." Upon his entrance into the city he had cleansed the Temple by driving out the money changers. The next day when he arrived at the Temple to teach, the Jewish leaders challenged him by asking what authority he had to do "these things." His answer found in Matt. 21:24-25 confounded them. Jesus then told the three parables: "*The Parable of the Two Sons,*" "*The Parable of Landowner,*" and the "*Parable of the Wedding Feast.*" All of these parables are about the unfaithfulness of the Jews and God's giving the inheritance to another people who would replace them.

In this context then, the *Parable of the Wedding Feast* was spoken primarily to the Jewish leaders. As we begin to look at the parable we notice that initially the King in the parable has an "invitation list" (the Jews), but those on the list are too busy to attend the banquet. Later the Jews mistreat and kill the slaves (the prophets and apostles) the King had sent to them (See Matt. 22:1-6). This obviously made the King angry, and we read:

The king was enraged, and he sent his armies and destroyed those murderers and set their city on fire. Then he said to his slaves, 'The wedding is ready, but those who were invited were not worthy. Go therefore to the main highways, and as many as you find there, invite to the *wedding feast*. (Matt. 22:7-9 NASB, emphasis mine)

From this passage we learn that in the first century, if the Jews had accepted Jesus as Messiah and King, they would have entered the *wedding feast* ("the wedding is ready"). The fact that the Jews did not resulted in the anger of the King and the destruction of Jerusalem and the Temple in AD 70. Additionally, the rejection of Jesus by the Jews resulted in the birth of the Church (the invitation of others to the *wedding feast*).

PARABLE OF THE TEN VIRGINS

Only a few days later as Jesus explained to the disciples the signs that would precede his return, he told another set of parables. The first was the *Parable of the Ten Virgins*. This parable also mentioned the *wedding feast* and a separation of those who were worthy from those who were not.

Those who were ready went in with him to the *wedding feast*; and the *door was shut*. Later the other virgins also came, saying, 'Lord, lord, open up for us.' But he answered, 'Truly I say to you, I do not know you.' (Matt. 25:12 NASB, emphasis mine)

As we examine this parable, we learn that the *wedding feast* begins with the return of Christ. The wise virgins go in with Jesus to the feast and he shuts the door behind them; effectively shutting out the foolish virgins. This "door" is an interesting symbol and it recalls two other famous "doors."

Those that entered, male and female of all flesh, entered as God had commanded him; *and the Lord closed it* (the door) behind him (Noah). (Gen. 7:15 NASB, clarification and emphasis mine)

He who is holy, who is true, who has the key of David, *who opens and no one will shut, and who shuts and no one opens*, says this: "I know your deeds. Behold, I have put before you *an open door which no one can shut*, because you have a little power, and have kept My word, and have not denied My name." (Rev. 3:7-8 NASB, emphasis mine)

In the account of Noah, God shut the door of the Ark and protected Noah and his family from the flood that lasted *one year and ten days*. Jesus will open the door of heaven (and close it behind the saints) at the Rapture and protect them from the *one year and ten day* Wrath of God that will be poured out. "Just as it happened in the *days* of Noah, so it will be also in the *days* of the Son of Man."(Luke 17:26 NASB, emphasis mine)

BE READY

Jesus also discussed a *wedding feast* in this other illustration in Luke.

Be dressed in readiness, and keep your lamps lit. Be like men who are waiting for their master when he returns (Gk: ANALUO, meaning "depart" or "return") from the *wedding feast*, so that they may immediately open the door to him when he comes and knocks. Blessed are those slaves whom the master will find on the alert when he comes; truly I say to you, that *he will gird himself to serve, and have them recline at the table, and will come up and wait on them*. Whether he comes in the second watch, or even in the third, and finds them so, blessed are those slaves. (Luke 12:35-38 NASB, clarification and emphasis mine)

This illustration contains a rather unfortunate translation. The Greek word ANALUO which in every other instance in the NT is given as "depart" (Phil. 1:23, Tim. 4:6) is rendered "return" here. If it is rendered "departs" the meaning is so much clearer. We are to be ready to *depart for the wedding feast*. The interesting facet of this illustration is that Jesus himself will wait on the guests.

TABERNACLES AND THE WEDDING FEAST

There are no records in the scriptures of an actual Jewish wedding ceremony. The consummation of the wedding took place during the Wedding Feast which was typically 7 days long (Judges 14:12); usually at the beginning. This seven day feast is reminiscent of the Feast of Booths or Tabernacles, where the Lord will dwell with his people. Returning to Rev. 7:9-17, palm branches are in the *hands* of the saints, now having resurrection bodies. In Jewish culture, palm branches are a symbol of rejoicing during the *Feast of Tabernacles* (Lev. 23:40, Neh. 8:15). This is a Feast that celebrates God dwelling with man, and obviously from this point on (after the Rapture), the saints will be with Jesus forever, even returning with him to the earth at the end of the 70th Week of Daniel.

In this passage in Rev. 7 there are even more references to the Feast of Tabernacles:

> And he (an elder) said to me, "These are the ones who come out of the *great tribulation*, and they have washed their robes and made them white in the blood of the Lamb. For this reason, they are before the throne of God; and they serve Him day and night in His temple; and He who sits on the throne will spread *His tabernacle* over them. They will hunger no longer, *nor thirst* anymore; nor will the sun beat down on them, nor any heat; for the Lamb in the center of the throne will be their shepherd, and will guide them to *springs of the water of life*; and God will wipe every tear from their eyes." (Rev. 7:14-17 NASB, clarification and emphasis mine)

Rev. 7:15 *directly* mentions that Jesus will spread his *tabernacle* (or booth) over them. The reference in verse 17 to *springs of living water* is a quote from John 8 and a statement Jesus made in the Temple during the Feast of Tabernacles:

> Now on the last day, *the great day of the feast*, Jesus stood and cried out, saying, "If anyone is thirsty, let him come to me and drink. He who believes in me, as the Scripture said, 'From his innermost being will flow *rivers of living water.* (John 7:37-38 NASB, emphasis mine)

Why do I bring these references to the Feast of Tabernacles to your attention? Some commentators who are attuned to the Hebrew roots of our Christian faith believe the final fulfillment of this Old Testament feast is the *Marriage Supper of the Lamb*, when Jesus and his Bride abide together and live as one, following the *Marriage of the Lamb* in heaven. I think this reference in Rev. 7:9-17 is that event. *The Marriage Supper of the Lamb* is referred to directly in Revelation 19:1-10 as well, and almost the same language is used:

> After these things I heard something like a loud voice of **a great multitude** in heaven, saying, "Hallelujah! **Salvation and glory and power** belong to our God . . . **And the twenty-four elders and the four living creatures fell down and worshiped God who sits on the throne** saying, "Amen. Hallelujah" . . . Let us rejoice and be glad and give the glory to Him, for the *marriage of the Lamb* has come and His bride has made herself ready." It was given to her to clothe herself in **fine linen, bright and clean**; for the fine linen is the righteous acts of the saints. Then he said to me, "Write, 'Blessed are those who are invited to the *marriage supper of the Lamb.*'" (Rev. 19: 1, 4, 7-9 NASB, emphasis mine)

> **A great multitude** which no one could count, from every nation and all tribes and peoples and tongues, standing before the throne and before the Lamb, **clothed in white robes**, and palm branches were in their hands; and they cry out with a loud voice, saying, "**Salvation to our God** who sits on the throne, and to

the Lamb." And all the angels were standing around the throne and around *the elders and the four living creatures; and they fell on their faces before the throne and worshiped God*, saying, "Amen, blessing and *glory* and wisdom and thanksgiving and honor and *power* and might, *be to our God* forever and ever. Amen." (Rev. 7:9-12 NASB, emphasis mine)

In both accounts we have *great multitudes*, they are *clothed in white linen*, and they cry out *"salvation," "power," and "glory."* We also see a near direct quote (the Greek words are in slightly different order in the two passages) involving the elders and the living creatures falling on their faces before God. This certainly appears to be the same event, which Revelation 19 clearly identifies as the *Marriage Supper of the Lamb*.

So in my opinion, the "marriage made in heaven" is actually *held* in heaven—the *Marriage of the Lamb* and the *Marriage Supper of the Lamb*. It occurs at the beginning of the *Seventh Year* of the 70th Week of Daniel, during the Feast of Tabernacles, which follows *Yom Teruah*, the day of the Rapture, by 15 days on the Jewish biblical calendar.

THE BRIDE

If it were only that easy! Revelation makes a further reference to *the Bride*:

And I saw the holy city, *New Jerusalem*, coming down out of heaven from God, *made ready as a bride* adorned for her husband. . . Then one of the seven angels who had the seven bowls full of the seven last plagues came and spoke with me, saying, "Come here, *I will show you the bride*, the wife of the Lamb." And he carried me away in the Spirit to a great and high mountain, and showed me the holy city, *Jerusalem, coming down out of heaven from God*. (Rev. 21:2, 9-10 NASB, emphasis mine)

The Bride is also the city of the New Jerusalem which comes down out of heaven *after* the Millennial Kingdom is over. This is a very different concept and timing than what we have just discussed. *The Bride* in this passage is obviously not the walls and the streets of the city, but rather it's the people who will inhabit it. This will include the Christians raptured during the 70th Week of Daniel and also the Jews and other Gentile survivors of the 70th Week who come to faith. The New Jerusalem will include all those who enter the Eternal State after the completion of the Millennial Kingdom.

The main Old Testament reference to the *Wedding Supper of the Lamb* also seems to indicate a wedding feast on earth at the completion of the Millennial Kingdom:

> The Lord of hosts will prepare a *lavish banquet* for all peoples on this mountain; A banquet of aged wine, choice pieces with marrow and refined, aged wine. And on this mountain He will swallow up the covering which is over all peoples, even *the veil which is stretched over all nations*. He will *swallow up death for all time*, and *the Lord God will wipe tears away from all faces.* (Isa. 25:6-8 NASB, emphasis mine)

The veil stretched over all nations reminds us of the veil that Moses wore to hide the Glory of God which reflected from his face. We also see that death will be defeated forever at this time and God will wipe away all tears. These three things are all mentioned in Rev. 21 which occurs at the same time the New Jerusalem descends after the Millennial Kingdom.

> Behold, *the tabernacle of God is among men, and He will dwell among them* (the veil will be lifted), and they shall be His people, and God Himself will be among them and *He will wipe away every tear from their eyes*; and *there will no longer be any death.* (Rev. 21:3-4 NASB, clarification and emphasis mine)

This re-enforces the timing that Isaiah 25:6-8 is a banquet after the end of the Millennial Kingdom.

ONE, TWO, OR THREE WEDDINGS

This analysis is very complex. We have already seen that the *wedding feast* begins upon the return of Jesus (Matt. 25:12), and yet Isa. 25:6-8 and Rev. 21:2, 9-10 seems to indicate it also occurs after the Millennial Kingdom is completed. The Word of God is inerrant, so both things must be true. I see two possibilities:

> 1) The wedding feast begins upon the return of Jesus at the *seventh seal*, but the wedding of the Lamb is not consummated until after the Millennial Kingdom, or
>
> 2) There is a wedding and a wedding feast after each of the three resurrections (*first fruits, the main harvest, and the gleanings harvest*).

The first option is possible, but unlikely in my opinion. The Jewish wedding feast was typically seven days long (Judges 14:12). This is a perfect match with the Feast of Tabernacles which is also seven days long. A *wedding feast* of a thousand years in length seems unlikely. Additionally, Rev. 19:7 states that the "*Wedding of the Lamb* has come." The same wedding cannot have "come" during the 70th Week of Daniel and a thousand years later.

That would necessitate that at least two Weddings of the Lamb occur, each with a seven day *wedding feast*. There may be three. Let me explain. In Chapter Five: "Signed, Sealed, and Delivered (Rev. 4-6)," we have learned that there will be three resurrections. The first of these, the *first fruits* resurrection, occurred at the time of Jesus's resurrection. We are told that "many saints" were resurrected at that time as well, and we purposed in that Chapter that these saints may be the *24 elders*. Interestingly in Rev. 4:4, we see that the *24 elders* are wearing white garments. This could be consistent with saints who were resurrected in the *first fruits* resurrection and who put on their white garments after a *Wedding of the Lamb* at that time.

In this Chapter, we have seen how it is very likely that a *Wedding of the Lamb* occurs after the *Seventh Seal* and the *Main Harvest* resurrection. These are the saints pictured wearing white garments in Rev. 7:9-17. Notice in Rev. 7:17, the passage mentions that Jesus "will wipe away every tear from their eyes." This direct quote of

Isa. 25:6-8 indicates to me that this wiping away of tears occurs at each of the three weddings. Both of the first two *Weddings of the Lamb* take place in heaven.

In Chapter Five: "Signed, Sealed, and Delivered (Rev. 4-6)" we also learned there will be a *Gleanings Harvest* at the end of the Millennial Kingdom. This resurrection is pictured in Rev. 20:5 and these saints are judged righteous in Rev. 20:11-15. It is immediately after this judgment that the New Jerusalem descends from heaven "as a bride." It is my opinion, that the saints judged righteous in the *Great White Throne Judgment* (those who came to faith in Jesus during the *seventh year* of the 70th Week and during the Millennial Kingdom) will be in that city as it descends. They will be the Bride at the third *Wedding of the Lamb* which is pictured in Isa. 25:6-8. This is the *wedding feast* that will include the Jewish remnant that comes to faith in Jesus upon his physical second coming. It is for this reason that the picture of this final wedding feast is included in the Old Testament.

THE MARK OF A HOLY ONE

Before he pours out the Wrath of God to stake his claim on the kingdoms of this world, Jesus removes his saints by means of the Rapture. The Jews, those of his chosen people who have not yet believed, are not raptured. They remain upon the earth. God protects and seals the righteous remnant of Jews prior to his pouring out his wrath:

> He cried out with a loud voice to the four angels to whom it was granted to harm the earth and the sea, saying, "*Do not harm the earth or the sea or the trees until we have sealed the bond-servants of our God on their foreheads.*" And I heard the number of those who were sealed, *one hundred and forty-four thousand* sealed from every tribe of the sons of Israel." (Rev. 7:2-4 NASB, emphasis mine)

144,000 Jews are sealed and protected. Thus God protects his people from his wrath—Christians by rapture and the Jewish remnant by sealing.

A frequent question I receive when teaching involves the 144,000 and their purpose. The vast majority of the Church considers them Messianic believers (Jewish Christians) and evangelists. A careful reading of the text in Revelation 7 and 14 (the other chapter where the 144,000 are found) doesn't support either theory. The idea that they are evangelists stems from the old *Pre-Tribulation Rapture* theory. In that theory, the Church is raptured prior to the 70th Week of Daniel. If that theory were true, evangelists would be needed during the "Tribulation Period" to help lead the lost to faith in Messiah. Believers in this false theory have chosen the 144,000 as the only group mentioned that could be these evangelists. The problem is that the text doesn't mention evangelistic activity of any kind for this group. The text simply says that these 144,000 are sealed and protected. We will learn in Chapter Eleven: "Event Four: Abomination and Death" that this sealing likely occurs in the *Fourth Year* of the 70th Week to protect them from both the *Great Tribulation* and the Wrath of God which is about to be poured out following the Rapture of those who have put their trust in Jesus for salvation.

The text also says nothing about them believing in Messiah prior to his physical return to the earth. In Rev. 14, we read the 144,000 follow the Lamb where ever he goes:

> Then I looked, and behold, the Lamb was *standing on Mount Zion*, and with Him *one hundred and forty-four thousand*, having His name and the name of His Father written on their foreheads . . . These are the ones who have not been defiled with women, for they have kept themselves chaste. These are the ones who *follow the Lamb wherever He goes*. (Rev. 14:1,4 NASB, emphasis mine)

At that point, Jesus is standing on the Mount of Olives. He has landed upon the earth. The *Seventh Trumpet* has already blown with the unleashing of the final seven bowl judgments, and the physical Second Coming to earth has occurred. This is the beginning of the *Eighth Year* following the 70th Week and is entirely consistent with what we know so far about the 70th Week of Daniel. At the end of the *Seventh Year*, the Jews will finally reach the end of their rope. They will cry out to God, gaze upon the one whom they have pierced (Jesus), repent, and all of Israel will be saved on that day (Zech. 12:10). It is only at *that point* that the 144,000 follow the Lamb everywhere he goes. We know from the vision in Rev. 14 that the remnant of the Jews *survive and come to faith.* Joel pictures this event on Mount Zion as well:

> And it will come about that *whoever calls on the name of the LORD* will be delivered; for on *Mount Zion* and in Jerusalem there will be those who escape as the LORD has said even among *the survivors* whom the LORD calls. (Joel 2:32 NASB, emphasis mine)

Furthermore, logically the 144,000 can't be Messianic believers during the 70th Week for another reason. If they were, why wouldn't they be raptured with the rest of the Church at the *Seventh Seal*?

After God protects his people, by the Rapture for those who have put their faith in Jesus for salvation and by his sealing of his righteous remnant of the Jews, he pours out his Wrath upon the earth.

RAPTURE AND WRATH

We have already shown the Rapture happens at the breaking of the *Seventh Seal*. In the *Olivet Discourse*, Jesus also tells us that his coming will be like the days of Noah:

> The coming of the Son of Man will be *just like the days of Noah.* For as in those days before the flood they were eating and drinking, marrying and giving in marriage, until the day that Noah entered the ark, and they did not understand until the flood came and took them all away; so will the coming of the Son of Man be. Then there will be two men in the field; one will be taken and one will be left. Two women will be grinding at the mill; one will be taken and one will be left. (Matt. 24:37-41 NASB, emphasis mine)

The "sense" of this verse (as a portion of "Sense and Reference") is that the *unrighteous* will be taken by complete surprise by the coming of Jesus. They will be living normal lives right up until the judgment sweeps them away. Is this all that Jesus meant by the passage or is there a "reference" to this passage as well? In order to understand the reference, we need to understand the account of Noah.

> The Lord saw that the *wickedness of man* was great on the earth, and that every intent of the *thoughts of his heart was only evil continually.* The Lord was sorry that He had made man on the earth, and He was grieved in His heart. The Lord said, "I will blot out man whom I have created from the face of the land, from man to animals to creeping things and to birds of the sky; for I am sorry that I have made them." But Noah found favor in the eyes of the Lord. (Gen 6:5-8 NASB, emphasis mine)

The account of the Flood is the first example of God pouring out his wrath upon the earth. Besides being an historical account that explains a great deal about the natural world, God gave us this description as a picture of his Wrath to come. The reason for the wrath is clearly stated related to Noah's day. At that time, *the hearts of the unrighteous conceived evil continually*. If Jesus's words are to be believed, this will also be the condition on the earth at the time of his second coming. The prophet Daniel also speaks of the growth of evil in men's hearts:

> And at the latter time of their kingdom, *when their sins are coming to the full (Gk: PLEROO, meaning "being made complete")*, there shall arise a king (the Antichrist) bold in countenance, and *understanding riddles.* And his power shall be great, and he shall destroy wonderfully, and prosper, and practice, and shall destroy mighty men, and the holy people. (Dan. 8:23-24 LXX, clarification and emphasis mine)

Ch. 14: Event Seven: Rapture and Wrath

We notice that the Antichrist will arise when the sins of his followers are "being made completely full"; when his subjects think of evil continuously. This is the first aspect of the "reference" to the days of Noah.

There are also a number of subtle details about the account of Noah that further picture the Rapture. Notice that God shuts the door of the Ark. Jesus references this similar event when he shuts the door to the *Wedding Supper of the Lamb* in his Parable of the Ten Virgins:

> And they that entered went in male and female of all flesh, as God commanded Noe (Noah), and *the Lord God shut the ark* outside of him. (Gen. 7:16 LXX, clarification and emphasis mine)

> Those who were ready went in with him to the wedding feast; *and the door was shut*. (Matt. 25:11 NASB, emphasis mine)

We also learn that at the very beginning of the narrative, God warns Noah that the flood is coming. He gives him a seven-day lead time to load the Ark. It is at that time that he and his household help load all the living creatures into the Ark:

> Then the Lord said to Noah, "Enter the ark, you and all your household, for you alone I have seen to be righteous before me in this time . . . For *after seven more days*, I will send rain on the earth forty days and forty nights; and I will blot out from the face of the land every living thing that I have made. (Gen. 7:1, 4 NASB, emphasis mine)

Will there be a prophetic fulfillment of this warning prior to the Rapture? Is this warning what Joel speaks about in his picture of the *Celestial Earthly Disturbance*?

> It will come about after this that *I will pour out my Spirit on all mankind*; and your sons and daughters will *prophesy*, your old men will *dream dreams*, your young men will *see visions*. Even on the male and female servants *I will pour*

278

out My Spirit in those days. I will *display wonders in the sky and on the earth,* blood, fire and columns of smoke. The sun will be turned into darkness and the moon into blood before the great and awesome day of the LORD comes. And it will come about that whoever calls on the name of the LORD will be delivered; for on Mount Zion and in Jerusalem there will be those who escape, as the LORD has said, even among the survivors whom the LORD calls. (Joel 2:28 – 32 NASB, emphasis mine)

Is this why Paul says, "But you, brethren, are not in darkness, that the day would overtake you like a thief" (1 Thess. 5:4 NASB)? Is it because God will individually alert the faithful to the timing of the great and awesome Day of the Lord? We can only speculate because scripture is not completely clear on this point. In my opinion, God will use the *Celestial Earthly Disturbance* and *visions* in conjunction to prepare his people.

THE *DAY OF THE LORD*

As we have discussed previously, the Resurrection, Rapture and the beginning of the Wrath of God all happen on *a single day* known as the *Day of the Lord*. In the first century, the believers in the Thessalonian church received a forged letter as if from Paul saying the *Day of the Lord* had already come. Paul wrote the epistle of 2 Thessalonians to answer their concerns which gives us a magnificent perspective on what occurs on this day. This forgery the Thessalonians seemed to receive is a blessing to us 2000 years later because Paul put in writing for all time these timeless truths he had only told the Thessalonians in person.

Paul's understanding of the events that will happen on the *Day of the Lord* came primarily from the *Olivet Discourse* given to us by the Lord himself as we will soon see.

For after all *it is only just for God to repay with affliction those who afflict you*, and to *give relief to you who are afflicted and to us as well when the Lord*

Jesus will be revealed from heaven with His mighty angels in flaming fire, dealing out retribution to those who do not know God and to those who do not obey the gospel of our Lord Jesus. These will pay the penalty of eternal destruction, away from the presence of the Lord and from the glory of His power, when He comes to be glorified in His saints on that day, and to be marveled at among all who have believed—for our testimony to you was believed. (2 Thess. 1:6-10 NASB, emphasis mine)

This passage describes the events of the *Day of the Lord*:

- The dual purpose of the *Day of the Lord* is stated: 1) Relief for the saints and 2) Affliction for the unrighteous. *This is a key insight*. The Day of the Lord has *two purposes* not just one.

- Second, Jesus will be revealed from heaven on that Day with his mighty angels in flaming fire. (This is further explanation of Jesus's description in Matt. 24:30-31). The sign of the Son of Man from this verse in Matthew refers to is his Shekinah Glory which is called *flaming fire* in 2 Thess. 1.

In regard to the *relief of the saints*, we see that this comes when Jesus is revealed with his mighty angels in Shekinah glory. It does not happen until that point. Notice it says it is relief for the Thessalonians and Paul as well. *These are both incredibly significant points*. Our relief does not come from a silent rapture. Jesus is revealed on the day that all will see him. Matt. 24:30 states "all the tribes of the earth will mourn." It is also the day of the Resurrection as well. Paul and the Thessalonians will receive their relief on the same day as all the saints throughout history. We know the Resurrection occurs *before* the Rapture (1 Thess. 4:16-17); thus the revealing of Jesus, the Resurrection and the Rapture all happen on this one day, at the start of the *Day of the Lord*.

Not only will relief happen on that day, but immediately after the Resurrection and Rapture, Jesus will begin to punish the wicked on that day as well. Jesus explains the dual nature of this day in Luke.

And just as it happened in the days of Noah, so it will be also in the days of the Son of Man: they were eating, they were drinking, they were marrying, they were being given in marriage, until the day that Noah entered the ark, and the flood came and destroyed them all . . . On the day that Lot went out from Sodom it rained *fire and brimstone from heaven and destroyed them all. It will be just the same on the day that the Son of Man is revealed.* (Luke 17:26-27, 29-30, emphasis mine)

Jesus is telling us that on the same day he is *revealed* (with his angels in flaming fire) and saves the righteous (pictured by Noah and Lot), punishment will be poured out on the wicked that includes fire and brimstone. The Genesis account gives us details about that time that are known as the *Days of Lot*:

Lot went out and spoke to his sons-in-laws, who were to marry his daughters, and said, "Up, get out of this place, for the Lord will destroy the city." *But he appeared to his sons-in-laws to be jesting.* When morning dawned, the angels urged Lot, saying, "Up, take your wife and your two daughters who are here, or you will be swept away in the punishment of the city." *But he hesitated.* So the men seized his hand and the hand of his wife and the hands of his two daughters, for the compassion of the Lord was upon him; and they brought him out, and put him outside the city. . . . Then the Lord rained on Sodom and Gomorrah brimstone and fire from the Lord out of heaven, and He overthrew those cities, and all the valley, and all the inhabitants of the cities, and what grew on the ground. *But his wife, from behind him, looked back, and she became a pillar of salt.* (Gen. 19:14-16, 24-26 NASB, emphasis mine)

God's Word said it will be "just like" this when the Day of the Lord comes. Notice how Lot's future son-in-laws think he is only jesting and how Lot himself hesitates. It appears that this type of hesitation may be a real possibility when the Rapture occurs. As we will learn later in this chapter, God transformed even the limestone of the towns of the valley into salt. For Lot's wife to be so transformed, it is likely she did more than just "look back." Might this mean she hesitated and attempted to grab some of her belongings and thus was caught in the judgment? Is this why Lot's wife was *behind him*? We can only surmise, but Jesus's warning seems to imply it:

> Whoever seeks to keep his life will lose it, and whoever loses his life will preserve it. I tell you, on that *night* (Jesus is indicating he will come at *night*) there will be two in one bed; one will be taken and the other will be left. There will be two women grinding at the same place; one will be taken and the other will be left. Two men will be in the field; one will be taken and the other will be left." And answering they said to Him, "Where, Lord?" And He said to them, "Where the body (Gk: SOMA, meaning "living body") is, there also the vultures (Gk: AETOI, meaning "eagles") will be gathered (Gk: EPISYNACHTHESONTAI, meaning "will gather together")." (Luke 17:33-37 NASB, clarification and emphasis mine)

There are those in the Church who say the ones "taken" in this passage are the ones taken to punishment. However, the analogy within the account of "the days of Lot" renders this meaning nonsensical. The ones taken are the ones *saved*. The ones left behind in Sodom faced fire and brimstone, just as those who will be left behind after the Rapture will face God's wrath.

The disciples then ask a question, "where Lord?" I *think* they meant "where will this separation of righteous and unrighteous take place?" Jesus answers this question with a strange, short parable which has perplexed the Church for centuries. Improper theology has led most commentators to assume that this parable is about Armageddon. This theory holds the *vultures* to be the birds who feast on the flesh of the Antichrist armies in Rev. 19:17-18. This interpretation has caused translators to claim the AETOI ("eagles") are *vultures* and the EPISYNACHTHESONTAI ("will gather together") is only a gathering of these vultures. *Eagles* can be both a predatory bird and a scavenger bird so the idea of calling them "vultures" is not outlandish. However, we must remember that this short parable or illustration does not have to be totally literal. It is a parable after all. The term AETOI only appears four other times in the New

Testament. It is found in the parallel passage in Matt. 24:28 and three times in Revelation (Rev. 4:7, 8:13, and 12:14.) In Revelation, all three uses of AETOI refer to *eagles* that are obviously actually *angels*. By claiming the AETOI are "vultures," traditional commentators on this short parable stress a minor portion of an eagle's behavior and ignore the sole use of the term AETOI (*angles*) in the New Testament.

EPISYNACHTESONTAI also appears in two of the most famous passages about the Rapture (Matt. 24:31 and 2 Thess. 2:1). In the Matthew reference, the *angels gather together* the living saints and the resurrected saints. The body (Gk: SOMA) in Luke's version of the parable is a living body. Interestingly, in a parallel account in Matt 24:28, the body is a dead body (Gk: PTOMA). In combination, the passages in Luke and Matthew give us the complete picture of the Body of Christ, both living and dead (soon to be resurrected.) By substituting the proper translations for the word "body" and "gather" into the passage, along with using the word "angels" for "eagles," we get this "modified" translation:

Where the Body (living and dead) is, there the angels will gather together.

Translated this way, the parable is obviously about the Rapture of the resurrected and the living survivors when the angels gather them! But does this modified translation hold up in context? In Luke, Jesus tells the parable after discussing the separating of the righteous from the unrighteous. After this, the disciples ask "where?" Maybe the disciples were worried this separation would only occur in Jerusalem or on the Mount of Olives, etc. In this brief parable, was Jesus telling them that where ever the Body of Christ is (in Luke he uses SOMA for body), there the angels will gather them together? I think so. The *living righteous* would have been the disciples' main concern not the unrighteous, and Jesus was telling them that they need not worry. Where ever the righteous will be on that Day, the angels will find them.

In Matthew, the contextual clues are even stronger. The parable occurs immediately after the *Sign of the Son of Man* found in Matt. 24:27 and is immediately followed by verses 29-31, which give the cosmic signs and Rapture. Completely surrounded by verses that concern the return of Jesus, the parable must by context also involve the return of Jesus. In the parable, the Lord uses the exact same word "gather together" for what the angels will do in verse 31. By using this exact same Greek word, Jesus is interpreting his short parable for the disciples so they don't misunderstand it. Since we see the parable in Luke as well (Luke 17), Jesus may have taught this illustration of the "Vultures" several times. Here, in Matthew's account (Matt. 24), Jesus wants to leave no doubt what it means so he says the "eagles gather together" in v. 28 and the "angels gather together" in v. 31.

In contrast, let's examine how an *Armageddon interpretation* for this short parable might look in context. We have already seen that traditional church theory considers the vultures (actually "eagles") are the birds who feast on the flesh of the Antichrist's armies. If this interpretation were true, the Luke passage makes no sense. First, it uses SOMA to mean a "living body." Scavenger birds wouldn't be feasting on the living. Second, the disciples ask the question "where?" meaning *where does the separation of the righteous and unrighteous take place?* An answer by Jesus of "where the birds eat the flesh of the Antichrist's armies" would be totally unacceptable. That might be an answer to "when" (an incorrect answer), but not an answer to the question the disciples actually asked which was "where." Separation of righteous and unrighteous will occur all over the world, not just near Armageddon.

If the Matthew account of the parable was about Armageddon, it would chronologically follow the return of Jesus in Matt. 24:30-31 just like the Wrath of God will follow the Rapture. But it doesn't, it precedes verse 31. Armageddon will not precede the return of Jesus coming on the clouds. Again, an interpretation of the short parable of the "Vultures" as being about Armageddon *fails* in the context of both passages where it occurs.

The reason this obvious interpretation of these passages is not commonly taught as the Rapture is that Matthew 24:28 shows the event clearly occurring *after* the *Great Tribulation*. Although this is proper theology, it flies in the face of the *Pre-Tribulation Rapture* theory. Additionally, *Post-Tribulation Rapture* theory wants to place the physical return of Jesus to the earth (the Second Coming) in Matthew 24:30-31. They also have a vested interest in wrongly assuming this parable concerns Armageddon.

WHEN DOES THE *DAY OF THE LORD* OCCUR?

We have already seen that the *Day of the Lord* contains both relief for the righteous (Resurrection and Rapture) and punishment of the wicked (God's Wrath beginning with fire and brimstone.) Paul continues to give the Thessalonians instruction on the signs to look for prior to the *Day of the Lord*:

> Now we request you, brethren, *with regard to the coming of our Lord Jesus Christ and our gathering together to Him,* that you not be quickly shaken from your composure or be disturbed either by a spirit or a message or a letter as if from us, to the effect that the day of the Lord has come. Let no one in any way deceive you, for *it will not come unless the apostasy comes first, and the man of lawlessness is revealed*, the son of destruction, who opposes and exalts himself above every so-called god or object of worship, so that he *takes his seat in the temple of God, displaying himself as being God.* (2 Thess. 2:1-4 NASB, emphasis mine)

Paul refers back to the coming of the Lord and our gathering together to him, which he mentioned in the previous few verses. This is obviously the *Rapture*. Notice how he also calls it the *Day of the Lord*. This is further proof that the Rapture occurs on the Day of the Lord. Paul then says *two things* must happen *prior* to the *Day of the Lord*:

1) The Great Apostasy
2) The Abomination of Desolation (which occurs as part of the revealing of the man of sin)

These *two major signs* are also taken directly from Jesus's *Olivet Discourse*:

> Then they will deliver you to tribulation, and will kill you, and you will be hated by all nations because of my name. *At that time many will fall away and will betray one another and hate one another.* Many false prophets will arise and will mislead many. Because lawlessness is increased, most people's love

will grow cold . . . "Therefore when you see the *abomination of desolation* which was spoken of through Daniel the prophet, standing in the holy place (let the reader understand), then those who are in Judea must flee to the mountains. (Matt. 24:9-12, 15-16, emphasis mine)

Returning to Thessalonians, we see that deception by the Antichrist is to be expected. Interestingly, this matches the Olivet Discourse as well!

The one whose coming is in accord with the activity of Satan, with *all power and signs and false wonders*, and with all the *deception of wickedness* for those who perish, because they did not receive the love of the truth so as to be saved. For this reason God will send upon them a *deluding influence* so that they will believe what is false. (2 Thess. 2:9-11 NASB, emphasis mine)

Many false prophets will arise and will *mislead many* . . . For *false Christs and false prophets will arise and will show great signs and wonders*, so as to mislead, if possible, even the elect. Behold, I have told you in advance. (Matt. 24:11, 24-25 NASB, emphasis mine)

These passages give us the "why" there will be a Great Apostasy. Churchgoers will be deceived by the Antichrist. As we can see, 2 Thess. is a restatement of the major themes of the *Olivet Discourse* with added information.

2 Thessalonians also allows us to perfectly time the *Day of the Lord* (and the Rapture!) We can immediately *eliminate* a *Pre-Tribulation* or *Mid-Tribulation* timing for the Day of the Lord because the Abomination of Desolation that comes at the *Midpoint* must come first. But interestingly, it also *eliminates* a *Post-Tribulation Rapture* because of what the related scriptures in Luke 17 and Rev. 8 have to say. *This is a very important nuance of interpretation that is not well understood.* Only a *Pre-Wrath Rapture* timing is consistent with all the scriptures.

From this study, we know that on the Day of the Lord, *fire will fall upon the earth.* This is confirmed in other verses throughout scripture:

But by His word the present heavens and earth are being reserved for *fire*, kept for the Day of Judgment and destruction of ungodly men. (2 Pet. 3:7 NASB, emphasis mine)

But a terrifying expectation of judgment and the fury of a *fire* which will consume the adversaries (Heb. 10:27 NASB, emphasis mine)

Upon the wicked He will rain snares; *Fire and brimstone and burning wind* will be the portion of their cup. (Psalm 11:6 NASB, emphasis mine)

He (those who take the Mark) also will drink of the wine of the wrath of God, which is mixed in full strength in the cup of His anger; and he will be tormented with *fire and brimstone* in the presence of the holy angels and in the presence of the Lamb. (Rev, 14:10 NASB, clarification and emphasis mine)

The following overwhelmingly awesome picture of the *Day of the Lord* shows deliverance in the midst of fire:

Then the earth shook and quaked; and the foundations of the mountains were trembling and were shaken, because He was angry. Smoke went up out of His nostrils, and fire from His mouth devoured; Coals were kindled by it. He bowed the heavens also, and came down with thick darkness under His feet. (Jesus coming on the clouds) He rode upon a cherub and flew; and He sped upon the wings of the wind. He made darkness His hiding place, His canopy around Him, darkness of waters, thick clouds of the skies. From the brightness before Him (Jesus's Shekinah glory) passed His thick clouds, *hailstones and coals of fire*. The Lord also thundered in the heavens, and the Most High uttered His voice, *hailstones and coals of fire*. He sent out His arrows, and scattered them and lightning flashes in abundance, and routed them. Then the channels of water appeared, and the foundations of the world were laid bare at your rebuke, O Lord, at the blast of the breath of your nostrils. He sent from on high, He took me; He drew me out of many waters. He delivered me from my strong enemy, and from those who hated me, for they were too mighty for me. They confronted me in the day of my calamity, but the Lord was my stay. (Psalm 18:7-18 NASB, clarification and emphasis mine)

I think it is universally accepted that Jesus will judge the world with *fire*. If we study Revelation carefully, however, there is only one place where fire comes down from heaven that could be the fire on the *Day of the Lord*: the *First Trumpet* Judgment.

> The first sounded (*First Trumpet*), and there came *hail and fire, mixed with blood*, and they were thrown to the earth; and a third of the earth was burned up, and a third of the trees were burned up, and all the green grass was burned up. (Rev. 8:7 NASB, clarification and emphasis mine)

The mixture of hail and fire is a direct reference to Psalm 18 above. The *Gog/Magog War passage in Ezekiel 38* also references hail and fire, and additionally adds the *blood*. "With pestilence and with *blood* I will enter into judgment with him; and I will rain on him and on his troops, and on the many peoples who are with him, a torrential rain, with *hailstones, fire and brimstone* (Ezek. 38:22, emphasis mine)." This book's *Pre-Wrath* position teaches the Resurrection/Rapture at the *Seventh Seal*. After the Rapture (on the same day) will come the Wrath of God. A "half an hour" (not necessarily literal) after the *Seventh Seal* is opened, the *First Trumpet* is blown. This is completely consistent with a *Pre-Wrath Rapture*. It is not consistent with a *Post-Tribulation Rapture* on the last day however. Nowhere in scripture is there a picture of fire falling on the last day.

How Long is the *Day of the Lord*?

The *Wrath of God* is a *year-long*. This is a source of eminence confusion as well. Most commentators believe Wrath of God and the *Day of the Lord* are only a day-long, yet scripture clearly defines it as a year.

> For the Lord has a *day of vengeance, a year of recompense* for the cause of
> Zion. (Isa. 34:8, emphasis mine)

God calls his Wrath both a *day of vengeance* and a *year of recompense* (Heb: SHILLUM, meaning "retribution"). Clearly his Wrath will begin on a specific day, the first day of the *Day of the Lord*, but last for an *entire year*. Later in Isaiah, God restates the purposes of this year:

> For the *day of vengeance* was in my heart, and my *year of redemption* (Heb: GAAL, meaning to "act as a kinsman redeemer") has come. (Isa. 63:4 NASB, clarification and emphasis mine)

In this verse we see that yes, it is a Day of *wrath and vengeance*, but it is also a time of *redemption*. Jesus will act as a "kinsman redeemer" to buy back the dominion of this world from Satan. He will restore the dominion to the rightful owners: Jesus and the saints. At the end of the *Sixth Year* of the 70th Week, Jesus will break the *Seventh Seal* on the *7 Sealed Scroll*. At that moment, Jesus will come upon the clouds of heaven and resurrect and rapture his Church. Then he will pour out his wrath and vengeance upon the unrepentant. During this year of wrath, he will also redeem or buy back his dominion. Upon the blowing of the *Seventh Trumpet*, God's plan to regain the dominion of the earth will be completed. In Revelation we read:

> Then the *seventh angel* sounded; and there were loud voices in heaven, saying,
> *"The kingdom of the world has become the kingdom of our Lord and of His*
> *Christ; and He will reign forever and ever."* And the twenty-four elders, who
> sit on their thrones before God, fell on their faces and worshiped God, saying,
> "We give You thanks, O Lord God, the Almighty, who are and who were,
> because You have taken Your great power and have begun to reign (Rev.
> 11:15-17 NASB, emphasis mine)

Ch. 14: Event Seven: Rapture and Wrath

At this moment when Christ assumes his great power, Satan will not surrender so easily. He is determined to put up one final struggle. Jesus commands his angels to pour out the final judgments upon Satan's forces who are still in rebellion in what is known as the *7 Bowl Judgments*. The trumpets and bowls are God's "Shock and Awe," bombarding the kingdoms of this earth prior to the invasion-force landing. That invasion force will be Christ, his Holy Angels and the Church physically descending during the Second Coming.

You may have a question at this point. As we have previously indicated, the time between the Rapture on Yom Teruah of the *Sixth Year* of the 70th Week and the physical return of Jesus at the Second Coming on Yom Kippur of the *Seventh Year* of the 70th Week is actually *one year and ten days*. The verses we have just looked at in Isaiah both indicate that the Day of the Lord will be *one year* long. To help explain the dichotomy, there is yet a third verse in Isaiah that clarifies why that year might be *a year and ten days long*:

> To proclaim *the favorable year of the Lord* and *the day of vengeance* of our God (Isa. 61:2 NASB, emphasis mine)

The first half of this verse from Isaiah 61 was quoted by Jesus in the synagogue in Nazareth. Most scholars associate "the favorable year of the Lord" with the *Jubilee year*. Interestingly, the *Jubilee year* starts on Yom Kippur (Lev. 25:9) rather than on Yom Teruah (also called Rosh Hashanah) as must Jewish years do. This makes the year *before* a Jubilee year *exactly one year and ten days long*. This is the length of time we propose for the Day of the Lord (God's Wrath). If God's Wrath occurs in a year immediately preceding a Jubilee year, it will be *one year and ten days* long. A Jubilee year beginning precisely at the Second Coming (on Yom Kippur) would indeed fulfill the promise inherent in a Jubilee of "setting the captives free." The Jews have been captive to sin, but the Jewish remnant will receive their salvation when Jesus is seen returning in the sky from heaven. These multiple puzzle pieces fitting together with such precision, truly makes me fall before my Savior in awe of the majesty of his perfect plan of salvation as recorded in his inerrant scripture.

SHOCK AND AWE

On March 20, 2003, President George Bush began Operation Iraqi Freedom (the Iraq War) by ordering an overwhelming show of military force nicknamed "Shock and Awe." The term was coined by military strategists Ulman and Wade at the Armed Forces University. Its purpose was to "a military strategy based on achieving rapid dominance over an adversary by the initial imposition of overwhelming force and firepower."[lxi] Americans who are old enough to remember the war were "treated" to nightly pictures of Iraqi targets bursting into flames as USA bombing runs destroyed significant amounts of the Iraqi infrastructure.

The Iraqi War will be nothing compared to the "shock and awe" Jesus will pour out on an unbelieving world. The Old Testament account of Lot and his escape from Sodom, mentioned in the Gospel of Luke, with God's Wrath then poured out on the sinful towns of the area, pictures this future event:

> It was the same as happened in the *days of Lot*: they were eating, they were drinking, they were buying, they were selling, they were planting, they were building; *but on the day that Lot went out from Sodom it rained fire and brimstone from heaven and destroyed them all. It will be just the same on the day that the Son of Man is revealed.* On that day, the one who is on the housetop and whose goods are in the house must not go down to take them out; and likewise the one who is in the field must not turn back. Remember Lot's wife. Whoever seeks to keep his life will lose it, and whoever loses his life will preserve it. (Luke 17:28-33 NASB, emphasis mine)

The Rapture happens at the appointed time on *Yom Teruah* (Feast of Trumpets) at the end of the *Sixth Year* of the 70th Week of Daniel, and the first of the 7 Trumpets begins blowing *on the same day*. In Luke 17:29, Jesus is clear that on the day he is revealed coming on the clouds, he will both rapture his Church and also begin to pour out his wrath. Although the saints will be entering a year of Sabbath rest in heaven after the Rapture, this *Seventh Year* of the 70th Week will be anything but restful for the unsaved. God's Wrath will begin with fire and brimstone poured out on a third of the earth, just as was poured out on *Sodom and the other Cities of The Valley* in Genesis. In Revelation we read:

> Then the angel took the censer and filled it with the fire of the altar, and threw it to the earth; and *there followed peals of thunder and sounds and flashes of lightning and an earthquake.* And the seven angels who had the *seven trumpets* prepared themselves to sound them. *The first sounded, and there came hail and fire, mixed with blood*, and they were thrown to the earth; and a third of the earth was burned up, *and a third of the trees were burned up, and all the green grass was burned up.* (Rev. 8:5-7 NASB, emphasis mine)

THUNDERING AND SEVEN THUNDERS

Thundering and lightning mark the transition between phases of God's redemption of the earth, described in Revelation. There are four sets of these events of *thundering and lightning* that are progressive in nature. The chart below describes the four references in Revelation (Figure 36: Timing of the Thunderings in Revelation):

Timing of Thundering, Lighning, Voices, and Earthquakes	Revelation	Specifics
Prior to the Seals	Rev. 4:5	Lightning, "peals of thunder," and seven lamps burning before the throne
Prior to the Trumpets	Rev. 8:5	Lightning, "peals of thunder," and an earthquake
Prior to the Bowls	Rev. 11:19	Lightning, "peals of thunder," an earthquake, and a hailstorm
After the Bowls	Rev. 16:18	Lightning, sounds, "peals of thunder," an earthquake that levels all the cities of earth, and 100 lb. hailstones

Figure 36: Timing of the Thundering in Revelation

When I say the "thunderings" are progressive, I mean that they become more intense with each time. Prior to the seals, we see only lightning and thunder. At each successive transition, we notice something new added: earthquakes, hailstorms, and "sounds." The intensity of the events increases as well. The final earthquake levels all the cities of the earth and the hailstones at that time will be 100 pounds each!

This "progressive" nature of God's judgments, worsening with time, is seen repeatedly throughout Revelation. For instance during the *Sixth Seal*, the islands and mountains are moved out of their places (Rev. 6:14), whereas at the *Seventh Bowl*, the islands and mountains were no more (Rev. 16:20). Additionally many of the trumpet judgments afflict 1/3 of the earth whereas the bowl judgments afflict the entire earth. The purpose of the progressive nature of judgment is God's mercy and compassion. He desires all to come to faith in him, so he gradually "turns up the heat" to give a maximum time for repentance and turning to him.

In addition to these transitional "thunderings," there are the mysterious *Seven Thunders*. The *Seven Thunders* speak, and what they say is the only portion of

Revelation that is "sealed." Let's look at the beginning of the passage in Revelation about these "Thunders."

> I saw another strong angel coming down out of heaven, clothed with a cloud; and the rainbow was upon his head, and his face was like the sun, and his feet like pillars of fire; and he had in his hand *a little book* which was open. He placed his right foot on the sea and his left on the land; and he cried out with a loud voice, as when a lion roars; and when he had cried out, the *seven peals of thunder* uttered their voices. (Rev. 10:1-3 NASB, emphasis mine)

Who is the "strong angel" pictured in this vision? Personally, I believe it is Jesus. He is clothed with a cloud (God appeared as a pillar of cloud during the Exodus, Jesus is seated on a cloud in Rev. 14, and he comes on the clouds in Matt. 24:30-31), his face is like the sun and his legs like pillars of fire (John's previous vision of Jesus shared these traits), and his voice is like a lion (Jesus is the Lion of Judah). The strong angel also holds the "small scroll" which is the *7 Sealed Scroll* [see Chapter Five: "Signed, Sealed, and Delivered (Revelation 4-5)"]. Jesus is the one who held this *Scroll* in his hand and opened it. In this vision we see that the *Scroll* is already open. The strong angel (who I assume is Jesus) then places his feet on the land and the sea. We know that when *the Beast* arose from the sea, the *Dragon* (Satan) stood on the seashore (Rev. 13:1) which is indicative of his dominion. By standing on the land *and* sea, Jesus is staking claim to the dominion Satan stole from Adam. He does this while roaring like the Lion of Judah. I assume this occurs immediately after the "little book (scroll)" is opened.

After Jesus stakes this claim, the *Seven Thunders* speak, and John is forbidden to write what the Thunders say:

> I heard a voice from heaven saying, "*Seal* up the things which the *seven peals of thunder* have spoken and *do not write them*." (Rev. 10:5 NASB, emphasis mine)

This is the only section of Revelation that is sealed. Obviously, Jesus is holding these *seven peals of thunder* (revelations) back until the time of the end. I notice with great interest that what the *Seven Thunders* spoke is *sealed*, and John is even prohibited from writing it down. We discussed in Chapter Five: "Signed, Sealed, and Delivered (Revelation 4-5)" that many commentators on Daniel believe the text of the *Book of Daniel* is sealed (Dan. 12:4). These commentators believe that God has caused us to not fully understand the text supernaturally. I do not believe that is correct. In this instance in Revelation, John is not permitted to write the material down. True sealing seems to involve not even recording the details of the sealed material.

Who are the *Seven Thunders*? We aren't told, but I surmise they are the seven angels who stand before the throne of God. At the end of the passage about the *Seven Thunders*, we are told the final one is the "seventh angel."

> *In the days* of the *voice* of the *seventh angel*, when he is about to sound (Gk: SALPEZEIN, meaning "to sound a trumpet"), then the mystery of God is finished, as He preached to His servants the prophets. (Rev. 10:7 NASB, clarification and emphasis mine)

We notice that it is in "the days of the *voice* of the seventh angel" that the mystery of God is finished (all revelations will have been revealed). We also notice that the seventh angel also sounds a trumpet. Are the *Seven Thunders* the voices of the seven angels sounding the seven Trumpet Judgments? I believe they are. In my opinion, God will reveal additional revelations to the unsaved with each successive Trumpet Judgment. Our God desires that none should perish. Even during his Wrath, he will still be appealing for the unsaved to repent. Why are these final seven revelations sealed? We cannot know God's ways and say for certain. God doesn't reveal the reason. If the thesis that the Thunders are sounded during the Wrath of God, the Church is already raptured. These messages are not for the Church, and we do not need to know them.

Finally, this verse from Revelation reveals an aspect of the *trumpet judgments* of which most are unaware. Rev. 10:7 mentions "in the days" of the voice of the seventh angel. Hence, it is assumed that the seventh angel's "thundering" lasts for multiple days. Also, he speaks before he blows the trumpet as the verse says his voice is "when he is about to sound."

THE SEVEN *TRUMPET JUDGMENTS*

Over the course of the final year, the *Seventh Year,* of the 70th Week of Daniel, *seven trumpets* will blow and judgments will befall the unbelieving, as summarized in the following chart (Figure 37: Seven *Trumpet Judgments*):

Trumpet	Judgment
One	Hail and Fire burns 1/3 of the land
Two	Mountain (?) falls into the sea and 1/3 of sea life dies
Three	A star falls named Wormwood and polutes 1/3 of the fresh water
Four	1/3 of the sun, moon, and stars are darkened
Five	Bottomless pit is opened and locut army tortures those with the Mark of the Beast
Six	1/3 of mankind is killed by 200 million man army
Seven	Second Coming. Kingdoms of this world become Jesus's. The Seventh Trumpet opens the seven bowl judgments

Figure 37: Seven Trumpet Judgments

THE *FIRST TRUMPET*

We have already seen that the *First Trumpet* judgment is hail, fire, and blood cast upon the earth that burns up a third of the trees and the grass. It should be noted that, initially, the first four trumpets of God's Wrath do not directly affect the *people* but the *earth* itself. This is God's overwhelming mercy, still hoping for repentance from the wicked. In Isaiah we see this motivation played out:

Woe to the proud crown of the *drunkards of Ephraim*, and to the fading flower of its glorious beauty, which is at the head of the fertile valley of *those who are overcome with wine*! Behold, the Lord has a strong and mighty agent; *as a storm of hail, a tempest of destruction*, like a storm of mighty overflowing waters, He has *cast it down to the earth* with His hand. (Isa. 28:1-2 NASB, emphasis mine)

The term "drunkards" does not refer to those drunk with physical wine, but rather to the members of the house of Israel (Ephraim) who have been overcome (Gk: NIKAO) with the *wine of the immorality of the Harlot*, which is clarified in the following passages in Revelation: "The great harlot who sits on many waters, with whom the kings of the earth committed acts of immorality, and those who dwell on the earth were made *drunk with the wine of her immorality*" (Rev. 17:1-2 NASB). In the next section, we will learn the Harlot is the religion of the people of the Antichrist. In the above passage in Isaiah we see God uses the *hail* as an agent to get the attention of those of the house of Israel who have been led astray. He is still patient; wishing them to come to repentance. In addition, we should note that the concept of "hail and fire" is a direct reference by John to Psalm 18:

He rode upon a cherub and flew; and he sped upon the wings of the wind. He made darkness His hiding place, his canopy around him, darkness of waters, thick clouds of the skies. From the brightness before Him passed His thick clouds, *hailstones and coals of fire*. (Psalm 18:10-12 NASB, emphasis mine)

This passage from Psalm 18 is obviously referring to the return of Christ coming on the clouds and the dual purpose of the day Christ returns. He will save the righteous upon the breaking of the *Seventh Seal* and punish the wicked at the blowing of the *First Trumpet*.

Some have claimed that the *hail, fire, and blood* are reminiscent of the debris field of a comet. This is possible. The word translated "blood" (Gk: HAIMATI) can

297

mean literal blood or it can mean the color of blood such as in a "blood moon." This later meaning is likely so this might be a mineral such as iron oxide which is common in comets and meteorites and has a red color. There are many passages that indicate that a great *drought* will occur during the final years of the 70th Week of Daniel (Rev. 11:6). If a comet debris field were to fall on the earth during a drought, it is entirely likely that a fire could be kindled that would burn vast amounts of forest and grasslands. If brimstone (elemental sulfur) were part of the comet field, the fire would spread uncontrollably as sulfur burns quickly, easily, and intensely.

SODOM AND GOMORRAH

Recent archaeological discoveries near the coast of the Dead Sea have revealed the remains of five ancient cities. We generically refer to these cities as Sodom and Gomorrah. Peter and Jude tell us that the *remains* of these cities are left to us as *examples* to live godly lives. As our nation and our world continue to run headlong toward the depravity of those ancient cities, we need to examine this teaching in depth. If the ruins of Sodom are an example, let's start by looking at the warnings of Jude where we find this truth:

> Sodom and Gomorrah and the cities around them, since they in the same way as these indulged in gross immorality and went after strange (unnatural) flesh, are *exhibited as an example* in undergoing the punishment of *eternal* (divine) *fire*. (Jude 1:7 NASB, clarification and emphasis mine)

Notice that these cities are *exhibited* as an example. Presenting something as an exhibit means physically displaying it. Despite the fact you probably haven't seen pictures of the modern remains of Sodom; they must be present if God's Word says they are exhibited—and they are! Also notice Jude calls the fire "eternal" fire. It's still not burning at the present time. A better translation may be a fire of divine origin, which will occur in the future.

Peter had this to say about Sodom and Gomorrah:

He condemned the cities of Sodom and Gomorrah to destruction by *reducing them to ashes*, having *made them an example* to those who would live ungodly lives thereafter; and if He rescued righteous Lot, *oppressed by the sensual conduct of unprincipled men* (for by what he saw and heard that righteous man, while living among them, felt his righteous soul tormented day after day by their *lawless deeds*), then the Lord knows how to rescue the godly from temptation, and to keep the unrighteous under punishment for the day of judgment, and *especially those who indulge the flesh in its corrupt desires and despise authority*. (2 Peter 2:6-10 NASB, clarification and emphasis mine)

First, notice God reduced the cities to ashes. He *didn't cover them* with ashes like Pompeii, He *turned them into ashes*. This is entirely consistent with the archeological findings near the Dead Sea that we will discuss in the next section.

Second, notice that the "remains" of the cities are given to us as an example of what will happen in the *future* judgment during the Day of the Lord. God's wrath on Sodom and Gomorrah is an example of "near/far" fulfillment, with partial fulfillment having occurred in history and a second fulfillment yet in the future. Peter says this warning is especially for those who indulge the flesh *and* despise the authority of God's Word. Isn't this exactly what we are experiencing in today's world? People are despising the Word of God because they love sin.

Third, notice the historical account of Lot's escape from Sodom is also given as an example for the righteous of God's ability to save us before the judgment. Jesus explained how this will occur in the last section. We have seen that during the *First Trumpet* judgment 1/3 of the earth is consumed by the divine fire. This will be massive destruction. It will take the world by complete surprise. They will be doing normal, earthly tasks of eating, drinking, buying, selling, etc. Paul, in his first letter to the Thessalonian church, even tells us they will be saying "Peace and safety" right before this horrible destruction:

For the Lord Himself will descend from heaven with a shout, with the voice of the archangel and with the trumpet of God, and the dead in Christ will rise first. Then we who are alive and remain will be caught up together with them in the clouds to meet the Lord in the air (the *Rapture*), and so we shall always be with the Lord. *Therefore **comfort** one another with these (following) words:* Now as to the times and the epochs, brethren, you have no need of anything to be written to you. For you yourselves know full well that the *day of the Lord* (God's Wrath) will come just like a thief in the night. While they are saying, "*Peace and safety!*" then destruction will come upon them suddenly like labor pains upon a woman with child, and they will not escape. *But you, brethren, are not in darkness, that the day would overtake you like a thief;* for you are all sons of light and sons of day. . . *Therefore **encourage** one another* and build up one another. (1 Thess. 4:16 - 5:5, 11 NASB, clarification and emphasis mine)

In most Bibles, this passage contains one of the most unfortunate chapter breaks in all of scripture which has caused this passage to be terribly misunderstood. Chapter breaks were not in the original manuscript. Paul wrote this as a continuous passage and it *should read just as it reads above.* Paul first describes the Rapture. He then relates the rest of the passage (1 Thess. 5:1-11) as the words of encouragement. The *Day of the Lord* (God's Wrath) comes *after* the Rapture. In Luke 17, Jesus tells us it happens *on the very same day.* At this time the unrighteous will be saying "peace and safety." The forces of the Antichrist will have finally finished "shattering the power of the holy people (Christians and Jews)" (Dan. 12:7 NASB), and the Antichrist and his followers will begin to relax, believing they have won. It is then that destruction will come upon them like a thief.

Finally, Paul (in the above 1 Thess. Chapter 4 and 5 verses) uses the *same* phrase (in the Greek) at the beginning and end of the encouragement passage (". . . comfort one another" and ". . . encourage one another") showing this is a unified thought. Unfortunately, this is yet another horribly unfortunate English translation. In the original Greek they are the identical word (PARAKALEITE) from which we get one of the names of the Holy Spirit, the Parakaleite: the Comforter.

The gross misunderstanding of this passage has led some to believe that all will be saying "peace and security" before the 70th Week of Daniel begins or at its *Midpoint*. Both are probably mistaken. It is the *unrighteous* saying "peace and safety." *Christians will know* when the Day of the Lord will come at that point in time. Paul tells us it *won't* come upon *them* as a thief in the night.

THE SINS OF SODOM

Before we move on and discuss some of the amazing archaeological discoveries in the area of Sodom and Gomorrah, let's take a brief look at the sins of Sodom that caused its downfall. They might surprise you.

> Behold, this was the guilt of your sister *Sodom*: she and her daughters had *arrogance*, abundant food and *careless ease*, but she *did not help the poor and needy*. (Ezek. 16:49 NASB, emphasis mine)

> Also *among the prophets* of Jerusalem I have seen a horrible thing: The committing of *adultery* and walking in *falsehood*; and they *strengthen the hands of evildoers*, So that no one has turned back from his wickedness. All of them have become to me like *Sodom*, and her inhabitants like *Gomorrah*. (Jer. 23:14 NASB, emphasis mine)

Wow! I bet you weren't expecting that. In addition to its more famous homosexuality transgressions of Sodom and Gomorrah; the sins of pride, adultery, lying, careless ease, and an unwillingness to help the poor were the ones God chose to mention in Ezekiel's and Jeremiah's passages. Many readers might not share the sin of homosexuality and feel insulated from the punishment of those cities, but many share these other sins. Notice the passage in Jeremiah is directed at men of God! Because of the sins of God's watchmen, no one repented from his sin. Many of us are not doing what we need to do to reconcile the culture to Christ. God is no respecter of persons. It is not just the homosexual he views as "Sodom"; he views *many of us* that way as well.

However, in today's "post-Christian" world where homosexuality is now not only legal, but openly embraced and encouraged, we must not totally disregard that aspect of Jesus's statement, "as in the days of Lot." This world-wide effort to empower homosexuality (even by a American President) is certainly a sign that the Master's return is at hand. The Book of Romans discusses how the rebellious got that way:

> For *the wrath of God is revealed* from heaven against all ungodliness and unrighteousness of *men who suppress the truth in unrighteousness*, because that which is known about God is evident within them; for God made it evident to them. For since the creation of the world His invisible attributes, His eternal power and divine nature, have been clearly seen, being understood through what has been made, so that they are without excuse. (Rom. 1:18-20 NASB, emphasis mine)

This passage from Romans states that the Wrath of God will be poured out on the unrighteous as it was on Sodom because they *suppress the truth*. They do this by committing their acts of unrighteousness. The committing of sins actually suppresses the truth in the conscious mind of the sinner. The passage states they know the truth and have no excuse before the Throne of God. Even though they know God exists, they choose to worship idols instead. Notice in the following passage from Romans that the primary god/idol listed is the "image" of corruptible man. *Secular humanism* is our modern term for this idolatry.

> For even though they knew God, they did not honor Him as God or give thanks, but they became *futile (Gk: MATAIOO, meaning "without purpose")* in their *speculations*, and their foolish heart was darkened. Professing to be wise, they became fools, and exchanged the glory of the incorruptible God for *an image in the form of corruptible man*. (Rom. 1:21-23 NASB, clarification and emphasis mine)

This exchange of idols for the one true God leads to futile thinking. The sinner develops "speculative" theories that exclude God (evolution, etc.). Finally, God "gave them over to a depraved mind" (Rom. 1:28). The Greek word for depraved is ADOKIMON which literally means "counterfeit money" or "worthless." The sinners develop a counterfeit reality, a way of thinking that seems correct to secular human thinking, but leads to destruction and God's wrath.

> For this reason God gave them over to degrading (Gk: ATIMIOS, meaning "dishonorable use") passions (homosexuality); for their women exchanged the natural function for that which is unnatural, and in the same way also the men abandoned the natural function of the woman and burned in their desire toward one another, men with men committing indecent acts and receiving in their own persons the due penalty of their error. And just as they did not see fit to acknowledge God any longer, *God gave them over to a depraved mind*, to do those things which are not proper . . . and although they know the ordinance of God, that those who practice such things are worthy of death, they not only do the same, *but also give hearty approval* to those who practice them. (Rom. 1:26-28 NASB, clarification and emphasis mine)

When the wicked no longer acknowledge God, *he gives them over to a depraved mind* that can no longer think logically. One cannot debate with this type of depraved mind. The *only* solution is the cross of Jesus—repentance and salvation. In cases of total rejection of God, the solution will be his Wrath.

Although homosexuality is not a "worse" sin than others (all sin is rebellion and breaking of God's Law), it is highlighted in this passage specifically as the first example of sin. In the passage, the word translated "degrading" is the Greek word ATIMIOUS which means "dishonorable use." *This word brings meaning to the entire passage in Romans 1*. Homosexuality is a very visible, symbolic "type" of sin in which the sinner uses his body which God made for honor in a dishonorable, non-productive way—basically, a perversion of God's creation. All the other sins in the continuation of this passage, "every kind of wickedness, evil, greed and depravity . . . envy, murder, strife, deceit and malice . . . gossips, slanderers, God-haters, insolent, arrogant and boastful; they invent ways of doing evil; they disobey their parents; they have no understanding, no fidelity, no love, no mercy" (Rom. 1:29-31 NASB) are further examples of using our created being in dishonorable (worthless, unproductive) ways. Homosexuality is symbolic of these sins because in the physical, it cannot be productive; it cannot result in children. In the same way, all of these sins will not produce the righteousness of God and are "worthless." All these sins are an affront to a holy God. Those who have rejected God and his Laws practice these types of sins and give "hearty approval" to others that do as well.

> There is a way which seems right to a man, but its end is the way of death.
> (Prov. 14:12 NASB)

Without repentance, these things eventually lead to God's Wrath. Only Jesus can save us from our sins, as He paid the price for our sins committed against a holy and righteous God by taking our just punishment of death upon himself, by the shedding of his blood. In this way through repentance and trusting in the sacrifice of Jesus for our sins, God fills us with his Holy Spirit, views us as having taken on the righteousness of Jesus, and we will be welcomed into God's presence for eternity. Praise God.

ARCHAEOLOGICAL DISCOVERIES

We learned earlier from Peter that the five cities destroyed by God (the most famous of which are Sodom and Gomorrah) were turned to ash, not covered with ash. If we look for these cities, we should expect to find remains of cities converted to ash. We learned from Jesus that "fire and brimstone" destroyed them. Brimstone is an old word for *sulfur*. We should expect to find elemental sulfur in the ruins as well. Because Jude told us these cities are "exhibited" or displayed for us as examples, they must exist. We need to look for them.

Josephus, the first century Jewish historian, visited and *saw* the ruins of Sodom, "There are still the remainders of the divine fire; and the traces of the five cities are still to be seen" (Josephus in his *Wars of the Jews*, Book IV, Chapter VIII). Obviously the ruins were visible in the first century.

Ron Wyatt, a noted Christian "archaeologist," was the *modern* discoverer of the ruins in the 1980's. Wyatt saw the very unusual formations of salt in this area. They have the appearance of weathered buildings, strikingly so, but are made of a salt-like material. The salt itself is *exactly* what you would expect if the Biblical account is correct. The primary building material used at that time was limestone because it was available and easy to cut and work with. If limestone (calcium carbonate) is burned at high temperatures with sulfur, it produces a calcium sulfate material, of which much of this ash is composed.[lxii]

Amazingly, embedded within the ash are *sulfur crystals*. This is what you'd expect if sulfur rained down. This sulfur is in a form unlike any sulfur found naturally on earth. Sulfur only crystallizes in this unique structural form in the presence of very high heat. Again, this is entirely consistent with the Biblical account. In 1924 William Albright and Melvin Kyle found pieces of brimstone at the southern end of the Dead Sea and stated, "A region on which brimstone was rained will show brimstone. Well, it does; we picked up pure sulfur, in pieces as big as the end of my thumb" (*Explorations at Sodom* by Dr. Melvin Kyle, 1928, pp. 52-53). In all, 800 square miles of the area around the Dead Sea exhibit these features. Once again, the biblical account is verified by archeological findings.

WHAT DO WE DO WITH THIS INFORMATION?

First, we should praise God. Only the God of the Bible could accomplish what is seen on the plain of the Jordan River at the southern end of the Dead Sea. But beyond this, Peter and Jude tell us these ruins exist as examples for us. How can we use them as examples and for whom? Certainly they should be examples for us personally to encourage us to live lives of holiness and thanksgiving before God. We should share the references above with our friends and families as well to help build their faith in God's Word and fear of the Lord.

"Fire and Brimstone" preaching has gone out of style, but discussing these findings with unbelievers as well is not out of the question. Unbelievers will immediately try to find natural explanations for the formations and chemical make-up of the cities of the plain of Jordan, but creating doubt about their world view in their minds is a good thing. We are to plant seeds. One never knows which ones will fall on good soil and grow with the work of the Holy Spirit.

THE SECOND TRUMPET

When the *Second Trumpet* will sound, "Something like a *great mountain* burning with fire was thrown into the sea; and a third of the sea became blood, and a third of the creatures which were in the sea and had life, died; and a third of the ships were destroyed" (Rev. 8:8-9 NASB; emphasis mine). With the *Second Trumpet*, we again see destruction of the earth not people. This time the destruction is aimed at the sea. Just as with the *First Trumpet*, there is a limit placed. Only 1/3 of the sea is damaged. God's patience still hopes for repentance and salvation of the lost.

Some have considered this flaming mountain to be an asteroid. It might be. The word "mountain" might also be a symbol for a kingdom. We have already seen that symbol used in Dan. 2. In Jeremiah, there is a passage that John might have been alluding to:

> But I will repay *Babylon* and all the inhabitants of Chaldea for all their evil that they have done in Zion before your eyes," declares the Lord. "Behold, I am against you, O *destroying mountain*, who destroys the whole earth," declares the Lord, and I will stretch out my hand against you, *and roll you down* from the crags, and I will make you a *burnt out* (Gk: EMPTUO meaning "set on fire") *mountain*." (Jer. 51:24-25 NASB, clarification and emphasis mine)

We can see that this passage identifies the mountain as *Babylon*. Might this be the famous "Mystery Babylon" found later in Revelation? Here is a passage which is specific about that famous city:

Then a strong angel took up a stone like a great millstone and *threw it into the sea*, saying, "So will *Babylon*, the great city, be *thrown down* with violence, and will not be found any longer. (Rev. 18:21 NASB, emphasis mine)

This appears to be a match to me; a mountain is set on fire and thrown into the sea. We know *the Beast* and the Ten Kings destroy *"Mystery" Babylon* (Rev. 17: 16). We know that they burn her up with fire and that she will never be inhabited again. Does *the Beast* use *nuclear weapons* to destroy the city, and does this pollute 1/3 of the sea? It is a possibility.

THE *THIRD TRUMPET*

When the *Third Trumpet* sounds, a "star" falls from heaven. "The third angel sounded, and a great *star* fell from heaven, burning like a torch (Gk: LAMPAS), and it fell on a third of the rivers and on the springs of waters. The name of the star is called *Wormwood*; and a third of the waters became wormwood, and many men died from the waters, because they were made bitter" (Rev. 8:10-11 NASB; clarification and emphasis mine). Although men are affected by the *Third Trumpet*, the primary target is the *earth*. This time it is the *fresh water* that is made bitter. Jeremiah refers to this:

Thus says the Lord of hosts, the God of Israel, "behold, I will feed them, this people, with *wormwood* and give them *poisoned water* to drink. I will scatter them among the nations, whom neither they nor their fathers have known; and I will send the sword after them until I have annihilated them." (Jer. 9:15-16 NASB, emphasis mine)

Just as we saw with the *First Trumpet*, the purpose of this trumpet is to wake up the wayward and cause them to repent.

THE *FOURTH TRUMPET*

> The fourth angel sounded his trumpet, and a third of the *sun* was struck, a third
> of the *moon*, and a third of the *stars*, so that a third of them turned dark. A third
> of the day was without light, and also a third of the night. (Rev. 8:12 NASB,
> emphasis mine)

The first three trumpets affected the land, salt water, and fresh water. This *Fourth
Trumpet* affects the skies, darkening 1/3 of the sun, moon, and stars. Similar to the
future prophetic statement in Revelation, there is also a similar prophetic statement in
the book of Ezekiel. God spoke these words through Ezekiel to Egypt:

> And when I extinguish you, I will cover the heavens and *darken their stars*; I
> will cover the *sun* with a cloud and the *moon* will not give its light. *All the
> shining lights in the heavens I will darken over you* and will set darkness on
> your land. (Ezek. 32:7-8 NASB; emphasis mine)

THE *FIFTH TRUMPET*: THE *FIRST WOE*

In his "progressive discipline," with the *Fifth Trumpet,* God moves from judgments that
primarily strike the earth to those that *directly punish men in their bodies.* The *Fifth
Trumpet* is also called the *First Woe* judgment, of which there are two others to follow,
at the *Sixth* and *Seventh Trumpet* judgments [total of three Woes (Rev. 8:13)]. The *First
Woe* (*Fifth Trumpet*) lasts *five months*:

> The fifth angel sounded his trumpet, and I saw *a star* that had fallen from the
> sky to the earth. The *star* was given the key to the shaft of the Abyss. When *he*
> opened the Abyss, smoke rose from it like the smoke from a gigantic furnace.
> The sun and sky were darkened by the smoke from the Abyss. *And out of the
> smoke locusts came down on the earth* and were given power like that of
> scorpions of the earth. They were told not to harm the grass of the earth or any

plant or tree, but only *those people who did not have the seal of God on their foreheads.* They were not allowed to kill them but only to torture them for *five months.* And the agony they suffered was like that of the sting of a scorpion when it strikes. During those days people will seek death but will not find it; they will long to die, but death will elude them. (Rev. 9:1-6 NASB, emphasis mine)

Is this *star* that falls from heaven the same star in the *Third Trumpet*? Are the clouds it produces those of the *Fourth Trumpet*? They very well may be. Is this "star" an asteroid or comet? Is it a nuclear explosion? Both are possible. However, please notice that the passage says, "When *he* opened the Abyss." Comets and nuclear explosions are not a "he." Is this fallen star *Satan* whom Michael casts out of Heaven? Does Satan use the opportunity of an asteroid or nuclear war to open the Abyss? Whatever the cause, a *hoard of demons that sting like locusts* are released and inflict so much pain that men seek death to relieve it. We know these are not natural locusts because they are held in the Abyss (the holding area for demons) and because of their bizarre appearance (Rev. 9:7-9; emphasis mine). Jesus interestingly linked the casting down of Satan with scorpions, "I saw Satan fall like lightning from heaven. I have given you authority to trample on snakes and *scorpions* and to overcome all the power of the enemy; nothing will harm you (Luke 10: 18-19 NASB; emphasis mine). Was Jesus speaking of the *Fifth Trumpet*? I think so. We also see these "locusts" have power in their tails:

They had tails with stingers, like *scorpions*, and in their tails they had power to torment people for five months. They had as *king over them* the angel of the Abyss, whose name in Hebrew is *Abaddon* and in Greek is *Apollyon* (that is, Destroyer). (Rev. 9:10-11 NASB, clarification and emphasis mine)

The first interesting observation from this passage is that the locusts are given the power to torment men. Death is said to have a "sting" (1 Cor. 15:54-56). Are these locusts the same ones who inflict that sting in Hades when the wicked are tormented? We can only surmise.

There is mercy embedded in this *First Woe* as well. The "victims" of this Woe still have the ability to repent. Interestingly, most seek death rather than repentance. That is how hard-hearted they will have become.

We also see the locusts are prevented from harming the 144,000 sealed by God. Anyone who repents and trusts in Jesus for salvation during this period will most likely be protected as well. We know that once a soul is saved, they are sealed by God (Eph. 1:13-14).

ABADDON, KING OF THE LOCUSTS

The locusts have a king as mentioned in the previous Revelation passage:

> They have as *king over them*, the angel of the abyss; his name in Hebrew is *Abaddon*, and in the Greek he has the name *Apollyon*. (Rev. 9:11 NASB, emphasis mine)

The question immediately arises, is this angel a fallen angel or one of God's Holy angels? This concept may stun you. Traditional theories have most frequently associated this figure with Satan himself or a fallen angel. That is not necessarily the case. The locusts are part of *God's Wrath* not Satan's wrath, and they exclusively torment those who are not sealed by God (God's servants). It is incredibly unlikely that Satan is their king. Why would he torment his own people and not the Jews and those who repent during the *Seventh Year*? At this point in the 70th Week, Satan is not yet confined to the Abyss. He is still the prince (Gk: ARKON) of *this* world.

So, who is this mysterious "angel of the abyss?" In my opinion he may be one of the seven angels that stand before God; the same angels who blow the seven trumpets and voice the seven thunders. His responsibility is the Abyss. It is likely he is also the angel who chains and seals Satan in the Abyss after the 70th Week (Rev. 20:1). The Hebrew name for this king is ABADDON. We find this same word in Job:

The departed spirits tremble under the waters and their inhabitants. Naked is Sheol before Him (God), and *Abaddon* has no covering. (Job 26:5-6 NASB, clarification mine)

In this passage the word ABADDON most likely refers to the pit itself rather than the king of the Abyss. The passage is referring to God being able to see the inhabitants of Hell and being able to observe what occurs there. A similar verse is found in Proverbs:

Sheol and *Abaddon* lie open before the Lord, how much more the hearts of men! (Prov. 15:11 NASB, emphasis mine)

THE *SIXTH TRUMPET*: THE *SECOND WOE*

After the sixth angel is authorized to blow his trumpet—this is the *Sixth Trumpet* (which is the *Second Woe*) —four angels are released to *kill 1/3 of mankind*. This is an incredibly severe judgment:

Then the sixth angel sounded, and I heard a voice from the four horns of the golden altar which is before God, one saying to the sixth angel who had the trumpet, "Release *the four angels who are bound* at the great river Euphrates." And the four angels, who had been prepared for the hour and day and month and year, were released, so that *they would kill a third of mankind*. (Rev. 9:13-15 NASB; emphasis mine)

As we saw with the *Fifth Trumpet*, this *Sixth Trumpet* judgment is *God's Wrath*, as are all the trumpet and bowl judgments. The angels who are overseeing the judgment, however, are bound. This leads me to believe these are *fallen angels* which God uses to carry out this judgment. God's word also gives us the location of these angels as the Euphrates River. This river flows through Turkey, Syria, and Iraq, which is consistent with an Islamic-centric basis for the Trumpet Judgments of God.

311

The four angels release an army of "twice ten thousand ten thousands" (Gk: DISMIRIADES MIRIADES MIRIADON) or *two hundred million*. The army is described as wearing breastplates of "fire, hyacinth, and brimstone." Fire is red, hyacinth is a deep smoky blue, and brimstone (sulfur) is yellow. It is interesting to see that, "A third of mankind was killed by these three plagues, by the fire and the smoke and the brimstone which proceeded out of their mouths" (Rev. 9:18 NASB). So the colors in the breast plates represent the means of killing. We also learn that the tails of the horses that this army rides are like serpents. This is another reference to Jesus's statement in Luke 10:19 that his followers will tread on serpents (*Sixth Trumpet*) and scorpions (*Fifth Trumpet*), and they will not harm them. This implies the people of God (Jews and those who repent in the *seventh year*) will be immune to this judgment as well.

We can try to surmise what this killing entails. The judgment may be similar to the fire and brimstone that rains on the earth during the *First Trumpet* or it may be nuclear fallout. The purpose of the judgment is to *lead to repentance*. Unfortunately, God's Word tells us this: "The rest of mankind, who were not killed by these plagues, *did not repent* of the works of their hands" (Rev. 9:20 NASB, emphasis mine).

THE *SEVENTH TRUMPET*: THE *THIRD WOE*

Upon blowing the *Seventh Trumpet* (this is the *Third Woe*) the *dominion of this world transfers to Christ Jesus:*

> Then the seventh angel sounded [the *Seventh Trumpet*]; and there were loud voices in heaven, saying, "*The kingdoms of the world* has become *the kingdom of our Lord* and of His Christ; and He will reign forever and ever." (Rev. 11:15 NASB; emphasis mine)

It is my theory that the *Seventh Trumpet* is blown on the fall Feast of the Lord of Yom Teruah of the *Seventh Year*, ten-days before the end of the 70th Week. As we learned earlier, the *Seventh Trumpet* is a "nesting doll" containing the seven bowls of wrath just as the *Seventh Seal* contains all the seven trumpet judgments. The bowl judgments are

God's *finale* of the "Shock and Awe" he pours out before Christ returns. If the *Seventh Trumpet* indeed blows on Yom Teruah, the bowls will be poured out during the *Days of Awe* (the ten days on the Jewish calendar between Yom Teruah and Yom Kippur).

Edward Chumney in his important book, *The Seven Festivals of the Messiah* (Shippensburg, PA, Treasure House —Destiny Image Publishers, Inc., 1994), in Chapter 7 on Rosh HaShanah (Yom Teruah, the Feast of Trumpets), has several interesting sections that support the blowing of the *seventh trumpet* on Yom Teruah. His understanding is that "on Rosh HaShanah [Yom Teruah] the *coronation* of the Messiah Yeshua [Jesus] as King will happen in Heaven . . . in preparation for His coming back to earth to reign as King Messiah (Messiah ben David) during the Messianic age, the Millennium . . ." (p. 115, clarification and emphasis mine). In addition, Chumney believes Psalm 47 and Dan. 7 both picture this coronation event:

> O, clap your hands all peoples; shout to God with the voice of joy for the LORD Most High is to be feared, **a great King over all the earth**. He subdues peoples under us and *nations under our feet* [we, as the Church, are in heaven; on earth the nations are beneath our feet]. He chooses our *inheritance* for us, the glory of Jacob whom he loves. Selah. God has ascended [to the throne] *with a shout, the LORD, with the sound of a trumpet* [the shout and trumpet of *Yom Teruah*]. (Psalm 47:1-5, NASB clarification and emphasis mine)

> One like a Son of Man was coming and *He came up to the Ancient of Days and was presented before Him. And to Him was given **dominion**, Glory and a **kingdom*** that all the peoples, nations and men of every language might serve Him. His **dominion** is an everlasting dominion which will not pass away. (Dan. 7:13-14 NASB, emphasis mine)

In Revelation we see this coronation event pictured in two parallel passages, in Rev. 11 and 15:

Then the *seventh angel sounded* (the *Seventh Trumpet*); and there were loud voices in heaven, saying, "***The kingdom of the world has become the kingdom of our Lord and of His Christ***; and He will reign forever and ever." And the twenty-four elders, who sit on their thrones before God, fell on their faces and worshiped God, saying, "We give You thanks, O Lord God, the Almighty, who are and who were, because You have taken Your great power and ***have begun to reign***. And the nations were enraged (reference to Psalm 2:1), and Your wrath came, and the time *came* for the dead to be judged, and ***the time to reward Your bond-servants the prophets and the saints and those who fear Your name*** [the Resurrection and Rapture], the small and the great, and to destroy those who destroy the earth." ***And the temple of God which is in heaven was opened***. (Rev. 11:15-18 NASB, clarification and emphasis mine)

And I saw something like a sea of glass mixed with fire, ***and those who had been victorious over the beast and his image and the number of his name***, standing on the sea of glass, holding harps of God. And they sang the song of Moses, the bond-servant of God, and the song of the Lamb, saying, "Great and marvelous are Your works, O Lord God, the Almighty; Righteous and true are Your ways, ***King of the nations***!" . . . After these things I looked, and ***the temple of the tabernacle of testimony in heaven was opened*** . . . Then one of the four living creatures gave to the seven angels seven golden bowls full of the wrath of God. (Rev. 15:2-3, 5, 7 NASB, emphasis mine)

These are obviously describing the exact same event: the *Coronation of Jesus* as King of the nations. We see three similarities: the presence of the saints, the proclamation of Jesus as King of the earth, and the Temple of heaven being opened. *The timing of this event is also clear—the Seventh Trumpet (the Coronation of Jesus as King) happens prior to the pouring out of the bowl judgments.* These parallel passages (Rev. 11:15-18 and Rev. 15:2-3, 5, 7) also follow one right after the other in the continuous narrative of Revelation. The fact that Rev. 12-14 occurs between them (between Rev. 11 and 15) is only an indication that, as we mentioned earlier in this book, Rev. 12-14 are parenthetical events and not part of the chronological "story" of Revelation.

These parallel passages also prove beyond a shadow of doubt that the saints have been raptured and are in heaven with Jesus *prior* to the *Seventh Trumpet and the bowl judgments*. We can see in the first passage (Rev. 11:15-19) that time had already passed (at the *Seventh Trumpet*) where the saints of God were judged (the Resurrection) and rewarded (the Rapture). In the second passage (Rev. 15:2-3), we are shown those same saints standing on the sea of glass prior to the bowls being given to the angels, to further pour out God's wrath upon the earth.

This concept of the *Seventh Trumpet* being blown on Yom Teruah (Rosh Hashanah) matches Jewish Rabbinic tradition perfectly. Yom Teruah is the day that Jews each year celebrate the coronation of God as the King of the Universe[lxiii]! This connection of God's kingship to the holiday comes from the Mishnah (*Rosh Hashanah* 4:5-6). Jews were unable to find a scriptural basis for this tradition, but suggest that it dates back to the days of a Temple-based festival in which God was (re)enthroned annually as king. Jews speculate that the sounding of trumpets on this day herald the coronation of the king as well.[lxiv] Is it possible that God himself recommended this festival on this exact feast day to the ancient Jews to foreshadow the coming *Coronation of Jesus* yet to come? I would think that it is likely, not only possible.

DIFFERENCES BETWEEN TRUMPETS AND BOWLS

After the *Coronation of Jesus*, the bowls are poured out. Each of the bowls can be considered similar to their respective trumpet judgment except on "steroids." Whereas, the trumpet judgments affect 1/3 of the earth (possibly just the Middle East), the bowls generally affect the *entire earth*. Due to the extreme severity of the bowls, it is obvious they are poured out in rapid succession during the last few days of the 70th Week or no life would survive. Here is a graphic (Figure 38: Trumpet and Bowl Judgments Comparison) comparing the trumpets with the bowls.

Scope of Judgment	Trumpet Judgments	Bowl Judgments
Earth	1st - hail, fire and blood destroy 1/3 of grass and trees	1st - sores poured out on those who have the Mark of the Beast
Sea	2nd - fiery mountain thrown into the sea kills 1/3 of sea life	2nd - sea becomes blood killing all sea life
Fresh Water	3rd - Wormwood star falls and causes 1/3 of fresh water to become bitter	3rd - all fresh water becomes blood
Sky and Lights	4th - 1/3 of sun, moon, and stars darkened	4th - sun scorches men
Torture	5th - locusts with scorpion tails torture those who have taken the Mark of the Beast	5th - darkness falls on Kingdom of the Beast resulting in sores
Euphrates River	6th - four angels unbound at the Euphrates lead army of 200 Million, 1/3 of mankind dies	6th - Euphrates River dries up preparing the way for the Kings of the East and Armageddon
Kingdoms of the World	Kingdoms of this world become Christ's	Earthquake levels all the cities of the world

Figure 38: Trumpet and Bowl Comparisons

Prior to the *Seventh Bowl*, Satan, the Beast, and the False Prophet gather all the kings of the earth to fight Jesus at *Armageddon*:

> And I saw coming out of the mouth of the dragon and out of the mouth of the beast and out of the mouth of the false prophet, three unclean spirits like frogs; for they are spirits of demons, performing signs, which go out to *the kings of the whole world*, to gather them together for the war of the great day of God, the Almighty. ("Behold, *I am coming* like a thief. Blessed is the one who stays awake and keeps his clothes, so that he will not walk about naked and men will not see his shame). And they gathered them together to the place which in Hebrew is called *Har-Magedon* (Armegeddon). (Rev. 16:13-16 NASB, clarification and emphasis mine)

Notice that Satan gathers the kings of the whole inhabited earth *prior* to Jesus physically returning after the *Seventh Bowl*. It is clear Jesus has not returned at this point because he states "I *am* coming." By not physically coming before the end of the bowl Judgments, Jesus protects his raptured Bride and fulfills his promise that she will not experience any part of God's Wrath.

Another interesting observation from this passage is that *Satan gathers his army to oppose Christ before the physical Second Coming*; Satan is anticipating the return before it happens. He knows the date. Many oppose the notion of Jesus rapturing his Church on Yom Teruah (one of the seven Feasts of the Lord per Lev. 23) and returning in the physical Second Coming on Yom Kippur (another Feast of the Lord) because they believe this would allow Satan to know and anticipate the date. They believe God will keep these dates completely secret. Obviously that is *not* the case because from this passage we can see *Satan does anticipate Christ's coming*. It is not a secret to him—he knows scripture, as evidenced by his quoting scripture when he tempted Jesus in the wilderness at Jesus first coming.

THE SECOND COMING: ARMAGEDDON

As the *Seventh Bowl* is poured out, a *massive earthquake* levels all the cities of the earth. This is a perfect fulfillment of the *Jericho Model* when the walls fall down. In my opinion, this is the moment that Jesus, his Holy Angels, and the saints physically return to earth to defeat Satan.

> And I saw heaven opened, and behold, a *white horse*, and He who sat on it is called Faithful and True (Jesus), and in righteousness He judges and wages war. His eyes are a flame of fire, and on His head are many diadems; and He has a name written on Him which no one knows except Himself. He is clothed with a robe dipped in blood, and His name is called The Word of God. And the armies which are in heaven, *clothed in fine linen, white and clean*, were following Him on *white horses*. From His mouth comes a sharp sword, so that with it He may

strike down the nations, and He will rule them with a rod of iron; and He treads the wine press of the fierce wrath of God, the Almighty. And on His robe and on His thigh He has a name written, "KING OF KINGS, AND LORD OF LORDS." (Rev. 19:11-16 NASB, clarification and emphasis mine)

THE WRATH OF GOD AND ARMAGEDDON

Ezekiel also provides one of the most detailed prophecies in the Bible of Jesus' victory over the Antichrist. It is known as the *Battle of Gog of Magog*. Although we are examining this prophecy in the section about Armageddon, many portions apply to other sections of the entire *last half* of Daniel's 70th Week. This is an incredibly important point so I will state it again. *Ezekiel 38 and 39 span the entire last half of the 70th Week of Daniel, not just the very end as is commonly taught.* This is an incredibly important nuance. We will provide a graphic at the end of this section showing how the various portions of the Ezekiel prophecy detail each of these years.

Additionally many other commentators erroneously think this battle occurs *before* the 70th Week of Daniel, and that Gog is not the Antichrist, but rather possibly a Russian. These commentators appear to be wrong on all counts. Author Joel Richardson has done extensive research on this in his book *Mideast Beast[lxv]*, and most of these insights come from that book. First let's examine why the *Battle of Gog of Magog* must occur *during* the 70th Week of Daniel:

- Israel is living in false security (Ezek. 38:11). Look at Israel today. It does not live securely. Only a deceptive peace treaty will fool them into doing so.

- God refers to Gog as "you are the one of whom I spoke in former days through my servants the prophets of Israel, who prophesied in those days for many years that I would bring you against them" (Ezek. 38:17 NASB). This can only refer to the *Antichrist*, and the Antichrist only arises and attacks Israel at the *Midpoint* of Daniel's 70th Week.

- God states that he will rain hail, fire, and brimstone on the forces of Gog. (Ezek. 38:22) This only occurs during the *First Trumpet* judgment as we learned in Chapter Fourteen: "Event Seven: Rapture and Wrath." This time-stamps that event as occurring at the beginning of the *Seventh Year* of the 70th Week of Daniel.

- After God defeats Gog and his army, God feeds them to the birds of the air (Ezek. 39: 17-20). This is an exact match with Rev. 19:17 -18 where God calls the birds to gather to feast on the bodies of the Antichrist forces after the *Battle of Armageddon*.

- God calls Gog's forces a cloud that covers the land which is a match with God's description of them in Joel 2:2.

- After the battle, the Jewish captives are released around the world and brought back to the land (Ezek. 39:25-28). This happens *after* the *Battle of Armageddon*, and cannot happen prior to that point according to all the other pictures of the 70th Week that we have studied. This passage also claims that from that day forward, God will not allow a single Jew to be left behind in the nations. This is rock-solid evidence that this can only refer to the end of the 70th Week.

- After this battle, God will not let his Holy Name be profaned any more (Ezek. 39:7). This can only happen at the conclusion of the 70th Week of Daniel. It is utter nonsense to believe that this can apply to a time *before* the 70th Week.

- After the Battle, Israel knows the Lord is God from that point on forever (Ezek. 39: 22). Again, this can only happen at the conclusion of the 70th Week.

- God announces that this "is the day of which I have spoken" (Ezek. 39:8 NASB).

- After the battle, God pours out his Spirit on Israel (Ezek. 39:29).

- Finally, in Ezek. 38:19-20 we learn that Jesus is physically present on the earth. As we have seen all of these aspects can only be fulfilled at the conclusion of Daniel's 70th Week and at no other time.

For all these reasons, the *Battle of Gog of Magog* can only be the *Battle of Armageddon*, and *Gog* can only be the *Antichrist*. This is important understanding, because in this passage, God's Word clearly identifies the *armies and Kingdom of the Antichrist*. All this indicates that we can conclude that the *Battle of Gog of Magog* does *not* occur before the start of the 70th Week but is the same as the *Battle of Armageddon* at the end of the 70th Week.

There are other things that can be said related to the nations and other aspects involved in the future *Battle of Gog of Magog*. The nations listed below in Ezekiel 38 are the names of grandsons and great-grandsons of Noah, and represent the names by which God calls the nations:

And the word of the Lord came to me saying, "Son of man, set your face toward *Gog of the land of Magog* (Turkey), the prince of Rosh (see explanation below), Meshech (Turkey), and Tubal (Turkey), and prophesy against him and say, 'Thus says the Lord God, "Behold, I am against you, O Gog, prince of Rosh, Meshech and Tubal. I will turn you about (remember Daniel 'you will turn back') and put hooks into your jaws, and I will bring you out, and all your army, horses and horsemen, all of them splendidly attired, a great company with buckler and shield, all of them wielding swords; Persia, Ethiopia (actually Sudan) and Put (Libya) with them, all of them with shield and helmet; Gomer (Turkey/Assyria) with all its troops; Beth-Togarmah (Turkey/Assyria) from the remote parts of the north with all its troops—many peoples with you. (Ezek. 38:1-6 NASB, clarification and emphasis mine)

Identifying these ancient named nations is quite a science. It is far beyond the scope of this book to accomplish the task. Rather, I refer you to *Mideast Beast* by Joel Richardson (WND Books, Washington D.C., 2012). In Chapter 15 of his book, Mr. Richardson does a phenomenal job of explaining why this list of ancient nation names refers to these *modern Islamic nations* led by Turkey. I heartily recommend his book and suggest you read this chapter as well as the whole book for a complete explanation.

The use of the word *Rosh* in the above passage has been the source of controversy for some time. Many commentators believe it refers to *Russia*. It may, but there are several good reasons[lxvi] to believe *it does not*:

- *Rosh* is a common Hebrew word that means "head or chief" in literal translation. The Jewish secular New Year, *Rosh* Hashanah meaning "head of the year," shows this common usage. If this is the meaning found in Ezekiel 38, then the use of "rosh" in the passage means "chief prince of Meshech and Tubal" and does *not* refer to a separate country.

- Rosh was not a grandson or great grandson of Noah like the name-sakes all the other nations were. Because of this, it does *not* qualify for God's definition of a nation based on bloodlines found in Genesis.

- Rosh is considered Russia only on the grounds that it grammatically sounds like Russia in *English*! No ancient documents containing this name have been found. Even the most scholarly, historic research on the history of the "Rosh" people is unable to locate them in Russia!

If you have additional questions on this topic, please refer to Mr. Richardson's book. It does an exhaustive study explaining why this and many other proofs clearly show that the Antichrist and his empire will be *Islamic*. This is an extremely important understanding.

WILL THE ANTICHRIST BE BURIED?

Knowing that *the Beast* is the *Antichrist possessed by a demonic ARCHON* helps us answer a question that has plagued commentators for some time. *Both* of the following verses from Ezekiel and Revelation are thought to refer to the Antichrist:

> On that day I will give *Gog* a burial ground there in Israel, the valley of those who pass by east of the sea, and it will block off those who would pass by. So *they will bury Gog* there with all his horde. (Ezek. 39:11 NASB, emphasis mine)

And *the beast* was seized, and with him the *false prophet* who performed the signs in his presence, by which he deceived those who had received the mark of the beast and those who worshiped his image; *these two were thrown alive into the Lake of Fire* which burns with brimstone. And the rest were killed with the sword which came from the mouth of Him who sat on the horse, and all the birds were filled with their flesh. (Rev. 19:20-21 NASB, emphasis mine)

Many ask how the Antichrist can be both *buried in Israel* and *thrown alive into the Lake of Fire*. If the Antichrist (Gog) is a man and *the Beast* and the *False Prophet* are demons this is easy to consider. The man is buried and the demons are thrown alive into the Lake of Fire.

SUMMARY OF GOG/MAGOG WAR

The following graphic (Figure 39: Battle of Gog of Magog) details the events found in Ezekiel Chapters 38 and 39, and how they align with the *Pattern of Seven Events*, which we have been building in this book:

Year of Daniel's 70th Week	Pattern of Seven Events	Events during Ezekiel 38 and 39
One	1) Deception by False Messiahs	Israel dwells securely (Ezek. 38:8,11)
Two	2) Blood, War, and Chaos	
Three	3)Famine	
Four	4) Abomination and Death	Gog's armies invade like a cloud covering the land (Ezek. 38:9)
		Gog invades because he desires spoil and plunder (Ezek. 38:12)
		Israel goes into captivity (Ezek. 39:23)
Five	5) Martyrdom	
Six	6) Heavenly Signs	
Seven	7) Rapture and Wrath	God will rain fire and brimstone and hail on Gog's forces [First Trumpet] (Ezek. 38:22)
Eight	Judgment	There will be a great earthquake, *every* wall will be thrown down [Seventh Bowl] (Ezek. 38:20)
		"Everyman's sword will be against his brother" [like Gideon account] (Ezek. 38:21)
		Gog's army will be given as food to the birds of the air (Ezek. 39:4, 17-20)
		Jesus's name will be known in the midst of his people Israel (Ezek. 39:7, 20)

Figure 39: Battle of Gog of Magog

SUMMARY

In this Chapter Fourteen with the breaking of the *Seventh Seal*, the scroll of *Mans' Inheritance* opens and the names of the righteous are revealed. Jesus then resurrects the dead in Christ and raptures his Church. After the Rapture, God sends his "Shock and Awe" attack upon the unrighteous as he pours out the Wrath of God in the form of the 7 trumpet judgments and 7 bowl judgments.

Ch. 14: Event Seven: Rapture and Wrath

Appendix A contains a graphic that highlights the most prominent aspects of the *Seventh Event* in the *Pattern of Seven Events*. Refer to this graphic as needed to re-enforce this Chapter

.

PART THREE:

The Book of Daniel:

Underpinning

Revelation

Chapter Fifteen

OVERCOMING LIONS

(DANIEL 1 - 12)

When my oldest daughter was four years old, we visited the zoo in Fort Wayne, Indiana. My family loves animals and zoos. We've visited a number of them over the years, but none of our visits were like the one to the Fort Wayne Zoo. My daughter's favorite exhibit was the open-air, walk-though Kangaroo Section. Although it wasn't a "petting zoo," we were able to enter the kangaroo habitat. We were advised not to pet them, but we could have. At that time, there were probably two dozen kangaroos hopping around the habitat within inches of us. Our daughter was enthralled, and frankly, so were we.

We were so enthralled we lost track of time. I looked down at my watch to notice the park would be closing in ten minutes. We hurried to the gate of the habitat only to discover it was already locked. Frantically, we looked around for a park employee. There were none as far as we could see. "Help, we're locked in," we yelled. Nothing; there wasn't a sound. We were trapped. Obviously the park employees didn't see us in the exhibit, and deciding it was close enough to quitting time, locked up and left!

I looked around at the kangaroos that a moment before seemed friendly and cute. Facing the prospect of spending the night with them reminded me they were wild animals. My wife was thinking the same thing and hugged our daughter to her side. I looked at what was our only means of escape. The habitat was built with what I remember as a 15 foot high fence. "Kangaroos hop," I told myself. "Naturally they'd build the fence high." What choice did I have? I started to climb. The fence was actually easier to climb than I expected. In a couple minutes I was running for the park entrance. In another couple minutes, I returned with an apologetic park employee who freed my wife and daughter. This story has become legend in the Walters' home.

Although my wife and I were relieved, I think my daughter would have loved to spend a night with the kangaroos.

The Prophet Daniel spent a night with lions. It has become the stuff of legend as well. It is probably the most well-known account about Daniel, and interestingly, it is considered a children's story. King Darius thought Daniel would be torn limb from limb. When Daniel survived, the government officials who plotted to take his life were thrown to the same lions and they *were* torn limb from limb. This story deserves an "R" rating for violence rather than a "G." I've taught this story a dozen times in Sunday School classes, and somehow, the kids catch the meaning of the story but miss the violence; just as my four-year old missed the danger of a night with kangaroos. I am thankful. The story is a nightmare waiting to happen.

THE *BOOK OF DANIEL*

As we learned in Chapter Four: "Bookends (Revelation 1-3)," the Apostle John's primary purpose in writing Revelation was to explain the *Book of Daniel*, and so prepare the Church for the last days. The *Book of Daniel* is divided into two sections. The *first six chapters* of Daniel contain narratives about the life of the Prophet and the exiles in Babylon. The *last six chapters* contain four visions. The entire book is prophetic. The narrative sections are all "pictures" of events that will occur during the 70th Week of Daniel. The visions all contain prophecies about this period as well. Is there a section that outlines the 70th Week of Daniel on a year-by-year basis and demonstrates the *Pattern of Seven Events*? There is. This section is found in Daniel's "*Great Vision Prophecy*" in Chapters 10 – 12.

In total, Daniel interpreted two dreams of King Nebuchadnezzar, interpreted the writing on the wall in King Belshazzar's banquet hall, and experienced four of this own visions found in Daniel 7, 8, 9, and the final vision found in Daniel 10, 11, and 12. These last 4 prophetic visions occurred over a period of 18 years. These visions in Daniel are summarized in the chart below (Figure 40: Daniel's Four Visions):

Vision (Chapter)	When Given	Year	Scope
4 Beasts (Ch. 7)	1st year of King Belshazzar	553 BC	Babylon to Millennial Kingdom
Ram and Goat (Ch. 8)	3rd year of King Belshazzar	550 BC	Great Sunni/Shia War to Millennial Kingdom
70 7's (Ch. 9)	1st year of King Darius	538 BC	From the Decree to rebuild Jerusalem to Millennial Kingdom
Great Vision (Chs. 10-12)	3rd year of King Cyrus	535 BC	From Persia to Millennial Kingdom

Figure 40: Daniel's Four Visions

A DRAGON AND FOUR BEASTS

Dan. 7 introduces us to *four beasts*. All four beasts resurface in Rev. 13 and (indirectly) in Rev. 17 along with a *Dragon*. We have already seen mention of the "Beast" in Chapter Seven: "A Horse of a Different Color (Rev. 6)." We need to fully understand these symbols to understand the 70th Week of Daniel.

"Progressive revelation" is a term used in Bible interpretation. It means that as more of the Bible was written, more is revealed. Utilizing this tool, we can know that what we learn in Daniel's *Great Vision Prophecy* (Dan. 10-12) reveals more than his earlier visions, and that what is revealed in Revelation reveals more than what is found in Daniel. Knowing this, let's start by looking at the *Dragon* in Rev. 12:

> Then another sign appeared in heaven: and behold, a great red (Gk: PYRROS, meaning "fiery red") *dragon* having seven heads and ten horns, and on his heads were seven diadems (Gk: DIADEMATA, meaning "kingly crowns") . . . And the great *dragon* was thrown down, the serpent of old who is called the

devil and Satan, who deceives the whole world. (Rev. 12:3, 9 NASB, emphasis mine)

From this passage we learn that the *Dragon* is Satan himself. He is identified as being "fiery red." In Chapter Seven: "Horse of a Different Color (Revelation 6)," we learned that this is the color associated with Esau and Edom. From the above verse in Rev. 12, we see he has seven heads and ten horns. He also has seven crowns. These crowns are not the same as the crown worn by the rider of the *white horse*. He had a victor's crown (STEPHANOS). These are crowns (DIADEMATA) of Satan's earthly dominion. Finally, we also see that the *Dragon* is "of old." He is the same creature who appeared as a *serpent* and deceived Eve in the Garden.

The second of these symbolic creatures is *the Beast*. He is nearly a mirror image of the *Dragon*:

> And the *dragon* stood on the sand of the seashore. Then I saw a *beast* coming up out of the sea, having ten horns and seven heads, and on his horns were ten diadems, and on his heads were blasphemous names. And the *beast* which I saw was like a leopard, and his feet were like those of a bear, and his mouth like the mouth of a lion. And the *dragon* gave him his power and his throne and great authority. (Rev. 13:1-2 NASB, emphasis mine)

> And he carried me away in the Spirit into a wilderness; and I saw a woman sitting on a scarlet (Gk: KIKKINON, meaning "scarlet") *beast*, full of blasphemous names, having seven heads and ten horns. (Rev. 17:3 NASB, emphasis mine)

The Beast and the *Dragon* are almost identical in appearance. There are a few subtle differences, however. First, the *Dragon* is *fiery red* while *the Beast* is *scarlet*. Scarlet is an interesting color and frequently associated with harlotry. We see the first mention of this color ("Law of Primacy") in the story of Tamar and Judah, a story of incest. Tamar was Judah's daughter-in-law. After Judah's son (her husband) died and left her childless, Jewish law dictated that her husband's brother was to become her new husband and give her a child. Judah relented to give her his youngest son as a husband. Tamar took matters into her own hands and dressed as a harlot and seduced Judah. The result of this relation was *twin boys*. When these boys were born *a scarlet thread* was tied around the hand of the one son:

> It came about at the time she was giving birth, that behold, there were *twins* in her womb. Moreover, it took place while she was giving birth, one put out a hand, and the midwife took and tied a *scarlet thread* on his hand, saying, "This one came out first." But it came about as *he drew back his hand* that behold, *his brother came out* (first). Then she said, "What a breach you have made for yourself!" So he was named *Perez*. *Afterward* his brother came out who had the *scarlet thread* on his hand; and he was named *Zerah*. (Gen. 38:27-30 NASB, clarification and emphasis mine)

Perez (first born) became the ancestor of Jesus not *Zerah*. The scarlet cord then, is a symbol of the lost kingship by the usurper (*Perez*), which rightly passed on to Jesus. Just as Esau lost his birthright, in a way so did *Zerah*. So *the Beast* is scarlet, in part, to symbolize his attempt to assume the dominion of the world that is rightly Jesus's.

A second mention of a *scarlet cord* is found in Leviticus 16 during the temple ceremonies occurring on the Day of Atonement (Yom Kippur). On that day, two goats were chosen. By lot, one was sacrificed to the Lord. The other had the sins of the people ceremoniously placed on it by the High Priest, and it was sent out as a scapegoat (Azazel goat) into the wilderness. A portion of a *scarlet cord* was traditionally tied to the Temple door in addition to this goat's horn (forever associating this goat with scarlet). The goat was then led out into the wilderness and thrown over a rocky precipice. Recorded Rabbinic Judaic tradition holds that after the death of this goat, the portion of the cord tied to the Temple door miraculously turned *white*, indicating God's acceptance of the blood sacrifice. "Though your sins are as scarlet, they will be as white as snow" (Isa. 1:18 NASB). Rabbinic sources claim this color change *ended* 40 years *before* the destruction of the temple[lxvii]. This date (30 AD) is strong evidence for one of the proposed dates for the death of Christ. Did God supernaturally change the color of the cord until Christ became our eternal atonement, and the "scapegoat" sacrifice was no longer needed? *The Beast* is scarlet as a symbol of sin that is *not redeemed.*

Another mention of a *scarlet cord* is found in the account of Jericho. Rehab the harlot (an ancestor of Jesus himself) placed a *scarlet chord* outside her window in Jericho as a sign of her later protection and salvation (Joshua 2:12-13, 18, 21; 6:22-25). It seems by using a *scarlet chord*, Rehab was acknowledging her sin. Upon the conquering of the city her acknowledgment of sin (and repentance) saved her. Finally, scarlet is the color of the Turkish flag. Why Turkey is important will be seen shortly.

The second difference between *the Beast* and the *Dragon* is that the diadem crowns of the *Dragon* are on the seven heads, and the diadem crowns of *the Beast* are on its ten horns. Why this is important will be seen shortly as well.

Finally, the third difference is that the *Dragon* is "of old," whereas *the Beast* came out of the sea as a combination of three other beasts: *a lion, a bear,* and a *leopard.* The other beasts are found in Daniel 7:

> The four winds of heaven were stirring up the great sea. And *four great beasts* were coming up from the sea, different from one another. The first was like a *lion* and had the *wings of an eagle.* I kept looking until its wings were plucked, and it was lifted up from the ground and made to stand on two feet like a man; a human mind also was given to it. And behold, another beast, a second one, resembling a *bear.* And it was raised up on one side, and *three ribs* were in its mouth between its teeth; and thus they said to it, 'Arise, devour much meat!' After this I kept looking, and behold, another one, like a *leopard,* which had on its back four wings of a bird; the beast also had *four heads*, and dominion was given to it. (Dan. 7:2-7 NASB, emphasis mine)

All the beasts arise out of the sea. We are told in Rev.17 that the sea or "waters" are "peoples and multitudes and nations and tongues." The *lion* with eagle's wings is Ancient Babylon. Jer. 4:6-7 is speaking of Babylon and the prophet calls it a *lion,* "A *lion* has gone up from his thicket, and a destroyer of nations has set out; he has gone out from his place to make your land a waste. Your cities will be ruins without inhabitant." In Ezek. 17:1-24, the prophet tells a parable of two eagles and a Cedar tree. The eagles are the kings of Egypt and Babylon and the Cedar is Israel. Combining these symbols, we have a *lion* with eagle's wings. In Ezekiel's parable the eagle uses his wings to fly to the top of the Cedar and carry off branches. This is a picture of Nebuchadnezzar carrying off the King of Israel and his royal court. If the wings of the lion are "plucked" off, this is a symbol of the *lion* being defeated and no longer being able to invade.

In Dan. 4, we see a dream of Nebuchadnezzar that was interpreted by Daniel. In that dream, Nebuchadnezzar was given a "beast's mind" (Dan. 4:16) and his hair and nails grew to be like an eagle's feathers and claws (Dan. 4:33). At the end of a seven-year period, Nebuchadnezzar's mind was restored to him, and of course he cut his hair and nails. This is a picture of the *lion* being given a human mind.

The *bear* that is raised up on one side is Persia. The Persian Empire at that time was the empire of the Medes and the Persians, but the Persians had become the stronger faction, thus the *bear* was "raised up" on one side showing the strength of the Persians. The *three ribs* were the three kingdoms the Persians had conquered: Babylon, Lydia, and Egypt.

The *leopard* with four wings and four heads is the Hellenistic Empire founded by Alexander the Great. After his death, it split into four sub-kingdoms, thus the *four heads*. These empires correspond to the first three kingdoms of the statue of *four metals* seen in Nebuchadnezzar's dream (Dan. 2): the head of gold (Babylon), the chest of silver (Medo-Persia), and the abdomen of bronze (Hellenistic). This is exactly the dream that John told us he would explain to us in Revelation [see Chapter Four: "Bookends (Revelation 1-3)"].

All three of these beasts first appear in the Book of Hosea, written two hundred years before Daniel, which foretells that these beasts will tear Israel apart:

> So I will be like a *lion* to them; like a *leopard* I will lie in wait by the wayside. I will encounter them like a *bear* robbed of her cubs, and I will tear open their chests; there I will also devour them like a lioness, *as a wild beast* would tear them. (Hos. 13:7 NASB, emphasis mine)

We have already learned that the final Beast Empire will be a combination of the Babylonian Kingdom, the Medo-Persian Kingdom, and the Hellenistic Kingdom. *Exactly how this happens in our modern era is detailed in Dan. 8.*

THE RAM AND THE GOAT

While Dan. 7 looks at the historic empires of Babylon, Persia, and the Hellenistic (Greece), Dan. 8 looks at the modern nations that have replaced them, and prophecies in this Dan. 8 are history written in advance.

The modern fulfillment of Dan. 8 may be shocking to you. Many believe that Dan. 8 was exclusively fulfilled thousands of years ago by the Persians and the Greeks because events then were similar to the prophecy. This close-but-not-quite fulfillment is known as a "foreshadow." What these expositors have missed are the following critical verses:

> He said to me, "Son of man, understand that the vision pertains to the *time of the end.*" Now while he was talking with me, I sank into a deep sleep with my face to the ground; but he touched me and made me stand upright. He said, "Behold, I am going to let you know what will occur at *the final period of the indignation,* for it pertains to *the appointed time of the end.*" (Dan. 8:17-19 NASB, emphasis mine)

The Angel Gabriel makes three separate references that this vision applies to *the time of the end* and the final indignation. What could be clearer? Mark Davidson in his landmark book *Daniel Revisited* (Westbow, 2014) was the first to realize the significance of these passages as they relate to the "here and now" in the Middle East. I remember the day I first read his writing. I figuratively fell on the ground just like the prophet Daniel! I was blown away. If you are unfamiliar with this prophecy, I bet you will be experiencing a similar feeling as you read on here.

In the vision, a *ram* head-butts its way westward, northward and southward (Dan. 8: 3-5). The ram is then attacked by a *shaggy goat* that defeats the ram (Dan. 8: 5-

7). *After* the Angel Gabriel informs Daniel that this vision applies to the *time of the end*, he identifies the ram and the shaggy goat (further proof this is end-time prophecy).

> The *ram* which you saw with the two horns represents the kings of Media and Persia. The *shaggy goat* represents the kingdom of Greece. (Dan. 8:20-21 NASB, emphasis mine)

These verses are one of the primary stumbling blocks of historic expositors. They see the names of ancient kingdoms and think, "Aha! This has an ancient fulfillment." Nothing could be further from the truth. One verse earlier Gabriel advised Daniel that the *entire vision* concerns the *appointed time of the end*. Media and Persia disappeared over a thousand years ago. So why did the angel use the names of these ancient kingdoms? The name "Iran" (which occupies the same land as ancient Media and Persia) would have meant nothing to Daniel who lived 2500 years ago. The angel gave Daniel names of the *ancient peoples* who occupied the piece of land that currently is Iran. Those names Daniel was familiar with. There is no doubt that if *Iran* "head-butts" west, north and south, it will fulfill Daniel 8.

Who is the *goat*? The Hebrew word translated "Greece" is actually YAVAN. Yavan were an ancient people that occupied eastern Greece and western Turkey. The principle city within the region is Istanbul. The Angel is not referring to Greece but rather to the land once occupied by the Yavan people who lived in *western Turkey!* Hence, *Turkey* is the *goat*.

This brings up an important point. There is some debate in Christian circles whether names of ancient peoples in the Bible like "Yavan" should prophetically apply to the *land masses* these peoples once occupied (that is my opinion) or to the *actual people* themselves, wherever they may be. For instance, some believe the current Turkish peoples migrated from China, so they are actually a Chinese people group. This thinking is very popular among those looking for the lost tribes of Israel.

In my opinion, the ancient people groups have intermarried and migrated so much over the thousands of years since they were established by Noah's grandchildren that they no longer exist. My wife, our three children, and I have the following ethnic backgrounds: Spanish, Mayan Indian, Italian, French, Irish, German, English, Welch, Swedish and Lithuanian. What ancient people group are we from? Exactly! We aren't part of any ancient people groups; we are a modern people group: we're Americans. The ancient peoples no longer exist (with the exception of the Jews). In my opinion, when we see the names of ancient peoples in prophecy, those names refer to the *land masses* the original people settled on. Yavan, for instance, refers to *eastern Greece and Western Turkey*. Now let's return to the prophecy.

Daniel has instructed us that a great war is about to take place between Iran and Turkey, and Turkey will ultimately prevail. It will be a war between *Shia Muslims* and *Sunni Muslims*. There have been wars throughout history. Why does scripture highlight this particular war? It is highlighted because it launches the career of the Antichrist!

> Out of one of them came forth a rather *small horn* which grew exceedingly great toward the south, *toward the east*, and toward the Beautiful Land. It grew up to the host of heaven and caused some of the host and some of the stars to fall to the earth, and it trampled them down. It even magnified itself to be equal with the Commander of the host; and it removed the regular sacrifice from Him, and the place of His sanctuary was thrown down. (Dan. 8:9-11 NASB, emphasis mine)

The *small horn* is the *Antichrist*. His coming is ushered in by this war we are about to witness. Some have claimed that even this verse was fulfilled in ancient times by Antiochus Epiphanes. However, Antiochus did not, obviously, cause the host and stars of heaven to fall. Additionally, Dan. 8:9 clearly states that the "small horn" will grow towards the east. This is something Antiochus never did; his empire grew towards the south and towards Israel only.

Every Christian needs to be aware of this prophecy in Dan. 8. Iran's invasion of countries to the west, north and south will mark the *beginning* of the rise to power of the Antichrist.

The war will also *facilitate the formation of the Empire of the Beast*. When Iran "head-butts west" it will overrun the former empire of Babylon (Iraq). Then when Turkey (Yavan) counterattacks, Turkey will re-conquer Babylon (Iraq) and conquer Persia (Iran). This will create an empire that is part *Lion*, part *Bear*, and part *Leopard* (referring to Rev. 13). *This is a key understanding.*

The Great Sunni-Shia War will probably be the next prophetic event to take place. As such it will be an amazing opportunity to show the unbelieving world the truth of God's Word. "God predicted it 2500 years ago and we are seeing it before our eyes," we can say. This technique is called *Apocalyptic Evangelism*, and we discuss it at length in Chapter Eighteen: "To Him Who Overcomes."

THE FOURTH TERRIFYING *BEAST*

We have examined the first three beasts described in Dan. 7. Daniel's primary interest was, and ours should be, with the final, fourth Beast, however. It is *this Beast* that will be led by the Antichrist, will conquer Jerusalem, and will persecute the Jews and Christians unto death.

> A *fourth beast*, dreadful and terrifying and extremely strong; and it had large iron teeth. It devoured and crushed and trampled down the remainder with its feet; and it was different from all the beasts that were before it, and it had *ten horns*. While I was contemplating the horns, behold, *another horn, a little one*, came up among them, and three of the first horns were pulled out by the roots before it; and behold, *this horn* (the *little horn*) possessed eyes like the eyes of a man and a mouth uttering great *boasts*. (Dan. 7:7-8 NASB, clarification and emphasis mine)

We looked at this passage in Chapter Five: "Signed, Sealed, and Delivered (Revelation 4-5)." We learned that these events occur before the opening of the *7 Sealed Scroll* and before the beginning of the 70th Week of Daniel.

Revelation actually speaks of two "beasts" and Daniel speaks of four "beasts," so we need to specify who *"the"* Beast is. In Revelation we learn there is a "beast from the sea" and a "beast from the earth," also known as the *False Prophet*.

> I saw *a beast* coming up out of the sea, having *ten horns and seven heads*, and on his horns were ten diadems, and on his heads were blasphemous names . . . Then I saw *another beast* coming up out of the earth; and he had two horns like a lamb and he spoke as a *dragon*. He exercises all the authority of the first beast in his presence. (Rev. 13:1, 11-12 NASB, emphasis mine)

In this above passage from Rev. 13, the "sea" symbolizes gentile nations and the "land" or "earth" is Israel. So, the first beast arises out of gentile nations and the *False Prophet* (who most likely will say he is the historic Jesus) will appear to be from Israel. It is the first "beast from the sea" that is the same as the fourth terrifying beast. He is *the Beast, the Antichrist.*

There are four, main relevant chapters in scripture that identify *the Beast*: Rev. 13, Rev. 17, Dan. 7 and Dan. 2. Proving these scriptures are all referring to the same Beast is an easy matter. First, he is identified by his *heads and his horns*:

> A fourth *beast*, dreadful and terrifying and extremely strong; and it had large iron teeth. It devoured and crushed and trampled down the remainder with its feet; and it was different from all the beasts that were before it, and *it had ten horns.* (Dan. 7:7 NASB, emphasis mine)

> Then I saw *a beast* coming up out of the sea, having *ten horns* and *seven heads*, and on his horns were ten diadems, and on his heads were blasphemous names. And the beast which I saw was like a *leopard*, and his feet were like those of a *bear*, and his mouth like the mouth of a *lion*. (Rev. 13:1-2 NASB, emphasis mine)

338

> I saw a woman sitting on a scarlet *beast*, full of blasphemous names, having *seven heads and ten horns*. (Rev. 17:3, emphasis mine)

We can also identify the fourth beast, "*the Beast*," by its actions:

> A *fourth beast*, dreadful and terrifying and extremely strong; and it had large *iron* teeth. It devoured and *crushed* and *trampled down the remainder with its feet*; and it was different from all the beasts that were before it, and it had ten horns. (Dan. 7:7 NASB, emphasis mine)

> Then there will be a *fourth kingdom* as strong as *iron*; inasmuch as iron *crushes* and *shatters* all things, so, like iron that breaks in pieces, it will crush and *break all these in pieces*. (Dan 2:40 NASB, emphasis mine)

From this analysis, we can see that these four chapters of the Bible are all describing the same thing: *the Beast*.

THE BEAST HAS A 3-PART NATURE

Identifying who *the Beast* is from scripture, however, is not as easy. Commentators have poured over the relevant scriptures for 2000 years, and there are still misunderstandings and questions. Part of the reason is that it appears that *the Beast* is multiplex; that it has various aspects to it all at the same time. I am presenting the theory here that *the Beast* is at once the following: 1) a spiritual *demonic being*: an ARCHON, 2) a political empire, and 3) a human ruler: the *Antichrist*. I think that scripture supports this 3-part make-up of *the Beast*. When scripture refers to "*the Beast*" it can be referring to any one aspect or all three aspects at one time. This causes the concept to be complex and leads to some of the confusion. The following discussion and scripture references given in the next paragraphs substantiate this view of the multiplex nature of *the Beast*.

Ch. 15: Overcoming Lions

In Daniel 7, we are first introduced to four beasts, the fourth of which is *"the"* *Beast*. We are immediately told what the four beasts are:

> These four beasts are *four kingdoms* that shall rise up on the earth. (Dan. 7:17 LXX, emphasis mine)

These same entities (the beasts) are described in Nebuchadnezzar's dream as *four kingdoms* as well.

An additional aspect of the *fourth Beast* of Daniel 7 is also mentioned in Rev. 17:

> The beast that you saw was, and is not, and is about to *come up out* of *the abyss* and go to destruction. (Rev. 17:8 NASB, emphasis mine)

From this passage in Rev. 17, we learn *the Beast* comes up out of the "abyss," which is a holding area for demons. It is referred to in this way in Luke 8:31, Rev. 9:11, Rev. 11:7, Rev. 20:1, 3 as well. Thus, *the Beast* is also a *demon*.

Finally, we see from the same passage in Rev. 17 that the Beast is also an *earthy king*:

> I saw a woman sitting on a scarlet beast, full of blasphemous names, having seven heads and ten horns . . . the seven heads are *seven mountains* on which the woman sits, and they are *seven kings* (Rev. 17:3, 9-10 NASB, emphasis mine)

The passage shows us that the *seven heads* of *the Beast* are symbolic; they are both "mountains" and they are *"kings."* This immediately proves the multiplex nature of the Beast; its heads are two things at once: "The seven heads are *seven mountains* and *seven kings*." As we know, this passage is explaining Daniel 2 and Nebuchadnezzar's dream of the statue composed of multiple metals. In Daniel 2:35 we learn that "mountain" is a symbol for kingdom. Therefore using the *direct reference* to Daniel 2, the passage in

Revelation is saying the *seven heads* are *seven kingdoms* and *seven kings*. This makes perfect sense because a "head" is a symbol of authority just as Jesus is the "head" of the church. Thus the heads of *the Beast* are its sources of authority which are *seven kingdoms* and *seven kings* who rule those kingdoms.

This is very straightforward analysis of the verses of Rev. 17:9-10. Unfortunately, historically many Bible scholars have claimed the seven mountains are seven "hills" and that the verses refer to Rome. Nothing could be further from the truth. Why a "head", which is a symbol of power and authority, could ever be considered a symbol of a "hill" is beyond me. But it is a commonly held misconception related to this passage in Rev. 17. The forced analogy was made because Rome is known as being founded on seven hills. This is, however, not the intended analogy.

As we have learned earlier in this Chapter Fifteen: "Overcoming Lions (Daniel 1-12)," scripture also describes *Satan* as having these same seven heads.

We now know *Satan* and *the Beast* each have seven heads which are seven kingdoms or empires that have existed on the earth and that have been used by them to further their evil purposes. A question must arise in your mind: "Why does *the Beast* exhibit the exact same seven heads as Satan when *the Beast* itself is only one of the heads?" This is a very good question. The answer is that *the Beast* incorporates all of Satan's previous kingdoms (heads) into one. We will explain that understanding below in more detail.

IDENTIFYING THE SEVEN HEADS

As we attempt to identify these *seven heads*, the problem is how to choose only seven kingdoms from the hundreds of earthly kingdoms that have dominated world affairs. Scripture must interpret scripture for us; the Bible must provide the answer. By referring back to Daniel 7, we will find the solution. In that chapter we have learned of *four wild beasts*. How many heads do these beasts have between them?

> And four great beasts were coming up from the sea, different from one another. The first (1st) was like a *lion* . . . And behold, another beast, a second

one (2nd), resembling a *bear*. . . and behold, another one (3rd), like a *leopard*, which had on its back four wings of a *bird*; the beast also had *four heads*, and dominion was given to it. After this I kept looking in the night visions, and behold, a *fourth beast* (4th). (Dan. 7:3-7 NASB, clarification and emphasis mine)

The Lion, the Bear, and the fourth Beast have one head each while the Leopard has four heads. Between them, the four Beasts have *seven heads*. These are the seven heads of *Satan* and *the Beast*. Bible teacher Mark Davidson in his landmark book, *Daniel Revisited*, has rightly shown that we can easily identify the heads of the Leopard. After the death of Alexander, the Hellenistic Kingdom (the Leopard) was divided into four sub-kingdoms: Macedonia (modern day Greece), Asia Minor (modern day Turkey), the Seleucid Empire (Syria and much of eastern Asia), the Ptolemaic Empire (modern Egypt). The final *seventh head* will be the future *Beast Empire*.

IDENTIFYING *THE BEAST* EMPIRE

The passage Rev. 17:9-10 also helps us identify the final head of Satan (and *the Beast*):

> The seven heads are seven mountains, on which the woman sits, and they are seven kings; *five have fallen, one is, the other has not yet come*; and when he comes, he *must remain a little while*. (Rev. 17:9-10 NASB, emphasis mine)

This passage gives us two clues. First, John writes that the final head of Satan (and *the Beast*) "must" remain a little while, and that implies that *this final head will be a long lasting kingdom*. Some commentators stress the word "little" and assume this verse means just the opposite—that the seventh head will last only a short time. I think the Greek word translated "*must remain*" implies the *longevity* of the Kingdom. You'd say "only for a little while" if you were trying to imply a short period. You would not say "*must remain* a little while." If my interpretation is true, one must ask why the verse contains the word translated "a little while?" It seems confusing. The Greek word OLIGON is utilized in many ways. Interestingly, when used in terms of time, it appears in 1 Pet. 1:6 and 1 Pet. 5:10. Both of these verses use the word in terms of *suffering*; that we must endure suffering for "a little while." Suffering may seem long but it will end, and that end will be for God's glory. Even more importantly, this phrase is found in these two key verses about the *Great Tribulation*:

> Come, my people, enter into your rooms and close your doors behind you; hide for *a little while* until indignation runs its course. (Isa. 26:20 NASB, emphasis mine)

> And there was given to each of them a white robe; and they were told that they should rest *for a little while* longer, until the number of their fellow servants and their brethren who were to be killed even as they had been would be completed also. (Rev. 6:11 NASB, emphasis mine)

So to me, this use of OLIGON ("a little while") in Rev. 17:10 is a reference to these two verses above, related to *suffering during the Great Tribulation* and *not a reference to short time at all*. Christians have endured the suffering caused by *the Beast* for "a little while" now (14 centuries!!), and they will continue to do so until the end of the *Great Tribulation*.

Second, related to the second clue about the final head of Satan (and *the Beast*), John writes in Rev. 17:9-10 that by his day "five have fallen, one is, and one has not yet come (total of *seven* kingdoms)." This information helps us further identify the seven heads. John wrote during the height of power of the Roman Empire, so we know that the *sixth empire* must be *Rome*. From our previous analysis of Dan. 7, we predicted the first six heads would be Babylon, Persia, and the Leopard (Greece, Turkey, Seleucid Empire and Ptolemaic Empire). However, there is a problem with this analysis. The Empire John told us "one is" (or was currently existing in John's day), according to common interpretation, was Rome. However, Rome does not exist on this list of six heads.

This dilemma is easily solved, however. As we discussed earlier, it is my opinion that when the Bible refers to an ancient empire or people group (other than the

Jews) in prophecy it is referring to the *land mass* that the empire or people group lived on. The ancient peoples have migrated and intermarried and the empires are no more, but the *land mass* is still there. The Roman Empire and especially the Byzantine Eastern Roman Empire occupied *Asia Minor (modern Turkey)* and this land mass *is* on the list of the first six heads of Satan and the Beast! Hence, we should freely substitute *Asia Minor* for the common understanding of "Rome" in the heads of Satan and *the Beast*.

In my opinion, there is a "special elegance" in the Bible using *Asia Minor* (modern *Turkey*) and not the entire Roman Empire as the sixth head of Satan and the Beast. Although it makes calculating the heads of Satan and *the Beast* a bit more complex, it more accurately describes the *land mass* that *the Beast* will occupy. It entirely eliminates the Western Roman Empire and the Holy Roman Empire from consideration as part of *the Beast*! This is another insight that refutes the "European Antichrist Theory," and gives further support for the Antichrist coming from the Middle East.

HISTORIC EMPIRE APPROACH

Another valid approach to determining the heads of Satan and *the Beast* is to examine all the historic empires of the world and logically choose six that appear to be the ones Satan has used throughout history to persecute the Jews and Christians and disrupt God's plan of redemption. I would choose the following six ancient kingdoms: Egypt, Assyria, Babylon, Persia, Hellenistic (Greece), and Rome. Just as we saw with Rome, many of these "logical" empires for the heads of Satan and the Beast don't match the heads from Daniel 7. But if we apply the same "land mass" theory we applied above to Rome, using "Asia Minor (modern Turkey)," an amazing thing happens—we have a perfect match! The following graphic (Figure 41: First Six Heads of *Satan* and *the Beast*, Modern Land Mass) provides us with a summary:

Historic Empire	Heads of Satan and the Beast	Modern Land Mass Area
Egypt	1) Ptolemaic	Egypt
Assyria	2) Seleucid	Syria and Eastern Asia
Babylon	3) Babylon	Iraq
Persia	4) Persia	Iran
Hellenistic	5) Macedonia	Greece
Rome	6) Asia Minor	Turkey

Figure 41: First Six Heads of Satan and the Beast

If we assemble these first six kingdoms in chronologic order and place them on a time line we discover a very interesting fact: *each of these kingdoms defeated and replaced the previous*. This cannot be coincidence. The fact that each historic empire defeated the previous one, and the fact that each of these empires occupied the land mass predicted by Daniel 7, leads us to the inescapable conclusion that these first six empires are the correct ones.

We are now prepared to search for the seventh head of Satan and the Beast. Just as each of the first six kingdoms defeated the previous, an Islamic Caliphate (the Ottoman Empire) defeated the last vestige of the Roman Empire (Byzantine) in 1453 AD. Thus the Caliphate fits this model as well. It also was a long lasting kingdom existing from AD 622 when Mohammed founded the first Caliphate until 1922. The following graphic is from my book *Are We Ready For Jesus* and details the applicable seven kingdoms:

Kingdom	Actions Taken to Thwart God's Plan of Redemption	Who Replaced Them
1) Egypt	Pharaoh attempted genocide by killing Jewish baby boys by throwing them in the Nile.	Assyria conquered Egypt in 701 BC (Isaiah 20:1–6).
2) Assyria	Conquered Israel and sent it into captivity, and nearly conquered Judah.	Babylon conquered Assyria in 612 BC.
3) Babylon	Conquered Judah and took them into captivity.	Medes and Persians conquered Babylon in 539 BC (Daniel 5).
4) Persia	Haman, in the Persian Court, attempted genocide of the Jews.	Greece conquered Persia in 324 BC.
5) Greece	Antiochus IV desecrated the temple and killed thousands of Jews who would not convert to paganism.	Rome conquered Greece (the Seleucid Empire) in 64 BC.
6) Rome	Rome crucified Jesus, killed Peter and Paul, killed numerous Christian martyrs, burned the temple and Jerusalem in AD 70, and sent the Jews into captivity.	Islam (the Ottoman Empire) conquered Rome in AD 1453.
7) Islamic Caliphate	Killed millions of Jews and Christians during empire-building jihads. Crushed the nations where Christianity began, converting them to Islam. Built the Dome of the Rock on the Temple Mount in Jerusalem.	The Allies divided the Ottoman Empire after WWI (1922).

Figure 42: The Seven Heads of Satan and the Beast (Seven Kingdoms)

These two proofs of the identity of the heads of *Satan* and *the Beast*, based on Daniel 7 and the historical record, give me great confidence these seven Kingdoms are the historical heads of authority of *Satan* and *the Beast*.

MAKE-UP OF *THE BEAST'S* TERRITORY

If *the Beast* is an empire, what will be the extent of its territory? We are told it will be made up of the *Lion*, the *Bear* and the *Leopard* from Dan. 7 and also from Rev. 13:1-2:

> Then I saw a beast coming up out of the sea, having ten horns and seven heads, and on his horns were ten diadems, and on his heads were blasphemous names. *And the beast which I saw was like a leopard, and his feet were like those of a bear, and his mouth like the mouth of a lion.* And the *dragon* gave

him his power and his throne and great authority. (Rev. 13:1-2 NASB,
emphasis mine)

As we have seen, these *first three beasts* (the Lion, Bear, and Leopard) of Daniel 7 encompass the following territories: Iraq, Iran, Egypt, Syria and eastern Asia, Turkey and Greece. This will be the territorial land mass of the *Beast Empire* based on these six heads. Of great interest to me is where Saudi Arabia is located in this analysis. The answer should be clear—Saudi Arabia is the *seventh head* of the Beast! It was Mohammed's original home and his base of operations from which he launched his empire-building jihads. So *Saudi Arabia* needs to be included in the geographical footprint of *the Beast*.

The Beast is not the United Nations nor is it the European Union. This should be clear from this analysis. No where do we see references to Western European countries or North or South American countries! Only Middle Eastern kingdoms (and Greece) are mentioned.

THE SEVENTH HEAD IS "SLAIN"

Although *the Beast* has seven heads, there are actually *eight kingdoms*. One of the first seven heads "dies," descends into the abyss, and then returns to the earth. "The beast that you saw was, and is not, and is about to come up out of the abyss and go to destruction . . . The beast which was and is not, is himself also *an eighth* and is *one of the seven*" (Rev. 17:8,11 NASB, emphasis mine). This apparent "death" of one of the heads (Kingdoms) of Satan is mentioned earlier in Revelation as well:

> *I saw one of his heads as if it had been slain*, and *his fatal wound was healed*. And the whole earth was amazed and followed after the beast. (Rev. 13:3 NASB, emphasis mine)

In November 1922, the seventh "head," the *Ottoman Empire* (the Islamic Caliphate that conquered Rome), was "slain" and dissolved by the Allied Powers that won World War

347

I. For decades, Satan has not had a "head" on this earth to disrupt the plan of redemption of our God. We know that an *Islamic Caliphate will return* according to the passage above; the fatal wound will be healed and the whole earth will be amazed. *This is an important prophecy insight* and is, certainly, timely for what we are seeing today in the Middle East.

At that point, Satan will transfer his power and authority to *the Beast*.

> And the dragon gave him (*the Beast*) his power and *his throne* and great authority. (Rev. 13:2 NASB, clarification and emphasis mine)

Where is Satan's throne? In Revelation 2: 13 we learn it is located in *Pergamum* in modern Turkey. This is yet another proof that the *Islamic Caliphate* (based in Turkey) will be the *Beast Empire*.

THE BEAST IS ALSO A DEMON

Up to this point, we have been referring to *the Beast* as a kingdom and it is. *The Beast* is also an individual, "*the beast* which was and is not, is *himself* also an eighth." How can this be? If *the Beast* is a demonic power behind and controlling an empire, it can be both an empire and an individual demon.

We know from Dan. 10 that several of the kingdoms making up the 7 Heads of Satan have had *demonic powers* controlling them:

> I will return to fight with the *prince of the Persians* (a demon): and I was going in, and the prince of the Greeks came. But I will tell thee that which is ordained in the scripture of truth: and there is no one that holds with me in these matters but Michael your prince. (Dan. 10:20-21 LXX, clarification and emphasis mine)

The Greek word translated "prince" three times above is the word ARCHON which means "spiritual ruler" and most often refers to angelic powers and rulers, both good and evil. You can see Michael is referred to as an ARCHON as well. If Persia and Greece had an ARCHON isn't it likely that *the Beast* does as well?

Interestingly, many Muslims believe a physical animal known as the "Daabba" will arise during the time of the end. This animal (beast) will *mark the foreheads of all believers in Islam* so they can be differentiated from "infidels." They even expect this "beast" will be able to speak. This bears a striking resemblance to both the *Image of the Beast* (which will speak) and the *Mark of the Beast*[lxviii]. Will Muslims construct a hologram of an animal or even a seven-headed creature that "talks?" Or will a demonic aberration inhabit a physical animal? Only time will tell, but keep these things on your "radar screen."

THE BEAST IS ALSO THE ANTICHRIST

Finally, most commentators also believe *the Beast* is embodied in the physical by the "man of lawlessness"—-the *Antichrist*.

> The seven heads are seven mountains on which the woman sits, and *they are seven kings; five have fallen, one is, the other has not yet come*; and when he comes, he must remain a little while. *The beast* which was and is not, is *himself also an eighth and is one of the seven*, and he goes to destruction. (Rev. 17:9-11 NASB, emphasis mine)

This is one of the most complex passages in the Bible and shows that the seven heads of *the Beast* are kingdoms and that each kingdom is associated with a king. We can only guess who these kings are, and frankly it is not that important. There is an *eighth king*, however. We are told *the Beast* himself (the demonic ARCHON) is the *eighth king*, and he was one of the seven. Does this mean that *this demon* possessed one of previous kings and will possess the final king, the Antichrist? I think that is exactly what it means.

We now know that *the Beast* is the *Islamic Caliphate*, so the king that *the Beast* possessed in the past must be *the most prominent of all Islamic kings*. In my opinion, it was *Mohammed*, and the *demonic spirit* of that evil individual will also possess the Antichrist. There is a great deal of evidence that Mohammad may have been demon possessed; in fact he even thought he was possessed himself! A "spirit being" dictated the Quran to Mohammad in a cave. During this dictation, the spirit choked or squeezed Mohammad forcibly three times. This experience so upset him he attempted to commit suicide. Only the intervention of this spirit prevented his death. The spirit claimed to be Gabriel and told Mohammad he would be an apostle of Allah. Despite this reassurance, Mohammad continued to have suicidal thoughts. This certainly sounds like a demonic encounter to me.[lxix]

Will the Antichrist not only be demon possessed but claim to be Mohammed himself? We know the restoration of the *Islamic Caliphate* will be the "healing of the fatal head wound" of Rev. 13:3. *Will the healing of the fatal head wound in the physical be the Antichrist claiming to be the resurrected Mohammed as well?* An interesting aspect of this theory is that it is easy to make the case that *only the return of Mohammed himself* could unite Sunni and Shia together in one religion. This is conjecturing at this point, but it something to consider. Will this be part of the *Great Delusion* prophesied by Paul in 2 Thess. 2: 10-11? Only time will tell if it is, but it is something to keep in mind and "watch" for this coming about.

WILL *THE BEAST* POLITICALLY CONTROL THE ENTIRE WORLD?

A frequent conception about the coming *Beast Empire* is that it will politically and militarily conquer the entire world. This understanding is based on two parallel verses in Rev. and Dan.

> The fourth beast shall be the fourth kingdom on the earth, which shall excel all other kingdoms, and shall devour (Gk: KATESTHEO) the *whole earth*, and trample and destroy it. (Dan. 7:23 LXX, clarification mine)

> It was also given to him to make war with the saints and to overcome (Gk: NIKAO, meaning to spiritually overcome) them, and *authority over every tribe*

and people and tongue and nation was given to him. (Rev. 13:7 NASB, clarification mine)

Certainly at first glance, both verses in Dan. 7 and Rev. 13 seem to imply a world political domination. A close examination of the Greek word KATESTHEO translated "devour" in the first verse has nothing to do with political or military efforts. This word primarily carries a *spiritual meaning*; either good or bad. For example, Luke 8:5 from the Parable of the Sower states that the birds "devour" the seed that falls on the hardened path. This represents Satan stealing the Word. In Luke 15:30 from the Parable of the Prodigal Son, the younger son was accused of "devouring" his inheritance on loose living. In John 2:17, Jesus claimed that zeal for the Temple "devoured" him. In Rev. 12:4, the dragon (Satan) attempted to "devour" the man child. As can be seen from these numerous examples, this is NOT a political or military word but has *spiritual meaning*.

Rev. 13:7 also seems to imply that *the Beast* will control the whole world, but that is *not necessarily so*. Let's explore this deeper. There are *two authorities* given to the Antichrist in this Chapter Fifteen: one from Satan and one from God himself, and we will consider these *two authorities* further in the following sections:

THE AUTHORITY GIVEN TO THE ANTICHRIST BY SATAN

Then I saw a beast coming up out of the sea, having ten horns and seven heads, and on his horns were ten diadems, and on his heads were blasphemous names. And *the beast* which I saw was like a leopard, and his feet were like those of a bear, and his mouth like the mouth of a lion. And *the dragon gave him his power and his throne and great authority*. I saw one of his heads as if it had been slain, and his fatal wound was healed. And the whole earth was amazed and *followed after the beast*. (Rev. 13:1-3 NASB, emphasis mine)

Ch. 15: Overcoming Lions

We learned in Chapter Five: "Signed, Sealed, and Delivered (Revelation 4-5)" that Satan is currently the ruler of this world. In that Chapter we studied Luke 4:5-7 where Satan offered Jesus the kingdoms of this world. The true Messiah turned down Satan's offer. The *false messiah* (*Antichrist*) will accept the offer. We also learned that the Messiah paid the price to redeem the world at the cross, but the control has not transferred and won't transfer until the *7 Sealed Scroll* is opened and the 7 Trumpets are blown during Daniel's 70th Week. That is when the "Kingdoms of this world have become the kingdoms of our Lord and of his Christ." Christ has won the right to the spiritual and political authority of the world, but won't stake his claim until the 7th Trumpet is blown. Prior to that event, the Antichrist will excise *Satan's authority*.

Satan's demonic authority over the world will be temporarily transferred to the Antichrist. Does this mean that the Antichrist will be the *political leader* of the all the nations? No, it does not. Satan is not the political leader of all nations now, but the Antichrist will have Satan's *spiritual authority* over the entire world. Satan's *political authority* over the world seems to be limited to the seven heads of the Beast. The geo-political extent of this empire was outlined earlier in this Chapter 10. Note that Rev. 13 also outlines the *physical borders* of this kingdom as being the Lion, the Bear and the Leopard (Turkey, Greece, Syria and eastern Asia, Egypt, Iran, and Iraq.)

We notice that after the Beast's head wound is healed, the *whole earth* is amazed and follows after the Beast. This statement doesn't mean that the Antichrist politically controls the whole world either. The Greek word translated "follow" in Rev. 13:3 is THAUMAZO which means "admire" or "be in awe of." So this verse means that *the whole world is in awe of the Beast* after the healing of its head wound.

So, in summary, *the Beast* will have Satan's *spiritual authority* over the whole world and the whole world will *be in awe* of *the Beast* after the healing of his head wound.

THE AUTHORITY GIVEN THE ANTICHRIST BY GOD

We also see the Antichrist will be given an authority to act for *42 months* (3 ½ years). This authority will be given to him *by God*, but has a time limit.

There was given to him a mouth speaking arrogant words and blasphemies, and authority to act for *forty-two months* was given to him. And he opened his mouth in blasphemies against God, to blaspheme His name and His tabernacle, that is, those who dwell in heaven. It was also given to him to make war with the saints and *to overcome* (Gk: NIKAO, meaning to "spiritually overcome") them, and authority over every tribe and people and tongue and nation was given to him. All who dwell on the earth will worship him, everyone whose name has not been written from the foundation of the world in the *book of life* of the Lamb who has been slain. (Rev. 13:5-8 NASB, clarification and emphasis mine)

The Beast will be permitted to war with the saints. This is a nearly direct quote from Dan. 7:21. The Greek word translated as "overcoming" in the above verse in Revelation 13: 7 is NIKAO, which we have already seen means a *spiritual overcoming*. This is the same word mistranslated "conquering and to conquer" in relation to the rider of the White Horse in Rev. 6:2. What this verse really says then is extremely important. This is not a physical war, it is a *spiritual war* and the Antichrist will overcome many of the saints. We call this the *Great Falling Away* or the *Great Apostasy*. The verse that clarifies those that are overcome immediately follows this verse:

And *authority over every tribe and people and tongue and nation* was given to him. All who dwell on the earth will worship him, everyone whose name has not been written from the foundation of the world in the *book of life* of the Lamb who has been slain. (Rev. 13:7-8 NASB, emphasis mine)

Now that we have learned the "overcoming" is *spiritual* not physical, the verse that follows Rev. 13:7 (the verse that has caused such controversy) takes on a completely new meaning. *Spiritual authority* is given to the Antichrist over individual members of all tribes, people, tongues, and nations (Gk: ETHNOS, meaning "people groups"). Rev. 13:7 and its mention of tribes, people, tongues, and nations is an exact quote of Rev. 5:9 that refers to *those that are the Messiah's*.

353

> Worthy are you to take the book and to break its seals; for you were slain, and
> purchased for God with your blood men from *every tribe and tongue and
> people and nation*. (Rev. 5:9, NASB emphasis mine)

This contrast between the people that the Antichrist is given authority over and those
Jesus is given only further re-enforces the concept that this authority given to the
Antichrist is a *spiritual authority*. Immediately after Rev. 13:7, we get confirmation
of this. All who dwell upon the earth will *worship* the Antichrist unless their names are
written in the *Book of Life*. Carefully re-examining the parallel passage in Rev. 5:9, we
see this same reference to the *Book of Life* with its seals!! (This is just one further
evidence that the *7 Sealed Scroll* contains the *Book of Life*.)

In summary, Rev. 13: 1-10 is primarily about the *spiritual authority* of the Antichrist,
not political authority.

OTHER REASONS THE ANTICHRIST MIGHT NOT POLITICALLY CONTROL THE WORLD

In Dan. 11, we are told that the Antichrist does *not* control the area that is modern day
Jordan.

> He will also enter the Beautiful Land, and many countries will fall; *but these
> will be rescued out of his hand: Edom, Moab and the foremost of the sons of
> Ammon*. (Dan. 11: 41 NASB, emphasis mine)

If the Antichrist doesn't control a country like Jordan, which is close to his base of
operations (Syria/Turkey/Iraq), it is likely there are many other countries that he doesn't
control as well. We also see the Antichrist *fighting wars* during the final 3 1/2 year
period (after the Abomination of Desolation.)

But rumors from *the East* and from the North will disturb him, and he will go

forth with great wrath to destroy and annihilate many. (Dan. 11:44 NASB,

emphasis mine)

Immediately, at the *Sixth Bowl*, before the Battle of Armageddon, we see that there are

still Kings in the East. This may be alluding to the war listed in Dan. 11:44:

The sixth angel poured out his bowl on the great river, the Euphrates; and its

water was dried up, so that the way would be prepared for the kings from *the*

east. (Rev. 16:12 NASB, emphasis mine)

Finally, at the battle of Armageddon, it appears the Antichrist must *convince* the kings

to do battle with our Messiah; it doesn't seem that he can order them to do so.

And I saw *coming out of the mouth* of the dragon and out of the mouth of the

beast and out of the mouth of the false prophet, three unclean spirits like

frogs; for they are spirits of demons, performing signs (to convince them),

which go out to the kings of the whole world, to gather them together for the

war of the great day of God, the Almighty. (Rev. 16: 13-14 NASB, clarification

and emphasis mine)

WHAT MIGHT THE ANTICHRIST CONTROL?

If the Antichrist is the *Islamic Mahdi*, he will have spiritual and political control of all

Muslims. These peoples are now seeded into nearly all the nations, so in that way he

will have potential control over a portion of the population of most nations. We are

already seeing a microcosm of this effect. ISIS controls radical Islamists in many

countries via social networking without physically controlling the countries. When the

Antichrist arises, it is likely he will control all Muslims (not just the current "radical"

ones. It is likely 1.6 billion followers will all become "radical" at that time in their desire to serve their *Mahdi*). When this occurs, *Islamic terrorism* will be epidemic around the world.

Additionally, Islam has the largest voting bloc in the UN via their OIC (Organization of Islamic Cooperation). It is likely this control will expand and be another source of power for the Antichrist. The Antichrist may even be made the Secretary-General of the UN.

We are not given a complete description of lands the Antichrist does and does not control at the end, but it certainly seems that the Antichrist does not have complete *political* control of the world at any point, just *spiritual* control.

NEBUCHADNEZZAR'S STATUE

In Dan. 2 we learn about Nebuchadnezzar's dream. Providing understanding of this dream is a primary focus of Revelation, and we are finally to the point of explaining it. Let's take a few moments to give some background. Nebuchadnezzar was the King of Babylon. He conquered Jerusalem and carried off Daniel and dozens of other Israelites of royal linage to serve him in his court. Nebuchadnezzar trained Daniel and his friends and "God gave them knowledge and intelligence in every branch of literature and wisdom; Daniel even understood all kinds of visions and *dreams*" (Dan. 1:17 NASB, emphasis mine).

During Daniel's time of study, Nebuchadnezzar had a disturbing dream. He called his wise men and advisors to him and asked for them to both tell him the dream and interpret it under penalty of death. No one was able to do that. Daniel, however, prayed to God and he showed Daniel both the dream and its interpretation. Because of this divine revelation, Daniel saved the lives of all the wise men and was appointed second in charge of Nebuchadnezzar's kingdom. This reminds us of Joseph in Egypt interpreting Pharaoh's dream, doesn't it?

Nebuchadnezzar's dream found in Dan. 2 was of a *statue* made of *four metals* and some clay. This statue was God's communication to Nebuchadnezzar (and future Bible students) of the kingdoms that would reign over *Babylon* from that point on throughout history. Of the *seven kingdoms* from Revelation 17, two (Egypt and

Assyria) existed *previous* to Babylon and weren't part of the statue in Nebuchadnezzar's dream, since only the additional kingdoms which *followed* Babylon are included in the dream. One future empire (Rome) would never rule over Babylon and wasn't intended to be included for that reason, although most commentators list Rome as the fourth kingdom of the statue.

The *fourth kingdom* of Nebuchadnezzar's statue is equivalent to *the Beast* of Revelation and Daniel's *fourth, terrifying beast*. It should be the focus of our study.

> Then there will be a *fourth kingdom* as strong as *iron*; inasmuch as iron *crushes* and shatters *all things*, so, like iron that breaks in pieces, it will crush and break *all these* in pieces. (Dan. 2:40 NASB, emphasis mine)

This verse makes it clear that the *fourth kingdom* will crush and break *"all these"* (the other three kingdoms) into bits and crush them. Rome did *not* do this to either Babylon or Persia. (Rome controlled Babylon for only one year and did not "crush" Babylon, and it never defeated Persia.) It is obvious then that the *Islamic Caliphates* which controlled both Babylon and Persia for nearly a thousand years and completely transformed the language, religion, and culture (broke Babylon into bits and crushed it) is, indeed, the fourth kingdom. Joel Richardson was the first to understand that the *Islamic Caliphate* is the fourth kingdom of Nebuchadnezzar's Dream. Please reference his landmark book, *Mideast Beast,* for more details.

After the *fourth kingdom*, a *fifth kingdom* will arise, a divided kingdom.

> In that you saw the feet and toes, partly of potter's clay and partly of iron, it will be a *divided kingdom*; but it will have in it the toughness of iron, inasmuch as you saw the iron mixed with common clay. *As* the toes of the feet *were* partly of iron and partly of pottery, *so* some of the kingdom will be strong and part of it will be brittle. And in that you saw the iron mixed with common clay, they will combine with one another in the seed of men; but they will not adhere to one another, even as iron does not combine with pottery. In the days of *those*

kings the God of heaven will set up a kingdom which will never be destroyed. (Dan. 2:41-44 NASB, emphasis mine)

This *"divided kingdom"* is the same as the *eighth kingdom* of Rev. 17, and is the final *Beast Empire* that will conquer Jerusalem and persecute the saints. We notice that there are ten "toes" on the statue in Dan. 2. In verse 44 we are told these "toes" are ten kings (*"those kings"*). We are told the toes are made of iron and pottery (earthenware). This is a direct reference to Psalm 2 and gives us a picture of what the *Beast Kingdom* will be like under the Antichrist:

> Ask of me, and I will surely give the nations as your inheritance, and the very ends of the earth as your possession. *You* shall break them with a rod of *iron*; you shall shatter them like *earthenware*. (Psalm 2:8-9 NASB, emphasis mine)

From this reference, we learn that iron will crush the nations of the world like earthenware. The use of "iron" and "earthenware" in Nebuchadnezzar's dream must therefore also have the same meaning. Half of the toes will crush the other half just as iron crushes earthenware. This image allows us a view of the future, that the coming *Beast Empire* will be made up of ten Islamic nations and that initially half of them will oppose the Antichrist, but *his portion* of the Empire will crush the other half.

Some teachers have considered that the iron and earthenware will be Shia and Sunni Islam respectively. This may be an *aspect* of what the iron and earthenware represents, but in my opinion it cannot be the sole meaning. We know from the vision in Dan. 8 that Shia Islam is defeated by Sunni Islam (led by Turkey) *prior* to the emergence of the Antichrist. It appears that after the war seen in Dan. 8, the revived Ottoman Empire is divided into *four nations*, and it is likely that the *ten kings* arise at that point. Could one of the "earthenware" kings include Shia Iran? Yes, Iran probably is one, but to me the "earthenware" toes (kings) will also include Sunni nations— Egypt, Libya and Sudan (English translations of Dan. 11: 43 renders this "Ethiopia"), included in all the "kings" that the Antichrist will crush.

Daniel and Revelation make two other references to the final Beast Kingdom having ten kings reigning simultaneously before the ascension of the Antichrist: Dan. 7:24, Rev. 17:12. In Rev. 17, these ten kings are symbolized by the ten horns on the heads of the *dragon* and *the Beast*. We notice that the crowns move *from the heads* on the dragon *to the horns* on *the Beast*. This shows that the authority of Satan was vested in the "heads" until *the Beast* arises. At that point, the authority will be given to the ten kings. Later *these kings* will give their authority to the *Beast* (Rev. 17: 12).

This *Kingdom of the Beast* will then be destroyed by Jesus, described as follows:

> A *stone* was cut out without hands, and it struck the statue on its feet of iron and clay and crushed them. Then the iron, the clay, the bronze, the silver and the gold were crushed all at the same time and became like chaff from the summer threshing floors; and the wind carried them away so that not a trace of them was found. But *the stone* that struck the statue became *a great mountain* and *filled the whole earth*. (Dan. 2:34-35 NASB, emphasis mine)

This is a picture of Jesus ("*the stone*") destroying the *Beast Kingdom* and God's Millennial Kingdom filling the entire earth.

I'm sure you have noticed that the vision Daniel was given in Dan. 7 is parallel to this interpretation of Nebuchadnezzar's Dream. The following graphic "Figure 43: Comparison of Dan. 2 and Dan. 7" presents some of these similarities:

Dan. 2	Dan. 7	Commonalities	Meaning
Head of Gold	Lion with Eagles Wings	Head leads the body Dan. 2:38; Lion is King of the Beasts Dan. 7:4	Babylonian Empire
Chest and Arms of Silver	Bear	Bear has "ribs" in mouth Dan. 7:5; Chest has ribs	Medo-Persian Empire
Belly and thighs of Bronze	Leopard	Bronze Kingdom rules over earth Dan. 2:39; Leopard is given dominion Dan. 7:6	Hellenistic Empire (Greece)
Legs of Iron	Fourth Terrifying Beast	Iron crushes Dan. 2:40; Fourth Beast crushes Dan. 7:7	Islamic Caliphate
Ten Toes	Ten Horns	Ten Toes on "feet" Dan. 2:33, Toes called "kings" Dan. 2:44; Beast with Ten Horns tramples under "feet" Dan. 7:7, Horns called kings Dan. 7:24	Beast Empire
Stone and Mountain	Kingdom Given to Jesus and Saints	Kingdom will never be destroyed Dan. 2:44; Kingdom is everlasting Kingdom Dan. 7:24	Jesus's Millennial Kingdom

Figure 43: Comparison of Dan. 2 and Dan. 7

We have now examined Daniel's prophetic visions in Dan. 2, 7, 8 and 9 and how they are linked and explained by Revelation. We are now ready to examine *Daniel's Great Vision Prophecy* (Dan. 10-12), which includes the chronologic *Pattern of Seven Events* that we have been studying throughout Part Two: "The *Pattern of Seven Events*."

ANALYSIS OF DANIEL'S *GREAT VISION PROPHECY*

This vision helps us further understand the nature of the eventual *Antichrist Kingdom*. It will have *ten kings*. Dan. 2 pictures these kings as *ten toes* of the metallic statue. Rev. 17 also mentions these *ten kings*. Might the *four kingdoms* (sub-kingdoms) seen in Dan. 8 be home to four of these ten kings? It is entirely probable. Many have tried to guess what the countries are that are ruled by these ten kings. I consider this an exercise in futility. The geo-political borders of the countries we now know in the Middle East will most likely be radically changed by the Sunni-Shia war (Dan. 8 prophecy) and attempts to guess at the borders of future countries is pointless.

We see that the Antichrist arises after the ten kings, *and* he is different from them. We also know from Dan. 7:20 that the Antichrist will be "more imposing" than the other ten kings. The Hebrew word for "imposing" is RAB which means "great, powerful or influential." In the *Septuagint* Greek, the word translated "imposing" means "big" in a physical sense, either taller or heavier. So might the Antichrist be a very tall (like King Saul?) or a heavy person? Perhaps.

Because as we will soon see, the Antichrist goes to war with many of his neighboring kings, it is likely this group of ten kings is a loose affiliation or league and not a single empire at first. The Antichrist will attempt to consolidate it into a single empire, and Rev. 17:13 tells us the kings will eventually give their power to the Antichrist.

SPIRITUAL WARFARE

If Daniel 9 that we discussed in Chapter Two: "Uncovering the Keys" is the central and foundational prophecy about the 70th Week, Daniel's *Great Vision Prophecy* found in Daniel 10-12 is of next importance. Did Satan fear this last vision so much that he tried to keep it secret? The story of how Satan tried to keep this final vision from being released to Daniel is one of the greatest examples of *spiritual warfare* in the Bible. In Daniel Chapter 10, the veil between the spiritual realm and the physical is drawn back, if only for a moment, to allow us to view the spiritual warfare occurring:

> Then he (an angel) said to me, "Do not be afraid, Daniel, for from the first day that you set your heart on understanding *this* and on humbling yourself before your God, your words were heard, and I have come in response to your words. But the *prince of the kingdom of Persia was withstanding me* for twenty-one days; then behold, Michael, one of the chief princes, came to help

me, for I had been left there with the kings of Persia. Now I have come to give you an *understanding of what will happen to your people in the latter days*, for the vision pertains to the days yet future." (Dan. 10:12-14 NASB, clarification and emphasis mine)

Prior to this amazing passage, we learn that Daniel had been fasting and seeking God for three weeks. From the first day Daniel began seeking God, this angel was dispatched to respond to Daniel's prayer. He didn't arrive for 21 days (Dan. 10:13)! The reason is an "evil" angel was "*withstanding,*" or "standing between," or "opposing" the messenger angel.

Daniel's Chapter 10 doesn't tell us what Daniel's prayer was that prompted the messenger angel, but we can deduce it from the vision the angel gives him and from comments he gave us previously in other chapters. The angel's answer is a detailed vision of what is to occur in the later days (literally the "end of days"). Previously, Daniel had three other visions (Dan. 7, 8, and 9). These three visions were perplexing to him. At the conclusion of the first two visions (Dan. 7, 8) he wrote:

At this point the revelation ended. As for me, Daniel, my thoughts were greatly *alarming me and my face grew pale*, but I kept the matter to myself." (Dan. 7:28 NASB, emphasis mine)

Then I, Daniel, was *exhausted and sick for days*. Then I got up again and carried on the king's business; but I was astounded at the vision, and there was none to explain it. (Dan. 8:26 NASB, emphasis mine)

We can see these previous visions of Dan. 7, 8 had made Daniel physically ill, and they confused him. It is very likely then that Daniel was seeking God's face so he could receive an explanation of the previous visions that he had received as long as 18 years earlier. In response, the angel gave Daniel a highly detailed vision that spans Dan. 10, 11 and 12 (*Daniel's Great Vision Prophecy*).

THE INVISIBLE WAR

Returning to the previous passage from Dan. 10, we see it is an *"evil"* angel that is *"withstanding"* or *"opposing"* the messenger angel for 21 days. This evil angel is given a most instructive name. He is called the *"prince of the kingdom of Persia."* In the Hebrew, the word translated "prince" is SAR which is primarily a term applied to angels meaning "captain or commander or general." In the *Septuagint* Greek, the word is ARCHON which is translated "ruler." In the Greek, this word equally applies to angels and religious leaders such as members of the Jewish Sanhedrin. Here are some angelic references that use this word, ARCHON in the New Testament:

> For our struggle is not against flesh and blood, but against the *rulers* (ARCHON), against the powers, against the world forces of this darkness, against the spiritual forces of wickedness in the heavenly places. (Eph. 6:12 NASB, clarification and emphasis mine)

> But the Pharisees were saying, "He casts out the demons by the *ruler* (ARCHON) of the demons." (Matt. 9:34 NASB, clarification and emphasis mine)

These passages imply a hierarchy of demonic powers. The evil angel in Daniel 10 is one of these ruler angels, and it appears he is in charge of the nation of Persia. Does Satan assign *demonic angels* to rule the nations? Obviously, it appears he does. Later in the passage, we learn that after the ARCHON of Persia, the ARCHON of Greece will arise. It is not directly stated, but we can assume the *demonic aspect* of *the Beast* of Rev. 13 is an ARCHON as well.

The passage in Dan. 10 also implies a hierarchy of *heavenly* angels. Michael is dispatched to help the messenger angel, and he is described as *one* of the ARCHON of the *Holy* angels (those that didn't fall in Satan's rebellion). Later in Dan. 10:21, we learn Michael is the ARCHON of the Jewish nation (Israel). Because he is listed as only *one* of the rulers, the passage implies there are more rulers like him. Perhaps the "sheep" nations of Matthew 25:31 have *Holy* rulers and the "goat" nations have *demonic* rulers? We don't know. It is not explained to us. Maybe all the nations have both. I suspect this is the case. This is something we may learn in the Millennial Kingdom under Jesus' teaching.

A question that came to my mind is how Satan has authority to assign demons to be in charge of nations? As we learned in Chapter Five: "Signed, Sealed, and Delivered (Revelation 4-5)," Satan currently has dominion over the earth and its nations (Luke 4:5-8 NASB). These *demonic* angels appear to be his means of administering his dominion.

AFTER THIS VISION DANIEL UNDERSTANDS

We know the message the angel brought to Daniel was so important that Satan feared it and tried to prevent its delivery. After Daniel received this vision, he was no longer confused about the meaning of his previous visions:

> In the third year of Cyrus king of Persia a message was revealed to Daniel, who was named Belteshazzar; and the message was true and one of great conflict, *but he understood the message and had an understanding of the vision.* (Dan. 10:1 NASB, emphasis mine)

If Daniel was confused about the meaning of his previous visions (Dan. 7-9) but understood this one (Dan. 10-12), the vision in subsequent verses of Dan. 11, 12 must be able to clarify questions he had (and that we have) about his previous visions in Dan. 7-9. This makes this final vision, *Daniel's Great Vision Prophecy* (Dan. 10-12), of extreme importance.

Most commentators of Daniel believe that *a portion* of Dan. 11 was historically fulfilled and that a portion will have a future fulfillment. Most of these commentators have stated specifically that Dan. 11: 1- 35 is prophecy *only* related to the past, and it was fulfilled historically by Persian and Greek kings. The final one of these kings detailed in this section was Antiochus Epiphanes, an individual many Bible scholars consider a foreshadow of the Antichrist. These same commentators also state that Dan.

11: 36 – 12:4 are prophecies related to the coming *Antichrist*. Unfortunately this "historic only" view of the first part of Daniel 11 is not entirely consistent with close examination of the entire passage itself as we will soon see. Indeed, there is a "near/far" fulfillment of this prophecy, partially fulfilled by Antiochus Epiphanes but to be ultimately fulfilled by the *Antichrist*.

THE CONSERVATIVE FUTURIST VIEW OF DANIEL 11

Nearly all commentators on Daniel believe that Dan. 11:36-45 (and all of Chapter 12 as well) apply to the *Antichrist* and the future. However, the *Conservative Futurist* view believes that Daniel 11: 21-35 will have a dual fulfillment ("near/far"). This view holds that it was fulfilled historically by Antiochus Epiphanes in ancient times *and* will be fulfilled by the Antichrist in the future. As we will see, this view is entirely supported by scripture, and I support that view.

In order to understand this scriptural support, we must view the *Scroll* of Daniel the way the ancients viewed it—as a single scroll without chapter divisions and without verse divisions. As we have seen, Daniel Chapters 10-12 represent *one vision* and we must not mentally separate them into three divided chapters. Chapter 10 is the introduction to the vision. The prophetic vision itself then occurs in Dan. 11:1 – Dan. 12:4 (notice the vision is continuous until verse 4). At that point (Dan. 12:5 and following), the angel interprets the vision to Daniel. This structure is consistent with all of Daniel's other visions. An angel gives a brief explanation after delivering each of the visions.

In the angelic explanation in Chapter 12, the angel gives Daniel some details about the timing of the events in the proceeding prophecy, and he *quotes* from the prophetic vision to show us where on the timeline those events fall. This is incredibly important information that is ignored by commentators looking at *only* a historic fulfillment. Bible teacher Joel Richardson has provided the Church with much of the following interpretation in an article, "Daniel's Final Vision and the Antichrist," found on his webpage[lxx]. Please feel free to access it to learn more about the *Conservative Futurist* position. Much of this sub-section is based on that article.

Ch. 15: Overcoming Lions

First, let's look at the timeline the angel gives Daniel:

> And one said to the man dressed in linen, who was above the waters of the river, "How long will it be until the end of these wonders?" I heard the man dressed in linen, who was above the waters of the river, as he raised his right hand and his left toward heaven, and swore by Him who lives forever that it would be for a *time, times, and half a time.* (Dan. 12:6-7 NASB, emphasis mine)

This angelic conversation states that the end of these wonders (the events in Chapter 11 and the beginning of Chapter 12) will be for a *"time, times and half a time."* This is one of the most famous phrases in prophecy, and it is understood to mean the 3 ½ year period of the second half of the 70th Week of Daniel, including the period of the *Great Tribulation* for believers (Matt. 24:21). We have learned Jesus termed this period "the *Times of the Gentiles.*" So the angel is saying that the wonders of this vision will cumulate in a 3 ½ year period of incredible tribulation by the Antichrist, then the resurrection and rapture of believers, and finally the physical return of Jesus at the very end of the 70th Week of Daniel. This will be further explained later.

The angel then immediately quotes from his own prophetic vision (Dan. 11) so that we can time-date the point at which the *Great Tribulation* starts in the vision! This is incredibly important, but often neglected interpretation. The first of these quotes is:

> As soon as they finish shattering the power of the holy people, all these events will be completed. As for me, I heard but could not understand; so I said, "My lord, what will be the outcome of these events?" He said, "Go your way, Daniel, for these words are concealed and sealed up until the end time. *Many will be purged, purified and refined*, but the wicked will act wickedly; and *none of the wicked will understand, but those who have insight will understand.*" (Dan. 12:7-10 NASB, emphasis mine)

This passage in the angel's explanation in Daniel 12 contains a direct quote from the vision in Daniel 11:

> ***Those who have insight*** among the people ***will give understanding to the many***; yet they will fall by sword and by flame, by captivity and by plunder for many days. Now when they fall they will be granted a little help, and many will join with them in hypocrisy. Some of those who have insight will fall, in order to ***refine, purge and make them pure*** until the *end time*. (Dan. 11:33-35 NASB, emphasis mine)

From this direct quote, we can see that we can apply the prophecy to the *Great Tribulation* and the Antichrist as far back as Daniel 11:33. The direct reference within the passage to the *"end time"* clearly shows this is "end time" prophecy. But can we go back further? The next verse in Dan. 12 (and its parallel verse in Dan. 11:31) gives us the answer:

> From the time that the ***regular sacrifice*** is abolished and the ***abomination of desolation*** is set up, there will be 1,290 days. (Dan. 12:11 NASB, emphasis mine)
> Forces from *him* will arise, desecrate the sanctuary fortress, and do away with the ***regular sacrifice***. And they will set up the ***abomination of desolation***. (Dan. 11:31 NASB, emphasis mine)

From this second direct quote we can clearly see that Chapter 11 refers to the Antichrist as far back as Dan. 11:31. Jesus confirms this futurist interpretation by referring to this same event (the *Abomination of Desolation*) in Matthew 24:15. Jesus was speaking 150 years *after* Antiochus set up the original *abomination of desolation*, yet Jesus was referring to a future event. Obviously this could only be referring to the *Antichrist* coming in the future.

Now that we know that Daniel 11:31-35 refers to *both* Antiochus and the Antichrist we have tremendous insight. In verse 31 we learn that "forces from *him* will arise." The "*him*" in this verse we now know refers to the *Antichrist*. This means that all previous references to *him* (this character) in Dan. 11 also refer to the Antichrist!!! Since this character (the contemptible person) enters the story in verse 21, we can safely say (under the laws of solid Biblical interpretation) that Daniel 11:21-35 *all refer to the Antichrist.*

This is of incredible importance. Daniel is giving us a great amount of detail about the career of the Antichrist. No wonder Satan attempted to prevent this prophecy from being given to Daniel. It is now available to us too.

> He will be succeeded by a *contemptible person* who has not been given the honor of royalty. He will invade the kingdom when its people feel secure, and he will seize it through *intrigue*. (Dan. 11:20-21 NIV, emphasis mine)

THE RADICAL FUTURIST VIEW OF DANIEL 11

A minority of commentators believe that all of Dan. 11 will have a near/far fulfillment. The prophecies of Dan. 11:2-35 were fulfilled in marvelous detail by Persian and Greek Kings prior to the birth of Christ. Although most modern commentaries claim that all the prophecies of Dan. 11:2-20 were completely fulfilled in antiquity, they were not. In the *Keil and Delitzsch Commentary on the Old Testament*, the authors highlight a number of inconsistencies between this detailed prophecy and the historic record[lxxi]. To me this may indicate that the historic record is incomplete or that a future fulfillment of all the prophecies is yet to come.

Dan. 11 also precedes the prophecy about the Antichrist with a prophecy about the leader who precedes him. To me personally, this is a huge clue that the vast majority of Dan. 11 may be yet future. Notice how it says "*his successor*" and "*he will be succeeded by.*" The entire chapter is a series of one leader succeeding another; it is a continuous narrative. It doesn't seem logical that the future aspects "just begin" in the middle of a continuous narrative.

Finally, when we compare the prophecies of Dan. 8 (which we know will have a near/far fulfillment from our study earlier in this Chapter) with those of Dan. 11, we find an incredible 22 fingerprint resemblances.

Daniel 8	Daniel 11
Persian Ram has second horn which becomes longer than the other v. 3	Fourth Persian King becomes richer than all the others v.2
"Conspicuous horn" (first king) of Yavan magnifies himself exceedingly vv. 5,8,21	A mighty king will rule with great authority and do as he pleases v.3
As soon as the Yavan Goat Kindgom is mighty, its first king is "broken" v.8	As soon as the mighty king has arisen, his kingdom is "broken" v.4
four horns (kingdoms) grow up towards the "four winds of heaven" (Heb: HASSA MAYIM RUHOWT LEARBA) v.8	The kingdom is parceled out to the "four winds of heaven" (Heb: HASSA MAYIM RUHOWT LEARBA) v.5
Little Horn (Antichrist) grows out of one of the four horns at the four winds of heaven v.9	A despicable person (Antichrist) becomes King of the "North" v.21
Little Horn grows exceedingly great towards the east, south and "Beautiful Land" v. 9	King of the North enters the "Beautiful Land" v. 41, gains control of Egypt, Libya, and Ethiopia (South) v. 43, rumors from the East disturb him v.44
Little Horn magnifies himself to be equal with the Commander of the Host and will oppose the Prince of Princes (Jesus) v.11,25	The King of the North will exalt himself above every god v.36
Regular sacrifice is removed v.11	Daily sacrifice is taken away v.31
Place of Jesus's Sanctuary is torn down v.11	Sanctuary fortress is desecrated v.31
The "transgression that causes horror" will trample the Holy Place v.13	The King's forces will set up the "Abomination that causes Desolation" v.31
The timing of the vision is for the "time of the end," the "final indignation," and the "appointed time of the end" v.17,19	the "end time," the "appointed time," and "until the indignation is finished" v.35, 36
The King is skilled at intrigue v.23	King will seize the kingdom by intrigue v.21
The King will be mighty but not of his own power v.24	The King takes action with the help of a foreign god
The King will prosper v.24	The King will prosper v.36
The King will do his will v.24	The King will do as he pleases v.36
The King will destroy to an extraordinary degree v.24	The King will destroy and annihilate many v.44
The King will destroy might men v.24	The King takes action against the strongest
The King will destroy the Holy people v.24	Some of those with insight will fall v.35
The King is shrewd v.25	The King will devise schemes v.24
The King causes deceit to succeed v.25	The King practices deception v.23
The King destroys many while they are at ease v.25	In a time of tranquility he enters the richest parts of
He will be broken without human agency v.25	He will meet his end in Israel v.45

Figure 44: Comparison of Dan. 8 and Dan. 11

This evidence supports a *"Radical Futurist"* position that all of Daniel 11 will have a near/far fulfillment. If the ultimate fulfillment is yet future, that is incredible because it will give us tremendous insight into the years before Antichrist arises. Perhaps I will address that in another book! In this book, let's look at what is rock-solid: the fact that Dan. 11:21-45 will have future fulfillment. It is one of the earliest and most meaningful pictures of the *Pattern of Seven Events*.

YEAR ONE: EVENT ONE (DECEPTION BY FALSE MESSIAHS)

Returning to Dan. 11, we are given an incredible picture of what occurs to the Antichrist after he arises as a leader and immediately before and during the *First Year* of the 70th Week of Daniel.

> Then an overwhelming army will be swept away before him (Antichrist); both it (the army) and a *prince of the covenant* will be destroyed. After coming to an agreement with him (the prince of the covenant), he (Antichrist) will act deceitfully, and with only a few people he will rise to power. (Dan. 11:22-23 NIV; clarification and emphasis mine)

This passage offers us astonishing insight. After coming to power in the new kingdom, the *Antichrist will defeat an overwhelming army led by an Israeli general* (a *prince of the covenant.*) *This is mind blowing.* It appears that after this military victory, the Antichrist signs *an agreement* with the Israeli leader which I believe is the famous *Covenant with Death* (also called the "Agreement with Sheol" and the *"Covenant with the Many"*), which marks the beginning of Daniel's 70th Week. Is this agreement preceded and prompted by an Antichrist military *victory*? Does this victory and agreement then lead to the Antichrist's rise to power?

In Isa. 28:16, God tells Israel in advance that the *only true foundation of hope is Jesus*, the stone laid in Zion, the precious cornerstone. Unfortunately, Israel will trust the Antichrist and learn the hard way. They will only come to faith in Jesus after suffering through the *Great Tribulation* and the *Day of the Lord*, God's wrath on earth (at the end of the 70th Week of Daniel), when Jesus physically returns and "They will look on me, the one they have pierced, and they will mourn" (Zech. 12:10 NIV).

The Antichrist's negotiation of a treaty with Israel will probably be an enormous event world-wide and especially in the Islamic realm. It is likely he will utilize this event to promote himself, ride a *"white horse,"* and present himself as a possible messiah. We learn from this passage in Dan. 11 that initially the Antichrist won't be successful in his bid to become a world leader. If he was successful initially, he wouldn't need to invade the richest parts of the kingdom or attack the King of the South (Egypt) in the *Second Year* of the 70th Week. These other countries would surrender peacefully if they considered him their rightful ruler. The fact that they don't surrender shows us that the Antichrist will still be the ruler of a single nation or a small group of nations at this point in his career.

Year Two: Event Two (War, Bloodshed, and Chaos)

Because the Islamic world does not immediately accept his rule, the *Antichrist* attempts to gain this position by force:

> When the richest *provinces feel secure*, he will invade them and will achieve what neither his fathers nor his forefathers did. He will distribute plunder, loot and wealth among his followers. (Dan. 11:24a NIV, emphasis mine)

First, we observe that some passage of time occurs for the richest provinces *to feel secure*. It is then that he strikes and takes "peace from the earth." This demonstrates that this is the *Second Year* of the 70th Week when the *Second Seal* breaks. Also notice that the term used for the areas he invades is *"provinces"* not nations or kingdoms. This implies to me that they are other regions close to the Antichrist's nation. Daniel 8 supports the idea of an invasion close to the Antichrist's home base:

> Out of one of them came another horn, which started small *but grew in power to the south and to the east and toward the Beautiful Land (Israel)*. (Dan. 8:9 NIV, clarification and emphasis mine)

The identity of these nations is not clear. South and east of Assyria are Iraq, Iran, the Arabian Peninsula, and Afghanistan and Pakistan. Certainly, Iraq and Saudi Arabia are *rich* with oil. These may be the nations involved. If the Arabian Peninsula is conquered, this would surely take "peace" (peace of mind) from the world. A Muslim leader conquering 2/3 of the Middle East and taking complete control of most of the oil fields would certainly upset the industrialized west, and with good reason!

> He will *plot* the overthrow of *fortresses*—but only for a time. With a large army he will stir up his strength and courage *against the king of the South.* (Dan. 11:24b -25 NASB, clarification and emphasis mine)

Also we notice that the Antichrist attempts to overthrown "fortresses" during the *Second Year* of the 70th Week. Are these the western nations? Is this the "chaos" and "disturbances" that Jesus refers to in Luke 21:9 [we will discuss this in depth in Chapter " At this time, he is unsuccessful. We also see he attacks the King of South (Egypt.) Jesus referenced the war by quoting Isaiah 19, "kingdom against kingdom;" this is what will be seen.

YEAR THREE: EVENT THREE (FAMINE AND ECONOMIC COLLAPSE)

References to the *Third Year* of the 70th Week are more subtle:

> The king of the South will mobilize an extremely large and mighty army for war; but he will not stand, for schemes will be devised against him. *Those who eat his choice food will destroy him*, and his army will overflow, but many will fall down slain. As for both kings, their hearts will be intent on evil, and they will speak lies to each other at the same table; but it will not succeed, for the end is still to come at the appointed time. Then he (the Antichrist) will return to his land with much plunder; *but his heart will be set against the holy covenant, and he will take action and then return to his own land.* (Dan. 11:26 – 28 NASB, clarification and emphasis mine)

Although it *may* be stretching details, I find it extremely interesting that food is mentioned in this passage about the *Third Year*. The term used is "choice food." The same term as used in Dan. 1:8 to describe the food served to Daniel and his friends by

Nebuchadnezzar. This is a marker to me that the forces of the King of the South are eating under the *Mark of the Beast* (Rev. 13:16-17). Is that an aspect of why they plot against their own king? It is possible that the Muslim military leaders of Egypt actually hold allegiance to the Antichrist and view him as *Mahdi* despite their position in the Egyptian military? It could be, but his is supposition.

We also see reference to an "*action*" being taken against Israel (Dan. 11:28). In Chapter Ten: "Event Three: Famine and Economic Distress," we learned that a siege against Jerusalem will begin in the *Third Year* of the 70th Week. Is this the "action" being referred to in Dan. 11? It most likely is.

Before we look at the fourth event, let's list the Antichrist's early exploits from the *first three years* that we have learned in detail from Daniel 11:

1) Antichrist negotiates and signs the *Covenant with the Many*
2) He invades the richest parts of the "Kingdom" and distributes the wealth among his followers
3) He plots the destruction of powerful nations
4) He attacks the King of the South (Egypt) but withdraws
5) He takes action against Israel but withdraws

This is why Satan opposed the sharing of this knowledge. *The incredible detail of these verses from Dan. 11 will allow Christians with this information to closely follow the prophetic path of the Antichrist.* This passage also matches the *Pattern of Events* that we are building about the 70th Week of Daniel.

YEAR FOUR: EVENT FOUR (ABOMINATION AND DEATH)

After this successful expansion of his realm in the *Second Year* of the 70th Week, the Antichrist attempts to destroy fortresses (the USA and Europe?), attempts to invade Egypt, and undertakes some sort of action against Israel. It appears none of these actions are completely successful *at that time*. At the very beginning of the *Fourth Year*, the Antichrist attempts to invade Egypt again:

At the *appointed time* he will *return* and come into the South, but this last time
it will not turn out the way it did before. For *ships of Kittim* (thought to be
"Cyprus") will come against him; therefore he will be disheartened. (Dan.
11:29 – 30 NASB, clarification and emphasis mine.)

First, all of these passages represent an extreme amount of warfare in just a short one or
two year period. The assumption that the Antichrist will be a man of peace is very
misguided. Initially, he appears a man of peace by signing the *Covenant with the Many*,
but starting in *Year Two* of the 70th Week of Daniel until the end, there will be constant
war.

I also want to mention the reference to "*ships from Kittim*" (this is thought to be
Cyprus).

The phrase "*ships from Kittim*" is a reference to a very ancient prophecy by Balaam,
who we discussed in Chapter Seven: "Horse of a Different Color (Revelation 6):"

But ships shall come from the coast of Kittim and they shall afflict *Ashur* and
will afflict *Eber*; so they also will come to destruction. (Num. 24:24 NASB,
emphasis mine)

Ashur is father of the Assyrian people who are the *people of the Antichrist.* By this,
Daniel is again signaling that the Antichrist will be *Islamic.* Eber is one of the great-
great grandsons of Noah. Tradition says that Eber (Gk: HEBER) rebelled against
Nimrod and refused to assist in building the Tower of Babel. As a reward, God did not
confuse his language (Hebrew). Ancient sources claim the descendants of Eber were
those who crossed the Euphrates (Abraham and Lot).[lxxii] Are the "*ships from Kittim*"
western warships? Most commentators think they are.

THE ABOMINATION (DAN. 11: 30-31)

Dan. 11: 31 ushers in the beginning of the last half (last 3 ½ years) of the 70th week of
Daniel:

> At the appointed time he will return and come into the South, but this last time it will not turn out the way it did before. For ships of Kittim will come against him; *therefore he will be disheartened* and will return *and become enraged at the holy covenant* and take action; so *he will come back and show regard for those who forsake the holy covenant.* Forces from him will arise, *desecrate the sanctuary fortress (the Temple), and do away with the regular sacrifice. And they will set up the abomination of desolation.* (Dan. 11:29-31 NASB, clarification and emphasis mine)

We already looked at these events in other chapters of this book. The events that clearly mark this as the *Fourth Year* of the 70th Week are the *desecration of the Temple* and the setting up of the *Abomination of Desolation.*

One factor that adds to our understanding is that the Antichrist is thwarted in his attack on Egypt by "western" warships. It is only then that he turns on Israel once again with his full fury. Notice how the western warships prevent him from conquering Egypt, but freely allow him to attack Israel!! This clearly demonstrates that the West most likely will have completely turned their backs on Israel by this time. It is a very sad commentary.

In the last section, we noted that the Antichrist will lose heart when the western warships oppose him, but then he "turns" and is finally able to defeat Israel. What changes, and what causes him to suddenly be successful? In Chapter Eleven: "Event Four: Abomination and Death," we discussed how it is at this very moment that Michael stands up, Satan is cast out of heaven, and *the Beast* enters and possesses the Antichrist. It is from this moment on that he is directly assisted in his evil endeavors by satanic forces. In just a few more verses we see that he is assisted by a "foreign god" (Dan. 11:39). This is the Muslim's god, *Allah* (Satan), who assists him, and it explains why in the first half of Daniel's 70th week he is somewhat unsuccessful, and why in the second half he is much more successful, due to this satanic assistance. A common theme in this book has been the Islamic nature of the Antichrist and his empire. Muslims are fully expecting demonic assistance in their assault on the world. They call these fallen angels *"jinn"* or *"djinn"* from which we get the word genie. [lxxiii]

Those who think the USA and western powers will be able to resist the Antichrist with their traditional armies forget this fact: that the Antichrist forces will be *demonically assisted*. It will not be a fair fight. However, of course, the Lord Jesus will physically return at the end of the 70th Week of Daniel and punish all the evil doers, *jinn* and human. Praise God!

YEAR FIVE: EVENT FIVE (MARTYRDOM AND APOSTASY)

After setting up the Abomination, the Antichrist will begin to intently and intensely persecute the Jews and Christians. Many will fall away at that time. Daniel tells us that the Antichrist will use *flattery* to corrupt many:

> With *flattery* he will corrupt those who have *violated the covenant*, but the people who know their God will *firmly resist him*. Those who are wise will *instruct many*, though for a time they will fall by the *sword or be burned or captured or plundered*. When they fall, they will *receive a little help*, and many who are not sincere will join them. Some of the wise will stumble, so that they may be *refined, purified and made spotless* until the time of the end, for it will still come at the appointed time. (Dan. 11:32-34 NIV, emphasis mine)

I absolutely love how the NIV phrases the reaction of true Christians; they will "*firmly resist him.*" Not only will they resist him, but they will "*instruct many*" during this time. But there will be a price to pay for their resistance as many will be martyred. One of the purposes of the persecution is made clear as well—-to refine and purify the Bride of Christ, the Church.

We also notice that that they will "receive a little" help. This implies that even unbelievers will come to their aid. In Matthew 25 we will see that during the *Sheep and Goats Judgment*, the nations will be separated based on whether they had helped the Christians and Jews during this time. Dan. 11:34 is telling us some will come to their aid.

Dan. 11:32-35 also says that many who are insincere will join the Jews and Christians. To me, this means that many will see the evil of the Antichrist, will see YHWH's Spirit in the lives of the wise that resist the Antichrist, but when faced with persecution themselves, they will commit apostasy as well. Falling away from the faith (apostasy) was a major discussion point of Jesus' sermon on how to prepare for his return (the *Olivet Discourse*).

> At that time *many will turn away from the faith* and will *betray and hate* each other, and many false prophets will appear and deceive many people. Because of the increase of wickedness, the *love of most will grow cold.* (Matt. 24:10-12 NIV, emphasis mine)

I read with sadness how betrayal of other fellow Christians will figure prominently in the prophesized time of apostasy.

HE WILL BLASPHEME GOD AND WORSHIP ALLAH

Daniel's vision of each successive year of the 70th Week of Daniel in Dan. 11 then pauses for a brief interlude in Dan. 11:36-45. At this point, in the first part of this interlude (in Dan. 11:36-38), the angel first shows Daniel the spiritual aspects of the Antichrist:

> The king will do as he pleases. *He will exalt and magnify himself above every god and will say unheard-of things against the God of gods.* He will be successful until the time of wrath is completed, for what has been determined must take place. *He will show no regard for the gods* (Heb. ELOHE, meaning one God not gods) *of his ancestors* or for the *one desired by women* (Jesus), *nor will he regard any god,* but will exalt himself above them all. Instead of them, *he will honor a god of fortresses* (Heb: MAOZ, meaning "strength" or "stronghold"); a god unknown to his ancestors he will honor with gold and

silver, with precious stones and costly gifts. (Dan. 11:36-38 NIV, clarification and emphasis mine)

The Antichrist will exalt himself over everyone except Allah and will blaspheme the one, true God. He will be allowed to do this until the Wrath of God is complete at the end of the 70th Week of Daniel. Daniel then clarifies who the Antichrist will *not* honor. The God of his ancestors (Ishmael and Esau) was initially YHWH ("Jehovah"). He also will not honor Jesus. Here the Messiah is pictured as the "one desired of women." Every Jewish girl dreamed of giving birth to Messiah. Some believe this passage says the Antichrist will be a homosexual. He may be, but this passage in Daniel is about his spiritual side, not his sexuality. Others claim this passage speaks of the Islamic disdain for women. Again this disdain is accurate, but the passage is about theology of the Antichrist.

Rather, the Antichrist will honor a god of "fortresses." The Hebrew word MAOZ translated fortresses means "strength or stronghold." The Antichrist will honor a god who values strength. Allah (Satan) values warfare and violence, so this supports the view that this reference is to *Allah*. The first use of this Hebrew word MAOZ (Law of Primacy) is found in Judges 6:25-26 where Gideon pulls down the altar of Baal. This altar is called a MAOZ or "stronghold." In Chapter Six: "The Walls Came Tumbling Down (Joshua 6, Judges 6-8)," we saw that *Baal* may very well be the same god as *Allah*. So this use of MAOZ further supports the theory that the Antichrist worships Allah, a god of "strongholds." What Dan. 11:36-38 clearly demonstrates is that the Antichrist honors this god of strength above himself.

It is a common assumption that the Antichrist will sit in the Temple of God and proclaim to be God. I think it is doubtful that the Antichrist will actually *proclaim* himself God.

In a parallel passage to Dan. 11:37-38 in 2 Thess., Paul says the Antichrist "opposes and exalts himself above every so-called god or object of worship, so that he takes his seat in the temple of God, *displaying* himself as being God" (2 Thess. 2:4 NASB, emphasis mine). Notice that the word Paul uses is "displaying." The Antichrist doesn't say he is a god, he *portrays* himself as God by sitting on God's throne in the Holy of Holies in the Temple of God.

Additionally, in Rev. 13: 4, 12, 15, we read that the *False Prophet* causes those on the earth to worship *the Beast*. The Greek word translated worship is PROSKUNEO which means to bow down and prostrate oneself before a superior. It does not mean worship a god.

THE ANTICHRIST WARS CONTINUE

The second aspect of the interlude of Dan. 11:36-45 (in Dan. 11:39-45) shows how the Antichrist will continue his pursuit of warfare during the *Great Tribulation* period. We have already seen that prior to being possessed by and aided by demons, the Antichrist will attempt to attack the strongest nations and Egypt. He will fail and be disheartened. Now, after he has *demonic assistance*, he will be successful:

> *He will attack the mightiest fortresses with the help of a foreign god* and will greatly *honor those who acknowledge him* (Antichrist and Allah). *He will make them rulers over many people and will distribute the land at a price.* At the time of the end the king of the South will engage him in battle, and the king of the North will storm out against him with chariots and cavalry and a great fleet of ships. He will invade many countries and sweep through them like a flood. He will also invade the Beautiful Land. Many countries will fall, but Edom, Moab and the leaders of Ammon will be delivered from his hand. He will extend his power over many countries; *Egypt will not escape.* He will gain control of the treasures of gold and silver and all the riches of Egypt, with the Libyans and Cushites in submission. But reports from the east and the north will alarm him, and he will set out in a great rage to destroy and annihilate many. *He will pitch his royal tents between the seas at the beautiful holy mountain.* (Dan. 11:39-45 NIV, clarification and emphasis mine)

If we look at the beginning of the passage, it implies the Antichrist gets assistance from two sources in his attack against the "strongest fortresses" (probably the western nations). He is helped by his "foreign god" (Allah/Satan), and he is helped by "those who acknowledge *him."* To my reading, the inclusion of this section within the attack on the western nations seems to imply he will get assistance from Muslims within those countries (those who acknowledge him). He may then place these Muslims as rulers over the western nations—"He will make them rulers over many peoples." We also see that Egypt attacks the Antichrist, but now that he is demonically assisted, the Antichrist prevails. This is in fulfillment of Isaiah 19:

> "I will hand the Egyptians over to the power of a cruel master, and a fierce king will rule over them," declares the Lord, the Lord Almighty. (Isa. 19:4 NIV)

We also see in this passage (Dan. 11:39-45) that armies from the north (Russia?) and the East (China?) come against him, and he strikes out to defend himself. Is this another view of Rev. 16:12 where the Euphrates River dries up to prepare the way for the Kings of the East? It's very possible.

After all of this, Daniel's vision tells us the Antichrist pitches his tent between Jerusalem (the Beautiful Mountain) and the sea (the Mediterranean Sea). It's here that he meets his end at *Armageddon*, the final battle of Jesus against Satan and his followers, at the end of the 70th Week when Jesus physically returns to earth. This is further explained later.

SPIRITUAL VIEW OF THE *GREAT TRIBULATION*

> Yet he will come to his end, and no one will help him. At that time Michael, the great prince who protects your people, will arise (*stand*). There will be a *time of distress such as has not happened from the beginning of nations until then.* (Dan. 11:45-12:1 NIV, clarification and emphasis mine)

We see that Michael will *stand,* and this standing leads to the *time of distress* that Jesus refers to as the *Great Tribulation* in Matthew 24. In my opinion, Michael is the "restrainer" of 2 Thess. 2. As we discussed in Chapter Eleven: "Event Four:

Abomination and Death," it appears he arises and casts Satan out of heaven at the *Midpoint* of the 70th Week.

An interesting phrase regarding the restrainer occurs in 2 Thessalonians and is often mistranslated like this:

until	**he be**	**(taken)**	**out of**	**the midst.**
HEOS	GENETAI		EK	MESOU

This is the phrase traditionally translated *"until he is taken out of the way."* This *mistranslation* has led many to believe the restrainer is the Holy Spirit. But that is *not* what the phrase says. The Greek word GENETAI actually means "becomes" or "is revealed" just as in the phrase "the Word *became* flesh and dwelt among us." Also notice the word *"taken"* doesn't appear anywhere in the passage. It was inserted by some translators.

The passage actually should be translated: "until he is revealed out of the midst (or middle)." It is speaking of the *Antichrist* not the restrainer, and means that the restrainer will restrain *the Beast* until the *Antichrist* arises (is revealed). No one is "taken out of the way." Michael (the restrainer) "withdraws" as we learned in Daniel 12:1. He withdraws to fight against Satan and his fallen angels as we learn in Revelation 12. It is at this point he no longer "holds fast" and no longer restrains the lawless one, *the Beast*/Antichrist. The word translated "midst" can also mean "middle." Perhaps this is in reference to the *Midpoint* or "middle" of the *70th Week of Daniel* which is the exact point the Antichrist is revealed.

The concept that the "restrainer" might be the Holy Spirit was concocted by those favoring a *Pre-Tribulation Rapture* position. Their erroneous conclusion was that the Holy Spirit would leave the earth when believers were raptured (assumed to be *before* the start of the 70th Week), because he lives within us. The Holy Spirit convicts us of sin and causes us to believe. How would the multitudes that come to faith in Jesus during what they call "the Tribulation" (something even the staunchest *Pre-Tribulation Rapture* proponent believes) without the Spirit? Let's look at Joel before we leave this important topic:

It will come about after this (after the *Great Tribulation*) *that I will pour out My Spirit* on all mankind; and your sons and daughters will prophesy, your old men will dream dreams, your young men will see visions. Even on the male and female servants I will pour out My Spirit in those days. I will display wonders in the sky and on the earth, blood, fire and columns of smoke. *The sun will be turned into darkness and the moon into blood before the great and awesome day of the LORD comes.* (Joel 2:28-31 NASB, clarification and emphasis mine)

We have already studied the second half of this wonderful section of scripture from Joel, and learned that Joel is prophesying about the *Celestial Earthly Disturbance* that we know happens during the *Sixth Year* of the 70th Week of Daniel. Now let's look at the first half of this passage related to God pouring out his Spirit. We know that the end of the passage is "time stamped" by the *cosmic signs* of the *Day of the Lord* (Joel 2:31). All these events (Joel 2:28-29) occur prior to this time. If we carefully look at the first verse of the passage we see a "time stamp" there as well: "it will come about after this." What events time stamps the beginning of this passage? What events come prior to the mass pouring out of God's Spirit? The beginning of Joel 2 pictures the invasion of Jerusalem at the *Midpoint* of the 70th Week of Daniel which ushers in the *Great Tribulation*. This is confirmed by the phrase, "There has never been anything like it, nor will there be again after it" (Joel 2:2 NASB), which is quoted by Daniel (Dan. 12:1) and Jesus (Matt. 24:21) when referring to the *Great Tribulation*. Thus, the massive pouring out of God's Spirit occurs *during the Great Tribulation*. It makes sense that during the time of greatest need, the greatest outpouring of God's Spirit occurs. Obviously, the Holy Spirit has not withdrawn from the earth during this time.

YEAR SIX: EVENT SIX (CELESTIAL EARTHLY DISTURBANCE)

Dan. 10-12 does not contain a reference to the *Celestial Earthly Disturbance,* but it contains the most direct reference in the Old Testament of the Resurrection that we will look at in the next section.

Year Seven: Event Seven (Rapture and Wrath)

Returning to Dan. 12, after the passage about the *Great Tribulation,* we see a reference to the resurrection:

> But at that time your people—everyone *whose name is found written in the book*—will be delivered. *Multitudes who sleep in the dust of the earth will awake*: some to everlasting life, others to shame and everlasting contempt. *Those who are wise will shine like the brightness of the heavens*, and those who lead many to righteousness, *like the stars for ever and ever*. (Dan. 12:1b-3 NIV)

The order of events is exactly as we see it in other scriptures such as Matthew 24, Luke 21 and Revelation 6. The Bible is consistent. The *Great Tribulation* comes first, then the righteous are resurrected/raptured. Daniel's vision is yet another confirmation that there is no *Pre-Tribulation Rapture*. Rather, this supports the *Pre-Wrath Rapture* position, with the resurrection/rapture occurring when the *Great Tribulation* is cut short just before the Day of the Lord (God's Wrath) begins. It should be noted that all these things occur *after* the *Midpoint* of the 70th Week.

We also know from 1 Thess. 4:16-17 that the rapture of believers occurs immediately after the resurrection of believers who have died, and Daniel's vision pictures it exactly this way: the *Book of Life* (the *7 Sealed Scroll*) is opened first, the resurrection of the righteous occurs next, and finally all believers are raptured together with Jesus to heaven. All of these events are pictured in this short passage *in order*; let me explain.

We already know from Chapter Five: "Signed, Sealed, and Delivered (Revelation 4-5)" that the "book" with names found in it here is the *Book of Life* (the *7 Sealed Scroll*). Once this *Scroll* is opened, upon the *Seventh Seal* at the end of the *Sixth Year* of Daniel's 70th Week, the dead in Christ will rise first. This is exactly what we see pictured in the passage above. Then from 1 Thess. 4:16-17, we know that those who survive will be caught up together in the air with the resurrected saints. This is also pictured, but you may not see it at first. We are told by Paul in 1 Corinthians that at the Rapture we shall be changed in a moment:

> Behold, I tell you a mystery; we will not all sleep, but *we will all be changed*, in a moment, in the twinkling of an eye, at the last trumpet (the last trumpet of Yom Teruah (the last shofar!); not the 7th Trumpet judgment); for the trumpet will sound and the dead will rise imperishable and *we will be changed*. (1 Cor. 15:52-53 NASB, clarification and emphasis mine)

What does "changed" mean? Might we, now with our resurrection bodies, begin to reflect the Shekinah glory of our Lord and begin to "shine?" Will this be a similar effect to what Moses experienced when he went up and received the Ten Commandments on the mountain of God (Gen. 34: 29-34)? After speaking with God, Moses's face glowed, and he had to wear a veil to hide the "shine." Is this why the angel tells Daniel twice that the righteous will "shine" like the brightness of heaven" and "like the stars?" I believe it is the exact reason. What other purpose does the angel have for placing this passage about "shining" immediately after the verse about the resurrection?

The Bible is clear that *our bodies will be transformed* into conformity with Jesus' resurrection body:

> Jesus Christ who will *transform the body of our humble state into conformity with the body of his glory*. (Phil. 3:20-21 NASB, emphasis mine)

We have seen in Chapter Four: "Bookends (Revelation 1-3)" that in the vision of Jesus seen by John that Jesus's body glowed like the sun. It is then highly likely that our "glorified bodies" will as well since "we will be like him" (1 John 3:2).

Interestingly, at the conclusion of Daniel's vision, he is instructed to *seal up the book* (the *7 Sealed Scroll*). He is then told that "many will go back and forth, and knowledge will increase" (Dan. 12:4 NASB). What does this mean? In my opinion, this means that believers will do exactly what you the reader are doing right now; they will *go back and forth throughout the books of the Bible to see what all the references in*

God's Word say about the end times. It is only then that knowledge of the end increases, as we see happening today. Praise God for what he has written for our benefit, even today and in the future.

JUDGMENT

> He (Antichrist) will pitch his royal tents between the seas at the beautiful holy mountain. Yet *he will come to his end,* and no one will help him. (Dan. 11:39-45 NIV, clarification and emphasis mine)

This reference to the Antichrist pitching his tent in the area of Armageddon where he will meet his end is the only reference to the *Seventh Year* of the 70th Week of Daniel in the vision. At the conclusion of the vision, however, the angel tells Daniel what the conclusion of these events will be:

> It would be for a *time, times, and half a time* (3 ½ years); and as soon as they finish shattering the power of the holy people, all these events will be completed. (Dan. 12:7 NASB, clarification and emphasis mine)

We have seen previously that this phrase *"time, times, and half a time"* is 1260 days (3 ½ years). This time period will mark the very end of the *Seventh Year* of the 70th Week, counting from the *Midpoint.* This is also the day that the Antichrist will meet his end. Later in the explanation of Daniel's vision, two other mysterious numbers of days are mentioned: 1290 (Dan. 12:11) and 1335 (Dan. 12:12). In Chapter Twenty-Three: "Appointments," we will discuss what these numbers might mean.

SUMMARY

Understanding the Book of Daniel and the prophecies that God gave him is essential to understanding the Book of Revelation. As we have already pointed out, one of the purposes of Revelation is to explain Daniel.

Daniel's prophecy of the 70 Weeks is the foundational prophecy about the final seven year period of time our culture calls the "Tribulation." Nebuchadnezzar's Dream of the metal statue and Daniel's visions in Dan. 7 and 8 assist us in understanding the Beast and the make-up of the coming Beast Empire. Finally, Dan. 10-12 provides us with an incredible prophecy about the *Pattern of Seven Events* with numerous unique insights.

In Part Four: "Letters to the Seven Churches," we will apply what we've learned from our study of the Pattern of Seven Events to these letters to discover their amazing prophetic meaning which has lain hidden beneath the topsoil of the last 2000 years.

PART FOUR:

Letters to the Seven

Churches

Chapter Sixteen

THE CHURCH OF EPHESUS
(REVELATION 2:1-7)

My wife and I dated long distance. We lived in cities that were four hours apart, but when you meet *the one* God has chosen for you, no sacrifice too big. Those were the days before cell phones and texting, but my wife did get one of the original "bag phones," so that she wouldn't ever be out of touch while traveling. The old bag-phones were huge, but they did work. There was no such thing as texting, however, back then.

When you are hours apart, you can't see each other as often as you like, and by necessity, you learn to write: cards, notes, and letters. I tried to send two or three every week. Writing letters is a lost art, but receiving one is more exciting than a phone call or text. Folks raised in the "texting generation" should pay attention. There is a romance about a letter.

Jesus's *Letters to the Seven Churches* in Revelation are his *love letters* to us, his bride. As we have stated before, one of the purposes of the 70th Week of Daniel is to prepare the *Bride of Christ* for the wedding—to refine her with fire like fine gold. When I read these letters from our Lord, I see the "romance" in them; he wants all of us to enter the wedding feast. These letters are his way of showing us how to "overcome" and join him in that feast, the *Wedding Supper of the Lamb*, which we have discussed.

It is our thesis that *each of the Seven Churches* represents the Church in one of the seven years of that period. The first letter is to the Church during the *First Year* of the 70th Week of Daniel, the second letter is to the Church during the *Second Year*, etc. We have already seen that scripture provides multiple *other* "pictures" of this seven-year period. Studying these *other scriptures* provides a stunningly consistent *Pattern of*

Seven Events: [1) Deception by False Messiahs, 2) War and Bloodshed, 3) Famine, 4) Abomination of Desolation, 5) Martyrdom and Apostasy, 6) *Celestial/Earthly Disturbance* and Rapture, and then the 7) Wrath of God/Day of the Lord].

I must stop and thank my fellow writer, Josh Word, for helping me discover how the *Letters to the Seven Churches* also matches this pattern. If you are still doubtful that these seven letters are *prophecy*, as we study them, the fact that they also match this seven-year pattern should be all the additional proof needed.

It should be duly noted that these letters are the *only prophecies written specifically for the Church* who will endure the 70th Week of Daniel; hence, they are key for our understanding about how the Church should prepare for events the Church will go through in the 70th Week. As such, they are of great, great value because they instruct us on *how to overcome* during this period. Can you now see how the *misinterpretation* of these letters takes the **single most important end-time instructions out of the hands of the Church**? If these Letters are truly guidelines on how to overcome in the 70th Week, we must share this information with the members of our churches. This is important and timely for the days upcoming.

This is a bit of a lengthy study, but it is highly recommended that you stay with it as it is extremely valuable to you. Remember, these *Letters to the Seven Churches* in Revelation are "love letters" to us, the Church, from Jesus, to help us overcome during the 70th Week.

THE STRUCTURE OF THE LETTERS

Not only do the letters match the seven-year pattern we have seen in the six other scriptural passages which we have covered, they also all have a somewhat complex internal structure which is consistent among each of the seven letters. This internal structure which is shared by all the letters helps the reader to compare and contrast how the environment surrounding the Church is changing during each year and how the Church is to react to this changing environment. Let's look at these basic elements of these seven letters in Figure 45: Structure of the Seven Letters:

Structural Section	Explanation
Church Name	Each Letter is addressed to a historical church from the first century. These church names have symbolic meaning
Address	Each letter is addressed to the "angel" of its respective church
Description of Jesus	Each letter gives an aspect of Christ's appearance, primarily from the visions given John and Daniel. These aspects of Christ's appearance also have *symbolic meaning*.
Condition of the Church	The letters contain a statement about current conditions.
Praise	Most churches receive praise.
Rebuke	Most churches are admonished for aspects where they are lacking.
Correction	Most churches receive suggestions for correction.
Call to Hear	All churches receive the same "call to hear," which is a direct quote from Luke 8.
Promise to the Overcomers	A promise is given to the ones who *overcome* each year of the 70th Week of Daniel.

Figure 45: Structure of the Seven Letters

Two elements are identical in all seven letters—they are all addressed to an "angel," and they all have the same "call to hear." We will examine these identical elements first, and then we will begin to study each of the individual letters.

"TO THE ANGEL OF THE CHURCH"

All seven letters are *addressed to the "angel" of each specific church*. This has been a problematic interpretation during the entire Church age. The word "angel" can mean a literal angel or it can mean "messenger." There have been *three main theories* about what John meant by "angel."

1) Seven literal angels who guard and protect the Church. Scripture tells us about seven angels who stand before the throne of God. Some consider John meant these as specific angels.

2) The seven pastors of the churches.

3) Seven messengers who perhaps were those who shuttled messages back and forth between the churches of Asia Minor and John while he was on Patmos, off the coast of western Turkey, where he wrote the Revelation.

Ch. 16: The Church of Ephesus

Let's look at the relevant passages in Revelation about each church and see which theory makes the most sense.

> The mystery of the seven stars that you saw in my right hand and of the seven golden lampstands is this: The *seven stars* are the *angels* of the seven churches, and the *seven lampstands* are the seven churches. (Rev. 1:20 NASB, emphasis mine)

John was given the interpretation of several aspects of the appearance of Christ from his first vision. He told us that the *seven stars* are the *seven angels* and the *seven lampstands* are the *seven churches*.

Stars occasionally refer to *angelic beings* in scripture (Job 38:7, Isa. 14:13, Jude 1:13). They also can refer to *saints* (Gen. 22:17, Dan. 12:3, Phil. 2:15). In the above references to angels, the passages claim the angels *are* stars. In the references to saints they shine *like* stars or are as numerous *as* stars but they are not called stars. This would seem to favor the interpretation that the stars are angels *except* this is a specific symbol given to a *specific group of angels* or messengers. In my opinion, the symbolism of "stars" is non-conclusive between the two choices.

> To the angel of the church in Ephesus *write*: (Rev. 2:1 NASB, emphasis mine)

We also see that John is commanded to *write* to the angels. I consider this much more conclusive evidence. Angels who stand before God himself have no need to have a human write to them. They hear from God directly. Human messengers need divine revelation, however, so this highly favors an interpretation that the "angels" are *human messengers* that relay God's instructions to his churches.

Are they *pastors*? This is traditional thinking, but we have already learned that traditional thinking on the *Letters to the Seven Churches* has been incorrect. In my humble opinion, the "angels" of each church are *those that bring the message of "overcoming"* to the Christians during each year of the 70th Week of Daniel. Many will

392

die and be martyred, so the "angels" may differ from year to year and place to place. They may be pastors and they may not. You and I may be among these "angels." These *messengers* will have an important role, and they will shine like the stars in leading and instructing us during this time of tribulation.

WHOEVER HAS EARS, LET HIM HEAR

Each of the letters also includes a *call to listen, "Whoever has ears to hear, let them hear."* This call to listen is a favorite phrase of Jesus that he included at the conclusion of many of his parables (Matt. 11:15, 13:9, 13:43; Mark 4:9, 4:23; Luke 8:8, 14:35). The extended *Parable of the Sower* in Luke 8 seems to give the best understanding of this phrase. I believe this is the primary reference Jesus was giving us when he used this phrase in each of the seven letters:

> "A farmer went out to sow his seed. As he was scattering the seed, some fell *along the path*; it was trampled on, and the birds ate it up. Some fell on *rocky ground*, and when it came up, the plants withered because they had no moisture. Other seed fell *among thorns*, which grew up with it and choked the plants. Still other seed fell on *good soil*. It came up and yielded a crop, a hundred times more than was sown." When he said this, he called out, *"Whoever has ears to hear, let them hear."* (Luke 8:5-8 NASB, emphasis mine)

This parable is about the possible results of *hearing* and doing the Word of God (the seed). Jesus then explains the meaning to his disciples and quotes Isaiah 6:9:

> His disciples asked him what this parable meant. He said, "The knowledge of the secrets of the kingdom of God has been given to you, but to others I speak in parables, so that, 'though seeing, they may not see; though hearing, they may not understand.'" (Luke 8:9-10 NASB)

In essence, Jesus was saying that Christians who hear or read the message of "overcoming" in the seven letters will react one of four ways based on the condition of their heart (symbolized by the four types of soil.) Jesus continued:

> This is the meaning of the parable: The seed is the word of God. Those *along the path* are the ones who hear, and then the devil comes and takes away the word from their hearts, so that they may not believe and be saved. Those on the *rocky ground* are the ones who receive the word with joy when they hear it, but they have no root. They believe for a while, but in the time of testing they fall away. The seed that *fell among thorns* stands for those who hear, but as they go on their way they are choked by life's worries, riches and pleasures, and they do not mature. But the seed on *good soil* stands for those with a noble and good heart, who *hear the word, retain it,* and *by persevering* produce a crop. (Luke 8: 11-15 NASB, emphasis mine)

By quoting the reference to this parable in each of the letters, Jesus is telling us that only a portion of the Christians will have a receptive heart (good soil) for his message. Notice those with good soil will *hear, retain, and persevere* and thus produce a crop. By including this call to *hear* in each Letter, Jesus was telling us that this situation will exist during *each of the seven years* of the 70th Week of Daniel. In the Letter to Philadelphia, Jesus tells us there will be a time of testing coming upon the whole earth. The Church will be tested as well, and it will be obvious what type of "soil" each human heart possesses.

We know from numerous passages we have already looked at in other Chapters of this book that there will be a "falling away" or a "rebellion from the faith." This parable in Luke 8 pictures *why* people fall away. Many have heard the Word of God and the Gospel of the Kingdom. One group hears but never believes. Another group hears gladly and does believe (the rocky soil), but Jesus tells us "in the time of testing they fall away." These churchgoers are unable to endure the persecution that will come. Others also believe (the weedy soil), but "they are choked by life's worries, riches and pleasures, and they do not mature." Are they the ones who take the *Mark of the Beast?*

Are they the ones who are unwilling to wean themselves from the buying and selling of the world economic system? In both of these later cases, the churchgoers had the beginnings of faith, but it did not mature into *saving faith*. By quoting from this parable (Luke 8:5-8) in each of the seven letters, Jesus is warning us there will be those *in each year* of the 70th Week that "fall away," and for Christians to be mindful of the snares the devil will set.

Now that we have examined the two common elements—they are all addressed to an "angel" and they all have the same "call to hear"—let's investigate each of the individual seven letters.

YEAR ONE: EVENT ONE (LETTER TO EPHESUS)

Each letter is written to a church that existed in Asia Minor (Turkey) during the First Century. It may only be a coincidence, but please notice that all seven churches are found in modern day *Turkey*. We saw in Chapter Fifteen: "Overcoming Lions (Daniel 1-12)," that it is likely that *Turkey will be the seat of power of the Antichrist*. Not only are the *Seven Letters* addressed to these churches, but all of the Book of Revelation is addressed to them as well: "I heard behind me a loud voice like a trumpet, which said: 'Write on a scroll what you see and send it to the seven churches: to Ephesus, Smyrna, Pergamum, Thyatira, Sardis, Philadelphia and Laodicea'" (Rev. 1:10-11 NASB).

In Chapter Two: "Uncovering the Keys," we have already shown conclusive evidence that the *Seven Letters* are prophecies and *not* letters to individual churches, types of churches, or Church Ages. If the letters are *prophecy*, then *the name given to each church may be symbolic of the general condition facing believers during that respective year of the 70th Week of Daniel*, and the *purpose of all of Revelation is to prepare and equip believers to overcome this time of trial*. Both of these aspects are profound understandings. As we examine the letters and the names of the churches, this will become apparent.

Related to the first letter, *Ephesus* means "the desired one." This name is highly reflective of the immense spiritual battle about to take place. God and Satan both desire the souls of believers. All of the 70th Week of Daniel will revolve around this battle symbolically played out in the conquest of Jericho. As we have learned in our previous pictures of *Year One* of this period, Satan's counterfeit messiah and *False Prophet* will burst upon the world scene. The conflict for the souls of believers will be between the false messiahs and the true Messiah, Jesus, who is the way, the truth, and the life. In Chapter Seven: "A Horse of a Different Color (Revelation 6)," we learned that the rider of the white horse comes to conquer (Gk: NIKAO) which literally means to overcome spiritually. The battle lines are drawn for the "desired one."

At the time John wrote Revelation, *Ephesus* was the "crown jewel of Asia Minor," a rich and highly pagan city. Their economy centered on worship of *Artemis*, the moon goddess (Allah is the moon god!) and goddess of fertility. She was also a huntress and skilled with a bow (recall that the rider of the white horse carries a bow).[lxxiv] The Temple of Artemis was one of the seven wonders of the ancient world.[lxxv] Many of her worshipers deposited their savings with the priests of Artemis, trusting that the goddess would protect them. It was an early form of banking. A robust industry of the manufacture of Artemis idols supported the town as well. At the center of the Temple of Artemis was her "image," a *black meteorite* that fell to the earth. It is mentioned in the book of Acts. "After quieting the crowd, the town clerk said, 'Men of Ephesus, what man is there after all who does not know that the city of the Ephesians is guardian of the temple of the great Artemis and of *the image which fell down from heaven*'" (Acts 19:35 NASB, emphasis mine)? In my previous book, *Are We Ready For Jesus?* we discussed how this very *meteorite* is likely currently on the Kaaba in Mecca. It is the most-holy item in Islam. We also discussed at length that this *black stone* (contrasted to the *white stone* of Jesus) will likely be the *image of the beast* mentioned in Revelation 13 and the Abomination of Desolation mentioned in Daniel, Matthew, and Mark.

We also learn from Acts that during Paul's time in Ephesus, his teaching so disrupted the trade of idols a great riot broke out. A silversmith named Demetrius said:

> "Men, you know that our prosperity depends upon this business. You see and
> hear that not only in Ephesus, but in almost all of Asia, this Paul has persuaded
> and turned away a considerable number of people, saying that gods made with

hands are no gods at all. Not only is there danger that this trade of ours fall into disrepute, but also that the temple of the great goddess *Artemis* be regarded as worthless and that she whom all of Asia and the world worship will even be dethroned from her magnificence." When they heard this and were filled with rage, they began crying out, saying, and *"Great is Artemis of the Ephesians!"* The city was filled with the confusion, and they rushed with one accord into the theater, dragging along Gaius and Aristarchus, Paul's traveling companions from Macedonia. (Acts 19:25-29 NASB, emphasis mine)

I can almost hear a modern crowd crying out *"Allah Akbar"* instead of *"great is Artemis"* when I read this passage. The parallels to Islamic Sharia blasphemy laws seem striking. Will Christians be dragged to the city courts for blasphemy against *Allah* during the *First Year* of the 70th Week of Daniel? Church history relates that Timothy, who was Bishop of Ephesus and the protégé of Paul, was martyred by *Artemis* worshipers chanting this very phrase, *"great is Artemis."*[lxxvi]

THE APPEARANCE OF JESUS IN THE LETTER TO EPHESUS

As we mentioned in Chapter Two: "Uncovering the Keys," the *attributes of Jesus's appearance* mentioned in the letter to each church is symbolic.

> The One who holds the seven stars in His right hand, the One who walks among the seven golden lampstands, says this: (Rev. 2:1 NASB)

Jesus himself has defined both of these aspects of his appearance for us. Earlier in this section, we learned the *seven stars* are the angels of each church. We also did an extensive analysis and determined the *angels* are most likely *human messengers delivering Jesus's instructions on how to overcome the 70th Week of Daniel*. He holds these angels in his right hand. The right hand is the hand of blessing. Israel blessed Ephraim with his right hand in Genesis 48:14. God's right hand is also a place of power, "Your right hand, O Lord, is majestic in power, Your right hand, O Lord, shatters the enemy" (Ex. 15:6 NASB). Jesus will use these angels to help shatter his enemies by the revelation of His Word, and he will bless these human messengers. What an awesome privilege and reward.

We have already learned in a previous section that the *seven lampstands* are the seven churches. The Greek word for lampstand is LYCHNION. These lampstands are patterned after the lampstand of the Tabernacle described in Exodus which was modeled after the one in heaven:

> Then you shall make a *lampstand* of pure gold. The lampstand and its base and its shaft are to be made of hammered work; its cups, its bulbs and its flowers shall be of one piece with it. Six branches shall go out from its sides; three branches of the lampstand from its one side and three branches of the lampstand from its other side. (Ex. 25:31-32 NASB, emphasis mine)

The lampstand was a collection of *seven individual lamps* joined into a single fixture much as the Church is a collection of individual believers joined into the Body of Christ. The *center lamp* of the seven lamps of a Menorah (lampstand) is considered by the Church to be the "Jesus candle," as Jesus is at the center of his Church. Interestingly, in the *Tabernacle* there was *one* lampstand. Note that in Solomon's *Temple*, there were *10 lampstands* in the Holy Place. Randall Price, in *Rose Guide to the Temple*, describes the Golden Lampstands (Menorahs) in Solomon's Temple as follows[lxxvii]:

> "Transferred from the tabernacle was the golden lampstand which had been beaten from a single piece of gold (Exodus 25:31-40). It is unclear exactly where the *tabernacle menorah* was placed in Solomon's temple, but it may have been hidden and stored in one of the temple chambers. Solomon had *10 new golden lampstands* made and positioned them five on the north side and five on the south side of the Holy Place (2 Chronicles 4:7 NASB, emphasis mine)."

Why did Solomon place *10 new lampstands* in the Temple instead of just bring in the *one lampstand* from the Tabernacle? Did Solomon do this on his own accord or was he instructed by God to do this? As God gave the detailed plans to David and Solomon, it can be assumed that God *directed* that *10 lampstands* be placed in the Temple for some reason.

Why are there *seven lampstands* mentioned in this section of Revelation? Why isn't there *only one* to represent the entire Church or 10 as were in Solomon's Temple? I don't have a good answer for this; perhaps you might. However, in my opinion, this is yet another proof that the Seven Churches are all pictures of the *one true Church* (as there was only *one lampstand* in the Tabernacle) —-as it endures each successive event in the *Pattern of Seven Events* during the seven years of the 70th week. In this way there is only *one lampstand* at a time upon the earth.

Notice that in the Letter to the Church of Ephesus, it is stated that *Jesus walks among the lampstands*. Jesus will be right there with us as we endure and overcome. "Lo, I am with you always, even to the end of the age" (Matt. 28:20 NASB). These aspects of Jesus's appearance are appropriate for the *First Year*. They are introductory and act as encouragement for all seven years of the 70th Week.

CONDITION OF THE CHURCH

In all *Seven Letters* after the address and the description of Jesus's symbolic appearance, he gives us a *brief description* of the Church. For most of the seven years, Jesus provides both positive and negative feedback. This is what our Lord says will be the positive aspects of the Church in the *First Year* of the 70th Week of Daniel:

> I know your *deeds and your toil and perseverance*, and that *you cannot tolerate evil men*, and *you put to the test those who call themselves apostles*, and they are not, and you found them to be *false*; and you have perseverance and have endured for my name's sake, and have *not grown weary*. (Rev. 2:2-3 NASB, emphasis mine)

Ch. 16: The Church of Ephesus

The primary condition of the world during this *First Year* will be *deception by false messiahs*. It appears from this passage that the Church is initially able to test and then recognize the false messiahs and false prophets as *liars* (the Greek word PSEUDEIS translated as "false" means "lying or liar.") This is the same root word as used in 1 John in this famous verse about the Antichrist, "Who is the *liar* but the one who denies that Jesus is the Christ? This is the *antichrist*, the one who denies the Father and the Son" (1 John 2:22 NASB, emphasis mine).

Jesus also commends the Church for hating the works of the Nicolaitans: "Yet this you do have, that you hate the deeds of the Nicolaitans, which I also hate" (Rev. 2: 6 NASB). We have seen in Chapter Seven: "A Horse of a Different Color (Revelation 6)" that the word "Nicolaitans" means *"overcoming the people of God"* and it is tied to the actions of the rider of the white horse whose "conquering" in Rev. 6:2 is a *spiritual overcoming*. By this, we determined the Nicolaitans here are the followers of the Antichrist, most likely *Muslims*.

Jesus also commends the Church for their *perseverance*. The Greek word for perseverance is HUPOMONE which is also sometimes translated *endurance*. This is the identical Greek word we just saw in Jesus's explanation of the *Parable of the Sower* which is critical to understanding Jesus's call to hear:

> But the seed in the *good soil*, these are the ones who have heard the word in an honest and good heart, and hold it fast, and bear fruit with *perseverance* (HUPMONE). (Luke 8: 15 NASB, emphasis mine)

Bearing fruit in the coming trial will require *endurance*. Additionally, the trial will help *produce* this endurance, "We also exult in our tribulations, knowing that *tribulation brings about perseverance* (HUPOMNE)" (Romans 5:3 NASB, emphasis mine). This is one purpose of Daniel's 70th Week—the refining of the Bride of Christ.

Jesus has one rebuke for the Church, and it's a big one:

> But I have this against you, that *you have left your first love*. Therefore remember from where you have fallen, and *repent and do the deeds you did at*

400

first; or else I am coming to you and will remove your lampstand out of its place—unless you repent" (Rev. 2:4-5 NASB, emphasis mine).

What is the Church's "first love?" In Matthew, Jesus tells us, "You shall *love the Lord your God* with all your heart, and with all your soul, and with all your mind. This is the great and foremost (*first*) commandment" (Matt. 22:37-38 NASB, clarification and emphasis mine). Bringing the Bride of Christ back into a love relationship is the *main purpose* of the 70th Week of Daniel. Jesus is clear that the Church will cease to be the Church if they don't *repent and act accordingly*. They will fall away and apostatize.

Entering the trial, the Church will do "works" and will "toil," for the Lord says, "I know your deeds and your toil" (Rev. 2:2 NASB). The Church will be expending effort, but it will not be done through the love of Jesus. Just a few verses later, we learn the Church's works are not adequate. Jesus wants the Church to "do the deeds you did at first" (Rev. 2:5 NASB). Even though Jesus is aware of the effort the Church is expending in "good deeds," these deeds are not done in the right spirit. In his first epistle, John teaches, "Beloved, let us love one another, for love is from God; and everyone who loves is born of God and knows God. The one who does not love does not know God, for God is love" (1 John 4:7-8 NASB). So love of God and works done through the love of Jesus are the way of *overcoming* (Rev. 2:2-3).

Let's look at a brief graphic (Figure 46: Ephesus Model) of how the Letter to Ephesus matches perfectly with the model of the *First Year* of the 70th Week of Daniel we have been constructing per the *Pattern of Seven Events*:

Year of the 70th Week of Daniel	Pattern of Seven Events	Letter to Ephesus
Enemy Identified		Artemis (goddess of Ephesus) was moon goddess, Allah (Islamic god) is moon god "Image" of Artemis now in Kaaba in Mecca
First Year	1) Deception	DECEPTION BY FALSE MESSIAHS AND PROPHETS Ephesians tested false apostles and found them to be liars. "Liar" is same root word as used in 1 John 2:22 in passage describing the Antichrist Ephesians hated the Nicolaitans (those who try to spiritually overcome the people) Artemis (goddess of Ephesus) was a huntress and carried a bow

Figure 46: Ephesus Model

After the deception of the *First Year*, the world is about to enter a most difficult time.

Chapter Seventeen

THE CHURCH OF SMYRNA

(REVELATION 2:8-11)

Related to the second letter, the Letter to Smyrna, *Smyrna* means "myrrh or death." The spice myrrh which was primarily used for embalming was the main export of the city. We know from the model we have been constructing of the 70th Week that the *Second Year* is a year of bloodshed, war, and chaos. Death is a main export of the *Second Year*.

The most famous saint from Smyrna was Polycarp[lxxviii], a disciple of John himself. Polycarp was martyred for his unyielding faith in Jesus by the apostate Jews and the Romans. They attempted to burn him at the stake, but the flames wouldn't touch him. Frustrated, the city's leaders killed him by running him through with a spear.

THE ATTRIBUTES OF JESUS IN THE LETTER TO SMYRNA

Revelation has this to say about Jesus in the Letter to Smyrna:

> The *first and the last*, who was dead, and *has come to life*, says this (Rev. 2:8 NASB, emphasis mine)

The statement *"first and the last"* is a paraphrase of Rev. 1:8 where Jesus claims to be the *"alpha and the omega"* (the first and last letters of the *Greek* alphabet.) It is interesting to note that these same two letters in the *Hebrew* alphabet are also used in the very first sentence of the *first* book of the Bible, Genesis! Unfortunately, this is not translated in English translations: "In the beginning God created the heavens and the earth." In the *Hebrew*, there is an *additional word* after "God," composed of two letters—*aleph and tav* (the first and last letters of the *Hebrew* alphabet)[lxxix]. This is referring to the same person as the *"alpha and the omega"* in Revelation; it is Jesus!

Jesus created all things (John 1: 2) at the beginning and will judge all things at the end. In Rev. 22: 13, the two concepts (the "first and the last," and the "alpha and the omega") are joined in a single verse showing they mean the same thing. This phrase is highly encouraging to those about to suffer. *Jesus* created all things and will judge all things in the end; between the two events, he is in control of all things. Nothing will happen to Christians that he does not work for their ultimate good.

The second phrase ("has come to life") is also encouraging. Jesus has conquered death. It is not what we should fear. Jesus said, "I say to you, my friends, do not be afraid of those who kill the body and after that have no more that they can do. But I will warn you whom to fear: fear the One who, after He has killed, *has authority to cast into hell*; yes, I tell you, *fear Him*" (Luke 12:4-5 NASB, emphasis mine). Those who have died to Jesus and live in him have nothing to lose or to fear. We are already "dead" to the old self and to this world and its evil system. We are alive in him.

> For to me, *to live is Christ and to die is gain*. But if I am to live on in the flesh, this will mean fruitful labor for me; and I do not know which to choose. But I am hard-pressed from both directions, having the desire to depart and be with Christ, for that is very much better; yet to remain on in the flesh is more necessary for your sake. (Phil. 1:21-24 NASB emphasis mine)

This should be the attitude of the saints facing the *Second Year* of the 70th Week as reflected in the attributes of Jesus in the letter to Smyrna.

CONDITION OF THE CHURCH IN THE *SECOND YEAR*

The condition of the Church in the *Second Year* is difficult, per the *Letter to Smyrna*:

> I know your *tribulation and your poverty* (but you are rich), and the blasphemy by those who say they are *Jews* and are not, but are a *synagogue of Satan*. (Rev. 2:9 NASB, emphasis mine)

We observed in the section about Ephesus that worship of the Antichrist's god may be tied to economic prosperity. In this section we notice that the Christians are *economically poor*. Unwillingness to compromise may have led to their poverty. We know from the model we are constructing of the 70th Week of Daniel, that there will be world-wide economic problems in *Year Three*. Perhaps these problems *begin* for the Christians in *Year Two*.

In the previous section on Ephesus, we also saw a focus on *Islam* as the spiritual challenge for the Church. In *Year Two*, from Rev. 2:9 we see that *apostate Judaism* is added. We know from Daniel 9:27 that the Antichrist eliminates sacrifices and offerings at the *Midpoint* of the 70th Week. This obviously indicates that prior to that time, sacrifices and offerings were occurring. We know that "It is impossible for the blood of bulls and goats to take away sins" (Heb. 10:4 NASB). Only Jesus's eternal blood sacrifice will take away sin. So when the Jews begin the practice of temple sacrifices again, it certainly is at the prompting of Satan; to take their eyes off their Messiah who alone can take away sin. God wants his Church to know these sacrifices are *blasphemy*.

Jesus then gives the Church an encouragement:

> Do not fear what you are about to suffer. Behold, the devil is about to *cast some of you into prison*, so that you will be tested, and you will have tribulation for *ten days*. Be faithful until death, and I will give you the crown of life. (Rev. 2:10 NASB, emphasis mine)

Although the Great Tribulation does not begin until the *Fourth Year, the Church experiences tribulation from the Second Year on.* We notice in this passage that many of the faithful will be placed in prison or prison camps. The length of time the Church will have tribulation is curious: *ten days*.

The *Days of Awe* are a ten-day period from Yom Teruah (Feast of Trumpets) until Yom Kippur (Day of Atonement). These are days of repentance. Jewish tradition teaches that those who repent during the *Days of Awe* will be written into the *Book of Life*. The meaning of this time seems such a perfect match with the purpose of the imprisonment ("to be tested"). We have also seen a *ten day* period in Daniel 1:12. It is the period of testing (note the similarities) when Daniel and his friends refused the Royal food and trusted God.

A major facet of the *Second Year* of the 70th Week that is *not* mentioned in the Letter to Smyrna is *warfare*. Why is that? The Letter to Smyrna is specifically for the Church, so it may be because Jesus has already instructed the Church in his *Olivet Discourse* to not be scared when the warfare begins: "You will be hearing of wars and rumors of wars. See that you are *not frightened*" (Matt. 24:6 NASB, emphasis mine). Jesus wants us to know that the wars of the *Second Year* are not war that leads to the invasion of Israel and the eventual Abomination.

Here is a brief graphic (Figure 47: Smyrna Model) showing how the Letter to Smyrna matches the model for the rest of *Year Two*:

Year of the 70th Week of Daniel	Pattern of Seven Events	Letter to Smyrna
Enemy Identified		Apostate Judaism will feature Temple sacrifices
Second Year	2) Bloodshed, War, and Chaos	BLOODSHED AND CHAOS Smyrna means "death" and second year is the beginning of bloodshed Believers will begin to be imprisoned Believers will be economically poor

Figure 47: Smyrna Model

Chapter Eighteen

THE CHURCH OF PERGAMUM
(REVELATION 2:12-17)

Related to the third letter, the Letter to Pergamum, some believe the name *Pergamum*[lxxx] may have been derived from the Greek word PURGOS meaning "tower." The city is believed to have been the citadel of Troy written about in Homer's *Iliad*, and the ruins of the city still dramatically overlook the Adriatic Sea. I'd like to suggest another meaning for the name Pergamum: *"all-surrounding marriage"* (Gk: PERI meaning "around or all-surrounding" and GAMOS meaning marriage). I rather like this later meaning. Abraham's union with Hagar in Genesis was improper, yet he felt forced into it because of a lack of faith in God and at the urging of Sarah. The perceived need for this marriage (to produce an heir) seemed to encompass him all around and *surround* him. In Chapter Two: "Uncovering the Keys," we learned the result of that union, *Ishmael*, has led to the conflict we currently see in the Middle East. That conflict will eventually lead to the events of the 70th Week of Daniel. The *Third Year* of the 70th Week will begin the improper, seemingly-forced "marriage" of many churchgoers to the Antichrist. As food becomes scarce, many will take the *Mark of the Beast* and suffer eternal condemnation, rather than trust God, because the threat of starvation will surround them.

In Biblical days, Pergamum housed one of the largest libraries of the ancient world. It was even said to rival the great library at Alexandria in Egypt. A third possible derivation of the name Pergamum is from the name of the type of parchment made there, PERGAMENA. It is more likely, however, that the parchment was named after the city rather than vice versa.[lxxxi]

The city was also a famed center of medicine and healing. A lavish spa, the shrine to *Asclepius* (the god of healing)[lxxxii], was world renowned. Asclepius's symbol was a staff wound with a serpent which is still the symbol of medicine world-wide. In

Ch. 18: The Church of Pergamum

Chapter 21 of Luke's Gospel, when Jesus is outlining the events that will occur during the 70th Week, he lists plagues and famines together. Up until this point in this book, we have assumed that plagues, sickness and disease begin in the *Fourth Year* because they are found in Psalm 14 (associated with the *Fourth Year*) and in the description of the Green Horseman (also associated with the *Fourth Year*).

Pergamum's world-wide renown for medicine coupled with Luke's Gospel which suggests that plagues and famine begin together, both suggest to me that the plagues may begin in the *Third Year* and carry over into the *Fourth Year*, but this is conjecture on my part.

Pergamum was also the *site of Satan's throne* according to Rev. 2:13, and at the Pergamon Museum in Germany[lxxxiii], a magnificent original archeological artifact, the Pergamon Altar (the altar of Zeus), is displayed. It is most probably the throne Jesus referred to. We can make a few interesting observations. First, Pergamum is a city in western Turkey. This is further evidence that the Antichrist's empire will be anchored there. Second, it is incredibly interesting to note that the Pergamon Museum is presently in Berlin, Germany, and that the stones of the Pergamon Altar were moved from Turkey by German archeologists and reconstructed by 1930 at the same time Adolph Hitler was rising to power. Was there a connection? In September, 2014, the Pergamon Museum closed the Pergamon Altar exhibit for five years. Is the Altar going to move again? Possibly back to Turkey in light of Dan. 8 prophecy involving Turkey? Will another world leader (Antichrist?) be assisted in his rise to power by this altar? This is highly speculative, but possible. I plan to keep an eye on the Pergamon Altar if it ~~moves.~~ is moved back to Turkey.

Around the time that Revelation was recorded by John, Antipas, the Bishop of Pergamum, was martyred.[lxxxiv] This cemented the satanic reputation of the city. Antipas is mentioned in the Letter to Pergamum (Rev. 2:13), and some accounts have that he was killed in AD 92 on the altar of Zeus, the same Pergamon Altar, previously described.

THE ATTRIBUTES OF JESUS IN THE *LETTER TO PERGAMUM*

In the *Letter to Pergamum*, Jesus is described this way, "The One who has the sharp *two-edged sword* says this" (Rev. 2:12 NASB, emphasis mine). In the *Second Year*, the rider of the *Red Horse* is given a "great sword." In the *Third Year*, Jesus counters with his *two edged sword*. Let us look at other references to this sword. The direct reference is made in John's vision of the risen Christ:

> In His right hand He held seven stars, and out of His mouth came a sharp *two-edged sword*; and His face was like the sun shining in its strength. (Rev. 1:16 NASB, emphasis mine)

Related to the Letter to Pergamum, it is likely Jesus also had this earlier stated reference to the *two-edged sword* in mind as well; however, in Hebrews we read yet another reference to a *two-edged sword*, this time referring to the Word of God:

> For if Joshua had given them rest, he would not have spoken of another day after that. So *there remains a Sabbath rest* for the people of God. For the one who has entered His rest has himself also rested from his works, as God did from His. *Therefore let us be diligent* to enter that rest, so that no one will fall, through following the same example of disobedience. For the *word of God* is living and active and *sharper than any two-edged sword*, and piercing as far as the division of soul and spirit, of both joints and marrow, and able to judge the thoughts and intentions of the heart. And there is no creature hidden from His sight, but all things are open and laid bare to the eyes of Him with whom we have to do. (Heb. 4:8-13 NASB, emphasis mine)

Most folks who have been around the church for a while know the verse Heb. 4:12 which refers to the *two-edged sword*. Most don't know the context. We have already looked at the beginning of this passage back in Chapter Two: "Uncovering the Keys." We discussed these verses in relation to God's way of telling time; that *a day equals a thousand years.* Those beginning verses speak of the *thousand year Millennial Kingdom* that is yet to come. Notice as the passage progresses that we are to be *diligent* to enter that rest. There is a risk of falling away if we follow the example of disobedience the Jews charted after Joshua's day. It is into this context that God's Word is compared to a *two-edged sword.* It appears that this verse is the reference Jesus wants us to consider in the Letter to Pergamum. He wants his Word to lay our intentions bare when faced with the choice of taking the *Mark of the Beast.* He does not want us to enter into an "improper marriage." Ultimately, it is this *sword* that comes out of Jesus's mouth (the Word of God) which will strike down the nations:

> From His mouth comes *a sharp sword,* so that with it He may strike down the nations, and He will rule them with a rod of iron; and He treads the wine press of the fierce wrath of God, the Almighty. (Rev. 19:15 NASB, emphasis mine)

Jesus also wants us to remember that Satan may appear to be winning, but He alone will ultimately triumph. The *Mark of the Beast* may provide a few morsels of food, but little else in this life, but eternal condemnation by God in the life to come. It can't be emphasized enough, *NEVER* take the *Mark of the Beast.*

CONDITION OF THE CHURCH OF PERGAMUM

We can see from what Jesus writes to the Church of Pergamum that the *persecutions* have already begun in the *Third Year*:

> I know where you dwell, where Satan's throne is; and you hold fast my name, and did not deny my faith even in the days of Antipas, my witness, my faithful one, *who was killed among you,* where Satan dwells. (Rev. 2:13 NASB, emphasis mine)

In our study of *Year Two* of the 70th Week (the Letter to Smyrna), we saw that imprisonment of Christians would begin that year, and that the imprisonments would eventually would lead to death. Now in *Year Three* we see that *martyrdom* has begun. The name "Antipas" means *"in place of all."* His martyrdom is a symbol of what is to come.

We also see that Satan's man (the Antichrist) is seated upon his throne—he is ruling. Revelation 13 shows us the Devil giving the Antichrist his throne, "And the beast which I saw was like a leopard, and his feet were like those of a bear, and his mouth like the mouth of a lion. And the *dragon gave him his power and his throne* and great authority" (Rev. 13:2 NASB, emphasis mine).

In the Letter to Pergamum, Jesus is also telling us that he sympathizes with us. He knows the tribulation Christians will be facing in those days, and he is pleased with the faith of those who stand fast. In the next verses, he also reveals that this is the point where some churchgoers, faced with the choice of taking the *Mark of the Beast*, will commit apostasy. He also shows that for some who have not taken the *Mark*, there is still time to repent:

> There some who hold the teaching of Balaam, who kept teaching Balak to put a stumbling block before the sons of Israel, to *eat things sacrificed to idols* and to commit acts of immorality. So you also have some who in the same way hold the teaching of the Nicolaitans. *Therefore repent.* (Rev. 2:14-16 NASB, emphasis mine)

Notice that Jesus uses names we have seen earlier in this book: Balaam and the Nicolaitans. We learned in Chapter Seven: "A Horse of a Different Color (Revelation 6)" that Balaam is a foreshadow of the *False Prophet* and the Nicolaitans are a symbolic word for followers of the Antichrist (Muslims). The sins that are listed: eating *food sacrificed to idols* and sexual immorality, are indicative of the *Third Year*. Christians are not under the Mosaic Law and can eat food sacrificed to idols, although many would certainly choose not to do so. This verse *is* talking about food, but the sacrifice isn't the sacrifice of bulls and goats, rather it is the *sacrifice of churchgoers' souls to Satan*. By taking the *Mark of Beast*, these churchgoers will be allowed to buy and sell and thus eat. They will *lose their salvation*, however——a terrible deal. This is especially true given the promise Jesus gives at the end of the Letter to Pergamum:

> To him who *overcomes*, to him I will give some of the *hidden manna* (Rev. 2:17 NASB, emphasis mine)

Obviously, this speaks of some kind of provision: spiritual, physical, or both. Manna was "hidden" in the Ark of the Covenant in Moses' day:

> There was a tabernacle prepared, the outer one, in which *were* the lampstand and the table and the sacred bread; this is called the holy place. Behind the second veil there was a tabernacle which is called the Holy of Holies, having a golden altar of incense and the ark of the covenant covered on all sides with gold, in which was *a golden jar holding the manna*, and Aaron's rod which budded, and the tables of the covenant (Heb. 9:2-4 NASB, emphasis mine)

We learned in Chapter Six: "The Walls Came Tumbling Down (Joshua 6, Judges 6-8)" that the Ark of the Covenant is a *symbol of Jesus*, so the manna is hidden "in Jesus." Will there be physical provision for those in Jesus during this time? I think there will be. In Matthew 25, Jesus judges the nations based on how they have provided and supported his household (Jews and Christians) during the 70th Week of Daniel:

> For *I was hungry*, and you gave Me something to eat; *I was thirsty*, and you gave Me something to drink; . . . Then the righteous will answer Him, 'Lord, when did we see You hungry, and feed You, or thirsty, and give You something to drink? (Matt. 25:35, 37 NASB, emphasis mine)

This passage is from the prophecy of the *Goat and Sheep Judgment*. Those being addressed by Jesus are human *survivors* of the 70th Week of Daniel. In *this passage*, Jesus is seated on his glorious throne in Jerusalem after the end of the 70th Week, judging *according to works*. Only *living survivors* of the 70th Week will be so judged. The *dead*, both unbelievers and believers, are judged according to faith, and for unbelievers this judgment will occur at the *Great White Throne Judgment* at the end of the Millennium. Notice the basis for the judgment at the *Goat and Sheep Judgment* will be how unbelievers cared for God's people. Obviously, some will be righteous and will provide for Jews and Christians during their time of need, perhaps literally *sharing* the manna which will be given to sustain believers. Of course, this is speculation.

As we also learned in Chapter Seven: "A Horse of a Different Color (Revelation 6)," Jesus has specifically commanded the "heads of his household" (pastors, etc.) to provide for his people during the appointed time of the end (Matt. 24:46), like Joseph did in Egypt. This implies storing food for the times to come. Today, I spent my lunch hour at Costco. I spend many lunch hours there, not to buy food for use now, but to buy it to store for the appointed time. This isn't food for just my family, but for God's entire household, as the Holy Spirit leads. God gave Joseph seven years of plenty to stock up for the seven years of famine. Are the years of famine approaching? I think they are. Let us all prepare for the food shortage of the appointed time.

God gave another wonderful picture of his provision in the account of *Elijah* the prophet. We first learn about Elijah in these verses from 1 Kings:

> Now *Elijah* the Tishbite, who was of the settlers of Gilead, said to Ahab, "As the Lord, the God of Israel lives, before whom I stand, surely there shall be neither dew nor rain these years, except by my word." The word of the Lord came to him, saying, "Go away from here and turn eastward, and hide yourself by the brook Cherith, which is east of the Jordan. It shall be that you will drink of the brook, and *I have commanded the ravens to provide for you there*." So he went and did according to the word of the Lord, for he went and lived by the brook Cherith, which is east of the Jordan. *The ravens brought him bread and meat in the morning and bread and meat in the evening*, and he would drink from the brook. It happened after a while that the brook dried up, because there was no rain in the land. (1 Kings 17:1-7 NASB, emphasis mine)

God commanded Elijah to stop the rain for 3 ½ years during the reign of the evil Israelite king Ahab. This is a foreshadow of what the *Two Witnesses* will do during the Great Tribulation. "These have the power to shut up the sky, so that rain will not fall during the days of their prophesying" (Rev. 11:6 NASB). The drought in the days of Elijah led to a famine. God miraculously led Elijah to the Brook Cherith where he was fed by ravens. The root meaning of the Hebrew word translated *ravens* (OREBH) is "to be black." This is another reference to the color black and the *black horse* of Rev. 6. Interestingly these birds seem to frequently be associated with food. In English, *ravenous*, means starving. In Luke, Jesus connected ravens with God's provision of food, "Consider the *ravens*, for they neither sow nor reap; they have no storeroom nor barn, and *yet* God feeds them; how much more valuable you are than the birds" (Luke 12:24 NASB).

Ravens, however, were "unclean" birds under Mosaic Law (Lev. 11:13-19). So how should we interpret this symbol? I think this is a symbol of God using *unbelievers* to feed Christians. Initially during the time of the *Mark of the Beast*, in my opinion, some unbelievers will take pity on the Christians who are starving and help them. Jesus's short illustration in Luke shows us that our ultimate provision is dependent on the Lord, and he can use "ravens." In the Elijah account, after a while the "brook dries up," and there was no more provision in the first location. Christians need to be aware that the source of provision may change during the famine. We need to be faithful and flexible and follow His leading.

After this, Elijah was sent to Zarephath which means "workshop for the smelting of metals." What an appropriate name for the village! Elijah was being refined like silver during the famine. Zarephath was in Sidon (a Philistine city). Again, Elijah is provided for by those not of the household of God. Jesus mentioned the town when preaching in the synagogue in Nazareth, "But I say to you in truth, there were many widows in Israel in the days of Elijah, when the sky was shut up for *three years and six months* (3 ½ years), when a great famine came over all the land; and yet Elijah was sent to none of them, but only to Zarephath, in the land of Sidon, to a woman who was a widow" (Luke 4:25-26 NASB, clarification and emphasis mine). It was this very account that caused the people of Nazareth to attempt to kill Jesus. They were angry because Jesus was saying that *Gentiles* could be saved as well as Jews. Not only did God provide for Elijah (the believer), but the *unbelieving Gentile widow* as well. Elijah was a witness to her. This is likely what will happen in the 70th Week. Believers will be cared for by some unbelievers and the unbelievers may be saved by the witness of the believers. Also notice Jesus confirms the account in 1 Kings that the time of the famine was *3 1/2 years*, the same length of the ministry of the *Two Witnesses* in Revelation (Rev. 11:3).

There is debate in the Church about the timing of the ministry of the *Two Witnesses*. Some claim it will be the first 3 ½ years of the 70th Week. Some claim it will be the last half of the 70th Week. I would like to suggest a third possibility. In my speculative opinion, the 1260 days of their ministry (Rev. 11:3) may not coincide exactly with either half of the 70th Week. Rather, it may *overlap* the two halves, starting during the *Third Year* and ending with the Resurrection/Rapture event at the end of the *Sixth Year*. Why do I suggest this? Here are some reasons:

- The *Two Witnesses* will be believers. In order for their ministry to encompass the entire second half of the 70th Week, they would have to endure the *Day of the Lord*/the Wrath of God; something God has said he will not do.

- If the *Two Witnesses* have their ministry entirely in the second half of the 70th Week (1260 days), they would then be resurrected *3 ½ days* (Rev. 11:11) *after Jesus returns to earth* with His Church at the end of the 70th Week—this would not make sense! Surely, these *Two Witnesses* will be part of His Church as believers and will be resurrected with all dead believers at the time of the Rapture and will return to earth with Jesus and the other members of the Church. Hence, they would not be resurrected 3 ½ days *after* Jesus physically returns at the end of the 70th Week, which negates the possibility of their ministry being entirely during the second half of the 70th Week.

- The rain of fire and brimstone that occurs at the *First Trumpet* judgment in the *Seventh Year* includes *hail*. This is a form of rain (frozen). This also precludes a ministry that includes the entire second half of the Week since the *Witnesses* prohibit rain for 1260 days (3 ½ years). It does support an idea, however, that the rain of hail is the *end* of the 1260 days.

- The death of the *Witnesses* results in world-wide celebration (Rev. 11:10). It is possible but unlikely that celebrations of this sort take place during the end of the second half of the week in the midst of the horrific Bowl Judgments, during the last 10 days of the *Seventh Year*.

- The *Witnesses* are resurrected and raptured 3 ½ days after their death (Rev. 11:11). If the *Witnesses* were resurrected after a ministry during the *first half* of the Week, this would mean *their* resurrection and rapture would precede *the* main harvest Resurrection and Rapture by 2 ½ years. This is not impossible scripturally, but seemingly unlikely; the better understanding is that they will be resurrected at the time of the main harvest of all believers at the end of the *Sixth Year* of the 70th Week.

The theory that best fits the evidence is a 1260-day ministry that begins at the middle of the *Third Year* and ends 3 ½ days prior to the Resurrection/Rapture event, close to the end of the *Sixth Year*. In this way, the *Two Witnesses* would be able to stop the rain from falling during the year of famine, throughout the *Great Tribulation*, and would be able to be resurrected in the Rapture with all of the others who died in Christ. This is my best guess, and it is logical and ties together all related scripture, a necessity to arrive at truth.

THE OTHER SIN

Returning to the Letter to the *Letter to Pergamum*, Jesus warned them of two sins, eating food sacrificed to idols and sexual immorality. Let's discuss the later sin. This book sets forth the theory that the Antichrist will be the *Mahdi*, the Muslim messiah. You may wonder how a Muslim can promote sexual immorality. In fact, sexual slavery and rape are a part of the Islamic law. Sharia Law allows Muslim men to take horrible advantage of non-Islamic women. I am writing this is 2016, and the Islamic State (ISIS) is engaged in the most horrendous sexual exploitation modern society has ever seen. It appears from the *Letter to Pergamum* that this practice will only increase in the 70th Week.

THE WHITE STONE

The symbol of a *white stone* at the end of the Letter to Pergamum has baffled commentators for years. This is what Jesus said:

> To him who overcomes, to him I will give some of the hidden manna, and I will give him a *white stone*, and a new name written on the stone which no one knows but he who receives it. (Rev. 2:17 NASB, emphasis mine)

I have heard at least six or seven theories about the meaning of the *"white stone."* The one I like best makes complete sense and is the only one that is directly connected to Pergamum. Ray Vander Laan of *That The World May Know* video series has shown that white stones with names on them still line the Sacred Way in Pergamum, a mile long road leading to the shrine of Asclepius, the god of healing[lxxxv]. After a person was supposedly healed by this god, they inscribed their name on one of these stones. In my opinion, Jesus is saying that there will be a sacred way in the Kingdom lined with *white stones* of those he eternally heals.

The aspect of a "new name" is intriguing. God gave Abram a new name: *Abraham.* He renamed Sarai: *Sarah.* He renamed a man named Hosea and called him Joshua. In Isaiah 62:2 he tells the city of Jerusalem that he will rename it. In Rev. 19:12 we learn Jesus has a name written on him that no one else knows. This last example is almost a direct quote of Rev. 2:17. When God changes someone, he renames him. I think these names inscribed on the white stones will be *our new names,* our new names that announce Jesus's victory.

The following graphic (Figure 48: Pergamum Model) highlights how the third church, *Pergamum,* fits into the model we have been constructing of Daniel's 70th Week, related to the *Pattern of Seven Events* in the *Third Year*:

Year of the 70th Week of Daniel	Pattern of Seven Events	Letter to Pergamon
Enemy Identified		Throne of Satan originally in what is now Turkey
Third Year	3) Famine and Economic Collapse	FAMINE Nicolaitans and followers of Balaam encourage eating food sacrificed to idols Jesus will provide "hidden manna" "Pergamos" means "improper marriage" which is what happens to those taking the Mark of the Beast Pergamum worshiped Asclepius: the god of healing, perhaps pestilence begins this year and many will trust medicine over God Pergamon Altar in Berlin now was perhaps the "throne of Satan" mentioned in the letter White stones with unknown names of those healed by Asclepius are found on the Royal Way in Pergamon. Will our names be inscribed on white stones after Jesus changes us?

Figure 48: Pergamum Model

Chapter Nineteen

THE CHURCH OF THYATIRA
(REVELATION 2:18-29)

Related to the fourth letter, the *Letter to Thyatira*, commentators are uncertain as to the meaning of the name *Thyatira*[lxxxvi]. Some have proposed that it is a Turkish word, not Greek. The Turkish equivalent of "Thyatira" means "graveyard on a hill." If this is the correct meaning, it fits perfectly with the *Fourth Year* of the 70th Week of Daniel—the year the *Green Horse* rides, signifying death.

Thyatira's most famous *biblical* resident was Lydia; a convert of Paul's who traded in purple dye. Thyatira was noted for its commercial trade guilds. These guilds were highly organized. They possessed property, made contracts, and wielded a wide influence. The dyer's guild was one of them. In Acts 16:14, Lydia, who was probably a member of this guild, met Paul in Philippi while there selling her dyes. The purple-color dye obtained by the use of the madder root is now called Turkish red.[lxxxvii] Each guild had its particular guardian god, and members were expected to attend all its functions and participate in its activities which included offerings, feasts and often immorality. Christians were torn between making a living on the one hand by being part of a guild and staying faithful to Christ.

A quick read of the *Letter to Thyatira* doesn't seem to give any obvious clues about why this letter applies to the fourth event in the *Pattern of Seven Events* and the *Fourth Year* of the 70th Week. But as we will soon learn, although the symbols are a bit obscure, they do have amazing correlation to the *Fourth Year*.

ATTRIBUTES OF JESUS IN THE *LETTER TO THYATIRA*

Both aspects of the appearance of Jesus given in this *Letter to Thyatira* involve fire and glowing. This is somewhat symbolic about the trial of fire that the Church is about to enter:

The *Son of God*, who has *eyes like a flame of fire*, and His feet are like burnished bronze, says this: (Rev. 2:18 NASB, emphasis mine)

I also notice with great interest that Jesus is listed as the *Son of God*. This is the only reference to this title in the Book of Revelation. It appears here to re-enforce the authority of Jesus. In the *Fourth Year*, the Antichrist will sit in the temple of God and proclaim to be God. He will speak great blasphemies against the Father and the Son (1 John 2:22), especially against Jesus's divinity.

This idea of Jesus being God's Son is found first in Psalm 2. Amazingly, at the conclusion of this Letter to Thyatira, Jesus quotes this *very Psalm*. This dual reference to Psalm 2 in this letter "time stamps" this Psalm as being primarily about the *Fourth Year*. Let's look at the quoted section:

He who sits in the heavens laughs, the Lord scoffs at them (the gentile nations). Then He will speak to them in His anger and terrify them in His fury, saying, "But as for Me, *I have installed My King upon Zion*, My holy mountain. I will surely tell of the decree of the Lord: He said to me, '*You are My Son*, today I have begotten you. Ask of me, and I will surely give *the nations as your inheritance*, and the very ends of the earth as your possession. You shall break them with a *rod of iron*; you shall shatter them like earthenware.'" (Psalm 2:4-9 NASB, clarification and emphasis mine)

This is an incredibly important section of scripture in relation to our understanding of the 70th Week of Daniel. We see God saying he has installed his Messiah (Jesus) as *King upon Zion*. We know during this *Fourth Year* that the Antichrist will take *his* seat in the Temple and proclaim *himself* god. God the Father is essentially saying, "No, you are not king and *not* God. I have a son, even if Muslims deny it, and his inheritance will be the entire earth and all nations." Psalm 2 is God's answer to the Antichrist's blasphemous statements. Furthermore, *Jesus* will rule with a rod of iron and not Antichrist.

In the Letter to Thyatira, Jesus quotes the conclusion of this passage but applies it to the Church as well:

> He who overcomes, and he who keeps My deeds until the end, *to him I will give authority over the nations*; and he shall rule them with a *rod of iron*, as the vessels of the potter are broken to pieces, as I also have received *authority* from My Father. (Rev. 2:26-27 NASB, emphasis mine)

Jesus's promise to the Church is that they will reign over the Kingdom of the Antichrist with Jesus. Even though authority has been given to the Antichrist for 42 months (Rev. 13:5), that authority will be taken from him and given to Jesus and the saints. This letter is Jesus's reminder to the Church that no matter how hopeless the *Fourth Year* looks, they are to know how the story ends.

This letter and Psalm 2 both reference *iron and earthenware* in the same verse, just as you remember the "toes" of the Statue in Nebuchadnezzar's dream:

> As the toes of the feet were *partly of iron and partly of pottery*, so some of the kingdom will be strong and part of it will be brittle. And in that you saw the iron mixed with common clay, they will *combine with one another in the seed of men*; but *they will not adhere to one another*, even as iron does not combine with pottery. In the days of those kings the God of heaven will set up a kingdom which will never be destroyed, and *that* kingdom will not be left for another people; it will crush and put an end to all these kingdoms, but it will itself endure forever. (Dan. 2:42-44 NASB, clarification and emphasis mine)

In Rev. 2, the *iron* is incorporated into the "rod" which represents the aspects of the Kingdom that will "crush"; the *earthenware* represents the weaker aspects of the kingdom that will be crushed. This weakness is similar to other references to saints being earthenware jars (Isa. 45:9, 2 Tim. 2:20, 2 Cor. 4:7). We know the "toes" in Nebuchadnezzar's dream are kings because we are told "in the days of those *kings*" God will set up his Kingdom. This combination is not one that "adheres" or endures. In the

421

dream of Nebuchadnezzar, God smashed the alliance of these ten kings with a rock (Jesus) and in Revelation 2 and Psalm 2 it is Jesus who smashes this alliance with his rod of iron; he will "crush" the kingdoms of man. In both cases the alliance of these kings (the *Beast Empire*) is destroyed to never rise again. This is wonderful encouragement to those living through the *Fourth Year* of the 70th Week.

AUTHORITY

"Authority" is a very important aspect of the *Fourth Year*. From a spiritual perspective it may be the principal, defining aspect of the *Fourth Year*. In Revelation 13 we see Satan giving *the Beast* his authority and his throne in this year:

> And *the beast* which I saw was like a leopard, and his feet were like those of a bear, and his mouth like the mouth of a lion. And *the dragon gave him his power and his throne* and great *authority*. (Rev. 13:2 NASB, emphasis mine)

In Revelation 13 we also learn that God places a time limit on the authority of *the Beast*:

> There was given to him a mouth speaking arrogant words and blasphemies, and *authority* to act for *forty-two months* was given to him. (Rev. 13:5 NASB, emphasis mine)

God also grants *the Beast* (the rider of the Green Death Horse) authority to kill in this *Fourth Year*:

> *Authority* was given to them over a fourth of the earth, to *kill with sword and with famine and with pestilence and by the wild beasts* of the earth. (Rev. 6:8 NASB, emphasis mine)

God also grants *the Beast* authority to war with the saints and defeat them. He also grants him authority over every tribe and people group:

> It was also given to him to make war with the saints and to overcome them, and *authority* over every tribe and people and tongue and nation *was given to him*. (Rev. 13:7 NASB, emphasis mine)

So, when Jesus writes that to him who overcomes he will give *authority* over the nations (Rev. 2:26), it is this same authority that is granted to *the Beast* for 42 months that Jesus will wrest from him and give to its rightful owners——the faithful. This wonderful encouragement is needed in the *Fourth Year* because it is at that time that the authority is temporarily given to *the Beast*. It will appear all is lost, but Jesus wants his Church to remember the end of the story, that ultimately the authority will be given back to Jesus and the redeemed.

THE APPEARANCE OF JESUS

The *two aspects of his appearance* Jesus mentions in the *Letter to Thyatira* are quoted from both visions of Jesus in Daniel and Revelation that we looked at in Chapter Two: "Uncovering the Keys." The *first aspect* of Jesus' appearance mentioned in the *Letter to Thyatira* relates to his *eyes*:

> His *eyes were like a flame of fire*. His feet were like burnished bronze, when it has been made to glow in a furnace. (Rev. 1:14-15 NASB)

> His *eyes were like flaming torches*, his arms and feet like the gleam of polished bronze. (Dan. 10:6 NASB)

In Daniel, Jesus's eyes are compared to flaming torches (Gk: LAMPAS). There is another reference to torches in Revelation that we need to examine:

423

And there were *seven lamps* (Gk: LAMPAS) of fire burning before the throne, which are the *seven Spirits of God*. (Rev. 4:5 NASB, emphasis mine)

Another reference tells us who these *seven spirits* are:

And I saw between the throne (with the four living creatures) and the elders a Lamb standing, as if slain, having seven horns and *seven eyes, which are the seven Spirits of God*, sent out into all the earth. (Rev. 5:6 NASB, emphasis mine)

So Jesus's "eyes" are the *seven Spirits of God* who are sent into all the earth. Zechariah mentions these as well:

"I am going to bring in my servant the Branch. For behold, the stone that I have set before Joshua; on *one stone are seven eyes*. Behold, I will *engrave an inscription on it,*" declares the Lord of hosts, "and I will remove the iniquity of that land in one day." (Zech. 3:8-9 NASB, emphasis mine)

Wow! This passage must have been almost undecipherable to the readers of Zechariah's day. But once Jesus gave us Revelation, the symbols become clear! From this passage in Zechariah we learn that *the stone (Jesus) has seven eyes*. We also see *an inscription engraved upon it*, just as we saw on the *white stone* in the *Letter to Pergamum* in Revelation.

From Revelation we know the seven eyes are the seven Spirits of God that stand before his throne and are sent through all the earth. Let's look at another grouping of seven who stand before the throne of God:

And I saw the *seven angels who stand before God*, and seven trumpets were given to them. (Rev. 8:2 NASB, emphasis mine)

Are the *seven angels* the *seven Spirits of God*? Although I am not sure, it is likely that they are. They are Jesus's servants. We see they pour out his wrath (the seven trumpets judgments and the seven bowl judgments). This explains why this aspect of Jesus's appearance is so important during the *Fourth Year*. It encourages the Church that Jesus's judgment is coming upon those who are persecuting them.

The *second aspect of Jesus's appearance* mentioned in this *Letter to Thyatira* (in addition to the aspect of his *eyes* covered in the above discussion) are his *feet of burnished bronze* that appear to glow "white hot" as if they had been heated in a furnace. Feet seem to be *symbolic of sinful uncleanliness*. In Solomon's Temple a great bronze sea was set up for the priests to wash their hands and feet. (2 Chron. 4:6). During the Last Supper, Jesus washed *the feet* of his disciples. (John 13:5) During the washing Jesus comments to Peter, "He who has bathed needs only to wash his feet, but is completely clean" (John 13:10 NASB). This means that once saved by faith, Christians only need forgiveness of their daily sins (their feet) not re-salvation. Feet therefore are a symbol of *uncleanliness*. Obviously the Holy Son of God not only has clean feet, but feet that glow "white hot" in purity.

CONDITION OF THE CHURCH OF THYATIRA

By the *Fourth Year*, many lukewarm Christians have fallen away. The Church, though smaller, is now stronger in their faith and in their deeds due to the refining of persecution. Jesus recognizes them for it in this *Letter to Thyatira*, "I know your deeds, and your love and faith and service and perseverance, and that *your deeds of late are greater than at first*" (Rev. 2:19 NASB, emphasis mine). The final phrase, *"your deed of late are greater than at first,"* is the opposite of what was said in the *First Year* in the Letter to Ephesus: *"repent and do the deeds you did at first."* The fire of the trial is refining the Church of Thyatira.

Jesus does rebuke the Church, however, for its relationship to "Jezebel":

Jezebel, who calls herself a *prophetess* (like Mohammed), and she teaches and leads my bond-servants astray so that they commit acts of immorality and eat things sacrificed to idols. (Rev. 2: 20 NASB, clarification and emphasis mine)

Who is *Jezebel*? In prophecy, *women* are used as symbols represent *religious systems*. The "woman" in Revelation 12 is Israel/Judaism, for example. The passage of Revelation 2 clearly states *Jezebel* is a "prophetess" (she *thinks* she hears from God) and she teaches this mistaken theology. Jezebel only *calls herself a prophetess*, however, and leads Christ's bond servants astray by encouraging them to sin by eating food sacrificed to idols and to committing acts of sexual immorality. Jezebel herself is not the "adulteress," but rather encourages believers to commit adultery. This is an important distinction. What religion is this? We know it isn't Judaism or apostate Christianity because if they are unfaithful to our Lord they would truly be committing adultery. That leaves *Islam* as the only remaining choice. Let's examine the account of Jezebel in the Old Testament to help determine if Islam truly is the religion represented by Jezebel:

Now Ahab the son of Omri became king over Israel in the thirty-eighth year of Asa king of Judah, and Ahab the son of Omri reigned over Israel in Samaria twenty-two years. *Ahab the son of Omri did evil in the sight of the Lord* more than all who were before him. It came about, as though it had been a trivial thing for him to walk in the sins of Jeroboam the son of Nebat, that *he married Jezebel* the daughter of Ethbaal king of the Sidonians, and *went to serve Baal and worshiped him*. (I Kings 16:29-31 NASB, emphasis mine)

We learn from this account that *Jezebel was the wife of Ahab*, who has the dubious distinction of being more evil than all the previous kings of Israel. The text says he acted as though it was trivial that he married an unbeliever and began to serve their god, *Baal*. This ancient god was the nemesis of Israel throughout most of its existence. Who was Baal? Is there a connection between *Baal* and *Allah*? There is speculation that they are the same. Numerous scholars support this theory.[lxxxviii] Mohammed was from the tribe of Quraysh. Most documents show their principal deity was *Hubal* that scholars have confirmed was the same deity known in northern countries as *Baal*. Other documents show that the principal deity was *Allah*. Since you can't have two principal deities, many scholars contend *Hubal*, *Baal*, and *Allah* are the same. Even if Baal and Allah are not the same god, it is rather obvious that Jezebel does *not* symbolize apostate Christianity. The historic *Jezebel* was *a pagan, not an apostate*. The only choice for the symbol *Jezebel* is *Islam*.

Now that we have come to the conclusion that *Jezebel* is a symbol for *Islam*, let us continue to examine the "career" of Jezebel. Her name means "where is the prince?" This was a ritualistic phrase called out by Baal worshipers during times of the year he was supposedly in the underworld. This phrase would be shouted to usher him onto the earth[lxxxix]. To Christians, this has an eerie similarity to *the Beast* that comes out of the abyss. As we discussed in Chapter Eleven: "Event Four: Abomination and Death," Michael stands up in the *Fourth Year* of the 70th Week to fight Satan and this releases *the Beast*.

In addition to requiring that Baal worship be recognized as the national religion of Israel, Jezebel was the first to persecute the people of God based on their faith in YHWH. Jezebel killed as many prophets of God as she could. Obadiah saved one hundred prophets and hid them in a cave from her wrath (1 Kings 18:4). This also has an eerie similarity to the persecution of the "woman" and Christians about to take place at the hand of the Antichrist during the Great Tribulation. God will hide *his remnant* in the "secret place" just as Obadiah did the prophets.

Jezebel also desired the vineyard of Naboth whose name means "fruit producer." She had two false witnesses accuse Naboth of blasphemy, and then had him stoned to death in order to acquire his vineyard (1 Kings 21:8-10). Isn't this also a perfect picture of the persecutions to come when Muslims will accuse faithful, "fruit producing" believers of blasphemy against Allah (Baal)?

We already saw in the last section how Elijah caused no rain to fall for 3 ½ years during the reign of Ahab. After God said he would restore rain to the land, Elijah challenged the prophets of Baal on Mount Carmel. In this famous confrontation, Elijah mocked the Baal prophets. After God caused fire to fall from heaven following Elijah's prayer, Elijah had the Israelites kill the 450 prophets of Baal (1 Kings 18:20-40). Furious at the loss of her prophets of Baal, Jezebel threatened to kill Elijah, who ran away from her into the wilderness (1 Kings 19:1-3). I anticipate that confrontations between God's *Two Witnesses* during the Great Tribulation and the Antichrist will mirror this confrontation.

In total, the career of Jezebel seems a perfect foreshadow of *Islam* during the *Fourth Year* of the 70th Week. By using this one symbol of Jezebel, Jesus has given us so much information. Let's return to the *Letter to Thyatira* and see what Jesus adds to this symbolic account:

> The woman Jezebel, who calls herself a prophetess, and she teaches and leads My bond-servants astray so that they *commit acts of immorality* and *eat things sacrificed to idols*. (Rev. 2:20 NASB, emphasis mine)

In this passage we see that *Islam* is going to lead churchgoers astray so they *eat food sacrificed to idols*. It is interesting that the Islamic system of Hallal, slaughtering and preparing meat for food, is all a sacrifice to their god, Allah (whom we know to be an idol.) Additionally in the last section, we learned how all food eaten under the system of the *Mark of the Beast* can be considered food sacrificed to this idolatrous religion.

Some consider the Christian free to eat all types of food, but the Apostles placed a restriction on gentile believers to "abstain from things contaminated by idols "(Acts 15:20). While the apostle Paul writes that we are free to eat all things, he pointedly makes the exception when the meat is said to be sacrificed to idols (1Cor 10:1-13) so our liberty does not create a stumbling block for weaker brothers.

The sexual immorality mentioned may be physical as we have discussed in previous sections or may be a spiritual unfaithfulness as believers fall away and commit apostasy rather than face death.

Jesus will begin to punish the *false religion of Islam* with pestilence in the *Fourth Year* as well:

I gave her time to repent, and she does not want to repent of her immorality. Behold, I will throw her on a bed of sickness, and *those who commit adultery with her* into *great tribulation*, unless they repent of her deeds. And I will kill her children *with pestilence*, and all the churches will know that I am He who searches the minds and hearts; and I will give to each one of you according to your deeds. (Rev. 2:21-23 NASB, emphasis mine)

If there is still doubt in your mind about the end-time fulfillment of the *Letters to the Seven Churches*, the following passage should finally help you overcome those doubts. Jesus uses the term *"great tribulation."* This phrase only occurs two other times in the New Testament (Matt. 24:21 and Rev. 7:9), and in both other instances it refers to the period of the tribulation by the Antichrist in the last half of the 70th Week of Daniel, as named by Jesus himself in the *Olivet Discourse*. Jesus and the disciples frequently use the term "tribulation" (Gk: THLIPSIN) to represent persecution during this life, but the term the *"Great Tribulation"* is specific to one future time. Completely consistent with our thesis, this term occurs in the letter about the *Fourth Year* of the 70th Week—-the year the *Great Tribulation* begins.

The passage has much more information than just a reference to the *Great Tribulation*. It says that Jesus has allowed "Jezebel" (Islam) time to repent. Most scholars date the beginning of Islam with the writing of the Quran in 609 AD. Jesus has given Jezebel (Islam) 1400 years to repent, but at some point, Jesus's long suffering patience with Islam will end. And that time won't be pretty.

We then see that *Islam* and her children will be thrown onto a bed of sickness. Jesus specifically says he will kill her children with pestilence, *and* that this will be cause for all the churches to know that Jesus is the one who searches minds and hearts. In my opinion, this implies that the pestilence will be of supernatural origin, and will specifically target *Muslims*. Psalm 91 states the following related to this pestilence:

You will not be afraid of the terror by night, or of the arrow that flies by day; or the *pestilence that stalks in darkness*, or of the destruction that lays waste at noon. A thousand may fall at your side and ten thousand at your right hand, *but it shall not approach you.* You will only look on with your eyes and see the recompense of the wicked. For you have made the Lord, my refuge, even the Most High, your dwelling place. No evil will befall you, *nor will any plague come near your tent.* (Psalms 91:5-10 NASB, emphasis mine)

The passage in Rev. 2:21-23 also says those that commit adultery with Jezebel (Islam) will be thrown into *great tribulation.* This passage specifically differentiates between those who commit adultery with Islam and her children. To me, *"those who commit adultery with her"* are not those who *convert* to Islam, which are her "children." Rather they are *those who do not actively oppose Allah and accept some of Islam's practices.* Jesus is clear that those people (Christians and non-believers alike) should not be fooled; they will not escape the wrath of Islam and they will be thrown into *great tribulation* by God. In other words, they will be persecuted unto death. Their passivity will not save them.

Jesus then addresses those who have remained true to the faith:

But I say to you, the rest who are in Thyatira, who do not hold this teaching, who have not known the deep things of Satan, as they call them—I place no other burden on you. Nevertheless what you have, *hold fast until I come.* He who *overcomes,* and he who *keeps my deeds until the end,* to him *I will give authority over the nations.* (Rev. 2: 24-26 NASB, emphasis mine)

We have now circled back to the promise of Jesus's authority being given to the saints. But carefully notice what the passage says, "hold fast until I come . . . he who *keeps my deeds until the end,* to him I will give . . ." Jesus makes this promise only to those who endure until the end. This implies that a significant trial is coming in which believers will have to hold fast. Jesus is encouraging the Church to do just that because he is coming with his reward *"to give authority over the nations"* during the Millennium. Approximately 2 ½ years from the *Midpoint* to the Rapture is not that long of a time to hold fast in relationship to all of eternity.

Finally, Jesus concludes the message with these words, "and I will give him (the one who *overcomes*) the morning star" (Rev 2:28 NASB, clarification mine). Who or what is the morning star? Jesus tells us later in Revelation, "I am the root and the descendant of David, the *bright morning star*" (Rev. 22:16 NASB, emphasis mine). This is an even better promise than the promise of his authority. Jesus is promising us himself!

This is a confusing passage for some in the Church because many think Satan is also referred to as the *"morning star"*:

> How you have fallen from heaven, *O star of the morning, son of the dawn!* You have been cut down to the earth, you who have weakened the nations! But you said in your heart, 'I will ascend to heaven; I will raise my throne above the stars of God, and I will sit on the mount of assembly in the recesses of the north. I will ascend above the heights of the clouds; I will make myself like the Most High.' (Isa. 14:12-14 NASB, emphasis mine)

This famous passage is about *Satan* (and the Antichrist by extension). It seems to say that Satan claims the title "star of the morning, son of the dawn" as well. But a wonderful analysis by Rodrigo Silva author of *The Coming Bible Prophecy Reformation* (Kingdom Publishers, 2014) shows that *this is not so*. If we look at the phrase "O star of the morning, son of the dawn" one of the Hebrew words is not translated.

HELEL	BEN	SACHER	YALAL
Lucifer	son	(of the) morning	

The Hebrew word HELEL which is translated "morning star" in the NASB is most frequently translated "Lucifer" or "shining one." However, it is also very similar to the Arabic HILAL which means "crescent" as in "crescent moon." Obviously, the crescent moon is a primary symbol of Islam. Thus Lucifer's very name is similar to the Arabic word for a primary Islamic symbol. The Hebrew word YALAL which is not translated at all in the NASB means "howling or to howl." When we plug this word into the phrase above we get: "Lucifer (crescent), son of the *howling* morning." Mr. Silva's theory is that the "howling morning" is the *Islamic call to prayer each dawn* that can even make dogs bark[xc]. In all instances, this phrase does *not* refer to Lucifer being a *morning star*, which is a *title for our Messiah*.

As we have been doing, let's present a graphic (Figure 49: Thyatira Model) of the model related to the *Pattern of Seven Events* we have constructed for the *Letter to Thyatira*, representing the *Fourth Year*:

Year of the 70th Week of Daniel	Pattern of Seven Events	Letter to Thyatira
Enemy Identified		Jezebel is symbol for Islam Baal and Allah may be the same god
Fourth Year	Abomination and Death	Jezebel (Islam) will persecute saints Jezebel (Islam) will try to tempt saints to eat food sacrificed to idols and engage in sexual immorality Islam will be thrown on bed of sickness that will not touch the Church as a sign to her Link to Psalm 2 showing that Jesus is the Son of God not the Antichrist Link of Psalm 2 encouraging saints that the authority given Antichrist is temporary and Jesus will give it to them after the 42 months Jesus references "Great Tribulation"

Figure 49: Thyatira Model

432

Chapter Twenty

THE CHURCH OF SARDIS

(REVELATION 3:1-6)

The fifth church letter is the *Letter to Sardis*, representing "martyrdom" in the *Pattern of Seven Events* and *Year Five*. The name of the town of Sardis comes from the Greek word SARDIUS which is an orange red gemstone. Similar related gemstones are SARDONYX and SARDION which is also called a carnelian. The Sardonyx is especially interesting because it is white streaked with red. What a perfect picture of the faithful Church, the pure (white) will be streaked with red (martyrdom.) Because the Church has missed the end-time prophetic meaning of the *Letters to the Seven Churches*, this meaning of this symbol has evaded them as well. But when you understand the true nature of the *Letters to the Seven Churches*, the symbols come into focus.

These gemstones appear throughout the Bible. The Sardonyx and the Sardius appear as foundations for the walls of the New Jerusalem. Sardonyx is the fifth foundation (*Fifth Year* of the 70th Week?) and the Sardius is the sixth foundation (Rev. 21:19-20). Does this imply that martyrdom of the saints that occurs in the *Fifth* and *Sixth Years* of the 70th Week are foundations the New Jerusalem is built upon? It is an intriguing theory. The *Throne of the Most High himself* is pictured as being like Jasper and Sardius in appearance as well. In Revelation 21:11 we are told that the Glory of God is like a stone most precious, like Jasper that is as clear as crystal. God is so pure. His Throne isn't a white stone streaked with red like the saints of the *Fifth Year;* his throne is clear as crystal with the red stone of sacrifice (Sardius) as well, obviously referring to Jesus's sacrifice. The first mention of Sardius (Law of Primacy) appears in Exodus:

And the Lord spoke to Moses, saying, Speak to the children of Israel, and take *first-fruits* of all, who may be disposed in their heart to give; and ye shall take my first-fruits. And this is the offering which ye shall take of them; gold and silver and brass, and blue, and purple, and double scarlet, and fine spun linen, and goats' hair, and rams' skins dyed red, and blue skins, and incorruptible wood, and oil for the light, incense for anointing oil, and for the composition of incense, *and Sardius stones*, and stones for the carved work of the breast-plate, and the full-length robe. And thou shalt make me a sanctuary, *and I will appear among you.* (Exod. 25:1-8 LXX, emphasis mine)

Other than the *Septuagint* (Greek) translation, the other Hebrew translations of this text miss that God is requesting a *first fruits* offering of Sardius stones and the obvious reference to the town of Sardis. In the Hebrew text this stone is referred to as SOHAM meaning "onyx stone." Isn't it interesting that the Hebrew refers to an onyx and the Greek translation to a "Sardius"? Together they form a "Sardonyx," the white and red striped stone of martyrdom.

Let's examine this amazing text from Exodus a little closer. God spoke to Moses and asked those "who may be disposed in their heart to give" to make *first-fruit* offerings. From these offerings, Moses was to make a sanctuary: the Tabernacle. This meaning is incredibly similar to the idea that the foundations of New Jerusalem will include Sardonyx and Sardius stones. The dwelling place of our Lord rests on the sacrifices and martyrdom of his people. Then the passage concludes with this promise "and I will appear among you." Jesus doesn't return until the *first-fruit* martyrdom of his people. In Chapter Twenty-Three: "Appointments," we will discuss an additional link between the Feast of the Lord, *First Fruits*, and the *Fifth Year* of the 70th Week. In total this greatly overlooked passage in Exodus 25 is a key to great understanding of the proper interpretation of various scriptures we are looking at.

It is truly amazing how all scripture ties together, and how all the bits and pieces need to be brought together to give the proper interpretation. Indeed, scripture interprets scripture to give proper understanding in all cases.

THE HISTORIC SARDIS

In the sixth century BC, Sardis was the capital of the Kingdom of Lydia. It was ruled by Croesus whose very name is associated with wealth ("as rich as Croesus"). The Lydians discovered the secret of separating gold and silver and producing metals of incredibly high purity.[xci] Isn't this also a perfect picture of what will occur during the *Fifth Year* of 70th Week? Jesus will use the "furnace" of great tribulation to refine his Bride like fine gold and silver. Jesus chose the symbol of this town with divine precision.

Returning to the narrative about ancient Sardis, the ability to refine gold made Croesus the richest man in the world. The purity of the gold and silver made coins minted in Sardis the standard currency world-wide. In today's vernacular, they had the "reserve currency." Prior to this advancement, merchants were never sure of the value of a coin. Sardis is known as the birthplace of modern currency.[xcii] I am writing this section of the book in June, 2015. World economies teeter on the brink of crashing. Will a new world currency emerge based on a gold and silver standard that merchants will be able to trust? Will the *Mark of the Beast* be tied to this new, probably digital currency? Will this currency emerge during the *Fifth Year* of the 70th Week; during the time described by the *Letter to the Church of Sardis*? Only time will tell.

Wealth made Croesus the envy of many other leaders of his day. The citadel of Sardis was set on high cliffs, inaccessible to attacking armies. The Persian king Cyrus the Great (who also conquered Babylon) attempted to overthrow the city but found the walls too high. One day, a chance accident led to the fall of the city. A Lydian soldier dropped his helmet from the wall. Not thinking that anyone was watching him, he climbed down to retrieve it using a secret narrow path. One of Cyrus's soldiers observed this, reported the path to Cyrus, and the Persian Army used the path to access and conquer the city[xciii].

This historic narrative is almost a mirror image of how Cyrus conquered Babylon. In that more famous account, Cyrus received a message from God showing him that if he dammed up the Euphrates River that ran under the wall and through the city of Babylon, his men could enter secretly *under* the gates that spanned the river.

435

Cyrus timed his attack to coincide with the Babylonian feast thrown by Belshazzar. Records of this conquest are also found on the famous Cyrus Cylinder now housed in the British Museum in London. Cyrus gives credit to "the supreme God" for allowing him to overthrow the tyranny of Babylon. This cylinder also tells how Cyrus decreed that all the captive nations be returned their holy objects (the Temple vessels of Jerusalem included). Cyrus returned them to their rightful owners and places of worship[xciv]. Amazingly, the coming of Cyrus and his victory was prophesied by the prophet Isaiah 150 years prior to the events:

> It is I who says to the depth of the sea, "Be dried up! and *I will make your rivers dry.*" It is I who says of *Cyrus*, "He is my shepherd! And he will perform all my desire. *And he declares of Jerusalem, 'She will be built,'* And of the temple, 'Your foundation will be laid.'" (Isa. 44:27-28 NASB, emphasis mine)

Isaiah is clearly telling us that Cyrus did the will of YHWH in capturing Babylon. Isaiah also tells us Cyrus is the one to declare that Jerusalem and the Temple will be rebuilt. Daniel's prophecy of the 70 Weeks contains this phrase that determines *when we should begin counting* the 70 Weeks: "*From the issuing of a decree to restore Jerusalem until Messiah*, the prince, there will be *seven weeks and sixty two weeks*" (69 x 7 years = 483 years) (Dan. 9:25 NASB, clarification and emphasis mine). Did the decree in Daniel's prophecy to restore Jerusalem come directly from *Cyrus*? My reading of scripture, independent of any mathematical calculations of looking at dates, says that it did.

Isaiah then continues:

> Thus says the Lord to *Cyrus* His anointed, "Whom I have taken by the *right hand*, to subdue nations before him and to loose the loins of kings; *to open doors before him so that gates will not be shut*: I will go before you and *make the rough places smooth*; I will shatter the doors of bronze and cut through their iron bars. I will give you the treasures of darkness and hidden wealth of secret places, so that you may know that it is I, the Lord, the God of Israel, who calls

you by your name. For the sake of Jacob My servant, and Israel My chosen one, I have also called you by your name; I have given you a title of honor though you have not known Me. (Isa. 45:1- 3 NASB, emphasis mine)

Although this is clearly written about *Cyrus the Great*, did you notice the multiple messianic references ("right hand," "open doors that none can shut," and "making the rough places smooth")? In addition to a prophecy about Cyrus, this passage also has a *near/far fulfillment.* It is also speaking of the future victory of our *Messiah* over the forces of the *Antichrist!* Jesus refers to this directly in the *fifth letter*, the *Letter to Sardis*:

Therefore *if you do not wake up, I will come like a thief,* and you will not know at what hour I will come to you. (Rev. 3:3 NASB, emphasis mine)

Cyrus's sneak attack up the hidden path to Sardis came as a *"thief in the night."* Jesus is saying that if churchgoers do not *wake up*, He will come as a thief to them as well. Indeed, we need to *wake up*! He is going to overthrow the world systems of wealth (Sardis) and false religion (Babylon/Baal/Islam) and only the faithful will be awake to anticipate it.

THE ATTRIBUTES OF JESUS IN THE *LETTER TO SARDIS*

Jesus describes the attribute of himself this way to the Church living through the *Fifth Year* of the 70th Week:

He who has the *seven Spirits* of God and the *seven stars*, says this. (Rev. 3:1 NASB, emphasis mine)

We have already discussed both of these symbols previously. We saw the *seven spirits* of God are most likely the *seven angels* who stand before the Throne of God and are Jesus's servants going to and fro throughout the earth. We saw in that discussion that

437

these *seven angels* blow the *seven trumpets* and pour out the *seven bowls* which constitute the Wrath of God. We also learned they are the "eyes" of Jesus that burn like torches. By using this symbol, Jesus is encouraging us to know that despite the great tribulation of the Church, Jesus sees and knows what is occurring and has *his angels* ready to avenge the persecution of his saints.

We studied the opening of the *Fifth Seal* on the 7 *Sealed Scroll* in Chapter Twelve: "Event Five: Martyrdom and Apostasy." This, of course, is a parallel passage and also describes the *Fifth Year* of the 70th Week. At that time we saw the saints beneath the Altar of God crying out:

> "How long, O Lord, holy and true, will you refrain from judging and avenging our blood on those who dwell on the earth?" And there was given to each of them *a white robe*; and they were told that they should rest for a little while longer, *until the number of their fellow servants and their brethren who were to be killed even as they had been, would be completed also.* (Rev. 6:10-11 NASB, emphasis mine)

Notice that the saints are asking when God will avenge their martyrdom, just as the reference to the seven spirits of God is a reference to God's coming wrath. I also notice with particular interest the mention of *"white robes."* At the conclusion of the *Letter to Sardis*, those who "overcome will thus be clothed in *white garments*" (Rev. 3:5 NASB, emphasis mine). This is yet another perfect fingerprint identification that the *Letters to the Seven Churches* and the *Seven Seals* are two different prophetic views of the *same events*.

As we learned in Chapter Fourteen: "Event Seven: Rapture and Wrath," the *white robes* are the righteous deeds of the saints (Rev. 19:8) which they obtain from washing the robes in the blood of the Lamb (Rev. 7:14). They are indicative of their salvation. I also believe they are symbolic of the new, changed, "Resurrection" bodies we receive upon the Resurrection and Rapture.

The second attribute of Christ found in this letter is that *he holds the seven stars*. We have also studied the meaning of this symbol previously and concluded that the "stars" refer to *human messengers* given to the churches to help convey Jesus's message in Revelation to them. If the seven Spirits of God give us encouragement of the coming end of *the Beast* system during the Wrath of God, the seven messengers (stars) help the churches interpret Jesus's revelations so they *can* overcome. This understanding of Jesus's revelations will never be more needed as during the *Great Tribulation*, before the resurrection/Rapture, followed by God's Wrath on earth.

THE CONDITION OF THE CHURCH OF SARDIS

Every commentary I've read claims Sardis was a dying church. When you view Jesus's instructions to the Church through the lens of advice to church types or Church Ages, this would be appropriate. However, viewed through the lens of an intended prophetic view of the *Fifth Year* of the 70th Week, Jesus's words take on a slightly new meaning—it is a *mostly dying* church:

> I know your deeds, that you have a name that you are alive, but *you are dead. Wake up*, and *strengthen the things that remain*, which were about to die; for I have not found your deeds completed in the sight of My God. So remember what you have received and heard; and keep it, and repent. Therefore if you do not *wake up*, I will come like a thief, and you will not know at what hour I will come to you. But you have *a few people* in Sardis who have not soiled their garments; and they *will walk with me in white*, for they are worthy. (Rev. 3:1-4 NASB, emphasis mine)

The *Fifth Year* is the *year of decision*. Churchgoers will stand up for Jesus and face persecution and martyrdom, or will commit apostasy. In Matthew 24, Jesus says the love of *"most"* will grow cold. To me that means *most* will commit *apostasy*. That is why at the end of this passage Jesus says the Church has only a few people whose garments aren't soiled. As the *Fifth Year* progresses, more and more of the true believers will lay their lives down for Jesus and His Word. By the end, the majority of those claiming to be "Christian," but who have committed apostasy, will vastly outnumber the dwindling number of true believers left. This is why Jesus says to this Church that they have a reputation for being alive but they're really dead. The *Sardis Church* is a mostly dead and dying Church. The true believers are mostly martyred. They are physically dead. The apostates still physically alive are, however, spiritually dead and dying.

Jesus instructs them to *wake up* because he is coming soon. What does the command to *"wake up"* mean? Jesus's main teaching on the sleeping Church is the *Parable of the Ten Virgins.* Jesus taught that "Now while the bridegroom was delaying, they *all* (all ten!) got drowsy and began to sleep" (Matt. 25:5 NASB, clarification mine). Jesus taught that the *entire church* will be *sleeping* at some point before his return. Most misread the passage, and think that only the foolish virgins are sleeping. That is not what Jesus is teaching. He is teaching the *entire Church is asleep.*

But then at "midnight," a cry goes out that wakes them up. What is "midnight?" Many teach this is the Rapture, but that is inaccurate. If we carefully read the passage after the "midnight cry," all the virgins light their lamps. The foolish virgins run out of oil and they are instructed to go and buy oil, but when they are gone, Jesus returns. That is a lot of activity for the midnight cry to come directly before the Rapture.

So what is "midnight?" It is the depth of the night; *the darkest hour.* That is a perfect symbol for the *Fifth Year* of the 70th Week. It will truly be *Great Tribulation*; the Churches' darkest hour. The fact that Jesus inserts the instruction to "wake up" into the *Letter to Sardis* tells me that the *Great Tribulation* is the *"midnight cry."* It appears that for some, however, even the Great Tribulation won't wake them up because Jesus further instructs, "if you do not wake up, I will come like a thief, and you will not know at what hour I will come to you" (Rev. 3:3 NASB). Paul taught on this same subject in the section of scripture about the Rapture:

Now as to the times and the epochs, brethren, you have no need of anything to be written to you. For you yourselves know full well that the day of the Lord will come just like a thief in the night. While they (non-Christians) are saying, "Peace and safety!" then destruction will come upon them suddenly like labor pains upon a woman with child, and they will not escape. But *you, brethren,*

440

are not in darkness, that the day would overtake you like a thief; for you are all
sons of light and sons of day. We are not of night nor of darkness; so then let us
not sleep as others do, but let us be *alert and sober.* (1 Thess. 5: 2-6 NASB,
clarification and emphasis mine)

This is pretty radical teaching to many who fully expect that Jesus will come upon them
(the Church) like a thief in the night (the "imminent" return of Christ). This is what has
been taught incorrectly to the Church. Scripture clearly teaches us that is *not* the case.
"But *you, brethren, are not in darkness, that the day would overtake you like a thief.*"
Paul is teaching us we will *know* the approximate timing of Jesus's return. Let's see
exactly what the passage is saying.

- Paul had just taught on the resurrection and Rapture in the previous verses.
  He then equates the timing of the Rapture with the timing of the *Day of
  Lord.* We have studied that previously. The *Wrath of God* on the *Day of
  the Lord* occurs immediately after the Church is raptured.

- Paul assumed his readers were aware of the "times" (Gk: CHRONON
  meaning sequence of events) of the end times. CHRONON is the word
  from which we get "chronology." Paul taught that his readers already knew
  the chronology of end time events. How did they know this? Jesus
  provided the chronology in the *Olivet Discourse*. He taught that the Church
  would *go through tribulation before his coming* as well as see other signs.

- Paul also taught that his readers knew the "epochs" (Gk: KAIRON meaning
  "appointed times") that would apply to Christ's return. "Appointed Times"
  can mean appointments. In Hebrew this same meaning is found in the word
  MO'EDIM which is also used for the *Jewish Feast Days* (Lev. 23). Was
  Paul saying that the *Jewish Feast Days* would be fulfilled at the coming of
  Christ? I believe he was. We will discuss this in depth in Chapter Twenty-
  Three: "Appointments." We will visit it again in the next section on the
  Letter to Philadelphia as well. There is value in understanding the Hebrew
  roots of our Christian faith, such as the Feasts of the Lord.

In regard to our discussion here, let it suffice to say that the readers of Paul's epistle knew the chronology of end time events and how the *Jewish Feast Days* would be fulfilled upon the coming of Jesus. Paul is teaching *only unbelievers* will be surprised by Jesus' return.

If we combine the teaching of Jesus in the *Parable of the Ten Virgins* with this teaching from Paul's epistle, we see three groups of persons. First, we see the unbelievers do not wake up at all to the reality that Jesus is about to return. Despite the *Great Tribulation* raging on about them, they attribute these events to the normal course of politics and economics. They are the *mockers* we learned about in Chapter Two: "Uncovering the Keys," who laugh at the notion that Jesus is about to return. They will be saying "peace and safety" when disaster comes upon them like a "thief in the night."

The second and third groups both wake up during the *Great Tribulation*. They are the *virgins of Jesus's Parable*. Now one must ask, why are they only waking up to the reality of Jesus's soon coming during the *Great Tribulation*? Will all the events we discussed in these many chapters of this book take place in the first 3 ½ years of the 70th Week of Daniel and they will miss them? In my opinion, *yes*, they will miss the fact that they are signs of Jesus's coming. The next obvious question is, "Why?" The vast majority of churchgoers today believe in a *Pre-Tribulation Rapture*. Those who believe in this theory will most likely continue to do so until great tribulation stares them in face. They will not "watch" for the signs and chronology (CHRONON) of Jesus's return because they have been taught that his return could happen a moment from now or a thousand years from now; they have been taught the non-biblical theory of the *"imminent return of Jesus"* (that He can come at any time without any prophesized events having to occur first—sounds "good" but there is only one problem—it is not a biblical teaching!). Most believers in a *Pre-Tribulation Rapture* don't believe we need to watch for "signs," as given in the *Olivet Discourse* by Jesus (Matt. 24). All of these churchgoers wake up, however, when severe persecution unto death begins. We will study what happens to the wise and the foolish virgins in the *Letter to Laodicea*.

Finally, let's return to the closing statement of Jesus in this fifth letter, the *Letter to Sardis*, the letter we are currently studying, relating to the *Fifth Year*:

He who overcomes will thus be clothed in white garments; and I will not erase his name from the book of life, and I will confess his name before My Father and before His angels. (Rev. 3:6 NASB, emphasis mine)

We have already seen that the *overcomers* receive white robes just as at the opening of the *Fifth Seal*. What is highly unusual, however, is what Christ says next. He says *he will not erase their names from the Book of Life*. This implies that at some point some people were written into the Book *and then later erased*. Were these never born-again believers? Is this the Great Falling Away, the *Great Apostasy*? I believe it is. I think the greatest majority of the Great Falling Away occurs during the *Fifth Year* of the 70th Week. When faced with the choice of physical death in this life or apostasy, unfortunately most churchgoers will choose *apostasy*.

Let's construct the model for Sardis (Figure 50: Sardis Model):

Year of the 70[t]Daniel	Pattern of Seven Events	Letter to Sardis
Fifth Year	5) Martyrdom and Apostasy	MARTYRDOM Name Sardis from Sardius stone (red) and Sardonyx (red and white streaked), both indicative of sacrifice Cyrus the Great conquered Sardis "like a thief in the night" Sardis was a materially wealthy city Overcomers receive white robes Great Falling Away pictured by names being erased from the *Book of Life* Sardis is a mostly "dead" church because the many of the righteous are martyred and physically dead; the apostates fall away and are spiritually dead

Figure 50: Sardis Model

Chapter Twenty-One

THE CHURCH OF PHILADELPHIA
(REVELATION 3:7-13)

The *Sixth Year* is represented by the *Letter to Philadelphia*. I'm sure the symbolism found in the names of most of the cities in the seven letters has been a bit obscure at first glance. Philadelphia is probably the exception. Philadelphia, "the city of brotherly love," is the motto of a large American city in the state of Pennsylvania on the east coast. The city's name is derived from the Greek PHILADELPOS meaning "love for a family member" or "love for a brother." This meaning is exactly what we'd expect given the city motto of the current city of Philadelphia. But what does it say about conditions in the Church of the same name during the *Sixth Year* of the 70th Week?

The *Fifth Year* of the 70th Week that we just studied relating to the *Church of Sardis* is the year of the *Great Falling Away*. Massive numbers of nominal churchgoers will turn away from the faith when faced with persecution. They will bow to *the Beast*, his name, and will take his number (the *Mark of the Beast*, likened to *666*). Numerous faithful Christians will not bow. They will resist *the Beast* and be martyred. What remains of the faithful Church will be bound in brotherly love by the persecution of earth-shaking proportions. These Christians will be living on the run or they'll go "underground;" totally weaned from the world economic system. Life in the *Sixth Year* of the 70th Week will be much like the First Century Church described in Acts—they'll have all things in common. Most will have lost family members, either to apostasy or martyrdom. They truly will be one family, the Family of God.

Little is known about the historic Church at Philadelphia. An interesting sidelight that we looked at in Chapter Four: "Bookends (Revelation 1-3)" is that Ignatius, an early Church Father, sent an epistle to Philadelphia that has survived over time. In that epistle, he was much more critical of the church than Jesus was in this letter. According to Ignatius, there were men among them who tried to lead him astray. These men thought only the Old Testament had God's authority behind it, not the Gospels[xcv]. This contradiction with Jesus's Letter to Philadelphia is troubling if Jesus's letter is thought to be addressing only the conditions in the First Century. If the *Letters to the Seven Churches* are prophetic of future events as I am proposing, no problem exists. Jesus is addressing conditions that *will occur* in the future. I think the inconsistency between Ignatius's epistle and Jesus's Letter provides significant evidence that Jesus's *Letter to Philadelphia* is prophetic in nature.

Another aspect of the historic church of Philadelphia is the area's propensity to earthquakes[xcvi]. At the end of the letter, Jesus says, "He who overcomes, I will make him a *pillar in the temple of My God*, and he will not go out from it anymore" (Rev. 3:12 NASB). In light of the damage Philadelphia sustained in the various earthquakes, this promise of being a *permanent* pillar in the "temple of My God" probably had very significant meaning to those that knew the city's earthquake history.

ATTRIBUTES OF JESUS IN THE *LETTER TO PHILADELPHIA*

In this *Letter to Philadelphia* Jesus is described by the following attributes:

> He who is *holy*, who is *true*, who has the *key of David*, who opens and no one will shut, and who shuts and no one opens, says this. (Rev. 3:7 NASB, emphasis mine)

The first attribute about Jesus noted is that Jesus is *Holy*. Throughout the Old Testament *God* is referred to as *Holy* (Isa. 1:4, 5:19, 6:3, 10:7, 12:6, Jer. 50:29, 51:5, Ezek. 39:7, Hos. 11:9, etc.) In all there are 416 separate references to holiness in the Old Testament. Saying that *Jesus* is also *Holy* is a reflection of *Jesus's divinity*. It is also a reflection of his separateness, his "otherness." At the end of the *Sixth Year* of the 70th Week, Jesus is coming to separate the elect from this world by means of the Rapture. Then they will be "like him."

The second attribute is that Jesus is *true*. In the *Letter to Philadelphia*, truth is contrasted with "lying." Jesus is true, those of the synagogue of Satan are liars (Rev. 3:9, 1 John 2:22). Jesus is the true light (John 1:9), the true vine (John 15:1), the true Bread (John 6:32), and the way, the truth and the life (John 14:6). This attribute being "true" is critical. Those in the *Sixth Year* of the 70th Week can trust Jesus that he will save them at the appointed time. His word is *true*.

The third attribute is the most intriguing. *Jesus has the key of David.* In the last section we saw a reference to doors that would open and not be shut in regard to Cyrus, who we learned is a type of Christ:

> Thus says the Lord to Cyrus His anointed, whom I have taken by the right hand, to subdue nations before him and to loose the loins of kings; *to open doors before him so that gates will not be shut*. (Isaiah 45:1 NASB, emphasis mine)

In Isaiah 22 we see another "type" of Jesus in the Old Testament, Eliakim:

> That I will summon my servant Eliakim the son of Hilkiah . . . Then I will set the *key of the house of David* on his shoulder, when he opens no one will shut, when he shuts no one will open. I will drive him *like a peg in a firm place*. (Isa. 22:20, 22-23 NASB, emphasis mine)

This is the direct reference Jesus uses in the *Letter to Philadelphia*. Eliakim had the *"key of David."* He controlled access to the king. Jesus controls access to God. This passage also indicates the steadfastness of Jesus. He is a *"peg in a firm place."* This statement was further encouragement for the earthquake-prone city of Philadelphia. Not only does Jesus open and shut the door, he *is* the door.

> He who does not enter by the door into the fold of the sheep, but climbs up some other way, he is a thief and a robber. But he who enters by the door is a shepherd of the sheep. To him the doorkeeper opens, and the sheep hear his

voice, and *he calls his own sheep by name and leads them out. . . I am the door*; if anyone enters through me, he will be saved, and will go in and out and find pasture. The thief comes only to steal and kill and destroy; I came that they may have life, and have it abundantly. (John 10:1-3, 9-10 NASB, emphasis mine)

This passage is an amazingly clear contrast between Jesus and the Antichrist (the thief). In the *Sixth Year* of the 70th Week, Jesus will use the *key of David* and open the door no one can shut, call to his sheep, and lead them out in the Rapture.

In the *Letter to Sardis*, we discussed the *Parable of the Ten Virgins*. This *Letter to Philadelphia* continues to explain that parable, especially in regard to the door that is shut. All ten virgins have lamps. The Greek word translated "lamps" is LAMPAS which is more properly translated "torches." This is the same word as found in the account of Gideon. In that account, the torches were covered with earthenware jars. On Gideon's command, the jars were broken and the torches were exposed. The torches represent our testimony of Jesus, His Spirit living within us. This testimony is fed by the Holy Spirit that is symbolized by the oil (the oil of anointing.) The foolish virgins don't have enough Holy Spirit oil to continue their testimony so they are told to "buy" some. One cannot "buy" this type of oil, but I find the suggestion ironic because without the *Mark of the Beast*, one cannot buy or sell in the 70th Week. When the foolish virgins are trying to find oil, Jesus returns.

It is at that moment the Messiah opens the door that no one can shut by using the *Key of David*, and grants the *wise virgins* access to God via the Rapture. He then shuts the door that no one can open. "Later the other virgins (the *foolish virgins*) also came, saying, 'Lord, Lord, open up for us," but they were too late. Who are the foolish virgins without oil for their lamps? Jesus referred to them earlier in his ministry in his Sermon on the Mount. Fellow teacher Phillip Brown demonstrated to me how this is a clear reference to the *Parable of the Ten Virgins*:

Not everyone who says to me, *'Lord, Lord,' will enter the kingdom of heaven*, but *he who does the will of my Father who is in heaven will enter*. . . And then I will declare to them, '*I never knew you*; depart from me, you who practice lawlessness.' (Matt. 7:21, 23 NASB, emphasis mine)

Later the other virgins also came, saying, '*Lord, Lord, open up for us.*' But he answered, 'Truly I say to you, *I do not know you.*' (Matt. 25:11-12 NASB, emphasis mine)

Matt. 7 then is the key to identifying the foolish, apostate virgins. Immediately following the passage in Matt. 7 above, Jesus told the familiar *Parable of the House upon the Rock*. In that parable Jesus made this key point:

Therefore everyone who hears these words of mine *and acts on them* may be compared to a *wise* man (wise virgin) who *built his house on the rock*. (Matt. 7:24 NASB, clarification and emphasis mine)

By contrast, the foolish virgins are those that build their house on sand by not "acting on" the Word. They may claim Jesus as Lord, but these are only words and their lives do not reflect the presence of the Spirit (oil) within them. When the storm of the *Great Tribulation* comes, their foundation will not be strong enough to stand up to the persecution. Acting on Jesus commands will require we love our Lord more than life or the things of this world. "If you love me, you will keep my commandments" (John 14:15 NASB). We will discuss the fate of the foolish virgins in the seventh letter, the *Letter to Laodicea*.

The *Key of David* appears in the sixth letter in the sequence of seven letters. The *Sixth Year* of the 70th Week is the year of the Rapture. This is the year the Lord opens the door of heaven for the wise virgins. It is another overwhelming support for the theory that the *Letters to the Seven Churches* are a prophetic section of scripture and each letter represents the events of each successive year of the 70th Week of Daniel.

Ch. 21: Church of Philadelphia

CONDITION OF THE CHURCH OF PHILADELPHIA

Jesus has nothing but complements for these survivors of the *Great Tribulation*, his faithful remnant represented in the *Letter to Philadelphia*:

> I know your deeds. Behold, *I have put before you an open door* which no one can shut, because you have a little power, and have kept my word, and have not denied my name. Behold, I will cause those of the synagogue of Satan, who say that they are Jews and are not, but lie—I will make them come and bow down at your feet, and make them *know that I have loved you.* (Rev. 3:8-9 NASB, emphasis mine)

Again, Jesus is telling the Philadelphia church that he is *opening the door of heaven for them*. He is doing it because they don't have the power to do it themselves (or the authority), and because *they have not denied him*. Interestingly *those that have denied Jesus* will bow before those that have overcome. This almost assuredly happens at the *Sheep and Goats Judgment*, before Jesus ushers in his Millennial Kingdom, at which time the previously raptured saints will be in glorified bodies, bright as the sun, and ruling ten cities (Luke 19:17).

Jesus then makes a statement that is related to the Rapture. This statement has been misconstrued by many—by believers in a *Pre-Tribulation Rapture* and those who don't believe in the Rapture at all. Only a proper theology of the Rapture—that it occurs at the end of the *Sixth Year* of the 70th Week, before the Wrath of God occurs (the *"Pre-Wrath Rapture"*)—makes proper sense of this passage:

> Because you have kept (Gk: TEREO, meaning to guard) the word of my perseverance (Gk: HYPOMONES, meaning endurance) also will I keep (Gk: TEREO, meaning to guard) you from the *hour of testing* (Gk: PEIRASMOU, meaning temptation, trial, or testing), that hour which is about to come upon the whole world, to test those who dwell on the earth. (Rev. 3:10 NASB, clarification and emphasis mine)

The context of this passage found in the *Letter to Philadelphia* means that it is related to the *Sixth Year* of the 70th Week. Second, what those who overcome are guarded against is an *"hour of testing"* or trial, not the entire 70th Week of Daniel. This is an important distinction. Let's look at other references to an *"hour"* in Revelation:

> I saw another angel flying in mid-heaven, having an eternal gospel to preach to those who live on the earth, and to every nation and tribe and tongue and people; and he said with a loud voice, "Fear God, and give Him glory, because the *hour of His judgment* has come; worship Him who made the heaven and the earth and sea and springs of waters." (Rev. 14:6-7 NASB, emphasis mine)

> Woe, woe, the great city, in which all who had ships at sea became rich by her wealth, for in *one hour* she has been laid waste. (Rev. 18:19 NASB, emphasis mine)

> And another angel came out of the temple, crying out with a loud voice to Him who sat on the cloud, "Put in your sickle and reap, for *the hour* to reap has come, because the harvest of the earth is ripe." (Rev. 14:15 NASB, emphasis mine)

The brief *hour of testing* the saints will be guarded from is the *Wrath of God* which occurs during the *Seventh Year* of the 70th Week. Note that all three references to "hour" above also refer to this time period. Jesus places a caveat on this promise, however, "hold fast what you have, so that no one will take your crown" (Rev. 3:11 NASB). There is yet time to fall away and lose their rewards.

Finally, let's return to take another look at the passage about the saints being made pillars in the Temple of God:

> He who *overcomes*, I will make him a *pillar in the temple of My God*, and he *will not go out from it anymore*; and I will write on him the name of My God, and the name of the city of My God, the new Jerusalem, which comes down out

of heaven from My God, and My new name. (Rev. 3:12 NASB, emphasis mine)

The earliest meaning of "pillar" was of a monument. The earliest pillars were a single stone or a pile of stones. In Gen. 28: 18, Jacob set up the stone he used as a pillow on the night he saw "Jacob's Ladder," and called the place "Bethel." In Jer. 1:18, God said he was making the prophet a "pillar of iron." (Remember iron is a symbol of authority). The apostles are said to be pillars in Gal. 2:9, and the Church itself is a pillar in 1 Tim. 3:15.

It was a common practice in ancient days to inscribe pillars with the names of important people or events. Three names will be inscribed on us as a witness of who we belong to: 1) the name of God (Num. 6:27); 2) the name of the New Jerusalem ("the name of the city from *that* day *shall be*, 'The Lord is there'" [Ezek. 48:35 NASB]); and 3) Jesus's new name ("He has a name written on Him which no one knows except Himself" [Rev. 19:12 NASB]). This is a further explanation of what we studied in the *Letter to Pergamum*: "I will give him a *white stone*, and a new name written on the stone which no one knows but he who receives it." Is this white stone the *"pillar in the temple of My God"*? I think it may be. If that is the case, our new names will be inscribed on it as well.

The idea in Rev. 3:12 of forever dwelling (*"not go out from it anymore"*) in God's Temple mirrors the summation statement of the well-known Psalms 23:

Surely goodness and loving kindness will follow me all the days of my life, and *I will dwell in the house of the Lord forever*. (Psalm 23:6 NASB, emphasis mine)

This concept of *always being with the Lord* should be familiar to us. We have already studied this in Chapter Five: "Signed, Sealed, and Delivered (Revelation 4-5)":

These are the ones who come out of the great tribulation, and they have washed their robes and made them white in the blood of the Lamb. For this reason, *they*

are before the throne of God; and they serve Him day and night in His temple.
(Rev. 7:14-15 NASB)

Then we who are alive and remain will be caught up together with them in the
clouds to meet the Lord in the air, and so *we shall always be with the Lord*. (1
Thess. 4:17 NASB)

As we have seen, both of these passages in Revelation and 1 Thessalonians refer to the
Resurrection/Rapture. They exactly parallel the passage in the *Letter to Philadelphia*,
and this is totally appropriate. The concepts of the Key of David, the pillars in the
Temple, and being kept from the hour of trial found in the letter are all references to the
Rapture, happening at the end of the *Sixth Year* of the 70th Week. All these concepts
occurring at the end of the *Sixth Year* are further support for the *Pre-Wrath Rapture* of
the Church, which is biblical and this book supports. The "Main Harvest" Resurrection
of the righteous that we learned about in Chapter Five: "Signed, Sealed, and Delivered
(Revelation 4-5)" will precede the Rapture. Then the resurrected and the living will be
caught up together in the air and will forever be with Christ.

Let's look at the graphic (Figure 51: Philadelphia Model) for the *Sixth Year*
found in the sixth letter, the *Letter to Philadelphia*:

Year of the 70ᵗʰ Week of Daniel	Pattern of Seven Events	Letter to Philadelphia
Sixth Year	6) Heavenly Signs	The COMING RAPTURE Jesus has the Key of David to open and shut the door of heaven Jesus will make the overcomers "pillars" so we will always be with Him in God's Temple The overcomers will be guarded from the "hour" of trial (the Wrath of God)

Figure 51: Philadelphia Model

Chapter Twenty-Two

THE CHURCH OF LAODICEA
(REVELATION 3:14-22)

efore we begin to look at this seventh letter, the *Letter to Laodicea*, in detail, I'm sure the first question that is burning in your mind is this: *If the Church has been taken in the Rapture at the end of the Sixth Year, why is there a letter to a Church applying to Year Seven?* This is a very good question. The sad answer is not all of the Church is in heaven with Christ during the *Seventh Year*. We need to revisit and complete our study of the *Parable of the Ten Virgins*.

In the *Letter to Sardis* and the *Letter to Philadelphia*, we learned that there are three groups of people: 1) those who have denied Jesus, 2) the foolish virgins, and 3) the wise virgins. Those who have denied Jesus never wake up spiritually, but all of the churchgoers wake up in the *Great Tribulation* as we learned in the *Letter to Sardis*. They then all light their torches. These torches are the righteousness and testimony of the saints that lead others to salvation. Isaiah speaks of Jerusalem as burning like a torch:

> Her righteousness goes forth like brightness and her *salvation like a torch that is burning.* (Isa. 62:1 NASB, emphasis mine)

These torches are fueled by the oil of the Holy Spirit. The *foolish virgins* run out of oil (they don't have the Holy Spirit) as we saw in our previous discussions. While they are trying to "buy" the Holy Spirit, Jesus comes in the Rapture and shuts the door of heaven, preventing them from entering:

> While they were going away to make the purchase, the bridegroom came, and those who were ready went in with him to the wedding feast; and *the door was*

shut. Later the other virgins also came, saying, "Lord, lord, open up for us." But he answered, "Truly I say to you, *I do not know you.*" (Matt. 25:10-12 NASB, emphasis mine)

The issue for the foolish virgins (churchgoers) is that Jesus does not know them. They didn't have a personal "born-again" relationship with him, with evidence of the Holy Spirit within them ("they did not have enough oil"). They may have known about him, but they had no intimacy with him. Head knowledge of Christianity and a "fire insurance" confession of Christ as Lord will not substitute for true salvation.

This understanding, that the *foolish virgins* are still on the earth during the Wrath of God in the *Seventh Year*, helps explain one of the most misunderstood passages in the *Letters to the Seven Churches*:

I know your deeds, that you are neither cold nor hot; I wish that you were cold or hot. So *because you are lukewarm, and neither hot nor cold*, I will *spit you out* of my mouth. (Rev. 3:15-16 NASB, emphasis mine)

Commentators have struggled with what this verse means. If the symbol "hot" means righteous and the symbol "cold" means unrighteous (Matt. 24: 12), why wouldn't Jesus prefer that the Laodiceans be "hot" (righteous)? Why does Jesus say he would even prefer these people to be "cold" over being "lukewarm?" It seems to make no sense if this letter is describing "Church Ages" or advice on Christian living. However, if this letter is understood in a proper prophetic-sense context, this passage takes on a whole new meaning—-one that makes complete sense.

As we stated above, upon Jesus's return there are three categories of people: 1) those who deny Jesus (the unrighteous represented by "cold"), 2) the *foolish virgins* (represented by "lukewarm"), and 3) the *wise virgins* (represented by "hot"). Jesus is about to pour out his wrath upon the earth. The righteous (*wise virgins*) are safe in heaven. The unrighteous deserve the wrath of God. The *foolish virgins* deserve the wrath of God because it is only faith through the Holy Spirit that saves, but it breaks Jesus's heart to see those who have resisted taking the *Mark of the Beast* still suffering through His Wrath unleashed on the earth. That is why Jesus writes "I wish you were hot or cold." Now, that makes perfect sense.

Is it possible for the *foolish virgins* to be saved? *Yes!* That is the purpose of the *Letter to Laodicea*. They will have missed the Rapture and the *Wedding of the Lamb* taking place in heaven during the *Seventh Year* [See Chapter Fourteen: "Event Seven: Rapture and Wrath"], but *they still can be saved if they repent*, just as the Jewish remnant alive at the time will be saved, at the very end of the 70th Week, when they see Jesus returning to earth and trust in Him. These *foolish virgins*, as will be the case with the Jewish remnant, will then go into the Millennium without resurrection bodies (unlike the *wise virgins* previously raptured and with resurrection bodies) and will await the "Gleanings Harvest" Resurrection at the end of the Millennium to receive their resurrection bodies.

THE CITY OF LAODICEA

We have now examined the symbolic meaning of the names of the first six cities of the *Seven Churches of Revelation*. Related to the seventh letter, it should come as no surprise then that the name of *Laodicea* has a symbolically significant meaning as well. Laodicea is a combination of two Greek words (LAO, meaning "God's people"; and DIKE, meaning "justice or judgment"). In combination the town's name means "judgment of God's people." DIKE is a legal term and can also be rendered "court decision." The *Seventh Year* of the 70th Week is the *legal trial*. This places the passage we looked at in the sixth letter, the *Letter to Philadelphia*, in a whole new light:

> I will also keep you from the *hour of trial* that is *going to come on the whole world* to test the inhabitants of the earth. (Rev. 3:10 NIV, emphasis mine)

The *foolish virgins* are now *on trial*. Notice in the attributes of Jesus given in this seventh letter, the *Letter to Laodicea*, Jesus is called "the faithful and true *witness*" (Rev. 2:14). From Matt. 25:12 Jesus is the *eyewitness* to the sin of the foolish virgins (*"I do not know you"*). Jesus later says "I *counsel you. . ."* (Rev. 3:18). Hence, he is the *counselor* (defense attorney) as well. These are all legal "trial" terminologies, which align with this *Seventh Year* being in a sense a legal trial related to the *foolish virgins*, as mentioned before.

The city of Laodicea was rich and relied on trade in exclusive black wool and a world-famous eye-salve. One thing they did not have was good water. Pipes in the archeological ruins of the town exhibit heavy calcium deposits. It is likely the "lukewarm" water tasted terrible. Many commentators believe the hard water of Laodicea was the basis of Jesus's metaphor discussed above about being "spit out" (Rev. 3:16).

ATTRIBUTES OF JESUS IN THE *LETTER TO LAODICEA*

The attributes of Jesus are described this way in the *Letter to Laodicea*:

> These are the words of *the Amen*, the faithful and true witness, the ruler of God's creation. (Rev. 3:14 NIV, emphasis mine)

"The Amen" is a title of Jesus only found in this letter. "Amen" is a Jewish word which means "verily or truly." This title re-enforces Jesus's position as a reliable witness. Jesus is also described as the ruler of God's creation. The Greek word used is ARCH which means "chief ruler." It is a variant of ARCHON which means "prince." In Chapter Fifteen: "Overcoming Lions (Daniel 1-12)," we discussed how the word ARCHON (from which we get the term *Arch*angel) is frequently used in the Bible to describe spiritual beings that control nations such as the "Prince of Persia" or "Michael, the great prince of your people." Satan is the ARCHON of this world. Jesus is the ARCHE or ruler of all ARCHON. He is the ultimate authority, and the *judge* over the trial, as well as being the *witness* and *defense attorney*.

Praise God for all of Jesus' roles.

CONDITION OF THE CHURCH OF LAODICEA

Jesus is highly critical of the *foolish virgins* in Laodicea:

458

You say, 'I am rich; I have acquired wealth and do not need a thing.' But you do not realize that you are wretched, pitiful, poor, blind and naked. I counsel you to *buy from me gold refined in the fire*, so you can become rich; and *white clothes to wear*, so you can cover your shameful nakedness; and *salve to put on your eyes*, so you can see. (Rev. 3: 17-18 NIV, emphasis mine)

This passage seems to imply that the *foolish virgins* left behind in the *Seventh Year* of the 70th Week have chosen worldly wealth over spiritual wealth from Jesus. They obviously still have a chance at salvation and thus can't have taken the *Mark of the Beast*, but yet in their ignorance they seem to think they have all they need. They have most likely weaned themselves from the world system and are still surviving and have what they "need" physically. Jesus counsels them that they are now in the "two minute warning;" that only a *single year* remains. He counsels them to *"buy from me"* gold refined in fire. He recommends giving up whatever comforts they have, to stop worrying about physical survival, and to spend what time they have left giving testimony to God's Kingdom.

    Jesus also uses symbols drawn from the historical city of Laodicea, and he counsels them to put on *white garments* as opposed to the black wool of Laodicea. White garments as we have seen previously imply *righteousness*. He also counsels them to *put salve on their eyes* (from him) so they can see what is happening right in front of them; that time is very short.

    Finally, the *Letter to Laodicea* ends with what is probably the most famous quote in Revelation:

Those whom I love, I reprove and discipline; therefore be zealous and repent. Behold, *I stand at the door and knock*; if anyone hears my voice and opens the door, I will come in to him and will dine with him, and he with me. He who *overcomes*, I will grant to him to sit down with Me on My throne, as I also overcame and sat down with My Father on His throne. (Rev. 3:19-21 NASB, emphasis mine)

Jesus is clear that he still loves the *foolish virgins* and wants them to repent. Their sin is so offensive it makes him want to vomit, but he still loves them. He is disciplining them in the midst of his wrath which is being poured out on the earth, but he desires them to repent and be saved. So he stands at their door and knocks. At the end of the *Parable of the Ten Virgins* (Matt. 25:1-13), the *foolish virgins* knocked on heaven's door, but it had already been shut after the Rapture. Now it is *Jesus who is knocking on the door* of the *foolish virgins*. If anyone hears Jesus's Word during the trial and *repents*, he will still save them. Although they have missed going to heaven and missed the *Wedding Supper of the Lamb*, he will still dine with them. Jesus walks among the seven lampstands (Rev. 2:1) and that includes Laodicea.

There is a parallel in the Song of Solomon, the book of the Bible following Ecclesiastes, as the bride searches for the Bridegroom, who was knocking at the door:

> I was asleep (all the virgins were asleep) but my heart was awake. A voice! *My beloved was knocking*: 'Open to me, my sister, my darling, my dove, my perfect one! For my head is drenched with dew, my locks with the damp of the night.' "I have taken off my dress ("you are wretched, pitiful, poor, blind and naked"), how can I put it on *again*? (Song of Solomon 5:2-3 NASB, clarification and emphasis mine)

Jesus then gives Laodicea a promise of a reward for those who are *overcomers:*

> He who *overcomes*, I will grant to him to *sit down with me on my throne*, as I also overcame and sat down with my Father on his throne. (Rev. 3:21 NASB, emphasis mine)

This is an older promise made in Jeremiah's day that the city of Jerusalem (a picture of the eternal Jerusalem) will be inhabited by the "high" and the "low" of people measured by earthly standards:

There will come in through the gates of this city *kings and princes sitting on the throne of David* (Jesus's throne), riding in chariots and on horses, they and their princes, the men of Judah and the inhabitants of Jerusalem, and *this city will be inhabited forever*. (Jer. 17:25 NASB, emphasis mine)

The reference to "sitting on David's throne" is a direct reference to the promise in the *Letter to Laodicea*, "He who overcomes, I will grant to him to sit down with me on my throne" (Rev. 3: 21 NASB).

Let's look at the graphic model of the *Letter to Laodicea* and what we have learned related to the *Pattern of Seven Events* for the *Seventh Year* of the 70th Week (Figure 52: Laodicea Model):

Year of the 70th Week of Daniel	Pattern of Seven Events	Letter to Laodicea
Seventh Year	7) Wrath	**GOD'S TRIAL OF HIS PEOPLE** Laodicea means trail of God's people Jesus is the faithful witness during the trial Jesus wishes the Laodiceans had been raptured or were unrighteous fully deserving of his wrath, rather than having to endure it Laodiceans are poor, blind, and naked, and Jesus desires they be refined like gold, put on white garments, and use eye salve to be able to see The foolish virgins had knocked on heaven's door and found it locked. Jesus now desires them to answer when he knocks on their door

Figure 52: Laodicea Model

SUMMARY OF THE *LETTERS TO THE SEVEN CHURCHES*

I am sure that you doubted when I first suggested the concept that the *Letters to the Seven Churches,* found in Revelation 2 and 3, were prophetic. Hopefully, now that you have reached the end of this section of our study, Chapter 12: "Love Letters (Revelation 2-3)," you are as amazed as I am at the detail that God's Word has placed within the names of the cities and the symbols contained in the *Seven Letters to the Churches*. From our study, there can be no doubt that the letters are prophetic of the Church related to *each of the seven years* of the 70th Week of Daniel, which is amazing in itself.

Not only are the letters prophetic, they are central to the message of Revelation. That is why they are positioned at the beginning of Revelation. It should be noted that they serve as a *central core* around which all the other prophecies are built. To say that the letters are important is an understatement. In Revelation 1, Jesus told John:

> Write in a book what you see, and *send it to the seven churches*: to Ephesus and to Smyrna and to Pergamum and to Thyatira and to Sardis and to Philadelphia and to Laodicea. (Rev. 1:11 NASB)

Now that we have reached this point in our study, we know that these churches are *not seven random churches in first century Asia*, but representative of *the* Church as it endures and overcomes *each year* of the 70th Week of Daniel. Wow! This places the Book of Revelation in an entirely new light. Revelation was written for the Church to use as a manual and guide as it passes through the 70th Week. This understanding that the *Letters to the Seven Churches* of Revelation are representative of *each of the last seven years* and the *Pattern of Seven Events* is an incredibly important insight to help the Church in the days ahead.

In the next section, Part Five: "Overcoming the 70th Week of Daniel," we will begin to unpack the specific instructions of Jesus to His Church.

PART FIVE:

Overcoming the 70th

Week of Daniel

Chapter Twenty-Three

APPOINTMENTS

I don't keep a written appointment book. All my appointments are kept on my computer in Outlook®. I find this software generally very convenient; however, a couple years ago I learned one of its great weaknesses. I was working part-time as a consultant for a large company. I mistakenly gave them access to my Outlook®, thinking that allowing them to make appointments directly on my appointment keeper would be an advantage. Within days all sorts of phone conference appointments started popping up. My part-time consulting position was quickly becoming "full" time—basically, full of useless appointments. Within a week, my experiment of letting others schedule directly on my Outlook® ended.

One of the other disadvantages of keeping appointments online is that they can be lost if your computer crashes. A skilled (and highly priced) computer technician can usually retrieve this data, but you may miss dozens of appointments in the meantime.

Our culture is built around our calendars and our schedules. What would happen if our seven-day week was disrupted and changed into say, a ten-day week? What if our current 12-month calendar was changed into a 15-month calendar of varying days each? How easy would it be for us to adjust to those changes? Would we be able to keep track of the dates of birthdays or Christmas; or would we be completely disoriented?

In the *Book of Daniel* we have learned that the Antichrist is planning on changing the "times:"

> And he shall speak words against the Most High, and shall wear out the saints of the Most High, and shall think to *change times* (Gk: Kairos, meaning "appointed times") and law. (Dan. 7:25 LXX, clarification and emphasis mine)

Ch. 23: Appointments

In Chapter Fifteen: "Overcoming Lions (Daniel 1-12)," we examined this verse and considered that the Antichrist may try to institute Islamic Law (*Sharia*) and an Islamic calendar. You might think that institution of an Islamic calendar is insignificant. It might be disruptive as we discussed above, but of no lasting consequence. After all you might say, "We aren't following God's calendar right now anyway." You would be correct. People in the western nations are following the *Gregorian calendar* established by Pope Gregory XIII in 1582. The *Biblical calendar* (or *Jewish calendar*), was established by God.

Even the *current* Biblical calendar is not the original one given to Moses. It was adjusted to account for the change from 360 days per year to the current year of approximately 365 days per year. The current Biblical calendar year contains twelve months in standard years and thirteen months in "leap years." There are seven "leap years" with an extra month in each cycle of nineteen years. These months on the Biblical calendar are based on the *lunar cycles*. Each month begins with the *new moon*. The extra "leap years" function to keep the *lunar cycles* in alignment with the *solar-year cycles*, which it does extremely well.

Basing the calendar on *lunar cycles* has an enormous advantage: *you always can know approximately the date during the lunar month by simply looking up at night at the phase of the moon.* I am writing this section during the biblical month of Av (the fifth month on the Jewish calendar). Last night there was a full moon. From this sighting of the full moon, I knew the date was either the 14th or the 15th of Av (full moons always occur at the middle of each lunar-based month). During the 70th Week of Daniel, Christians and Jews will always be able to know the approximate biblical date by watching the *lunar cycle*. Even if the "times" (the calendar) are changed by the Antichrist, Christians and Jews will always know the biblical date within a the month if they observe the phase of the moon. The Antichrist will not be able to change the moon.

Why are Biblical dates important? I am sure you are thinking to yourself, *I have lived my entire life not needing to know the biblical date. Why will I need to know it during Daniel's 70th Week?* The reason is that God has set appointments for us—specific dates in the future when important events are most likely going to take place. If

466

we know these dates, we can watch for them and prepare for them. Of course, all these future appointment dates are based on the *Biblical calendar*.

The most important of these events will likely fall on the *"Feasts of the Lord"* as listed in Leviticus 23. Other events will likely happen on the anniversaries of other important dates in Jewish history. We know that it is likely that future events will be fulfilled on these *"Feasts"* and historic dates because throughout biblical history, other events of significance like Jesus' crucifixion and resurrection, as well his sending the Holy Spirit were all fulfilled on *Feasts of the Lord* days. If God had chosen to fulfill events of this magnitude on His Feasts in the past, it is likely he will do so in the future.

If the *"Feasts of the Lord"* are this important, let's examine them. There are seven Feasts of the Lord (or MO'EDIM in the Hebrew, KAIRON in the Greek). These were instituted by God, and given to Moses and the Israelites (Lev. 23) prior to their entering the Promised Land, and they played prominent roles in the Tabernacle and later in the Temple services.

> These are the *appointed times* (MO'EDIM meaning "appointed times") of the Lord, holy convocations (Heb.: MIQRA meaning "*assembly* or *rehearsal*") which you shall proclaim at the times appointed (Heb. MO'EDIM meaning "appointed times") for them. (Lev. 23:4 NASB, clarification and emphasis mine)

God established these *"appointed times"* as *"rehearsals"* of the great redemptive events in the life of Jesus. The celebration and symbolism of each "Feast" foretold the redemptive event. These Feasts are divided into four "spring" Feasts during the spring of the year and three "fall" Feasts during September and October.

The *primary* prophetic meanings of the "spring" Feasts have already been fulfilled by Jesus at His *First Coming*. Most Christians are familiar with *Passover*, the first of the four spring Feasts, and how it prefigured the death of Jesus on the cross. The blood of the sacrificial lamb which was spread on the Jewish doorframes in Egypt to protect them from the Angel of Death foreshadowed the blood of Jesus, the sinless Lamb of God.

As we know, Jesus was the perfect, sinless, blood-sacrifice uniquely acceptable to God. Only his death could pay the substitutionary judgment required by the Holy God for atonement of the sins of those who put their trust in him. Sacrificial lambs did not accomplish this. But why was this *sacrifice of Jesus* absolutely required by God and needed for forgiveness of our sins? Only Jesus, being the sinless Son of God, was forever acceptable as the sacrifice to take upon himself God's punishment for our sins—-in God's eyes our sins were transferred onto Jesus, and his death, and his death alone, paid our sin-debt before God. This is all pictured in *Passover* and is the primary and initial step in God's plan of redemption.

The three other spring Feasts prefigured the other redemptive works of Jesus at his *First Coming*. The second Feast, the *Feast of Unleavened Bread,* foretold the burial of Jesus, and *First Fruits* foretold the resurrection of our Lord. *Shavuot* (Pentecost) foretold the coming of the Holy Spirit and the birth of the Church.

In addition, there are three Feasts of the Lord that have *not yet* been fulfilled, the "fall" Feasts—-*Yom Teruah* (Feast of the Blowing of Trumpets), *Yom Kippur* (Day of Atonement), and *Sukkot* (Feast of Tabernacles). All of these fall Feasts occur in September/October on our Gregorian calendar and occur in the seventh month, *Tishri,* on the Jewish calendar each year. All these will be fulfilled related to Jesus' *Second Coming*. In Chapter Fourteen: "Event Seven: Rapture and Wrath," we examined how this final Feast, the Feast of Tabernacles, will most likely be celebrated by the Church in the *Marriage Supper of the Lamb* in heaven after the Rapture. We have also briefly indicated in Chapter Two: "Uncovering the Keys" that *Yom Teruah* is the expected date of the Resurrection/Rapture (*Tishri 1* on the Jewish calendar).

In their classic book, *The Last Shofar!* by Lenard and Zoller (Xulon Press, 2014), the authors propose that the fall feasts will be literally fulfilled at the *Second Coming* of Jesus with the same precision of timing as the spring feasts have been related to his *First Coming*. The Resurrection and Rapture will occur on *Yom Teruah* at the end of the *Sixth Year* of the 70th Week, and Jesus will physically land upon the earth in power and glory at the physical *Second Coming* on *Yom Kippur* on the final day of the *Seventh Year* of the 70th Week. This is incredibly startling and important information. Not only does this understanding absolutely shatter the theory of the "imminent" return of Jesus at the Rapture (held by the *Pre-Tribulation Rapture* position, which states that Jesus can come at "any time;" instead, he comes at the "appointed time"), but it gives additional support for the *Pre-Wrath Rapture* position, in that it provides a chronology for the Rapture, in line with all scripture, within the *second half* of the 70th Week of Daniel.

We have previously seen that Jesus made this well-known statement related to the Rapture:

> *But of that day and hour no one knows,* not even the angels of heaven, nor the Son, but the Father alone. (Matt. 24:36 NASB, emphasis mine)

As we have already learned, the words of these passages don't appear to say that we can't know the *approximate* timing of Christ's return. Paul has clearly stated in 1 Thess. 5:1-4 that Christians will *not* be surprised by the Day of the Lord, and by extension, the Rapture. He is stating that we will know the date on the Jewish calendar:

> Now as to the times (Gk: CHRONON, meaning "chronologies") and the epochs (Gk: KAIRON, meaning "appointed times"), brethren, you have no need of anything to be written to you. For you yourselves know full well that the day of the Lord will come just like a thief in the night. While they (the unrighteous) are saying, "Peace and safety!" then destruction will come upon them suddenly like labor pains upon a woman with child, and they will not escape. *But you, brethren, are not in darkness, that the day (Day of the Lord) would overtake you like a thief.* (1 Thess. 5:1-4 NASB, clarification and emphasis mine)

In Part Four, we studied this exact passage. Paul is saying that Christians will *know* the chronologies of the 70th Week (CHRONON), the fulfillment of the "appointed times" (KAIRON), and that *they would not be surprised by the Rapture/start of the Day of the Lord (God's Wrath).*

We know from Chapter Fourteen: "Event Seven: Rapture and Wrath" that the *Day of the Lord* (God's Wrath on the earth) begins on the same day as the Rapture. The

Day of the Lord extends from *Yom Teruah* of the *Sixth Year* of the 70th Week until *Yom Kippur* at the end of *Year Seven*. That period is *one year and ten days*. This is supported by the witness of Isaiah: "For the Lord has a day of vengeance, *a year* of recompense for the cause of Zion" (Isa. 34:8 NASB, emphasis mine). The *ten days* between *Yom Teruah* and *Yom Kippur* are known as the *Days of Awe*. These are ten days of introspection and repentance for Israel as they prepare for the *Day of Atonement* (*Yom Kippur*). We have seen that Daniel and his friends were *tested* for *ten days* when they didn't eat the King's food. In Chapter Seventeen, we saw that the believers in Smyrna will be imprisoned for *ten days* as well. Both of these are allusions to this time of repentance. It is incredibly likely that the seven *Bowl Judgments* we discussed in Chapter Fourteen: "Event Seven: Rapture and Wrath" will happen during these *ten days* during *Year Seven,* immediately before the end of the 70th Week.

Interestingly, Noah was in the Ark for exactly *one year and ten days* (calculated from Gen 7:11, Gen. 8:14). This is not a coincidence. In Chapter Fourteen: "Event Fourteen: Rapture and Wrath" we learned that Jesus told us the Rapture of the Church will be *"like the 'days' of Noah."* The Church will most likely be off the earth in Heaven for the identical time that Noah was raised above the earth in the Ark: *one year and ten days*. Additional support for this timeframe is a verse in Deuteronomy, which states that Hebrew men are not permitted to go to war for *one year* after marriage (Deut. 24:5). Jesus will marry his Bride (the Church) in heaven, immediately after the Rapture. Definitely, this Jewish marriage commandment further supports the idea that the Rapture occurs slightly more than *a year* before Jesus returns to destroy the Antichrist, because Jesus will follow the prescription of the Law and avoid war for *"one year."* Amazing how scripture ties together!

On *Tishri 10*, the Jews celebrate the *Day of Atonement* (*Yom Kippur*) which is often referred to simply as "The Day." Prophetically on this day, Jesus will triumph over evil, destroy the Antichrist, and redeem the Jewish remnant who will repent. He will "atone" for their sins. This will be at the physical Second Coming of Jesus to the earth (with his Church), when Jesus's feet touch down on the Mount of Olives.

From this analysis we have established two relatively firm dates, both fulfilled on "Feasts of the Lord" days. The Rapture will likely occur on *Yom Teruah* of the *Sixth*

Year of Daniel's 70th Week and the physical *Second Coming* will likely occur on *Yom Kippur* of the *Seventh Year* at the end of Daniel's 70th Week. God has given us the evidence for this case in his Word.

FULFILLMENT ON HISTORIC DATES

This brief, but very important analysis we just undertook about the *Feasts of the Lord* has shown us that it is likely God will fulfill events of eternal significance on future occurrences of these Feasts. We also mentioned that other dates from Jewish history may also be "fulfilled" again in the future. There are certain dates in Jewish history that seem to continually have events of significance occurring on them.

One of these dates is the *17th of Tammuz* (the fourth month on the Jewish calendar—*June/July* on our Gregorian calendar). It is considered one of the *darkest days* in Jewish history. These following historic events all occurred on this date:

- Worship of the golden calf and Moses' destruction of the stone tablets of the Ten Commandments,
- The daily *Tamid* ("constant") offering ceased in Temple during the Babylonian siege of Jerusalem,
- An idol was erected in the Temple during the Babylonian invasion of Jerusalem,
- The walls of Jerusalem were breached by the Roman armies in AD 70, and
- A Roman leader burned a Torah scroll prior to the Bar-Kokhba Revolt in AD 132-136.

The *9th of Av* (the fifth month on the Jewish calendar—*July/August* on the Gregorian calendar) is another one of the *darkest days* of enormous historic importance. Events that occurred on this date include the following:

- The ten spies sent by Moses encouraged the Israelites not to enter the promised land,
- The destruction of the First Temple in 586 BC, and
- The destruction of the Second Temple in AD 70.

The *9th of Tammuz* is the historic date the walls of Jerusalem were breached during the Babylonian invasion of Jerusalem. Interestingly, in modern times this is the exact Biblical date (in 2015) that the United States Supreme Court breached the "walls of morality" in that country (U.S.A.) and sanctioned marriage between members of the same sex, in defiance of God's biblical plan. Later that same week, a sign of biblical proportions appeared in the night sky—the planets Jupiter and Venus came into one degree of conjunction (they appeared to "touch"). This sign had not been seen since 3 BC, and is the same sign some believe was the Star of Bethlehem. Was God signaling that the second advent of his Son was upcoming?

As we can see from these several examples, certain specific dates in Jewish history have had significant events fulfilled on them. In the future, events during the 70th Week of Daniel may also have significant events fulfilled on Jewish historic dates as well.

TIMING OF THE SEVEN SEALS

In Chapter Six: "The Walls Came Tumbling Down (Joshua 6, Judges 6-8)," we discussed a theory that all the seals on the *7 Sealed Scroll* may be opened on the *Feasts of the Lord* days. We have already shown that it is incredibly likely that the Resurrection and Rapture (which occur at the *Seventh Seal*) will occur on *Yom Teruah* (*Feast of Trumpets*) which is one of the seven *Feasts of the Lord*, or *appointed times,* in the fall. Let's investigate the possibility that *all* the other seals will be opened on Feast days as well *during each of the seven years* of the 70th Week. I must thank Joseph Lenard, co-author of *The Last Shofar!,* for his assistance in helping me make this case.

We are now fairly sure of the case that the Rapture will ~~occur~~ happen on *Yom Teruah,* occurring close to the end of the *Sixth Year,* and that the physical *Second Coming* (and the end of the 70th Week of Daniel) will happen on *Yom Kippur,* occurring at the very end of the *Seventh Year*. If the 70th Week of Daniel begins exactly seven years before its completion (on *Yom Kippur* of the *Seventh Year*), that means that the 70th Week will also begin on a *Yom Kippur*—the *Yom Kippur* at the very start of the *First Year*. *Yom Kippur* is, of course, a *Feast of the Lord* (the seventh Feast!), and an

472

interesting pattern has developed. If the seven seals truly are opened chronologically on each of the seven Feasts of the Lord, and if the *First Seal* is opened on *Yom Kippur* of the *First Year*, then all the seals could be opened in successive chronologic order in each of the seven years and end with the *Seventh Seal* opened on *Yom Teruah* of the *Sixth Year*, which we already know is its proper date of fulfillment.

It is really quite amazing how the events happening in each of the seven years align with the events and symbols of the seven *Feasts of the Lord*. This is further indication that God has ordained significant happening to occur on the appointed times of the Feast days and shows his omnipotent hand. Let's look at a chart (Figure 53: Fulfillment of the Seals on *Feasts of the Lord* Days) of what that future fulfillment *might* look like:

Year of the 70th Week of Daniel	Seal	Feast of the Lord
One	First	Yom Kippur
Two	Second	Tabernacles
Three	Third	Passover
Four	Fourth	Unleavened Bread
Five	Fifth	First Fruits
Six	Sixth	Shavuot
Seven	Seventh	Yom Teruah

Figure 53: Fulfillment of the Seals on Feasts of the Lord days

The assumption that it is likely that two seal fulfillments (the Rapture and the physical return of Jesus to earth/repentance and salvation of the Jewish remnant) will fall on Feast Days is interesting, but not completely convincing of a more extensive alignment within the whole 70th Week. Is there any Biblical support for *other* Feast Day fulfillments shown on this chart? Interestingly, there is! As we know from our previous study of Chapter Thirteen: "The Celestial Earthly Disturbance," the *Sixth Seal* is the *Celestial Earthly Disturbance Event*. Based on this model above, we are predicting that it will be fulfilled on *Shavuot* (Pentecost). As we have covered in this Chapter Thirteen, the initial primary fulfillment of *Shavuot* occurred when the Holy Spirit came upon the disciples in Jerusalem and they spoke in other languages to the listeners in Jerusalem. Peter then delivered the famous sermon found in Acts 2 to those listeners, and 3000 people were saved and baptized. In that sermon, Peter quoted Joel 2:30-31 which directly references the *Celestial Earthly Disturbance Event*!

> And I will grant wonders in the sky above and signs on the earth below, blood, and fire, and vapor of smoke. *The sun will be turned into darkness and the moon into blood* (part of the *Celestial Earthly Disturbance Event*), *before* the great and glorious *day of the Lord* shall come (starts later on *Yom Teruah*, on the same day as the Rapture). (Acts 2: 19-20 NASB, clarification and emphasis mine; Peter is quoting from Joel 2:31)

Stay with me on this explanation. Peter was openly linking the *Celestial Earthly Disturbance Event* with *Shavuot* (Pentecost) and with the later Rapture/start of the *Day of the Lord* (on *Yom Teruah*). This cannot be a coincidence. Although Peter was no doubt quoting Joel's mention of the *darkening of the sun and moon* to remind his listeners of events during and after Jesus's crucifixion (Matt. 27:45), which happened on *Passover* (about 50 days before Pentecost). The Holy Spirit was also linking the ultimate fulfillment of *Shavuot* (Pentecost, the day on which Peter was speaking) with the *ultimate darkening of the sun and moon* as part of the future *Celestial Earthly Disturbance Event* at the *Sixth Seal* (Joel 2:31 and Rev. 6:12)—and also linking the Rapture/start of the *Day of the Lord* on *Yom Teruah* (the Feast of Trumpets), to follow shortly after that time (*Yom Teruah* occurs about four months after Pentecost). This is extremely strong evidence that this *Sixth Seal* will open on *Shavuot* (Pentecost), and by extension, from other correlations we have already noted, that *all the seals* will be fulfilled on the sequential Feasts' dates. This is speculation, but a logical case is building for this happening as such. As you can see, knowing the *Hebrew roots of our Christian faith* is important in correctly interpreting much of scripture.

USE OF THE TERM *"APPOINTED TIME"* IN SCRIPTURE

The Bible includes hundreds of references to the term *"appointed time(s)"* (Gk: KAIRON, Heb: MO'EDIM). Traditionally, Bible translators and commentators have looked at the use of this word to mean "a time God has specifically set aside" and this is the true meaning of the word. But, what if in certain instances, the Bible is referring specifically to the *Feasts of the Lord* when using this term? If we closely examine these scriptures containing *"appointed time(s)"* with an understanding that the *seven seals* might be fulfilled at *these* times, numerous scriptures take on new prophetic meaning in an instant.

One of the most iconic uses of *appointed time* (Gk: KAIROS) in scripture is in the phrase *"time, times, and half a time"* found in Dan. 7:25, Dan. 12:7, and Rev. 12:14. The Greek word translated *"time"* or *"times"* in each of its uses in this phrase is KAIROS (KAIRON) or *appointed time(s)*. We know from our study of this phrase (*"time, times, and half a time"*) in other chapters of this book that the phrase refers to a period of time equal to 1260 days, 42 months, or 3 ½ years, all of which are equal in length (based on a 360-day prophetic year). As we have already seen, this phrase is used as a synonym for the *last half* of Daniel's 70th Week. This phrase has become so familiar to those who study biblical prophecy that the true meaning may have been overlooked. The translated phrase actually means *"appointed time, appointed times*, and half an *appointed time."* By using this particular translation of the phrase, was the angel telling Daniel and John that *time* during the 70th Week of Daniel (or at least the last half of the "week") will be measured by the passing of the *Feasts of the Lord (appointed times)*? There is scriptural evidence which supports this understanding and is included below.

As we continue to examine scriptures containing the Greek word KAIROS (*"appointed time"*), several contain the plural form of the word and may be related to the fulfillment of the *entire* 70th Week of Daniel (which would include fulfillment of all seven *appointed times—Feasts of the Lord*). These passages containing KAIROS follow:

- "It is not for you to know times or epochs (KAIRON: appointed times) which the Father has fixed by His own authority." (Acts 1:7 NASB, clarification mine)

- "Now as to the times and the epochs (KAIRON: appointed times), brethren, you have no need of anything to be written to you." (1 Thess. 5:1 NASB, clarification mine)

- "But realize this, that in the last days difficult times (KAIRON: appointed times) will come." (2 Tim. 3:1 NASB, clarification mine)

- "The vision which this man sees is for many days, and he prophesies for times (KAIRON: appointed times) afar off." (Ezek. 12:27 LXX, clarification mine)

- "With a view to an administration suitable to the fullness of the times (KAIRON: appointed times), that is, *the summing up of all things in Christ,* things in the heavens and things on the earth." (Eph. 1:10 NASB, clarification and emphasis mine)

I think this brief study of scripture of the use of "*appointed time(s)*" has indicated to me at least that there is a high likelihood that scriptures containing this word (KAIRON), that we have not to this point in time considered to be related to the *Feasts of the Lord*, actually may be related. At the conclusion of each of the following sections (about the fulfillment of each of the seals on Feast days), we have included a collection of relevant scriptures (in the shaded text box) which contain KAIROS ("*appointed time*") for your examination. We will leave it to the reader to decide if they are related to the fulfillment of each *Feast of the Lord/Seal*. We certainly believe that the case is strong for that. Now let's examine each *Feast of the Lord* and its related *Seal* to see if there are further connections.

YEAR ONE: EVENT ONE

FIRST SEAL FULFILLED ON *YOM KIPPUR*

In Part Four, we have already discussed how the Temple celebration of *Yom Kippur* (Day of Atonement) involved two goats. One was sacrificed for YHWH and one for Azazel. The goat "for Azazel" was the *scapegoat* and was released into the wilderness. Eventually this goat was thrown into a deep valley (signifying the Abyss?). When the *First Seal* opens, the false messiah will come forth to deceive the world. Just as *Yom Kippur* features two goats, the *First Seal* features a true Messiah (Jesus) and a false messiah (Antichrist). This false messiah will present Israel with a deceptive peace treaty. In Isaiah 28:15-18, God contrasts this covenant with Sheol with the precious cornerstone (Jesus). Initially during this *First Year* of the 70th Week, Israel will make the wrong choice and will trust the "goat for Azazel"—the *Antichrist* and his covenant.

"For the time (KAIROS: appointed time) will come when they will not endure sound doctrine; but wanting to have their ears tickled, *they will accumulate for themselves teachers in accordance to their own desires*" (2 Tim 4:3 NASB, clarification and emphasis mine)

YEAR TWO: EVENT TWO

SECOND SEAL FULFILLED ON TABERNACLES

Celebration of the *Feast of Tabernacles,* as of are all the other Feasts, is given as a command in the book of Leviticus:

> Again the Lord spoke to Moses, saying, "Speak to the sons of Israel, saying, 'on the fifteenth of this seventh month (Tishri) is the Feast of Booths (Heb: SUKKAH) *for seven days* to the Lord. *On the first day is a holy convocation; you shall do no laborious work* of any kind. For *seven days* you shall present

an offering by fire to the Lord.'" (Lev. 26: 33-36, clarification and emphasis mine)

The Feast of Tabernacles is itself a mini-picture of the 70th Week of Daniel. It is a *seven-day* Feast which reminds us of the *seven years* of the 70th Week (just as Jericho was a *seven-day* battle). The Feast of Tabernacles occurs five days after Yom Kippur. The Jews construct "booths" out of branches and live outside their homes for the duration of the Feast. This is a picture of the Jews who will flee to the wilderness during the *Time of Jacob's Trouble* or be sent to captivity. Finally, notice that "no work" is to be done on the first day of the Feast. The *First Year* of the 70th Week is a year in which a false peace pervades the earth. In the *Second Year* of the 70th Week, the false peace will be broken and the *"laborious work"* of tribulation will begin. The Antichrist will take *"peace"* from the earth:

> When He broke *the second seal*, I heard the second living creature saying, "Come." And another, a red horse, went out; and to him who sat on it, it was granted *to take peace from the earth.* (Rev. 6:3-4 NASB, emphasis mine)

There is also an element of "preparation" embedded in the instructions for the Feast of Tabernacles (Feast of Booths) as well:

> You shall celebrate the Feast of Booths seven days *after you have gathered in from your threshing floor and your wine vat.* (Deut. 16:13 NASB, emphasis mine)

Based on information we learned in Part Two: "The *Pattern of Seven Events*," we know that the *Third Year* of the 70th Week involves economic distress and famine. The Feast of Tabernacles is celebrated *after* provisions are stored up for the time before the next harvest/the coming famine.

At the completion of each "shabua" (7-year economic cycle), the Torah is read during this Feast of Tabernacles. In the 70th Week, this will be a time of *spiritual preparation* as well for the coming trial.

478

At the *end of every seven years*, at the time of the year of remission of debts (the seventh year of the seven-year cycle of rest for the land and cancelling debts—the *Shmitah*), at the *Feast of Booths (Tabernacles)*, when all Israel comes to appear before the Lord your God at the place which He will choose, you shall *read this law in front of all Israel* in their hearing. (Deut. 31:10-11 NASB, clarification and emphasis mine)

The Feast of Tabernacles is perfectly appropriate for the breaking of the *Second Seal* in the *Second Year* which *takes peace from the earth* because Tabernacles marks a point of spiritual and physical preparation for what lies ahead, when "all Israel will live in booths."

"Allow both to grow together until the harvest; and in the time (KAIROS: appointed time) of the harvest (Tabernacles) I will say to the reapers, '*First gather up the tares and bind them in bundles to burn them up; but gather the wheat into my barn*' [this may refer to the *Sheep and Goats Judgment*]." (Matt. 13:30 NASB, clarification and emphasis mine)

YEAR THREE: EVENT THREE
THIRD SEAL FULFILLED ON PASSOVER

Passover has already had a major fulfillment during Jesus' First Coming: the death of our Savior on the cross. It appears likely, however, that this "spring" Feast will be used again to mark the opening of the *Third Seal* during the *Third Year* of the 70th Week. Passover is a specific day on the Biblical calendar: *Nisan 14* (*Nisan* is the first month of the Jewish religious calendar; happening on March/April on the Gregorian calendar). Preparation begins earlier, however, on *Nisan 10*: "On the *tenth of this month* they are each one to take a lamb for themselves, according to their fathers' households" (Ex. 12:3 NASB, emphasis mine). This day was fulfilled by Jesus when he was chosen to die for the nation and he rode into Jerusalem on a donkey. In the 70th Week of Daniel, the whole world will have to choose a "lamb." They will either choose *Jesus* or *the Beast* with "two horns *like a lamb*, but (who) spoke like a dragon" (Rev. 13:11 NASB, clarification and emphasis mine).

We know from our study in Part Two: "The *Pattern of Seven Events*" that the *Third Seal* breaks during the *Third Year* of the 70th Week. The breaking of this seal will *begin famine, drought, and economic chaos*. While physical provision is at that time will be at a minimum, *Passover* reminds us that Jesus will provide spiritual "food" for us (the sacrament of the "Last Supper," communion—which comes from the Jewish *Passover Seder*).

> And when He had taken some bread and given thanks, He broke it and gave it to them, saying, "This is my body which is given for you; do this in remembrance of me." And in the same way He took the cup after they had eaten, saying, "This cup which is poured out for you is the new covenant in my blood." (Luke 22:19-20 NASB)

The bread eaten at Passover is *unleavened bread*. This is a *highly significant* symbol for the *Third Year* of the 70th Week. During that time, the *Mark of the Beast* will likely be offered as the only means to buy and sell "bread." But those enduring the *Third Year* are not to eat this "leavened" (symbol of sin) bread from the Antichrist. "You shall not offer the blood of my sacrifice with leavened bread" (Ex. 34:25 NASB). Rather, God will use this period to wean us from the world system. Paul speaks of the purity of *unleavened* bread:

> *Clean out the old leaven* so that you may be a new lump, just as *you are in fact unleavened*. For Christ our Passover also has been sacrificed. (1 Cor. 5:7 NASB, emphasis mine)

In Chapter Six: "The Walls Came Tumbling Down (Joshua 6, Judges 6-8)," we learned that prior to fighting the battle of Jericho, all of Israel consecrated themselves and were circumcised. It is highly significant that this happened on *Passover* (Jos. 5:10). The breaking of the *Third Seal* on Passover of the *Third Year* of the 70th Week will signify the time for those enduring this period to *sanctify themselves and wean themselves from the world system* in preparation for what lies ahead.

"Who then is the faithful and sensible slave whom his master put in charge of his household to give them their *food* at the proper time (KAIROS: appointed time)." (Matt 24:45 NASB, clarification and emphasis mine)

"And thou shalt eat thy *food by weight*, twenty shekels a day: from time (KAIROS: appointed time) to time (KAIROS: appointed time) shalt thou eat them. And thou shalt *drink water by measure*, even from time (KAIROS: appointed time) to time (KAIROS: appointed time) thou shalt drink the sixth part of a hin." (Ezek. 4:10-11 LXX, clarification and emphasis mine)

Year Four: Event Four

Fourth Seal Fulfilled on Unleavened Bread

The seven-day *Feast of Unleavened Bread*, which starts the day after Passover, has also already had a major fulfillment. It marks the beginning of the time when Jesus lay 3 days and 3 nights in the grave. In the *Fourth Year* of the 70th Week, it will mark the beginning of the *Time of Jacob's Trouble*; the 3 ½ years the Jews will spend in "*affliction*" (and the 2 ½ years the Church will spend in great tribulation). God's command to Moses regarding this feast was:

> You shall eat unleavened bread with it, that is, *the bread of affliction (for you came out of the land of Egypt in haste)*, that you may remember the day in which you came out of the land of Egypt. (Deut. 16:3 NKJV, clarification and emphasis mine)

When the *Fourth Seal* is broken, the Antichrist and his armies will occupy Jerusalem and the Temple at the *Midpoint* of the 70th Week. It is at that point that Jesus commands those in Judea to flee to the mountains (Matt. 24:15-16). Notice in the above passage that the Feast of Unleavened Bread symbolizes coming out of Egypt *in haste*:

> And thus you shall eat it: with a belt on your waist, your sandals on your feet, and your staff in your hand. So you shall eat it *in haste*. (Ex. 12: 11 NASB, emphasis mine)

When the *Fourth Seal* breaks at the *Midpoint* of the 70th Week, those in Judea need to be ready to flee. This flight of the woman (Israel) is pictured in Rev. 12 which describes a woman clothed in the sun, the moon at her feet and with a crown of 12 stars. Who is this enigmatic figure—the woman of Rev. 12? What does this strange description mean?

    Many believe this woman pictured in Rev. 12 is Mary. Some believe she is Israel. Others believe she is the Bride of Christ. Scripture will not leave us without an answer. The search for the correct answer begins in the very first verses of Rev. 12:

> *A great sign appeared in heaven*: a *woman* clothed with the sun, and the moon under her feet, and on her head a crown of twelve stars; and she was with child; and she cried out, being in labor and in pain to give birth . . . *And she gave birth to a son, a male child, who is to rule all the nations with a rod of iron* (Jesus); and her child was caught up to God and to His throne. (Rev. 12:1-2, 5 NASB, clarification and emphasis mine)

The *woman* appears as a "great sign" in heaven. This tells us she is *symbolic* of other things, not a literal woman. We see immediately that she gives birth to the Messiah who rules the nations with a rod of iron. This is obviously Jesus. The Church did not give birth to Jesus; rather Jesus started the church! This eliminates the Church being the *woman* from contention. Israel symbolically gave birth to the Messiah and Mary literally did, so they are both still possible correct answers.

    The second clue is the woman's odd wardrobe of a sun, moon, and stars. These symbols are emblematic and found in Joseph's dream about his family:

I have had still another dream; and behold *the sun and the moon and eleven stars* (Joseph was the twelfth star) were bowing down to me." He related it to his father and to his brothers; and his father rebuked him and said to him, "What is this dream that you have had? Shall *I and your mother and your brothers actually come to bow ourselves down* before you to the ground?" (Gen. 37:9-10 NASB, clarification and emphasis mine)

Jacob interprets the dream for Joseph. The sun, moon, and stars are *Jacob's family*; the first family of Israel. *This clearly identifies the woman as Israel.* She is not just the Jews because they are the tribe of Judah, only one tribe. She is *all of Israel*, all twelve tribes. Some have tried to stretch the symbolism of the sun, moon, and stars to mean Mary, but none of these are biblically based. John uses direct Old Testament and New Testament references in Revelation to telegraph his meaning; it is a "Revelation Key." Mary is *not* the woman of Rev. 12. She fulfilled some of these roles in a prophetic way (giving birth to Jesus, fleeing to Egypt), but she is *not* the focus of this portion of scripture. Hence, the correct answer is that the *woman* is symbolic of *all of Israel.*

Let's continue to examine the passage from Rev. 12 for more clues:

Then *another sign* appeared in heaven: and behold, a great red dragon having seven heads and ten horns, and on his heads were seven diadems. And his tail swept away a third of the stars of heaven and threw them to the earth. And the dragon stood before the woman who was about to give birth, so that when she gave birth he might devour her child. And she gave birth to a son, a male child, who is to rule all the nations with a rod of iron; and *her child was caught up to God and to His throne. Then the woman fled into the wilderness* where she had (literal: has) a place prepared by God, so that there she would be nourished for one thousand two hundred and sixty days (1260 days = 3 ½ years). (Rev. 12: 3-6 NASB, clarification and emphasis mine)

This passage also clearly shows that the *woman* is not Mary. Notice the woman's child (Jesus) is caught up (Gk: HARPAZO, meaning "caught up or raptured") into heaven *and then* the woman flees into the wilderness. This cannot be Mary. Mary fled into Egypt long before Jesus was caught up into heaven. Once again, it is shown that the correct answer is that the *woman* in Rev. 12 is symbolic of *Israel*.

THE WOMAN PERSECUTED

At the *Midpoint* of the 70th Week of Daniel, we know that Michael stands up (Dan. 12:1) and fights a war with Satan and casts him out of heaven (Rev. 12:7-12). It is then that Satan begins the most intense persecution in all of history which we call the *Great Tribulation* (Dan. 12:1, Matt. 24:15).

> And when the dragon saw that he was thrown down to the earth, he persecuted the woman who gave birth to the male child. But the *two wings of the great eagle were given to the woman*, so that she could fly into the wilderness to her place, where she was (literally: will be) *nourished for a time and times and half a time*, from the presence of the serpent. And *the serpent poured water like a river out of his mouth after the woman*, so that he might cause her to be swept away with the flood. But the earth helped the woman, and *the earth opened its mouth and drank up the river* which the dragon poured out of his mouth. (Rev. 12:13-16 NASB, emphasis mine)

Israel is able to flee with the help of two wings of a great eagle. There has been much speculation about these wings of the great eagle, whether they are an airplane, a symbol of the USA, etc. As with all the symbolism in Revelation, the Bible interprets it. Here are other scripture verses which use a similar phrase *"eagles' wings:"*

> You have seen what I did to the Egyptians, and how I bore you on *eagles' wings* and brought you to myself. (Exod. 19:4 NASB, emphasis mine)

> But those who wait on the Lord Shall renew their strength; they shall mount up with *wings like eagles*, They shall run and not be weary, They shall walk and not faint. (Isa. 40:31 NASB, emphasis mine)

The first reference in the Bible to *"eagles' wings"* (Law of Primacy) is found in the story of the Exodus. The flight of Israel in the last days (in Rev. 12:13-16) is being compared to the flight of Israel in the Exodus. The very next few verses in the Revelation passage confirm this:

> And *the serpent poured water like a river out of his mouth after the woman*, so that he might cause her to be swept away with *the flood*. But the earth helped the woman, and *the earth opened its mouth and drank up the river* which the dragon poured out of his mouth. (Rev. 12:15-16 NASB, emphasis mine)

The picture of the *flood of water* attempting to carry away the *woman* is very similar to the Egyptian army pursuing Israel after the Passover except in this account it is sort of a "reverse" parting of the Red Sea. In the Exodus account, the Red Sea separated, Israel escaped through it, and the *Egyptians* were *swept away* when the *waters flooded back*. In this account in Revelation, Israel will be spared again, but when the *earth* swallows up the flood. Will this be a miraculous swallowing of a pursuing army (by the flood), just as in the Passover account? I believe it very well might be. Remember that the original parting of the Red Sea happened during the seven day *Feast of Unleavened Bread*. The future protection of Israel during the seven-year 70th Week of Daniel will most likely fulfill the Feast in this regard yet again.

Notice in the above passage from Revelation that, after the remnant of Israel is protected, Satan becomes enraged and vents his anger against the Christians. The following scriptures are applicable to the events at this time of the *Fourth Year* of the 70th Week:

> "And at that time (KAIROS: appointed time) *Michael the great prince shall stand up, that stands over the children of thy people: and there shall be a time of tribulation, such tribulation as has not been from the time that there was a nation on the earth until that time* (KAIROS: appointed time)." (Dan. 12:1 LXX, clarification and emphasis mine)

485

"Those on the rocky soil are those who, when they hear, receive the word with joy; and these have no firm root; they believe for a while, and in *time* (KAIROS: appointed time) *of temptation fall away."* (Luke 8:13 NASB, clarification and emphasis mine)

"They will fall by the edge of the sword, and will be led captive into all the nations; and Jerusalem will be trampled underfoot by the Gentiles until the times (KAIRON: appointed times) of the Gentiles are fulfilled." (Luke 21:24 NASB, clarification mine)

"And you know what restrains him (the Antichrist) now, so that in *his time* (KAIROS: appointed time) he will be *revealed."* (2 Thess. 2: 6 NASB, clarification and emphasis mine)

"At the set time (KAIROS: appointed time) he (the Antichrist) shall return, and shall come into the south, but the last expedition shall not be as the first. For the Citians (Ships of Kittam) issuing forth shall come against him, and he shall be brought low, and shall return, and shall be incensed against the holy covenant: and he shall do thus, and shall return, and have intelligence with them that have forsaken the holy covenant. And seeds shall spring up out of him, and *they shall profane the sanctuary of strength, and they shall remove the perpetual sacrifice, and make the abomination desolate."* (Dan. 11:29-31 LXX, clarification and emphasis mine)

This directly leads to the next fulfillment of a Feast —*First Fruits*, during *Year Five* of the 70th Week.

YEAR FIVE: EVENT FIVE

FIFTH SEAL FULFILLED ON FIRST FRUITS

First Fruits, as a "spring" Feast, has ~~also~~ had a major fulfillment already as the resurrection of our Lord and Savior occurred on this Feast during his *First Coming*. "Christ has been raised from the dead, the *first fruits* of those who are asleep" (1 Cor. 15:20 NASB, emphasis mine). In Chapter Five: "Signed, Sealed, and Delivered

(Revelation 4-5)," we discussed that this *First Fruits Harvest* was the first of three resurrection harvests to take place. This was also pictured in God's instructions to Moses regarding this Feast:

> When you enter the land which I am going to give to you and reap its harvest, then you shall bring in the sheaf of the *first fruits* of your harvest to the priest. He shall wave the sheaf before the Lord *for you to be accepted.* (Lev. 23:10-11 NASB, emphasis mine)

We are *accepted* because of Jesus's sacrifice (Jesus, in addition to being the *Passover Lamb*, was, in a sense, the *First Fruits* offering), and he is the *first fruits* of the resurrection. In the *Fifth Year* of the 70th Week, the *Fifth Seal* on the Scroll will be broken. It will also fulfill this ancient *Feast of First Fruits.* When the *Fifth Seal* breaks, the martyrs under the altar will cry out to God:

> When the Lamb broke the *fifth seal,* I saw underneath the altar *the souls of those who had been slain* because of the word of God, and because of the testimony which they had maintained; and they cried out with a loud voice, saying, "How long, O Lord, holy and true, will you refrain from *judging and avenging our blood* on those who dwell on the earth?" (Rev. 6:9-10 NASB, emphasis mine)

They are told to wait a bit longer for God to avenge the blood of the martyrs, "until the number of their fellow servants and their brethren who were to be killed even as they had been, would be completed also" (Rev. 6:11 NASB). So these souls of the martyrs under the altar are *first fruits*, the first to offer their lives as a sacrifice of faith to their God during the *Great Tribulation* of the 70th Week. In Romans, Paul shows that even while we are alive, the Spirit within us causes us to groan, to cry out to God, in anticipation of the redemption of our bodies to come:

And not only this, but also we ourselves, having the *first fruits* of the Spirit, even we ourselves *groan* within ourselves, *waiting eagerly for our adoption as sons, the redemption of our body* (to receive resurrection bodies). For in hope we have been saved, but hope that is seen is not hope; for who hopes for what he already sees? But if we hope for what we do not see, with perseverance we wait eagerly for it. (Rom. 8:23-25 NASB, clarification and emphasis mine)

The following scripture passages also relate to this period of the *Fifth Seal* fulfilled on First Fruits in *Year Five,* related to the *Great Tribulation* that the Church will undergo, demonstrating their sacrifice of faith to God during this period:

"But the Spirit explicitly says that in later times (KAIRON: appointed times) some will *fall away from the faith,* paying attention to deceitful spirits and doctrines of demons." (1 Tim. 4:1 NASB, clarification and emphasis mine)

"And some of *them that understand shall fall, to try them as with fire,* and to test them, and that they may be manifested at the time (KAIROS: appointed time) of the end, for the matter is yet for a set time (KAIROS: appointed time)" (Dan. 11:35 LXX, clarification and emphasis mine)

The fulfillment of First Fruits is one of anticipation of the next Feast, the *Feast of Shavuot* (Feast of Weeks; Pentecost).

SIXTH YEAR: SIXTH EVENT

SIXTH SEAL FULFILLED ON SHAVUOT

At the beginning of this section, we have already seen how Peter's Sermon on *Shavuot* (Pentecost) forever linked it with the future *Celestial Earthly Disturbance Event.* The happenings of that fulfillment in the First Century also forever linked the Feast to the coming of the Holy Spirit.

In the *Sixth Year* of the 70th Week of Daniel when the *Sixth Seal* is broken, these two aspects (linkage of the *Shavuot* to the *Celestial Earthly Disturbance* and the Holy Spirit) will again be seen. Prophetic hints of this are found in Moses's command to the Israelites regarding this Feast:

> You shall count *seven weeks* for yourself; you shall begin to count *seven weeks* from the time you *begin to put the sickle to the standing grain.* Then you shall celebrate the *Feast of Weeks* (*Shavuot*; Pentecost) to the Lord your God with a tribute of a freewill offering of your hand, which you shall give just as the Lord your God blesses you; *and you shall rejoice before the Lord your God*, you and your son and your daughter and your male and female servants and the Levite who is in your town, and the stranger and the orphan and the widow who are in your midst, in the place where the Lord your God chooses to establish His name. You shall remember that you were a slave in Egypt, and you shall be careful to observe these statutes. (Deut. 16:9-12 NASB, emphasis mine)

Notice that the "counting" begins when the sickle is put to the "*standing grain*," when the *first fruits* harvest of the early barley crop was harvested in Jerusalem. In the days of the Temple, Jews verbally counted the 49 days (known as "Counting the Omer") between the wave sacrifice of an "omer" of barley which has been *ground down to fine power* on First Fruits (always on "Sunday," the 7th day on the Jewish calendar) until *Shavuot* (Pentecost).[xcvii]

In the 70th Week, Christians and Jews will be counting the 42 months (3 ½ years) of authority that will be given to the Antichrist. As we learned in Chapter Fifteen: "Overcoming Lions (Daniel 1-12)," God has established an exact number of days that the Antichrist will have authority (3 ½ years, 42 months, or 1260 days; all of which are equivalent). During this time, the believers will be *counting* these days because the saints ("*standing grain*") will be "*cut down*" (martyred) and "*ground down*" (persecuted) during this entire period.

The *Celestial Earthly Disturbance Event* that occurs at the *Sixth Seal*, however, will mark a time of rejoicing for the saints ("*you shall rejoice before the Lord your*

God"). We know from Jesus's words in Luke that at this time Christians are to *"straighten up and lift up your heads, because your redemption is drawing near"* (Luke 21:25 NASB). Christians will also rejoice because this event (the *Sixth Seal*) will be *a sign* marking the end of the *Great Tribulation* and the end of the persecution for them. "But immediately *after the tribulation* of those days the *sun will be darkened, and the moon will not give its light, and the stars will fall from the sky, and the powers of the heavens will be shaken*" (Matt. 24:29 NASB).

Why will the *Great Tribulation* end with this sign of the *Celestial Earthly Disturbance Event*? It is a sign of the upcoming Rapture and subsequent *Day of the Lord*, God's Wrath. Revelation shows us that while Christians are lifting their heads in joy, the forces of the Antichrist are hiding in caves:

> Then the kings of the earth and the great men and the commanders and the rich and the strong and *every slave and free man hid themselves in the caves and among the rocks of the mountains*; and they said to the mountains and to the rocks, "Fall on us and *hide us from the presence of Him who sits on the throne, and from the wrath of the Lamb; for the great day of their wrath has come*, and who is able to stand?" (Rev. 6: 15-17 NASB, emphasis mine)

The Antichrist's forces will be focused on self-preservation and not persecution immediately after the *Sixth Seal* is broken, when they see the celestial signs form God, because the Lord is soon coming on the clouds to rapture his Church and to bring his Wrath upon the earth (the *Day of the Lord*).

The time after the *Sixth Seal* will probably also be a time when the *Holy Spirit* is poured out to comfort his Church in the midst of the persecution. The following scriptures speak of the *need to be awake and alert* for the *coming* resurrection/rapture of the Church, which also follows *after the Sixth Seal*:

"At that time (KAIROS: appointed time) thy people shall be delivered, even every one that is written in the book. And *many of them that sleep in the dust of the earth shall awake, some to everlasting life*, and some to reproach and everlasting shame. And *the wise shall shine as the brightness of the firmament* and some of the many righteous as the stars for ever and ever." (Dan. 12:1-3 LXX, clarification and emphasis mine)

"And thou, Daniel, close the words, and seal the book (*Book of Life*) to the time (KAIROS: appointed time) of the end." (Dan. 12:4 LXX, clarification and emphasis mine)

"Take heed, keep on the alert; for you do not know when the *appointed* time (KAIROS: appointed time) will come . . . Therefore, *be on the alert*—for you do not know *when the master of the house is coming*, whether in the evening, at midnight, or when the rooster crows, or in the morning." (Mark 13:33,35 NASB, clarification and emphasis mine)

"Keep the commandment without stain or reproach until *the appearing of our Lord Jesus Christ*, which He will bring about at the proper time (KAIROS: appointed time)." (1 Tim. 6:14-15 NASB, clarification and emphasis mine)

Seventh Year: Seventh Event

Seventh Seal Fulfilled on *Yom Teruah*

We have discussed this fulfillment of *Yom Teruah* (Feast of Trumpets) by the resurrection/Rapture at length in this chapter (Chapter 13: "Appointments") as well as other chapters in this book. Although there is very little to add, I'd like to share another scripture about the *silence in heaven and joy on the earth* upon the breaking of the *Seventh Seal*:

> There will be *silence* before you and *praise in Zion*, O God, and to you the vow will be performed. O *you who hear prayer, to you all men come*. Iniquities prevail against me; as for our transgressions, you forgive them. How blessed is the one whom you choose and bring near to you to *dwell in your courts*. (Psalms 65:1-4 NASB, emphasis mine)

In Heaven there will be *silence* before the Father. "When the Lamb broke the *seventh seal*, there was *silence in heaven* for about half an hour" (Rev. 8:1 NASB, emphasis mine), but on the earth there will be great *rejoicing* at Jesus returning to rapture his saints. Silence in heaven is unusual as the angels are continually lifting their voices in praise of God. What would cause the silence in heaven? Perhaps, it is due to Jesus leaving heaven to return to earth to meet the Church in the air at the Rapture.

During this period of time, the prayers for deliverance of the saints will rise before God like incense. "Incense was given to him, so that he might add it to the prayers of all the saints on the golden altar which was before the throne. And the smoke of the incense, with the prayers of the saints, went up before God out of the angel's hand" (Rev. 8:3-4 NASB). And God will hear them, and the "blessed ones" will come to "*dwell in his courts.*"

On the same day of the Rapture, Jesus will begin to pour out his wrath:

> It is only just for God to *repay with affliction those who afflict you* (God's Wrath), and to give relief to you who are afflicted and to us as well *when the Lord Jesus will be revealed* from heaven with His mighty angels in flaming fire (Shekinah Glory), dealing out retribution to those who do not know God and to those who do not obey the gospel of our Lord Jesus (pouring out his Wrath). (1 Thess. 1:6-8 NASB, clarification and emphasis mine)

The following scripture passages also allude to this time of the resurrection/rapture of the saints (at the end of *Year Six*) and the ensuing wrath of God unleashed upon the earth (during *Year Seven*):

"And they (the demons) cried out, saying, 'What business do we have with each other, Son of God? Have you come here to *torment us before the time* (KAIROS: appointed time)'" (Matt. 8:29 NASB, clarification and emphasis mine)

"And the nations were enraged, and *your wrath came*, and the time (KAIROS: appointed time) came for the *dead to be judged, and the time to reward your bond-servants the prophets and the saints* and those who fear your name, the small and the great, and to destroy those who destroy the earth." (Rev. 11:18 NASB, clarification and emphasis mine)

"And one week shall establish the covenant with many: and in the midst of the week my sacrifice and drink-offering shall be taken away: and on the temple shall be the abomination of desolations; and at the end of time (KAIROS: appointed time) *an end shall be put to the desolation.*" (Dan. 9:27 LXX, clarification and emphasis mine)

"In those days and at that time (KAIROS: appointed time) they shall call Jerusalem the throne of the Lord; and all the nations shall be gathered to it: and they shall not walk any more after the imaginations of their evil heart." (Jer. 3:17 LXX, clarification and emphasis mine)

"The Ancient of days came, and he gave judgment to the saints of the Most High; and the time (KAIROS: appointed time) came on, and the saints possessed the kingdom" (Dan. 7:22 LXX, clarification mine)

The following chart (Figure 54: Biblical Feast Dates for the Seals During the Seven Years), displaying the possible biblical dates for all the *Feasts of the Lord* (and the fulfillment of the seven seals) during each of the seven years of the 70th Week. In addition, Figure 57 at the end of this Chapter presents these dates in graphic form, shown to scale.

Year of the 70th Week of Daniel	Seal	Feast of the Lord	Biblical Date
One	First	Yom Kippur	Tishri 10
Two	Second	Tabernacles	Tishri 15-21
Three	Third	Passover	Nisan 14
Four	Fourth	Unleavened Bread	Nisan 15 - 21
Five	Fifth	First Fruits	Range From Nisan 15- 21
Six	Sixth	Shavuot	Range From Sivan 5 - 11
Seven	Seventh	Yom Teruah	Tishri 1

Figure 54: Biblical Feast Dates for the Seals during the Seven Years

I hope you have noticed that not only has this section established the *chronological timeline* for the breaking of the seals, it has also given us another beautiful picture of the *Pattern of Seven Events* during the 70th Week of Daniel——a picture painted in the fulfillment of the seven *Feasts of the Lord*. This understanding too will help the Church during their tribulation to know the *timeframe* of the persecution.

THE MYSTERIOUS "DAYS" OF DANIEL

In the *Book of Daniel* there are *four mysterious numbers of days* which have puzzled Bible scholars for thousands of years. What do these mystic numbers (*1260, 1290, 1335*, and *2300*) mean? Is there a link between these numbers of days and the *Feasts of the Lord* as well?

We will discuss the first three of these *mysterious numbers of days* (*1260, 1290, and 1335*) in this section. The mysterious number 2300 is covered in the later section "Other Dates."

All of these numbers of days are calculated from the setting up of the Abomination of Desolation at the *Midpoint* of the 70th Week, at which time the *Great Tribulation* also begins. These counts of days are the God-ordained time limit for the desolation and desecration that the Antichrist will inflict on the Temple and God's people. The first "number" is *1260 days.* From Revelation we see that this is equivalent to 42 months and 3 ½ years. First, we see that the time period *"time, times and half a time"* is equal to *1260 days*:

> Then the woman fled into the wilderness where she had (literally "has") a place prepared by God, so that there she would be *nourished* for *one thousand two hundred and sixty days* (*1260 days*). (Rev. 12:6 NASB, clarification and emphasis mine)

> But the two wings of the great eagle were given to the woman, so that she could fly into the wilderness to her place, where she was (literally "will be*")* *nourished for a time and times and half a time* (3 1/2 years). (Rev. 12:14 NASB, clarification and emphasis mine)

These two passages show the *woman* (Israel) is *nourished* for a given time period of *1260 days*. Since two different ways of expressing that period are given, they must be equivalent. Next, we see from Daniel and Revelation that *"time, times and half a time"* is also equal to *42 months,* and both are described as the *period of the Antichrist's authority*:

> They (the saints) will be given into his hand for *a time, times, and half a time* (3 1/2 years). (Dan. 7:25 NASB, clarification mine)

There was given to him a mouth speaking arrogant words and blasphemies, and authority to act for *forty-two months* (42 months) was given to him. (Rev. 13:5 NASB)

These last two references show us that the three ways the Bible designates this period (*1260 days*; 42 months; 3 1/2 years) are all equivalent, *and* they are equal to (omit space)the reign of the Antichrist. This gives us a fixed point (the time from the *Midpoint* of the 70th Week to the end of the reign of Antichrist) from which we can surmise what all the other mysterious days may involve.

Do Daniel's days (*1260, 1290, 1335,* and *2300*) fall on the *Jewish Feasts*? I would like to purpose a theory that *all or most of the mysterious number of days in Daniel are linked to the fulfillment of the Feasts of the Lord or other important days in Jewish history*. This is further developed in the following sections.

There are seven Feasts of the Lord. These were instituted by God, and given to Moses and the Israelites prior to entering the Promised Land. We studied these at length in the previous section. Now, we will tie these Feasts to the *mysterious days* of Daniel.

DAYS OF DANIEL TIMELINE

We already have two firm dates on our timeline related to the 70th Week: *Tishri 1 (Yom Teruah; Feast of Trumpets)* of *Year Six* (the Rapture), and *Tishri 10 (Yom Kippur; Day of Atonement)* of the end of *Year Seven* (the physical Second Coming). To this we can add *Tishri 15-21 (Sukkot; Tabernacles)* of *Year Six* (the *Wedding Supper of the Lamb*)——as we studied in Chapter Fourteen: "Event Seven: Rapture and Wrath." In addition, we can add *Tishri 1-10* (the ten *Days of Awe*) of *Year Seven* (the bowl judgments).

As we continue to build this thesis, let's assume that *Tishri 10 (Yom Kippur; Day of Atonement)* of the end of *Year Seven* will be Daniel's mysterious *1260th day*. Starting at the *Midpoint*, the Antichrist is given authority for 42 months ("time, times, and half a time"). We have already shown both of these are equivalent to *1260 days*. It makes sense that ~~his~~ Antichrist's reign ends when Jesus is present upon the earth, which occurs at the very end of the 70th Week. There can only be one King of the

Earth. That will be Jesus instantly upon his descent to earth, when he will defeat Satan with a Word from His Mouth.

The next number on Daniel's timeline is *1290 days*. Daniel describes it this way:

> From the time that the regular sacrifice is abolished and the abomination of desolation is set up, there will be *1,290 days*. (Dan. 12:11 NASB, emphasis mine)

This date (related to *1290 days*) is *thirty days after the physical Second Coming*, which occurs on *Yom Kippur* (Day of Atonement, *Tishri 10* [day *1260*]). If our theory is correct, the biblical date for *1290 days* will be the date *Cheshvan 10* (*Heshvan* 10) on the Biblical calendar. Historically, this is the day that Noah and his family entered the Ark. We know from Chapter Six: "The Walls Came Tumbling Down (Joshua 6, Judges 6-8)" that every Ark in the Bible is symbolic of Jesus. What event might occur *thirty days* after the physical Second Coming where the human survivors of the 70th Week of Daniel take shelter in Jesus? (The *saints* have been sheltered in Jesus since the Rapture.) Could the *Sheep and Goat Judgment* be the event that is foretold by the mysterious *1290 days*? It appears to be.

> When the Son of Man comes in His glory, and all the angels with Him, then He will sit on His glorious throne. *All the nations will be gathered before Him*; and *He will separate them from one another*, as the shepherd *separates the sheep from the goats*; and He will put the sheep on His right, and the goats on the left. (Matt. 25:31-33 NASB, emphasis mine)

We know that the *goats* (the *unrighteous* survivors of the 70th Week) are severely judged and thrown into the *Lake of Fire* along with the *Antichrist* and the *False Prophet* (Matt. 25:41, 46). It is at this judgment (*Sheep and Goat judgment*) that Jesus removes all the remaining wicked from the earth. It will be the official last day of the rebellion that started with the setting up of the Abomination of Desolation. The *righteous* survivors of the 70th Week will take shelter in King Jesus (the Ark). It seems a perfect fulfillment of *Cheshvan 10*. In the days of Noah, the wicked and righteous were separated when God closed the door of the Ark. After the 70th Week of Daniel, they will be forever separated in the *Sheep and Goat Judgment*.

What about the mysterious *day 1335*? This date is *75 days after the physical Second Coming*. The Biblical date will be *Kislev 25*. There is already a Jewish Feast on that date: *Hanukkah*. Daniel has this to say about that date:

> How blessed is he who keeps waiting and attains to the *1,335 days*! (Dan. 12:12 NASB, emphasis mine)

Hanukkah is the feast that celebrates the rededication of the temple after it was desecrated by the first Abomination of Desolation set up by Antiochus Epiphanes (a foreshadow of the Antichrist) in the second century BC. . In my opinion, the *1335th day* will be another rededication of the Temple (on *Hanukkah*), which is rebuilt by Jesus after he returns, after the final Abomination of Desolation at the *Midpoint*. If this is correct, we should add another date to our timeline, *Cheshvan 23*. This is the day when the polluted stones (the Abomination) were removed from the Temple in the second century BC. In my opinion, it is highly likely that the upcoming event in the 21st century will mirror this ancient cleansing of the Temple.

I would like to add one final date to our timeline. Although the *Marriage Supper of the Lamb* in Heaven occurs in *Year Seven* of the 70th Week on the *Feast of Tabernacles*, I believe the final fulfillment of this Feast will occur five days following *Year Seven* of the 70th Week, in *"Year Eight,"* after the physical Second Coming. It is at that point both the Jews and the Christians, God's entire household, will sit together with Jesus as he "tabernacles" with us. It will be a glorious eight-days celebration with Jesus during the *Feast of Tabernacles* (*Tishri* 15-22). In the *Letter to Laodicea*, Jesus knocks on the door of the *foolish virgins* and promises to come in and dine with them if they open the door. I believe it is this final fulfillment of the *Feast of Tabernacles* that Jesus spoke of.

OTHER DATES

If we know that *Tishri 10* of *Year Seven* is exactly *1260 days* after the *Midpoint* of the 70th Week, we *should* be able to calculate the *Midpoint* as well. There are several factors that make this a bit tricky, however. First, present Jewish calendar years have a varying number of days, depending if they have twelve or thirteen months (in seven years of each 19-year cycle). Second, in Chapter Thirteen: "Event Six: The Celestial Earthly Disturbance," we learned that upon the *Celestial Earthly Disturbance*, the earth *may* return to a 360-day year. This is a factor to consider. These potential complications may be a reason why Daniel says that the events are "sealed."

> Go your way, Daniel, for *these words* (the mysterious number of days) are concealed and sealed up until the end time. (Dan. 12:9 NASB, clarification and emphasis mine)

This may also be why, in the *Olivet Discourse*, Jesus gives us the *Abomination of Desolation* as a "sign" to look for: "Therefore when you *see* the *Abomination of Desolation*" (Matt. 24:15 NASB, emphasis mine). If we were able to calculate the exact *Midpoint* during the first half of the 70th Week, Jesus would have no need to tell us to watch for it as a *sign*. Once this dreadful abomination is set up, however, it will be a marker, and we will be able to calculate the rest of the Days of Daniel (*1260, 1290, 1335*, and *2300*) going forward. Is this why Paul assumes we will *not* be taken by surprise by the Day of the Lord? "But you, brethren, are *not* in darkness, that the day would overtake you like a thief" (1 Thess. 5:4 NASB, emphasis mine).

For these reasons, I'm choosing to look at several possible dates in the month of Nisan of *Year Four* of the 70th Week (approximately *1260 days* prior to the physical Second Coming) for the *Midpoint* rather than trying to calculate a date, if that is not possible due to several factors mentioned previously. I am trusting scripture that this date of the *Midpoint* truly is *sealed* at least from *viewing it from the first half* of the 70th Week, so perhaps looking at possible historic dates on the Jewish calendar will give us a better sense of what that date might be:

- *Nisan 10*: This is the date that the Lamb was selected to be observed for blemishes before being sacrificed on Passover. It was also the day of

Jesus's triumphant entrance into Jerusalem on Palm Sunday. Additionally, *if* the calendar will already be set to a 360 day year, Nisan 10 will be exactly *1260 days* prior to the physical Second Coming on *Tishri 10*—this supports this date as being at the *Midpoint* of the 70th Week.

- *Nisan 17*: This is the historic date that God parted the Red Sea and protected the fleeing Hebrews from Pharaoh.
- *Nisan 26*: This is "Holocaust Day" in modern Israel

We know from our previous study on the *seven seals* that the *Fourth Seal* breaks during the *Feast of Unleavened Bread*. Of these proposed dates, only Nisan 17 occurs during this Feast (Nisan 15-21), and we also know from that earlier study that the parting of the Red Sea will be prophetically fulfilled again in the flight of the "woman" (Israel). For these reasons I am "guessing" that the *Midpoint* might be *Nisan 17*, but I really can't say with certainty. *Nisan 10* being the *Midpoint* also has great matching attributes, being the day that the Passover lamb was selected, just as *Antichrist* will set himself up in the Temple at the *Midpoint* to be "selected" and worshiped as the Passover lamb. However, since he, upon inspection, is the blemished, unacceptable lamb, he is the *abomination that causes desolation*. The fact that *Nisan 10* lies outside of the seven-day *Feast of Unleavened Bread* may not be important. *The Midpoint of Daniel's 70th Week and the breaking of the Fourth Seal may not be the same day.* They may be two separate events, and the *Midpoint* may not correlate to the date of the *Feast of Unleavened Bread*—some other event might. Only time will show the true date of the *Midpoint*.

Daniel has one more "mysterious day" remaining, related to the number 2300 days:

How long will the vision about the regular sacrifice apply, while the transgression causes horror, so as to allow both the holy place and the host to be trampled?" He said to me, "For *2,300 evenings and mornings*; then the holy place will be *properly restored*." (Dan. 8:13-14 NASB, emphasis mine)

There are two questions to answer here. Is it *2300 evenings plus mornings* (1150 days) or 2300 evenings and mornings (*2300 days*)? The second question is what does *"properly restored"* mean?

We already know that Jesus doesn't return until *1260 days* after the Abomination of Desolation is set up. The smaller figure (1150 days) is therefore impossible to relate to this time period. The phrase *"evenings and mornings"* is a traditional Jewish phrase for *"day"* ("There was evening and morning, day one"), so this larger figure (*2300 days*) must be correct.

In terms of what *"properly restored"* means related to the holy place (Temple), let's look at what the Hebrew and Greek words translated *"properly restored"* mean. The Hebrew word translated *"properly restored"* is TSADEQ which means "make righteous." The Greek word for this same phrase is KATHARIZO which means to "make clean." Obviously, it is going to take *1040 days* after Armageddon (1260 + 1040 = *2300 days* from the *Midpoint*) for the Temple to be completely cleansed and made righteous. What that cleansing entails is not completely obvious. It might even necessitate the construction of an entirely new Temple.

What is certain is this final cleansing of the Temple happens *1040 days* (approx. 2 yrs. 10 mos.) after *Tishri 10* (*Yom Kippur*) of the very end of the *Seventh Year*. Assuming a 360-day year, as Daniel did in his prophecies including the 70th Week of Daniel, this date would fall on *Elul 1*. *Elul* is currently the month of repentance in the Jewish calendar. After the physical Second Coming, the Jews will be using the Temple for purposes other than forgiveness of sin (their faith in Jesus will have removed the need for redemptive sacrifices), but perhaps it will be used for ritualistic cleansing from recurring sin in order to be in the *presence* of a Holy God——Jesus.

My understanding is that when Jesus physically returns, the remnant of the Jews will come to faith in their Messiah and be saved, but they will still have human physical bodies (not resurrection bodies); hence, they can and will still sin——just as we are presently saved but we still sin with our physical non-resurrection bodies. Hence, the Temple might still have a purpose for "redemptive sacrifices" for *ritualistic cleansing* for the remnant Jews as well as their progeny during the Millennium, to be in the presence of a Holy God. This makes sense of the Temple animal sacrifices.

The foreshadowing of atonement in future *Yom Kippurs* which is a current function of Elul will be unnecessary as the Jews' "atonement" (Jesus) will live among them. In my mind that makes *Elul 1* an incredibly likely date for this final mysterious number of days. The month of *Elul* will be given a new and more glorious meaning in the Millennial Kingdom if this understanding is correct. We know that there will be a Temple during the Millennium, and its purpose might very well be as a memorial reminder of the work of redemption of Jesus as well as for ritualistic cleansing.

Let's assemble all these mysterious dates of Daniel onto a single timeline. The following chart (Figure 55: Days of Daniel and Alignment with *Feasts of the Lord Days*) does that:

Prophetic Event	Symbolic Event	Year of the 70th Week of Daniel	Hebrew Feast or Historic Event	Hebrew Date	Days of Daniel
Day of the Lord (Rapture and Wrath)	7th Seal	Sixth	Yom Teruah	Tishri 1	
Wedding Supper of the Lamb		Seventh	Tabernacles	Tishri 15-21	
Coronation of Jesus as King	7th Trumpet	Seventh	Yom Teruah	Tishri 1	
Bowl Judgments		Seventh	Days of Awe	Tishri 2-9	
Second Coming (Armageddon)	7th Bowl	Seventh	Yom Kippur	Tishri 10	1260
Feast of Tabernacles			Tabernacles	Tishri 15-21	
Goat and Sheep Judgment			Noah Enters the Ark	Cheshvan 10	1290
Rededication of the Temple			Hanukkah	Kislev 25	1335
New Temple?				Elul 1	2300

Figure 55: Days of Daniel and Alignment with Feasts of the Lord Days

TIMELINE OF RESURRECTIONS AND JUDGMENTS

Now that we have uncovered probable explanations of the *mysterious days of Daniel*, we are ready to undertake a very worthwhile analysis. In Chapter Five: "Signed, Sealed, and Delivered (Revelation 4-5)," we learned that there will be three resurrections (First Fruits, Main Harvest, and Gleanings). We have also learned of two judgments: a judgment of the living (*Sheep and Goats*) and a judgment of the dead (*Great White Throne)* Assembling all of these onto a single Timeline will help us understand how Jesus will administer his righteous mercy and rewards and punishments. The graphic which follows (Figure 56: Resurrections and Judgments) displays these three resurrections and two judgments:

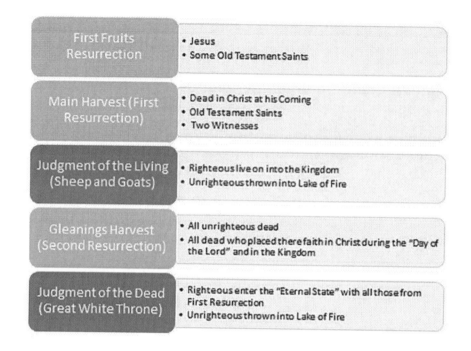

First Fruits Resurrection
- Jesus
- Some Old Testament Saints

Main Harvest (First Resurrection)
- Dead in Christ at his Coming
- Old Testament Saints
- Two Witnesses

Judgment of the Living (Sheep and Goats)
- Righteous live on into the Kingdom
- Unrighteous thrown into Lake of Fire

Gleanings Harvest (Second Resurrection)
- All unrighteous dead
- All dead who placed there faith in Christ during the "Day of the Lord" and in the Kingdom

Judgment of the Dead (Great White Throne)
- Righteous enter the "Eternal State" with all those from First Resurrection
- Unrighteous thrown into Lake of Fire

Figure 56: Resurrections and Judgments

In the first two resurrections, only the righteous are resurrected. These individuals are raptured into heaven by Jesus and are married to Jesus at the *Wedding of the Lamb* as we saw in Chapter Fourteen: "Event Seven: Rapture and Wrath." At the physical Second Coming, Jesus and his Bride return to the earth. The righteous (the *Bride of Jesus Christ*) had previously been given immortal, resurrection bodies, like the resurrection body of Jesus. After Armageddon, there will also be human, mortal survivors of the 70th Week of Daniel. Jesus will then judge these living based on their *works* not on faith. His basis of judgment will be on how well they treated "the least of these my brothers" (the Jews and Christians persecuted in the 70th Week). This first judgment, the "*Sheep and Goats Judgment,*" will be for the living only. Those Jesus deems worthy (the remnant of Jews who come to faith and are "saved" when Jesus physically returns, as well as those judged as "Sheep" in the *Sheep and Goats Judgment*) will enter the Kingdom in their human bodies (not resurrection bodies). Some of these (other than the remnant of Jews) will not have placed their faith in Jesus yet. Jesus's sole criterion at the *Sheep and Goats Judgment* seems to be how the living treated his "brothers."

> Then the King will say to those on His right, "Come, you who are blessed of My Father, inherit the kingdom prepared for you from the foundation of the world . . . Truly I say to you, to the extent that you did it to one of these brothers of Mine, even the least of them, you did it to Me." (Matt. 25:34, 40 NASB)

The unrighteous, who mistreated Jews and Christians, will we thrown into the *Lake of Fire* with the *Antichrist* and *False Prophet*, for eternal punishment.

> Then He will also say to those on His left, "Depart from Me, accursed ones, into the *eternal fire* which has been prepared for the devil and his angels . . . Truly I say to you, to the extent that you did not do it to one of the least of these, you did not do it to me." (Matt. 25:41,45 NASB)

Jesus will then also *imprison* Satan for 1000 years (in the *Abyss*; Rev. 20:3) and later release him "for a short time" during which he will lead yet one more rebellion against God, of the unrighteous on earth. He will be defeated yet again. Then will come the *Great White Throne Judgment*, after which Satan and all the resurrected unrighteous from all ages [as well as the unrighteous still alive at the end of the Millennium (per Rev. 20:15)] will be thrown into the *Lake of Fire* for eternity.

> Then I saw an angel coming down from heaven, holding the key of the abyss and a great chain in his hand. And he laid hold of the dragon, the serpent of old, who is the devil and Satan, and *bound him for a thousand years; and he threw him into the abyss,* and shut it and sealed it over him, so that he would not

deceive the nations any longer, until the thousand years were completed; *after these things he must be released for a short time*. (Rev. 20:1-3 NASB)

The Millennial Kingdom will then begin. On the earth will be Jesus, the *Bride of Christ* in resurrection bodies, the Jews who were all saved in a day when Jesus physically returns, and human survivors of the 70th Week who have had righteous works (the "Sheep" from the *Sheep and Goats Judgment*). The Jews and the Gentile human survivors of the 70th Week will not have resurrection bodies, but will go into the Millennium along with the *Bride of Christ*. The *Bride of Christ* will rule and reign with Christ: "Behold, a king will reign righteously and princes will rule justly" (Isa. 32:1 NASB). The human survivors, who have been judged on works and found righteous, will live longer lives:

> No longer will there be in it an infant who lives but a few days, or an old man who does not live out his days; for the youth will die at the age of one hundred and the one who does not reach the age of one hundred will be thought accursed. (Isa. 65:20 NASB)

Even though all these human survivors will have had their works judged righteous and even though Satan is bound, they will not all behave righteously. Notice some are thought accursed. That is why Christ rules with a *rod of iron* in the Kingdom. All of these human survivors and their offspring (note the reference above to infants) will eventually die; and all men will eventually be judged on *faith alone in Jesus alone* at the end of the Millennium, at the *Great White Throne Judgment*.

After the 1000 years are completed, Satan is loosed from his chains:

> When the thousand years are completed, *Satan will be released from his prison*, and will come out to deceive the nations which are in the four corners of the earth, Gog and Magog, to gather them together for the war; the number of them is like the sand of the seashore. And they came up on the broad plain of the earth and surrounded the camp of the saints and the beloved city, and fire came

down from heaven and devoured them. And the devil who deceived them was *thrown into the Lake of Fire and brimstone*, where the beast and the false prophet are also; and they will be *tormented day and night forever and ever.* (Rev. 20:7-10 NASB, emphasis mine)

The end of the Millennial Kingdom and the judgment of Satan mark the end of God's *Great Creation Prophecy.* The 7000 year rebellion will be over and man and God will be ready to reside together in the eternal state; it will be a return to Eden so to speak. Prior to this, God has one last resurrection and one last judgment to perform.

The *rest of the dead did not come to life until the thousand years were completed* . . . Then I saw a *great white throne* and Him who sat upon it, from whose presence earth and heaven fled away, and no place was found for them. And I saw the dead, the great and the small, standing before the throne, and books were opened; and another book was opened, which is the *book of life*; and the dead were judged from the things which were written in the books, according to their deeds. And the sea gave up the dead which were in it, and death and Hades gave up the dead which were in them; and they were judged, every one of them according to their deeds. Then death and Hades were thrown into the *Lake of Fire*. This is the second death, the Lake of Fire. And if anyone's name was not found written in the *book of life*, he was thrown into the *Lake of Fire*. (Rev. 20:5, 11-15 NASB, emphasis mine)

The resurrection after the Millennial Kingdom is known as the "Gleanings Harvest" or "*Second Resurrection.*" Everyone who died and who was *not* resurrected in the *Main Harvest* or *First Resurrection* (end of the *Sixth Year* of the 70th Week) will be resurrected at this time. Most of these will be the unrighteous dead from the Fall of Adam until the end of the Kingdom. Additionally, there will be some righteous dead. These will include those who placed their faith in Jesus during the *Day of the Lord* (Jewish remnant and some Gentiles) and all who placed their faith in Jesus (those without resurrection bodies) during the Millennial Kingdom. Those without saving faith in Jesus will be thrown into the *Lake of Fire* with the Devil.

Finally at this point, all unrighteousness will have been purged from the earth. God the Father (who cannot be present with unrighteousness) will come to dwell with Jesus and with their people in the *New Jerusalem* for eternity. Praise God.

> Then I saw a new heaven and a new earth; for the first heaven and the first earth passed away, and there is no longer any sea. And I saw the holy city, *New Jerusalem*, coming down out of heaven from God, made ready as a bride adorned for her husband. And I heard a loud voice from the throne, saying, "Behold, the tabernacle of God is among men, and He will dwell among them, and they shall be His people, and God Himself will be among them, and He will wipe away every tear from their eyes; and there will no longer be any death; there will no longer be any mourning, or crying, or pain; the first things have passed away. (Rev. 21:1-4 NASB, emphasis mine)

SUMMARY

What would the comprehensive timing of the 70th Week of Daniel look like in approximate scale? The following summary graphic [Figure 57: The 70th Week of Daniel and Alignment of Seals, Trumpets, and Bowls (Enhanced *Pre-Wrath Rapture* position)], might be described as an *Enhanced Pre-Wrath Rapture* position, with the integration of this specific chronology. This graphic illustrates the fulfillment of the seals, trumpets, and bowls during the seven years of the 70th Week of Daniel, according to our interpretation found in this Chapter 13 and other Chapters of this book:

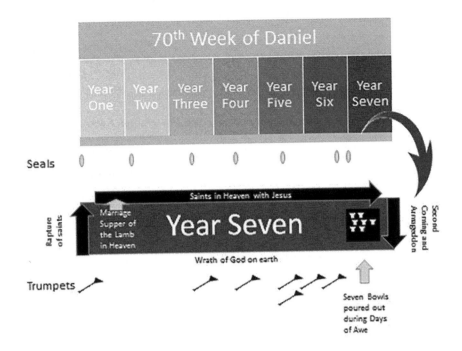

Figure 57: The 70th Week of Daniel and Alignment of Seals, Trumpets, and Bowls

Chapter Twenty-Four
TO HIM WHO OVERCOMES

Bethany Hamilton is a professional woman's surfer (and a Christian). At thirteen she endured a vicious shark attack that cost her an arm and almost took her life. Only one month later, she was back in the water relearning to ride a surfboard. Two years after that she had won first place in the Women's Division of the NSSA National Competition. Her valiant efforts to *overcome* have been seen by millions in the movie *Soul Surfer* (Film District and TriStar, 2011), which I highly recommend.

President Theodore Roosevelt, who also knew something about *overcoming*, had this to say:

> "It is not the critic who counts, nor the man who points out how the strong man stumbled, or where the doer of deeds could have done them better. The credit belongs to the man who is actually in the arena, whose face is marred by dust and sweat and blood; who strives valiantly; who errs and comes short again and again; who knows great enthusiasms, great devotions; who spends himself in a worthy cause; who, at the best, knows in the end the triumph of high achievement, and who, at the worst, if he fails, at least fails while daring greatly, so that his place shall never be with those timid souls who know neither victory nor defeat."
>
> ~Theodore Roosevelt~

The greatest *overcomer* in world history is the Messiah of Israel and our Lord and Savior, *Jesus*:

> These things I have spoken to you, so that in me you may have *peace*. In the world you have *tribulation*, but *take courage*; I have *overcome* the world. (John 16:33 NASB, emphasis mine)

Ch. 24: To Him Who Overcomes

In the 70th Week of Daniel, we will be able to *overcome* the *tribulation* of those days precisely because Jesus has already overcome the world. No matter what we will endure, we can *take courage* and have *peace*. We will *overcome* because he has already *overcome*, and he has sent us the *Holy Spirit* to be with us to help guide and comfort us in everything we go through.

PRAYER AND *THE LORD'S PRAYER*

As we begin our exploration into how to apply what we have learned, I would like to start with *prayer*. Frankly, nothing we can do on our own will accomplish anything. It is only through the power of God that the Church will *overcome*.

So let's begin with *prayer*; and not just any prayer, but with the *Lord's Prayer* itself. But before we begin, first let me share the account of how this prayer is linked to my interest in and knowledge of the end times. One day in my earlier years, when I had no interest in end times at all, I was reading the Book of Matthew during my quiet time. It dawned on me that the *Model Topical Prayer* given to us by Jesus in Matt. 6:9-13 (*the Lord's Prayer*) could be applied to the end times; that the topics of this prayer closely matched what would occur before the return of our Lord. These topics included the need for food, the establishment of Jesus's Kingdom on earth, protection from Satan, etc. I then began the daily practice of praying these topics as they would apply to the end times. From that moment on, the Spirit began to reveal things to me about the time of Jesus's return that continues to this day.

What I have realized only upon the writing of this book is that the topics covered in the *Lord's Prayer* actually mirror the *exact sequence* of the *Pattern of Seven Events* that describe the *seven years* of the 70th Week of Daniel that we have spent a majority of this book detailing. The six lines of the *Lord's Prayer* and the seven events and the *Pattern of Seven Events* (and the seven years of the 70th Week) relate together in that the *Prayer* covers the first six years, the time of persecution of the Church—the time that the Church is on the earth before the Rapture. This is incredible. This re-enforces in my mind that although Jesus gave this *Model Topical Prayer* to the Church for all of its ages, this is *the prayer* for the saints to follow as we prepare for and endure the 70th Week. This sheds a whole new light on this model prayer by our Lord.

Before we explore the *Lord's Prayer* as an end-times prayer, let's discuss what a *Model Topical Prayer* is. This type of prayer functions as a mnemonic or a "memory helper" to assist us in remembering what topics to pray for. Each line or topic in this type of prayer should spark our memories and cause us to pray a number of separate praises and requests related to that topic. For instance, when we pray *"Our Father who art in heaven, hallowed be thy name,"* this is a mnemonic to begin our prayer with praise and thanksgiving; to recall the power of God, his sovereignty, his majesty, his grace, his mercy, etc. Each succeeding line should function similarly to remind us to pray for that topic.

When one of Jesus's disciples asked, "Lord, teach us to pray" (Luke 11:1 NASB), Jesus responded with the *Model Topical Prayer* we know as the *Lord's Prayer*. Most of us have memorized this prayer, which is highly recommended. Essentially, he was saying *pray these topics in this order*. As we are about to find out, incredibly, *this sequence is the Pattern of Seven Events that comprise the 70th Week of Daniel!*

First, here is a full presentation of the *Lord's Prayer* in the translation used in this Chapter 14: "To Him Who Overcomes," and used as Section titles, from each of the six lines of the prayer which follows (the lines are numbered):

1) OUR FATHER IN HEAVEN, HALLOWED BE YOUR NAME
2) YOUR KINGDOM COME, YOUR WILL BE DONE ON EARTH AS IT IS IN HEAVEN
3) GIVE US THIS DAY OUR DAILY BREAD
4) FORGIVE US OUR DEBTS AS WE FORGIVE OUR DEBTORS, AND DO NOT LEAD US INTO TEMPTATION
5) DELIVER US FROM EVIL
6) FOR YOURS IS THE KINGDOM AND THE POWER AND THE GLORY FOREVER, AMEN.

(MATT. 6:9-13 NASB)

Ch. 24: To Him Who Overcomes

1) Our Father in heaven, hallowed be Your name

As we stated above, this topic in the *Lord's Prayer* reminds us to begin all our prayers with praise and thanksgiving. It also reminds me to pray to overcome the hallmark of the *First Year* of the 70th Week—*deception*. On the day Peter and John were examined before the Sanhedrin for healing the man crippled from birth, Peter boldly stated, "And there is salvation in no one else; for there is *no other name* under heaven that has been given among men by which we must be saved" (Acts 4:12 NASB, emphasis mine).

During that *First Year*, the *deception* will intensify. The rider of the *white horse* will be a different messiah with a *different name* offering a worldly "salvation." I pray that God's Church will continue to honor and proclaim the Holy *Name* of Jesus (Yeshua) throughout all the challenges and persecutions that lay ahead until "at the *name* of Jesus every knee will bow, of those who are in heaven and on earth and under the earth, and that every tongue will confess that Jesus Christ is Lord, to the glory of God the Father" (Phil. 2:10-11 NASB, emphasis mine).

2) Your Kingdom Come, Your Will be Done on Earth as it is in Heaven

The second topic in the *Lord's Prayer* reminds us to pray for God's Kingdom to come upon the earth. As we learned in Chapter Six: "The Walls Came Tumbling Down (Joshua 6, Judges 6-8)," *working to advance the coming Kingdom is our primary focus in the days ahead.* We are to circle the world showing them the Ark of the Covenant (Jesus). This is our primary weapon: *displaying the love of Christ.* At this point in my praying the *Lord's Prayer*, I pray for all aspects of the advance of the Kingdom: missions, the awakening of the Church, divine guidance for the leaders of the nations, etc.

It is also the point in the prayer where I pray against the advancement of the kingdom of evil. In the *Second Year* of the 70th Week, the Antichrist will mount a *red horse* and take peace from the earth. He will attempt to advance *his* kingdom through bloodshed and chaos. We need to pray for God to impede the advancement of the kingdom of evil, yet *God's Will* be done as he is advancing the world toward his agenda and timeframe.

3) GIVE US THIS DAY OUR DAILY BREAD

Did you notice how the provision of food is the third topic of the *Lord's Prayer*, just as "famine" is the hallmark of the *Third Year* of the 70th Week? This is the point in the prayer where we should pray for our physical and emotional needs and the needs of others (not just the need for food). It is appropriate that we pray for our needs *after* we pray for the Kingdom. "Seek *first* His kingdom and His righteousness, and all these things will be added to you" (Matt. 6:33 NASB, emphasis mine). During this part of the prayer, I also ask God for our future provision. I pray that he raises up *"Josephs"* among his church to provide food during the appointed time to come; that he inspires them to make provision now for the days to come. Additionally, I pray for the unsaved who will support the remnant of Christians and Jews during their persecution.

4) FORGIVE US OUR DEBTS AS WE FORGIVE OUR DEBTORS, AND DO NOT LEAD US INTO TEMPTATION

Forgiveness is one of the most difficult aspects of the Christian life for non-believers to understand. It is also one of the most difficult aspects for Christians to apply. Yet when we pray as Jesus instructs, we petition God to forgive us *as* we forgive others. This can be a frightening request.

During the *Fourth Year* of the 70th Week, the persecution of the Church will begin in earnest. We have learned that family, friends, and fellow churchgoers will betray us. We are to forgive them. The forces of the Antichrist will kill and torture our loved ones. We are to forgive them. They may kill and torture us as well. All of this persecution will be *unjust*. We will need to be praying this daily reminder to *forgive* during the 70th Week because the temptation to hate will be great. I have begun praying for the *ability to forgive* these things now; before they happen.

We also will need to pray to overcome the temptation to apostatize once the *Abomination of Desolation* is set up at the *Midpoint* and all are required to worship the

Beast. Most of the world will follow the *broad way* that leads to destruction. It will be very difficult to stand for Jesus in those days. Even today (in 2015), we are starting to see the persecutions and apostasy beginning.

The Greek word translated "temptation" is PEIRASMON which more correctly means "trials." The prayer for God to not lead us into trials is similar to Jesus's prayer in the garden on the night of his arrest: *"If it is possible, let this cup pass from me; yet not as I will, but as you will."* (Matt. 26:39 NASB, emphasis mine). In God's sovereign will, some will be lead away from trials, and others will be given the strength and faith to endure them.

5) DELIVER US FROM EVIL

The word translated "evil" in Matthew 6:13 is PONEROS. This Greek word is derived from PONOS which can be translated "pain, laborious toils, and agony," all of which accompany evil. The *Fifth Year* of the 70th Week will be marked by all these things as God's saints endure the tribulation of the Antichrist and his minions. This same word PONEROS is found in the Beatitudes: "Blessed are you when people insult you and persecute you and falsely say all kinds of evil (PONEROS) against you because of me. Rejoice and be glad, for your reward in heaven is great; for in the same way they persecuted the prophets who were before you" (Matt. 5:11-12 NASB, clarification mine). During this point in my prayer, I pray for God's protection now and in the future for his saints. I pray for their strength and faithfulness as they endure.

6) FOR YOURS IS THE KINGDOM AND THE POWER AND THE GLORY FOREVER

And with this sixth line, the *Lord's Prayer* ends. As some of you may already be aware, the earliest Greek manuscripts do not include this last phrase of the *Lord's Prayer*: "for yours is the *Kingdom* and the *power* and the *glory* forever" (Matt. 6:13 NKJV, emphasis mine). Certain translations omit the phrase entirely[xcviii].

Most scholars believe that this phrase was added by later-day translators (in the pattern of many Jewish prayers of that day) to make the *Lord's Prayer* usable in liturgy.

Despite this, I find it fascinating that this phrase fits perfectly into the *Pattern of Seven Events* of the 70th Week. In Chapter Fourteen: "Event Seven: Rapture and Wrath," we learned that at the end of the *Sixth Year* of the 70th Week, "The sign of the Son of Man will appear in the sky, and then all the tribes of the earth will mourn, and they will see the Son of Man coming on the clouds of the sky with *power* and great *glory*" (Matt. 24:29 NASB, emphasis mine).

The *Lord's Prayer* ends here, as the Church is raptured to Heaven to be with Jesus, away from the Wrath of God unleashed on earth during the *Seventh Year* of the 70th Week. The *Lord's Prayer* will have accomplished its purpose of helping the Church during the period of trials on earth. Praise God, the Church is now in heaven.

After rapturing his Church in the *Sixth Year* of the 70th week, Jesus physically returns at the conclusion of Daniel's 70th Week, at the very end of *Year Seven*, to usher in the *Kingdom*.

My intercession during this section of the prayer is quite simple, "Despite all the tribulation yet to befall your Church, come quickly Lord Jesus; bring your *Kingdom*."

WE AND US IN *THE LORD'S PRAYER*

The final point about the *Lord's Prayer,* the *Model Topical Prayer*, is that the intercessions are not individualized, they are *community based*: "give *us* this day," "lead *us* not," "deliver *us*," etc. The "us" in this case is the *Church*. We are to pray for the *entire Church* and its well-being, and we are to work to achieve that well-being as well. The 70th Week of Daniel is *a time for the Church to become one*:

> I have other sheep, which are not of this fold; I must bring them also, and they will hear my voice; and they will become *one flock* with one shepherd. (John 10:16 NASB, emphasis mine)

> I do not ask on behalf of these alone, but for those also who believe in Me through their word; *that they may all be one*; even as You, Father, are in Me

and I in You, that they also may be in Us, so that the world may believe that You sent Me. (John 17:20-21 NASB, emphasis mine)

Neither of these passages has yet been fulfilled, but during the 70th Week, they will be. We can now look at *each of the successive years* of the seven years of the 70th Week to see correlations to our discussion of the events, as related to the *Lord's Prayer* and the things that will help the Church "become one" and *overcome* the events of the 70th Week.

YEAR ONE: SPIRITUAL PREPARATION

(*FIRST PRINCIPLE* OF OVERCOMING THE 70TH WEEK)

If we stopped right here after learning about how to pray for the end times; almost nothing else really would be required. Jesus, after all, *has* overcome the world and *will* overcome the 70th Week of Daniel. His grace will allow us to also *overcome* as well. Jesus's key instructions to his Church found in the *Letters to the Seven Churches*, however, must not be ignored. Not surprisingly, the instructions of Christ in his *Letters* follow the *Pattern of Seven Events* that we studied throughout this book. We can call these the *Seven Principles of Overcoming* the 70th Week of Daniel, as found in the *Seven Letters to the Churches*. We will look at this relationship on a Year by Year basis, starting with *Year One* of the 70th Week.

In the first letter, the *Letter to Ephesus*, Jesus admonished his readers and gave them a promise:

But I have this against you, that you have left your *first* (Gk: PROTOS, meaning first) *love*. Therefore remember from where you have fallen, and repent and do the deeds you did at first . . . To him who *overcomes*, I will grant to eat of the tree of life which is in the Paradise of God. (Rev. 2:4-6 NASB, clarification and emphasis mine)

518

The promise for those who *"overcome"* (Gk: NIKAO) by returning to their *first love* is that they will eat of the tree of life. This is a direct reference to the final chapter of Revelation:

> Then he showed me a river of the water of life, clear as crystal, coming from the throne of God and of the Lamb, in the middle of its street. On either side of the river was *the tree of life*, bearing twelve kinds of fruit, *yielding its fruit every month*; and *the leaves of the tree were for the healing of the nations*. (Rev. 22:1-3 NASB, emphasis mine)

In Chapter 12: "Love Letters (Revelation 2-3)" we further defined what the *first love* was that we need to aspire to:

> One of the scribes . . . asked Him, "What commandment is the *foremost* (Gk: PROTOS, meaning first) of all?" Jesus answered, "The *foremost* (Gk: PROTOS) is, 'Hear, O Israel! The Lord our God is one Lord; and you shall *love the Lord your God with all your heart, and with all your soul, and with all your mind, and with all your strength.' The second is this, 'You shall love your neighbor as yourself.'* There is no other commandment greater than these." (Mark 12:28-31 NASB, clarification and emphasis mine)

This is the *first love*: love of Jesus and love of others that we are being called back to having. Love isn't something you can manufacture or produce by works. It only comes through *relationship*. Relationship is formed by spending time with the one(s) you love; spending time in God's word, spending time in two-way prayer, and spending time working alongside Jesus in serving his children.

Most Christians know that Peter denied Jesus three times on the night he was betrayed. After Jesus's resurrection, he restored Peter in a passage where he asked him three times whether Peter loved him. Let's look at the specific passage because it discusses the *kind of love* that will be required in the end times:

So when they had finished breakfast, Jesus said to Simon Peter, "Simon, son of John, do you love (Gk: AGAPAS) me more than these?" He said to Him, "Yes, Lord; you know that I love (Gk: PHILO) you." He said to him, "Tend My lambs." He said to him again a second time, "Simon, son of John, do you love (Gk: AGAPAS) me?" He said to Him, "Yes, Lord; you know that I love (Gk: PHILO) you." He said to him, "Shepherd My sheep." He said to him the third time, "Simon, son of John, do you love (Gk: PHILEIS) me?" Peter was grieved because He said to him the third time, "Do you love (Gk: PHILEIS) me?" And he said to Him, "Lord, You know all things; you know that I love (Gk: PHILO) you." Jesus said to him, "Tend My sheep." (John 21:15-17, NASB)

Notice the Greek words translated "love" give this passage an incredibly different meaning in the Greek as opposed to the English. The words that Jesus used for the first two occurrences of "love" are more intense (AGAPAS) than Peter's (PHILO). AGAPAS can be thought of as "Godly love" while PHILO can be thought of as "brotherly love." The first two times Jesus asked Peter if he loved him, Jesus used AGAPAS, but Peter only replied that he loved Jesus with a brotherly love. Most likely, Peter was embarrassed by his failure and didn't want to claim the higher level of love Jesus was asking. Finally, on the third question, Jesus lowered the standard of love he asked about. This third time, he asked Peter if he loved him like a brother. Peter became angry at this lowering of the standard and told Jesus, "You know I love you like a brother." Jesus then explained to Peter that *he was going to need a higher standard of love* if he was not going to fall away again.

Truly, truly, I say to you, when you were younger, you used to gird yourself and walk wherever you wished; but when you grow old, you will stretch out your hands and someone else will gird you, and bring you where you do not wish to go." Now this He said, signifying by what kind of death he would glorify God. And when He had spoken this, He said to him, "Follow Me!" (John 21:18-19 NASB)

In this way, Jesus was telling Peter that PHILO love would not be enough. AGAPAS love was going to be necessary in the future in order for Peter to *overcome* and become victorious.

As we know, Peter became a leader of the Church, a great evangelist, and a writer of two epistles that bear his name. He also overcame his trial at the end of his life. Tradition tells us that he was crucified upside down on a Roman cross.

We need to pray that we will all be filled with AGAPAS love to the point where we lay our own interests aside to think more highly of the interests of others (Phil 2:1-4). Someday, this AGAPAS may be necessary for us to overcome our own trial like Peter's. On that day, events may ask "Do you love Jesus?" Let us all prepare *now* to be able to answer, "You know I AGAPAS you Lord" with our actions.

As we prepare to face the 70th Week of Daniel, nothing is more important that forming a deep, abiding, *love relationship* with our coming King, Jesus.

Christians will not "overcome" without this proper *love relationship* with Jesus.

If we truly love others as ourselves, we will also encourage them to aspire to this same deep relationship with the Savior. As we learned in the previous section, the 70th Week of Daniel is not about just "me" overcoming, but about all of "us" overcoming. Everything we do and say needs to be focusing on the *community of saints*.

YEAR TWO: EMOTIONAL PREPARATION
(SECOND PRINCIPLE OF OVERCOMING THE 70TH WEEK)

Fear is an over-riding emotion. God anticipates that *we will be fearful* from the *Second Year* of the 70th Week on. That is why he instructs us, "See that you are not frightened, for those *things must take place* (Gk: DEI GENESTHAI)" (Matt. 24:6 NASB, clarification and emphasis mine). Notice in his instruction, Jesus quotes Dan. 2:29, 45 just as we learned John does in Rev. 1:1 and Rev. 22:6! Jesus is telling us that he has all things under his control; that these *things must take place* before the Kingdom is ushered in.

Ch. 24: To Him Who Overcomes

Fear of pain and death are at the top of the list of our human fears. In the *Letter to Smyrna*, Jesus lays these fears wide open; he tells us we should anticipate *prison and death*:

> *Do not fear what you are about to suffer.* Behold, the devil is about to cast some of you into *prison*, so that you will be tested, and *you will have tribulation for ten days. Be faithful until death, and I will give you the crown of life* . . . He who *overcomes* will not be hurt by the *second death.* (Rev. 2:10-11 NASB, emphasis mine)

Jesus has let us know these are *things that must take place.* At the conclusion of our own *Days of Awe* (*ten days* for repentance), we will receive the crown of life. "Blessed is a man who *perseveres under trial*; for once he has been approved, he will receive *the crown of life* which the Lord has promised *to those who love Him*" (Jam. 1:12, emphasis mine). Those who wear this crown won't face the second death:

> But for *the cowardly* and unbelieving and abominable and murderers and immoral persons and sorcerers and idolaters and all liars, their part will be in the *lake that burns with fire and brimstone*, which is the *second death.*" (Rev. 21:8, emphasis mine)

Notice that the very first category of those who will face the second death are the *cowardly.* This is incredible! How many Christians in our western churches are *expecting* to lay their lives down for Jesus and the Gospel? How many will be *afraid* and *frozen* from proper action when the time comes to choose life or faithfulness? Jesus expects us to follow his command and *love him more than our own life.* "For whoever wishes to save his life will lose it, but whoever loses his life for my sake, he is the one who will save it" (Luke 9:24 NASB). God expects us to *bring his Gospel to a dying world* regardless of the cost.

> **In the 70th Week of Daniel, we are not to be "survivalists" but "revivalists."**

God also expects us to *comfort our fellow travelers* through the tribulation of the 70th Week:

> Comfort, O *comfort my people*," says your God . . . A voice is calling, "Clear the way for the Lord in the wilderness; make smooth in the desert a highway for our God. Let every valley be lifted up, and every mountain and hill be made low; and let the rough ground become a plain, and the rugged terrain a broad valley." *Then the glory of the Lord will be revealed, and all flesh will see it together.* (Isa 40:1, 3-5 NASB, emphasis mine)

This famous passage was quoted by John the Baptist, but look carefully at the final line. All flesh has *not yet seen* the glory of the Lord, hence, it is *future*. That will happen at the *Celestial Earthly Disturbance Event*. This powerful passage is our instruction—we are to comfort and prepare the people of God as we prepare the way of the Lord. We are to prepare for our own martyrdom and that of our family, friends, and our church. We may face tribulation during our own "personal *Days of Awe*," but Jesus will *revive* us. We can truly face these things without fear with the help of the *Holy Spirit* within us.

YEAR THREE: PHYSICAL PREPARATION
(THIRD PRINCIPLE OF OVERCOMING THE 70TH WEEK)

If it is likely that we are to enter martyrdom, why do we need to *physically prepare*? Let's see what Jesus has to say in his third Letter, the *Letter to Pergamum*:

> But I have a few things against you, *because you have there some who hold the teaching of Balaam*, who kept teaching Balak to put a stumbling block before the sons of Israel, to eat things sacrificed to idols and to commit acts of

immorality. So you also have some who in the same way hold the teaching of the Nicolaitans. (Rev. 2:14-15 NASB, emphasis mine)

What God will hold against us is that *some of us* will give in and accept the *Mark of the Beast* to be able to continue to buy and sell within the world economic system and be able to eat the Antichrist's food. In addition, God will hold us responsible for the rest of his household, not just for ourselves. The *Third Year* of the 70th Week will present many unprepared Christians and Jews with a great temptation. If we are able to come along side of them with food of God's Word as well as physical food, they may be able to "overcome" the temptation rather than give in. Jesus has said, "It is written: 'Man shall not live on bread alone, but *on every word that comes from the mouth of God*'" (Matt. 4:4 NIV, emphasis mine). This is what I think Jesus was implying in the *Olivet Discourse*:

> Who then is the faithful and sensible *slave whom his master put in charge of his household* to give them their *food* at the proper time (Gk: KAIROS, meaning "appointed time")? (Matt. 24:45 NASB, emphasis mine)

God has called faithful and wise slaves to provide both spiritual and physical food for his household (Jews and Christians) at the appointed time (perhaps *Passover* of the third year of the 70th Week).

We need to prepare now to be "Joseph" to God's household at the appointed time.

Jesus has promised those who *overcome* in this way "I will give some of the *hidden manna*" (Rev. 2:17 NASB, emphasis mine). The little boy who packed two fish and five loaves on the day Jesus fed the five thousand did not expect a miracle, but *in faith gave all he had to Jesus*. It was then that Jesus multiplied his simple "lunch" by thousands. When Jesus fed the five thousand, *twelve baskets* were left over. (Does this represent how he will provide for the twelve tribes of Israel?). When Jesus fed the four thousand, *seven baskets* were left over. (Does this represent how he will provide for the Seven Churches during each year of the 70th Week?) Jesus is not bound by our earthly economies. We will need faith to pack a small "lunch" now to provide for Jesus's household at that time, and allow Jesus to provide *hidden manna* as well.

FOURTH YEAR: WATCHFULNESS
(FOURTH PRINCIPLE OF OVERCOMING THE 70TH WEEK)

In the three versions of Jesus's *Olivet Discourse* in the various gospel accounts (Matthew, Mark, and Luke), he instructed us with over thirty commands to be *observant*, to *see*, and to be *watchful*[xcix]. The reason he instructs us to be *watchful* is because in the *Olivet Discourse* he gives us a number of signs. We will only *see* them if we watch. The most significant sign is the *Abomination of Desolation* that occurs in the *Fourth Year* of the 70th Week of Daniel:

> Therefore *when you see the abomination of desolation* which was spoken of through Daniel the prophet, standing in the holy place (let the reader understand), then those who are in Judea must flee to the mountains. (Matt. 24:15-16 NASB, emphasis mine)

Jesus wants us to be *watchful* so we can *see* the signs he has warned us about. These signs form a chronology (Gk. CHRONOS) which Paul assumes Christians will understand (1 Thess. 5:1). Paul assumes we will be familiar with the chronology of the end times because it was given to us by Jesus in the *Olivet Discourse*. Paul expects us to have committed these signs to memory. The *Pattern of Seven Events* and its relationship to the *Feasts of the Lord* and to the *Lord's Prayer* forms a powerful mnemonic. I encourage you to memorize all aspects of it.

In the *Letter to Thyatira*, which relates to the *Fourth Year* of the 70th Week, we are given another sign to watch for in that year:

Behold, I will throw her (Jezebel, meaning *Islam*) on a bed of sickness, and those who commit adultery with her into great tribulation, unless they repent of her deeds. And *I will kill her children* (Muslims) *with pestilence*, and *all the churches will know that I am* He who *searches the minds and hearts*. (Rev. 2:22-23 NASB, clarification and emphasis mine)

This sign during the *Fourth Year* of the 70th Week that only *Muslims* will be killed by this *specific pestilence* is a signal to the Church that God is still in control. Only God himself could specifically target a group of people based on the unbiblical beliefs they hold in their *hearts and minds*. The purpose of this sign is to embolden the Church to *endure* and *overcome* the trial ahead. That is the primary purpose of all the signs in the chronology Jesus has given us—so that Christians can anticipate the events that will occur during the 70th Week and prepare to *overcome*.

A second purpose is to *use the prophetic signs in evangelism*. We call this *"apocalyptic evangelism."* Peter used this technique in his sermon in Acts Chapter 2, after Pentecost. In that sermon he referenced a prophecy found in the Book of Joel:

And it shall be in the last days God says, "That *I will pour forth of My Spirit* on all mankind; *And your sons and your daughters shall prophesy*, And your young men shall see visions, And your old men shall dream dreams; Even on My bond slaves, both men and women, I will in those days pour forth of My Spirit And they shall prophesy. And I will grant wonders in the sky above and signs on the earth below, blood, and fire, and vapor of smoke. *The sun will be turned into darkness and the moon into blood*." (Acts 2: 17-20 NASB, emphasis mine)

Peter's quoting of Joel's prophecy (Joel 2:31) in his sermon was incredibly successful as 3000 people were saved that day. Why did this quote have such an impact on the listeners? It was so successful because the listeners had just experienced these things and they knew them to be true. They had seen the sun darkened on the day Jesus was crucified. They *may* have seen a full lunar eclipse (a "blood moon") on that same night following Passover. They certainly also witnessed the outpouring of the Holy Spirit as the disciples spoke in other languages. The net effect of witnessing prophecy being fulfilled before their eyes led to repentance and salvation. This same effect will happen in 70th Week of Daniel if believers know the prophecies, see them being fulfilled during each of the years, and use them in this same way in their witnessing to others.

Believers need to know the chronology of the prophetic signs, and they need to watch for their unfolding, to *use them in witnessing*.

The world will *see* the Antichrist assume great authority during the *Fourth Year*. The Church needs to remind itself and those it witnesses to that this authority of Antichrist is only temporary. What they *see* with their eyes is only illusion. Within 42 months (3 ½ years) this authority will transfer to Jesus and his saints. "He who *overcomes* and he who keeps My deeds until the end, to him I will give *authority over the nations*; and he shall rule them with a rod of iron, as the vessels of the potter are broken to pieces, as I also have received authority from My Father" (Rev. 2:26-27 NASB, emphasis mine).

YEAR FIVE: ENCOURAGEMENT AND WITNESS
(*FIFTH PRINCIPLE* OF OVERCOMING THE 70TH WEEK)

The *Fifth Year* of Daniel's 70th Week will be one of the most significant years of world history. It will be *a year of decision*. The *eternal destiny* of much of the world will hang in a balance. Most Christians will be forced to choose between physical death (and spiritual life) or physical life (and spiritual death). This will be a monumental choice. How Christians handle this public decision will have an *eternal impact* on those watching: both unbelievers and those whose faith might be weak. In the *Letter to Sardis*, with application to the Church in *Year Five*, Jesus addresses this concern:

> Wake up, and *strengthen the things that remain, which were about to die*; for *I have not found your deeds completed in the sight of My God*. So remember

what you have received and heard; and keep it and repent. (Rev. 3:2-3 NASB, emphasis mine)

Jesus's command is to *strengthen the things that were about to die*. This may have a personal application (strengthening our own faith), but it also has a corporate application. By the testimony of our words and deeds (martyrdom), we can strengthen the resolve and faith of those watching; both unbelievers and believers. It will be the greatest time of witness the world has ever seen. Christians may have been through a lot during the first four years of the 70th Week, but God's Word is telling them that their *deeds are not completed.* They still need to witness during this most significant year, the *Fifth Year,* during the *Great Tribulation.* That witness may include *martyrdom.*

This idea of *strengthening* those who are weak is a direct reference to the book of Hebrews, which teaches on the purpose of suffering, even unto death:

> You have not yet *resisted to the point of shedding blood* in your striving against sin; and you have forgotten the exhortation which is addressed to you as sons, "My son, do not regard lightly the *discipline of the Lord,* nor faint when you are reproved by Him; for those whom the Lord loves He disciplines, and He scourges every son whom He receives (direct quote of Prov. 3:7)." It is for discipline that you endure; God deals with you as with sons; for what son is there whom his father does not discipline? But if you are without discipline, of which all have become partakers, then you are illegitimate children and not sons. Furthermore, we had earthly fathers to discipline us, and we respected them; shall we not much rather be subject to the Father of spirits, and live? For they disciplined us for a short time as seemed best to them, *but He disciplines us for our good, so that we may share His holiness.* All discipline for the moment seems not to be joyful, but sorrowful; yet to those who have been trained by it, afterwards it yields the peaceful fruit of righteousness. Therefore, *strengthen the hands that are weak.* (Heb. 12:5-12 NASB, clarification and emphasis mine)

God disciplines us so we can become *holy* as he is Holy. It is interesting that this passage also references *resisting to the point of shedding blood,* which occurs during the *Fifth Year* of the 70ᵗʰ Week, and strengthening the weak.

> **God's purpose for the Church during the 70ᵗʰ Week is *to witness to the lost and to encourage those with weaker faith*. This may occur through *Martyrdom.***

God's promise of *reward* to those that suffer is great. "He who overcomes will thus be *clothed in white garments*; and I will *not erase his name* from the *book of life*, and *I will confess his name before My Father and before His angels*" (Rev. 3:5 NASB, emphasis mine). These are the ones who will participate in the *Wedding Supper of the Lamb*. A momentary trial that is overcome will lead to this greatest of rewards.

THE SIXTH YEAR: PROPER RAPTURE TIMING
(SIXTH PRINCIPLE OF OVERCOMING THE 70ᵗʰ WEEK)

The *Sixth Year* of the *70ᵗʰ Week of Daniel* reminds us dramatically that the *Pre-Tribulation Rapture Theory* is a false and dangerous theory which has the potential to lull the Church to sleep. Sleeping saints cannot be watchful, and as we have seen in Part Four the time to "wake up" is not during the *Great Tribulation* when the choice of life and death is set before them. The time to wake up is *now* so that they (we) can help awaken the Church.

Ready for Jesus Ministries is dedicated to *awakening the Church*. I highly advise you volunteer to join this worthy effort at www.arewereadyforjesus.com.

> **The time to awaken the Church from the error of the *Pre-Tribulation Rapture Theory* is now.**

Proper understanding of the Rapture and its timing *now* at the present time, may lead a person to strengthen their faith and to actually participate in the Resurrection and

Rapture *later*. As has been mentioned previously in this book, I highly recommend Alan Kurschner's book, *Antichrist Before the Day of the Lord—What Every Christian Needs to Know About the Return of Christ* (Eschatos Publishing, Pompton Lakes, NJ, 2013), which makes the biblical case for the *Pre-Wrath Rapture* position. This is the biblical Rapture position taken in this book.

SEVENTH YEAR: WEANED FROM THE WORLD SYSTEM
(SEVENTH PRINCIPLE OF OVERCOMING THE 70TH WEEK)

Although true sons of the Father will not have to endure the *Seventh Year* of the 70th Week, as they will be raptured to Heaven with Jesus, there is a lesson in the passage of the *Letter to Laodicea* that is applicable to us today:

> You say, "*I am rich, and have become wealthy, and have need of nothing*," and you do not know that you are wretched and miserable and poor and blind and naked. I advise you to *buy from Me gold refined by fire* so that you may become rich, and *white garments so that you may clothe yourself*, and that the shame of your nakedness will not be revealed; and *eye salve to anoint your eyes so that you may see*. (Rev. 3:17-18 NASB, emphasis mine)

In the western world, we have allowed our wealth to blind us to our need to rely on God alone. We need to repent of our love of money and reliance on money. Instead, we need to view money as it truly is—a tool that God has given us to do his will. In the 70th Week of Daniel, true Christians will have no choice but to wean themselves from the *Mark of the Beast* economic system that then exists. Now is the time to *see* things as they truly are and begin to wean ourselves from the love of money so that at *the appointed time* we are ready to *overcome*.

Yesterday, my thirteen-year-old daughter and I walked around an antique car show. My first car was a used Ford Mustang that I restored from a "beater" (slang for an old car that you can "beat" by running it hard) into a car one could be proud of. I cannot see cars from that era and not remember my Dad teaching me to restore cars.

Each spring he'd buy a rusted car which we'd restore together. Then in the fall, he'd sell it for a profit. This is one of my favorite "Dad/son" memories. So when I see restored Mustangs, it always reminds me of Dad and also of my teenage years.

For most of my life, the *"lust of the eyes"* (1 John 2:16, emphasis mine) enticed me to desire to possess another restored Mustang to relive those memories. One of the cars at the show had the license plate "Mine Agin" (mine again). I smiled knowing the owner of that car probably felt as I once did about a model of car he once possessed and now did again.

As we left the car show and walked through the parking lot, my daughter commented about all the expensive cars that the attendees of the show had driven to get there. It gave us a wonderful time to talk about what truly matters in life and what does not, and how at one time I was overcome by these things and how I've changed.

> For all that is in the world, the *lust of the flesh* and the *lust of the eyes* and *the boastful pride of life*, is not from the Father, but is from the world. (1 John 2:16 NASB, emphasis mine)

Now is the time to wean ourselves from the world system: *the lust of the flesh, the lust of the eyes, and pride.*

Once the *70th Week of Daniel* begins, it may be too late wean ourselves from the world system. We need to start today.

SUMMARY AND EPILOGUE

All of *Revelation Deciphered*, and really all of the Book of Revelation, has been building to this simple summary. The *Seven Principles of Overcoming* the 70th Week of Daniel found in the *Seven Letters to the Churches* and stated in the preceding seven sections of this Chapter 14: "To Him Who Overcomes" are the purpose and heart of both Daniel and Revelation. The Church's current blindness to the *Pattern of Seven Events* (see *Appendix A* for a summary description) and prophetic nature of the *Letters to the Seven Churches,* as well as the prophetic nature of the *Lord's Prayer,* is tragic. Without a proper understanding of these prophetic elements, the Church languishes and is largely ill-prepared for the 70th Week. This is a serious problem and places the Church in a position to be *blindsided* by events and by the Antichrist.

Now that you and I are aware of these biblical prophetic elements and principles, we must inform the Church and prepare as many as possible. Are we up to the task? Frankly, on our own, we aren't. But in the power of the *Holy Spirit,* we can do all things. God has prepared the way before us: "For we are His workmanship, created in Christ Jesus for good works, which *God prepared beforehand* so that *we would walk in them*" (Eph. 2:10 NASB, emphasis mine). He prepared the way before us so that we can help to prepare the way for his return!

God has allowed us to see the *Pattern of Seven Events* so we could recognize it in the *Lord's Prayer* and pray for the Church and the coming trial using that *Model Topical Prayer.* He also allowed us to see that pattern so we could uncover the important *Seven Principles of Overcoming* found in the *Letters to the Seven Churches* of Revelation 2-3. The graphic below (Figure 58: *Seven Principles of Overcoming* from the *Letters to the Seven Churches*) provides a summary of these seven important principles of overcoming:

Seven Principles of Overcoming	Based on the Letter to the Church
1) Spiritually prepare by loving and trusting Jesus alone and displaying that love to the world. *Love the Lord your God with all your heart, and with all your soul, and with all your mind, and with all your strength.' The second is this, 'You shall love your neighbor as yourself. (Mark 12:30-31 NASB)*	Ephesus
2) Emotionally prepare for tribulation (imprisonment and martyrdom). *Do not fear what you are about to suffer . . . Be faithful until death, and I will give you the crown of life (Rev. 2:10 NASB)*	Smyrna
3) Prepare now to be "Joseph" to provide food at the "appointed time." *Who then is the faithful and sensible slave whom his master put in charge of his household to give them their food at the proper time? (Matt. 24:45 NASB)*	Pergamum
4) Be watchful of the chronologic signs of Jesus's return and use in evangelism. *Keep watching and praying that you may not enter into temptation; the spirit is willing, but the flesh is weak. (Matt. 26:41)*	Thyatira
5) Use our response to tribulation as a means of witness to the unsaved and encouragement to the weak in faith. *He disciplines us for our good, so that we may share His holiness. All discipline for the moment seems not to be joyful, but sorrowful; yet to those who have been trained by it, afterwards it yields the peaceful fruit of righteousness. Therefore, strengthen the hands that are weak. (Heb. 12:10-12 NASB)*	Sardis
6) Awaken the Church from the error of the *Pre-Tribulation Rapture* Theory *But the Spirit explicitly says that in later times some will fall away from the faith, paying attention to deceitful spirits (1 Tim. 4:1 NASB)*	Philadelphia
7) Wean ourselves from the world system. *For all that is in the world, the lust of the flesh and the lust of the eyes and the boastful pride of life, is not from the Father, but is from the world. (1 John 2:16 NASB)*	Laodicea

Figure 58: Seven Principles of Overcoming from the Letters to the Seven Churches

These *Seven Principles of Overcoming* from the *Letters to the Seven Churches* are a radical departure from what most of our churches expect from the end times and from how they are currently living. However, armed with these principles and empowered by the Holy Spirit, together we can work to radically transform the Church—from one of weakness and sin to one of righteousness and preparation.

Of course, for most Churches to change, pastors need to change their frame of mind and receive and incorporate these insights. A start might be to pray for our Churches and pastors. Perhaps, God might use your giving a copy of this book, *Revelation Deciphered*, as well as my first book, *Are We Ready for Jesus?* to your pastors and encouraging them to read them. Also available is a short two-minute video *teaser* on my first book, which can be given to your pastor as a link on my website (www.areweready for jesus.com); it provides a good short video introduction. My first book was designed to be a first resource to introduce pastors to the need to *wake up* the Church and *get ready* for coming events; it also includes instruction on the dangers to the Church of the *Pre-Tribulation Rapture* position, which is probably the teaching your pastor has received and has fully bought-into. Other good books presenting the biblical case for the *Pre-Wrath Rapture* position taught in this book have been given in Chapter Two: "Uncovering The Keys." All these are resources for you to use.

This work to transform our Churches will be well-pleasing to God:

> A fragrant aroma, an acceptable sacrifice, *well-pleasing to God.* And my *God will supply all your needs* according to His riches in glory in Christ Jesus. (Phil. 4:18-19 NASB, emphasis mine)

Good and acceptable service for our Lord in this life will yield our Lord's pleasure and eternal rewards with him. He will supply everything we need to accomplish this task. Prayerfully, we will stand before him together and hear, *"well done, good and faithful servant"* (Matt. 25:21, 23). With all my heart I want that, and I believe you do too. Praise God that in him we can be an *overcomer* in this life and praise him and enjoy him for eternity.

Appendix A:

The *Pattern of Seven Events*

Appendix A

APPENDIX A: THE *PATTERN OF SEVEN EVENTS*

The Pattern of Seven Events is an essential and critical prophetic construction. In **Revelation Deciphered** we demonstrate how this pattern of events is the "roadmap" of the 70th Week of Daniel allowing Christians to know where they are in the "Week," what to anticipate next, what the timing of those events will be, and most importantly how to "overcome" during the trials that are to come. This pattern of events is found in Joshua, Judges, Psalms, Daniel, Ezekiel, the Gospels of Matthew and Luke, in the *Letters to the Seven Churches*, the *Seven Seals*, and in the meaning and order of the *Feasts of the Lord*.

Each event of the Pattern of Seven Events, during each of the seven years ("Year One," etc.) of the 70th Year of Daniel, is summarized in the following seven charts (Figure 59 — 65)

YEAR ONE: EVENT ONE
DECEPTION BY FALSE MESSIAHS AND PROPHETS

Aspect	Description
Deception	Will Mislead Many (Matt. 24:5)
	NIKAO: meaning "Spiritual overcoming"(Rev. 6:2)
	Will deceive many because of the signs (Rev. 13:14)
	Ephesians tested false apostles and found them to be liars. "Liar" is same root word as used in 1 John 2:22 in passage describing the Antichrist (Rev. 2:2)
	Nicolaitans ["overcomers of God's people] (Rev. 2:6)
False Messiah, False Prophets	Many coming in Jesus's Name (Luke 21:8)
	Claiming "I am he and the time is near" (Luke 21:8)
	Claiming: "I am the Messiah" (Matt. 24: 5)
	False Prophets and Christs arise (Matt. 24:24)
	Will show Great Signs and Wonders (Matt. 24:4)
	Will Perform Great Signs (Rev. 13: 13)
	Rides a White Horse (like Jesus's) (Rev. 6:2)
	Wear's a Victor's Crown (Rev. 6:2)
Deceptive Covenant	Antichrist strengthen Covenant with the Many (Dan. 9:27)
	Antichrist signs agreement with Israeli Leader after defeating him (Dan. 11:23-24)
	False Prophets claim peace when there is no peace (Ezek. 13:10)
	Antichrist attacks those who are defenseless (Ezek. 38:11-121)
	Rider of White Horse carries a "bow" [deceptive covenant] (Rev. 6:2)
	Artemis, Goddess of Ephesians carried a "bow"
	Wicked bend the "bow" (Psalm 11:2)

Figure 59: Year One, Event One Model

YEAR TWO: EVENT TWO
WAR, BLOODSHED, AND CHAOS

Aspect	Description
War	Wars and Rumors of War (Matt. 24:6)
	Nation against Nation (Matt. 24:7)
	Kingdom against Kingdom (Matt. 24:7)
	Great Sword was given to him (Rev. 6:4)
	"Who is like the beast, and who is able to wage war with him?" (Rev. 13:4)
	In time of tranquility invades the riches provinces (Dan. 11:24)
	Destroys many while they are at ease (Dan. 8:24)
	Plots against strongholds (Dan. 11:24)
	Attacks the King of the South (Dan. 11:25)
Disruptions and Chaos	Disruptions [Chaos] (Luke 21:9)
	Antichrist will take peace from the earth (Rev. 6:4)
	Flattery, Betrayal, and Vileness exalted (Psalm 12:2-8)
	Believers will be imprisoned (Rev. 2:10)
Bloodshed	Men will slay one another (Rev. 6:4)
	Destroys to an extraordinary degree (Dan. 8:25)
	Smyrna means "death"

Figure 60: Year Two, Event Two Model

YEAR THREE: EVENT THREE
FAMINE AND ECONOMIC COLLAPSE

Aspect	Description
Famine and Pestilence	Famine (Matt. 24:7)
	Daniel refuses to eat "king's food" and tested 10 days (Dan. 1: 12-16)
	Plagues (Luke 21:11)
	Eat bread by weight (Ezek. 4:16)
	God provides "bountifully", weans us from the world system (Psalm 13)
	Wise slave provides food at the appointed time (Matt. 24:45)
	Encourage eating food sacrificed to idols (Rev. 2:14)
	Jesus will provide "hidden manna" (Rev. 2:17)
	Pergamum worshiped Asclepius: the god of healing, perhaps pestilence begins this year and many will trust medicine over God
Economic Collapse	Price Setting for food (Rev. 6:7)
	Mark of the Beast (Rev. 13;16-17)
Siege of Jerusalem	Antichrist takes action against Israel and begins siege (11:28)
	Siege against Jerusalem 430 days (4:4-8)

Figure 61: Year Three, Event Three Model

Year Four: Event Four
Abomination and Death

Aspect	Description
Beginning of Great Tribulation (Death)	Authority was given to kill with sword and with famine and with pestilence and by the wild beasts of the earth. (Rev. 6:7-8 NASB) He who sat on it had the name Death; and Hades was following with him (Rev. 6:6-7) They will deliver you to tribulation, and will kill you, and you will be hated by all nations because of My name. (Matt. 24:9-10) Cause as many as do not worship the image of the beast to be killed. (Rev. 13:15) Michael "stands up" at beginning of Great Tribulation (Dan. 12:1) With "smooth words" Antichrist will convince many to leave faith (Dan. 11:32) Daniel placed in lion's den (6:1-28)
Abomination of Desolation	When you see the abomination of desolation which was spoken of through Daniel the prophet, standing in the holy place (Matt. 24:15) It was given to him to give breath to the image of the beast, so that the image of the beast would even speak (Rev. 13;15) Antichrist sets up Abomination (Dan. 9:27) Nebuchadnezzar's Golden Statue (Dan. 3:1-30) Antichrist forces desecrate Temple and set up Abomination (11:31)
Invasion of Jerusalem	Antichrist breaks the covenant, sacrifice ended (Dan. 9:27) Sealing of the 144,000 (Ezek. 9:3-6) Worst of nations desecrate the temple (Ezek. 7:21-24) 1/3 of Jerusalem will die by plague and starvation; these will then be burned with fire. Another 1/3 will die by sword (Ezek. 5:1,2,12) When you see Jerusalem surrounded by armies (Luke 21:20)

Figure 62: Year Four, Event Four Model

YEAR FIVE: EVENT FIVE
MARTYRDOM AND APOSTASY

Aspect	Description
Martyrdom	Saints given into Antichrist hands for "time, times, and half a time" (Dan. 7:25)
	Many fall by flame, captivity, sword and plunder (Dan. 11:33)
	Those with insight will fall to refine them, purge and purify them (Dan. 11:35)
	Name Sardis from Sardius stone (red) and Sardonyx (red and white streaked), both indicative of sacrifice
	Overcomers in Sardis receive white robes (Rev. 3:4)
	Sardis is a mostly "dead" church because the many of the righteous are martyred and physically dead; the apostates fall away and are spiritually dead (Rev. 3:1)
	Saints help overcome Satan with their testimony and blood (Rev. 6:9)
	They receive white robes (Rev. 6:11)
Captivity of Israel	Israel taken captive into all nations. (Luke 21:24)
	Israel captive in all nations (Ezek. 39:25-28)
Apostasy	Many will fall away and will betray one another and hate one (Matt. 24: 10)
	Many will betray by hypocrisy (Dan. 11:34)
	Great Falling Away pictured by names being erased from the Book of Life (Rev. 3:5)

Figure 63: Year Five, Event Five Model

YEAR SIX: EVENT SIX
HEAVENLY SIGNS

Aspect	Description
Heavenly Signs	Great earthquake, sun black, moon like blood, stars fall, sky like a scroll rolled up, every mountain and island moved (Rev. 6:12-14)
	Unrighteous hide in caves (Rev. 6:15)
	After the Tribulation the sun will darken, moon not give light, stars fall, power of heavens shaken (Matt. 24:29)
	Signs in the sun, moon and stars, roaring of the seas (Luke 21:25)
	People fainting with fear (Luke 21:26)
	Powers of the heavens shaken (Luke 21:26)
	Sun, Moon, and Stars darkened over Egypt (Ezek. 32:7,8)
Filling of Holy Spirit	Lord gives counsel, in the night my heart instructs me (Psalm 16:7)
	Pour our spirit on all flesh (Joel 2:28)

Figure 64: Year Six, Event Six Model

YEAR SEVEN: EVENT SEVEN
RAPTURE AND WRATH

Aspect	Description
Resurrection	Resurrection of the righteous whose names written in Book of Life (Dan. 12:2) Resurrection of the righteous; the dry bones vision(Ezek. 37:7-14)
Rapture	Son of Man comes on the clouds (Dan. 7:13) Righteous changed and made to "shine" (Dan. 12:3) Jesus has the Key of David to open Heaven's door (Rev. 3:7) Jesus will keep the righteous from his wrath (Rev. 3:10) Jesus will come on the clouds and send angels to gather the saints (Matt. 24:30-31) As the Days of Noah so will be the days of the Son of man (Luke 17:26) The sign of the son of man will be like lightening flashing (Luke 17:24) When the lamb broke the seventh seal there was silence in heaven for a half hour (Rev. 8:1)
Wrath	Court will sit in judgment and the dominion of Satan and the Antichrist will be taken from them (Dan. 7:26) Complete destruction poured out on Antichrist (Dan. 9:27) Antichrist will be broken without human agency (Dan. 8:25) Body of the Beast burned with fire (Dan. 7: 11) Dominion given to the saints (Dan. 7:25) God rains fire, hail, and brimstone on Gog (Ezek. 38:22) Laodicea means trail of God's people Jesus is the faithful witness during the trial (Rev. 3:14) Those God loves he disciplines (Rev. 3:19) Day son of man revealed will be just like the day Lot went out of Sodom (Luke 21:29) God defeats Gog and feeds his army to birds (Ezek. 39:17-20) God will remove Israel's heart of stone and give heart of flesh (Ezek. 11:17-20) God pours out spirit on Israel (Ezek. 39:27) 7 Trumpets: Fire, Mountain cast into Sea, Fresh water made bitter, sun and moon darkened, supernatural locusts, 200 Million man army, 7 Bowls poured out, Second Coming (Rev. 8-11)

Figure 65: Year Seven, Event Seven Model

Endnotes

Endnotes

END NOTES

Chapter One

[i] Ed Catmull, *The Global Leadership Summit*, Aug. 6, 2015

[ii] "Breaking Germany's Enigma Code," *BBC*, last modified Feb. 17, 2011, accessed June 21, 2015, http://www.bbc.co.uk/history/worldwars/wwtwo/enigma_01.shtml

Chapter Two

[iii] "Talmudical Hermeneutics'" *Kehill at Israel*, last modified Unknown, accessed June 21, 2015, http://kehillatisrael.net/docs/learning/txt/i_TalmudicHermeneutics.pdf

[iv] "Loving God with All Your Mind: Logic and Creation" *Creation.com*, last modified Unknown, accessed March 3, 2015, http://creation.com/loving-god-with-all-your-mind-logic-and-creation

[v] "God Created Land and Plants", *Mission Bible Class*, last modified unknown, accessed May 24, 2015, http://missionbibleclass.org/old-testament-stories/old-testament-part-1/creation-through-noah/day-3-god-created-land-and-plants/

[vi] "*Ezekiel 4: The Master Key to Unlock the Bible's Chronology*," *Ezekiel Master Key*, last modified Oct. 2, 2015, accessed Oct. 3, 2015, http://www.ezekielmasterkey.com/ (Very good chronology of the Bible information, but some of the presentation in the "Summary" at the end of the manuscript is hereby disclaimed.)

[vii] "Interpretation of the Bible," *Theopedia*, last modified Unknown, accessed May 30, 2015, http://www.theopedia.com/interpretation-of-the-bible

[viii] "What Was Koine Greek?" *Orville Jenkins*, last modified June 7, 2014, accessed March 3, 2015, http://orvillejenkins.com/languages/koinegreek.html

[ix] "An Historical Account of the Septuagint", *Bible Researcher*, last modified unknown, accessed March 3, 2015, http://www.bible-researcher.com/brenton1.html

[x] "Why the Greek Septuagint?" *2001Translation.com*, last modified , accessed March 3, 2015, http://www.2001translation.com/Septuagint.htm#_2

[xi] Ibid.

[xii] Ibid.

[xiii] "Evangelical Beliefs and Practices" *Pew Research Center*, last modified June 22, 2011, accessed March 7, 2015, http://www.pewforum.org/2011/06/22/global-survey-beliefs/

Chapter Three

[xiv] John Walvoord, Mark Hitchcock, and Phillip Rawley, *Revelation*, (Moody Publishers, Chicago, 2011), Chapter 6

[xv] Andreas J. Köstenberger, L. Scott Kellum, and Charles L Quarles, The Cradle, the Cross, and the Crown (B&H Academic, Nashville, 2009), p. 834.

[xvi] "A Comparison of the Olivet Discourse and Revelation," Pre-Trib. Research Center, last modified: unknown, accessed April 7, 2016, http://www.pre-trib.org/articles/view/comparison-of-olivet-discourse-and-book-revelation

[xvii] "Rapture Debate between Alan Kurschner (Pre-Wrath) and Thomas Ice (Pre-Trib.)," Eschatos Ministries, last modified September 27, 2015, accessed April 6, 2016, http://www.alankurschner.com/2015/09/27/rapture-debate-between-alan-kurschner-prewrath-and-thomas-ice-pretrib/ TIME: 1:17:15.

[xviii] William Jack Kelly, *Shadow of Things to Come*, (Westbow Press, Bloomington, 2013), p.42.

[xix] "Matthew 24 – Post Tribulation Rapture," Deep Truths, last modified: 1998, accessed April 24, 2016, http://deeptruths.com/letters/matthew24.html

[xx] "Seals, Trumpets, Bowls in the Book of Revelation: Concurrent-Recapitulation or Consecutive-Progressive? (Part 1 of 2) – Ep. 36," Escathos Ministries, last modified May 28, 2015, accessed October 11, 2015, http://www.alankurschner.com/2015/05/28/seals-trumpets-bowls-in-the-book-of-revelation-concurrent-recapitulation-or-consecutive-progressive-part-1-of-2-ep-36/

Chapter Four

[xxi] "Ha Dei Genesthai," *Blogspot*, last modified May 15, 2006, accessed April 11, 2015, http://ntrevelation.blogspot.com/2006/05/ha-dei-genesthai.html

[xxii] "To the Philadelphians," *Silouan*, last modified unknown, accessed July 18, 2015, http://silouanthompson.net/library/early-church/ignatius/to-the-philadelphians/

[xxiii] "NT Commentary - Henry Alford," *Preceptaustin*, last modified February 21, 2015, accessed July 26, 2015, http://www.preceptaustin.org/nt_commentary-henry_alford.htm

Chapter Five

[xxiv] "Ten Bizarre Cases of Amnesia," *Listverse*, last modified October 13, 2013, accessed April 12, 2015, http://listverse.com/2013/10/13/10-bizarre-cases-of-amnesia/

[xxv] "Revelation 5:1," *Bible Hub*, last modified 2014, accessed October 18, 2015, http://biblehub.com/commentaries/revelation/5-1.htm

[xxvi] "Faith the Title Deed," *Free Bible Studies Online*, last modified 2012 , accessed March 14, 2015, https://freebiblestudiesonline.wordpress.com/treasures/faith-the-title-deed/

Chapter Six

[xxvii] "Close Encounters of the Third Kind" *IMDB,* last modified unknown, accessed March 7, 2015, http://www.imdb.com/title/tt0075860/

[xxviii] Dr. Warren A. Gage, *Gospel Typology in Joshua and Revelation: A Whore and Her Scarlet, Seven Trumpets Sound, A Great City Falls* (St. Andrews House, 2013), p.1

[xxix] "Midian and Midianites," *Jewish Encyclopedia*, last modified unknown, accessed April 4, 2014, http://www.jewishencyclopedia.com/articles/10804-midian-and-midianites

[xxx] "Amalek," *Jewish Virtual Bible*, last modified 2016, accessed February 7, 2016, http://www.jewishvirtuallibrary.org/jsource/History/Amalek.html

[xxxi] Edward Chumney, *The Seven Festivals of the Messiah* (Shippensburg, PA: Treasure House, an Imprint of Destiny Image Publishers, Inc. 2001), pp. 92-93.

Chapter Seven

[xxxii] "How to Survive as a Dictator – a Ten Step Guide," *Popular Social Science*, last modified October 1, 2013, accessed July 26, 2015, http://www.popularsocialscience.com/2013/10/01/how-to-survive-as-a-dictator-a-10-step-guide/

[xxxiii] "Four Horsemen of the Apocalypse," *Wikipedia*, last modified March 25, 2015, accessed March 29, 2015, http://en.wikipedia.org/wiki/Four_Horsemen_of_the_Apocalypse

[xxxiv] "Nicolaitans," *Theopedia*, last modified: unknown, accessed March 29, 2015, http://www.theopedia.com/Nicolaitans

[xxxv] Mark Davidson, *Daniel Revisited* (Bloomington, In. Westbow Press 2013), pp.128-132.

Chapter Eight
[xxxvi] "10 Secrets Behind Houdini's Greatest Illusions," *ListVerse*, last modified Nov. 2, 2014, accessed August 31, 2016, http://listverse.com/2014/11/02/10-secrets-to-harry-houdinis-greatest-illusions/
[xxxvii] "Messiah," *New World Encyclopedia*, last modified October 17, 2014, accessed April 28, 2015, http://www.newworldencyclopedia.org/entry/Messiah
[xxxviii] "Moshiach 101," *Chabad.org*, last modified unknown, accessed April 28, 2015, http://www.chabad.org/library/moshiach/article_cdo/aid/101747/jewish/Appendix-II.htm
[xxxix] "Isa Son of Mary," *Answering Islam*, last modified: unknown, accessed April 28, 2015, http://www.answering-islam.org/Index/J/jesus.html
[xl] "A/RES/181(II) of 29 November 1947", *United Nations, 1947.*, accessed September 11, 2015, http://www.un.org/en/ga/search/view_doc.asp?symbol=A/RES/181(II)

Chapter Ten
[xli] Yves Peloquin, pp. 13-147.
[xlii] Ibid., pp. 4-19.

Chapter Eleven
[xliii] "The Futurist Interpretation of Luke's Version of the Olivet Discourse", *Joel's Trumpet,* last modified August 20, 2014, accessed March 29, 2015, http://www.joelstrumpet.com/?p=6920

[lv] Yves Peloquin, p. 328

Chapter Twelve
[xliv] "Dunkirk Evacuation," *Encyclopedia Britannica*, last modified unknown, accessed April 6, 2015, http://www.britannica.com/event/Dunkirk-evacuation
[xlv] "Battle of the Bulge," *Encyclopedia Britannica*, last modified unknown, accessed April 6, 2015, http://www.britannica.com/event/Battle-of-the-Bulge
[xlvi] Ibid.
[xlvii] Ibid.
[xlviii] "General Statistics and Facts About Christianity" *Christianity Today*, last modified 1/1/2015, accessed April 6, 2015, http://christianity.about.com/od/denominations/p/christiantoday.htm

Chapter Thirteen
[xlix] "An Ideal Earth Year of 360 Days?" *Ancient World Mysteries*, last modified 2015, accessed April 7, 2015, http://www.ancient-world-mysteries.com/360-days-earth-year.html
[l] "Prophetic Year," *Bible Study Tools*, modified 2014, accessed April 7, 2015, http://www.biblestudytools.com/commentaries/revelation/introduction/prophetic-year.html
[li] "360 Day Year," *Christadelphian Books Online*, last modified unknown, accessed April 7, 2015, http://www.christadelphianbooks.org/agora/art_less/num17.html
[lii] *Ancient World Mysteries*
[liii] "The 360 Day Year: No Coincidence," Examiner, last modified April 20, 2013, accessed August 3, 2015, http://www.examiner.com/article/360-day-year-no-coincidence
[liv] Immanuel Velikovsky, *Worlds in Collision*, Paradigma, Ltd., 2009
[lv] "The 360 Day Year: No Coincidence," Examiner, last modified April 20, 2013, accessed August 3, 2015, http://www.examiner.com/article/360-day-year-no-coincidence

[lvi] "The 360 Day Prophetic Year in the Books of Daniel, Revelation and Genesis," *Watchman Bible Studies*, last modified July 31, 2013, accessed April 7, 2015, http://www.watchmanbiblestudy.com/*biblestudies*/Definitions/360PropheticYear.htm

Chapter Fourteen

[lvii] "Evangelism Explosion," *Evangelism Explosion*, last modified 2015, accessed June 7, 2015, http://evangelismexplosion.org/

[lviii] "Revelation 8," *The Pulpit Commentary*, last modified 2010, accessed April 8, 2015, http://biblehub.com/commentaries/pulpit/revelation/8.htm

[lix] "Revelation 8:1 Commentaries," *Bible Hub*, last modified unknown, accessed April 8, 2015, http://biblehub.com/commentaries/revelation/8-1.htm

[lx] Ibid.

[lxi] "Shock and Awe," *Oxford Reference*, last modified unknown, accessed April 10, 2015, http://www.oxfordreference.com/view/10.1093/oi/authority.20110803100502693

[lxii] "Sodom and Gomorrah," *Ark Discovery*, last modified unknown, accessed May 26, 2015, http://www.arkdiscovery.com/sodom_&_gomorrah.htm

[lxiii] "What is Rosh Hashanah," *Chabad.org*, last modified September 7, 2015, accessed November 15, 2015, http://www.chabad.org/holidays/JewishNewYear/template_cdo/aid/4762/jewish/What-Is-Rosh-Hashanah.htm

[lxiv] "God's Coronation on Rosh Hashanah," *The Torah*, last modified unknown, accessed November 15, 2015,http://thetorah.com/coronation-on-rosh-hashanah-what-kind-of-king/

[lxv] *Mideast Beast*, Joel Richardson (WND Books, Washington, D.C. 2012), Chapter 15

[lxvi] *Mideast Beast*, Joel Richardson (WND Books, Washington, D. C. 2012), Chapter 15.

Chapter Fifteen

[lxvii] "Azazel," *Jewish Encyclopedia*, last modified unknown, accessed July 12, 2015, http://www.jewishencyclopedia.com/articles/2203-azazel

[lxviii] "The Daabba," *Discovering Islam*, last modified July 8, 2015, accessed September 7, 2015, http://www.discoveringislam.org/daabba.htm

[lxix] "Mohammad and the Demons," *Answering Islam*, last modified October 10, 2001, accessed December 28, 2015, http://www.answering-islam.org/Silas/demons.htm

[lxx] "Daniel's Final Vision and the Antichrist," Joel's Trumpet, last modified unknown, accessed May 16, 2015, http://www.joelstrumpet.com/wp-content/uploads/2014/01/Daniel-11-Abomination1.pdf

[lxxi] "Keil and Delitzsch Commentary on the Old Testament," StudyLight.org, last modified 2016, accessed January 25, 2016, http://www.studylight.org/commentaries/kdo/view.cgi?bk=26&ch=11

[lxxii] "A Short History of the Hebrew Language" *Ancient Hebrew Research Center*, last modified 2015, accessed May 16, 2015, http://www.ancient-hebrew.org/language_history.html

[lxxiii] "Jinn," *Bloomsbury Companion to Islamic Studies*, edited Clinton Bennett, (Bloomsbury Academic, New York, 2013), p. 346

Chapter Sixteen

lxxiv Mythology of Artemis," *Ephesus*, last modified 2015 , accessed June 8, 2015, http://www.ephesus.us/ephesus/mythology_of_artemis.htm

lxxv "Temple of Artemis, Ephesus" *Sacred Destinations*, last modified 2015 , accessed June 8, 2015, http://www.sacred-destinations.com/turkey/ephesus-temple-of-artemis

lxxvi "Apostle Timothy of the Seventy," *Orthodox Church in America*, last modified January 22, 2013, accessed June 8, 2015, http://oca.org/saints/lives/2013/01/22/100262-apostle-timothy-of-the-seventy

lxxvii Randall Price, *Rose Guide to the Temple*, Rose Publishing, Inc., 2012, p. 30

Chapter Eighteen
lxxviii "Polycarp's Martyrdom," *Christian History Institute*, last modified unknown, accessed July 19, 2015, https://www.christianhistoryinstitute.org/study/module/polycarp/

lxxix Yacov. A Rambsel, *Yeshua—-The Hebrew Factor* (Companion Press, Shippensburg, PA, 1996), p. x.

Chapter Nineteen
lxxx "Ancient Pergamon," Bible History Daily, last modified Nov. 11, 1014, accessed June 9, 2015, http://www.biblicalarchaeology.org/daily/biblical-sites-places/biblical-archaeology-sites/pergamon-2/

lxxxi "The Church at Pergamum," *Answers in the End Times*, last modified Mar. 1, 2011, http://www.answersintheendtimes.com/Sunday-School-Lessons/Pt-17-The-Church-at-Pergamum

lxxxii "Pergamon," *Ancient History Encyclopedia*, last modified June 14, 2015, accessed June 15, 2015, http://www.ancient.eu/pergamon/

lxxxiii "The Seat of Satan – Nazi Germany," *CBN*, last modified unknown, accessed June 9, 2015, http://www1.cbn.com/700club/seat-satan-nazi-germany

lxxxiv "Ancient Pergamon," *Bible History Daily*, last modified Nov. 11, 1014, accessed June 9, 2015, http://www.biblicalarchaeology.org/daily/biblical-sites-places/biblical-archaeology-sites/pergamon-2/

lxxxv *Early Church* by Ray Vanderlaan (Zondervan Publishing House, Grand Rapids Michigan, 2000), p. 90

Chapter Twenty
lxxxvi "Thyatira," Bible History Online, last modified unknown, accessed June 10, 2015, http://www.bible-history.com/isbe/T/THYATIRA/

lxxxvii Ibid.

lxxxviii "Who is Allah?" *The Plain Truth About Islam*, last modified unknown, accessed June 11, 2015, http://www.british-israel.ca/Islam.htm#.VXo-aPlViko

lxxxix The Oxford Guide to People & Places of the Bible. Hackett, Jo Ann; Metzger, Bruce M; Coogan, Michael D, eds.(Oxford University Press, 2004). pp. 150–151.

xc "Lucifer, Son of the Howling Morning," *The Coming Bible Prophecy Reformation*, last modified July 11, 2015, accessed September 14, 2015, https://thecomingbibleprophecyreformation.wordpress.com/2015/07/11/lucifer-the-son-of-the-howling-morning/

Chapter Twenty-One

Endnotes

[xci] "Croesus," *Ancient History Encyclopedia*, last modified September 2, 2009, accessed June 14, 2015, http://www.ancient.eu/croesus/

[xcii] Ibid.

[xciii] *Early Church*, p. 52

[xciv] "Cyrus Takes Babylon: the Cyrus Cylinder," *Ancient Warfare*, last modified unknown, accessed June 14, 2015, http://www.livius.org/ct-cz/cyrus_I/babylon05.html

[xcv] "Revelation 3," *Bible Hub*, last modified 2010, accessed June 15, 2015, http://biblehub.com/commentaries/pulpit/revelation/3.htm

[xcvi] Ibid.

[xcvii] "Counting of the Omer," *Judaism 101*, last modified 2011, accessed August 2, 2015, http://www.jewfaq.org/holidayb.htm

Chapter Twenty-Four

[xcviii] "Matthew 6:13," *Bible Hub*, last modified 2014, accessed August 15, 2015, http://biblehub.com/commentaries/matthew/6-13.htm

[xcix] Nelson Walters, *Are We Ready For Jesus*, (Seraphina Press, 2015, pp. 108-111)